Handbook to the

Ferns of British India

Handbook to the

Ferns of British India

Ceylon and the Malay Peninsula

with Supplement

Colonel **R. H. Beddome, F. L. S.**

GYAN

Published by

GYAN

Gyan Publishing House
5, Ansari Road
Daryaganj, New Delhi-110002
Phone: 011-47034999, 9811692060
E-mail: books@gyanbooks.com

Distribution Network
gyanbooks.com
India, USA, Canada, UK, Australia, France

ISBN: 978-81-212-8353-3 (HB)
First Published, 1883

2nd Impression 2023

Printed at: Gyan Press, Delhi.

HANDBOOK TO THE FERNS OF BRITISH INDIA
Author: R. H. BEDDOME

Handbook to the
Ferns of British India

Handbook to the
Ferns of British India
Ceylon and the Malay Peninsula
with Supplement

Colonel **R. H. Beddome, F. L. S.**

GYAN

Published by

Gyan Publishing House
5, Ansari Road
Daryaganj, New Delhi-110002
Phone: 011-47034999, 9811692060
E-mail: books@gyanbooks.com

Distribution Network
gyanbooks.com
India, USA, Canada, UK, Australia, France

ISBN: 978-81-212-8352-6 (PB)
First Published, 1883

2nd Impression 2023

Printed at: Gyan Press, Delhi.

HANDBOOK TO THE FERNS OF BRITISH INDIA
Author: R. H. BEDDOME

FERNS OF BRITISH INDIA.

No. 300

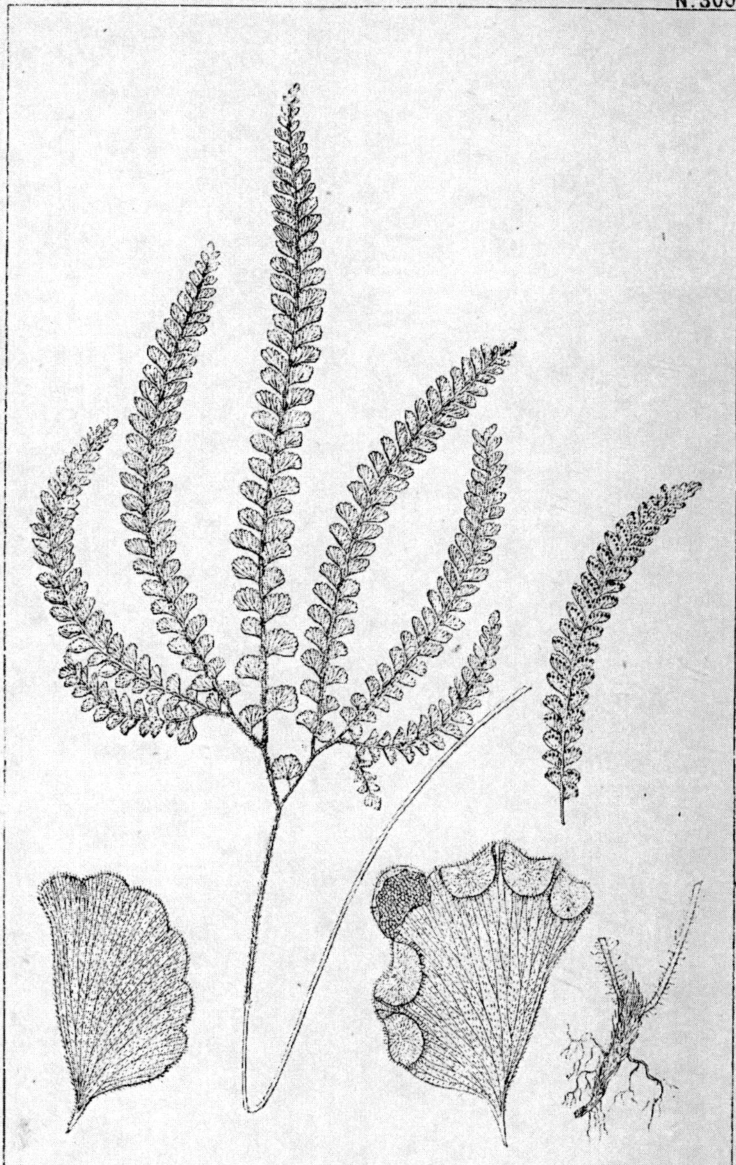

ADIANTUM HISPIDULUM. (*Sw.*)

Handbook to the
Ferns of British India
Ceylon and the Malay Peninsula

With Supplement

By

Colonel R. H. Beddome, F.L.S.

Late Conservator of Forests, Madras
Author of "The Ferns of British India"

With Three Hundred Illustrations

Calcutta

Thacker, Spink, and Co.

Bombay: Thacker & Co., Lim.; Madras: Higgingbotham & Co.
London: W. Thacker & Co.

1892

PREFACE.

THIS handbook is a digest of the information on Indian Ferns contained in Sir W. Hooker's "Species Filicum," the "Synopsis Filicum," Mr. J. Smith's "Historia Filicum," also of Mr. Clarke's "Ferns of Northern India," and of the author's works, "The Ferns of Southern India" and "The Ferns of British India."

The author's former works were compiled in India, without access to libraries or to any herbarium with typical specimens. He has now had the advantage of going thoroughly through the Wallichian ferns at the Linnæan, the large collections at Kew and in the British Museum, and of comparing his own collections with typical forms; he is, besides, indebted for much assistance to Messrs. Baker and Clarke, especially in the determination of all critical forms, so that he has been able, he believes, to clear up many doubts and to correct many errors.

The generic nomenclature is, with few exceptions, that of the "Synopsis Filicum," but the sub-genera have been raised to the rank of genera; this avoids the inconvenience of double generic names, and may be admitted on this score even by those who do not consider the wide difference in habit of such genera as Phegopteris, Polypodium, Pleopeltis, and Drynaria of any value generically, and who base their genera on the sori alone, without reference to habit, venation, or vernation.

The geographical limits of the work comprise the whole of British India, Ceylon and the Malay Peninsula.

WEST HILL, PUTNEY,
May, 1833.

TABLE OF THE

ORDERS, TRIBES, AND GENERA OF FERNS

AS FOLLOWED IN THIS WORK.

ORDER FILICES.

SUB-ORDER I.—GLEICHENIACEÆ.

	Genus.	Page.
Capsules opening vertically, surrounded by a broad transverse complete ring	1 Gleichenia .	2

SUB-ORDER II.—POLYPODIACEAÆ.

Capsules surrounded by a jointed, vertical and elastic ring.

A. Involucratæ. *Sori with an indusium, except in Alsophila.*

TRIBE I.—CYATHEÆ.

Sori globose, capsules sessile or stalked, often on a raised receptacle. Indusium (wanting in Alsophila) inferior, including the sorus, lateral and resembling a scale, or cup-shaped, often when young enveloping the sorus, eventually opening at the summit, or breaking down with a more or less regular margin, caudex generally arborescent.

	Genus.	Page.
Receptacle elevated, indusium globose, inferior, quite covering the sorus when young	2 Cyathea . .	5
Indusium a cup-like scale below the sorus, but never quite covering it, veins free	3 Amphicosmia .	8
Indusium none	4 Alsophila .	11
Receptacles not elevated, indusium inferior globose .	5 Diacalpe . .	13
Indusium umbrella-shaped, six-lobed . . .	6 Matonia . .	19

	GENUS.	PAGE.
TRIBE II.—DICKSONIEÆ.		
Sori globose, indusium inferior, subglobose, free, sometimes covering the whole sorus, closed, at length bursting irregularly, more frequently cup-shaped entire or with two lips.		
Fertile fronds contracted with revolute margins, indusium hemispherical, very fugacious or wanting, veins free	7 STRUTHIOPTERIS	20
Indusium thin, subglobose, open at the top and laciniate	8 WOODSIA	20
Indusium medial on a vein, thick globose pedicellate, bursting into two lips	9 PERANEMA	22
Indusium apical on a vein, two-valved	10 CIBOTIUM	24
Indusium apical on a vein, cup-shaped	11 DENNSTÆDTIA	24
TRIBE III.—HYMENOPHYLLEÆ.		
Filmy ferns, indusium inferior, apical on a vein, two-lipped or tubular.		
Indusium more or less two-lipped	12 HYMENOPHYLLUM	28
Indusium tubular, the mouth truncate or slightly two-lipped	13 TRICHOMANES	36
TRIBE IV.—DAVALLIEÆ.		
Indusium squamiform, suborbicular or tubular, open at the apex, fastened broadly at the base, and sometimes at the sides.		
Indusium apical on a vein, suborbicular coriaceous, attached by a broad base, the sides free	14 HUMATA	46
Indusium as in Humata, but thin and smaller and narrower	15 LEUCOSTEGIA	48
Indusium a subcylindric cyst formed of the substance of the frond, apical on the veins	16 PROSAPTIA	56
Indusium apical, tubular, attached by the base and sides	17 DAVALLIA	58
Indusium apical, half cup-shaped, attached by the base and sides	18 MICROLEPIA	62

	GENUS.	PAGE.
Indusium apical, compound, suborbicular, only open at the top	19 STENOLOMA	. 68
Indusium medial on a vein membranaceous, hood-like	20 CYSTOPTERIS	. 70

TRIBE V.—LINDSAYEÆ.

Indusium apical on the veins, in a continuous or interrupted line, the outer valve being the margin of the frond, the inner membranaceous.

Veins free	21 LINDSAYA .	. 72
Veins anastomosing	22 SCHIZOLOMA	. 77

TRIBE VI.—PTERIDEÆ.

Indusium oblong or linear, formed of the more or less changed and reflexed margin of the frond, opening inwardly.

Indusium globose to linear usually many and distinct, sometimes confluent and continuous, bearing the capsules on its under side, veins free	23 ADIANTUM	. 82
Indusium roundish and distinct, or more or less confluent but not continuous, capsules on the frond .	24 CHEILANTHES	. 88
Indusium as in Pteris, the ultimate segments of fronds small and very narrow	25 ONYCHIUM	. 95
As in Pellæa, but fronds dimorphic	26 CRYPTOGRAMME	98
Indusium quite continuous, sori at first dot-like, but soon running into a line	27 PELLÆA .	. 98
Indusium quite continuous, sori linear continuous, occupying a slender filiform receptacle in the axis of the indusium, veins free	28 PTERIS .	. 104
As in Pteris, but lowest veins meeting and forming an arch	29 CAMPTERIA	. 116
As in Pteris, but veins all anastomosing without free included veinlets	30 DORYOPTERIS	. 120
As in Pteris, but veins all anastomosing with some free included veinlets	31 LITOBROCHIA	. 120

TRIBE VII.—BLECHNEÆ.

Indusium linear or oblong parallel with the midrib and opening towards it, not near the margin.

TRIBE VIII.—ASPLENIEÆ.

Indusium linear or oblong or horseshoe-shaped, opening towards the midrib, sometimes double, sori attached to the veins.

	Genus.	Page.
TRIBE IX.—ASPIDIEÆ.		
Indusium superior, elliptical, subglobose or reniform fixed either by the centre or a sinus.		
Indusium elliptical, emarginate at the base, attached longitudinally to the linear receptacle, veins free .	47 DIDYMOCHLÆNA	199
Indusium of Didymochlæna habit and venation of Nephrodium	48 MESOCHLÆNA	199
Indusium orbicular, veins free	49 POLYSTICHUM	201
Indusium orbicular, veins generally anastomosing acutely with free veinlets from their junction . .	50 CYRTOMIUM	211
Indusium peltate orbicular, or reniform, veins copiously anastomosing with free included veinlets .	51 ASPIDIUM	212
Indusium reniform, veins only slightly anastomosing .	52 PLEOCNEMIA	223
Indusium reniform, veins free	53 LASTREA	228
Indusium reniform, one or more of the lower veinlets anastomosing with the corresponding one of the next group	54 NEPHRODIUM	267
As in Lastrea, but always simply pinnate, the pinnæ articulated and furnished with white dots above .	55 NEPHROLEPIS	282
As in Lastrea, but wide creeping and scandent with jointed stems and entire fronds	56 OLEANDRA	285
B. EXINVOLUCRATÆ.—*Sori without an indusium.*		
TRIBE X.—POLYPODIEÆ.		
Sori on the back of the lobes, round or rarely somewhat oblong.		
Stipes continuous with the caudex, habit of Lastrea, veins free	57 PHEGOPTERIS	288
Stipes continuous with caudex, venation and habit of Nephrodium	58 GONIOPTERIS	296
Stipes continuous with caudex, venation and habit of Aspidium	59 DICTYOPTERIS	298
Stipes articulated with caudex, veins free	60 POLYPODIUM	302
Veins forming regular areoles, the lower one or more with a free included soriferous veinlet . . .	61 GONIOPHLEBIUM	316

	Genus.	Page.
Areoles copious, each with two or more sori, fronds always simple and woolly beneath	62 Niphobolus	. 324
Fronds flabellate in two halves, veins copiously anastomosing	63 Dipteris .	. 334
Fronds either with the base oak-leaf-like, or with separate sterile oak-leaf-like small fronds . . .	64 Drynaria .	. 338
Fronds various, veins copiously anastomosing with free included veinlets	65 Pleopeltis	. 344

TRIBE XI.—GRAMMITIDEÆ.

Sori on the back of the lobes more than twice as long as broad, usually linear.

As in Cheilanthes, but without an indusium, sori though oblong or roundish at first, soon confluent into a continuous line	66 Notholæna	. 373
Sori linear, close to midrib on both sides, fronds grass-like	67 Monogramme	. 375
Sori linear or linear-oblong, otherwise as in Phegopteris	68 Leptogramme	. 377
As in Nephrodium, but sori linear	69 Stegnogramme.	380
Habit of Cheilanthes, sori linear, veins free . .	70 Gymnogramme.	380
Habit of Polypodium, sori linear, veins generally united by transverse veinlets near margin . .	71 Syngramme	. 384
As in Pleopeltis, with copiously anastomosing veins, sori linear, stipes articulate with caudex . .	72 Selliguea	. 389
As in Selliguea, but stipes not articulate and fronds leathery	73 Loxogramme	. 392
Anomalous, veins arcuately anastomosing at the base, forming costal areoles	74 Brainea .	. 395
As in Goniopteris, but sori elongated or confluent .	75 Meniscium	. 397
Sori carried along the veins imperfectly articulated, fronds simple	76 Antrophyum	. 401
Grass-like ferns, sori in continuous marginal lines, veins free	77 Vittaria .	. 404

	GENUS.	PAGE.
Sori in a continuous linear, or interrupted central or submarginal line, veins reticulated, fronds pinnate.	78 TÆNITIS	410
As in Tænitis, but fronds simple and dimorphous	79 DRYMOGLOSSUM	410
Veins copiously reticulated and completely soriferous.	80 HEMIONITIS	413

TRIBE XII.—ACROSTICHEÆ.

Sori not confined to the veins, but spread entirely over the frond beneath.

Fronds simple, veins free	81 ELAPHOGLOSSUM	416
Fronds pinnate, Lomaria-like, veins all simple or sometimes arcuate at the base; scandent ferns	82 STENOCHLÆNA	421
Fronds pinnate, not Lomaria-like, veins all simple; not scandent	83 POLYBOTRYA	424
Similar to Elaphoglossum, but with a connecting vein running round the margin	84 ACONIOPTERIS	427
Veins copiously anastomosing with free included veinlets	85 GYMNOPTERIS	429
Veins copiously anastomosing without free included veinlets. Sea-coast fern	86 ACROSTICHUM	440
Drynaria-like fronds, pinnæ articulated, but stipe adherent to caudex	87 PHOTINOPTERIS	442
Fronds with stag's-horn-like divisions, vernation articulate, sori in large patches only on the fertile fronds	88 PLATYCERIUM	444

SUB-ORDER III.—OSMUNDACEÆ.

Capsules two-valved, opening across the apex, furnished with a short horizontal ring	89 OSMUNDA	447

SUB-ORDER IV.—SCHIZÆACEÆ.

Capsule two-valved, opening down the side, crowned by a complete operculiform ring.

Capsules sessile in 2-4 rows on one side of close spikes	90 SCHIZÆA	452

SUB-ORDER V.—MARATTIACEÆ.

Capsule opening by a slit down one side or a pore at the apex, without a ring.

SUB-ORDER VI.—OPHIOGLOSSACEÆ.

Capsules deeply two-valved, opening down the side nearly to the base, without a ring.

No. 296

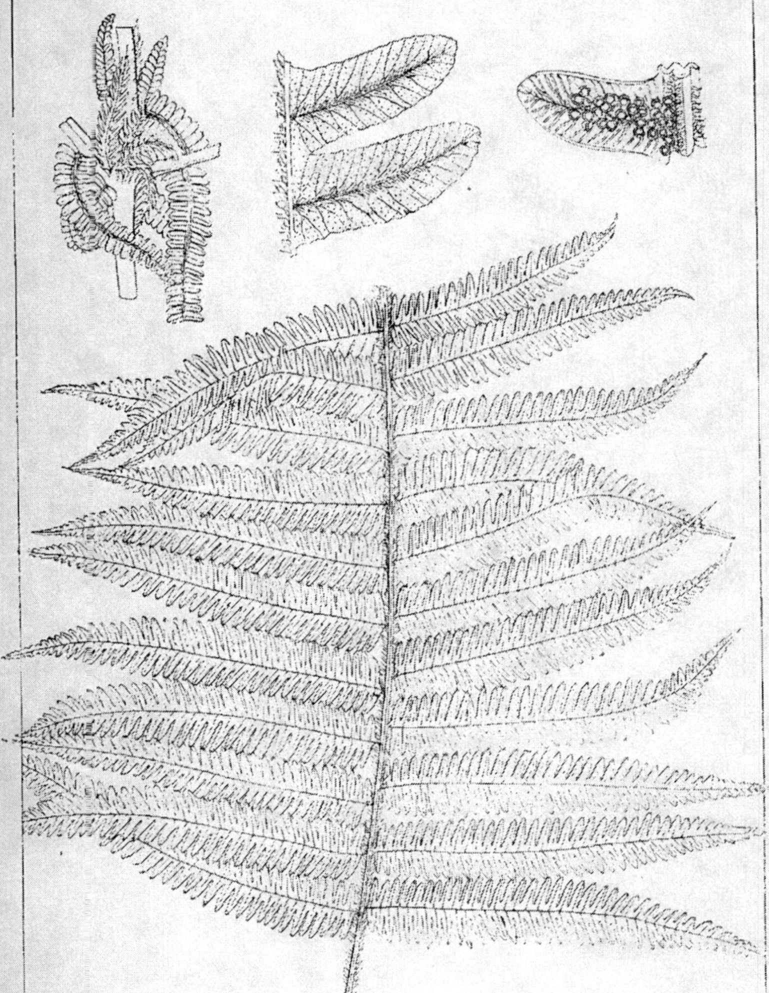

A. S. Cattell & Co, Engrs

GLEICHENIA GLAUCA. (*Hook.*)

Nº 297.

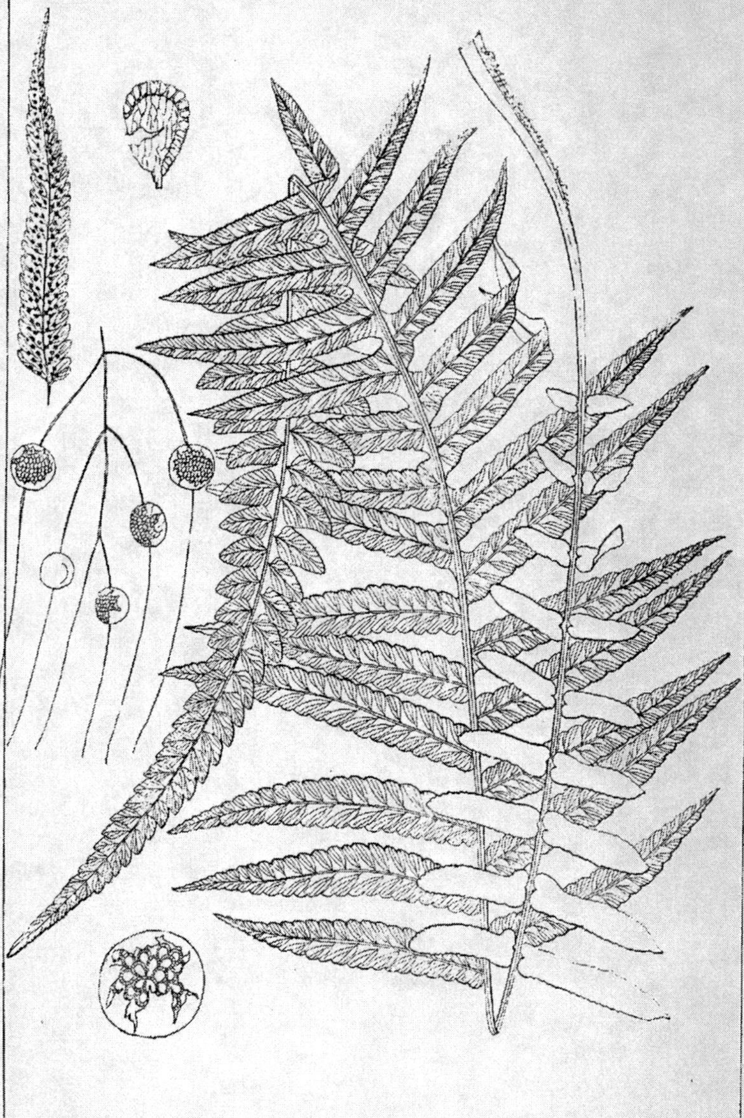

A. S. CATTELL & Cº, ENGRAᵛ

CYATHEA HOOKERI. (*Thw.*)

HANDBOOK TO THE
FERNS OF BRITISH INDIA, CEYLON,
AND THE
MALAY PENINSULA.

ORDER FILICES.

CAPSULES (sporangia) one-celled, usually membranaceous and dorsal (on the back of the frond), or marginal, encircled by a complete or incomplete, jointed, elastic ring, collected in clusters (sori) of a definite but varied form, with or without a covering (indusium) or panicled or spicate, rarely laxly scattered; or the capsules have the ring obsolete, or none, or the ring is confined to the apex of the capsule, where it forms a longitudinally striated crown, bursting vertically; or the capsules are sunk in a many-celled, fleshy or corky receptacle of varied forms, opening by pores or clefts on the upper surface; spores minute, various in form; vernation generally circinate, rarely erect.

SUB-ORDER I.—GLEICHENIACEÆ.

Sori dorsal; of few (2–10) capsules; capsules opening vertically surrounded by a broad, transverse, complete ring; indusium none; caudex generally creeping; stipes often dichotomous; fronds rigid, generally large, and dichotomously branched, frequently bearing axillary buds; vernation circinate.

GENUS I.—GLEICHENIA. (*Smith.*)

(In honour of Gleichen, a German botanist).

Sori of few sessile capsules, situated on a lower exterior veinlet; caudex generally creeping; frond rarely unbranched, generally dichotomously divided, often proliferous from the axils of the forks; pinnæ deeply pinnatifid, with the segments small and concave, sub-orbicular, or pectinate with elongated lobes.

§ Sori solitary at the apex of a veinlet.

1. GLEICHENIA CIRCINATA. (*Sw.*) Fronds dichotomous, divaricated, lobes of the pinnules bead-like, ovate, or subrotund, the margins slightly recurved; capsules 3–4; branches and rachis glabrous, or more or less scaly. *Bedd. F. B. I. t.* 177, as semivestita Labill. *Hook. Sp. Fil. p.* 11.

Malacca.

(Also in Australia, Tasmania, New Zealand, and New Caledonia.)

§ Sori near the middle, or at the forking, of the veinlets.

2. GLEICHENIA GLAUCA. (*Hook.*) A large straggling fern many feet long; stipes stout forked; primary pinnæ opposite, secondary pinnæ alternate, close, 6–8 inches long by 1–2 broad, lanceolate, acuminate, pinnatifid nearly to the rachis, the segments or pinnules oblong-lanceolate, but obtuse, more or less glaucous beneath, glabrous or tomentose, and paleaceous on the stipes and rachis; capsules 3–5, often mixed with hairs. *Bedd. F. B. I. t.* 30, as gigantea Wallich. G. longissima, *Bl. Hook. Sp. Fil. p.* 12. G. gigantea, *Wall. Cat.* Polypodium glaucum, *Thunb. Fl. Jap.* 338, which is the oldest specific name.

Bhotan and Sikkim, alt. 4,500–7,500 feet. Very common about Darjeeling, Khasya, 3,500–5,000. Common in Nepal, Malay Peninsula.

(Also in China, Japan, the Malay Islands, Sandwich Islands, Tropical Australia, Polynesia, West Indies, and Tropical America.)

3. GLEICHENIA NORRISII. (*Mett.*) Branches of the frond one-jugate, oblong-lanceolate, 2–3 feet long, pinnæ lanceolate, the lower distinctly stalked, spreading, 6–9 inches long, cut down to a narrow

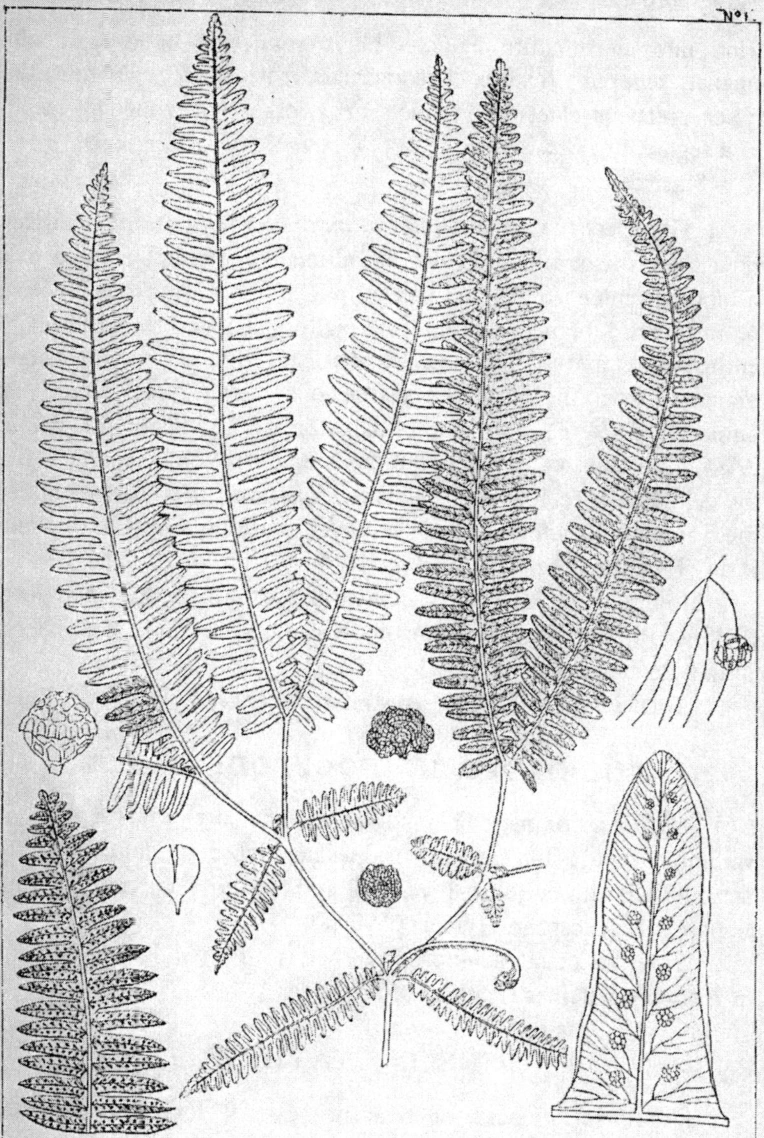

GLEICHENIA LINEARIS (*Burm.*)

wing into close entire ligulate blunt segments, upper gradually smaller, reflexed; texture subcoriaceous, both surfaces glabrous, the lower green or glaucous; veinlets once forked; sori medial, 12–20 to a segment. *Bedd. F. B. I. t.* 346. *Hook. Sp. Fil. p.* 449.

Malacca.

4. GLEICHENIA LINEARIS (*Burm. under Polypodium*). Stipes zigzag, repeatedly di- or trichotomous, the ultimate branches bearing a pair of forked pinnæ; a distinct pair of pinnæ also arises from the base of the forked branches, pinnules usually glaucous beneath, usually entire with recurved margins, texture hard, veinlets usually three-branched from the base, the centre one being often forked or pinnate. *Bedd. F. S. I. t.* 74, as dichotoma. Gl. dichotoma, *Willd. Hook. Sp. Fil. p.* 15. Polypodium lineare, *Burm. Fil. Ind.* 235, *t.* 67, fig. 2, oldest specific name. This fern has long been known under the name of dichotoma, which, however, must be dropped, as there is an older specific name.

Mountains of southern India and Ceylon, up to 6,000 feet, Sikkim, Bhotan, Nepal, Kumaon, Khasya, &c., up to 5,000 feet. Malay Peninsula.

(Also in Japan, Tropical Australia, America, Polynesia.)

SUB-ORDER II.—POLYPODIACEÆ.

Sori dorsal or marginal, subglobose, of many capsules, with or without an indusium, usually pedicellate, more or less completely surrounded with a jointed vertical and elastic ring, and bursting transversely (except in Hymenophylleæ).

A.—INVOLUCRATÆ.—Sori furnished with an indusium (except in Alsophila), Tribes Cyatheæ to Aspidieæ.

TRIBE I.—CYATHEÆ.

Sori dorsal, globose, often at or near the forking of a vein; capsules numerous, often very compact sessile or stalked, generally on an elevated receptacle, often mixed with hairs, obovate usually with a broad, vertical, or sub-oblique elastic ring; indusium (none in

Alsophila) inferior, including the sorus, lateral and resembling a scale on the under side of the sorus, or cup-shaped, often when young enveloping the sorus, eventually opening at the summit, or breaking down with a more or less regular margin ; caudex very often arborescent.

GENUS II.—CYATHEA. (*Smith.*)

(*Kyathos*, a cup — the form of indusium.)

Sori on a vein, or in the axil of the forking of a vein, receptacle elevated, globose, or elongated; indusium globose inferior, covering the whole sorus, afterwards breaking at the summit, and forming a more or less persistent cup, even or irregular, at the margin ; generally arborescent ; stipes often aculeated ; fronds simple, pinnate, or decompoundly pinnate.

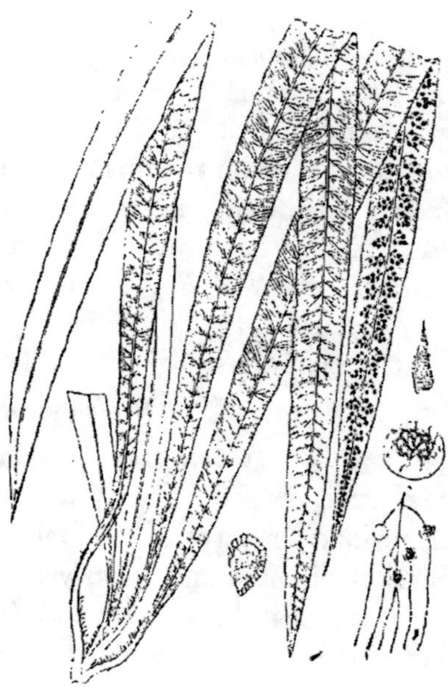

No. 2.

CYATHEA SINUATA. (*Hook.*)

* *Fronds undivided.*

1. CYATHEA SINUATA. (*Hook. and Grev.*) Caudex erect, 2–4 ft. long, about 1 inch in diameter ; frond simple, 2–3 ft. long, 1 2½ inches wide, elongate-lanceolate, sinuate, acuminate, tapering at the base ; veins pinnate ; veinlets soriferous near middle. *Bedd. F. S. I. t.* 259 ; *Hook. Sp. Fil. p.* 16.

Ceylon, in the Singhe-Rajah Forest.

** *Fronds pinnate.*

2. CYATHEA BRUNONIS. (*Wall.*) Stipes 12 feet long ; fronds 2–3 ft. long, pinnate glossy ; pinnæ 6–14 inches long, alternate, between membranous and coriaceous, oblong-lanceolate, acuminate with a long narrow point obliquely truncated at the base and shortly

petiolate, sinuate-crenate; veins three-branched or pinnate, the veinlets occasionally anastomosing amongst themselves, or with the next group; sori medial on the veinlets; indusium very persistent. *Bedd. F. B. I. t.* 87; *Hook. Sp. Fil. p.* 16.

Penang and Malacca.

(Also in the Malay Islands.)

3. CYATHEA HOOKERI. (*Thw.*) Small, but with a trunk-like caudex 1½ inch thick; stipes short black, muricated at the base and sub-paleaceous; fronds coriaceo-membranaceous, 2–3 feet long, 4–5 inches wide, elongate-lanceolate, acuminate, pinnate pinnatifid at the apex; pinnæ from a broad base, which is more or less auricled, lanceolate acuminate, sessile or sub-sessile, coarsely dentate-pinnatifid, more or less entire towards the apex and base, and the lower ones gradually diminishing in size and obtuse at their apex; veins pinnate; sori medial on the veinlets; indusium soon breaking up and becoming cup-like. *Bedd. F. B. I. t.* 260. *Thw. En. Pl. Zy. p.* 396. *Hook. Sp. Fil. p.* 16.

Ceylon, in the Singhe-Rajah Forest.

*** *Fronds decompoundly pinnate.*

4. CYATHEA SPINULOSA. (*Wall.*) A tall tree fern; stipes and main rachis beneath, strongly aculeate, dark purple; fronds glabrous, tripinnatifid; main rachis and rachis of pinnules ferruginous above; rachis of pinnules and main vein of segments scaly below, but the latter glabrous above; segments falcate-oblong acute, serrulate, the margin more or less recurved; veinlets once-forked, or more rarely three-branched; sori copious near the costules or main veins; indusium completely covering the sorus when young, soon breaking irregularly. *Bedd. F. S. I. t.* 57. *Hook. Syn. Fil. p.* 23.

The Wynad at 3,000 feet elevation, North and South Canara Coorg, Jeypore Hills (Vizag), Nepal, Jaintea Hills. The Wynad specimens are in every way identical with those from Northern India collected by Wallich, and Mr. Clarke is in error in stating that the South Indian plant is a Hemitelea, as on comparing with him the specimens he had examined at Kew I found that they were "Alsophila latebrosa," and that this Cyathea was not represented

No. 3

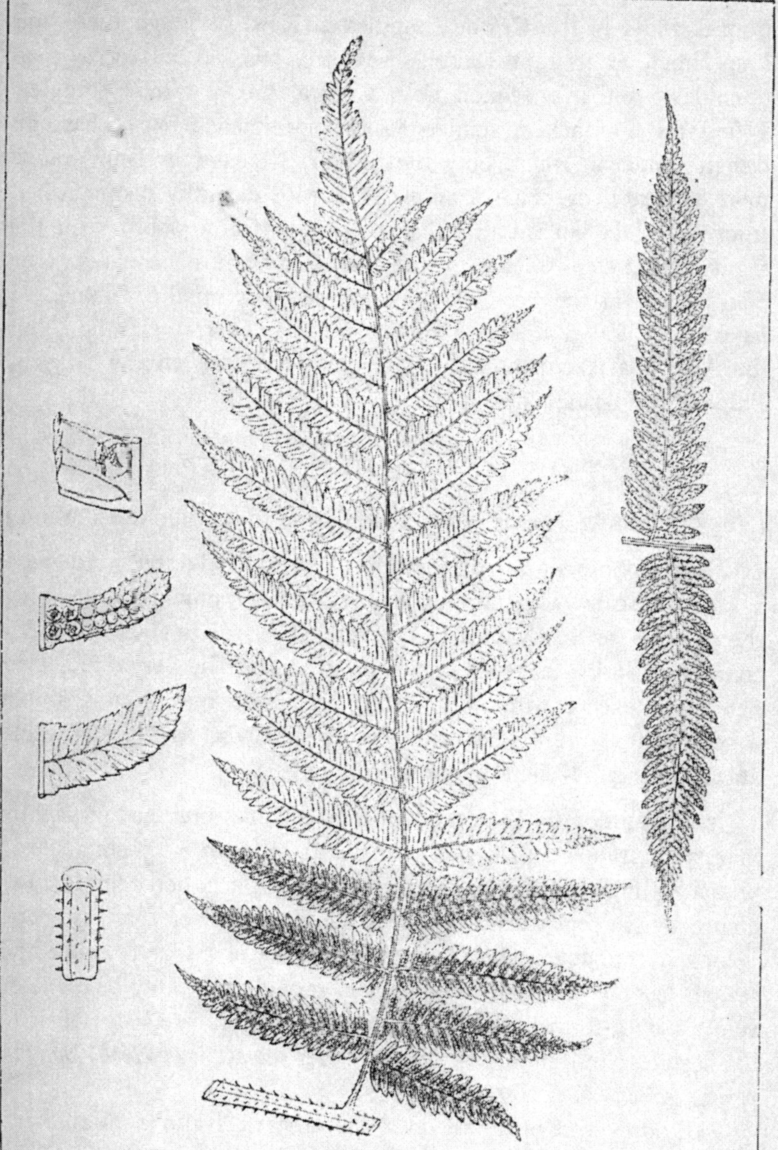

CYATHEA SPINULOSA. (*Wall.*)

from S. India in the Cyathea bundles at Kew, although there was a specimen of it from Dalzell elsewhere, labelled "Lastrea alsophiloides," and a specimen from Canara, mixed with Hemitelea. I find no 3-branched veinlets in my specimens; but I have no barren pinnæ in which only they occur. Except in being much more aculeate, over-ripe examples are with difficulty distinguished from Alsophila latebrosa; it is however perfectly glabrous on the segments beneath, whereas in the Alsophila there is generally some pubescence on the costules, and minute hairs on the veinlets. I have never found this fern much above 3,000 feet elevation, but the Alsophila is common at the highest altitudes on the Nilgiris, Pulneys and Anamallays.

GENUS III.—AMPHICOSMIA. (*Fée.*)

(*Amphi*, around; *kosmos*, world; in allusion to its wide distribution.)

Sori globose, dorsal, on a veinlet; receptacle elevated; indusium a cup-like scale below the sorus, but never completely covering the capsules as in Cyathea. Arborescent ferns like Cyathea, and a connecting link between that genus and Alsophila, very difficult to determine except with unripe sori; veins all free; fronds ample decompound. (Hemitelea only differs in having the costal veins anastomosing. None are found in India.)

1. AMPHICOSMIA WALKERÆ. (*Hook.*) Stipes unarmed or slightly muricate; fronds ample bi-tripinnate, thick, firm, very coriaceous; primary pinnæ 1½ foot long, secondary pinnæ rather remote, 3–4 inches long, deeply, nearly to the costa pinnatifid, or again pinnate, oblong, narrow-acuminate; the costa, as is the rachis, hairy above and scaly below; pinnules or lobes oblong, very obtuse, entire or crenate; veinlets once-forked, three-branched or even pinnate; sori close to the costules; indusium cup-shaped under the sorus. *Hook. Sp. Fil. p.* 30. *Bedd. F. S. I. tab.* 261.

Ceylon, centre of the island at the higher elevations. Var. *β tripinnata* has the ultimate pinnules lobed, but there are intermediate forms.

No. 4.

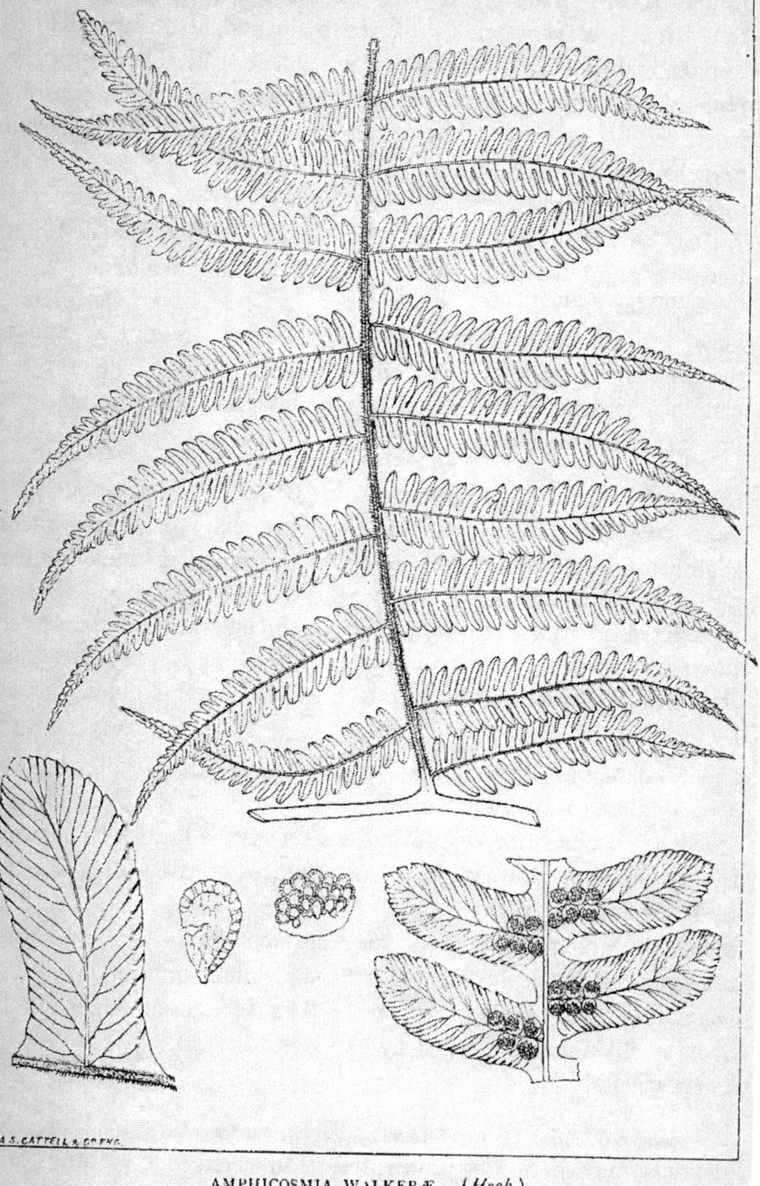

A. S. CATTELL & CO ENG.

AMPHICOSMIA WALKERÆ. (*Hook.*)

2. AMPHICOSMIA DECIPIENS. (*J. Scott*, under Hemitelea.) A lofty tree fern, very prickly on the main and secondary rachises, tertiary rachis (that of the pinnules) bullate-scaly, not pubescent; pinnules glabrous, or nearly so, segments sometimes much narrowed where fertile; veinlets forked, or often three-branched and even four-branched in the sterile portions; sori in two rows close along the main veins or costa of the segment; involucre a hemispheric cup. *J. Scott, in Lin. Trans.* xxx. 33, *t.* 14. *Bedd. F. B. I. t.* 311. Shows the veins and bullate scales correctly, but not the involucre.

Sikkim and Bhotan, 1,000–4,000 feet. Khasya below Nungklow. Differs from the next in being much more prickly and in the segments being generally longer and narrower. I do not feel certain it is distinct from Cyathea spinulosa, as I have not seen the involucre in very young state.

3. AMPHICOSMIA BRUNONIANA. (*Wall.* under Alsophila.) A large tree fern; main rachis somewhat prickly, secondary rachis slightly muricated or smooth; rachis of the pinnules crisped-pubescent; segments minutely hairy on the veinlets (under the lens), not contracted in fruit; veinlets forked, or three-branched veinlets very rare; sori and involucre as in the last. *Clarke, p.* 430. Alsophila Brunoniana, *Wall.* Alsophila latebrosa, var. hemitelioides, *J. Scott*, l. c. 34.

Sikkim and Bhotan, 4,000–7,500 feet; East Nepal; Khasya 3,000–5,000 feet, very common.

The specimen for which Mr. Clarke gives the locality "Deccan" is a specimen of Cyathea spinulosa, collected at Mendeb in Canara by Dr. Richie.

Mr. Clarke's variety β *Scottii*, "segments of the fertile pinnules unusually large, deeply crenated, with many three-branched veinlets," is founded on a single pinna in the Kew Herbarium, collected by Scott in Sikkim and labelled by him latebrosa, var. β; it is perhaps a new species.

4. AMPHICOSMIA ALTERANS. (*Hook, under Alsophila.*) Rachis glabrous, smooth, turning brown; fronds subcoriaceous, glabrous, sub-

tripinnate; primary pinnæ short, petiolate very remote, 10–14 inches long, 2–3 inches wide, oblong acuminate, deeply pinnatifid, pinnate near the base; segments 1–1½ inch long, oblong acute subfalcate entire or serrate, all horizontal, the extremity suddenly pinnated with oblong undivided sessile pinnules serrated at the margin; veins once forked (rarely twice-forked); sori in the axil of the fork, or in the lower veins, considerably above it; involucre a hemispherical cup completely surrounding the base of the sorus. *Bedd. F. B. I. t.* 236, under Alsophila. *Hook. Syn. Fil. p.* 41.

Penang. My specimens distinctly show the indusium.

GENUS IV.—ALSOPHILA. (*Brown.*)

(*Alsos*, grove; *phileo*, to love.)

Sori globose, dorsal, on a vein or at the forking of a vein; receptacle generally elevated, often villous; involucre none, but the bullate scales along the costa of the segments may often be mistaken for such. Arborescent ferns; fronds decompoundly pinnate; veins never anastomosing, simple forked or pinnate.

1. ALSOPHILA LATEBROSA. (*Hook.*) A lofty tree fern; stipes aculeate at the base, muricated upwards, dark mahogany-brown; primary pinnæ oblong acuminate, 12–24 inches long, 6–8 inches wide; pinnules lanceolate-acuminate, 3–4 inches long, cut down nearly to the rachis into linear-oblong, blunt slightly-toothed segments on each side; rachis of pinnules beneath glabrous or pubescent; veins generally minutely hairy (under the lens); veinlets forked; numerous bullate scales along the costa of the segments beneath and also along the rachis of the pinnules; sori occupying the lower two-thirds of the segment. *Bedd. F. S. I. t.* 58. *Hook. Syn. Fil. p.* 43.

Nilgiris and all the western mountains in the Madras Presidency and the Shevaroys, up to 7,000 feet; but often found as low as 3,000; Sikkim, Bhotan and Khasya, 3,500–5,000 feet; also throughout the Malay Peninsula and Penang. I cannot distinguish the two varieties given by Mr. Clarke. The South Indian specimens vary from quite or nearly quite glabrous to as pubescent as those from Sikkim, and the Penang specimens seem quite identical.

2. ALSOPHILA GLAUCA. (*J. Sm.*) A lofty tree fern; more or less prickly; fronds subcoriaceous, glabrous, glaucous beneath; pinnæ 2–3 feet long, pinnules 4–5 inches long, ½ to 1 inch broad, deeply, nearly to the costa pinnatifid; segments linear-oblong subfalcate, when fertile often contracted, entire or distantly crenulate; veins forked, and often three-branched; receptacle naked or hairy. *J. Sm. in Hook. Jour. Bot.* iii. 419. *Bedd. F. B. I. t.* 86 (as A. Brunoniana). Alsophila contaminans, *Hook. Syn. Fil. p.* 41. Chnoophora glauca, *Bl. En. Fil. Jav.* 443.

Sikkim, Bhotan, Assam, Khasya, Cachar, Sylhet, Chittagong, Burmah and Malay Peninsula, up to 4,000 feet.

(Also in the Malay Islands.)

3. ALSOPHILA ORNATA. (*J. Scott.*) A lofty tree fern; stipes paleaceous at the base, slightly muricated, and, as well as the main rachises, glossy purplish-brown; fronds herbaceous-membranaceous; primary pinnæ oblong-lanceolate, rather abruptly contracted into a short, deeply pinnatifid apex; pinnules nearly all petiolate lanceolate, oblong acuminate, deeply, nearly to the costa pinnatifid; segments ovate in the sterile, narrow oblong in the fertile, slightly falcate, serrated; costa of the pinnules somewhat hairy above and scaly below; veinlets forked or a few three-branched. *J. Scott, in Trans. Lin. Soc*, xxx. 36, *t.* 16 A. *Bedd, F. B. I. t.* 342

Sikkim, on the banks of the Rungbee, below the Government Cinchona plantation, at 2,500 feet elevation, called Dang pashin by the Lepchas.

4. ALSOPHILA ANDERSONI. (*J. Scott*) A tall tree fern; stipes muricated and rough, clothed more or less with lanceolate subulate deciduous scales; rachises tawny villous below, somewhat scabrous above; fronds ovate-lanceolate, herbaceous-membranaceous, pilose; primary pinnæ oblong-lanceolate acuminate; pinnules pinnatifid nearly to the rachis with an attenuated serrated apex; segments broad-oblong, slightly falcate, sharply serrated; veinlets simple or

once forked, 10–12 pair to each segment, all except the upper two or three with a single sorus a little below the middle; the costules, veins, and veinlets beneath all furnished with long weak white hairs, which are also present in a less degree on the upper surface. *J. Scott, in Trans. Lin. Soc.* xxx. *t.* 17. *Bedd. F. B. I. t.* 310.

Sikkim, in the tropical valleys below the Government Cinchona plantation, alt. 1,000–2,500 feet. Khasya. Called Pulai-nock by the Lepchas.

5. ALSOPHILA OLDHAMI. (*Bedd.*) A tree fern, 6–10 feet, unarmed; principal rachises half an inch thick, deep purple, asperous; fronds herbaceous - membranaceous; primary pinnæ about 2 feet long by 8–9 inches broad, oblong acuminate; secondary 4–5 inches long by about 1 inch broad, lanceolate acuminate; cut down nearly to the rachis into numerous linear oblong blunt-toothed segments on each side; costa hairy above, scaly below; veins simple, or once-forked; sori in two parallel rows below the middle of the veinlets. *Bedd. F. B. I. t.* 343, Alsophila comosa, *Scott, l. c. t.* 16 *B.*, not *Wall.*

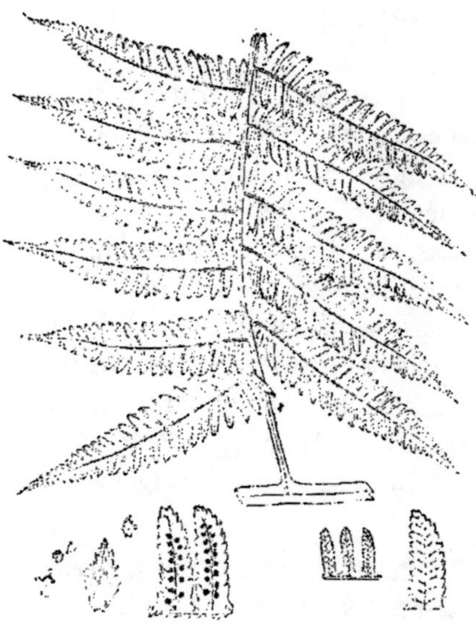

No. 5.

ALSOPHILA OLDHAMI. (*Bedd.*)

Khasya hills; Sikkim, in the forest between Darjeeling and Surail, 5,000–6,000 feet; Moulmein.

6. ALSOPHILA COMOSA. (*Hook.*) A tree fern, unarmed; stipes paleaceous, with long linear-subulate scales, pale brown, as well as the rachises, which are tawny-villous on the upper side; fronds

herbaceous, glabrous, and scaleless; primary pinnæ 14–16 inches long, 6–8 inches wide; pinnules oblong-acuminate from a rather broad and truncated sessile or shortly petioled base, serrated two-thirds of the way to the costule, pinnatifid with very narrow sinuses; lobes close-placed, oblong, serrated; veins, simple or rarely forked; sori about half-way between the margin and the costule; receptacle small, very slightly elevated. *Hook. Syn. Fil. p.* 41. *Bedd. F. B. I. t.* 84.

Singapore.

(Also in the Malay Islands.)

7. ALSOPHILA COMMUTATA. (*Mett.*) A tree fern; stipes paleaceous, at the base tuberculate-asperous; fronds bi-pinnate, partial rachis slightly squamose; pinnules all petiolate, sterile ones oblong-lanceolate, fertile portions often contracted, coriaceous, glossy as if varnished, ending in an acuminated serrulated point, pinnatifid scarcely half-way down to the rachis; segments ovate-obtuse, serrate, the margins thickened, or very slightly recurved; veins simple or often forked; sori frequently confined to the lower part of the pinnules, and a little distant from the costa of the segments. *Hook. Syn. Fil. p.* 43. *Bedd. F. B. I. t.* 235 (as squamulata.)

Malacca, on Mount Ophir.

8. ALSOPHILA GLABRA. (*Hook.*) A tree fern; stipes asperous, paleaceous at the base, the rachises purple-ebeneous, polished, glabrous, or with a few scales, or with adpressed pubescence; fronds subcoriaceous-membranaceous; primary pinnæ 1½–2½ feet long, deeply pinnatifid at the apex; pinnules, upper ones sessile, lower ones petiolate from a truncated base, oblong acuminate, 3–6 inches long, 5–9 inches wide, pinnatifid ¼ to ½ way to the costule, sometimes more in Himalayan examples; segments triangular or rounded, rarely ovate, serrated; veinlets all simple; sori arranged in the shape of a V inverted, not extending to the apex of the lobe. *Hook. Syn. Fil. p.* 43. *Bedd. F. S. I. t.* 60.

All the western hills of the Madras Presidency up to 4,000 feet;

Nº 6.

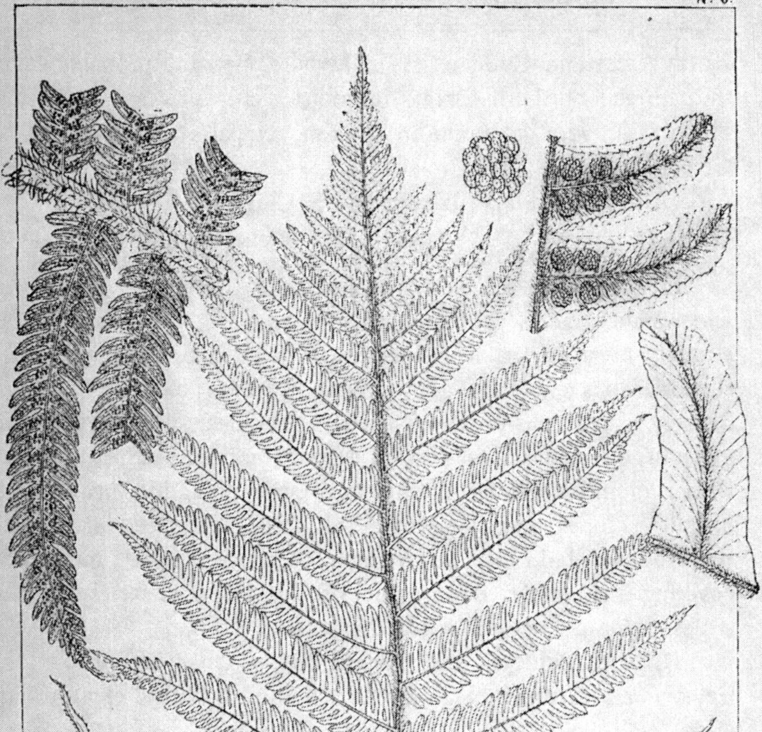

A.S.CATTELL & Cº ENG.

ALSOPHILA CRINITA. (*Hook.*)

North Arcot and Cuddapa Hills, Jeypore, &c., and probably general through the northern Circars in moist shady places on the hills; Himalayas, very common in Sikkim, Nepal, &c.; Burmah and Ceylon.

(Also in the Malay Islands and S. China.)

The hairs of the rachis are exaggerated in my figure quoted above.

9. ALSOPHILA CRINITA. (*Hook.*) A lofty tree fern; stipes and main rachis stramineous, brown, hispid-paleaceous, and strongly muricate; spines short, tipped with a black gland; fronds subcoriaceous; rachises above pilose, beneath and on the costæ densely paleaceous-crinite; scales sometimes short and minute, generally elongate and adpressed; primary pinnæ 2 feet long, 10 inches wide; pinnules oblong acuminate, sessile pinnatifid nearly to the costules; lobes narrow-oblong, sub-obtuse, falcate, the margins recurved, serrated; costa and veins often pilose; veinlets forked; sori covering the whole under side of the lobes mixed with ciliate scales. *Hook. Syn. Fil. p.* 42. *Bedd. F. S. I. t.* 59.

Nilgiris, Pulneys, and Anamallays, 5,000–7,000 ft. elevation. Ceylon central provinces. By far the most beautiful of all the tree ferns.

10. ALSOPHILA ALBO-SETACEA. (*Bedd.*) Main rachis purplish, muricated, and (in age) only slightly scaly; pinnæ long petioled; rachis of pinnæ very scaly; pinnules with the one-two lowest segments free, the rest cut down nearly to the rachis, oblong subfalcate, slightly crenate; veinlets all forked from near the base, one branch often (or both rarely) again forked; costæ sparingly clothed beneath with long white setaceous hairs, which are also present in a less degree on the costa and costules above; costules beneath furnished with deciduous bullate scales, which often have a hyaline setaceous point at the apex; sori copious. *Bedd. Supplmt. to Ferns, p.* 2 (not figured).

Nicobar Islands (Kurz).

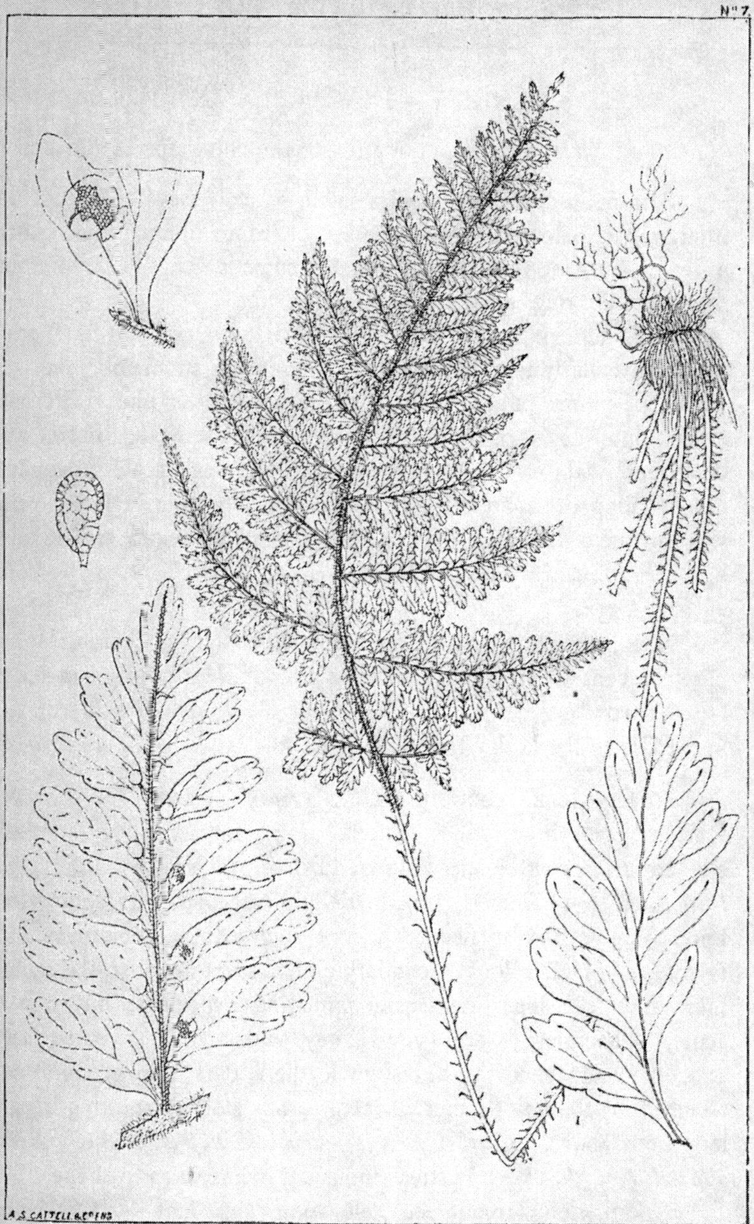

DIACALPE ASPIDIOIDES. (*Bl.*)

3

GENUS V.—DIACALPE. (*Bl.*)

(*Dia* and *kalpe*, a vessel, in allusion to the cup-shaped indusium.)

Sori globose, the receptacles small, scarcely elevated; indusium inferior (*i.e.*, below the sorus), globose, hard-membranaceous, entire, a length bursting very irregularly at the summit; capsules numerous, nearly sessile, ring broad, veinlets simple, free.

1. DIACALPE ASPIDIOIDES. (*Bl.*) A large compound fern; stipe scaly, particularly near the base; fronds tripinnate, submembranaceous, rachis of pinnæ pubescent with adpressed scales; pinnæ alternate or sub opposite, segments of pinnules oblong-cuneate, lobed, and decurrent, glabrous, or furnished with long weak scales; veinlets not reaching the margin; sori medial on the anterior lower veinlets, involucre bursting irregularly, or sometimes into two regular lips. *Bl. En. Pl. Jav. Fil.* 241. *Hook. Syn. Fil. p.* 45. *Bedd. F. S. I. t.* 257.

Nepal to Bhotan, Khasya, 4,000–6,000 feet. Ceylon, higher parts of central provinces. Tenasserim on Mooleyit 5,000–6,000 feet. Tavoy.

(Also in the Malay Islands.)

2. DIACALPE FŒNICULACEA. (*Hook. under Polystichum.*) Rhizome creeping; stipes tufted, 6–12 inches long, densely clothed below with lanceolate reddish-brown scales; fronds 1-2 feet long, 9–12 inches broad, deltoid-lanceolate, 4–5-pinnatifid, lower pinnule 6–8 inches long, 3–4 inches broad, pinnules subdeltoid, 2–3 inches long, secondary pinnules cut down to the rachis, their lower divisions often again pinnatifid; segments linear, very acute, subcoriaceous and very glossy, with a few scattered long scale-like hairs beneath; indusium leathery, dark purple, spherical, attached by the point under its centre, not stalked, splitting irregularly from above. *Clarke, p.* 434. *Hook. Syn. Fil. p.* 256. *Bedd. F. B. I. tab.* 36, under Lastrea (indusium incorrect as to shape).

Sikkim, 7,000–10,000 feet elevation, abundant at Buckeem; Upper Ratong, 8,000–9,000 feet.

GENUS VI.—MATONIA. (*Br.*)

(After Dr. Maton, a London physician.)

Receptacle of the sori expanded into a firm membranaceous, umbrella-shaped obscurely six-lobed stipitate involucre, which covers and encloses six large sessile capsules; veins forked free, except those round the sori, which are closely reticulated.

1. MATONIA PECTINATA. (*Br.*) Rhizome creeping; stipe slender, 6–8 feet high; fronds fan-like, conjugate-subpedately-flabellate, the pinnæ produced on the anterior or upper side of the divergent branches, rigid-coriaceous, linear, pinnatifid nearly to the costa, glabrous, often glaucous beneath, 1–2 feet long; sori situate at the posterior base of the segments. *Br. in Wall. Pl. As. Rar.* 1, *t.* 16. *Hook. Syn. Fil. p.* 45. *Bedd. F. B. I. t.* 186.

Malacca, on Mount Ophir; one of the rarest and handsomest of ferns.

(Also in Borneo.)

Nº 3

MATONIA PECTINATA. (*Br.*)

TRIBE II.—DICKSONIEÆ.

Sori globose, on the back or apex of a vein; indusium inferior, subglobose, free, sometimes covering the whole sorus, closed, or at length bursting irregularly; more frequently cup-shaped, entire, or with two lips; caudex arborescent in Cibotium; veins free, or anastomosing.

GENUS VII.—STRUTHIOPTERIS. (*Willd.*)

(*Struthios* ostrich, the fronds like feathers of the bird.)

Sori dorsal on the veins of the changed and contracted pinnæ of the fertile frond, and quite concealed by the revolute margins; indusium very thin hemispherical, very fugacious, or wanting; caudex erect or creeping; fronds stipitate, dimorphous, fertile ones pinnate; pinnæ torulose or flattish; veins all free pinnate. (Differs from Onoclea in having free veins.)

1. STRUTHIOPTERIS ORIENTALIS. (*Hook.*) Fronds ovate-oblong, not attenuated at the base; fertile ones oblong, contracted; pinnæ linear-oblong, flattened, two-edged, the broad refracted margins covering the whole back, dark brown, glossy, at length spreading, and torn at the margin. *Hook. Syn. Fil. p.* 46. *Bedd. F. B. I. t.* 171.

Sikkim, elevation 900–1,200 feet, Khasya, Assam.

(Also in Japan and Western China.)

GENUS VIII.—WOODSIA. (*Br.*)

(In honour of Joseph Wood, a British botanist.)

Sori globose; indusium inferior, soft, membranaceous, calyciform, or more or less globose, and sometimes enclosing the sorus, at length opening at the top, the margin laciniate or fringed; veins free, simple, or forked. Small herbaceous ferns, the stipes tufted, often jointed.

1. WOODSIA HYPERBOREA. (*Br.*) Glabrous, or with the stipes, rachis and costa beneath slightly hairy and scaly; fronds 5 inches long by ½ inch broad, linear-lanceolate, pinnate; pinnæ cordate-ovate, pinnatifid, with few broadly obovate entire lobes, the lower ones distinct; indusium smaller than the sorus, but fringed with long hairs which extend beyond it. *Hook. Syn. Fil. p.* 46. *Clarke, p.* 434.

Kashmir, Sind Valley, elevation 8,000 feet; collected only by Mr. Levinge.

(Also in Alpine and Arctic Europe and North Asia.)

No 9.

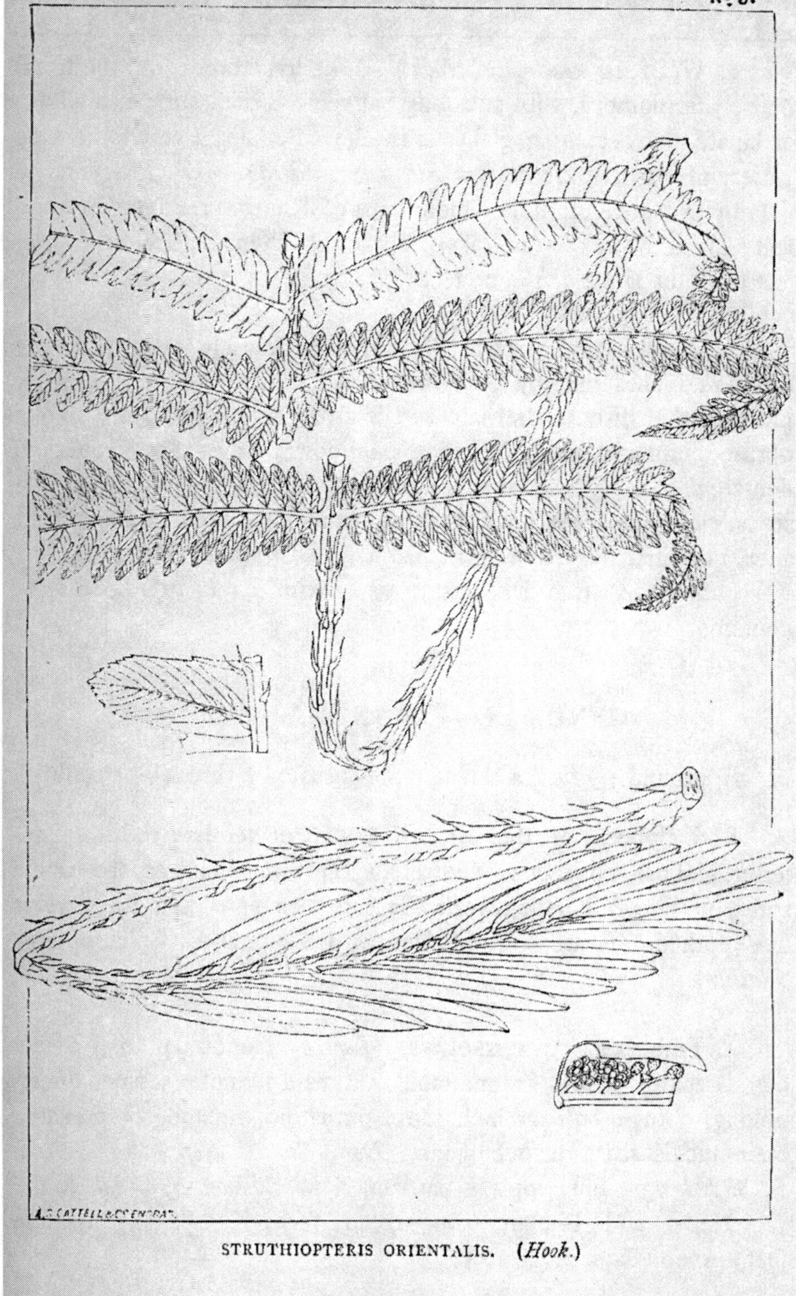

STRUTHIOPTERIS ORIENTALIS. (*Hook.*)

2. WOODSIA LANOSA. (*Hook.*) Like hyperborea, but the frond densely ferruginous, with soft long hairs and scales, stipe also villous or lanate, but becoming glabrous in age. Perhaps a very tomentose variety of No. 1. *Hook. Syn. Fil. p.* 47. *Bedd. F. B. I. t.* 341.

Only in Northern India—mountains of Kumaon; Pindari, 12,000 feet; above Namik, 11,600 feet; Sikkim Lachen, 14,000 to 16,000 feet; Mount Donkia, 18,000 feet.

3. WOODSIA ELONGATA. (*Hook*) Glandulosely pilose; fronds up to 12 inches long by 1–1½ inch broad, narrow oblong pinnate, pinnæ rather distant alternate sessile from a broadish base, oblong obtuse, pinnatifid not more than half down, lobes short, rounded, dentate; sori globose, much elevated; indusium larger than the sorus, very membranaceous, globose, soon bursting with a lacerated apex, not ciliated. *Hook. Syn. Fil. p.* 47. *Bedd. F. B. I. t.* 14.

Himalayas, from Dhurmsala to Sikkim, 8,000 to 12,000 feet; common.

GENUS IX.—PERANEMA. (*Don.*)

(*Peri*, around; *nema*, a thread; the sorus on a thread-like stalk.)

Sori globose, on the back of a vein or veinlet; indusium inferior, globose, coriaceous, pedicellate, at first enclosing the whole sorus, at length bursting vertically into two spreading lips; veins free, forked, clavate; fronds large, decompound. Sphæropteris, *Wallich.*

1. PERANEMA CYATHEOIDES. (*Don.*) Fronds up to 4–6 feet high, stipate, deltoid decompound, ultimate pinnules sessile, linear-oblong, obtuse, half an inch long, pinnatifid, repand, or crenate; main rachis scaly or pubescent. *Don. Pr. Fl. Nep. p.* 12. *Bedd. F. S. I. t.* 73. Sphæropteris barbata, *Wall. Hook. Syn. Fil. p.* 49.

Nepal and Bhotan, 6,000–10,000 feet; Khasya, 4,500–6,000 feet; Anamallays, 6,000 feet.

No. 10

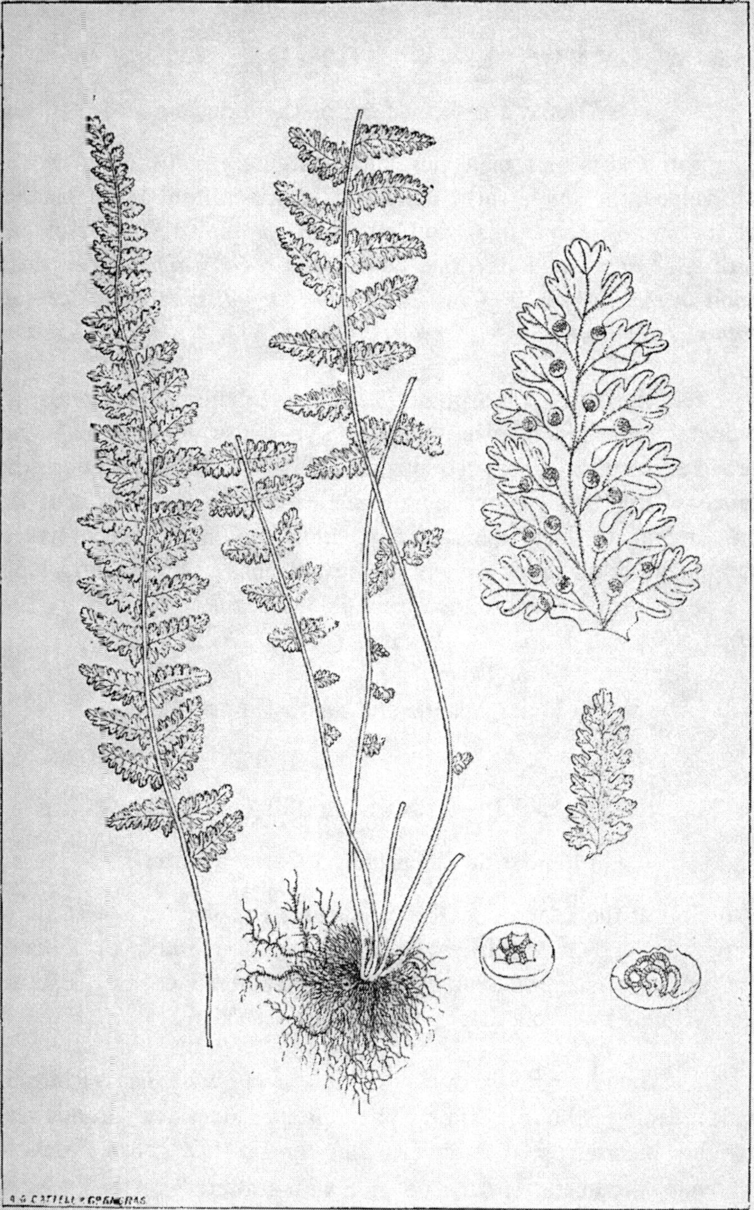

WOODSIA ELONGATA. (*Hook.*)

GENUS X.—CIBOTIUM. (*Kaulf.*)

(*Kibotos*, a casket—form of the indusium.)

Sori at the apex of a vein, intra-marginal; indusium distinctly two-valved, the outer valve coriaceous, distinct from the substance of the frond; veins free, simple, forked, or pinnate; arborescent, with large decompound coriaceous fronds. *Only differs from Dicksonia in the outer valve of the indusium being distinct from the substance of the frond.*

1. CIBOTIUM BAROMETZ. (*Link.*) Arborescent; fronds tripinnate, lower pinnæ ovate-lanceolate, 1–2 feet long, 6–12 inches broad; pinnules linear-acuminate, cut down within a short distance of the rachis above, and sometimes quite down to it at the base, segments linear-oblong, acute, subfalcate, upper surface naked, shining, lower glaucous, sometimes furfuraceous; sori 2–12 to a lobe; the valves nearly equal, transversely oblong. *Link, Fil. Sp. p.* 166. *Hook. Syn. Fil. p.* 49. C. glaucum, *Bedd. F. B. I. t.* 83.

Mishmee, Assam, Tavoy.

(Also in the Malay Islands and South China.)

GENUS XI.—DENNSTÆDTIA. (*Bernh.*)

(In honour of Dennstadt, a German writer.)

Sori at the apex of a vein; indusium cup-shaped, not at all, or very indistinctly, two-valved; veins free, simple, forked, or pinnate; not arborescent; fronds herbaceous or membranaceous. Patania Presl. a name of later date. Dicksonia Sec. Patania. *Hook.*

1. DENNSTÆDTIA SCABRA. (*Wall. under Dicksonia.*) Rhizome wide-creeping, villous; main rachis scabrous, often wavy; fronds very variable in size, up to 2½–3 feet long, and 2 feet broad; deltoid or ovate, bipinnate, surface beneath with scattered glistening hairs,

No. 11.

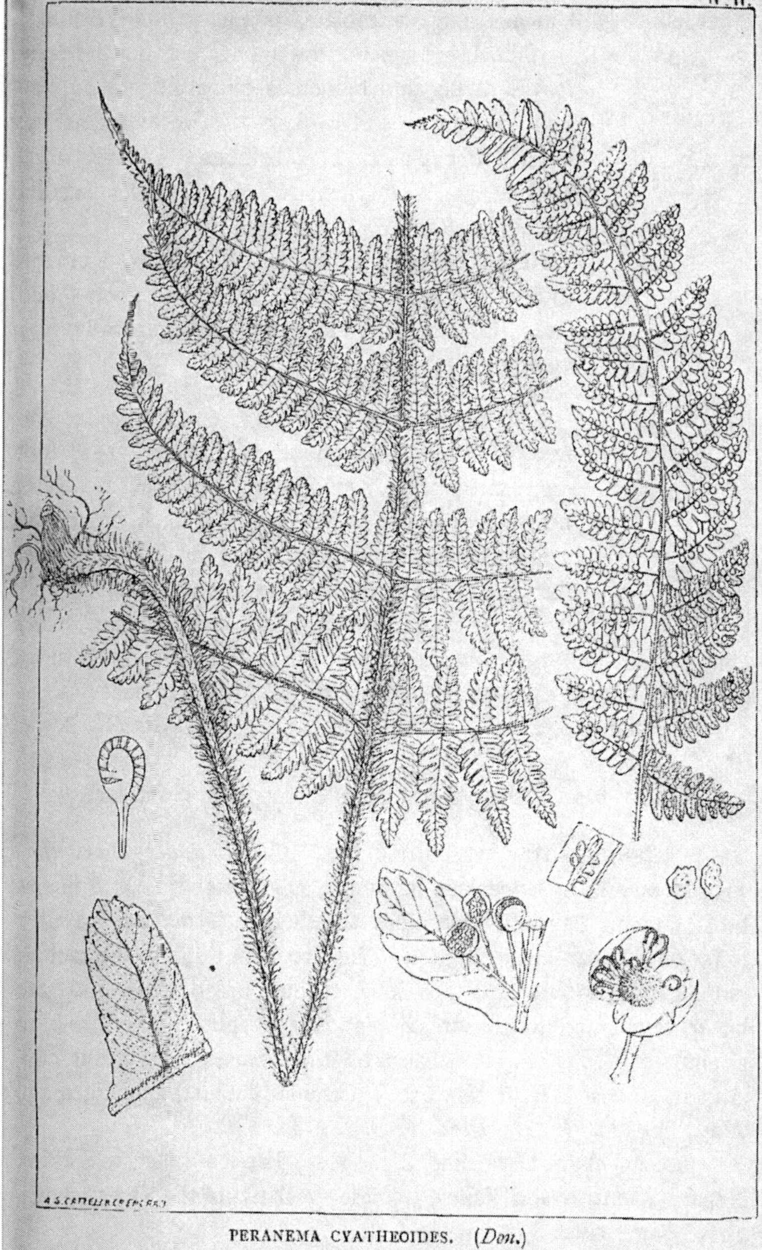

PERANEMA CYATHEOIDES. (*Don.*)

lower pinnæ 4–8 inches long, lanceolate, pinnules quite distinct, $1–1\frac{1}{2}$ inches long, the lower ones cut down nearly to the rachis into numerous pinnatifid oblong deltoid segments; sori 2–6 to the lower segments; indusium cup-shaped, subglobose. *Wall. Cat.* Dicksonia, *Hook. Syn. Fil. p.* 54. Dennstædtia deltoidea, *Bedd. F. S. I. t.* 258.

No. 12
DENNSTÆDTIA SCABRA. (*Wall.*)

Ceylon, central provinces; Himalayas, Kumaon to Bhotan, 4,000–8,000 feet; Khasya, 4,000–6,000 feet; Birma and the Malay Peninsula generally, very common.

2. DENNSTÆDTIA ELWESII. (*Baker, under Patania.*) Fronds lanceolate, tripinnatifid, $1–1\frac{1}{4}$ foot long; rachis stramineous glabrous; pinnæ lanceolate, nearly sessile, 3–4 inches long, $\frac{3}{4}–\frac{7}{8}$ inch broad, the rachis flattened; pinnules 20–30-jugate, lanceolate, sessile cuneate at the base, $1\frac{1}{2}–2$ lines broad, deeply pinnatifid; segments ligulate, erecto-patent, many entire parallel, lowest on the upper side often bifid, both sides glabrous; veins solitary in the centre of each segment; sorus covering the entire apex of the segment. *Hook. Syn. Fil. p.* 54. *Bedd. Suppl. to Ferns, t.* 347.

Sikkim, near Lachen, 8,500 feet; Choongtam, 9,000 feet.

3. DENNSTÆDTIA APPENDICULATA. (*Wall. under Dicksonia.*) Fronds oblong or lanceolate, bipinnate, 12–18 inches long, 6 inches broad; rachis hairy; pinnæ close together, their rachises parallel, lower ones linear-lanceolate, 3–4 inches long, cut down to the rachis; pinnules linear-oblong, $\frac{1}{2}$ inch long, 2 lines broad, pinnatifid into linear segments, under surface glandulosely pilose; sori 2–6 to a pinnule placed at the base of the sinuses; indusium cup-shaped, globose. *Wall. Cat.* 65. Dicksonia (Patania) appendiculata. *Hook. Syn. Fil. p.* 54. *Bedd. F. B. I. t.* 82.

Senchal above Darjeeling, 8,500 feet; Lachen Valley, in Sikkim, Nepal; Kumaon Gori Valley, 5,500 feet; Banks of the Vishnugunga, above Panchkisar, 8,000–9,000 feet.

No. 3.

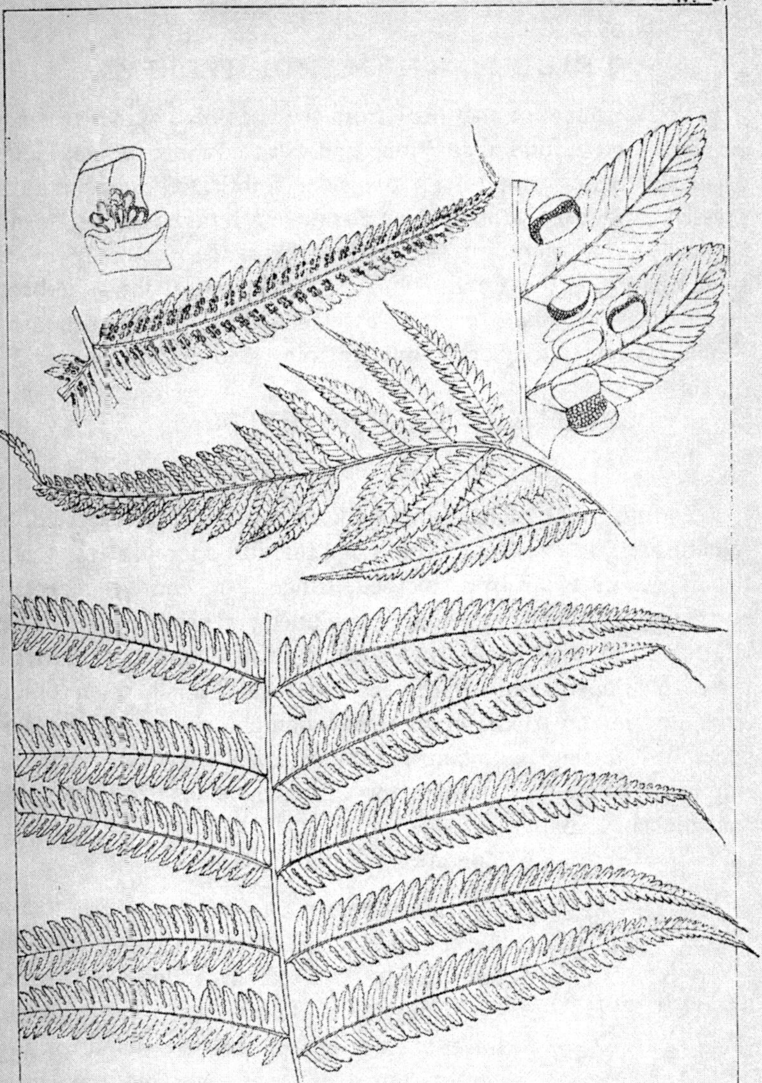

J. C. CATTELL & CO. ENGRAVERS.

CIBOTIUM BAROMETZ. (*Link.*)

TRIBE III.—HYMENOPHYLLEÆ.

Sori terminal or marginal from the apex of a vein; receptacle elongated, often filiform and long, and exserted more or less, clothed especially below with sessile orbicular imbricated subpeltate compressed capsules, surrounded by a complete transverse ring, opening vertically; indusium inferior, various in shape, generally of the same texture as the frond. Small, often epiphytal ferns, herbaceo-membranaceous, more or less laxly cellular, variously costate and veined. Caudex frequently long, creeping, and filiform.

GENUS XII.—HYMENOPHYLLUM. (*L.*)

(*Hymen*, membrane; *phyllon*, leaf.)

Sori marginal, more or less sunk in the frond or exserted, terminating a costa or vein; indusium inferior, more or less deeply two-lipped or two-valved, toothed, fringed, or entire; receptacle elongated, columnar, exserted, or included; capsule mostly orbicular, depressed, attached by the centre, furnished with a broad transverse ring, opening irregularly at the apex. Small, often minute ferns, growing on trunks of trees and damp rocks in moist places, generally on the mountains; fronds delicately membranaceous, simple or compound, costate, or with simple or branched, never anastomosing, veins.

* Margin of the frond entire.

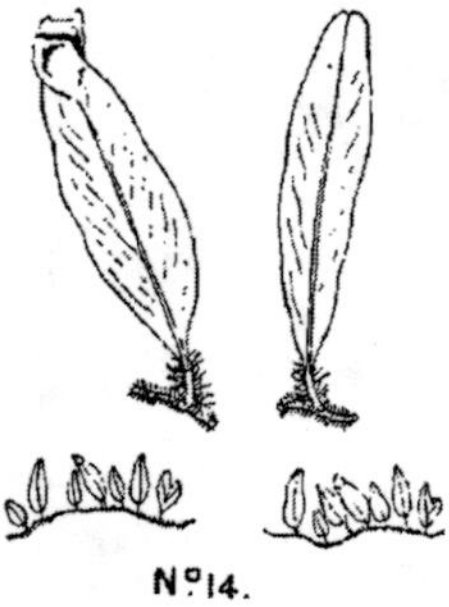

No. 14.
HYMENOPHYLLUM PARVIFOLIUM. (*Baker.*)

1. HYMENOPHYLLUM PARVIFOLIUM. (*Baker.*) A very tiny species, rhizome slender, creeping, tomentose; stipes about 1 line long; frond very minute, 2–3 lines long, 1 line broad, linear-oblong, margin entire; simple or 2–3-cleft at the apex, sometimes half-way down, furnished only with a central costa and a few faint, irregular, free spurious venules, the margin not thickened; sori solitary, terminal, the cuneate base sunk in the frond divided

No.

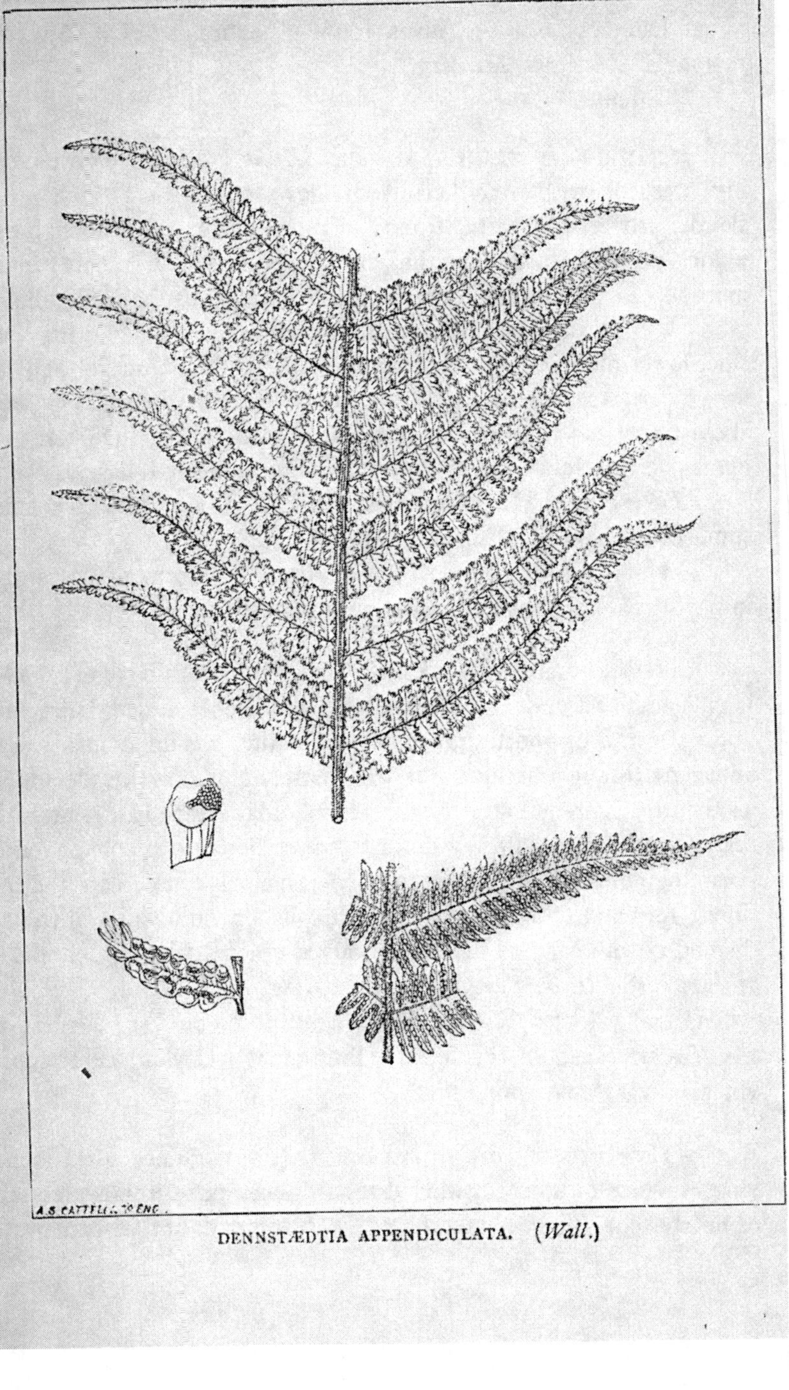

DENNSTÆDTIA APPENDICULATA. (*Wall.*)

about half way down; valves rounded entire. *Baker, Syn. Fil. p.* 56. *Bedd. F. B. I. t.* 225.

Moulmein.

2. HYMENOPHYLLUM TENELLUM. (*Kuhn.*) Rhizome wide-creeping hairy or with fine hair-like scales; stipes ½–1½ inch long; slender, somewhat hairy, fronds 1–2 inches long, ¾–1 inch broad, oblong to deltoid, tripinnatifid, margin entire, main rachis winged, more or less furnished beneath with ferruginous hair-like scales; pinnæ 4–6 jugate, deltoid, cuneate-truncate at the base on the lower side, lower pinnules 1–2, cleft at tip with ligulate blunt lobes, ½ line broad, partial rachises and veins more or less hairy beneath, glabrous above; sori 2–6 to a pinna, terminal in the lobes; involucre with hemispherical lobes, and a cuneate entire immersed base. *Baker, Syn. Fil. p.* 57. H. polyanthos, *Bedd. F. S. I. t.* 267. H. emersum, *Baker, Syn. Fil. 1st ed. p.* 457.

Ceylon. (C. P. 3,360.) Differs from any form of polyanthos in having the rachises and veins hairy beneath.

3. HYMENOPHYLLUM EXSERTUM. (*Wall.*) Stipe 1–2½ inches long, slender; fronds 2–6 inches long, 1–2 inches broad, lanceolate-oblong, ovate or short triangular bipinnatifid; main rachis winged above or throughout, more or less densely clothed with deciduous ferruginous hairs; lower pinnæ rhomboidal, lanceolate-acuminate, divided more than half way down to the rachis into simple or forked linear pinnules, slightly hairy on the principal veins; sori 2–8 to a pinna, terminal or axillary in the segments on both sides, involucre divided down nearly to the base; valves oblong, bluntly denticulate at the apex. *Hook. Syn. Fil. p.* 58. *Bedd. F. S. I. t.* 9.

Himalayas and Khasya Hills, 2,000 to 9,000 feet; Birma; all the Western Ghats of the Madras Presidency; Ceylon, central provinces. Very common.

4. HYMENOPHYLLUM POLYANTHOS. (*Sw.*). Stipes 2–3½ inches long, wingless or narrowly winged towards the apex; fronds glabrous, or nearly so, 2–8 inches long by 1–3 inches broad, not crisped, ovate-

No. 16

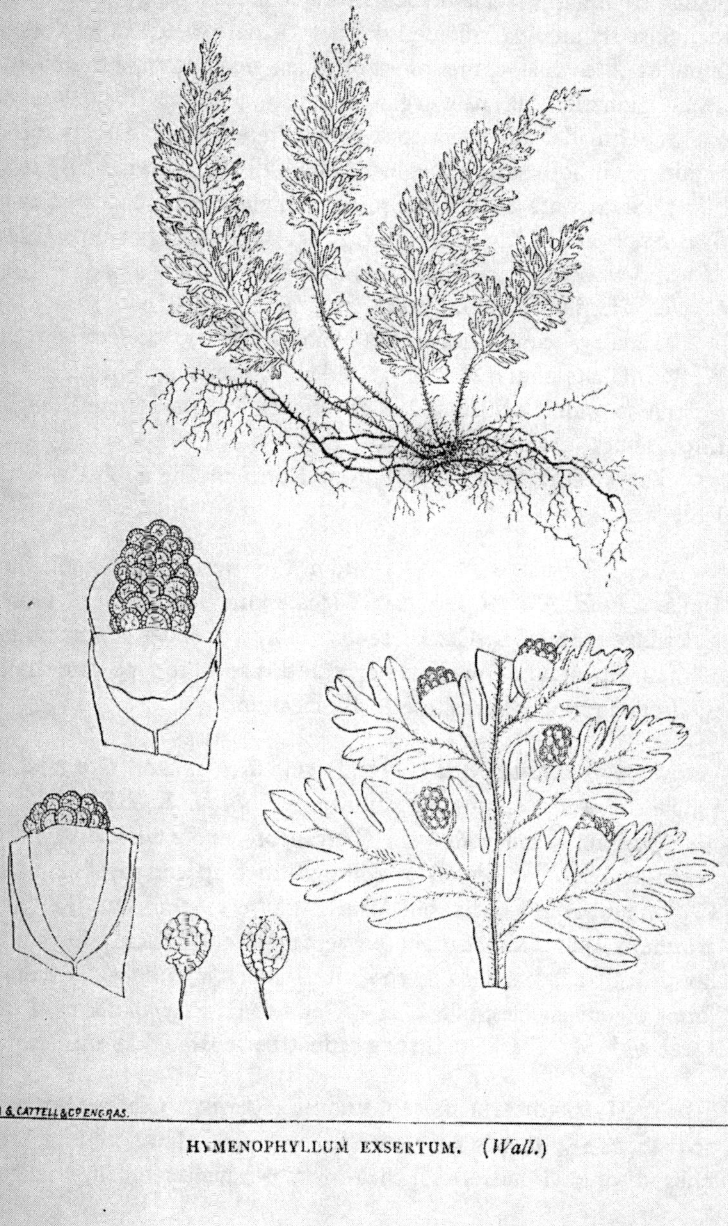

A. & CATTELL & CO. ENGRAS.

HYMENOPHYLLUM EXSERTUM. (*Wall.*)

oblong tripinnatifid; main rachis with a narrow wing; lower pinnæ triangular-rhomboidal, divided down to a narrow centre into several pinnules on each side, the lowest of which are cuneate or rhomboidal, deeply pinnatifid, ultimate segments linear, 1–1½ line long, less than ½ a line broad; sori 2–12 to a pinna, terminal or axillary on the segments on both sides; involucre small, divided down nearly to the base; valves ovate or rounded entire or slightly denticulate. *Swartz, Syn. Fil. t.* 149. *Hook. Syn. Fil. p.* 60. H. microglossum, *V.D.B. Hook. Syn. Fil. p.* 59. H. polyanthos β. minor. *Bedd. F. B. I. t.* 306. H. Blumeanum, *Spreng. Bedd. F. S. I. t.* 266.

Himalayas and Khasya mountains, 1,000–12,000 feet elevation. Western Ghats of the Madras Presidency; Ceylon; Birma.

(Also widely distributed in all tropical and subtropical regions throughout the world.)

The typical form is only from Northern India, and is a very large fern.

VAR. β MICROGLOSSUM is from the western ghats of South India. *Bedd. F. B. I. t.* 306. A small form with the stipe more or less winged; but Mr. Clarke sends me a fern under this name from Bhotan, which is intermediate between this and the type with some of the fronds running very close to Blumeanum.

VAR. γ BLUMEANUM. Fronds very narrow and elongate, and pinnæ sometimes simply pinnatifid only. *Bedd. F. S. I. t.* 266.

Ceylon; Tinnevelly and Travancore mountains. This has generally been considered a quite distinct species by botanists in Ceylon and South India, but Mr. Clarke says it runs into the type in Northern India, and cannot be separated. With only Ceylon and South Indian specimens in view, it is difficult to consider them all forms of one species, but after seeing the Himalayan forms, I quite agree with Mr. Clarke that they cannot be separated as species.

5. HYMENOPHYLLUM JAVANICUM. (*Spreng.*) Glabrous or nearly so; stipe 2–4 inches long, erect, margined above with a broad, crisped wing; fronds 4–8 inches long, 3–4 inches broad, triangular,

tripinnatifid; main rachis with a broad crisped wing; lower pinnæ $1\frac{1}{2}$–2 inches long, triangular-rhomboidal, erect-patent, divided down to a narrow crisped centre into several plane or slightly crisped pinnules on both sides, the lower of which are several times deeply pinnatifid; sori 6–20 to a pinna, terminal and axillary on the segments on both sides; involucre about as broad as the segments, divided down nearly to the base; valves orbicular, entire, or denticulate. *Spreng. Syst.* iv. 132. *Hook. Syn. Fil. p.* 60. H. crispatum (Wall.), *Bedd. F. S. I. t.* 207.

Himalayas, Nepal, and Bhotan, 5,000–8,000 feet; Khasya, 3,500–5,500 feet; Western Ghats of the Madras Presidency; Ceylon, central provinces; Birma and Malay Peninsula.

(Also in Australia, New Zealand, Mauritius, Bourbon, and the Philippines.)

VAR. β BADIUM. (*Hook. and Grev.*) Frond hardly or not at all crisped. H. badium, *Hook. Syn. Fil. p.* 60. *Bedd. F. B. I. t.* 282.

Sikkim, Malay Peninsula, Tenasserim on the Mooleyit Mountain.

6. HYMENOPHYLLUM CILIATUM. (*Sw.*) Stipe 1–2 inches long, furnished with tufts of stellate hairs, decurrently winged above; wing ciliate; frond oblong, acuminate, tripinnatifid, 2–6 inches long, 1–2 inches broad at the centre; main rachis broadly winged throughout ciliated and hairy like the stipe; lower pinnæ oblong or rhomboidal, with a broad central undivided portion, and numerous erect-patent simple or forked ciliated linear segments 2–3 lines long; sori 2–12 on a pinna, placed at the end of the lateral segments on both sides, involucre immersed suborbicular; valves divided about halfway down, and conspicuously ciliated. *Hook. Syn. Fil. p.* 63. *Bedd. F. B. I. t.* 305.

Sikkim.

(Also in tropical America from Cuba and Mexico to Chili and South Brazil; Tropical Africa, Mauritius, Madagascar, Bourbon, Seychelles and Johanna Island; New Zealand.)

Mr. Clarke seems to doubt the Sikkim locality, but my specimens received from Dr. Jerdon quite agree with the type.

** Margin of the frond serrulate.

7. HYMENOPHYLLUM SIMONSIANUM. (*Hook.*) Stipe slender, wiry or winged, naked or with a few ferruginous hairs, 1–2 inches long; fronds linear-oblong, 2–6 inches long, up to 1½ inch broad, pinnatifid to the winged rachis; the primary segments fan-shaped, 1–6 lobate, ultimate segments broadly oblong, serrulate; sori 1–4 terminal on the divisions of the upper pinnæ, involucre broadly oblong, divided nearly to the base; valves serrulate. *Hook. Syn. Fil. p.* 68. *Bedd. F. B. I. t.* 281.

Sikkim, 4,000–10,000; common. Khasya Hills.

8. HYMENOPHYLLUM SMITHII. (*Hook.*) Stipe 1–2 inches long, wiry naked or slightly tomentose; fronds oblong-acuminate, 3–8 inches long, 2–3 inches broad, bipinnatifid; rachis winged above, ciliated below; pinnæ oblong-triangular, with a winged rachis and simple or 1–4 times forked linear-serrulate segments; sori 1–4 terminal on the segments of the pinnæ on both sides; involucre oblong, small, divided half down; valves entire. *Hook. Syn. Fil. p.* 69. *Bedd. F. B. I. t.* 277.

Malacca and Penang.

(Also in Philippines and Java.)

9. HYMENOPHYLLUM DENTICULATUM. (*Sw.*) Stipe 1–2 inches long, erect, ferruginously hairy or naked, often winged towards the apex; rachis winged throughout; fronds 2–3 inches long by 1 or more broad at the base, ovate to narrowly oblong, glabrous, or with scattered hairs, slightly crisped, pinnatifid to the rachis; primary segments pinnatifid, secondary ones oblong, sometimes again divided, serrulate on the margin, involucre ovate, glabrous or scabrous, or rarely slightly hairy; valves serrulate, or pectinate. *Swartz, Syn. Fil. t.* 148 *and* 375. *Hook. Syn. Fil. p.* 70. *Bedd. F. B. I. t.* 278. *Clarke, Ferns of North India, p* 438.

Khasya hills, about Cherra Poonjee, 4,000–5,000 feet; Bhotan, Birma, Moulmein mountains, 7,000 feet.

(Also in Java.)

VAR. β FLACCIDUM. Main rachis often with much ferruginous hair beneath; fronds flaccid, hardly at all crisped, ultimate segments slightly serrulate in their upper portion only, the main rachis quite entire, valves of the involucre slightly serrulate at the summit. H. Khasianum, *Hook, Syn. Fil. p.* 464. *Bedd. F. B. I. t.* 276. *Clarke, l. c., p.* 438.

Khasya Hills, growing with the type. Mr. Clarke, who has seen it growing, considers it only a variety of denticulatum.

10. HYMENOPHYLLUM NEESII. (*Hook.*) Stipe 2–1 inches long, naked, or slightly winged, with a crispate margin on both sides; frond ovate, about 2 inches long, ¾–1 inch broad, tripinnatifid; rachis winged throughout, the wing and pinnæ much crisped; pinnæ with distant, narrow, simple or 1–3 times deeply forked, deeply toothed segments; sori small, usually single, supra-axillary on the upper pinnæ; involucre subcylindrical below, divided more than half-way down, with two acute spinulose-dentate valves. *Hook. Syn. Fil. p.* 71. *Bedd. F. S. I. t.* 279. Hymenophyllum Tunbridgense, *Bedd. F. S. I t.* 265.

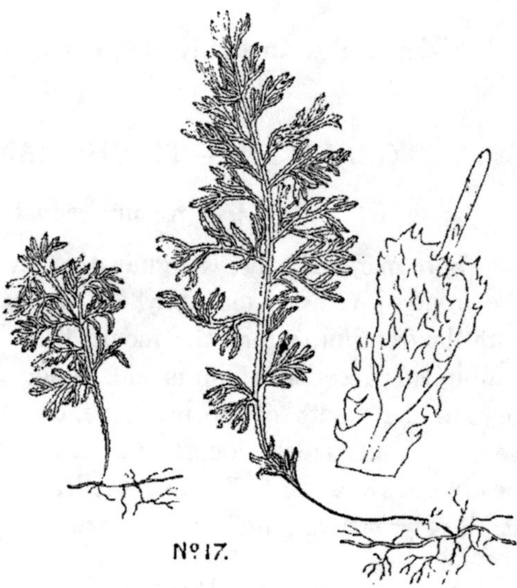

No. 17.

HYMENOPHYLLUM NEESII. (*Hook.*)

Ceylon, central provinces; Tinnevelly on the Chokampatty hills, 5,000 feet; Penang.

(Also in Java, Borneo, Fiji, and Philippines.)

11. HYMENOPHYLLUM LEVINGII. (*Clarke.*) Very delicate in texture; stipe 1 inch, with moniliform hairs; frond 1–2 inches long, more or less covered with moniliform hairs, narrowly oblong, not crisped, pinnatifid to the winged rachis; primary segments 1–4 lobate, ultimate segments oblong, remotely serrate, their midrib with many hairs and lanceolate scales of the same texture as the frond; involucres usually 1–2 at the end of the segment, small glabrous subquadrate; valves separating nearly to the base entire or slightly toothed at the apex. *Clarke, F. of North India, p.* 439. *t.* xxix. *fig.* 3.

Sikkim; Yoksun and Neebay, 7,000 feet elevation.

GENUS XIII.—TRICHOMANES. (*Smith.*)

(*Thrix*, a hair; *manos*, soft.)

Sori marginal, always terminating a vein, more or less sunk in the frond, involucre monophyllous, tubular, closely corresponding with the frond in texture, the mouth truncated or winged, or slightly two-lipped; receptacle filiform, elongated, often considerably exserted beyond the mouth of the involucre, capsuliferous principally at the base; capsule sessile, depressed, surrounded by an entire broad nearly transverse ring, bursting vertically. Like the last genus in habit of growth and delicacy of texture.

1. TRICHOMANES MOTLEYI. (*V. D. B.*) Rhizome creeping, more or less tomentose; fronds very small, sessile, or shortly stalked, about ¼ inch broad, cordate-orbicular, sometimes somewhat lobed, sterile ones nearly entire, fertile ones with a deep apical sinus; veins in the sterile fronds radiating from the base without any distinct central costa, but a distinct costa is present in the fertile fronds; spurious veins indistinct, a distinct marginal band; involucre

stalked, proceeding from the base of the sinus, the mouth spreading and much dilated. *Hook. Syn. Fil. p.* 73. T. Henzaiense, *Bedd. F. B. I. t.* 183.

Tenasserim, Andamans, Ceylon.

(Also in Borneo and New Caledonia.)

2. TRICHOMANES EXIGUUM. (*Bedd. under Hymenophyllum.*) Rhizome wide-creeping; stipe very short; frond ¼ to ½ inch linear-oblong, narrowed at the base, blunt repand, rarely somewhat pinnatifid; veins pinnate from a central costa, simple or forked, spurious venules few but nearly as prominent as the veins, not reaching the costa, and often not touching the margin; involucre solitary, terminal, the base sunk in the frond; valves entire, large and spreading; receptacle exserted or included. *Bedd. F. B. I. t.* 275. *Hook. Syn. Fil. p.* 464.

Wynaad and Coorg, 3,000–4,000 feet; Ceylon.

3. TRICHOMANES NEILGHERRENSE. (*Bedd.*) Rhizome creeping more or less tomentose; stipe 3–6 lines long, glabrous or tomentose, fronds glabrous, very small up to 1 inch long, ovate to elliptic lanceolate or linear, entire or somewhat lobed; veins from a more or less distinct central costa, spurious venules numerous, a marginal band generally present; involucres terminal, 1–2 sunk in the frond, the mouth exserted, more or less two-lipped; receptacles exserted. *Bedd. F. S. I. t.* 6. *Hook. Syn. Fil. p.* 74.

Nilgiris, abundant about Walaghat, 3,000–4,000 feet; Anamallay hills, Tinnevelly and Travancore hills; Ceylon, central provinces.

4. TRICHOMANES HENZAIANUM. (*Parish.*) Rhizome creeping, tomentose; stipe from obsolete up to ½ inch long; frond ¼–½ inch each way, very thin, orbicular to obovate-cuneate, more or less lobed, central costa present or often obsolete, except towards the base, above which it branches off into veins; veins prominent and distinct, spurious venules copious, marginal band absent or inconspicuous; involucres 1–6 sunk in the frond; the mouth two-lipped.

Parish in Hook. 2 *Cent. Ferns, t.* 1. *Hook. Syn. Fil. p* 75. *Bedd. F. B. I. t.* 303.

Moulmein and Pegue, on trees.

5. TRICHOMANES MUSCOIDES. (*Sw.*) Frond stalked, 1–3 inches long, by ¼–½ inch broad, linear-oblong to suborbicular, entire or variously lobed, spurious venules copious ; sori 1–8, terminal on the lobes, the tube sunk in the frond, the mouth free, dilated, but usually scarcely two-lipped. *Hook. Syn. Fil. p.* 75. *Bedd. F. B. I. t.* 304.

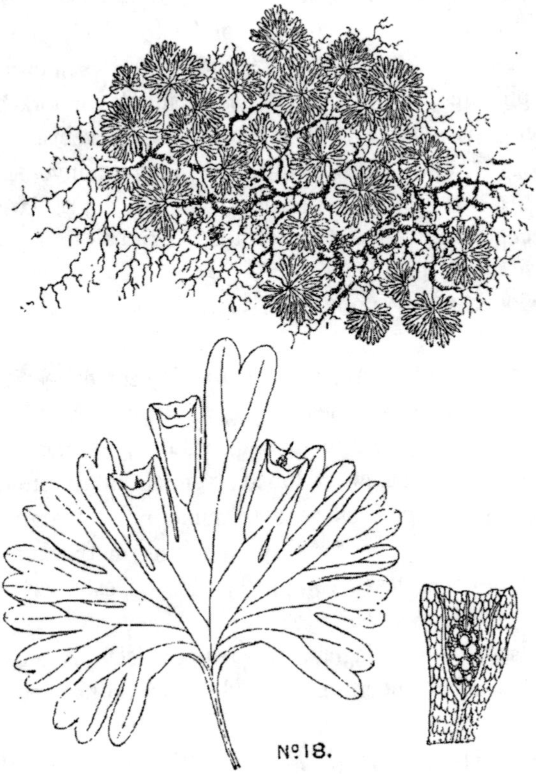

Nº 18.

TRICHOMANES PARVULUM.
(*Poir.*)

Northern India (received from Dyas) ; Khasya.

(Also in tropical America and Africa, Polynesia, &c.)

Mr. Clarke states that the typical form is not found in Northern India, but only the variety sublimbatum, distinguished by having no trace of a marginal band, but in Griffith's specimen collected on the Khasya hills, this marginal band is more or less present in some fronds, and I do not think it can be separated as a variety. This species, as I understand it, is not present in Ceylon or S. India, the Ceylon plant being identical with the Nilgiri T. neilgherrense.

6. TRICHOMANES PARVULUM. (*Poiret.*) Rhizome wide-creeping, interlaced; stipe 1 inch long, wiry, slender, tomentose below; frond ¼ to ½ inch each way, orbicular in general outline, cuneate or truncate at the base, flabellately cut about half-way down from the outer edge in the direction of the base into narrow irregular segments; veins close, prominent, so that the frond, when dry, appears channelled; dichotomous at a very small angle; spurious venules numerous; sori 4–6, terminal on the central segments, the tube quite sunk in the frond, the mouth dilated at the sides. *Hook. Syn. Fil. p.* 75. *Bedd. F. S. I. t.* 179.

Nilgiris.

(Also in Japan, China, Java, Polynesian Islands, Madagascar, Johanna Island, and the Moluccas.)

7. TRICHOMANES PROLIFERUM. (*Blume.*) Rhizome wide-creeping, interlaced; stipe 1–2 inches long, slender, bearing 1–3 deeply divided fronds about 1 inch broad each way, ovate-lanceolate to roundish; segments narrow dichotomously branched, divided down nearly to the central rachis; veins numerous, irregular; sori 4–12, terminal, the tube quite sunk, the mouth obscurely two-lipped; receptacles exserted. *Hook. Syn. Fil. p.* 76. *Bedd. F. S. I. t.* 262.

No. 19.
TRICHOMANES DIGITATUM.
(*Sw.*)

Nilgiris, west slopes, 3,000 feet; Travancore Hills, Ceylon.

(Also in Java and the Philippine Islands.)

8. TRICHOMANES DIGITATUM. (*Swartz.*) Stipe very slender, naked, ½ inch long; frond 1–2 inches long, ½–1 inch broad, irregular in general outline, divided down nearly to the base, or a broadly-

winged rachis into long broadly-linear dichotomous segments, sometimes ciliate, with only a central costa in each; sori 2–6, terminal on the segments; involucre cup-shaped, quite sunk, the mouth broadly dilated, slightly two-lipped. *Hook. Syn. Fil. p.* 76. T. corticola, *Bedd. F. S. I. t.* 264.

Ceylon, Ambagamwa district; also collected by Griffith either in North India or the Malay peninsula.

(Also in Mauritius, Bourbon, Java, and the Polynesian Islands.)

9. TRICHOMANES KURZII. (*Bedd.*) Rhizome slender, wide creeping; stipe very short; frond not 1 inch long, cuneate below, deeply pinnatifid, primary segments 1–3 lobate, ultimate segments linear, texture thick, surface somewhat undulated, margin bounded by a thickened line, a central vein only in each segment; sori 1–2 to a frond, subterminal, the involucre turbinate, sunk in the frond, the mouth dilated but without lips. *Bedd. F. B. I. t.* 286. Trich. nanum, *Hook. Syn. Fil. p.* 77. Crepidomanes nanum, *V. D. B. Hymen. Suppl. p.* 122. *Clarke, F. N. I. p.* 440.

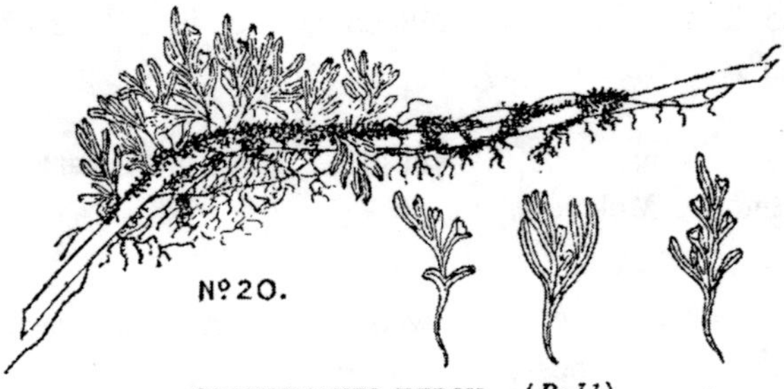

TRICHOMANES KURZII. (*Bedd.*)

Assam, Andaman Islands; Malabar, at Poodoopady, foot of the Tambacherry Ghat.

10. TRICHOMANES VIRIDANS. (*Mett.*) Rhizome creeping, tomentose; fronds with a broadly winged stipe $\frac{1}{2}$–1 inch long, very irregular in outline, more or less deeply pinnatifid nearly down to the midrib; segments again more or less deeply divided, obtuse and rounded at the apex of the lobes; veins erect-patent from a central costa one to each lobe of the segments; spurious venules lineolate, numerous, very short and detached; sori numerous, terminal

at the apex of the lobes, tube almost entirely exserted, only the base being sunk in the margin of the frond, the mouth dilated. *Kuhn, Lin.* 35, *p.* 389. T. pusillum, *Bedd. F. B. I. t.* 302. (*Not of Swartz.*)

Moulmein.

11. TRICHOMANES INTRAMARGINALE. (*Hook and Grev.*) Rhizome slender, creeping, tomentose; stipe short; frond 1–2 inches long, ¼–½ inch broad, tapering below, erect pinnatifid, central portion 1 line broad, segments few, erect, simple, forked or pinnate, subcoriaceous, opaque, the apices retuse, a central costa only in each segment, but the margin thickened; involucres 1–4 to a frond, subcylindric, tapering at the base, sunk entirely in the apex of the segments; receptacles protruding. *Hook. Syn. Fil. p.* 79. *Bedd. F. S. I. t.* 208.

Sivagiri Hills (Tinnevelly district); Malabar plains, foot of the Bhagamandal Ghat, which descends from Coorg; Ceylon, in the Ambagamwa district.

12. TRICHOMANES PALLIDUM. (*Blume.*) Rhizome creeping, slender, tomentose; stipe 1–3 inches long, wiry, slender; fronds 2–6 inches long by 1–1½ inch broad, ovate to lanceolate bipinnatifid, divided down to a narrowly winged rachis, glauco-fuscous when dry, primary divisions broad-lanceolate, the segments all acute-linear, simple or forked; veins broad and few; sori 1–4 to a pinna, superaxillary on short segments partially sunk, short cylindrical, attenuated at the base, the mouth broad-spreading, but scarcely two-lipped. *Blume Hook. Syn. Fil. p.* 80. T. glauco-fuscum, *Hook. Sp. Fil.* 1, *p.* 128. *Bedd. F. S. I. t.* 263.

Ceylon, Ambagamwa district; Penang.

(Also in the Pacific Islands, and the Philippines.)

13. TRICHOMANES BIPUNCTATUM. (*Poir.*) Rhizome wide-creeping, tomentose, rather slender, stipes 1–2 inches long, naked slightly winged above; frond 1–4 inches long, 1½–2 inches broad,

ovate, tripinnatifid, main rachis with a very narrow wing or free below; pinnæ ovate-rhomboidal, pinnatifid down to a narrowly-winged rachis; the lower pinnule again deeply pinnatifid; ultimate segment linear; texture firm, membranaceous; a central costa in each segment, spurious venules none or indistinct; sori 1–4 to a pinna, axillary or terminal on the segments; tube sunk or some what exserted; the mouth very distinctly two-lipped, the lips sub-triangular with a rounded apex. *Poiret in Encyc. Méth. Bot.* viii. 69. Trich. Filicula, *Bory. Hook. Syn. Fil. p.* 81. *Bedd. F. B. I. t.* 283.

Himalayas and Khasya hills, up to 6,000 feet; all the western forests of the Madras and Bombay Presidencies, up to 8,000 feet; Ceylon; Birma.

(Also throughout the tropics of the whole world.)

VAR. β INSIGNE. (*V. D. B.*) A narrower more slender form. *Bedd. F. B. I. t.* 284.

N. W. Himalaya.

VAR. γ PLICATUM. (*V. D. B.*) Ultimate segments of the pinnules very narrow and acute; wing of the rachis somewhat crisped. *Bedd. F. B. I. t.* 285.

Birma.

14. TRICHOMANES PYXIDIFERUM. (*L.*) Rhizome wide-creeping, tomentose, rather slender; stipe 1–2 inches long, naked, winged above; frond 1–6 inches long, 1–1½ inch broad, ovato-oblong, tripinnatifid, main rachis with a very narrow wing; pinnæ ovate-rhomboidal, pinnatifid down to a narrowly-winged rachis, with the lower pinnule again deeply pinnatifid; ultimate segment linear, often emarginate at the apex; texture membranaceous; a central costa in each segment; spurious venules none or indistinct; sori 1–4 to a pinna, axillary, tube more or less winged, mouth broadly dilated but scarcely two-lipped; receptacle filiform, exserted. *Hook. Syn. Fil. p.* 81. *Bedd. F. S. I. t.* 7. *F. B. I. t.* 301. A small variety.

Scarcely distinguishable from No. 13, except by the involucre.

South Indian forests, Ceylon, Birma, Eastern Bengal.
(Also in the tropics throughout the world.)

VAR. β LIMBATUM. Fronds up to 8–10 inches long, by $1\frac{1}{2}$–2 inches broad, flaccid, and larger and less cut than the type. *Bedd. F. B. I. t.* 348.

Khasya Hills, 6,000 feet.

15. TRICHOMANES BIRMANICUM. (*Bedd.*) Rhizome thick, wiry, wide-creeping, tomentose; stipe 1–3 inches long, winged throughout; frond 2–7 inches long up to $2\frac{1}{2}$ inches broad, ovate, rachis winged; pinnæ very compound, very minutely furfuraceous (under the lens), the ultimate segments very narrow, $\frac{1}{4}$ line broad, a single costa to each ultimate segment; sori copious, supra-axillary, much exserted, the mouth truncated. *Bedd. F. B. I. Suppl. t.* 349.

Birma, common on the Mooleyit mountain, 5,000–6,000 feet.

16. TRICHOMANES RADICANS. (*Sw.*) Rhizome wiry, wide-creeping, tomentose; stipe strong, up to 6 inches long, naked or nearly so; fronds up to 12 inches long and 6 inches broad, 3–4-pinnatifid, main rachis naked or winged sometimes to the base of the stipe, lower pinnæ 1–4 inches long, ovate-rhomboidal, ultimate segments oblong, one-nerved, texture firm, membranaceous; sori lateral, 1–4 to a pinnule, the tube small, subcoriaceous, more or less exserted, the mouth slightly lipped or altogether truncated, receptacle slender, elongated. *Swartz, Fl. Ind. Or.* 1736. *Hook. Syn. Fil. p.* 81. *Bedd. F. B. I. t.* 181. T. umbrosum, *Wallich.*

Himalayas from Nepal to Bhotan, 2,000–7,000 feet; common in Khasya, 2,000–5,500 feet; Mergui.

(Also scattered throughout warm, temperate regions of both hemispheres, and known as the Irish fern.)

Mr. Clarke says it often climbs to the height of 10 feet, and is 1–2 pinnate with finely divided fronds, in which state it is very distinct; but it also varies so as to be with difficulty distinguished from pyxidiferum on one hand and auriculatum on the other.

VAR. β ANCEPS. (*Wall.*) Frond smaller; stipe often winged to the base, primary segments pinnatifid or somewhat 2-pinnatifid; lips of the involucre slightly broader than the tube. *Clarke, F. N. I. p.* 441.

Sikkim and Khasya, frequent.

17. TRICHOMANES AURICULATUM. (*Blume.*) Rhizome strong, wide-creeping, tomentose; frond nearly sessile, 1–2-scarcely 3-pinnatifid, 6–12 inches long, 1–2 inches broad, rachis more or less winged, pinnæ shortly stalked, ovate-rhomboidal, obliquely cuneate at the base, irregularly pinnatifid half down or more, ultimate segments ovate entire with flabellate nerves, or narrowly oblong one-nerved, texture subcoriaceous; sori 2–12 to a pinna, the tube nearly or quite exserted, the mouth truncate. *Blume, Fl. Jav. Fil. p.* 225. *Hook. Syn. Fil. p.* 82. *Bedd. F. B. I. t.* 182.

Sikkim, Bhotan, 2,000–7,000 feet, frequent; Khasya, 3,000–5,500 feet, common; Cachar.

(Also in Japan, Formosa, Philippines, Java, and Guiana.)

18. TRICHOMANES JAVANICUM. (*Blume.*) Caudex tufted with strong wiry roots; stipe 1–4 inches long, wiry, erect, naked, or villous; fronds 2–8 inches long, 1–2 inches broad, ovate-lanceolate, acuminate, simply pinnate, pinnæ oblong serrate, or linear fimbriate, texture subcoriaceous; veins numerous, close, central costa not clearly marked or continuous to the apex; sori 1–4, placed in the axils of the linear segments on the upper side of the pinnæ; tube free, the mouth broadly dilated, but not two-lipped, receptacle much exserted. *Bl. En. Pl. Jav. Fil.* 224. *Hook. Syn. Fil. p.* 83. *Bedd. F. B. I. t.* 180.

Chittagong, up to 1,000 feet; Cachar; Malay peninsula.

(Also in Borneo, Java, Polynesian Islands, and Madagascar.)

19. TRICHOMANES RIGIDUM. (*Swartz.*) Stipe tufted, erect, wiry, 2–8 inches long, naked or very slightly winged above; fronds 2–8 inches long, 2–6 inches broad, deltoid or ovate, acuminate, 3–4 pinnatifid, the main rachis usually only slightly winged towards

No. 21.

TRICHOMANES JAVANICUM. (*Bl.*)

the top; lower pinnæ 2–3 inches long, erect-patent, ovate or lanceolate-rhomboidal cut down the rachis; pinnules deeply pinnatifid with deeply toothed or pinnatifid linear lobes, texture subcoriaceous, colour dark green, nearly black when dry, nearly naked, often slightly crisped; sori 2–16 to a pinnule, small axillary, the tube more or less exserted, the mouth slightly dilated. *Hook. Syn. Fil. p.* 86. *Bedd. F. S. I. t.* 8.

Common in the moist forests on the western mountains of the Madras Presidency, 2,000–4,000 feet elevation, and in Ceylon and the Malay Peninsula.

(Also in tropical America and the West Indies, Polynesian Islands, New Zealand, Japan, South China, South Africa, Angola, Fernando Po, and the Mascareen Islands.)

TRIBE IV.—DAVALLIEÆ.

Sori marginal or submarginal, roundish, covered by a reniform or suborbicular, squamiform indusium, which is open at the apex, fastened broadly at the base, open or free at the sides.

GENUS XIV.—HUMATA. (*Cav.*)

(*Humatos*, humid, in opposition to *Adiantum.*)

Sori intra- or sub-marginal, globose, indusium coriaceous suborbicular or reniform, attached by a broad base, the apex and sides free; fronds articulated upon the rhizome, coriaceous, small usually deltoid, more or less dimorphous, the barren ones less cut; veins always free, rhizome creeping, growing on trees or rocks.

1. HUMATA HETEROPHYLLA. (*Smith.*) Rhizome wide-creeping, scaly; frond shortly stalked, 3–6 inches long, 1 inch broad, glabrous; the sterile ones ovate-lanceolate entire or slightly lobed at the base, the fertile ones narrower, deeply sinuate-pinnatifid; sori 2–10 to a lobe. *Hook. Syn. Fil.* 88. *Bedd. F. B. I. t.* 100.

Singapore, Penang, and the Malay Peninsula.

(Also in the Polynesian Islands.)

2. HUMATA ANGUSTATA. (*Wall.*) Rhizome wide-creeping, scaly; fronds subsessile or shortly stalked, 3–8 inches long, $\frac{1}{4}$–$\frac{5}{8}$ inch broad, linear, slightly and irregularly crenate at the margin, rarely once forked; both surfaces naked; veins parallel, simple or forked thickened; sori in a row along the edges, indusium small, transversely oval. *Hook. Syn. Fil. p.* 88. *Bedd. F. B. I. t.* 237.

The Malay Peninsula, Malacca, &c.
(Also in the Malay Islands.)

3. HUMATA PARALLELA. (*Wall.*) Caudex creeping, paleaceous; fronds, 4–8 inches long, $1\frac{1}{2}$–2 inches broad, stipitate, coriaceous, ovate-lanceolate, acuminate, deeply pinnatifid nearly to the rachis; segments close, parallel, horizontally patent, linear or linear-oblong subfalcate entire, the lowermost pair sometimes with a solitary obtuse lobe at the base beneath, rarely more; involucres semiorbicular copious marginal, but all pointing towards the apex of the segments in two close parallel lines (not pointing towards the margins); veins thickened sunk. *Hook. Syn. Fil.* 89. *Bedd. F. B. I. t.* 99.

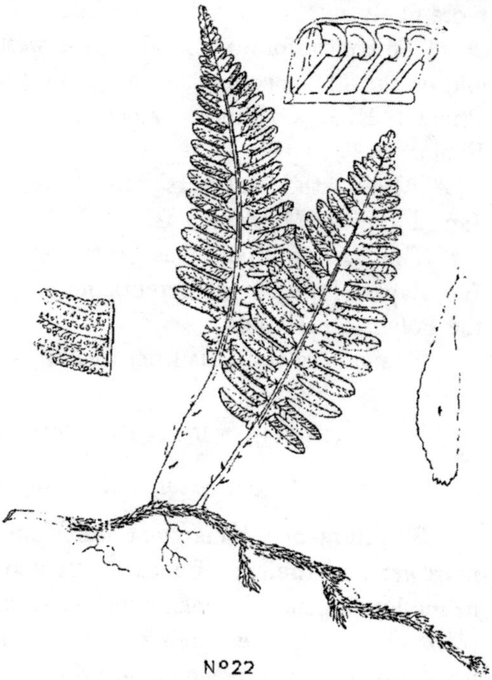

N°22
HUMATA PARALLELA. (*Wall.*)

Birma and the Malay Peninsula.
(Also in the Polynesian Islands.)

4. HUMATA PEDATA. (*Smith.*) Rhizome creeping, scaly; stipe 2–4 inches long, fronds 2–8 long, by 1½–4 inches broad, deltoid in outline, cut down nearly or quite to the rachis, the lower pair of segments or pinnules larger than the others, and more compound, deeply pinnatifid, with the segments crenated, or more or less pinnatifid; sori in rows on the teeth on both sides of the lobes. *Smith, Tentam Gen. Fil.* 15. *Hook. Syn. Fil. p.* 89. *Bedd. F. S. I. t.* 12. H. alpina, *Blume*, is a smaller, more finely cut variety, which is found in the Himalayas as well as Mergui. H. vestita (Bl.), *Bedd. F. S. I. t.* 253, has a longer stipe, is more lanceolate in shape, and more finely cut, but is said to run into typical "pedata."

The typical form is found on the western slopes of the Nilgiris, and on the Travancore Ghats, at 3,000–4,000 feet elevation; Sikkim, Bhotan, Khasya, Jaintea, 4,000 feet; Ceylon; and the Malay Peninsula.

(Also in the Malay Islands, North Australia, South China, in Japan, and the Mascareen Islands.)

The variety alpina has been received from the north west Himalayas (Dyas), and Mergui, and also inhabits Java, Azores, and the Polynesian Islands.

The variety vestita is from Ceylon, and also occurs in Java.

GENUS XV.—LEUCOSTEGIA. (*Presl.*)

(From *leucos*, white; *stegos*, a cover.)

Sori intra- or sub-marginal, indusium as in Humata, but smaller, narrower and thinner; fronds articulated upon the rhizome (except in nodosa), generally membranaceous and flaccid, generally 3–4-pinnatifid or pinnate, rarely only bipinnatifid; veins forked, venules free; rhizome long, creeping, growing generally on trees and rocks.

1. LEUCOSTEGIA HYMENOPHYLLA (*Parish MS.*) Caudex creeping, furnished with numerous long wiry roots, stipe slender, 3–4 inches long; fronds subglabrous, membranaceous, very flaccid and transparent, ovate, or deltoid-ovate pinnate; lower pinnæ deeply pinnatifid with the lower basal segments much the largest, and again

Nº 23.

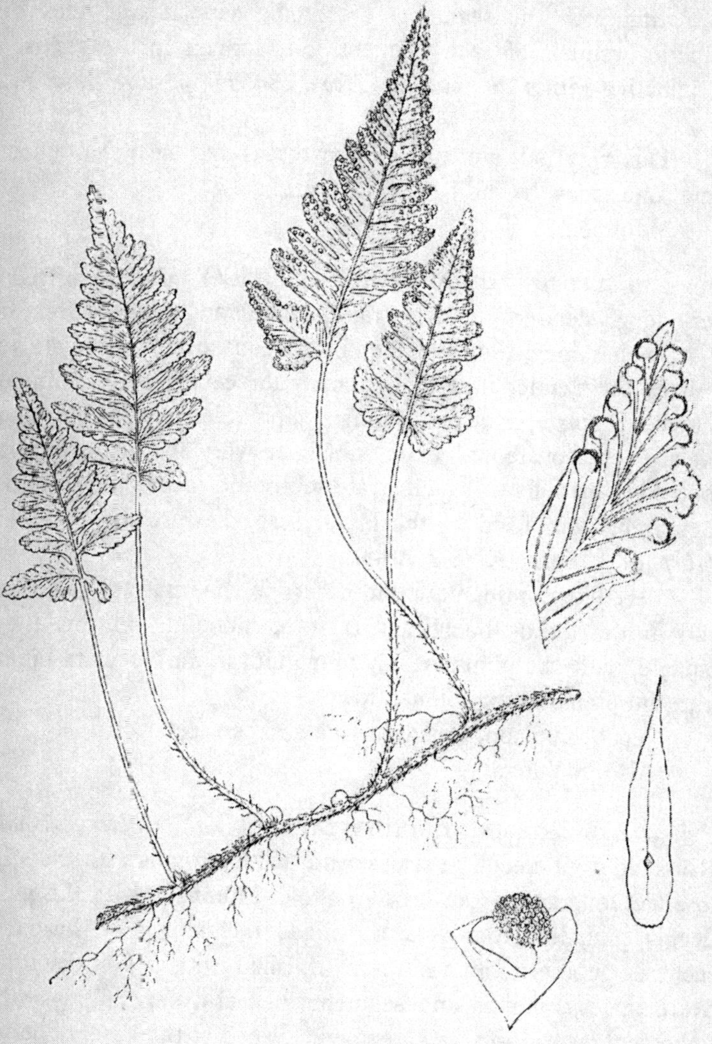

A.S. CATTELL & Co ENGRAS.

HUMATA PEDATA. (*Sm.*)

pinnatifid with the segments entire or crenated, the remaining pinnæ pinnatifid with the segments crenated; sori at the apex of the superior veinlets of each segment, indusium as in the genus, veins terminating within the margin. *Hook. Syn. Fil. p.* 90. *Bedd. F. B. I. t.* 96.

This very delicate species was discovered near Moulmein, on limestone rocks, by the Rev. C. S. Parish.

Moulmein.

2. LEUCOSTEGIA MEMBRANULOSA. (*Wall.*) Caudex hispid, with very long, slender, subulate, rigid, membranaceous scales; fronds 9–15 inches long, thin and membranaceous ovate-lanceolate and as well as the slender stipe and rachis pubescent-hirsute, bipinnatifid; pinnæ lanceolate, their rachis winged; pinnules lanceolate pinnatifid, the segments ovate-lanceolate subfalcate, very acute entire or rarely toothed; involucres small, ovate-subrotund acute, very thin and membranaceous fixed by the broad base, the rest free. *Hook. Syn. Fil. p.* 91. *Bedd. F. B. I. t.* 98.

Very like multidentata, but differs in the scales of the rhizome, and in the fronds being much less compound; in this they are pinnate, with the pinnæ deeply pinnatifid, in multidentata bipinnate, with the pinnæ deeply pinnatifid.

Nepal, Kumaon, Moharguri Pass, 6,500 feet.

(Also in Yunan.)

3. LEUCOSTEGIA MULTIDENTATA. (*Wall. under Aspidium.*) Rhizome stout-creeping; scales ovate-acute; fronds with the stipe up to 2 feet long and 1 foot broad, deltoid, bipinnate, with the pinnules deeply pinnatifid, down to a winged rachis, texture herbaceous; rachises pubescent above, often furnished with a few distant large ovate scales, rachises and segments beneath, generally glandularly pubescent; sori 2–12 to a segment, placed at the base of its teeth, on the upper side of the central vein. *Wall. Cat.* 346. Microlepia pteropus. *Bedd. F. B. I. t.* 313. *Hook. Syn. Fil. p.* 91.

Himalayas, Nepal and Bhotan, 5,000–8,000 feet; Khasya, 4,000–5,000 feet, common.

4. LEUCOSTEGIA ASSAMICA. (*Bedd. under Acrophorus.*) Rhizome creeping, covered with numerous imbricated chaffy golden, ovate-acute scales; fronds glabrous, shining, 8–14 inches long (including the stipe, which is 2–3 inches), 2–3 inches broad, subcoriaceous lanceolate, pinnate with the primary pinnæ alternate or opposite, pinnatifid almost to the rachis, lower ones petiolate, upper ones decurrent so as to form a regular wing to the rachis, pinnules pinnatifid, segments toothed, each bearing one sorus, veins terminating within the margin; involucres as in the genus, as broad as deep. *Bedd. F. B. I. t.* 94. *Hook. Sp. Fil. p.* 467.

Bhotan, Mishmee, and by the Dihong.

No. 24.

LEUCOSTEGIA ASSAMICA. (*Bedd.*)

5. LEUCOSTEGIA IMMERSA. (*Wall.*) Rhizome creeping stout, fibrillose; stipe 4–8 inches long, strong, erect; fronds 12–18 inches long, 6–9 inches broad, deltoid, tripinnate, glabrous; lowest pinnule lanceolate and deltoid, 2–3 inches long, 1 inch broad, with broad segments, which are obliquely truncate at the base below, and roundly lobed with the lobes again crenate above; texture herbaceous; sori large, impressed, clearly visible from the upper side, 1–6 to a segment, oblique; involucre broader than long. *Hook. Syn. Fil. p.* 91. *Bedd. F. S. I. t.* 11.

Madras Presidency on the Western mountains; very abundant in Coorg, growing on trees. Himalayas, from Mussorrie to Bhotan, 3,000–6,000 feet. Sikkim, Khasya, Parasnath, and the Malay Peninsula.

(Also in Java.)

6. LEUCOSTEGIA HOOKERI. (*Moore, under Acrophorus.*) Rhizome stout; scales dense, lanceolate, golden; stipe up to 6 inches long slender often scaly at the base; fronds deltoid up to 10 inches long, 3–4 pinnatifid; lower pinnæ opposite or alternate, lanceolate or deltoid, 1–2 inches broad; pinnules deltoid, ultimate segments ligulate, acute, 1-veined, ½–1 line broad texture; membranaceous; sori at the base of the ultimate lobes; involucre persistent, membranaceous, broader than long. Davallia Clarkii, *Baker. Syn. Fil. p.* 91.

Himalayas, Lachen, and Sirmur, 8,000–12,000 feet elevation. Sundukphoo, near Darjeeling, 11,000 feet.

Very like Polypodium dareæforme, Hook., but with acute segments, and differing somewhat in the scales of the rhizome. Indian botanists, not having seen this plant, have quoted Hookeri of Moore (Clarkii of Baker) as a synonym of dareæforme, and united the two under the name of Leucostegia dareæformis. Mr. Levinge has lately gathered this species at Sundukphoo, but the Kew specimens from Lachen and Sirmur were gathered by Thomson in 1849. I have examined a great many specimens of dareæforme in the Kew Herbarium, and can find no trace of an indusium, so I retain it in Polypodium; but it is very likely that there is a fugacious indusium, and that it is a Leucostegia nearly allied to this species.

7. LEUCOSTEGIA PULCHRA. (*Don. under Davallia.*) Rhizome wide-creeping, clothed with broad-obtuse, often peltately attached scales; stipe 4–6 inches long, naked; fronds 9–15 inches long, 4–8 inches broad, lanceolate-deltoid, 3–4 pinnatifid, lowest pinnule 1–2 inches long, 1 inch broad, cut down to a narrowly-winged rachis into deeply pinnatifid segments, ultimate lobes narrow lanceolate, not distant, not very acute; texture thin, rather flaccid; sori copious, usually as broad as the segment at the base of the teeth of which it is placed; involucre prominent. *Don. Prod. Fl. Nep.* 11. *Bedd. F. S. I. t.* 10 (under Acrophorus).

Madras Presidency, Western mountains, very common on rocks and trees; Ceylon, central provinces, 3,000–5,000 feet; Himalayas, Nepal, and Bhotan, 2,000–9,000 feet; Khasya; Moulmein.

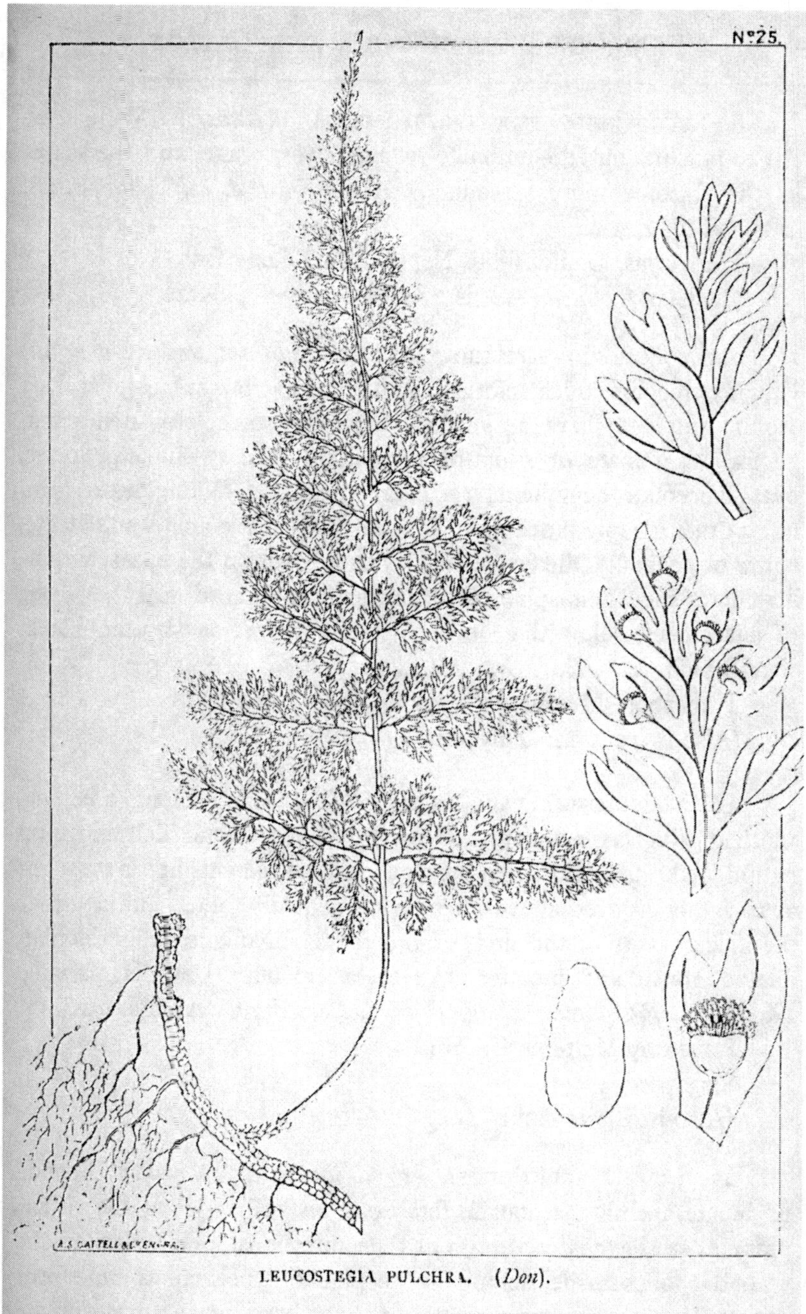

LEUCOSTEGIA PULCHRA. (*Don*).

8. LEUCOSTEGIA PSEUDO-CYSTOPTERIS. (*Kunze.*) Very similar to pulchra, but the ultimate segments very acute, and the scales of the rhizome more spreading. *Kunze in Bot. Zeit.* 1850, *p.* 68. *Bedd. F. B. I. t.* 92.

Himalayas, Dalhousie to Nepal, 4,000–8,000 feet.

Mr. Clarke considers it is a variety only of pulchra.

9. LEUCOSTEGIA HYMENOPHYLLOIDES. (*Blume, under Davallia.*) Caudex creeping, thick, clothed with long narrow subulate scales; fronds ample, tall, 12–24 inches long, ovate-lanceolate, membranaceous, 3–4 pinnate or supra-decompound; primary pinnæ petiolate, ovate-lanceolate acuminate, secondary petiolate oblong-ovate; pinnules ovate, deeply pinnatifid; the segments ovate acute, subfalcate, entire or generally (the fertile ones) with a tooth on the inner margin; involucres small hemispherical or subreniform, placed near the centre of a segment below the sinus of the tooth; veins slender, black. Davallia affinis. *Hook. Syn. Fil. p.* 92. *Bedd. F. S. I. t.* 252.

Travancore Mountains, Ceylon, 3,000–4,000 feet.

(Also in Java and Polynesia.)

10. LEUCOSTEGIA PARVULA. (*Wallich.*) Caudex long, creeping, clothed with lax subulate scales; frond very small deltoid-tripinnatifid, glabrous, rigid (from the stout costa), segments linear throughout, slightly grooved above when dry, unequally forked and acute at the apices; sori at the sinus of the forks; involucres suborbicular, dilated above, and broader than the segments. Davallia parvula, *Hook. Syn. Fil. p.* 92. *Bedd. F. B. I. t.* 97 (under Acrophorus).

Placed by Mettenius in Humata.

Singapore.

(Also in Borneo and Java.)

11. LEUCOSTEGIA NODOSA (*Presl. under Acrophorus.*) Fronds tripinnate, membranaceous furfuraceous on both sides of the veins; pinnules sessile (chaffy beneath at their insertions), oblong-lanceolate, secondary ones sessile, oblong obtuse, pinnatifid; segments cuneiform obtuse, lowest ones inciso-serrate or at the base again sub auriculate

No 26.

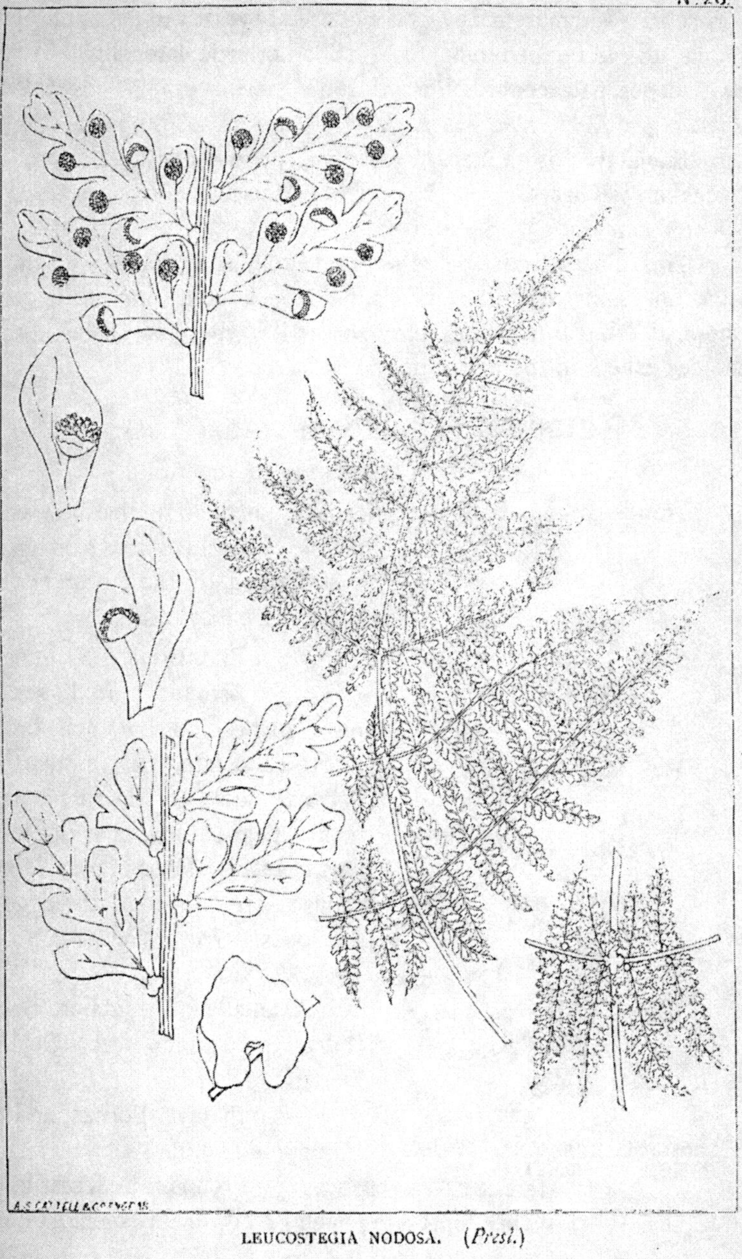

LEUCOSTEGIA NODOSA. (*Presl.*)

sori solitary submarginal; rachis nodose above at the insertion of the pinnæ and ferrugineo-tomentose; stipe not articulate, slightly rough or glabrous, paleaceous below; rhizome short-creeping. *Presl. Tent. Pter. t.* 3. *Hook. Syn. Fil. p.* 92. *Bedd. F. B. I. t.* 93.

Himalayas, from Nepal to Bhotan, 3,000–7,000 feet, abundant in Sikkim; Khasya, 3,000–6,000 feet; Malacca.

(Also in Java.)

This differs from the other Leucostegias in habit, and in the stipe not being articulate, and should be kept distinct as a genus under its original name of Acrophorus; it is very like Diacalpe aspidioides except in the indusium.

GENUS XVI.—PROSAPTIA. (*Presl.*)

(Sori immersed in the margin of the frond.)

Fronds contiguous, linear-lanceolate, pectinate-pinnatifid; veins simple, free; involucre a marginal cyst formed of the substance of the frond subcylindric.

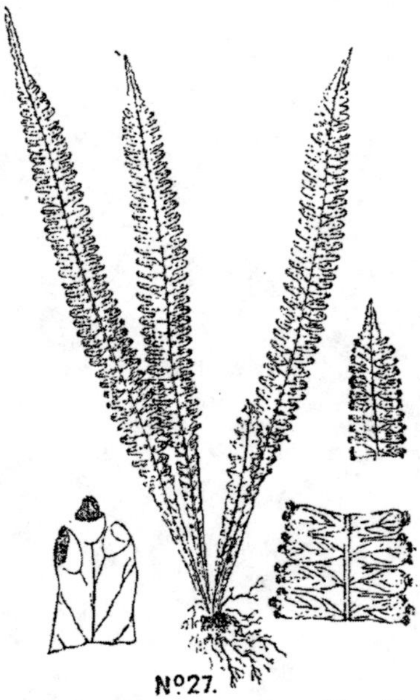

No. 27.
PROSAPTIA EMERSONI. (*Presl.*)

1. PROSAPTIA EMERSONI. (*Presl.*) Fronds tufted, sessile, 6–12 inches long, 1 inch broad, linear-lanceolate, cut more than half-way down to the rachis into many linear-oblong, or at the lower part triangular lobes; texture coriaceous; sori 1–6 round the edge of the lobes. *Hook. Syn. Fil. p.* 94. *Bedd. F. S. I. t.* 20.

Anamallay Mountains, South India, 3,000–4,000 feet; Ceylon; Penang.

(Also in Java, Borneo, and the Philippine Islands.)

2. PROSAPTIA CONTIGUA. (*Swartz.*) Fronds tufted, sessile, or nearly so, 12–18 inches long, 1–1½ inch broad, linear-lanceolate, cut

N° 28.

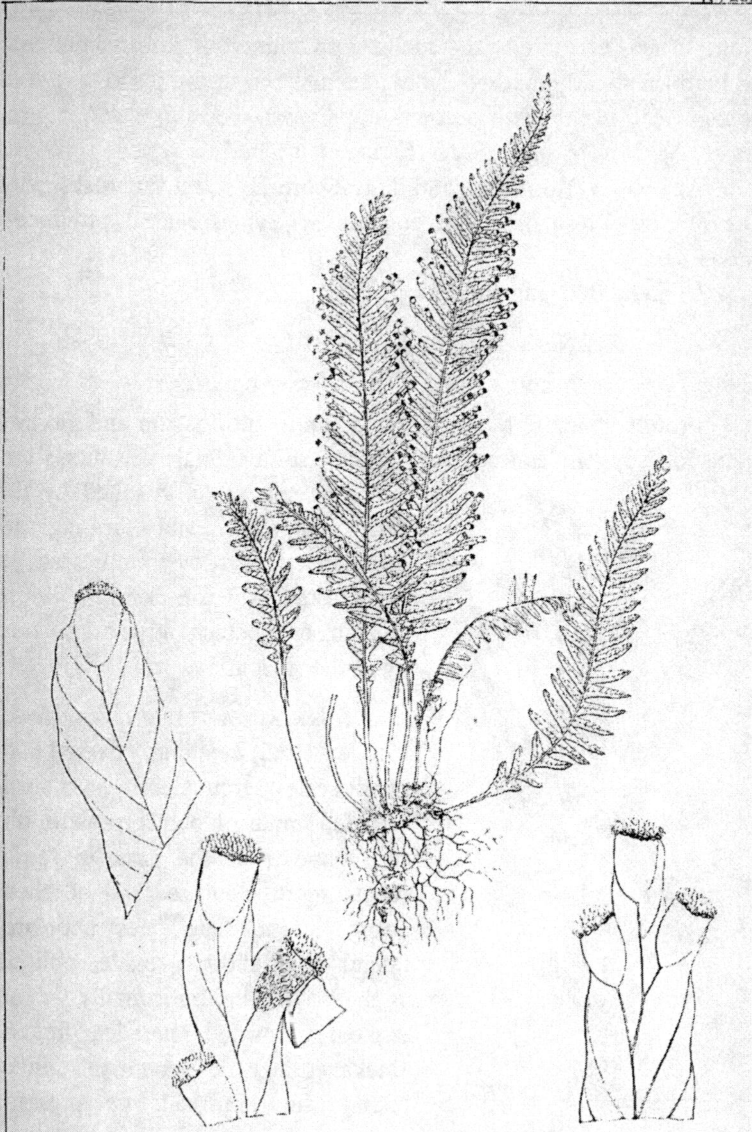

PROSAPTIA CONTIGUA. (*Sw*)

down nearly or quite to the rachis into numerous linear-acuminate or bluntish slightly-toothed lobes; texture coriaceous; sori 2–8 to a lobe, placed in the teeth on their upper part. *Sw. Syn. Fil. p.* 130. *Hook. Syn. Fil. p.* 94. *Bedd. F. S. I. t.* 19.

Anamallay Mountains and Travancore Hills, on the west side of the Madras Presidency, not common; Ceylon, central provinces, 5,000 feet.

(Also in Java and the Philippines.)

GENUS XVII.—DAVALLIA. (*Smith.*)

(In honour of Davall, a Swiss botanist.)

Fronds pinnate, bipinnate, or deltoid-multifid, firm and glossy; veins forked, venules free; sori intra- or submarginal; involucres terminal on the veins, attached by the base and sides, and forming an urceolate tabular cyst impressed in the substance of the frond; rhizome creeping or suberect; stipe articulated upon the rhizome.

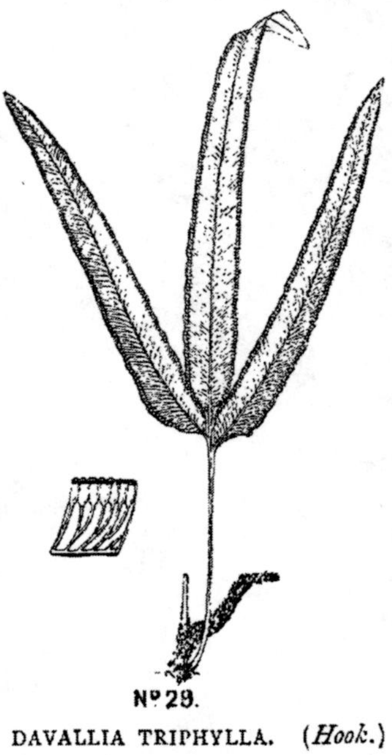

Nº 29.

DAVALLIA TRIPHYLLA. (*Hook.*)

1. DAVALLIA TRIPHYLLA. (*Hook.*) Caudex stout, creeping, covered with chaffy scales; fronds coriaceous small ternate, pinnæ oblong-lanceolate, obtuse cuneate at the base, in fertile plants more elongated, all of them entire, intermediate ones petiolate, lateral ones shorter, sessile, oblique at the base, veins horizontally patent, copious, crowded, parallel, forked, thickened, flat (not prominent); involucres semicylindrical, compressed, crowded so as to form an uninterrupted marginal line the whole length of the pinnæ. *Hook. Sp. Fil.* i. 162, and *Syn. Fil. p.* 94. *Bedd. F. B. I. t.* 105.

Singapore.

2. DAVALLIA SOLIDA. (*Swartz.*) Tall, caudex stout, creeping, clothed with densely imbricated scales, fronds coriaceous trisub-quadripinnate, pinnæ acuminate; pinnules trapeziform acuminate, pinnatifid, many-veined, terminal ones crenate-serrate coadunate into an acuminated point; involucres linear-oblong, sunk in a tooth or segment having a narrow wing on each side or entire. *Hook. Sp. Fil.* i. 163. *Sw. Syn. Fil. pp.* 132 *and* 345. *Hook. Syn. Fil. p.* 95. *Bedd. F. B. I. t.* 104. The width of the pinnules and the amount of cutting differ considerably. Davallia ornata (*Wall.*) is a variety with the pinnules very wide.

Birma; Penang; and Singapore.

(Also in Java and the Polynesian Islands.)

N° 30.
DAVALLIA SOLIDA. (*Sw.*)

3. DAVALLIA ELEGANS. (*Sw.*) Rhizome stout, creeping, clothed with woolly fibres; stipe firm, erect, 4–8 inches long; fronds 1–2 feet long, 9–15 inches broad, deltoid-tripinnatifid; main rachis slightly winged towards the apex; pinnules of the lower pinnæ 2–3 inches long, 1 inch wide, deltoid-lanceolate, cut down quite to the rachis in the lower part, with oblong-deltoid segments, which are slightly toothed and obliquely truncate at the base on the lower side; texture coriaceous; venation close, prominent, irregular, many spurious venules between the veins proper; sori several to a segment, marginal, but the sharp teeth projecting beyond them at the edges; involucre half cup-shaped. *Hook. Syn. Fil. p.* 95. *Bedd. F. S. I. t.* 18.

Western mountains of Madras; Ceylon, 2,000–3,000 feet elevation; Malay Peninsula.

(Also in China, Java, Borneo, Tropical Australia, Polynesian Islands, Madagascar, Angola, Fernando Po, and Johanna Island.)

4. DAVALLIA EPIPHYLLA. (*Blume.*) Rhizome thick, fibrillose; stipe 4–6 inches long, erect, firm; fronds 12–15 inches long, 6–9 inches broad, deltoid-lanceolate, tripinnatifid; main rachis hardly at all winged; pinnules of the lowest pinnæ lanceolate, 1½ inch long, ½ inch broad; segments narrow, mucronate, sharply toothed; texture coriaceous; veins not immersed, one or two carried into each tooth; sori small, submarginal, half cup shaped, with the sharp mucro of the tooth extending beyond them. *Hook. Syn. Fil. p.* 96. *Bedd. Suppl. to Ferns, t.* 350.

Malay Peninsula.

(Also in Java.)

5. DAVALLIA DIVARICATA (*Blume.*) Rhizome creeping, clothed with long lanceolate-caudate chestnut scales; stipe firm, erect, 6–12 inches long; fronds 2–3 feet long, tripinnatifid; lower pinnæ often 12 inches long by 6 inches broad; segments deltoid, cut down to the rachis in the lower part, with linear-oblong, sharply-toothed lobes; texture coriaceous; veins uniform, not conspicuous; sori half cup-shaped, placed obliquely as regards the central veins in the teeth at some distance from the edge; involucres as long as broad. *Hook. Syn. Fil. p.* 96. D. polyantha (Hook), *Bedd. F. B. I. t.* 107.

Sikkim, Mishmee, Khasya; Malay Peninsula.

(Also in South China and Java.)

6. DAVALLIA GRIFFITHIANA. (*Hook.*) Rhizome creeping, stout, clothed with long lanceolate-caudate white or yellowish scales; stipe erect, wiry, 4–6 inches long; fronds 9–12 inches long, 4–8 inches broad, deltoid 3–4-pinnatifid; pinnules of the lower pinnæ lanceolate-deltoid, 2–3 inches long, 1 inch or more broad; lower segments toothed on the barren fronds, cut down nearly to the rachis in the fertile; texture coriaceous; sori large, submarginal or marginal; involucres cup-shaped, very shortly attached on the sides. *Hook. Syn. Fil. p.* 96.

Bedd. F. B. I. t. 106. The texture and habit of Davallia, but the indusium is nearer that of Leucostegia.

Bhotan and Mishmee, Khasya and Jaintea, 3,000–5,000 feet. (Also in South China.)

7. DAVALLIA LORRAINEI. (*Hance.*) Rhizome thick as a quill; scales linear-subulate, nearly black, densely grey ciliated; stipe 3–4 inches long, naked brownish; fronds ½–1 foot long, deltoid, 4-pinnatifid; pinnæ stalked deltoid, lowest largest produced on the lower side, their rachises winged to base; pinnules and segments subsessile, crowded deltoid much reduced on lower side; final lobes ligulate, ¼–⅓ lines broad, with sorus at base of inner side; texture subcoriaceous; surfaces naked; barren lobes 1-veined; involucre subcylindrical, ½ line long. *Hance. Ann. Sc. Nat. Ser. V. vol.* v. *p.* 254. *Hook. Syn. Fil. p.* 469. *Bedd. F. B. I. Suppt. p.* 4. *t.* 351.

Malay Peninsula.

8. DAVALLIA BULLATA. (*Wall.*) Rhizome creeping, stout, densely clothed with hair-pointed chestnut scales; stipe strong, erect, 3–4 inches long; fronds 8–12 inches long, 4–8 inches broad, deltoid, 4-pinnatifid; pinnules of the lower pinnæ lanceolate, 2–3 inches long, 1 inch broad, with deeply inciso-pinnatifid oblong rhomboidal segments; texture coriaceous; sori deeply half cup-shaped, occupying the greater part of the tooth in which they are placed, marginal, with usually a horn on the outside. *Hook. Syn. Fil.* 97. *Bedd. F. S. I. t.* 17.

All the Western Ghats of Madras and Bombay Presidencies; Himalayas, Nepal to Bhotan, 2,000–6,000 feet; Khasya; Ceylon; Birma, and Malay Peninsula.

(Also in Japan, South China, and the Malay Islands.)

9. DAVALLIA SPECIOSA. (*Mett.*) Rhizome wide-creeping, 2 lines thick, scales ferruginous dense linear-subulate; stipe 3–5 inches, naked, brown, stramineous; frond deltoid, 4-pinnatifid, 1–1¼ foot long; rachis winged in upper half, pinnæ lanceolate-deltoid, long-stalked, lowest largest 3–4 inches broad; pinnules and segments

deltoid, with rachises winged to base, cuneate-truncate on lower side, final lobes lanceolate-falcate under 1 line broad, with sorus on upper side at base; texture subcoriaceous; surfaces naked; involucre cup-shaped, broader than deep, ½ line broad, oblique, close to final sinuses. *Hook. Syn. Fil.* 469. *Bedd. F. B. I. Suppt. t.* 352.

Moulmein.

GENUS XVIII.—MICROLEPIA. (*Presl.*)

(*Micros*, small; *lepis*, a scale, the small indusium.)

Fronds pinnate or variously compound; texture various; veins simple or pinnately forked; venules free; sori intra- or sub-marginal; involucre membranaceous, half cup-shaped, attached at the sides as well as the base; rhizome creeping; stipe continuous with the caudex.

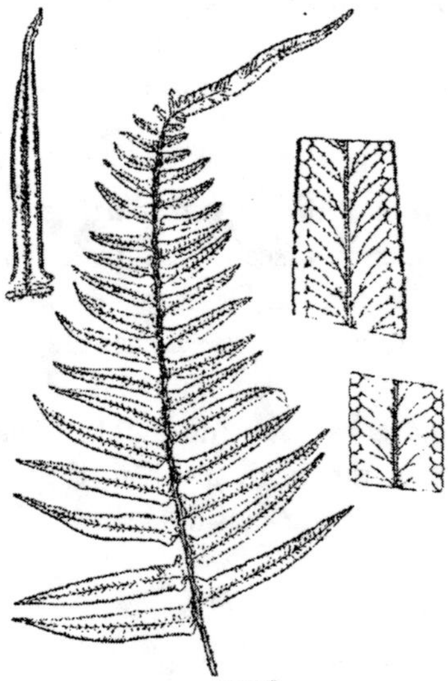

No 32

MICROLEPIA HOOKERIANA (*Wall.*)

1. MICROLEPIA HOOKERIANA. (*Wall.*) Stipe a foot and more long, pubescent, at length glabrous; rachis hirsute-pubescent; fronds lanceolate pinnate; pinnæ subpetiolate lanceolate from a broad hastate base, gradually acuminated submembranaceous, duplicate-crenated, sparingly hairy on the costa and veins beneath; veins parallel, dichotomous; sori approximate, forming a continued line at the base of the crenatures of the margin; involucres half cup-shaped; stipes and rachis pubescent-hirsute. *Hook. Syn. Fil. p.* 97. *Bedd. F. B. I. t.* 101.

Sylhet, Upper Assam, Khasya and Mikir Hills.

(Also in Hong Kong.)

N°31.

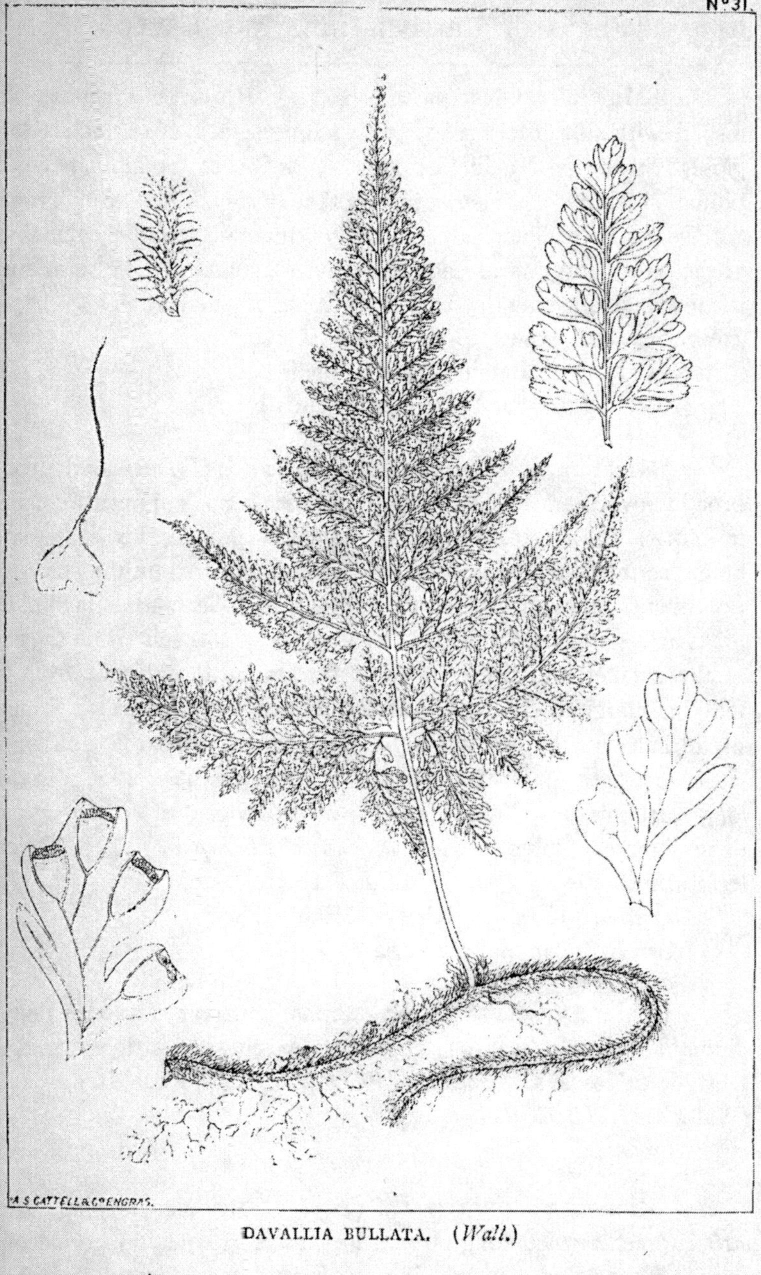

DAVALLIA BULLATA. (*Wall.*)

2. MICROLEPIA PINNATA. (*Cav.*) Rhizome creeping, furnished with fibrillose scales; stipe strong, erect, 6–12 inches long, glossy; fronds 9–15 inches long, 4–8 inches broad, lanceolate-pinnate, glabrous; pinnæ slightly toothed, 6 inches long, ¼ inch broad, coriaceous, linear-lanceolate, gradually acuminate, obliquely acuminate at the base; sori one to each tooth, small, submarginal; veins sunk, inconspicuous, generally forked; involucres small, half-cup-shaped. *Hook. Syn. Fil. p.* 98. *Bedd. F. S. I. t.* 14.

Anamallay Mountains; Malay Peninsula.

(Also in Java and Polynesian Islands.)

3. MICROLEPIA MARGINALIS. (*Thunb. under Polypodium.*) Fronds broadly ovate-lanceolate, firm, membranaceous; pinnæ elongate, lanceolate, subfalcate, acuminate, pinnatifid-lobate, the acuminated apices serrated, pubescent-villous beneath, most so on the costa and prominent veins, unequally cuneate at the base, and subpetiolate; lobes acute crenate-dentate; veins pinnated; sori solitary in the axils of the smaller and upper lobes or serratures, and distant from the margin, marginal on the small teeth of the larger lobes; involucres broad half-cup-shaped, densely villous; rachis and stipe downy, the latter at length glabrous; rhizome creeping, villous; stipe 1–2 feet long, erect, strong; fronds 18–24 inches long, 9–15 inches broad, once pinnate. Polyp. marginale, *Thunb. Fl. Japan, p.* 337. Microlepia scabra, *Don. Bedd. F. B. I. t.* 102.

Nepal and Kumaon, Khasya, Mikir Hills.

(Also in Japan and Formosa.)

VAR. β CALVESCENS. (*Hook.*) Pinnæ narrower and more deeply pinnatifid, nearly glabrous beneath, except the strigose midrib. Davallia calvescens. *Hook. Sp. Fil. I. p.* 172, *t.* 48 B. D. urophylla (Wallich), *Bedd. F. B. I. t.* 103.

Kumaon.

4. MICROLEPIA UROPHYLLA. (*Hook.*) Rhizome creeping; stipe strong, erect, 2–3 feet long; fronds bipinnate, tripinnatifid, coriaceous, shining above and beneath, but pubescent on the rachises below;

N° 33.

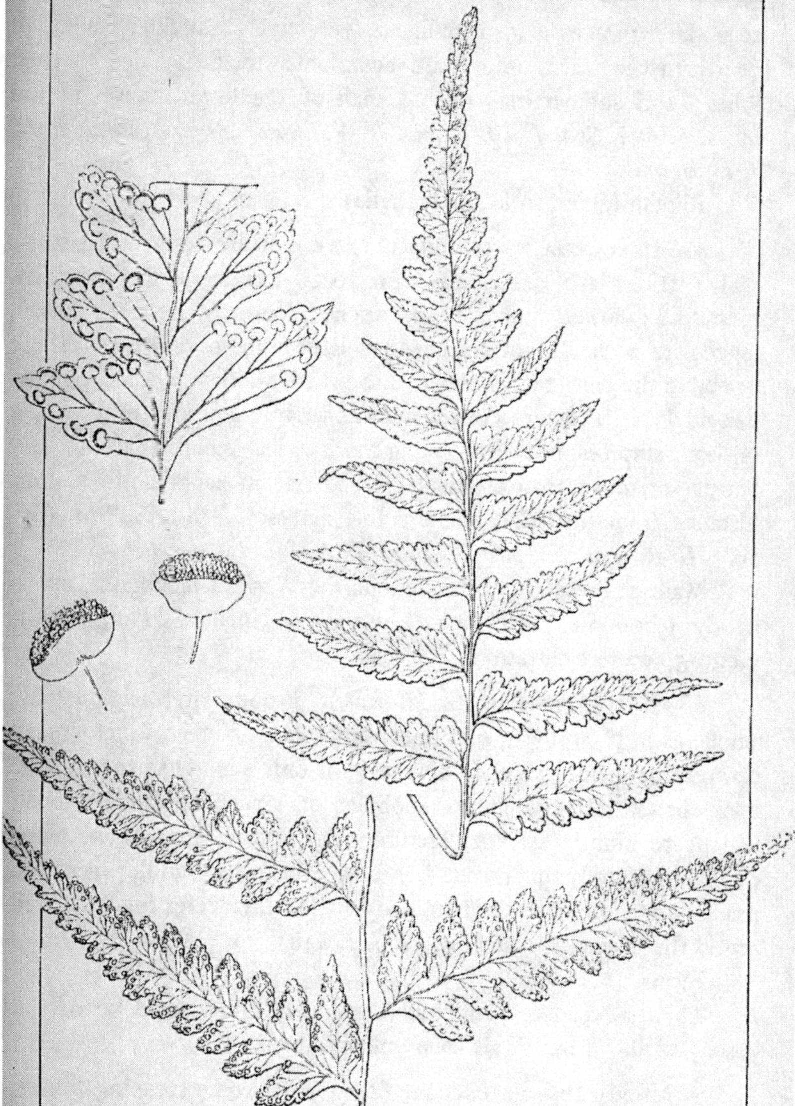

A. S. CATTELL & C° ENG.

MICROLEPIA PLATYPHYLLA. (*Don.*)

secondary pinnæ lanceolate-linear, very finely caudate, cut down nearly to the rachis into ovate acuminate, unequal sided toothed lobes; sori submarginal, one to each of the lower sinuses of the lobes. *Hook. Syn. Fil. p.* 99, *not of Wallich or Bedd. Clarke, F. N. I. t.* 50.

Bhotan (allied to M. platyphylla).

5. MICROLEPIA PLATYPHYLLA. (*Don.*) Rhizome creeping, stout, scaly; stipes 2–3 feet long, firm erect; frond 3–4 feet long, tripinnatifid; lower pinnæ 12–15 inches long, 6–9 inches broad, lanceolate with distant linear-lanceolate pinnules, which are cut nearly to the wavy rachis below, into broad, bluntish toothed, oblong-deltoid lobes; texture coriaceous when adult, glabrous and shining on both surfaces, but when young more or less membranaceous and hairy; sori 2–12 to a segment, placed one in each tooth, a short distance from the edge, about a line across. *Don. Fl. Prod. Nep.* 10. *Hook. Syn. Fil. p.* 99. *Bedd. F. S. I. t.* 13.

Madras Presidency, throughout the Western mountains, up to nearly 6,000 feet; Ceylon; Himalaya's, Nepal, Sikkim, Bhotan 3,000–5,500 feet elevation; Khasya.

6. MICROLEPIA KURZII. (*Clarke.*) Fronds large tripinnatifid; pinnæ as in platyphylla, with linear-lanceolate pinnules, which are cut down to its rachis (which is not wavy, or only slightly so towards the apex) below into triangular subobtuse or lanceolate-caudate lobes, which are bluntly serrate; texture not so coriaceous as in platyphylla, uniformly pubescent beneath, even when adult; venation much less prominent than in platyphylla; involucres finely ciliated round the margin. *Clarke F. N. I. p.* 446.

Birma.

This is very like platyphylla, and may turn out to be only a variety of it. I have only seen one specimen.

7. MICROLEPIA MAJUSCULA. (*Lowe.*) Rhizome creeping, tomentose; stipe 6–12 inches long, erect naked; fronds up to 3 feet long lanceolate-deltoid, tripinnatifid; lower pinnæ 9–12 inches long, 3–4 inches broad, lanceolate; pinnules lanceolate acuminate, cut down

nearly or quite to the rachis into blunt slightly crenated oblong lobes, rachis and both surfaces slightly hairy, the upper bright green, shining; texture subcoriaceous; sori small submarginal, 2–12 to a segment. *Hook. Syn. Fil. p.* 99. Microlepia proxima (Thw.), *Bedd. F. S. I. t.* 254.

Ceylon, Rangbodde, 3,500 feet elevation.

8. MICROLEPIA STRIGOSA. (*Swartz.*) Fronds tall, lanceolate, bipinnate; stipes elongated; rachis and veins pubescent-hispid, primary pinnæ petiolate, lanceolate-acuminate, secondary (or pinnules) mostly petiolate, subdimidiate-ovate, obtuse pinnatifid, chiefly on the upper edge, lower lobes obovate deep, the rest short, all of them angulate-dentate, veins pinnated, furnished with a few long scattered hairs both above and beneath (the remaining surface of the frond beneath being sometimes furnished with numerous small hairs, or sometimes glabrous as is the upper surface); involucres hairy, small, half cup-shaped. *Hook. Syn. Fil. p.* 98. *Bedd. F. S. I. t.* 255.

Tinnevelly and Travancore Mountains, South India; Ceylon; Himalayas; and Malay Peninsula.

(Also in Japan, South China, Sandwich and Fiji Islands.)

Mr. Clarke considers this a variety, or rather only a young state of speluncæ, as he states it develops into this more compound form; as far as the South Indian and Ceylon forms are concerned, this is never more than bipinnate, whereas speluncœ is 3–4 pinnate; it has been for years in cultivation in ferneries, at Ootacamund, and is quite constant.

9. MICROLEPIA SPELUNCÆ. (*Linn.*) Rhizome creeping; stipes strong, 1–1½ foot long; fronds up to 6 feet long, rarely more, and 2 feet broad, ovate to deltoid, 3–4-pinnatifid, more or less hairy, strigose or villous, or with few or many long glistening scale-like flaccid hairs, rarely sub-glabrous; texture membranaceous, or flaccid, pinnules from oblong or ovate to linear-lanceolate, ultimate segments entire or subentire and rhomboid, or irregularly inciso-obate or pinnatifid; sori large 1–5 to the entire segments, more copious on the lobed segments; involucre half cup-shaped, hispid or rarely glabrous; veins more or less prominent beneath. Polypodium speluncæ, *Lin. Sp. Pl.* 1555.

The Himalayas from Kumaon eastwards; Khasya; Chittagong; Madras, Western mountains; Ceylon; Malay Peninsula.

(Also in China, Japan, Malay Islands, Polynesia, and Tropical America.)

TYPE. Ultimate segments rhomboidal, subentire, or slightly crenated. Davallia rhomboidea, *Wall. Cat.* 257.

VAR. β HIRTA. Ultimate segments more or less deeply cut.

Rhomboidea (Microlepia polypodioides, *Bedd. F. S. I. t.* 15) can easily be picked out in the herbarium: it is very uniform in character, and does not run into hirta in cultivation; it is very common throughout India and in Ceylon.

The variety hirta (*Bedd. F. S. I.* 256) is a much more variable plant, and I refer to this *Wall. Cat.* 262 puberula; 263 pilosula; 264 virens; 2,218 Roxburghii, and 261 pyramidata. These are all so closely allied that it is impossible to keep them up as separate varieties, and they besides run one into the other. There are two varieties in Southern India and Ceylon: one very hairy and the other nearly quite glabrous, but differing in no way beyond the pubescence. The supposed species, flaccida (*Bedd. F. Sup. t.* 353) I now consider only a form of hirta, as I cannot distinguish it in the herbarium, it is said to be very flaccid, and to have fronds ten and twelve feet long. I have seen no forms anything like so large in Southern India or Ceylon, yet some Ceylon and South Indian specimens are referred to it. Wallich's pyramidata has the pinnules closer together and more elongated than any of the other forms, but otherwise it is quite like hirta.

GENUS XIX.—STENOLOMA. (*Fée.*)

(*Stenos*, narrow; *loma*, border.)

Fronds bi-tripinnatifid, ultimate segments cuneiform, growing gradually wider from the base to the apex; veins dichotomously forked, venules free; indusium terminal on the segments, forming a compressed suborbicular, or cup-shaped pouch, only open at the top; rhizome creeping; stipes tufted, not articulated upon the rhizome.

No. 34.

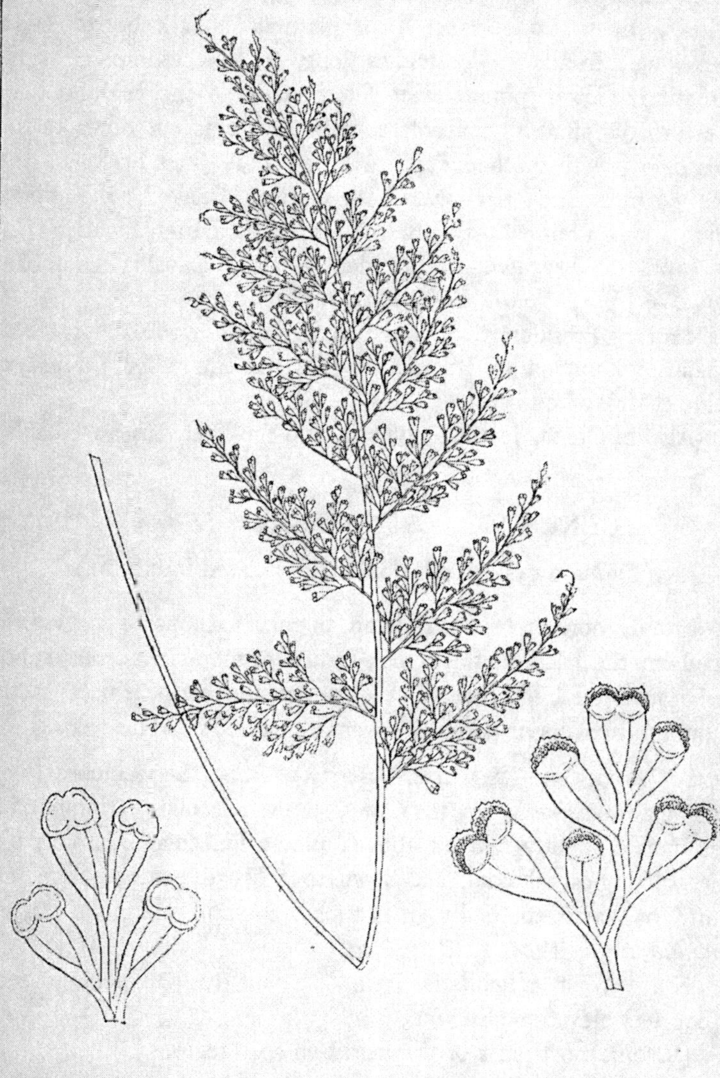

A. C. CATTELL & Co ENGRAS.

STENOLOMA CHINENSIS. (*Sw.*)

1. STENOLOMA CHINENSIS. (*Swartz.*) Rhizome stout, densely fibrillose; stipes strong, erect, polished, naked, dark brown, 6–12 inches long; fronds 12–18 inches long, 6–9 inches broad, ovate, 4-pinnatifid; lower pinnæ ovate-lanceolate, 4–6 inches long, 2–3 inches broad; pinnules lanceolate, their segments cut down to the rachis below, with toothed cuneate lobes, 1–1½ lines across at the apex; texture subcoriaceous, both surfaces naked, the upper shining; sori terminal, usually solitary, often rather broader than deep. *Swartz Syn. Fil.* 133 (under Davallia) Davallia tenuifolia, *Hook. Syn. Fil. p.* 102. *Bedd. F. S. I. t.* 16.

Madras Presidency, Western mountains, 3,000–6,000 feet: Himalayas, Kumaon to Bhotan, up to 1,000–4,000 feet; Khasya; Ceylon; Malay Peninsula.

(Also in China, Japan, Polynesia, and the East African Islands.)

GENUS XX.—CYSTOPTERIS. (*Bernh.*)

(*Cystos*, a cyst, in allusion to the inflated indusium.)

Fronds more or less compound, membranaceous; sori globose, placed on the back of the veins; indusium membranaceous, suborbicular inserted by its broad base, under the sorus, which, at the beginning it covers or partially covers like a hood; veins free.

1. CYSTOPTERIS FRAGILIS. (*Bernh.*) Stipes 2–12 inches long; fronds glabrous, weak, up to 1 foot, ovate-lanceolate, tripinnatifid; main rachis slightly winged above; pinnæ lanceolate-deltoid; pinnules oblong-rhomboidal, cut down to a broad central space into bluntly or sharply-toothed segments; sori 2–12 to a pinnule. *Hook, Syn. Fil.* 103. *Bedd. F. B. I. t.* 91.

North West Himalayas, from Kashmir to Kumaon, 10,000–15,000 feet elevation; Sikkim.

(Also in most parts of the world, in cold regions.)

2. CYSTOPTERIS SETOSA. (*Bedd.*) Caudex erect; stipes 1 foot long, sparsely covered with small flaccid subulate light-brown scales; fronds tufted 3–3½ feet long, tripinnate, pinnæ 8–10 inches long, lowest

No. 35.

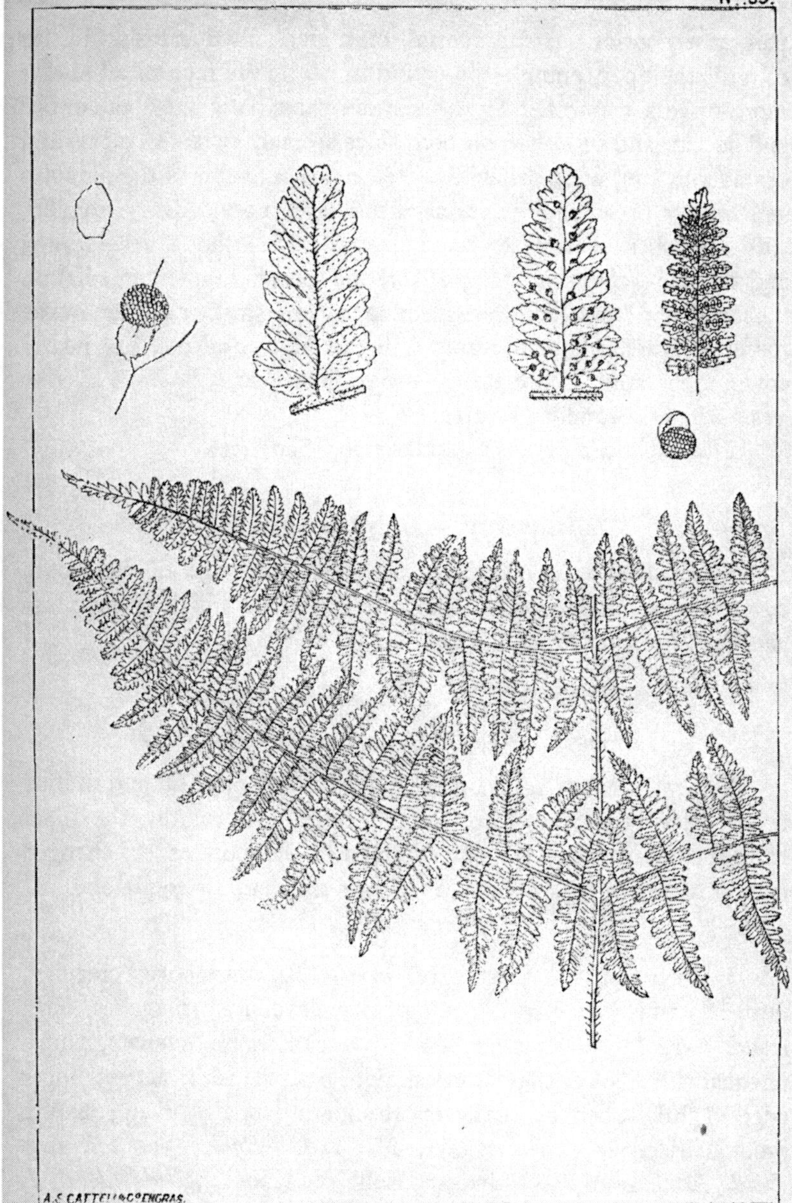

CYSTOPTERIS SETOSA. (*Bedd.*)

pair nearly as long as the central ones, gradually decreasing in size towards the apex, pinnules pinnatifid to nearly the rachis, but always more or less connected by a decurrent wing, very membranaceous and flaccid, and furnished on both sides sparsely (as is the rachis and costa) with long weak pellucid jointed setæ; segments of the pinnules generally as broad at the apex as at the base, more or less pinnatifid, with the lobes obtusely rounded or variously toothed; veins forked and simple reaching the margin; sori one to each segment, medial on the lower vein; involucre very membranaceous, small scale-like, ovate, roundish ovate, or oblong, from a broad base fornicate, not nearly covering the sorus, fimbriate or entire, fugacious. *Bedd. F. B. I. t.* 312; *also t.* 262, under Lastrea.

Moulmein Mountains; Sikkim 5,000–8000 feet.

TRIBE V.—LINDSAYEÆ.

Sori placed in a line, at or very near the edge of the frond, covered with an involucre, the inner valve of which is membranaceous, the outer formed of the margin of the frond.

GENUS XXI.—LINDSAYA. (*Dryand.*)

(In honour of Dr. Lindsay, a writer on Ferns.)

Sori marginal or submarginal, placed to the apex of, and uniting two or more veins; involucre double, opening outwardly, the inner valve membranaceous, the outer formed of the more or less changed margin of the frond; veins free; pinnæ unilateral or equilateral.

§ *Pinnæ unilateral.*

1. Lindsaya cultrata. (*Swartz.*) Rhizome wiry, creeping, furnished with linear scales, stipes wiry flexuous, 3–6 inches long; fronds 6–12 inches long, about 1 inch broad, simply pinnate, pinnæ unequal-sided, lower edge nearly straight near the main nerve; upper edge slightly lobed or nearly entire; lower pinnæ stalked; texture rather coriaceous. *Swartz. Syn. Fil.* 119. *Hook. Syn. Fil.* 105. *Bedd. F. S. I. t.* 23. Lindsaya Lobbiana (Hook.), *Bedd. F. B. I. t.* 28. A variety with rounded pinnæ, and a 4-winged rachis.

No. 36.

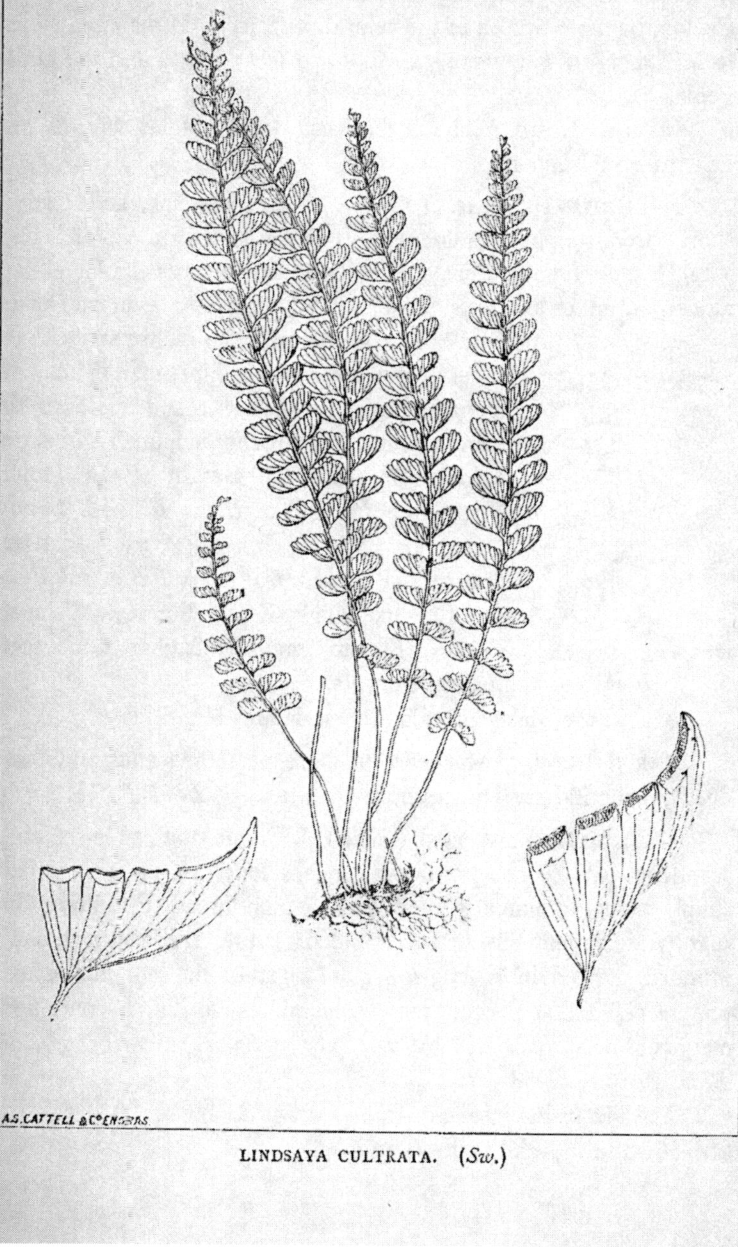

LINDSAYA CULTRATA. (*Sw.*)

Very common on the western side of the Madras Presidency, up to 6,000 feet, called the hay-scented fern, from its scent when drying. Ceylon, higher altitudes in the central provinces. Himalayas, Nepal, to Mishmee and Chittagong, up to 4,000 feet; Birma and the Malay Peninsula.

(Also in North Australia, Formosa, Japan, Malay Islands, and East African Islands.)

2. LINDSAYA REPENS. (*Thw.*) Caudex creeping, scaly; stipes short; fronds rigid, membranaceous linear-lanceolate, 10–18 inches long, ½ inch broad, pinnate attenuated at the base; pinnæ very numerous, 40 or more pair, half deltoid-ovate obtuse or sub-acute, base nearly parallel with the rachis, and with the lower margin quite entire, upper margin lobulate-crenate, costa parallel with and close to the margin; veins simple or forked, free; sori short, oblong, one near the margin of each lobule. *Thw. En. Pl.* 388. *Bedd. F. S. I. t.* 209. Odontoloma, *Hook. Syn. Fil. p.* 93. Lindsaya pectinata (Blume), *Hook. Syn. Fil. p.* 106.

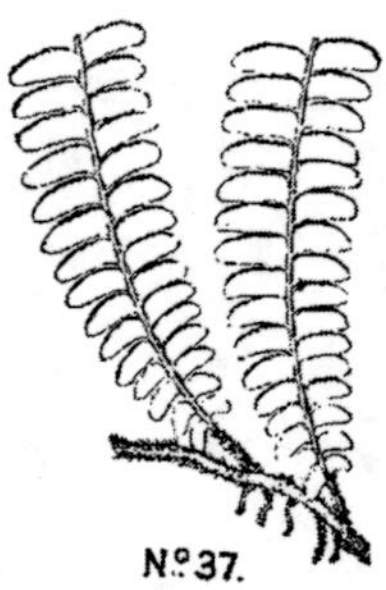

No. 37.

LINDSAYA SCANDENS. (*Hook.*)

Ceylon, Singhe-Rajah Forest; Mishmee, Khasya, Sikkim-Terai, Dulkajhar 1,000 feet; Malay Peninsula.

Also in the Malay Islands, Polynesia and Mauritius.)

VAR. β MINOR. A smaller form, more membranaceous, and more deeply pinnatifid; sori much shorter. *Thw. l. c.* *Bedd. F. S. I. t.* 214.

3. LINDSAYA SCANDENS. (*Hook.*) Rhizome stout, wide-creeping, scandent, paleaceous; frond 9–12 inches long, 1½–1¾ inch broad, simply pinnate; pinnæ ¾ inch long, ½ inch broad, the lower line slightly decurved, the upper rounded, entire, the point broadly rounded, placed in a long row close together, but not imbricated; texture pellucid-herbaceous; costa marginal; sori in a continuous marginal line. *Hook. Sp. Fil. i. p.* 205, *t.* 63 *B.; Syn. Fil. p.* 106. *Bedd, F. B. I. t.* 298.

The Malay Peninsula.

(Also in the Philippine Islands.)

4. LINDSAYA ORBICULATA. (*Lam. under Adiantum.*) Rhizome creeping; stipes tufted, generally elongated, fronds linear-lanceolate and pinnate or deltoid and bipinnate; pinnules approximate shortly petiolate, rather rigid flabellate, and approaching to lunate or sub-rhomboid, with the sides unequal, the base obliquely cuneate, sometimes the upper ones are confluent, the superior margin crenulate or soriferous; no distinct midrib; sori continuous or interrupted; involucres toothed. *Hook. Syn. Fil.* i. 211. L. flabellulata, *Hook. Syn. Fil. p.* 107. *Bedd. F. B. I. t.* 216.

Davallia trichomanoides, *Bedd. F. B. I. t.* 178 (not Blume) an abnormally cut variety. D. schizophylla, *Hook. Syn. Fil. p.* 468.

VAR. β TENERA. Pinnules of thinner texture, and obtusely rounded in outline. *Bedd. F. S. I. t.* 24. This is the only form found in the Madras Presidency.

Western Forests of Madras; Ceylon; Khasya, Assam, Jaintea; Malay Peninsula.

(Also in South China and Australia.)

5. LINDSAYA LANCEA. (*L. under Adiantum.*) Rhizome creeping; stipes strong, up to 12 inches long; frond up to 15 inches long, bipinnate; pinnæ, several pairs erect-patent; pinnules about 1 inch long, by ¼–½ inch deep, the lower line nearly straight, the upper rounded entire; texture pellucid-herbaceous; sori in a continuous line round the upper margin. Adiantum Lanceum. L. Lindsæa trapeziformis (Dry.), *Hook. Syn. Fil.* 107. L. caudata (Hook.), *Bedd. F. S. I. t.* 217. Mr. Wall sends from Ceylon a form with numerous pinnæ, which taper away into a long caudate apex, the lower pinnules being obovate from a longish stalk, and much smaller than in the type; the upper pinnules very small and tongue-shaped.

Ceylon; Malay Peninsula.

(Also in Tropical America, the West Indies, and the Malay Islands.)

6. LINDSAYA RIGIDA. (*J. Sm.*) Rhizome wide-creeping, stipes 4–6 inches long, rigid, erect, prickly towards the base; fronds with a long unbranched central point, and 1–4 pair of flexuose lateral

branches, 4–8 inches long; pinnules 3–4 lines broad, 2 lines deep, the lower edge often falcate, the upper 3–4 times bluntly, not deeply lobed, close together, but not imbricate; texture very thick, coriaceous; veins prominent; sori in a marginal line on the lobes. *Hook. Syn. Fil. p.* 108. *Bedd. F. B. I. t.* 166.

Malacca, on Mount Ophir.

§§ *Pinnæ equilateral.*

7. LINDSAYA WALKERÆ. (*Hook.*) Rhizome creeping, thicker than a crow's quill, ferruginous with scale-like hairs. Stipes very long, often 1 foot, and as well as the rachis dark purple, glossy; fronds lanceolate, pinnate, 6 inches to 1 long, pinnæ 6–9 pairs, with a terminal one, which is sometimes confluent with one or both of the upper pair, coriaceous, subopposite, remote, lanceolate or linear-lanceolate, equal, costa central, veins copious, almost parallel with the costa; sorus marginal, continuous on both sides. *Hook. Sp. Fil.* i. 209. *Syn. Fil.* 109. *Bedd. F. S. I. t.* 215.

Ceylon, Hinidoon Corle in swamps.

(Also the island of Banca, east of Sumatra.)

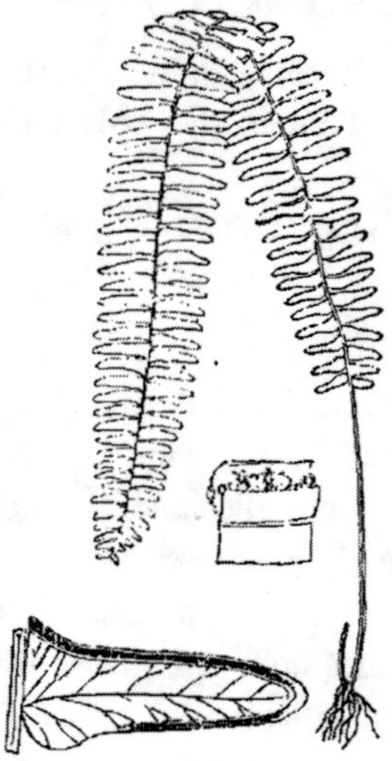

N°38.
LINDSAYA DIVERGENS.
(*Wall.*)

8. LINDSAYA DIVERGENS. (*Wall.*) Rhizome creeping; stipes and rachis ebony-black, glossy; fronds lanceolate-pinnate; pinnæ approximate, crowded, horizontal-lanceolate, obtuse, subsemihastate at the base, glaucous beneath, the sides equal; costa central; veins oblique, once forked, distant, internal, obscure; sorus marginal and continuous on both edges and at the apex. *Hook. Sp. Fil.* i. 210; *Hook. et Grev. Ic. Fil. f.* 226. *Bedd. F. B. I. t.* 250. Vittaria divergens, *Herb. Roxb. Wall. Cat. n.* 2191.

Malacca.

(Also in Borneo.)

9. LINDSAYA LANUGINOSA. (*Wall.*) Rhizome creeping, stout, clothed with fibrillose scales; stipes stout, erect, 4–6 inches long; fronds 12–24 inches long, 3–4 inches broad, simply pinnate; pinnæ 1½–2 inches long, ¼–½ inch broad, linear entire or very slightly toothed towards the point, which is acute in the fertile, bluntly rounded in the barren frond; texture coriaceous; rachis pubescent; sori in a continuous line along both edges. *Hook. Syn. Fil. p.* 110. *Bedd. F. B. I. t.* 140.

Birma and the Malay Peninsula.

(Also in Tropical Australia, Mauritius, and Tropical Africa.)

10. LINDSAYA HETEROPHYLLA. (*Bedd.*) Glabrous, fronds, 10–20 inches high; deltoid-bipinnate, in the lower portion, sometimes tripinnate, simply pinnate at the apex; lower pinnæ 4–6 inches long, upper ones gradually smaller and less compound, pinnules numerous, as many as 20, very variable in form, subrotund, rhomboidal or lanceolate, margin entire; veins simple or forked, all free; sori continuous round the whole margin except at the base, the larger pinnules have a distinct midrib. *Bedd. F. S. I. t.* 206.

This is more compound than any of the Indian forms of Schizoloma heterophylla; but there is a form of that plant from Hongkong in the Kew Herbarium very like this in outline, but with the veins anastomosing. I have examined many fronds of this plant, and the veins never anastomose, and if it be lumped with Schizoloma heterophylla, it at once does away with that genus or subgenus. I am, however, inclined to consider it a distinct species more allied to L. orbiculata var. tenera than to Schizoloma heterophylla.

Shevaroy Hills (on the Green hills), Tinnevelly Mountains.

GENUS XXII.—SCHIZOLOMA. (*Gaud.*)

(*Schizo*, I cut; *loma*, margin.)

As in Lindsaya, but veins more or less anastomosing.

1. SCHIZOLOMA LOBATA. (*Poir.*) Rhizome short-creeping; stipes 6–9 inches long, firm, erect; fronds pinnate; pinnæ 1–6 pairs, erect-patent, 3–6 inches long; pinnules about ½ inch long, ¼ inch

No. 39.

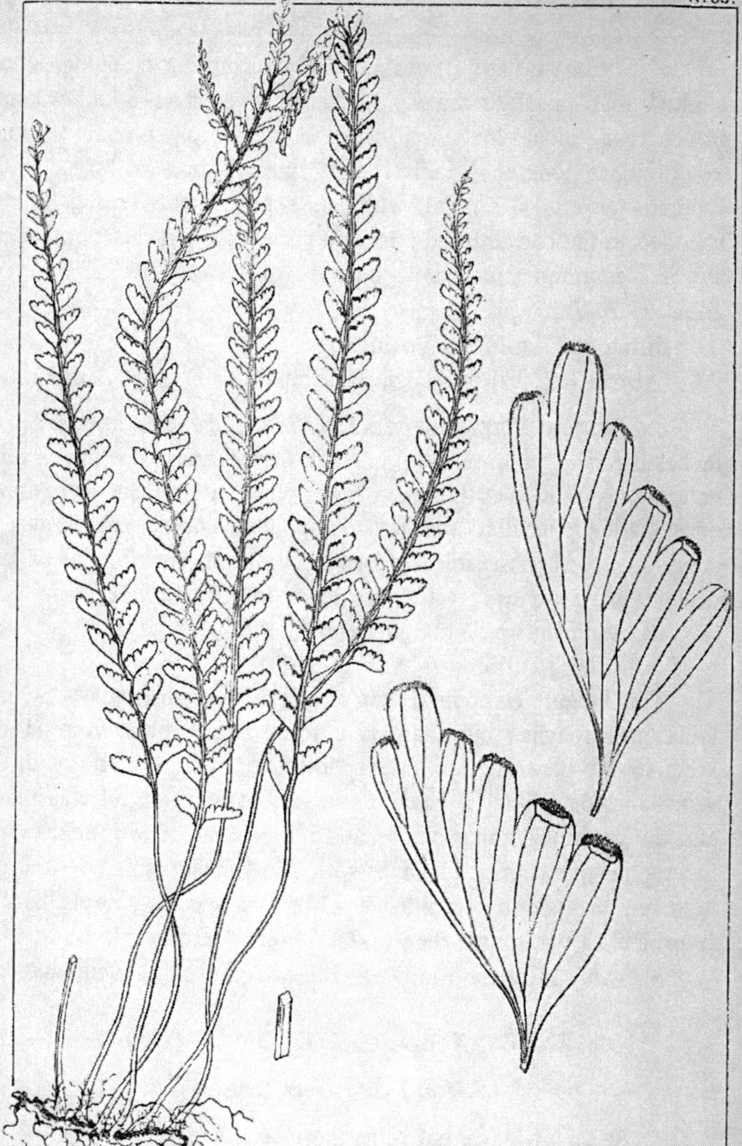

SCHIZOLOMA LOBATA. (*Poir.*) VAR. MALABARICA.

broad, recurved, rounded, the upper margin with broad, shallow lobes, texture thin pellucid-herbaceous; veins anastomosing in the upper portion of the pinnules; sori marginal in the lobes, the inner valve of the involucre narrow and membranous, the edge of the frond produced beyond it, and scarcely altered. *Hook. Syn. Fil. p.* 111. S. recurvata (Wall.), *Bedd. F. S. I. t.* 27. L. nitens, *Blume.*

Malabar and Travancore Mountains, Ceylon.

(Also in Queensland and the Polynesian Islands.)

VAR. β MALABARICA. (*Bedd.*) Fronds always simply pinnate; rachis tetragonous; pinnules erect, not recurved, upper margin more deeply lobed; veins less anastomosing. *Bedd. F. B. I. t.* 268.

Perhaps a distinct species.

Malabar and South Canara.

2. SCHIZOLOMA DAVALLIOIDES. (*Bl.*) Rhizome short-creeping; stipes 6–12 inches long, firm, erect; fronds pinnate, pinnæ 2–3 pairs, erect-patent, 4–8 inches long, pinnules 4–6 lines long, 2–3 lines broad, the lower margin straight or slightly curved, the upper with 4–6 regular rounded but not deep lobes, texture pellucid-herbaceous; veins anastomosing at the base of the lobes; sori marginal in the lobes. *Hook. Syn. Fil. p.* 111. *Bedd. F. B. I. t.* 141. (Closely allied to lobata.)

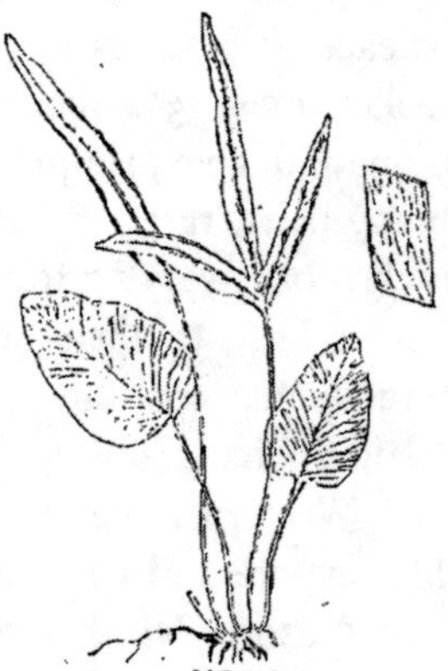

No. 40

SCHIZOLOMA CORDATA. (*Gaud.*)

Malacca.

(Also in the Malay Islands.)

3. SCHIZOLOMA CORDATA. (*Gaud.*) Rhizome short-creeping; stipe 3–6 inches long, slender, erect, wiry; barren frond 2–3 inches long, 1–1½ inch broad, cordate-oblong, quite entire, fertile one 3–6 inches long, linear entire or forked; texture coriaceous; sori in a continuous marginal line; veins anastomosing. *Hook. Sp.* i. *p.* 219, *t.* 66 *A.*; *Syn. Fil. p.* 111. *Bedd. F. B. I. t.* 299.

Malay Peninsula.

4. SCHIZOLOMA GUERINIANA. (*Gaud.*) Rhizome creeping, paleaceous; stipes 4–6 inches long, articulate with the rachis; fronds 6–9 inches long, oblong-lanceolate, simply pinnate, pinnæ ½–¾ inch long, ovate or oblong, nearly entire, horizontal or falcate, slightly auricled at the base on the upper edge; texture subcoriaceous; sori in a continuous line along both margins. *Syn. Fil. p.* 111; *Hook. Sp. Fil.* i. *p.* 221. *Bedd. F. B. I. t.* 340.

Malacca.

(Also in the Malay Islands.)

5. SCHIZOLOMA ENSIFOLIA. (*Swartz.*) Rhizome creeping, stout, paleaceous; stipes 6–9 inches long, wiry, flexuose; fronds 6–12 inches long, 3–4 inches broad, with a linear-lanceolate simple or pinnatifid apex, simply pinnate below, pinnæ herbaceous, usually in many pairs, rarely reduced to one, all stalked, 1½–6 inches long, ¼–1 inch broad, varying from linear-acuminate to lanceolate, sterile ones only a little toothed; veins copiously anastomosing; sori in a continuous marginal line. *Hook. Syn. Fil. p.* 112. *Bedd. F. S. I. t.* 24. (Griffithiana (Hook.), *Bedd. F. B. I. t.* 29 is a simple form.)

Western mountains of Madras; Ceylon; Himalayas, Sikkim to Muneypore and Chittagong up to 4,000 feet; Birma.

(Also in North Australia, Tropical Africa and its eastern islands, Polynesia.)

6. SCHIZOLOMA HETEROPHYLLA. (*Dry.*) Rhizome creeping; stipes 4–8 inches long, firm, naked, erect; frond 6–12 inches long, 3–6 inches broad, lanceolate or oblong, deltoid, varying from simply-pinnate with large linear-lanceolate entire pinnæ, to bipinnate with erect-patent branches 3–4 inches long, with oblong-lanceolate blunt pinnules ½–1 inch long ¼ inch broad, texture herbaceous; sori in continuous marginal lines. *Hook. Syn. Fil. p.* 112. *Bedd. F. S. I. t.* 25.

Malabar Mountains, Travancore; Ceylon; Malay Peninsula.

(Also in Mauritius, Hong-kong, and Malay Islands.)

No. 41.

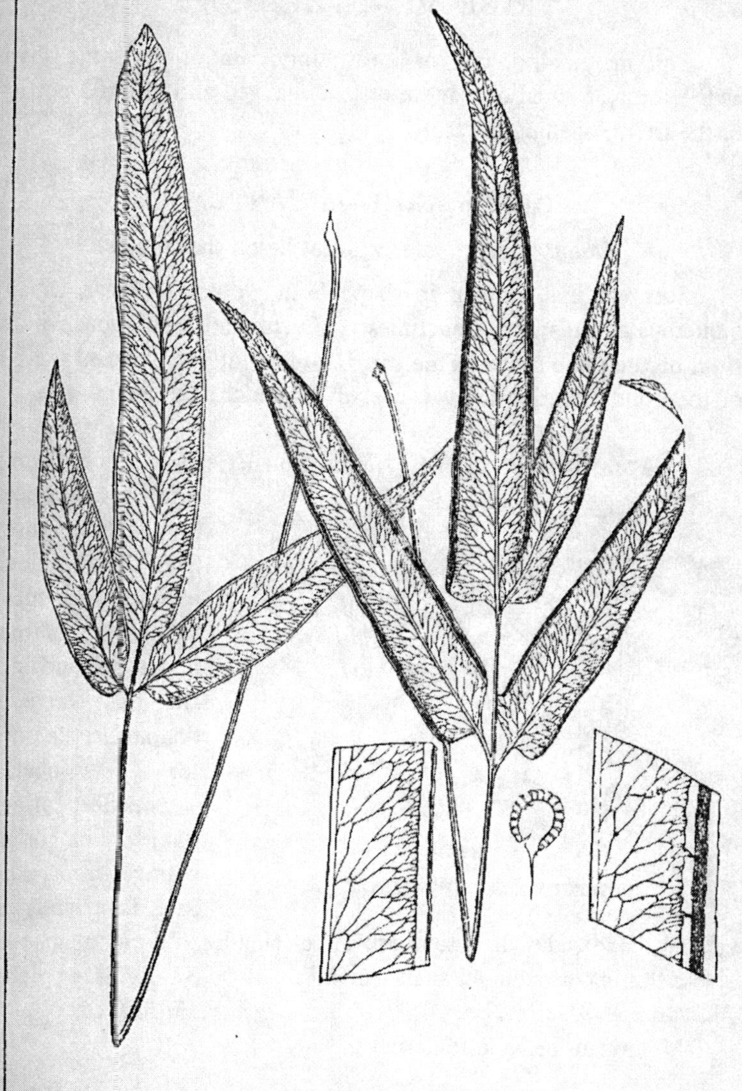

SCHIZOLOMA ENSIFOLIA. (*Sw.*)

TRIBE VI.—PTERIDEÆ.

Sori marginal, oblong, or linear; indusium of the same shape as the sorus, formed of a more or less changed and reflexed portion of the frond, opening inwardly.

GENUS XXIII.—ADIANTUM.

(*Adiantos*, dry; water will not lie on the fronds.)

Sori marginal, varying in shape from globose to linear, usually numerous and distinct, sometimes confluent and continuous; indusium of the same shape as the sorus, formed of the reflexed margin of the fronds, bearing the capsules on its under side; veins free.

1. ADIANTUM PARISHII. (*Hook.*) Small, cæspitose; no distinct caudex; roots few, fibrous, tomentose; fronds about 1 inch each way, orbicular, flabellate, membraneous, pellucid, sterile ones crenate-dentate, fertile ones few (3–5) lobate; sinuses deep soriferous; veins originating from the base, flabellately-divergent, repeatedly dichotomous; stipes slender, filiform, ebeneous, black, shining, articulated at the summit. *Hook. Sp. Fil.* ii. 237, and *Fil. Exot.* i. *pl.* 51; *Syn. Fil. p.* 114. *Bedd. F. B. I. t.* 16.

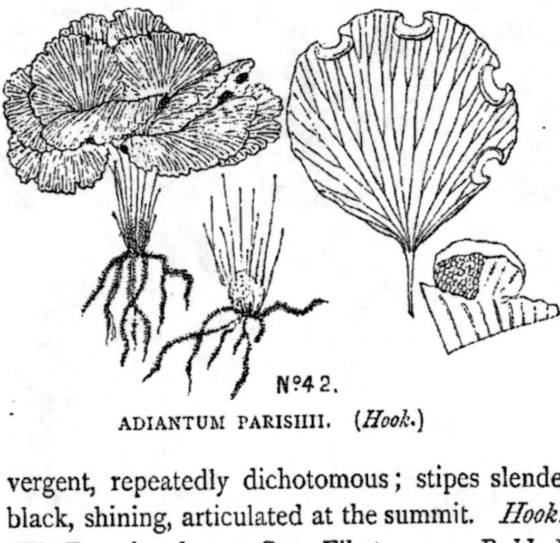

No. 42.

ADIANTUM PARISHII. (*Hook.*)

Moulmein, on limestone rocks.

2. ADIANTUM LUNULATUM. (*Burm.*) Stipes 4–6 inches long, tufted, wiry, naked, polished dark chestnut-brown; fronds 6–12

inches long and 3 inches broad, simply pinnate, often elongated and rooting at the apex; pinnæ subdimidiate, the lower edge nearly in a line or oblique with the petiole, the upper edge rounded and like the bluntly-rounded sides usually more or less lobed; petioles of the lower ones spreading $\frac{1}{4}$–$\frac{1}{2}$ inch long, texture herbaceous; the rachis and both surfaces naked; sori in continuous lines along the edge *Burm. Fl. Ind. p.* 235. *Hook. Syn. Fil. p.* 114. *Bedd. F. S. I. t.* 1.

Throughout Northern India in moist places; South India, very general on the western side in the plains and lower slopes of the hills; Ceylon; Birma.

(Also in the tropics of nearly the whole world.)

VAR. β METTENII. (*Kuhn.*) Stipes and rachis winged, not polished, petioles winged, very short, otherwise as in lunulatum (type). *Kuhn, Fil. Af. p.* 65. *Bedd. Ferns Suppl. t.* 354. A. pteropus, *R. Br.*

Travancore Mountains, in dense evergreen forests between Courtallum and Quilon, 1,000–2,000 feet. Perhaps a distinct species.

(Also in Tropical Africa.)

No. 43.
ADIANTUM LUNULATUM.
VAR. METTENII. (*Kuhn.*)

3. ADIANTUM CAUDATUM. (*L.*) Stipes 2–4 inches long, tufted, wiry, spreading, dark chestnut-brown, tomentose; fronds 6–12 inches long, simply pinnate, often elongated and rooting at the extremity, pinnæ $\frac{1}{2}$–$\frac{3}{4}$ inch long, $\frac{1}{4}$ inch deep, dimidiate, nearly sessile, the lower line straight and horizontal, the upper rounded, more or less cut, often deeply and repeatedly, the point usually blunt, the lower ones slightly stalked; texture coriaceous; the veins prominent; the rachis and both surfaces of the frond villose; sori roundish or transversely oblong on the edge of the lobes. *Hook. Syn. Fil. p.* 115. *Bedd. F. B. I. t.* 2.

Throughout India, Ceylon, and the Malay Peninsula, in the plains and on lower slopes of the hills.

(Also in South China, Tropical Africa, the Malay Islands, Java, Mauritius, and Cape Verde Islands.)

VAR. β EDGEWORTHII. Pinnæ and rachis glabrous; pinnæ less cut on the upper margin. Adiantum Edgeworthii. *Hook. Sp. Fil.* ii. 14. *Bedd. F. B. I. t.* 17.

Nepal, Mooltan, Gurwhal. Perhaps a distinct species.

Clarke refers this to rhizophorum Wall. Cat. 82, but that plant has the rachis scabrous above, and is one of the forms of typical caudatum.

VAR. γ SOBOLIFERUM. Stipes petioles and rachis winged. *Hook. Sp. Fil.* ii. 13. *Bedd. F. B. I. t.* 19.

Birma.

4. ADIANTUM CAPILLUS VENERIS. (*L.*) Stipes suberect, rather slender, 4–9 inches long, polished, blackish, naked; fronds bipinnate, with a short terminal pinna and numerous erect-patent lateral ones on each side, the lowest slightly branched again; segments ½–1 inch broad, the base cuneate, the outer edge rounded, deeply lobed from the circumference in the direction of the centre, and the lobes again bluntly crenated, lowest petioles ¼ inch long, texture pellucid-herbaceous, thin; rachis and both surfaces naked; sori roundish or obreniform, placed in the roundish sinuses of the crenations. *Hook. Syn. Fil. p.* 123. *Bedd. F. S. I. t.* 4.

Madras Presidency, west side, common on banks of rivers in the plains, and up to 5,000 feet on the mountains; Ceylon; North India, in many localities.

(Also in Europe, Africa, America, and Australia.)

5. ADIANTUM ÆTHIOPICUM (*L.*) Stipe 6–9 inches long, rather slender, erect, dark chestnut brown, polished, naked; fronds up to 18 inches long, 6–9 inches broad, deltoid in outline, 3–4-pinnate; lower pinnules 3–4 inches long, 2–3 inches broad, deltoid; ultimate segments ¼–½ inch across, suborbicular, straight or subcuneate or rounded at the base, the upper part broadly not deeply lobed; texture thinly pellucid-herbaceous; rachis and surfaces naked; sori in several roundish or transversely oblong patches in rounded hollows

N°44

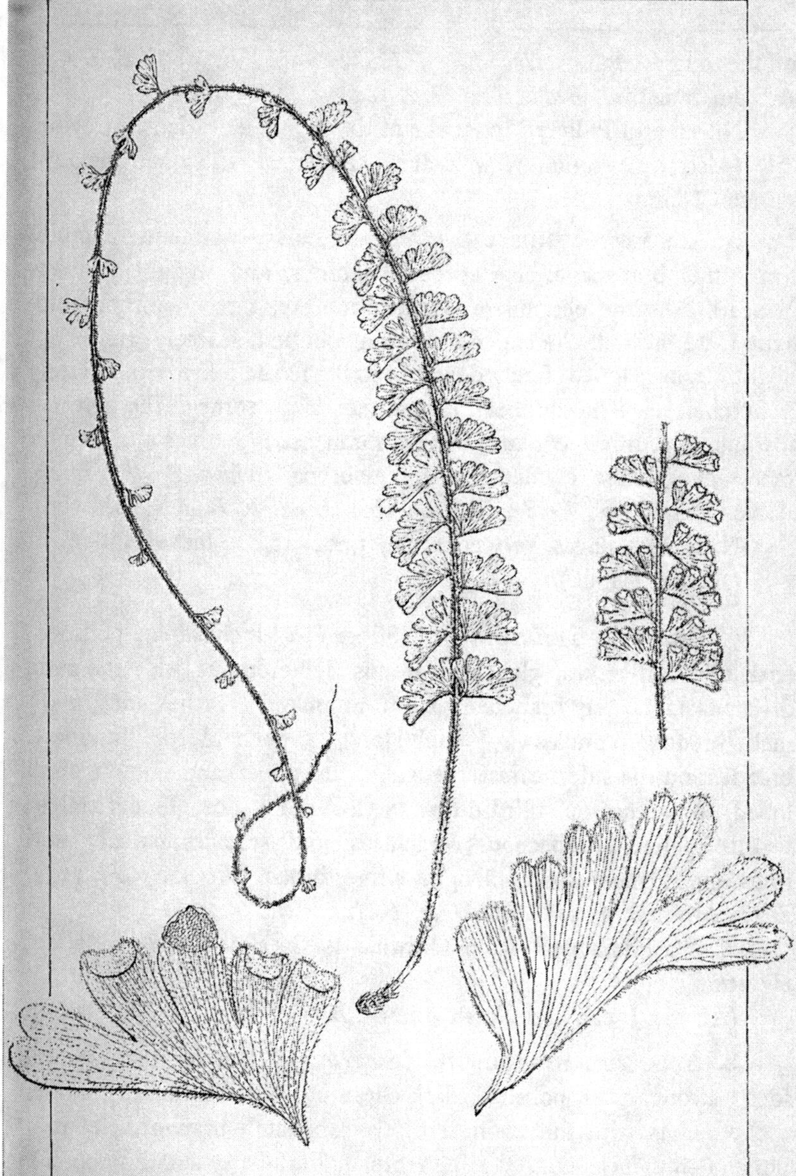

ADIANTUM CAUDATUM. (*Linn.*)

of the outer edge. *Hook. Syn. Fil. p.* 123. *Bedd. F. S. I. t.* 5. Ad. emarginatum, *Bedd. F. B. I. t.* 18.

Nilgiri and Pulney Mountains at the higher elevations. Ceylon.

(Also in Australia, New Zealand, America, Africa and the East African Islands.)

6. ADIANTUM VENUSTUM. (*Don.*) Fronds 3–4-pinnate; pinnules firm, membranaceous-chartaceous, glabrous, and slightly glaucous beneath, shortly petiolulate obovate-cuneate, rarely subrhomboid-acuminate, striated, the superior margin rounded, scarcely ever or but slightly 2 or 3 lobed, finely dentate-serrate, fertile lobes with 2, rarely 3 notches, each notch bearing a rather large sorus at the bottom; involucres reniform-cordate, submembranaceous; stipes and slender rachis everywhere ebeneous-glossy, glabrous. *Hook. Sp. Fil.* ii. 40. A. venustum, *Don Prodr. Fl. Nep.* 16. *Bedd. F. B. I. t.* 20.

N. E. Himalayas, very common, 3,000–10,000 feet elevation.

(Also in Cabul.)

7. ADIANTUM PEDATUM. (*L.*) Stipes 6–12 inches long, polished, dark chestnut-brown, glabrous; fronds dichotomous, with the main divisions flabellately branched; central pinnæ 6–9 inches long, 1–1½ inch broad; pinnules ½–¾ inch long, ¼ inch deep, dimidiate, broadest on the side nearest the stem, the upper and outer margin lobed, sometimes one-third down, the lowest on short slender stalks; texture pellucid-herbaceous; rachises and surfaces naked; sori roundish or transversely oblong, 1–2 lines broad. *Linn. Sp. Pl.* 1557. *Hook. Syn. Fil. p.* 125. *Bedd. F. B. I. t.* 167.

N. W. Himalayas, from Gurwhal to Sikkim, 6,000–9,000 feet elevation.

(Also in Japan and North America.)

8. ADIANTUM HISPIDULUM. (*Swartz.*) Stipes up to 15 inches long; strong, erect, polished, dark chestnut-brown, scabrous; fronds dichotomous, with the main divisions flabellately branched; central pinnæ 6–9 inches long, ½–1 inch broad, dimidiate, sub-rhomboidal, rather broader on the side nearest the stem, hispid on both sides, the outer edge bluntly rounded or oblique, upper and outer margin

No. 45.

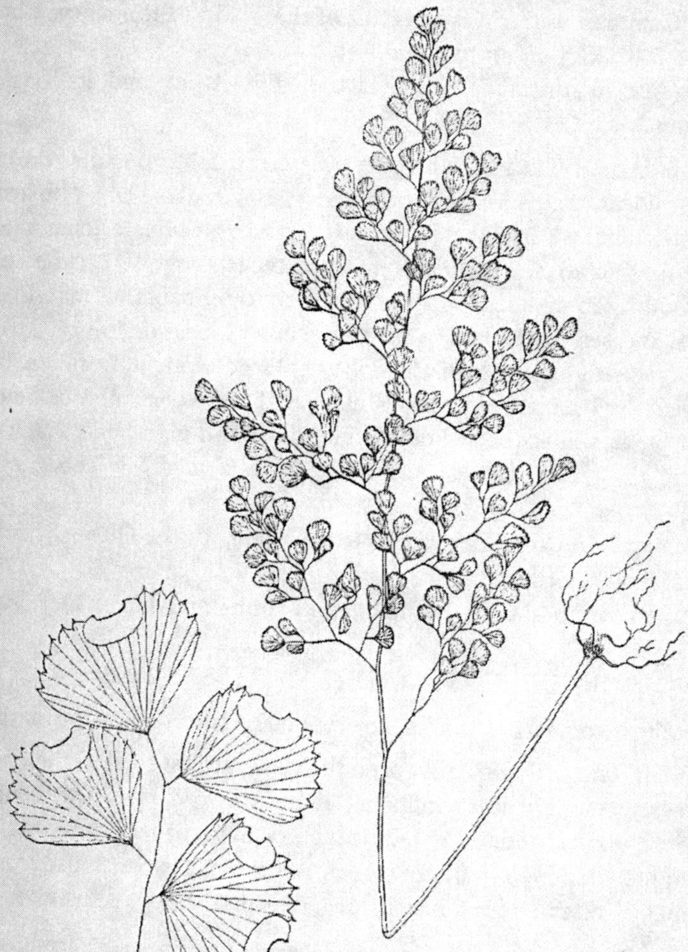

A. S. LATTEY & Co. ENGRAS.

ADIANTUM VENUSTUM. (*Don.*)

finely toothed, lower ones slightly stalked; texture subcoriaceous; sori roundish, numerous, contiguous round the upper and outer edge. *Hook. Syn. Fil. p.* 126. *Bedd. F. S. I. t.* 3.

Common in the Western Hills of the Madras Presidency, 3,000–5,000 feet; Ceylon up to 4,000 feet.

(Also in Australia, New Zealand, Fiji, Africa and its Eastern Islands.)

9. ADIANTUM FLABELLULATUM. (*L.*) Scales on the rhizome long, linear, lax, chestnut coloured; fronds flabellate, bipartite-pedately divided, tripinnate; secondary pinnæ lanceolate-acuminated; pinnules glabrous, subcoriaceous-chartaceous, obliquely cuneate or semi-orbicular-cuneate, superior base truncate, superior margin 2–4 lobed and serrate-dentate in the sterile one; lobes soriferous; involucres large, the breadth of the lobe, oblong, straight, rarely a little curved, hard coriaceous; stipes elongated ebeneous-scabrous below; the rest, as well as the slender rachis, glossy and glabrous. *Hook. Sp. Fil.* ii. 30. *Linn. Sp. Fil. p.* 1558. *Hook. Syn. Fil. p.* 126. *Bedd. F. S. I. t.* 218.

Nepal, Assam, Khasya, Sylhet; Ceylon, in the Ouvah district; he Malay Peninsula.

(Also in the Malay Islands, South China and Japan.)

GENUS XXIV.—CHEILANTHES. (*Swartz.*)

(*Cheilos*, lip or margin; *anthos*, flower; the fructification on the margin).

Sori terminal, or nearly so, on the veins, at first small, subglobose, afterwards more or less confluent; indusium formed of the changed reflexed margin, roundish and distinct, or more or less confluent, but not quite continuous; fronds subcoriaceous in texture, mostly under 12 inches, often under 6 inches long, 3–4-pinnatifid; veins free.

1. CHEILANTHES FRAGRANS. (*Swartz.*) Stipes cæspitose, wiry, 1–3 inches long, densely clothed with reddish-brown linear scales; fronds 2–3 inches long, about 1 inch broad, ovate-acuminate, bi- or tripinnatifid; pinnæ opposite, $\frac{1}{2}$–$\frac{3}{4}$ inch long, $\frac{1}{4}$–$\frac{3}{8}$ inch broad, deltoid, cut down to the rachis below into several sinuate-pinnatifid linear-

oblong lobes; texture subcoriaceous; rachis polished but slightly scaly, both surfaces green and naked; sori small, copious; involucre light brown, membranaceous, toothed. *Hook. Syn. Fil. p.* 134; *Sp. Fil.* ii. 81. Polypodium fragrans (Linn.), *Bedd. F. B. I. t.* 338.

Murree, 4,000–5,000 feet; Mountains of Kashmir; Kishtwar, 3,500–5,000 feet.

(Also in Cabul, and all round the Mediterranean, Canaries, Madeira.)

2. CHEILANTHES SZOVITZII. (*Fisch and Meyer.*) Stipes densely tufted, erect, wiry, polished, brown, thinly coated, as is the rachis, with spreading woolly hairs and linear scales; fronds 3–6 inches long, 1–1½ inch broad, ovate-lanceolate, bipinnate to tripinnate; pinnæ in opposite pairs, the lower ones deltoid; pinnules linear-oblong, contiguous, cut down to the rachis below into small round bead-like segments, ⅛ inch in diameter, subcoriaceous, above green slightly tomentose, below covered with white woolly hairs, which arise from the sori, the margins much incurved; sori copious, marginal. *Fisch and Meyer in Bull. Soc. Mosc.* 1838, *p.* 241. *Hook. Syn. Fil. p.* 139. *Bedd. F. B. I. t.* 145.

Kashmir and Baltistone, 5,000–7,000 feet, common; Kulu.

(Also in Cabul, Asia Minor, Persia, and South Europe.)

3. CHEILANTHES MYSORENSIS. (*Wallich.*) Roots densely cæspitose, the fibres very woolly, stipes slightly scaly below, short, 1–2 inches, and as well as the main rachises, deep glossy-ebeneous, rigid; fronds a span or more long, in outline narrow oblong, acute, tapering below by the diminishing of the pinnæ, glabrous, membranaceous but firm, bipinnate; lower pinnæ very small, all of them oblong-ovate, sessile, frequently opposite pinnate below, the upper half pinnatifid; pinnules or segments linear-oblong, plane (much incurved if dried without pressure), toothed or lobate-pinnatifid, each tooth or lobe bearing one or two subconfluent, small, whitish, suborbicular sori. *Hook. Sp. Fil.* ii. *p.* 94; *Syn. Fil. p.* 135. *Bedd. F. S. I. t.* 190.

South India, common in dry, rocky places in the plains and lower slopes of the hills; Ceylon, at low elevations.

(Also in China and Japan.)

No. 46.

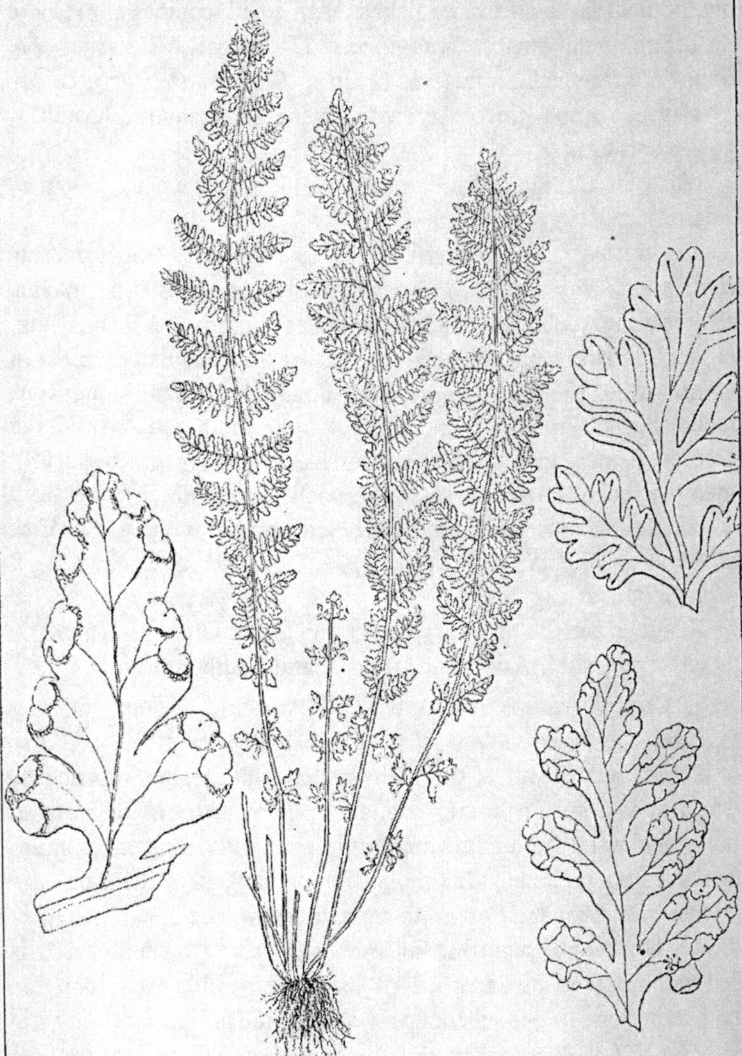

A. S. CATTELL & Co. ENGRAS.

CHEILANTHES MYSORENSIS. (*Wall.*)

4. CHEILANTHES FRAGILIS. (*Hook.*) Caudex none except the copious tufted wiry fibres, from which the stipes arise in tufts; main rachis and slightly scaly stipes (3–5 inches long) clothed with a greyish glandulose tomentum; fronds of an opaque brownish-green colour, submembranaceous, 8–15 inches long, erect, rather stiff but fragile, oblong-lanceolate, pinnate with the pinnæ pinnatifid; pinnæ alternate distant, horizontal up to 2 inches long, pinnatifid nearly to the rachis (which is furnished with subulate scales); segments crenated; lobes obtuse and partially ciliated at the margin; veins pinnated, simple or forked; sori approximate roundish; involucres ciliated, formed of the slightly changed lobes of the margin. *Hook. Fil. Exot. t.* 96; *Syn. Fil. p.* 135. *Bedd. F. B. I. t.* 223.

Perhaps only a form of No. 3.

Moulmein, on limestone rocks.

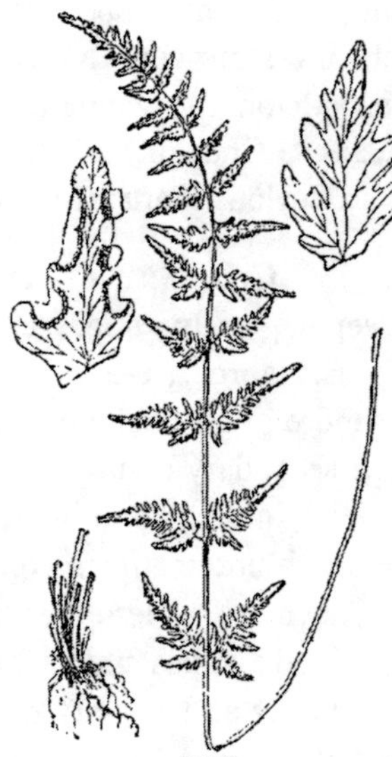

No. 47.

CHEILANTHES VARIANS. (*Wall.*)

5. CHEILANTHES VARIANS. (*Wall. under Pteris.*) Root tufted; stipes 4–6 inches long, slender, ebeneous-glossy, plane and margined on the upper side, obsoletely setose-paleaceous; fronds sub-membranaceous, glabrous, about a span long, long-lanceolate, the pinnatifid apex acuminated, pinnated above, bipinnate below; primary pinnæ distant, spreading or a little curved upwards, sessile, superior ones lanceolate, acuminate sinuate-pinnatifid at their base, and somewhat auricled at the upper base, lower ones deltoid acuminate pinnate at their base, pinnatifid acuminated (caudate) in the upper half; pinnules lanceolate acuminate or acute pinnatifid below, the lowest inferior pinnæ the longest. *Hook. Sp. Fil.* ii. *p.* 89; *Syn. Fil. p.* 136. *Bedd. F. S. I. t.* 189.

East Bengal plains from Assam to Chittagong; Khasya Hills, 2,000 feet; South India (Anamallay Hills); Birma.

(Also in South China and Luzon.)

6. CHEILANTHES LAXA. (*Moore.*) Stipes densely tufted, chestnut coloured, shining up to 8 inches long, sparsely clothed towards the base with lanceolate scales; fronds narrow-lanceolate up to 20 inches long by 3 inches broad, bipinnate or tripinnatifid; rachis naked, or nearly so; pinnæ distant, subsessile, deltoid, lower ones reduced; pinnules blunt, upper adnate entire, lower free lanceolate, bluntly lobed, texture very thin; surfaces naked; dull green, slightly farinose beneath on the young fronds; involucre narrow. *Moore Ind. Fil. p.* 245. Cheilanthes Thwaitesii, *Mett. Hook. Syn. Fil. p.* 457.

Ceylon, Kurunagalla and Kallupahane.

7. CHEILANTHES TENUIFOLIA. (*Sw.*) Annual, caudex short-creeping, scaly; stipes elongated, rarely scaly; frond submembranaceous, glabrous, 3–4 inches to a span and more long, ovate acuminate, or more or less deltoid, subtripinnate, ultimate lobes of the primary and secondary divisions the largest, more or less pinnatifid; pinnules elliptic, oblong or oblong-lanceolate subpinnatifid or crenate, with broad blunt teeth; involucres mostly elongated, more or less confluent, more or less crenated or denticulate, sometimes transversely wrinkled; stipes and rachis purple-black, main rachis winged above, secondary and tertiary rachises all with a narrow wing. *Hook. Sp. Fil.* ii. *p.* 82, *t.* 87*c. Syn. Fil. p.* 138. *Bedd. F. S. I. t.* 188.

Madras Presidency, common in the plains and on low hills up to 4,000 feet: Bengal, plains in Assam, Chittagong, Dacca, Chota Nagpore; Khasya, up to 3,500 feet; Sikkim; Malay Peninsula.

(Also in China, Australia, New Zealand, Polynesia, Uruguay, and the Malay Islands.)

8. CHEILANTHES FARINOSA. (*Kaulf.*) Roots tufted; stipes more or less elongated, ebeneous-glossy, deciduously scaly; fronds subcoriaceous, from a span to a foot long, deltoidly lanceolate, or lanceolate glabrous, white and powdery beneath, pinnate, the apex

pinnatifid, acuminate, pinnæ mostly lanceolate pinnatifid, the one or two lowermost pair more or less half deltoid bipinnatifid below; involucres brown, scariose, rounded, sometimes confluent, and then waved or lobed, the margin entire or toothed and jagged. *Hook. Sp. Fil.* ii. *p.* 77; *Syn. Fil. p.* 142. *Bedd. F. S. I. t.* 191 *and* 192 (*bullosa*).

Throughout North India, in the hills up to 5,000 feet; Madras Presidency, in the plains and up to 8,000 feet on the hills; Ceylon; Birma.

(Also in Tropical America, Java, Philippines, East Africa and its Islands, and Arabia.)

VAR. β DALHOUSIÆ. (*Hook.*) Pinnæ (even when young) without hairs, scales or powder underneath; involucres deeply crenulate toothed or lacerate on the margin. *Clarke, F. N. I. p.* 459, *and t.* 51. P. Dalhousiæ, *Hook. Sp. Fil.* ii. *p.* 10; *Syn. Fil. p.* 137.

West Himalaya, from Kashmir to Kumaon, 6,000–9,000 feet, Sikkim, Lachen, 10,000 feet.

VAR. γ FLACCIDA. Ultimate pinnules very flaccid, and generally broader than in the type, the white powder sparse on young fronds, altogether absent on mature ones; stipes and rachis weak and often wavy. Cheilanthes Dalhousiæ, *Bedd. F. S. I. t.* 192.

Nilgiris, in woods near Makoorty Peak, 7,000 feet, Anamallays, open grassy places on Ponachy Hill, 6,000 feet.

VAR. δ CHRYSOPHYLLA. Powder beneath of a bright golden colour; fronds with quite the outline of typical farinosa, but smaller. *Hook. Fil. Exot. t.* 95, *fig.* 1. Cheil. argentea var. chrysophylla, *Hook. Syn. Fil. p.* 142.

Khasya, 5,000 feet; Cheilanthes argentea var. sulphurea, *Clarke, F. N. I. p.* 458, is only the young undeveloped frond of this.

9. CHEILANTHES SUBVILLOSA. (*Hook.*) Stipes densely tufted, 2–4 inches long, polished, naked, bright chestnut coloured, rather brittle, clothed with lanceolate acuminate scales below, main rachis glabrous beneath, the partial rachises with crisped woolly salmon-coloured hairs beneath; fronds 6–12 inches long, 2–3 inches broad,

elongate-lanceolate tripinnatifid; pinnæ 8–10 pairs, the lower ones distant, 1½ inch long, more than 1 inch broad, deltoid; pinnules on the lower side the largest, sometimes 1 inch long oblong-lanceolate, cut down to the rachis below into oblong lobes; texture herbaceous, upper surface naked, lower villose, especially on the costa; involucre continuous, slightly crenulate, not fimbriate on the margin. *Hook. Syn. Fil. p.* 137; *Sp. Fil.* ii. *p.* 87, *t.* 98 *B. Bedd. F. B. I. t.* 142. *Clarke, F. N. I. p.* 456.

Mr. Clarke says that the involucre is that of Pellœa, to which genus this might be referred.

N. W. Himalayas, Palur Valley, and Kitghur, near Simla.

10. CHEILANTHES ALBO-MARGINATA. (*Clarke.*) Rhizome with tufts of hair-pointed scales, stipes up to 10 inches, shorter or longer than the frond; glabrous, reddish-brown, shining, furnished, particularly below and when young, with lanceolate white-margined scales; fronds deltoid to deltoid-lanceolate, when very young completely covered beneath with lanceolate brown scales, and with yellowish or whitish powder, in age glabrous except the partial rachises and costa, which are scaly; lowest pair of pinnæ half deltoid, and with their lower pinnules much more developed than in the others (as in farinosa); involucres lacerate on the margins. *Clarke, F. N. I. p.* 456, *t.* 52. Perhaps only a form of farinosa.

N. W. Himalayas, Kashmir, Basaoli, 5,000 feet; Dalhousie, 6,000 feet; Simla, 7,000 feet; Gurwhal, 2,000–9,000 feet.

11. CHEILANTHES RUFA. (*Don.*) Stipes tufted, up to 6 inches long, densely clothed with rusty brown, woolly tomentum; fronds 6–10 inches long, bipinnatifid, from deltoid with the lower pinnæ much developed (like farinosa) to lanceolate with the lower pinnæ dwindling down; whole frond woolly beneath, with crisped hairs; texture herbaceous, white powder present below on the young fronds; involucre ciliated. *Don. Prod. Fl. Nep.* 16. *Hook. Syn. Fil. p.* 141. *Bedd. F. B. I. t.* 144.

Very near the last species, only tomentose. I have some specimens from Gurwhal, I hardly know which to refer to, the tomentum being present, but very sparse; the difference between the two is only a question of the tomentum, and both may well be varieties of farinosa.

Khasya, 4,000 feet, plentiful on limestone; Sikkim, 5,000 feet; Gurwhal, 2,000–4,000 feet; Dalhousie.

12. CHEILANTHES ARGENTEA. (*Kunze.*) Stipes densely tufted, 3–6 inches long, thick, dark brown, polished, clothed at the very base with linear scales; fronds 3–4 inches long by 2 inches broad, triangular or deltoid, tripinnatifid, lowest pinnæ much the largest but not cut down to the rachis, tripinnatifid; rachis and costa polished like the stipe, upper surface naked, green, lower covered with white powder; involucres crenate or fimbriate. *Kunze. Linnæa*, 1850, *p.* 242. *Hook. Syn. Fil. p.* 142. *Bedd. F. B. I. t.* 143. (The lowest pair of pinnæ is rarely almost quite free, the decurrent wing on the rachis from the next pair being very narrow; the pinnæ are generally broadly decurrent, so that the frond is not cut down nearly to the rachis.)

No. 48.
CHEILANTHES ARGENTEA
(*Kunze.*)

Birma; Khasya, 3,000–5,000 feet.
(Also in Siberia, Japan, and China.)

GENUS XXV.—ONYCHIUM. (*Kaulf.*)

(*Onychion*, a little nail; resemblance to the fertile segments of the frond.)

Sori placed upon a continuous linear receptacle, which connects the apices of several veins; indusium parallel with the margin of the segments, linear, opposite, pressed down over the sori, the edge nearly or quite reaching the midrib. Closely allied to Pteris and referred to that genus by Mettenius.

1. ONYCHIUM AURATUM. (*Kaulf.*) Stipes 6–12 inches long, stout, erect, naked, straw-coloured or pale brown; fronds 12–18 inches long, about 6 inches broad, ovate, 4-pinnatifid; lower pinnæ subdeltoid, erect-patent; pinnules and segments numerous, usually deltoid; ultimate divisions of the sterile frond often obovate-cuneate, trifid at the apex, about 1 line long, $\frac{1}{3}$–$\frac{1}{4}$ line broad when entire, coriaceous in texture, fertile segments pod-like, $\frac{1}{2}$–1 inch long, $\frac{1}{8}$ inch broad; rachis and both surfaces naked, the membranous involucres and copious sori a rich golden yellow. *Kaulf. En. Fil. p.* 144. *Hook. Syn. Fil. p.* 143. *Bedd. F. S. I. t.* 30.

Plains of East Bengal, from Nepal to Assam, up to 4,000 feet; Birma; (once received from the Paulghaut Hills in Southern India, but as it has not been detected since, it was probably from a cultivated specimen).

(Also in New Guinea and the Malay Islands.)

2. ONYCHIUM JAPONICUM. (*Kunze.*) Stipes tufted, 6–12 inches long, stout, erect, straw-coloured or pale brown, scaly at the base; fronds subcoriaceous when mature, shining on both surfaces, 12–18 inches long, ovate, 4-pinnate, lower pinnæ lanceolate-deltoid; pinnules and segments numerous, usually deltoid, the copious linear-mucronate ultimate divisions 1$\frac{1}{2}$–2 lines long, nearly uniform in the barren and fertile segments; rachis and both surfaces naked; indusium pale, membranaceous, ripe capsules deep brown. *Kunze in Sch. Fil. Suppl. p.* 11. *Hook. Syn. Fil. p.* 143. *Bedd. F. B. I. t.* 21.

Himalayas, Gurwhal to Mishmee and Khasya, 3,000–6,000 feet; Birma.

(Also in Japan and China.)

Mr. Clarke makes two varieties besides the type: 1st. *multisecta,* fertile frond, very finely cut, herbaceous, hardly shining, often 5-pinnate, ripe capsules straw-coloured, not numerous; involucre remaining closed over the ripe capsules. 2nd, *intermedia;* fronds lax, more coarsely cut; involucres often $\frac{1}{4}$ inch; to this 2nd variety he

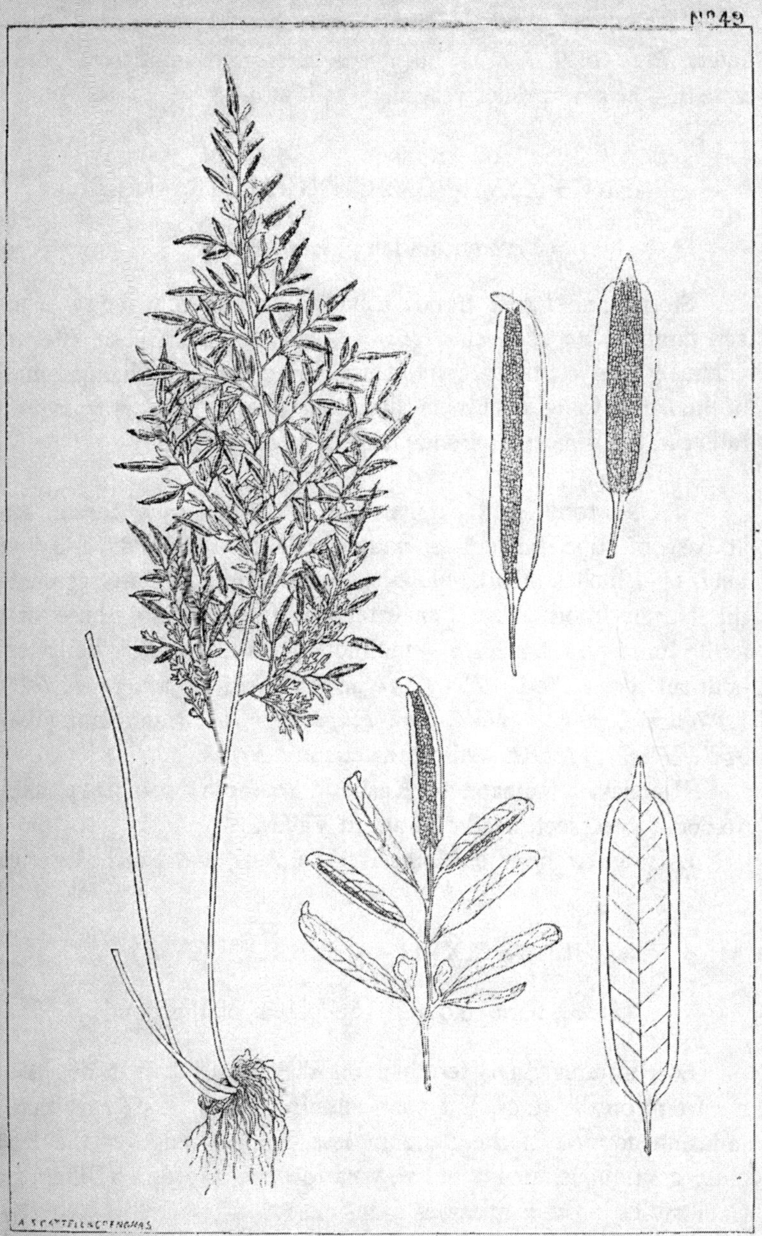

ONYCHIUM AURATUM. (*Kaulf.*)

refers, *Bedd. F. B. I. t.* 21, but it was taken from multisecta; the two varieties, however, differ very slightly, if at all.

GENUS XXVI.—CRYPTOGRAMME. (*R. Br.*)

(*Kryptos*, hidden; *gramme*, a line.)

Sterile and fertile fronds usually different from the same root; sori terminal on the veins, at first separate, subglobose, afterwards confluent, the continuous indusium formed of the changed margin of the frond, rolled over them till full maturity. (Differs from Pellæa rather in the dimorphic fronds than in anything else.)

1. CRYPTOGRAMME CRISPA. (*R. Br.*) Glabrous, tufted, scales at base of stipe, lanceolate, acute, pale-brown; fronds 2–4 inches long, 1½–2 inches broad, oblong, 3–4-pinnatifid; ultimate segments of the barren frond obovate-cuneate, deeply pinnatifid, those of the fertile frond pod-shaped, ¼–⅜ inch long; texture thickly herbaceous, both surfaces naked. *R. Br. in Richardson's Appen. to Franklin's 1st Journal, p.* 54. *Hook. Syn. Fil. p.* 144. C. Brunoniana (Wall.), *Bedd. F. B. I. t.* 164. Allosorus crispus, *Bernh.*

Himalayas, Kumaon to Kashmir, 10,000–15,000 feet; Sikkim, 10,000–14,000 feet, head of Lachen Valley.

(Also in Arctic and Alpine Europe, Asia, and North America.)

GENUS XXVII.—PELLÆA. (*Link.*)

(*Pellos*, dark coloured, the colour of the fronds.)

Sori intramarginal, terminal on the veins, at first dot-like or decurrent on the veins, but soon running into a line; involucre or indusium formed of the more or less changed edge of the frond, quite continuous, sometimes very narrow; veins free. (Differs from Cheilanthes in the continuous indusium.)

§ *Veins clearly visible; indusium broad.*

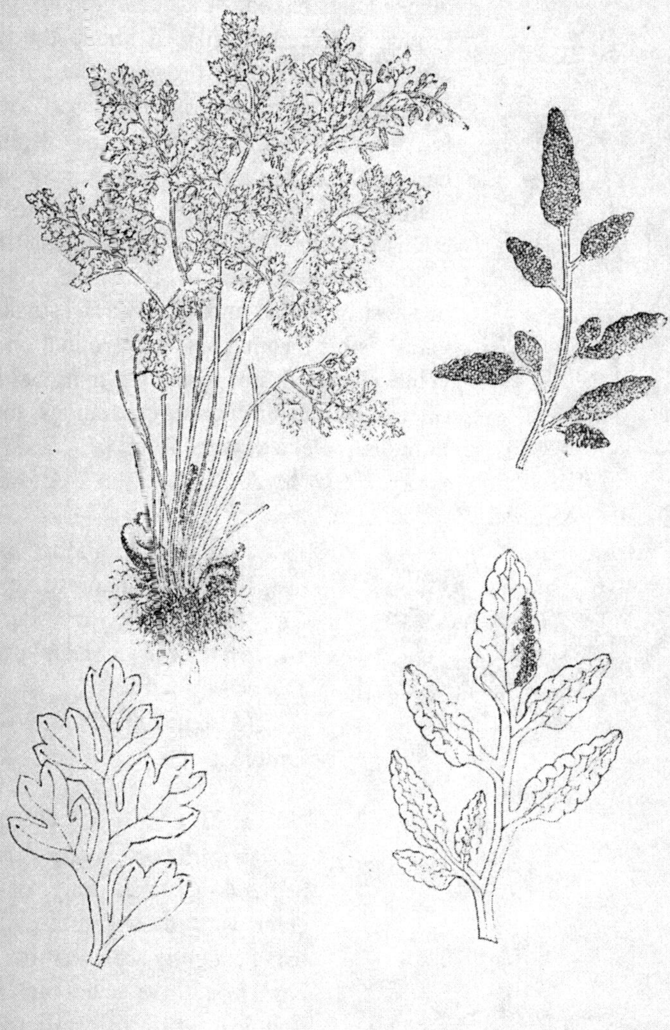

A. S. CATTELL & Co. ENGRAS.

CRYPTOGRAMME CRISPA. (*R. Br.*)

1. PELLÆA STELLERI. (*Gmelin under Pteris.*) Rhizome wiry, creeping; stipes scattered, slender, 2–3 inches long, naked, straw-coloured or pale-brown, polished, furnished about the base with few linear pale brown scales; fronds 2–4 inches long, 1–2 inches broad, ovate bi-tripinnatifid, often with the lowest pinnæ barren, the upper fertile; pinnæ lanceolate-deltoid, 1–2 inches long, cut down to the rachis; lower pinnule again sometimes slightly divided; texture thinly herbaceous or flaccid; rachis and both surfaces naked; veins visible; young sori subterminal on the veins, clustered, not forming a marginal line till old; indusium broad, continuous, membranous. Pellæa gracilis, *Hook. Syn. Fil. p.* 145. *Clarke, F. N. I. p.* 460. Allosorus gracilis (Rup.), *Bedd. F. B. I. t.* 73.

N°.51.
PELLÆA STELLERI. (*Gmel.*)

Himalayas, Baltic, 9,000 feet, Kumaon, Champua, 10,000 feet, Kashmir, Pir Punjul, 11,000 feet; Karakorum, 11,000–13,000 feet.

(Also in Canada and North United States.)

N°.52.
ELLÆA CONCOLOR. (*Langs and Fisch.*)

2. PELLÆA CONCOLOR. (*Langs and Fisch. under Pteris.*) Stipes 6–9 inches long, naked, erect, wiry, brownish black, polished, slightly scaly towards the base; fronds 2–4 inches each way, deltoid, cut down nearly to the rachis into 3–4-pinnæ on each side, of which the lowest pair is much the largest, with the

pinnules on the lower side much larger than the others, and deeply lobed with linear-oblong segments; rachis and costa dark coloured and polished like the stipe; texture herbaceous, lateral veins once forked; sori in broad marginal lines. *Langs and Fisch. Ic. t.* 21. Pteris geraniifolia, *Bedd. F. S. I. t.* 37. Pellæa geraniifolia, *Hook. Syn. Fil. p.* 146.

Western forests of the Madras Presidency, and in Ceylon up to 4,000 feet, very common.

(Also in Tropical America, Polynesian Islands, North China, Cape Colony, and the Mascareen Islands.)

3. PELLÆA TAMBURII. (*Hook.*) Stipes 6–9 inches long, erect, naked, chestnut-brown, polished; fronds about 6 inches each way, subcoriaceous, whitened beneath, deltoid, with three principal lobes, the terminal one cut down nearly to the rachis into several broad opposite lanceolate segments, of which the upper ones are entire and the lower ones larger and sinuated; lateral lobes with the segments on the upper side nearly entire, but those on the lower side prolonged and again deeply lobed, the largest entire divisions about 1 inch deep, ½ inch broad at the base; rachis polished; indusium brownish, continuous, but regularly crenated along the outer edge. *Hook. Syn. Fil. p.* 146; *Sp. Fil.* ii. *t.* 129A.

Tambur Valley, East Nepal.

§§ *Veins not perceptible; indusium broad, conspicuous.*

4. PELLÆA NITIDULA. (*Wall. under Pteris.*) Caudex short-creeping, stout; stipes 2–5 inches long, very numerous and crowded, hispid, with subulate deciduous chaffy dark brown scales, and as well as the rachis (which is downy on one side) ebeneous; fronds 3–4 or rarely 5 inches long, subdeltoid-oblong acuminate (sterile ones broader), coriaceous, shining beneath, glabrous, pinnate-pinnatifid, below subbipinnate; pinnæ approximate, nearly opposite, broad-lanceolate dimidiate (the inferior half broadest), deeply pinnatifid nearly to the rachis, lowest pair again subpinnate and the secondary pinnæ pinnatifid; lobes all oblong entire or sinuate, gradually coming to a sharp point, the lower base decurrent, the lowest inferior lobes

the longest; involucres subintramarginal, continuous or here and there interrupted, broad, flat, membranaceous, brown, close-pressed, frequently lobed and crenated and transversely wrinkled. *Wall. Cat. p.* 89. Cheilanthes nitidula, *Hook. Sp. Fil.* ii. *p.* 112; *Syn. Fil. p.* 149. *Bedd. F. B. I. t.* 222. (The involucres are sometimes continuous as in Pteris, sometimes interrupted and quite like Cheilanthes.)

Kashmir, 3,000–6,000 feet, frequent and plentiful to Chumba, scarce eastwards to Kumaon.

5. PELLÆA BOIVINI. (*Hook.*) Stipes 4–8 inches long, erect, naked, black, polished, very brittle; fronds 6–9 inches long, 4–6 inches broad, deltoid to lanceolate, pinnate to tripinnate; pinnæ erect-patent or spreading gradually smaller upwards; ultimate pinnules broadly ovate in the more simple forms and linear-lanceolate in the more compound, cordate or rounded at the base, very coriaceous, pale and dull beneath; both surfaces naked; veins sunk in the frond; sori in a continuous line round the segments; involucre membranous, ½ a line broad. *Hook. Syn. Fil. p.* 149. *Bedd. F. S. I. t.* 36 (under Pteris).

Nilgiris, Sispara and on the ghat, 4,000–5,600 feet; Anamallays, 4,000 feet, dry rocky places; Travancore and Tinnevelly Mountains; Ceylon. The Nilgiri and Anamallay plant is the more simple form (pinnate or bipinnate), as represented in the figure; the Travancore plant is much larger and more compound, being tripinnate.

(Also in Madagascar and the Mauritius.)

§§§ *Veins usually hidden; indusium so narrow as to be soon hidden by the sori.*

6. PELLÆA FALCATA. (*Fée.*) Rhizome wide creeping; stipes 3–6 inches long, strong, erect, more or less pubescent and scaly; fronds 6–18 inches long, 1–2 inches broad, linear-oblong, simply pinnate; pinnæ 10–20 on each side, nearly sessile, ½–1 inch long, ¼–½ inch broad, lanceolate or lanceolate-oblong, usually mucronate, often slightly falcate, cuneate, or dilated and cordate at the base;

No 53.

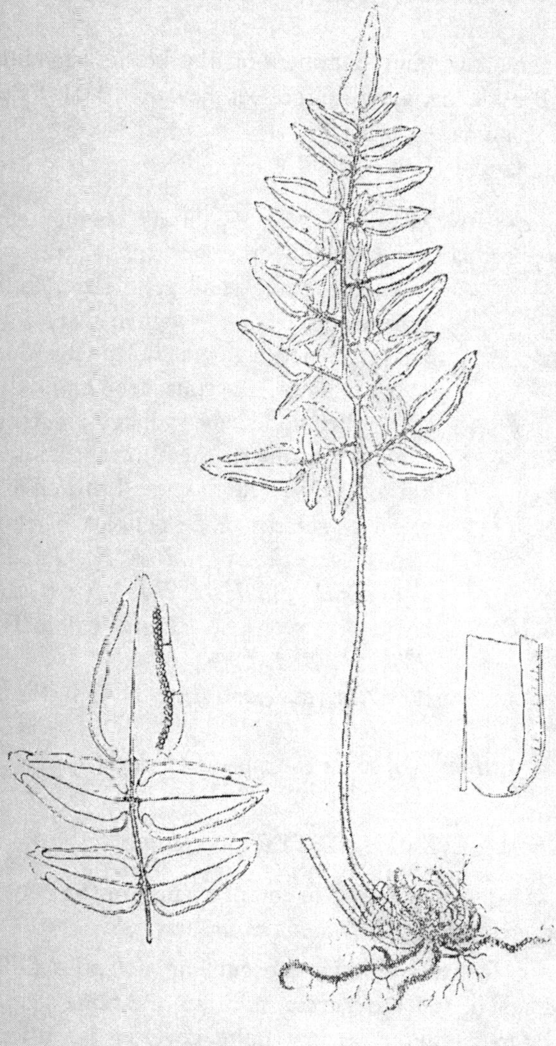

A. S. CATTELL & GRENGRAS.

PELLÆA BOIVINI. (*Hook.*)

texture coriaceous; rachis densely scaly and tomentose, with surfaces nearly naked; veins not visible; sori in broad marginal lines, soon hiding the narrow involucre. *Hook. Syn. Fil. p.* 151. *Bedd. F. S. I. t.* 22 (under Platyloma).

Nilgiris, Anamallays, and elsewhere on the Western mountains of the Madras Presidency, 2,000–4,000 feet elevation, Malay Peninsula; Ceylon, Telgamma.

(Also in Australia and New Zealand.)

7. PELLÆA CALOMELANOS. (*Link.*) Glabrous, caudex short, thick, very scaly; fronds cæspitose, subcoriaceous, oblong-triangular, bipinnate, pinnules all petiolulate, cordate- (rarely subhastate-) triangular, very obtuse, entire, sometimes subtrilobate or sinuate at the margin; the sinus deep and narrow; veins dichotomously radiated; sori continuous; involucres membranaceous; stipes short, scaly at the base, and as well as the slender rachises and petioles black-ebeneous, very glossy. *Hook. Sp. Fil.* ii. *p.* 140. *Link. Fil. Hort. Berol. p.* 61. *Hook. Syn. Fil. p.* 152. Pteris calomelanos, *Bedd. F. B. I. t.* 22.

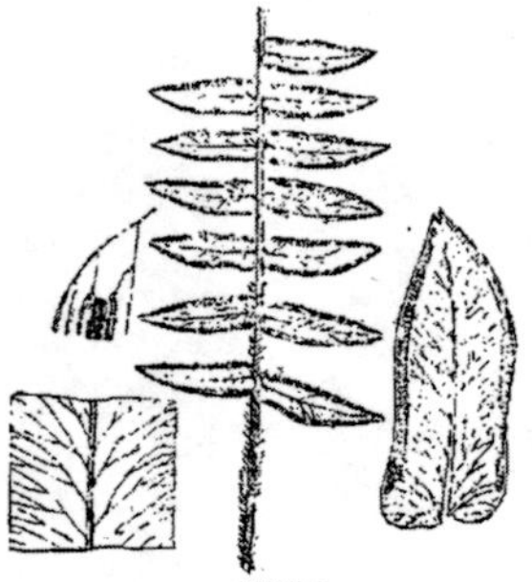

No. 54.

PELLÆA FALCATA. (*Fée.*)
Base of frond.

N. W. Himalayas, below Almora, 4,000 feet, Tikri in Sirmow, 5,000–6,000 feet.

(Also in Africa, from Abyssinia to Cape of Good Hope.)

GENUS XXVIII.—PTERIS. (*Linn.*)

(From *pteryx*, a wing; the supposed likeness to wings in the branches of the common *Pteris aquilina* or Bracken.)

Sori marginal, linear, continuous, occupying a slender filiform receptacle in the axis of the indusium; indusium the same shape as the sorus, usually membranous, at first quite covering it, at length more or less spreading.

N°. 55.

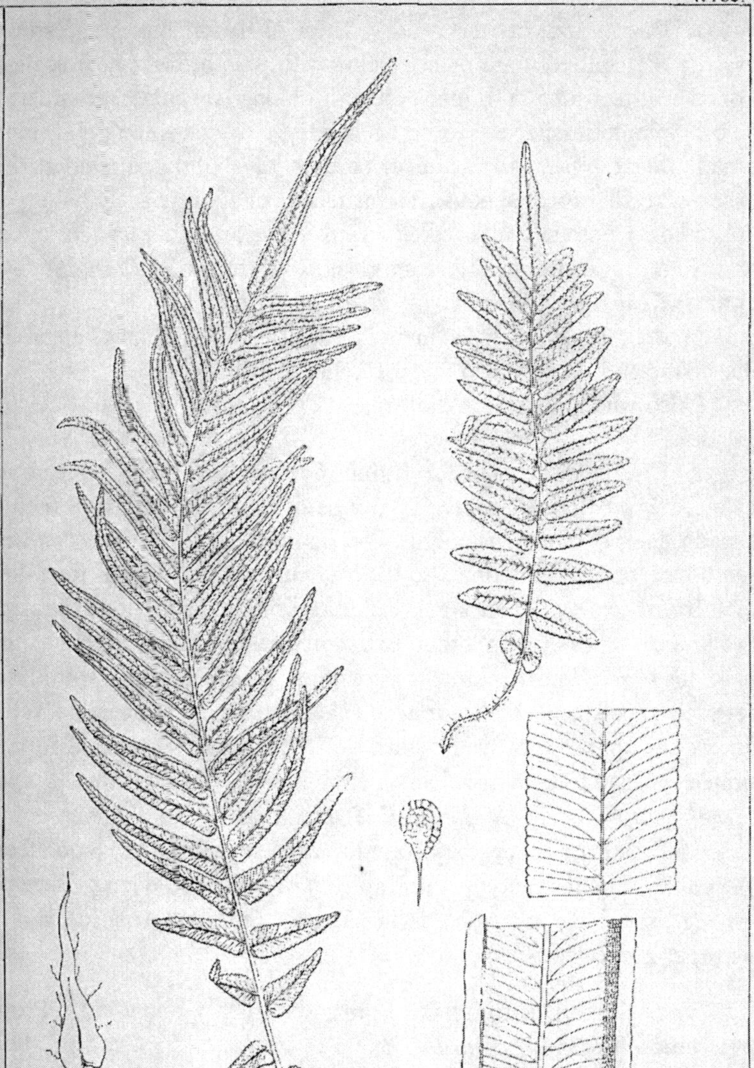

A. S. LAYTELL & Co. ENGRAV.

PTERIS LONGIFOLIA. (*L.*)

1. PTERIS LONGIFOLIA. (*L.*) Stipe 6–12 inches long, stout, erect, pale, clothed more or less below with pale brown linear scales; fronds 1–2 feet long, 4–9 inches broad, oblong-lanceolate, attenuated below; pinnæ sessile, 20–30 on each side, 3–6 inches long, $\frac{1}{8}$–$\frac{3}{8}$ inch broad, linear, entire, truncate or cordate or slightly auricled at the base; texture subcoriaceous; rachis naked or slightly scaly below or throughout; both surfaces naked; veins close and fine, usually once-branched; indusium membranous, yellowish-brown. *Linn. Sp. Pl.* 1531. *Hook. Syn. Fil. p.* 153. *Bedd. F. S. I. t.* 33.

Madras Presidency, in many localities; throughout Bengal in the plains and up to 5,000 feet; Ceylon; Birma.

(Also widely distributed all round the world.)

2. PTERIS CRETICA. (*L.*) Stipes 6–12 inches long, erect, wiry, naked, straw-coloured, polished; fronds 6–12 inches long, 4–8 inches broad; lateral pinnæ usually in 2–6 opposite sessile pairs, of which the upper one is sometimes a little decurrent, 3–6 inches long $\frac{1}{8}$–$\frac{3}{4}$ inch broad, the sterile ones generally the broadest, spinulose-serrated, the lowest or even 1–4 other pairs often cleft down nearly to the base into 2–3 linear pinnules; margins, where barren, spinulose-serrate; rachis and both surfaces naked; texture coriaceous; veins fine, close, parallel or wide apart in the narrow-segmented forms, simple or once-forked; involucre membranous. *Linn. Mant. p.* 130. *Hook. Syn. Fil. p.* 154. *Bedd. F. S. I. t.* 39.

Madras Presidency, very common from sea-level up to 8,000 feet; Bengal Presidency, very general up to 9,000 feet; Ceylon; Birma.

(Also widely distributed in Africa, Tropical America, South Europe, and elsewhere.)

VAR. β HETEROMORPHA. Pinnæ abnormally pinnatifid. Pteris heteromorpha, *Hook. Syn. Fil. p.* 156. *Bedd. F. B. I. t.* 89. This is, I think, only a variety of cretica, not a distinct species.

Birma.

(Also in the Philippine Islands.)

3. PTERIS PELLUCIDA. (*Presl.*) Stipes 1 foot or more long,

erect, naked; fronds 12–18 inches long, ovate-lanceolate, pinnate; pinnæ acute, sometimes many, sometimes 7, 5, 3, or 1, all simple, or the lowest pair 2-fid, often 1 inch broad or rather more; margins where barren, entire, undulate, crisped or crenulate; rachis naked; texture coriaceous, surfaces bright green often glossy; veins fine close, simple or forked at right angles from the midrib; indusium membranous. *Presl. Rel. Hænk.* 55. *Hook. Syn. Fil. p.* 154. *Clarke, F. N. I. p.* 462. *Bedd. F. S. I. t.* 38.

Plains and hills of Bengal up to 3,000 feet elevation, Western forests of Madras Presidency; Birma.

(Also in Malay Islands, and Guinea Coast.)

VAR. β STENOPHYLLA. Pinnæ 3–4 or sometimes 2–1 subdigitate, fertile pinnæ very long and narrow. *Hook. and Grev. Ic. Fil. t.* 130.

Gurwhal and Nepal, 3,000–4,000 feet.

4. PTERIS HOOKERIANA. (*Agardh.*) Stipes 6–12 inches long, naked, erect, pale; fronds coriaceous, opaque, pinnate or bipinnate, 9–12 inches long, 6–9 inches broad, with 2–6 pairs of sessile or stalked alternate or opposite entire pinnæ, the largest of which is about 6 inches long, ¾–1¼ inch broad, the 2–4 lower pairs more or less pinnatifid; rachis and both surfaces naked; veins about 1 line apart at the base, simple or once-forked, conspicuous above, but scarcely visible beneath; sori slightly intermarginal; indusium narrow. *Hook. Syn. Fil. p.* 155. *Bedd. F. S. I. t.* 40.

Ceylon, Adam's Peak, about 2,000 feet elevation, and the Southern provinces at low elevations.

5. PTERIS DACTYLINA. (*Hook.*) Stipes 6–9 inches long, slender, wiry, naked; fronds digitate, coriaceous, consisting of 3–7 (usually 5) linear glabrous pinnæ, 2–6 inches long by 1½–2 lines broad, the barren margins serrate; veins wide apart, thick and conspicuous, simple or forked; indusium broad. *Hook. Syn. Fil. p.* 155. *Bedd. F. B. I. t.* 23.

Khasya, 4,200 feet elevation; Sikkim.

6. PTERIS ENSIFORMIS. (*Burm.*) Stipes up to 10 inches long,

naked; fronds subcoriaceous, more or less dimorphous, up to 12 inches long by 3–6 inches broad, fertile ones with a long terminal pinna, and 2–4 pairs of lateral ones which are simple, forked, trifid or even more compound, the lateral lobes being pinnatifid, the segments very narrow, $\frac{1}{4}$ inch or less broad, entire; sterile fronds generally smaller, more compound, the lateral pinnæ being pinnate, sharply toothed, and much broader than in the fertile; veins forked or simple, diverging at about two-thirds of a right angle from the midrib, very close together. *Burm. Fl. Ind. p.* 230. *Hook. Syn. Fil. p.* 155. Pteris crenata (Sw.), *Bedd. F. S. I. t.* 35.

N° 56

PTERIS DACTYLINA. (*Hook.*)

Malabar, rare; Hills of Vizagapatam district, common; plains of East Bengal, Bhotan to Chittagong; Ceylon; Birma; and Malay Peninsula.

(Also in Tropical Australia, China, and Polynesia.)

VAR. β GREVILLEANA. Margin of the frond, where barren, with some spinulose teeth, lowest pinnæ in the barren frond often pinnate, the segments or pinnules acute. *Clarke, F. N. I. p.* 464. This was included under cretica in the Kew Herbarium, but Mr. Clarke has referred it here on account of the venation, and much divided lower pinnæ; it has more the habit of cretica, I think, than of ensiformis.

Sylhet, Mishmee, Khasya, Chittagong Hills.

7. PTERIS GRIFFITHII. (*Hook.*) A foot and more high, slender graceful; caudex none; roots of tufted fibres; frond ovate-lanceolate, submembranaceous pinnate, upper pinnæ simple, 2 or 3 of the lower pairs again pinnated simple; pinnæ and pinnules exactly linear, $\frac{1}{2}$–$1\frac{1}{2}$ inch long, obtuse, mostly opposite, everywhere

entire sessile, with the base adnate and decurrent, so as to form a narrow wing to the rachis; lowest pinnules of the inferior pinnæ sometimes again divided, terminal pinnule always elongated; veins distant, once-forked, veinlets divaricating; sori continuous, involucres sub-intramarginal, membranaceous, not reaching to the apex; stipes slender, longer than the fronds, stramineous-brown and a little scaly at the base. *Hook. Sp. Fil.* ii. *p.* 170, *t.* 123A. *Bedd. F. B. I. t.* 24.

Mishmee.

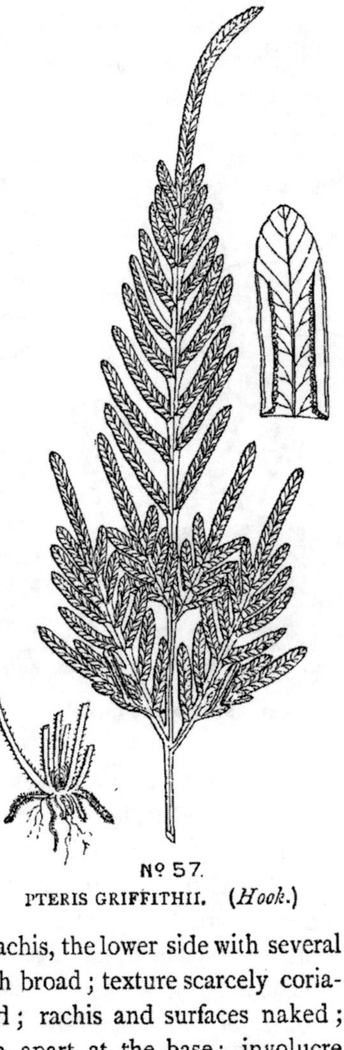

Nº 57.

PTERIS GRIFFITHII. (*Hook.*)

8. PTERIS SEMIPINNATA. (*L.*) Stipes strong, erect, dark brown, polished, hispid at the base, and then furnished with linear scales; fronds 12–18 inches long, 6–9 inches broad, ovate-lanceolate, the upper part cut down nearly to the rachis into numerous close entire linear lobes, the largest of which are 1½–3 inches long, ¼–½ inch broad, the lower two-thirds with 6–8 pairs of opposite distantly placed pinnæ, with long linear entire points and a broad entire wing on the upper side of the rachis, the lower side with several linear pinnules 1–2 inches long, ¼ inch broad; texture scarcely coriaceous; barren segment finely serrated; rachis and surfaces naked; veins simple or once-forked, ⅛ inch apart at the base; involucre membranous. *Hook Syn. Fil. p.* 157. *Linn. Sp. Pl.* 1534. *Bedd. F. S. I. t.* 34.

East Bengal, Assam to Chittagong, up to 1,000 feet; Travancore Hills; Birma.

(Also in Malay Islands, China, and Japan.)

In Indian examples the pinnæ are always semipinnate, but in Chinese and Japanese forms the upper margin of the pinnæ is also pinnatifid.

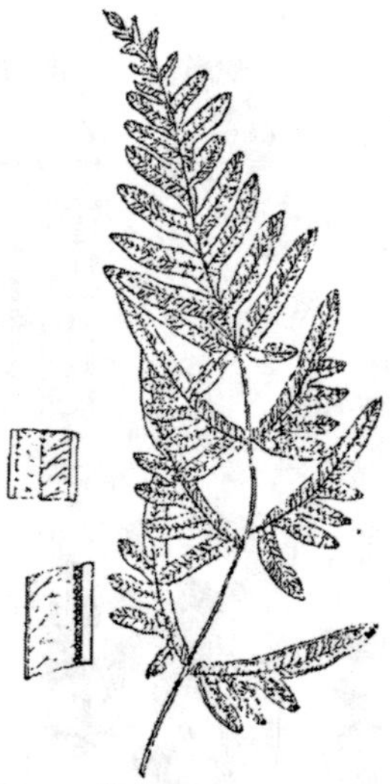

N°58.

PTERIS SEMIPINNATA. (*L.*)

9. PTERIS DALHOUSIÆ. (*Hook.*) Stipes strong, erect, about 1 foot high, polished, naked; fronds 2–3 feet long, 12–18 inches broad, 3–4 pinnatifid; upper pinnæ linear, unbranched decurrent down to the next pair, lower ones sometimes 1 foot long, deltoid; pinnules with simple or branched linear segments, the longest undivided ones 6 inches long, $\frac{1}{4}$–$\frac{3}{8}$ inch broad, those of the pinnæ with usually about 1 inch between them; the margins very slightly serrated; texture subcoriaceous; rachis and surfaces naked; veins fine, simple, or once-forked; indusium narrow-membranous. *Hook. Syn. Fil. p.* 157. *Bedd. F. B. I. t.* 191.

Penang.

10. PTERIS QUADRIAURITA. (*Retz.*) Stipe glabrous or scabrid; fronds very variable in size and texture, lanceolate or ovate-lanceolate, with 3–11 subopposite pairs of pinnæ; in the typical form all except the lowest pair are narrowly oblong acuminate or caudate, and cut down nearly to the rachis into many uniform segments, which are obtuse or acute entire or serrated, and the lowest pair bipartite; but in some forms several or nearly all the pinnæ are bipartite, and the lowest or two lower pairs have several pinnæ descending from the lower side, and in one form the lowest pair is completely bipinnate with five pinnæ on each side of the rachis; veins conspicuous,

usually once-forked; lowest veins reaching the margin above the sinus when very deeply cut, at the sinus when less deeply cut; sori generally partial on the segments, rarely continued to the apex. *Retz. Obs.* vi. 38. *Hook. Syn. Fil. p.* 158. *Bedd. F. S. I. t.* 31.

Throughout India, Ceylon, and the Malay Peninsula, from the plains up to 8,000 feet, very common.

(Also all round the world throughout the tropics and a little beyond them.)

The following varieties are tolerably constant even in cultivation:

VAR. β ARGENTEA. Like the type, but with broad white bands down the centre of the pinnæ.

Nilgiris and Western mountains of the Madras Presidency only at high altitudes; much in cultivation even in England.

VAR. γ ASPERICAULIS. Rachis and nerves red; stipe and rachis asperous, generally very rigid, coriaceous, and shining. (Often called rubro-nerva.)

Wynaad, Coorg, and elsewhere on the western side of Madras Presidency, 3,000–4,000 feet elevation.

VAR. δ SETIGERA. Rachises and costules setigerous, very membranaceous in texture, nearly all the pinnæ bipartite, the lowest pair with sometimes several pinnæ descending along the lower side. *Bedd. F. B. I. t.* 202.

Coorg and Malabar: Moulmein on limestone rocks.

VAR. ε LUDENS. Pinnules very abnormally cut, sometimes only with a waved margin for the greater length, then developing normal segments, then again narrowing into only the waved margin. *Bedd. F. S. I. tabs.* 41 and 219 (under Otaria.)

Malabar, Quilon; Ceylon.

Mr. Clarke gives the following varieties for Northern India:

VAR. ς KHASIANA. The lowest pinnæ with 5 secondary pinnæ

on each side of the rachis (*i. e.* completely bipinnate), those of the upper margin little smaller than those of the lower.

Khasya, 3,000 feet elevation.

Mr. Clarke says it graduates into the type.

VAR. η BLUMEANA. Lateral pinnæ with 50–60 segments, which are 1 inch long by $\frac{1}{6}$ inch broad, equally wide throughout or broader at apex, not falcate, obtuse, rounded, entire or crenulate at the barren apex. A very large fern. *Clarke, F. N. I. t.* 55.

Chittagong; Tenasserim; Singapore.

Much the habit of longipinnula.

VAR. θ SUBINDIVISA. (*Sp. Clarke.*) Small, with only 3 pinnæ, terminal one 6 inches long, with many segments, lateral pair hardly longer than the segments of the terminal pinna, or subobsolete.

Bhotan, Sikkim bed of the Teesta, 1,000 feet elevation.

Mr. Clarke has constituted this a species in his work on the "Ferns of Northern India," but he now agrees that it is only a variety of quadriaurita. *Clarke, F. N. I. t.* 56.

(Mr. Clarke's variety major has arched veins and is Campteria biaurita.)

11. PTERIS GREVILLEANA. (*Wall.*) Dimorphic, barren stipe shorter, winged towards the apex; barren frond pedately 5-fid, scarcely pinnate, margin spinulose-serrate; fertile frond with 5 pinnæ, the lower pair bipartite, veins exceedingly obscure. *Wall. Cat.* 2,680. *Agardh, Recens. Gen. Pter.* 23. *Clarke, t.* 54.

Sylhet, Cachar, Shapoor.

Suspiciously like quadriaurita, except that the fronds are dimorphic. Mr. Clarke thinks it is more nearly allied to ensiformis.

12. PTERIS LONGIPINNULA. (*Wall.*) Stipes erect, naked, 2–3 feet; fronds up to 3 feet long, and 18 inches broad, pinnate; pinnæ about 5 pairs, large, rather distant, deeply pinnatifid, segments entire, blunt, falcate, not distant, $1\frac{1}{2}$–$2\frac{1}{4}$ inches long, $\frac{1}{4}$–$\frac{1}{2}$ inch broad, apex usually barren, crenate, or subentire, the lowest pair undivided, or rarely bi-partite; texture subcoriaceous; rachis and surfaces naked;

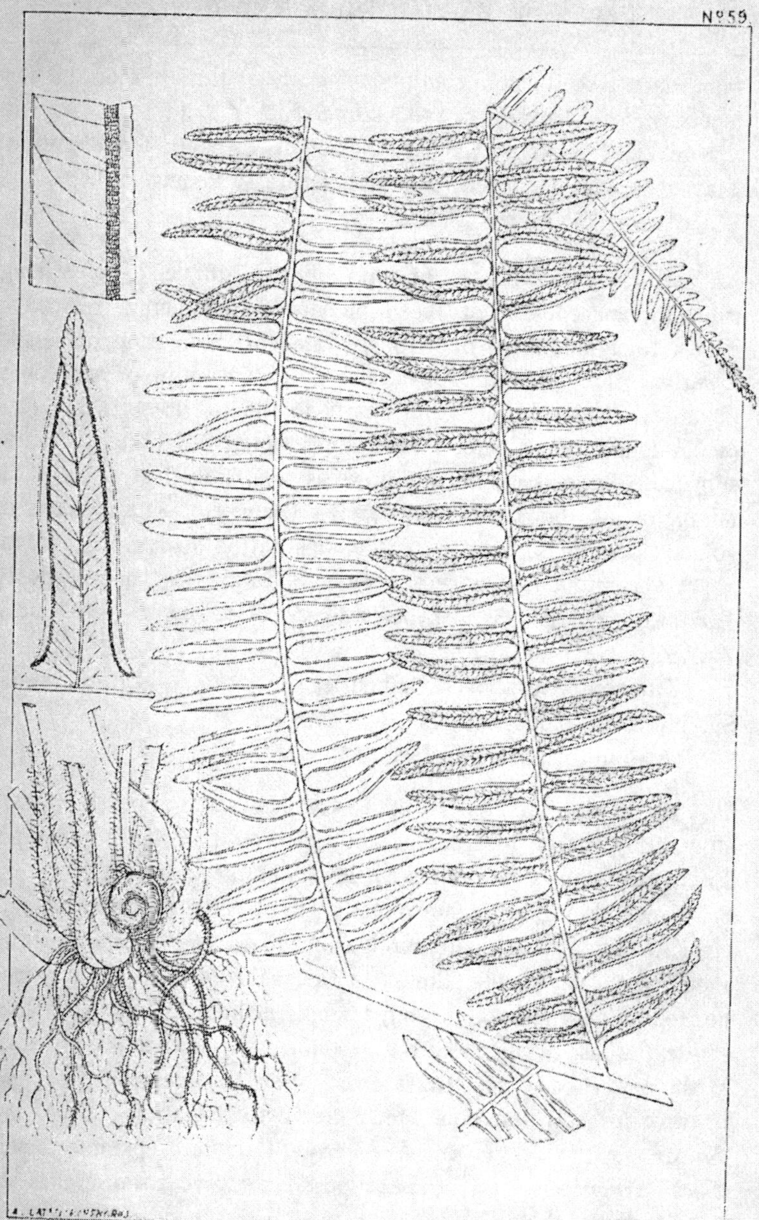

PTERIS PATENS. (*Hook.*)

veins once forked; sori continuous nearly to the apex of the segments. *Hook. Syn. Fil. p.* 158. *Bedd. F. S. I. t.* 43.

Sikkim; Khasya; Cachar; Sylhet up to 3,000 feet elevation; Travancore and Tinnevelly Mountains; Malay Peninsula.

(Also in the Malay Islands.)

13. PTERIS EXCELSA. (*Gaud.*) Fronds ample, 5–6 feet long, submembranaceous, light green, pinnate; pinnæ large, remote, 6 inches to a foot long, numerous, ovate-lanceolate caudate sessile, lower ones long-petiolate, lowest pair of pinnæ entire, or sometimes bipartite, all deeply pinnatifid nearly to the costa; segments (2–4 inches long) from a broad base, linear-lanceolate obtuse serrated subfalcate, lower base decurrent, veins free, forked at or near the middle or 3–4 branched; very rarely a few veinlets anastomose; involucres continuous from the base almost to the apex, rather broad; stipes very stout and flexuose; rachises bright castaneous glossy. *Hook. Sp. Fil.* ii. 183. *Gaud. in Fréyc. Voy. Bot. p.* 388. *Bedd. F. B. I. t.* 218.

Kumaon, Gurwhal; Dalhousie, 4,000–8,000 feet elevation; Sikkim, 8,000–9,000 feet; Nynee Tal.

(Also in the Sandwich Islands.)

14. PTERIS PATENS. (*Hook.*) Caudex erect; stipes numerous, stout, scaly at their base, rachis stout, glabrous; fronds ample, erect, strict, membranaceous, pinnate; lower pinnæ bi-tripartite; pinnæ 8–16 inches long, strict horizontally patent, numerous approximate, elongate oblong, acuminate, rarely subcaudate, sessile or lower ones shortly petiolate, deeply (almost to the rachis) pinnatifid; segments horizontal, very uniform, linear, scarcely acuminate, serrulate where sterile, the base dilated decurrently-confluent on both sides, especially at the lower base, sometimes apart; veins all free, simple or once or twice forked; sori continuous nearly to the apex. *Hook. Syn. Fil.* ii. 177. *Bedd. F. S. I. t.* 205. Campteria patens, *Baker. Hook. Syn. Fil. p.* 165. (The supposed narrow costal arches are only a wing to the rachis.)

Madras Presidency, Carcoor ghat, Wynaad and Travancore Hills,

2,000–2,500 feet elevation; Ceylon, Dodawilla, Matele and Mooroowa forests, above 2,000 feet elevation.

(Also in Borneo, Philippines and Society Islands.)

15. PTERIS LONGIPES. (*Don.*) Fronds membranaceous, furnished above with a few subulate scales on the rachis of the pinnæ, and with hairs on the rachis of the segments, ternately divided, or subpedately divided into 5–7 segments, lateral divisions multipinnate; pinnæ short, petiolate or subsessile lanceolate acuminate, deeply pinnatifid to the apex, or with the apex long caudate, segments oblong obtuse subtruncate, serrated at the sterile portions of the apex; sori lateral on the segments, never extending to the apex or base; veins rather remote, all forked, basal ones arising from the axil of the costule, and extending to the margin much above the sinus. *G. Don. Prod. Fl. Nep.* 15. Pteris pellucens, *Agardh, Sp. Gen. Pter.* 43. *Hook. Sp. Fil.* ii. 191. *Bedd. F. S. I. t.* 32. (South Indian examples are always ternately divided, but those from N. India have often 5, rarely 7, pinnæ.)

All the western hills of the Madras Presidency, 2,000–5,000 feet elevation; Ceylon; Birma; Sikkim, Bhotan; and Khasya 1,000–5,000 feet elevation.

(Also Guinea coast and Guatemala.)

§ *Stipes distant from a long creeping rhizome, indusium double.*
(*Genus Pæsia and Ornithopteris of authors.*)

16. PTERIS AQUILINA. (*L.*) Rhizome stout, creeping underground; stipes about 1 foot long, strong, erect, naked; fronds 2–6 feet long, 1–2 feet broad, subdeltoid in outline, only the uppermost pinnæ simple, the next lanceolate cut down nearly or quite to the rachis into short triangular or linear pinnules, the lowest long-stalked, 1 foot or more long, with ample lanceolate pinnules which are cut down to the rachis into numerous lanceolate segments, which are again fully pinnate; largest entire ultimate segments 1 inch long, 2 lines broad; texture thin or subcoriaceous; rachis and surfaces naked or pubescent; veins close, conspicuous, often twice forked; involucre double, or the

inner obsolete. *Hook. Syn. Fil. p.* 163. *Linn. Sp. pl.* 1533. *Bedd. F. S. I. t.* 42.

Throughout India, Ceylon, and the Malay Peninsula on the mountains, 2,000–8,000 feet elevation.

(Also throughout the whole world, except the Arctic zones and temperate South America.)

VAR. β ESCULENTA. Ultimate segments distant, linear and elongated. Moulmein and the Malay Peninsula southwards.

GENUS XXIX.—CAMPTERIA. (*Presl.*)

(*Kamptos*, arched; the lowest veins meeting and forming an arch.)

As in Pteris, but the lowest veinlets from the base of the vein or costule of each segment united with the veinlet from the next costule, and forming long arches along the costa of the pinnæ; upper veinlets free.

1. CAMPTERIA BIAURITA. (*Linn. under Pteris.*) Quite similar to Pteris quadriaurita, except that the costules of the segments are connected by a long arching veinlet; the pinnæ are generally less deeply divided, and the plant is generally larger and coarser, but these two latter differences cannot be relied on. *Linn. Sp. Pl.* 1534, under Pteris. *Hook. Syn. Fil. p.* 164. *Bedd. F. S. I. t.* 44.

Western parts of Madras Presidency up to 6,000 feet; not common. Pretty general throughout Northern India from the plains up to 6,000 feet. Ceylon; Malay Peninsula.

(Also in Malay Islands, China, tropical Africa, and Australia.)

2. CAMPTERIA KLEINIANA. (*Presl.*) 4–6 feet high; fronds very large, sub-membranaceous, pedately ovate, pinnate; pinnæ sub-sessile lanceolate with a long acumination; lowest pair with two large pinnæ descending from the lower margin of the costa; all the pinnæ deeply pinnatifid (leaving a broad margin on each side of the costa); segments falcate oblong, sterile ones broadly crenated, and fertile ones

N°60

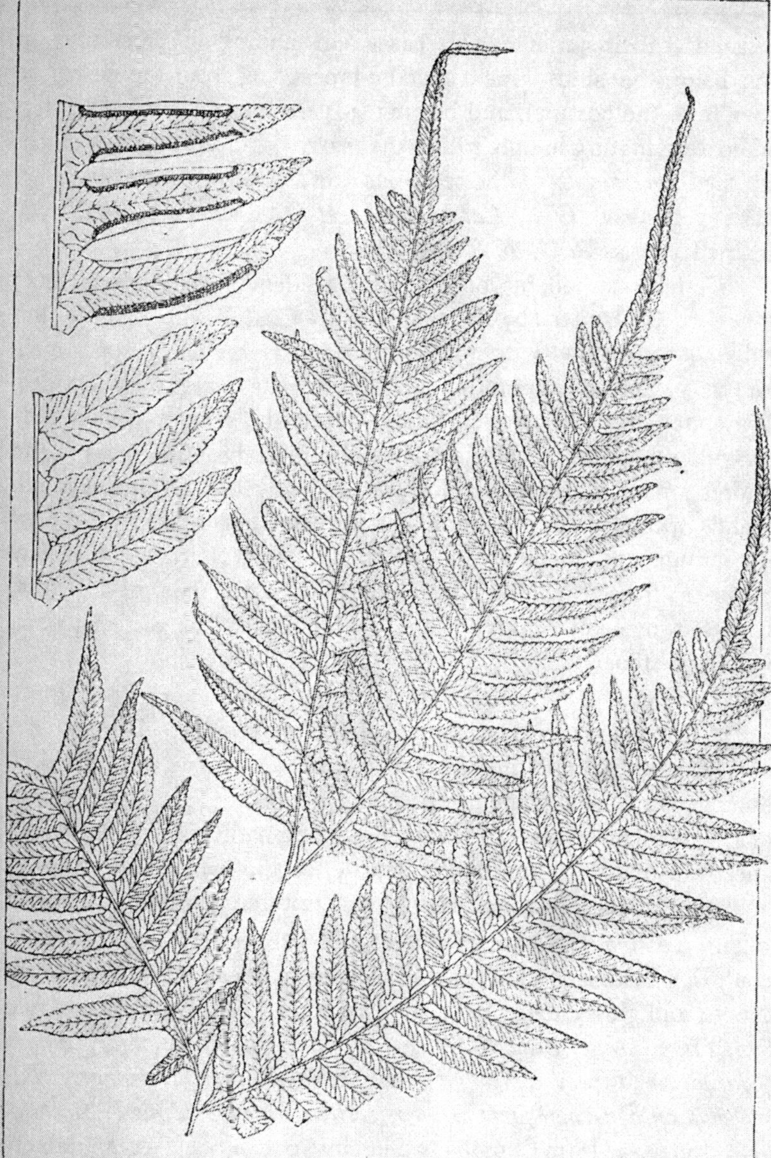

A. S. CATTELL & Co. ENGRAV.

CAMPTERIA KLEINIANA. (*Presl.*)

crenated at their sterile apices; basal veins uniting in pairs into an arch below the sinus (one generally proceeding from the costa, the other from the costule), and bearing 3–4 free veinlets; other veinlets forked, terminating in dots within the margin; indusium never reaching the base or apex of the segments. *Klein. Tent. Pter.* 147. *t.* 5. Pteris geminata, *Wall. Cat.* 2180. *Hook. Syn. Fil.* 164. *C.* Anamallayensis, *Bedd. F. S. I. t.* 45.

Western mountains of Madras Presidency 2,000–4,500 feet; rather rare. United by Hooker and by Clarke with biaurita but really quite distinct; its thin texture and very wavy appearance are very unlike any form of biaurita; its margin is, besides, always crenated, and the veins never reach the margin, which they always do in biaurita. It is one of the most beautiful ferns in the Madras forests, and has been for years in cultivation at Ootacamund. Wight's specimens from Courtallum are named geminata in the Kew Herbarium, and there are no specimens from N. India; there are specimens from Johanna Island; also from the Isle of Mayotta, (collected by Lady Barkly), named by Mr. Baker Campteria maxima. *Sp. Fil. p.* 480.

3. CAMPTERIA WALLICHIANA. (*Ag.*) Fronds ample, glabrous, submembranaceous, 3-partite, lateral branches compoundly divided, terminal one elongated, pinnated; pinnæ numerous, sessile, 4–6 inches long, linear-lanceolate acuminate, deeply pinnatifid; segments linear-lanceolate obtuse, sterile ones serrulate, all approximate, about ½ an inch long; basal veins monarcuate, the rest free and forked, rarely a solitary areole at the base of the costule; stipes very long, 5–6 feet; stout, rich castaneous, and, as well as the paler-coloured rachises, very smooth and glossy. *Ag. Sp. Gen. Pter. p.* 69. *Hook. Sp. Fil.* ii. 206. *Syn. Fil. p.* 165. *Bedd. F. B. I. t.* 25 *and* 217. *Var. quadripinnata (Clarke) is a very compound form with the pinnæ tripinnate; it is probably an abnormal form or monstrosity which would not be constant.*

Himalayas from Chumba to Bhotan 3,000–8,000 feet, abundant; Khasya.

(Also in the Philippines, Java, and Samoa.)

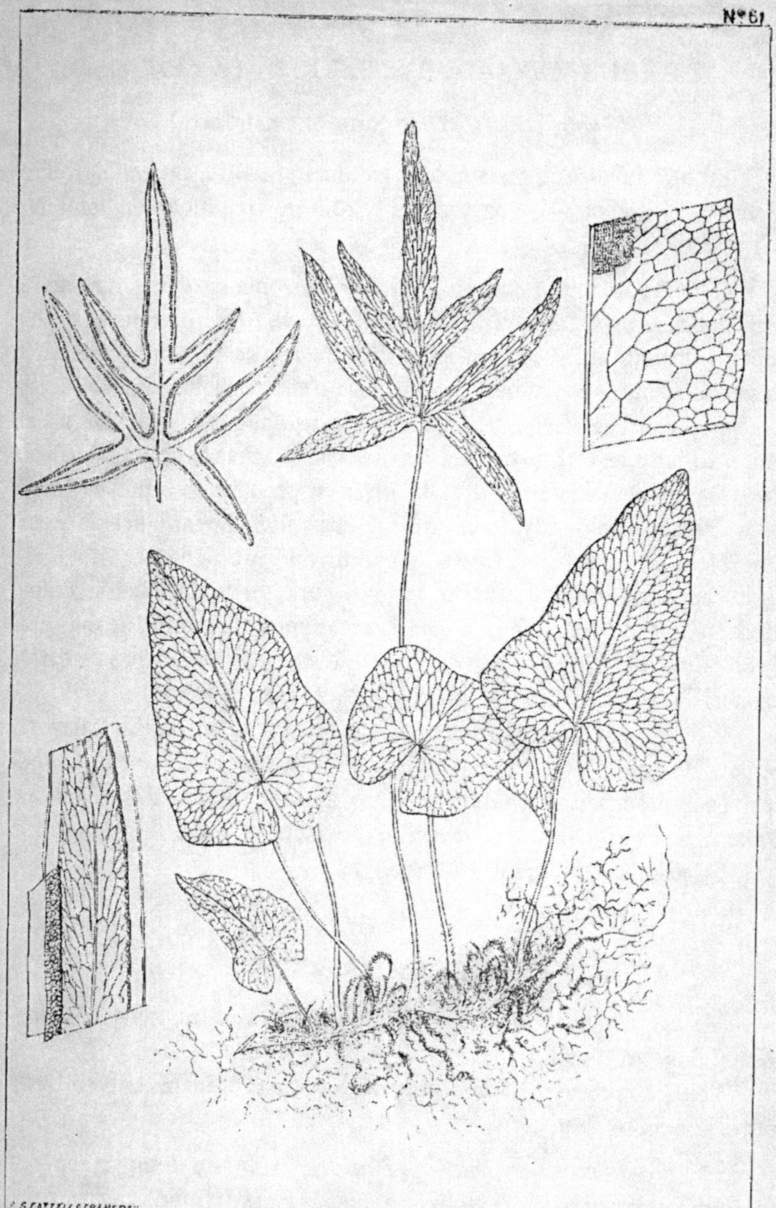

DORYOPTERIS LUDENS. (*Wall.*)

GENUS XXX.—DORYOPTERIS. (*J. Smith.*)

(*Dory*, spear; *pteris*, form of the fronds.)

Fronds small, sub-pedate or sagittate, in texture and colour like Pellæa; veins copiously anastomosing, without free included veinlets; the rest as in Pteris.

1. DORYOPTERIS LUDENS. (*Wall.*) Rhizome creeping, furnished with linear adpressed brown scales which have white margins; stipes solitary distant, polished, sometimes with a few scales, and often with dusky sub-tomentose pubescence at base and apex; barren frond on a stipe 3–4 inches long, triangular with two slightly deflexed basal lobes, to hastate with two basal and two large spreading lateral lobes, the margin entire; fertile frond, on a stipe often 12 inches long, 4–6 inches each way, cut down into five linear-lanceolate or lanceolate lobes, one erect, two spreading and two deflexed, of which all except the last are sometimes again forked; texture coriaceous, costa polished, veins hidden; sori continuous all round the margin. *Wall. Cat.* 88. *Hook. Syn. Fil.* 166. *Clarke, F. N. I.* 470. Litobrochia ludens and pedata, *Bedd. F. N. I. t.* 26 *and* 27.

Chittagong Hills up to 1,000 feet elevation; Orissa, on the Balasore Hills; Birma. (A specimen in Wight's herbarium of this or an allied species is supposed to be from the Dindigul mountains in the Madras Presidency; but it has never been found there of late.)

(Also in the Philippine islands.)

GENUS XXXI.—LITOBROCHIA. (*Presl.*)

(*Lithos*, a stone; *brocha*, spots; the areoles of the net-like veins resembling pavement.)

Veins copiously anastomosing with some free included veinlets; otherwise as in Pteris.

1. LITOBROCHIA INCISA. (*Thunb.*) Caudex long creeping, subterraneous; stipes and rachis castaneous glossy; fronds ample, sub-

N°62

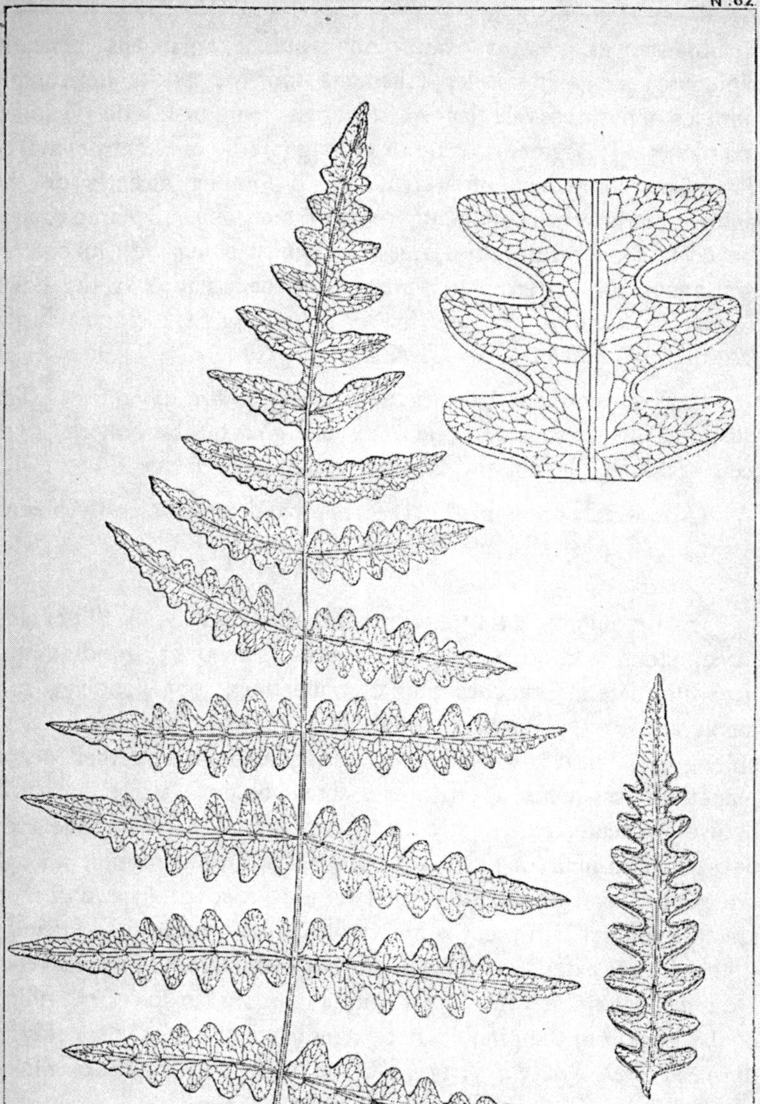

LITOBROCHIA INCISA. (*Thunb.*)

membranaceous, distant ovate, long stipitate, glaucous beneath, tripinnate; pinnæ all sessile, subadnate mostly opposite horizontal; pinnules opposite sessile, lanceolate obtuse, more or less deeply lobed and pinnatifid; segments ovate or oblong (sterile ones subsinuate) or triangular, lowest one often remote and forming auricles on the rachis, superior ones confluent; veins all anastomosing, areoles next the costa and costules the largest and most elongated; involucres continuous or interrupted, membranaceous entire at the edge. *Thunb. Pr. Fl. Cap.* 171. *Hook. Syn. Fil. p.* 172. Litobrochia aurita, *Hook. Sp. Fil.* ii. 231. *Bedd. F. S. I. t.* 221.

Ceylon, central and southern provinces, above 3,000 feet. Travancore Hills 3,000–4,000 feet. Sispara ghat on the Nilgiris, 4,500 feet. Sikkim, Bhotan, and Khasya, 3,000–6,500 feet.

(Also widely distributed in the tropics and sub-tropics of America, Africa, Asia, Australia, and Polynesia.)

2. LITOBROCHIA MARGINATA. (*Bory, under Pteris.*) Stipes elongated, stout, and with the rachis sub-castaneous; fronds ample, tripartite, lateral branches pinnate, spreading, long petiolate, submembranaceous, glabrous; pinnules 4–6 inches or more long, linear-oblong or linear-lanceolate sub-sessile, acuminate, rather deeply pinnatifid; segments approximate, linear-oblong falcate (upwards) obtuse or acute, entire or scarcely serrated and only at the apex, nearly half an inch long; sinuses obtuse; basal veins forming a single arc parallel with the costa; veins forming a series of two or more areoles (parallel with the costule), from which proceed free veinlets which do not extend to the margin but terminate with a thickened apex just within it; involucres continuous on the lower two-thirds of the margin of the pinnules not extending to the apex. *Bory. Voy.* 2. *p.* 192. *Hook. Syn. Fil. p.* 172. Pteris tripartita, *Hook. Sp. Fil.* ii. 225. Litobrochia tripartita, *Bedd. F. S. I. t.* 220.

Ceylon, common about Galle and the central provinces; Madras Presidency, much cultivated, and said to be found wild in the Cochin forests; Malacca.

(Also in West tropical Africa, the East African Islands, Queensland, the Philippines, and Polynesia.)

GENUS XXXII.—CERATOPTERIS. (*Brong.*)

(*Keras, keratos*, a horn ; *pteris*, a fern: the horned fern.)

Sori placed on two or three distantly anastomosing veins which run down the frond longitudinally, and are parallel both with the edge and midrib ; veins of the sterile fronds articulated in oblique oblong hexagonal areoles. Capsules scattered on the receptacles, sessile, subglobose, with a ring which is either complete or more or less partial or obsolete. Indusium formed of the reflexed margin of the fronds, those of the two sides meeting against the midrib. A very anomalous genus, regarded by some as a distinct order; it is very unlike Pterideæ, and should be placed in a distinct tribe.

1. CERATOPTERIS THALICTROIDES. (*Lin.*) Stipes tufted, thick inflated, filled with large air-cells; fronds succulent in texture, the barren ones floating or erect, simple or slightly divided when young, bi-tripinnate with narrow linear segments when mature, fertile ones bi-tripinnate ; ultimate segments podlike. *Hook. Syn. Fil. p.* 174. *Bedd. F. S. I. t.* 75. Acrostichum thalictroides, *L. Sp. Pl.* 1527.

Throughout India, Ceylon, and the Malay Peninsula up to 3,000 feet elevation; common in tanks, ditches, and swampy places, or even dry ground during the rains. Mr. J. Smith says it is an annual, but I do not think it is so in cultivation, if kept in water or very moist, as I had the same plant growing for some years at Ootacamund.

(Also in the tropics of the whole world.)

N°83.

A.S. CATTELL & Co

CERATÓPTERIS THALICTROIDES. (*L.*)

GENUS XXXIII.—LOMARIA. (*Willd.*)

(*Loma*, fringe or border; relating to the indusium.)

Sori linear continuous, parallel with the midrib and occupying the whole, or nearly the whole, of the space between it and the edge; indusium membranous, formed of the revolute edge of the frond. Fronds dimorphous, usually once or twice pinnatifid or pinnate, rarely simple or bi-pinnate; veins free; ring of capsule vertical.

1. LOMARIA PATERSONI. (*Spreng.*) Rhizome short-creeping; stipes 2–3 inches long, wiry, erect, rather scaly below; sterile frond simple, about 1 foot long and 1 inch broad, narrowed at both ends, or pinnatifid, 2 feet or more long, cut down nearly to the rachis into 6–12 segments on each side, which are often 6–9 inches long and nearly 1 inch broad, and suddenly decurrent at the base; texture coriaceous; fertile fronds simple and only $\frac{1}{8}$ inch broad, or pinnatifid with numerous segments on each side, 6 inches long by $\frac{1}{8}$ inch broad; or the fronds are sometimes in part sterile, in part fertile; veins prominent in the young sterile fronds, inconspicuous in mature fronds, forked, thickened at the apex close to the margin; sori covering the whole space between midrib and margin. *Spr. Sys. Veg.* iv. 62. *Hook. Syn. Fil.* 174. L. elongata (Blume), *Bedd. F. S. I. t.* 28, 28A.

Nilgiris and Anamallays 5,000–8,000 feet elevation. Ceylon, 4,000 feet and upwards. Nilgiris examples have the fertile fronds always pinnatifid as far as I have observed, and the sterile ones generally so. From Ceylon I have examples with the sterile and fertile both quite simple.

(Also in the Philippines, Fiji, New Zealand, S. Australia, and Tasmania.)

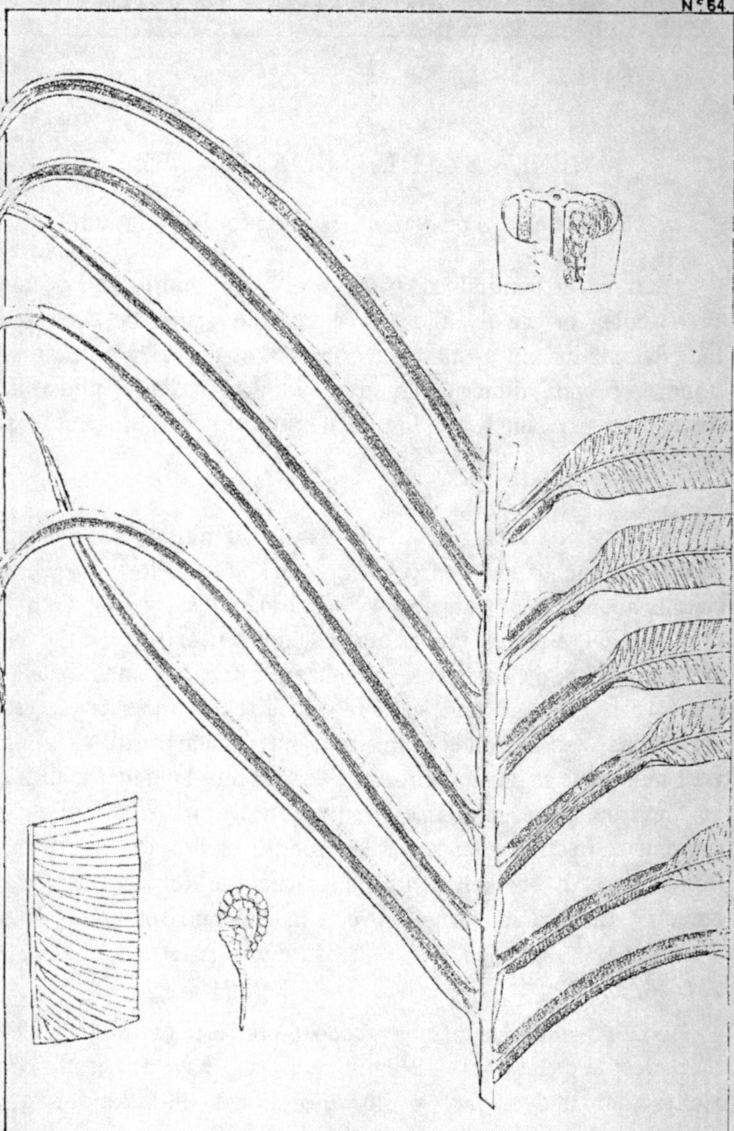

LOMARIA PATERSONI. (*Spr.*)

GENUS XXXIV.—PLAGIOGYRIA. (*Kunze.*)

(*Plagios*, oblique; *gyros*, a circle; the oblique ring of the capsule.)

As in Lomaria, except that the capsules have an oblique ring, and the base of the stipe is suddenly dilated, fleshy, triquetrous, and furnished with large spongy glands.

1. PLAGIOGYRIA ADNATA. (*Blume.*) Caudex stout short; stipes cæspitose, elongated, brown, triquetrous; a span to 1½ foot long; slender, naked at the base, dilated and subcarnose, furnished with orbicular spongy glands; fronds a foot and more long, ovate-lanceolate, chartaceous-membranaceous, sterile ones pinnatifid almost to the rachis, below pinnated, but all the pinnæ united by a narrow wing; segments mostly opposite distant lanceolate, much acuminated, more or less falcate, the inferior base round, superior base extended upwards, the margins entire or obscurely toothed, the apex strongly serrated; fertile fronds pinnated; pinnæ alternate distant linear sessile, rather obtuse; sori covering the whole under side between the costa and the brown membranaceous very distinct involucre. *Bl. En. Fil. Jav. p.* 205. *Hook. Sp. Fil.* iii. 19. *Bedd. F. B. I. t.* 51.

Khasya, 4,000–5,000 feet elevation.

(Also in Japan and Java) Mr. Clarke thinks it possible that this is not the same as Blume's Java plant, as the only example of that is a portion of a fertile frond.

2. PLAGIOGYRIA GLAUCA. (*Bl.*) Caudex stout erect; stipes elongated, subcompressed tetragonous with two furrows in front, the base dilated triquetrous on the anterior face bearing spongy depressed glands, fronds ovate-oblong 1–2 feet long, pinnated; sterile pinnæ numerous, 3–5 inches long, chartaceous, horizontally spreading, sessile, or very nearly so, lanceolate, acuminated at the base, truncated beneath, having a gland as much attached to the rachis as to the very short petiole; the margins finely dentate-serrulate, rather

No. 65.

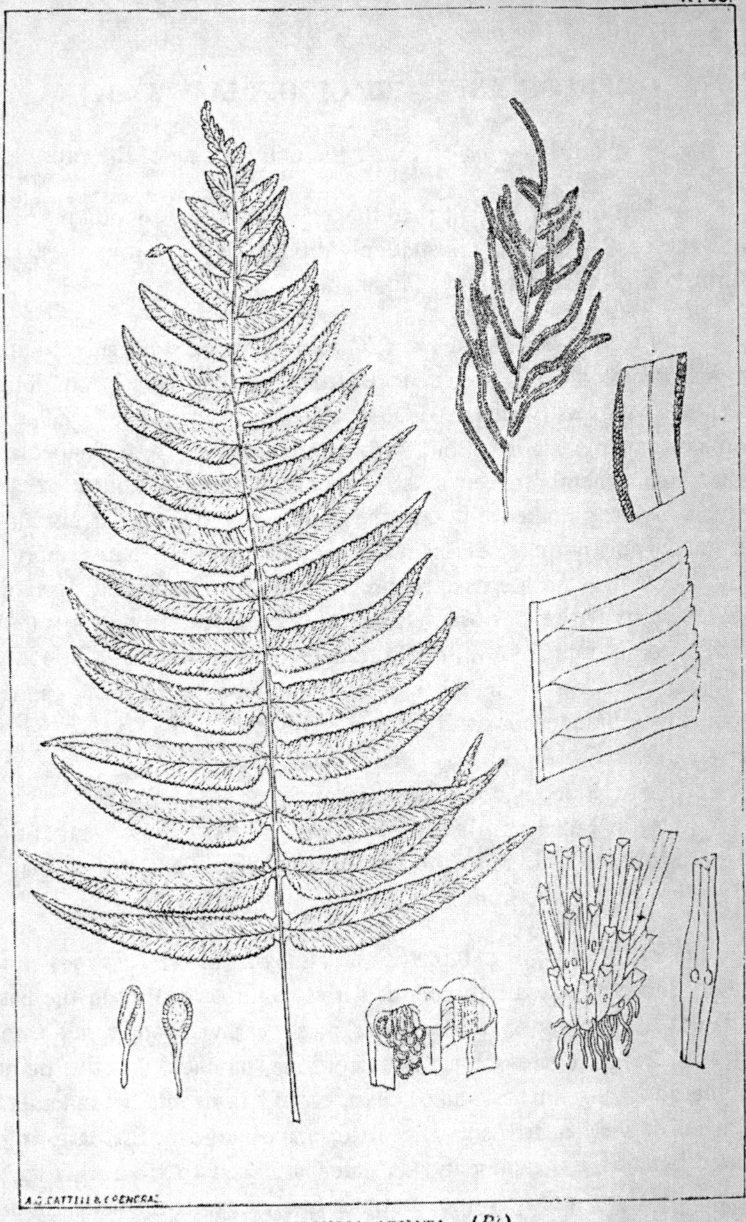

PLAGIOGYRIA ADNATA. (*Bl.*)

more strongly at the apex, white and almost powdery beneath, green above with a tinge of red; veins copious, compact, simple and forked; ultimate short pinnæ confluent into a pinnatifid and lobed caudate apex, fertile pinnæ narrow-linear obtuse erect-patent on very short petioles, which sometimes bear a gland beneath; sori and involucres as in other Plagiogyriæ. *Bl. En. Fil. I. p.* 204. Lomaria (Plagiogyria) glauca, *Hook. Sp. Fil.* iii. 22. *Bedd. F. B. I. t.* 90.

Khasya, 4,000–5,000 feet elevation. (*Probably only a variety of pycnophylla.*)

(Also in Java.)

3. PLAGIOGYRIA PYCNOPHYLLA. (*Kunze.*) Caudex stout, erect, very woody, and having many wiry roots; fronds fascicled; stipes sub-quadrangular 2-furrowed in front (as is the rachis), at the base dilated fleshy, triquetrous, bearing spongy glands; fronds 1–2 and more feet long, sterile ones, sub-chartaceous opaque, brown when dry, oblong-ovate pinnated for its whole length, except that the small terminal ones are confluent into a lobed (or pinnatifid) and finely acuminate and serrated apex, pinnæ horizontally patent sessile or very nearly so, numerous, approximate, narrow oblong-lanceolate very finely almost caudately acuminate, the base very obtuse and truncate (neither dilated nor contracted), at the base beneath furnished with one or two prominent glands (sometimes wanting); the margin very minutely serrulate, the caudate apex strongly serrated; veins numerous, closely placed, simple and forked; fertile fronds narrower pinnated; pinnæ linear obtuse on very short petioles with a gland on the under side; involucre at first vaulted, conspicuous, membranaceous, brown, at length forced back by the capsules. *Kze. in Bot. Zeit.* iv. *p.* 143. *Hook. Sp. Fil.* iii. 21. *Bedd. F. B. I. t.* 52.

Nepal and Bhotan, 6,000–11,000 feet; very common at 7,000–8,000 feet. Khasya, 4,000–6,000 feet; Malay Peninsula.

(Also in Java.)

4. PLAGIOGYRIA EUPHLEBIA. (*Kunze.*) Caudex stout woody elongated; stipes 1 foot or more long, naked erect, triquetrous below,

fronds ovate-lanceolate, 1–2 feet long, 6–12 inches broad; pinnæ 1 inch or more apart at the base, all stalked except towards the apex, erect-patent, linear, 4–6 inches long, $\frac{1}{4}$–$\frac{3}{4}$ inch broad, narrowed at the base on both sides, and at the apex, where it is toothed; texture subcoriaceous; veins prominent; fertile fronds similar, but the pinnæ more distant and narrowly linear; rachis erect naked. *Kze. in Bot. Zeit.* 1848, *p.* 521. *Hook. Syn. Fil. p.* 183. *Bedd. F. B. I. t.* 165.

Nepal, Khasya, 4,000–6,000 feet.

(Also in Japan and N. Australia.)

TRIBE VII.—BLECHNEÆ.

Sori linear or oblong dorsal, parallel with the midrib and edge of the segments, not close to the latter; indusium the same shape as the sorus, superior, opening towards the midrib.

GENUS XXXV.—BLECHNUM. (*L.*)

(One of the Greek names for a fern.)

Sori linear, continuous, or nearly so, parallel with and usually contiguous to the midrib; indusium membranous, distinct from the edge of the frond; fronds uniform or only slightly dimorphous, generally pinnate or pinnatifid; veins free.

1. BLECHNUM CARTILAGINEUM. (*Swartz.*) Caudex oblique, densely clothed at the crown with blackish fibrillose scales; stipes strong erect scaly and muricated in the lower part; fronds ovate-oblong, 1–2 feet long, 6–9 inches broad, pinnatifid and pinnate towards the base; pinnæ numerous erect-patent linear, 4–6 inches long, $\frac{1}{4}$–$\frac{1}{2}$ inch broad, narrowed gradually upwards, margin serrulate; the lowest pinnæ linear distant, narrower than those above, but not reduced to mere auricles. *Sw. Syn. Fil.* 114 *and* 312. *Clarke, F. N. I. p.* 473. *Hook. Syn. Fil.* 184.

Mishmee.—Mr. Clarke refers Griffith's solitary specimen to this species, which is Australian. Hooker referred it to nitidum, an

N°66

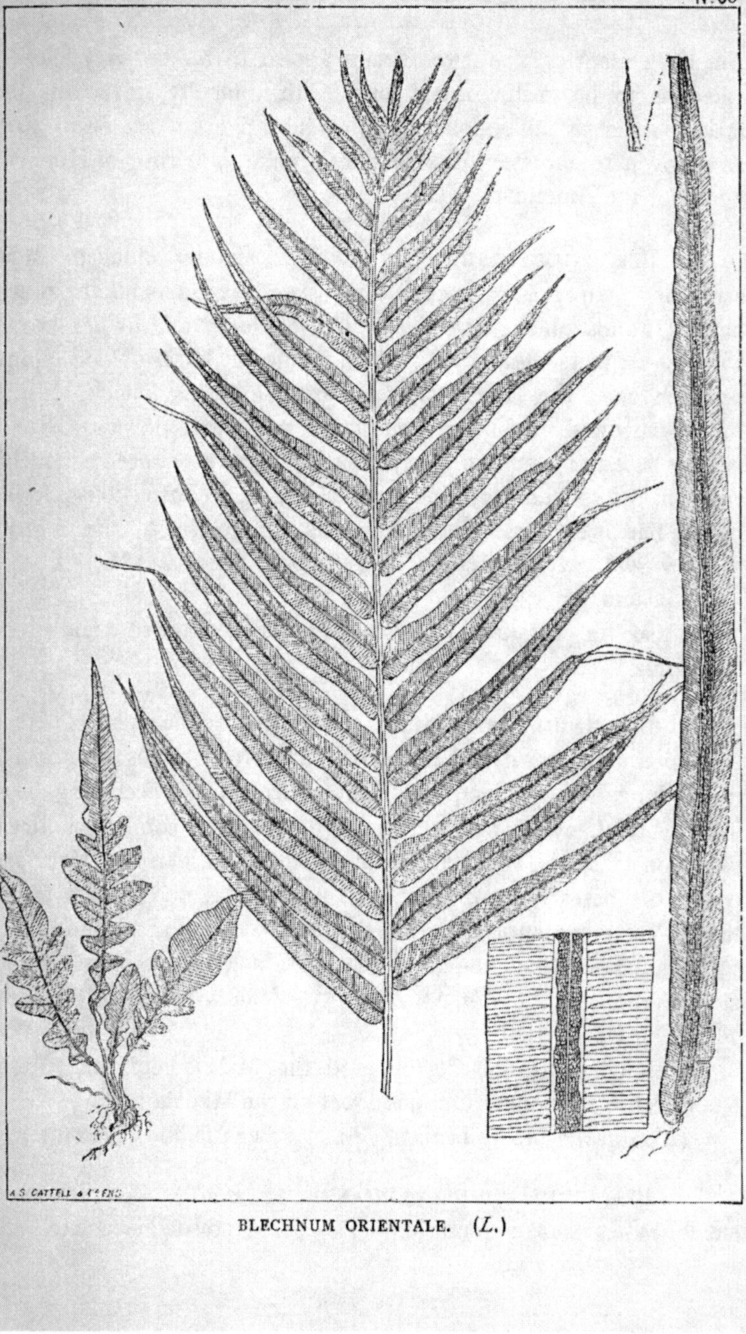

BLECHNUM ORIENTALE. (*L.*)

American plant. The two species appear to me so very closely allied as to be distinguished only with difficulty, if at all; the rachis is slightly puberulous in both. The figure *t.* 49, *Ferns Brit. Ind.*, given to represent the Mishmee plant, is a copy of Hooker's figure of the American species.

2. BLECHNUM SERRULATUM. (*Rich.*) Caudex elongated stout ascending; stipes 6–12 inches long, strong, erect, smooth, nearly naked; fronds oblong acuminate, 1–2 feet long, 6–9 inches broad, with 12–24 pairs of quite distinct articulated linear-oblong pinnæ on each side, the largest of which are 4–5 inches long, ½–¾ inch broad, narrowed gradually towards the point and downwards to a narrow base; the margin finely incised; texture coriaceous; rachis rigid naked; veins very fine and close, not conspicuous; fertile pinnæ narrower; sori in a continuous line close to the midrib. *Rich. in Act. Soc. Nat. Par.* i. 114. *Hook. Syn. Fil.* 186.

Malacca.

(Also in tropical America, Australia, Borneo, and New Caledonia.)

3. BLECHNUM ORIENTALE. (*Linn.*) Caudex stout erect, clothed at the crown with fibrillose dark brown scales; stipes 4–8 inches long, strong, erect, scaly below; fronds 1–5 feet long, 6–36 inches broad, ovate, with very numerous nearly contiguous linear pinnæ on each side, which are about ¾ inch broad, narrowed to a long point, the bases quite distinct, the upper ones decurrent, a few of the lowest mere auricles; texture subcoriaceous; rachis and both surfaces naked; veins fine and close; sori in a long continuous line close to the midrib. *Lin. Sp. Pl.* 1535. *Hook. Syn. Fil.* 186. *Bedd. F. S. I. t.* 29.

Throughout India, Ceylon, and the Malay Peninsula, up to 6,000 feet in the south, and 4,000 feet on the Himalayas.

(Also in the Malay Islands, China, Polynesia and Australia.)

4. BLECHNUM FINDLAYSONIANUM. (*Wall.*) Caudex very small; stipes short; frond ample, 2–4 feet, ovate-lanceolate, sub-

coriaceous, pinnated; pinnæ erect-patent, rather distant, 6–12–14 inches long, 1–1¾ wide, oblong or elongate-oblong, sessile, obliquely cuneate at the base, entire, upper ones much decurrent, but (except the two upper ones) not coadunate; the apex suddenly and sharply acuminated; several of the lowest pairs abortive, reduced to small hard scales; the surface glossy; veins obscure, compact, parallel; sori close to the costa continuous, narrow-linear; involucres also very narrow and indistinct. *Wall. Cat. n.* 2172. *Hook. Sp. Fil.* iii. 53, and *Syn. Fil. p.* 187. *Bedd. F. B. I. t.* 249.

Penang and the Malay Peninsula. (*Perhaps only a very broad-leaved form of orientale.*)

GENUS XXXVI.—BLECHNIDIUM. (*Moore.*)

(Resemblance to Blechnum.)

Like Blechnum, but the veins anastomosing and forming large arched areoles.

1. BLECHNIDIUM MELANOPUS. (*Hook. under Blechnum.*) Stipes black erect, 6 inches long, naked; fronds broadly falcate-lanceolate, glossy, sub-coriaceous, pinnate; pinnæ very approximate from a rather broad adnate base, linear-oblong falcate, somewhat acute, the margin entire, narrowly revolute, uppermost ones gradually confluent into a lanceolate elongated lobe, the lowest 3–4 pair suddenly diminished, short, very obtuse, sub-auriculate at the superior base; veins internal reticulated, forming large angled areoles next the costa, narrower oblique ones often extending to the margin; ultimate veinlets free and clavate at their apex just within the margin; sori quite close to the costa, continuous, not reaching to the apex of the pinnæ, lower half of the rachis beneath black. *Hook. Sp. Fil.* iii. 64. *Syn. Fil. p.* 186. *Bedd. F. B. I. t.* 50.

Khasya Hills.

N°67

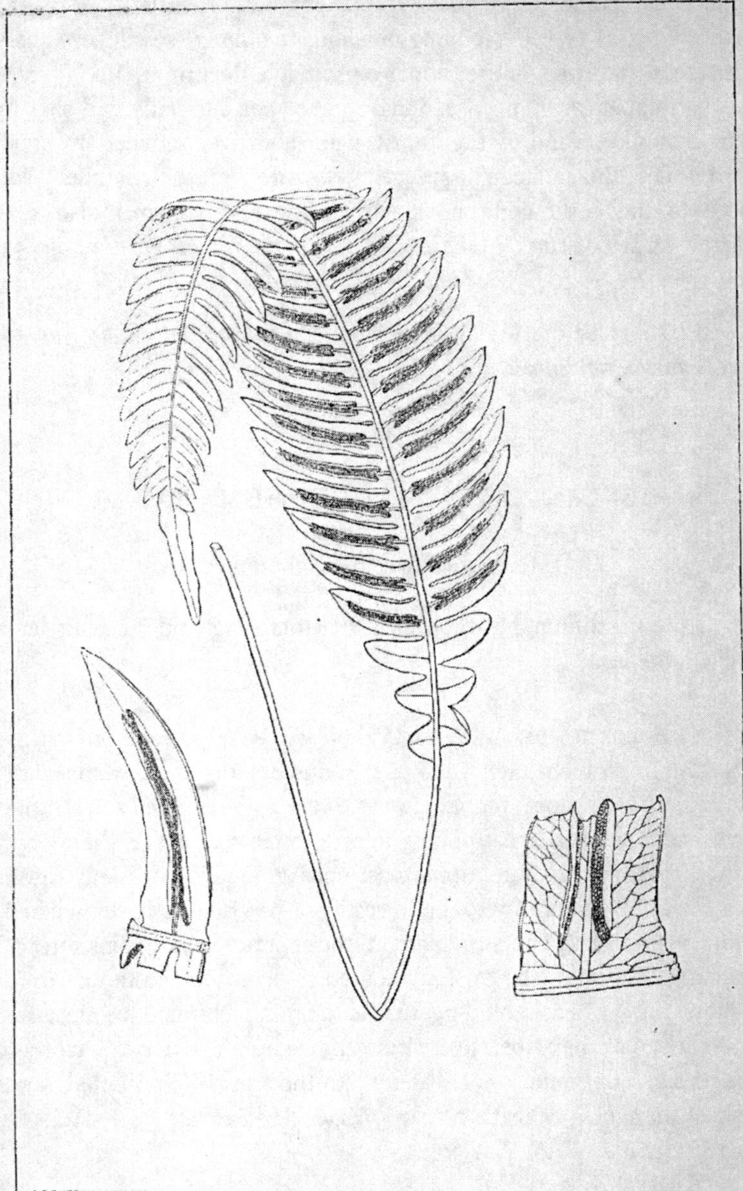

BLECHNIDIUM MELANOPUS. (*Hook.*)

GENUS XXXVII.—WOODWARDIA. (*Smith.*)

(In honour of T. J. Woodward, an English Botanist.)

Sori linear or linear-oblong, sunk in cavities of the frond, placed in single rows parallel with and contiguous to the midribs of the pinnæ and pinnules; indusium sub-coriaceous, the same shape as the sorus, closing over the cavity like a lid; veins forming a series of costal arches; the rest free or anastomosing; fronds ample and bi-pinnatifid.

1. WOODWARDIA RADICANS. (*Smith.*) Stipes elongate, with large lanceolate acuminate paleaceous scales at the base; fronds ample, pinnate, subcoriaceous; pinnæ distant, often a foot or more long, petiolate, deeply pinnatifid broad-lanceolate acuminate; laciniæ ovate-lanceolate, acuminate, subfalcate, spinulose-serrate towards the apex; veins reticulate towards the main costa (of the pinnæ), a single series of areoles outside of the sori thence free to the margin; sori parallel with and near to the costule, short oblong, sunk in the cavity of the sorus, which has an elevated margin; involucre vaulted coriaceous; rachis here and there producing large scaly germinating gemmæ at the base of some of the pinnæ. *Smith, Act. Taur.* v. *p.* 4–12. *Hook. Sp. Fil.* iii. 66. *Syn. Fil.* 138. *Bedd. F. B. I. t.* 88.

Himalayas, from Kashmir to Bhotan, 3,000–8,000 feet elevation; common in Khasya, 4,000–5,000 feet.

(Also in Java, S. Europe, Macaronesia, California and Mexico.)

GENUS XXXVIII.—DOODIA. (*R. Br.*)

(In honour of Samuel Doody, a British cryptogamist.)

Sori oblong or sub-lunulate, in one or more series, arranged transversely with the veins forming areoles which are superficial, not sunk; involucres membranaceous, of the same form as the sori, opening towards the costa and lying parallel with it; veins uniform, the

N°68

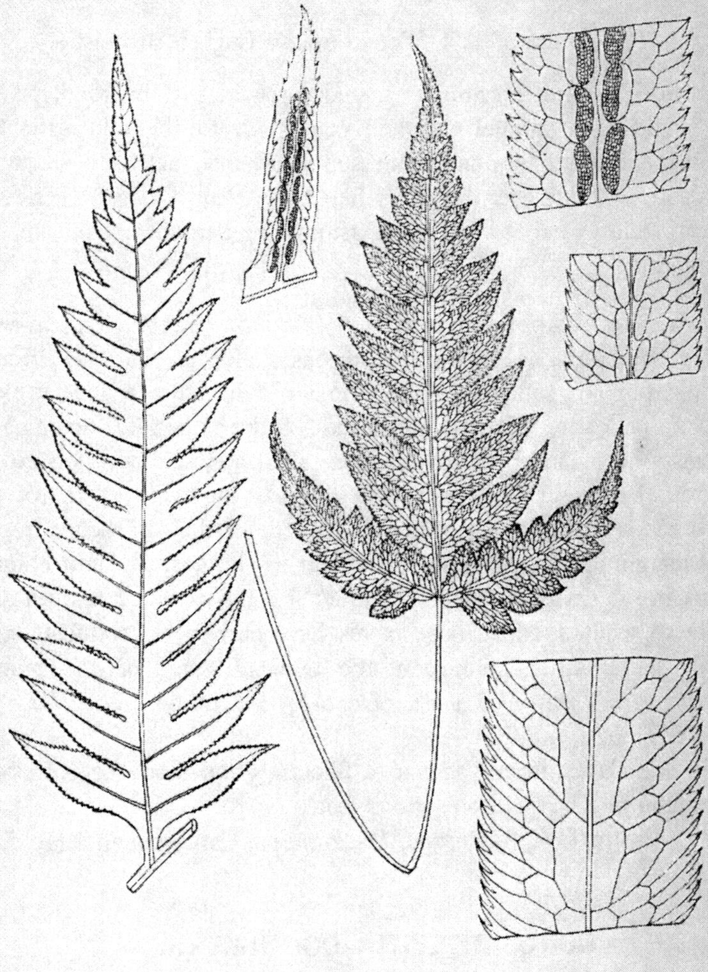

S. CATTELL & Co. ENGRAS.

WOODWARDIA RADICANS. (*Sm.*)

lower ones arcuately anastomosing, forming elongated costal areoles (one or more series), the marginal venules free; fronds pinnate or pinnatifid; segments or pinnæ sharply serrated, rhizome sub-globose.

1. DOODIA DIVES. (*Kunze.*) Rhizome obliquely ascending, paleaceous, rootlets clothed with black fibre; stipes angled brown, very paleaceous near the base; fronds coriaceous, glabrous ovate-oblong, long caudate at the apex, pinnate at the base, with some of the lower pinnæ auricled, pinnatifid above; pinnæ and segments patently divergent, oblong, margins pungently serrated; pinnæ or segments of the fertile fronds often distant; sori in one or two series on each side of the costa of the pinnæ and segments, and also on the wings of the rachis, lunate, often more or less confluent. *Kze. in Schk. Fil. Suppl.* ii. *p.* 12. *t.* 185. *Hook. Sp. Fil.* iii. 73. *Syn. Fil.* 189. *Bedd. F. S. I. t.* 222.

Ceylon, Hackgalla and the central provinces above 4,000 feet elevation.

(Also in Java.)

TRIBE VIII.—ASPLENIEÆ.

Sori attached to the veins, oblique with regard to the costa or occasionally sub-parallel with it, linear or oblong or horseshoe-shaped; indusium the same shape as the sorus, when single opening towards the midrib, sometimes double.

GENUS XXXIX.—THAMNOPTERIS. (*Presl.*)

(*Thamnos*, a thicket; *pteris*, fern.)

Sori unilateral linear; indusium linear, straight, single, free exteriorly; veins forked; venules parallel; their apices combined by a transverse continuous marginal vein; fronds undivided, simple, narrow-lanceolate to broad-lanceolate.

1. THAMNOPTERIS NIDUS. (*Linn.*) Fronds very variable in length and breadth, lanceolate acute or acuminate at the apex, taper-

No. 69.

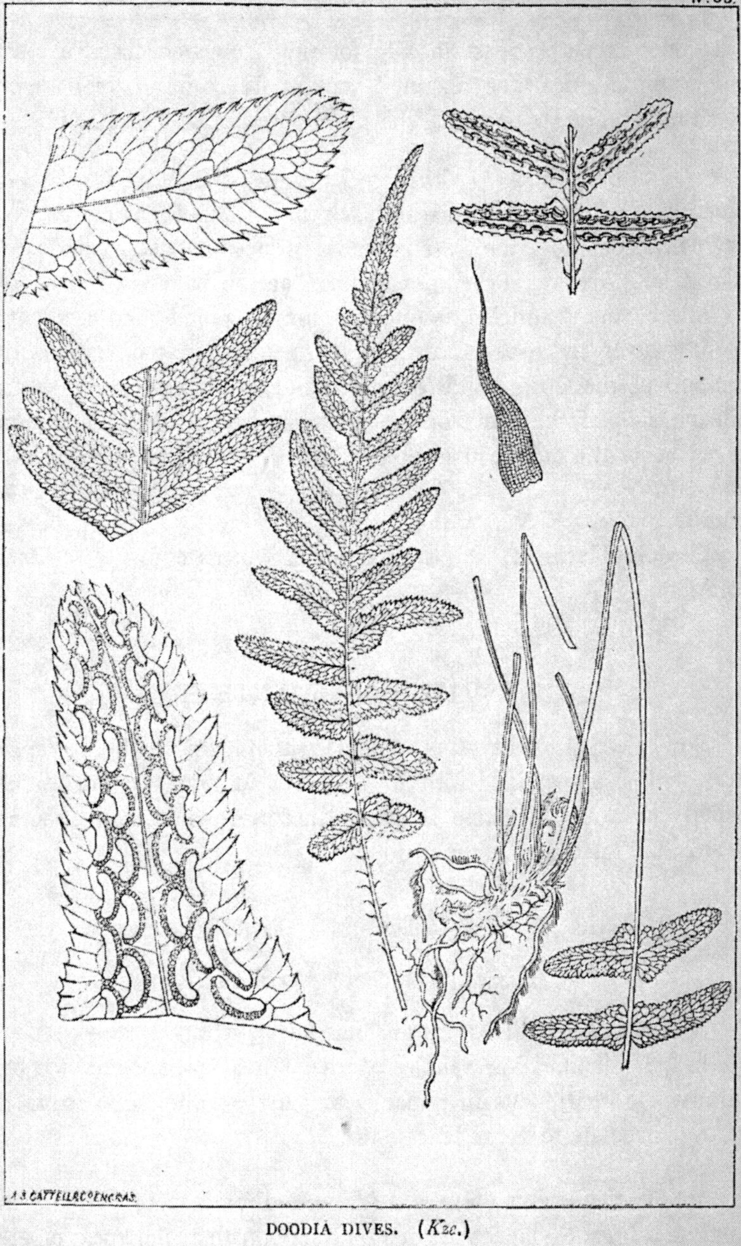

DOODIA DIVES. (*Kze.*)

ing gradually into a short stem, the edge entire, the midrib rounded on the back; texture coriaceous; veins fine and parallel, half a line apart; sori reaching about half-way towards the margin. *Lin. Sp. Pl.* 1537. *Hook. Syn. Fil.* 190. *Bedd. F. B. I. t.* 197.

North India; the Malay Peninsula; Ceylon.

(Also pretty general throughout tropical Asia, Mauritius, Madagascar, &c.)

Typical Nidus has the fronds up to 6 feet long and 5–6 inches wide, and has not been found in the Madras Presidency.

VAR. β MUSÆFOLIA. (*Mett.*) Fronds up to 6 feet long and 1 foot broad; sori extending nearly to the margin. *Mett. Asp. p.* 85. *Hook. Sp. Fil.* iii. 78.

Malacca, Singapore.

(Also in the Philippines.)

VAR. γ PHYLLITIDIS. (*Don.*) Fronds up to 2 feet long and 2, rarely 3 inches broad. *Don. Prod. Nep.* 7. *Hook. Sp. Fil.* iii. 80. *Bedd. F. S. I. t.* 123.

Western forests of the Madras Presidency, very common; Himalayas; Khasya; Malay Peninsula.

(Also in Java Luzon, and Samar.)

The above have been considered three different species by many botanists, they are now generally all united under Nidus; there appears to be no real difference except as to size, and it is doubtful if this is constant, or that the supposed varieties do not run into each other.

2. THAMNOPTERIS GREVILLEI. (*Wall.*) Fronds 12–18 inches long by 2–3 broad, lanceolate-spathulate, narrowed to an acute apex and suddenly below to a broad wing to the stipe, which grows very gradually narrower downwards, the margin entire; texture coriaceous; midrib keeled below; veins nearly horizontal, those in the body of the frond about ½ line apart; sori on most of them extending within a short distance of the edge. *Wall. Cat.* 1036. *Hook. Sp. Fil.* iii. 80. *Bedd. F. B. I. t.* 66.

No. 70

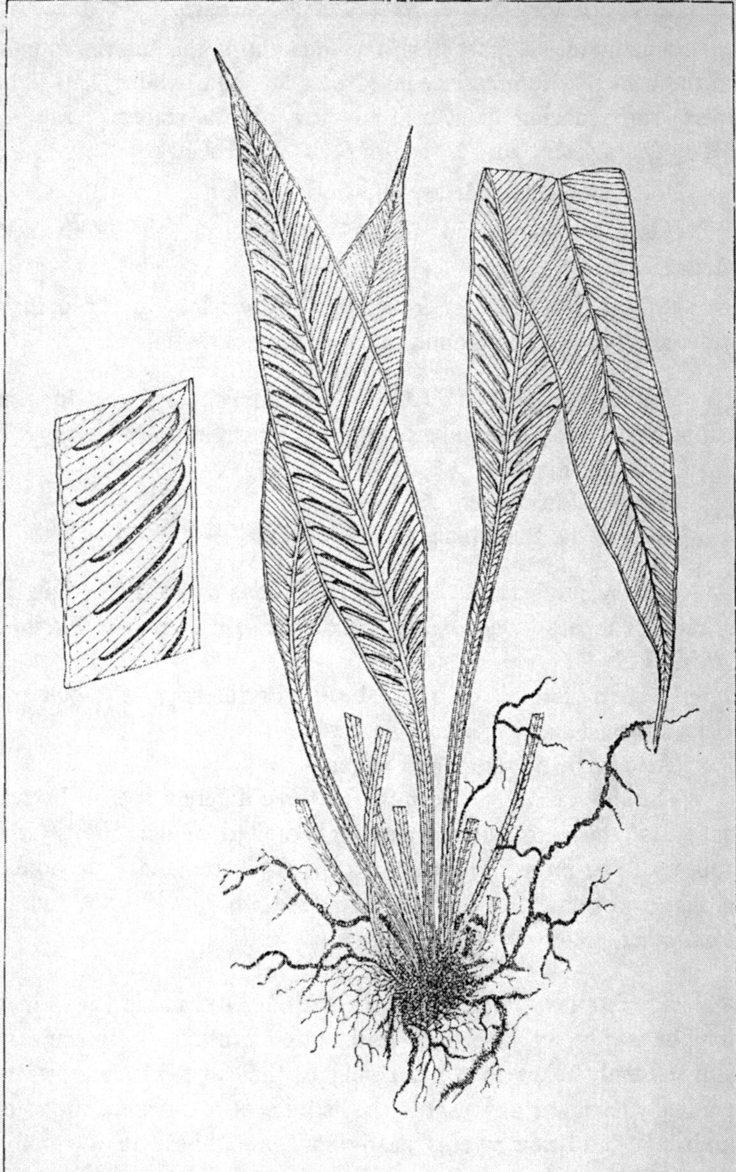

THAMNOPTERIS GREVILLEI. (*Wall.*)

Birma and Mishmee.

The spathulate fronds with the winged stipe give this fern a very different appearance to any form of Nidus.

3. THAMNOPTERIS SIMONSIANA. (*Hook.*) Fronds 12–18 inches long, 1–1½ inch broad, tapering above into an acuminated point, and very gradually below into a short stem, the margin nearly entire; midrib only rounded and prominent below; texture coriaceous; veins erect-patent, about ½ line apart; sori copious, reaching from the midrib to within a short distance of the edge. *Hook. Syn. Fil.* 191. *Bedd. F. B. I. t.* 247.

Khasya and Jaintea hills up to 4,000 feet; Chittagong; Madras Presidency, on the hills west of Vizagapatam, 3,000 feet.

Mr. Clarke is in error in saying that it is found in Malabar; he unites it with Nidus, but it would hardly be safe to do so unless it be proved to vary in cultivation.

GENUS XL.—ASPLENIUM. (*Linn.*)

(*A*, privative; *splen*, spleen; in allusion to its medical properties.)

Sori dorsal or sub-marginal, linear or oblong; indusium similar in shape, straight, single, plane or tumid, bursting along the outer edge; veins free.

* *Fronds quite entire.*

1. ASPLENIUM ENSIFORME. (*Wallich.*) Stipes tufted 1–3 inches long, firm, erect, scaly below; fronds 8–20 inches long, ⅜–⅞ inch broad, much acuminated; margin entire or nearly so, the lower part of frond very gradually narrowed; texture coriaceous; veins immersed, inconspicuous, erect-patent, usually once forked; sori broad, reaching nearly to the midrib and margin. *Wall. Cat.* 200. *Hook. Syn. Fil. p.* 191. *Bedd. F. S. I. t.* 125. A. stenophyllum, *Bedd. F. B. I. t.* 147.

Himalayas; Gurwhal to Bhotan, 4,000–9,000 feet elevation; Ceylon; Birma; Western forests of Madras Presidency. The South Indian, Ceylon, and Birma plant has fronds generally about 8 inches long and nearly 1 inch wide. Some Himalayan examples have very long and very narrow fronds, but they cannot be separated as varieties, as there are intermediate forms from the Himalayas; they both stain the paper they are dried in, a bright pink colour.

2. ASPLENIUM GRIFFITHIANUM. (*Hook.*) Stipes tufted, erect short; fronds lanceolate, 4–12 inches long, ¾–1 inch broad, the point acuminate, narrowing below very gradually; the margin undulate, crenate; texture subcoriaceous; veins distant, obscure, usually once forked; sori reaching from the midrib two-thirds of the way to the margin. *Hook. Syn. Fil.* 193. *Bedd. F. B. I. t.* 58.

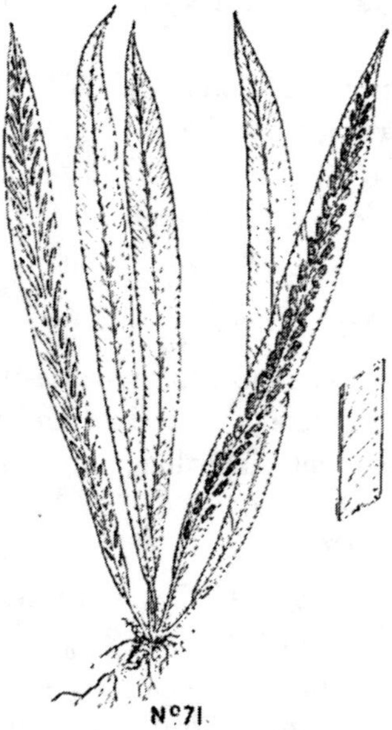

No. 71.
ASPLENIUM ENSIFORME.
(*Wallich.*)

Sikkim, below Darjeeling, 4,000 feet elevation, scarce; Mishmee; Khasya, 4,000–5,000 feet elevation, Mergui and Tavoy.

There is also, in the Kew Herbarium, a fern from Penang, which quite agrees with this, except that it has a slender stipe 6–9 inches long.

* * *Fronds lobed or pinnatifid.*

3. ASPLENIUM ALTERNANS. (*Wall.*) Caudex short, descending, copiously rooting, squamose with subulate scales as is the very short (rarely an inch long) stipe, and base of the costa beneath; fronds cæspitose, about a span long, chartaceous, very opaque pale rusty green beneath, glabrous, lanceolate, scarcely acuminate attenuated below, deeply and regularly pinnatifid throughout; lobes ovate or triangular-oblong with wide sinuses, obtuse, quite entire; veins subflabellate, all free; sori copious on all the lobes in two rows, linear-oblong erect-patent, the superior basal one parallel with the costa. *Wall. Cat.* 221. *Hook. Sp. Fil.* iii. 92. *Syn. Fil. p.* 194. *Bedd. F. B. I. t.* 59.

N. W. Himalayas, very common 3,000–9,000 feet elevation,

extending to west frontier of Kashmir, and eastward to Sikkim, where it is rare.

(Also in Abyssinia.)

* * * *Fronds pinnate.*

4. ASPLENIUM VIRIDE. (*Hudson.*) Stipes densely tufted; often brown or blackish, 2–4 inches long, naked; fronds 4–6 inches long, ½ inch broad with 12–20 sub-sessile pinnæ on each side, which are ovate or elliptic, the upper edge narrowed suddenly at the base, the lower obliquely truncate, the outer part deeply crenated; texture herbaceous; rachis naked green; veins sub-flabellate; sori copious linear-oblong oblique. *Huds. Fl. Ang.* 453. *Hook. Syn. Fil.* 195. *Bedd. F. B. I.* 64.

Kashmir, 12,000–13,000 feet; Gulmurg, Tilail, Kumaon.

(Also in Europe, Asia, and N. America in Arctic and Alpine regions.)

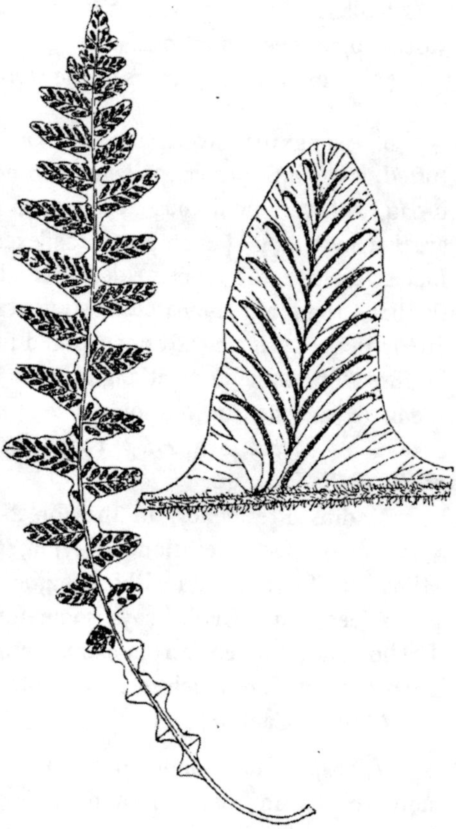

N°72.
ASPLENIUM ALTERNANS. (*Wall.*)

5. ASPLENIUM TRICHOMANES. (*Linn.*) Stipes densely tufted, 1–4 inches long, naked glossy brown or black; fronds 6–12 inches long, about ½ inch broad, with 15–30 opposite pairs of sessile horizontal pinnæ, which are ¼–⅜ inch broad, 1½–2 lines deep, the edge slightly crenate, the two sides unequal, the upper one the

broadest and narrowed suddenly at the base; texture sub-coriaceous; veins pinnate, inconspicuous; rachis polished; sori linear oblong, 3–6 on each side of the midrib. *L. Sp. Fil. p.* 1540*a*. *Hook. Syn. Fil.* 196. *Bedd. F. S. I. t.* 147.

Kulhatty on the Nilgiris; Himalayas, Kashmir to Kumaon, 5,000-10,000 feet elevation.

(Also in all four quarters of the world, Australia and Polynesia.)

6. ASPLENIUM NORMALE. (*Don.*) Stipes 4–6 inches long, tufted, wiry, dark purple, polished; fronds 8–15 inches long, 1½ inch broad, with very numerous close placed pinnæ, the lower ones, which are ¾–1 inch long, ¼ inch broad, deflexed; the apex obtuse, the edge incised-crenate, the upper side auricled and narrowed suddenly at the base, the lower truncate in a straight line; texture sub-coriaceous; rachis glossy; veins mostly once forked; sori in two rows, very various in direction, some at right angles with the veins, some parallel with them, or in one row, or only 1–2 to each pinna. *Don. Prod. Fl. Nep. p.* 7. *Hook. Syn. Fil. p.* 197. Asplenium multijugum (Wall), *Bedd. F. S. I. t.* 133.

Madras Presidency, in the forests of the Western mountains, 3,000–6,000 feet elevation; Ceylon, above 4,000 feet elevation Himalayas from Nepal to Bhotan, 4,000–8,000 feet; Khasya, 3,000-5,000 feet. Mr. Clarke says some forms are nearly allied to A. Trichomanes, others to monanthemum, a Madeira fern; Himalayan examples are much more variable than those from South India.

(Also in Canton.)

VAR. β. Pinnæ more numerous and overlapping each other, more regular in shape, forming almost parallelograms; sori 1–6, generally confined to the apex, and parallel with the veins, one sorus on the upper auricle close to the rachis and parallel with it.

Anamallays, 4,000 feet elevation.

7. ASPLENIUM SUBAVENIUM. (*Hook.*) Stipes tufted, 2–3 inches long, wiry, blackish, densely fibrillose; frond a span long, lanceolate coriaceous, very opaque, pinnated; pinnæ ¾ of an inch long,

numerous, approximate, horizontal sessile, oblong obtuse, upper half, obscurely serrated, cuneate at the base, superior base truncated subauriculate, inferior margin cut off as it were by a straight line; terminal pinna elongated, pinnatifid below; costa and veins sunk, obsolete; sori 2–6, oblong oblique, occupying the disc of the frond between the middle and the apex; involucre firm, membranaceous; rachis ebony-black, terete, rigid, sparsely setose. *Hook. Sp. Fil.* iii. 143. *Syn. Fil. p.* 198. *Bedd. F. B. I. t.* 288.

Penang.

8. ASPLENIUM SEPTENTRIONALE. (*Lin. under Acrostichum*). Small caudex creeping, densely radiculose scarcely paleaceous; stipes numerous, tufted, 3–6 inches high, erect, flexuose, green brown at the base; fronds 1–2 inches long, coriaceous, glabrous, pinnated; pinnæ $\frac{3}{4}$–1 inch long; long-petioled, linear or linear-lanceolate, subunguiculate, often very acute or acuminate, rarely solitary, generally 2–3, alternate entire or forked; lateral segments small subulate, rarely laciniated (2–3 acuminate segments); veins forked parallel; sori very long; involucres also much elongated, attached near the margin. *Hook. Sp. Fil.* iii. 174. *Syn. Fil. p.* 198. *Bedd. F. B. I. t.* 60. Acrostichum septentrionale, *Linn. Sp. Pl.* 1524. Acropteris, *Link.*

Northern India, Kashmir, 9,000–12,000 feet elevation; Gurwhal 8,000 feet.

(Also in Arctic and Alpine Europe, Asia, and America.)

9. ASPLENIUM LONGISSIMUM. (*Blume.*) Rhizome short-creeping; stipes tufted 3–12 inches long, strong erect, blackish, nearly naked; fronds 2–8 feet long, linear or lanceolate elongate, proliferous and rooting at the apex; pinnæ horizontal, very numerous, 2–4$\frac{1}{2}$ inches long $\frac{1}{4}$–$\frac{3}{8}$ inch broad, acuminate, the two sides nearly equal, with a distinct central midrib, the edge slightly toothed, the base on both sides often auricled; texture herbaceous; rachis dark-coloured strong, slightly scaly; veins forked oblique; sori numerous in two regular rows on each side the midribs, and reaching nearly to the edge. *Blume, En. Plant. Jav. Fil.* 178. *Hook. Syn. Fil.* 199.

Sylhet, abundant; Malay Peninsula from Moulmein southwards. (Also in Mauritius and the Malay Islands.)

10. ASPLENIUM WIGHTIANUM. (*Wall.*) Stipes tufted 6–9 inches long, green, naked; fronds up to 2 feet long, 6–8 inches broad, oblong-lanceolate with 6–12 subopposite or alternate pairs of pinnæ on each side, distinctly stalked, the lower ones rather distant, linear with a long acumination, ½–1 inch broad, the base gradually truncate-cuneate, often a little unequal, the margin coarsely toothed; colour pale green; texture coriaceous or subcoriaceous; veins simple, or once forked; sori very regular and parallel, not reaching the margin; indusium broad, pale. *Wall. Cat.* 2215. *Hook. Syn. Fil.* 199. *Bedd. F. S. I. t.* 126. A. Vulcanicum (Blume), *Hook. Syn. Fil.* 201.

(*The sterile fronds are rarely deeply and irregularly pinnatifid, with the segments serrated.*)

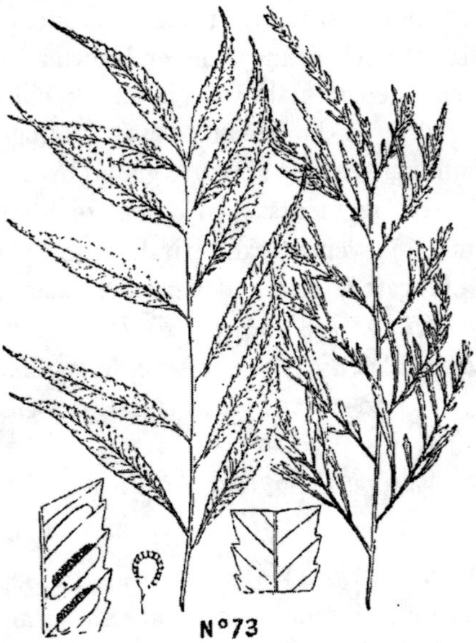

N°73

ASPLENIUM WIGHTIANUM. (*Wall.*)

Ceylon; South Indian mountains, Pulneys, Anamallays, Bolampatty Hills, 2,000–4,000 feet elevation; Malay Peninsula.

In South Indian examples the serratures are rather deep and the veins generally all simple, in a specimen from Birma the serratures are very shallow and sharp and the veins once forked.

(Also in the Malay Islands.)

VAR. β MICROPHYLLUM. Pinnæ much smaller, with a more unequal cuneate base, scarcely acuminated at the apex; serratures obtusely rounded, upper basal serratures larger than the others and bifid; fronds about 10 inches long by 2 inches broad. *Bedd. F. S. I. t.* 127.

Anamallays; banks of Toracadu and elsewhere. I believe this to be only a form of Wightianum, though Mr. Baker is inclined to regard it as a distinct species.

11. ASPLENIUM TENERUM. (*Forst.*) Stipes tufted, firm, erect, greyish, naked, 4–11 inches long; fronds 8–15 inches long, 3–4 inches broad, oblong-lanceolate; pinnæ numerous on each side, stalked, horizontal, $\frac{1}{4}$–$\frac{3}{8}$ inch broad, more or less bluntly rounded at the apex, the edge rather deeply crenated all round, the two sides unequal, the upper one narrowed, almost at a right angle, sometimes auricled, the lower one obliquely truncate; texture herbaceous; rachis compressed; veins all simple except the lowest superior one, which is always forked except in the uppermost pinnæ; sori numerous, regular, parallel, not reaching the margin or midrib. *Forst. Prod. p.* 80. *Hook. Syn. Fil. p.* 201. Asp. elongatum (Sw.), *Bedd. F. S. I. t.* 224.

Ceylon; at Oodawella and Matale East, not common. *Mr. Wall sends a specimen with most of the pinnæ pinnatifid in their lower half nearly to the rachis.* Singapore, Penang.

(Also in the Philippines, Borneo, Java, Marianne Islands, Taheiti, and New Guinea.)

No. 74
ASPLENIUM TENERUM.
(*Forst.*)

12. ASPLENIUM LUNULATUM. (*Sw.*) Stipes tufted, 2–4 inches long, firm, nearly naked, grey or ebeneous; fronds 8–18 inches long, $1\frac{1}{2}$–3 inches broad, narrowly lanceolate-oblong, with many horizontal pinnæ on each side, which are $\frac{1}{4}$–$\frac{1}{2}$ inch broad, bluntish or acute at the apex, more or less deeply crenate throughout, the two sides unequal, the upper one at the base narrowed suddenly at about

a right angle, the lower one obliquely truncate; lower pinnæ often deflexed; texture herbaceous; veins simple or once forked; sori falling short of both edge and midrib. *Sw. Syn. Fil.* 80. *Hook. Syn. Fil.* 202. Asplenium erectum, *Bory.*

VAR. β CAMPTORACHIS. Fronds 12–14 inches long; rachis winged; pinnæ 30–40 pair, alternate or subopposite, about ¾ inch long, rounded at the apex, lower ones often reduced to auricles. Asplenium camptorachis, *Kze.* Asplenium brasiliense (Raddi), *Bedd. F. S. I. t.* 135.

N° 75.

ASPLENIUM ZENKERIANUM. (*Kze.*)

Western parts of the Madras Presidency, Nilgiris, &c., at high elevations; Ceylon, central provinces.

VAR. γ TRAPEZIFORME Fronds about 14–20 inches long; rachis not winged; pinnæ about 15–20 pair, the lowest the largest, 1½ inches long; apex attenuated. Aspl. trapeziforme (Roxb.), *Crypt. p.* 497. *Bedd. F. S. I. t.* 134.

Nilgiris and Anamallays in Southern India.

Unless a distinct species, which it probably is, I consider this a variety of lunulatum, and not of unilaterale (resectum), to which it is referred by Hooker and Clarke, as the pinnæ are never unilateral. Mr. Clarke also alludes to it under longifolium, as closely allied to that species, but it is nothing like it, either in texture or cutting.

13. ASPLENIUM ZENKERIANUM. (*Kze.*) Stipes 6–9 inches long, tufted, slightly scaly; fronds oblong-lanceolate, 1–3 feet long, gene-

rally proliferous at the apex; pinnæ distant, alternate, 15–20 pair, stalked, ligulate-lanceolate acuminate, 3–5 inches long, 1–1¼ inch broad, crenate, broadly rounded on the upper, cuneate-truncate on the lower side at the base; lowest rather reduced; texture firm; surfaces naked, dark green; veins erect-patent, fine distant, forked; sori regular, parallel, 3–4 lines long, scarcely produced more than half-way to the margin; indusium firm, broad, *Kze. in Lin.* xxiv. *p.* 259. *Hook. Syn. Fil.* 484. Asp. persicifolium (Hook.), *Bedd. F. S. I. t.* 127.

Nilgiris and Pulneys at the higher elevation; Ceylon at Newera Elya, &c., above 5,000 feet elevation.

14. ASPLENIUM HIRTUM. (*Kaulf.*) Stipes tufted, 2–4 inches long, strong, erect, brownish, deciduously scaly; fronds 12–24 inches long; pinnæ very numerous, horizontal, 1–3 inches long, ¼–⅜ inch broad; the apex rounded or acute; the margin broadly not deeply toothed, the base on the upper side conspicuously auricled, on the lower side rather suddenly but obliquely narrowed; texture coriaceous; rachis dark-coloured, strong, more or less fibrillose; veins oblique, inconspicuous; sori in two regular rows which do not reach the margin. *Kaulf. En. Fil.* 169. *Hook. Syn. Fil. p.* 205. *Bedd. F. B. I. t.* 194.

Sikkim at Lingtam near Darjeeling; Moulmein.

(Also in the Mascareen Islands, Hong Kong, Philippines, and Solomon Islands.)

15. ASPLENIUM AURITUM. (*Sw.*) Stipes tufted, 4–8 inches long, firm, erect, grey, naked; fronds 3–12 inches long; pinnæ 10–20 distinctly stalked, horizontal, 2–3 inches long, the apex acute or blunt, either deeply pinnatifid or pinnate throughout, or only sharply toothed or variously lobed, especially on the upper side towards the base; texture very coriaceous; rachis firm, erect, naked; veins close, oblique, inconspicuous; sori in two broad rather oblique rows. *Sw. Syn. Fil.* 78. *Hook. Syn. Fil.* 208. *Bedd. F. S. I. t.* 137.

South India, rare; Conoor, on rocks 5,600 feet elevation; Anamallays, bed of the Toracadu river, 4,000 feet.

(Also throughout Tropical America and the West Indies, and in the Mascareen Islands.)

16. ASPLENIUM CRINICAULE. (*Hance.*) Stipes furnished with hair-like scales, densely tufted, 3–4 inches long, erect, dark-brown; fronds 6 inches to 2–3 feet long, $1\frac{1}{2}$–$4\frac{1}{2}$ inches broad; pinnæ 9–25 pairs, opposite, sub-opposite or alternate, lanceolate, sub-falcate, with a blunt or acuminated apex, the margins deeply incised, often the upper base and sometimes both the upper and lower base much auricled, giving the pinna a hastate shape, the lower base often obliquely truncate; texture coriaceous; rachis firm, fibrillose like the stipes; midrib rather indistinct; veins subflabellate; sori linear oblique. *Hance, in Ann. Sc. Nat. Ser.* v. 254. *Hook. Syn. Fil. p.* 208. Asp. Beddomei, *Mett. in Linnæa*, 36, 93. Aspl. falcatum, *Bedd. F. S. I. t.* 141.

Madras Presidency, on the Anamallays and in Coorg, 3,000–4,000 feet elevation; Sikkim, Jaintea hills 4,000–5,000 feet, nearly allied to the next species, and probably only a variety of it.

(Also in China.)

17. ASPLENIUM FALCATUM. (*Lam.*) Stipes tufted, 6–9 inches long, erect, greyish, glabrous, or more or less scaly; fronds 6 inches to 2 feet long or more, 4–8 inches broad; pinnæ stalked, 6–20 pair, alternate, sub-opposite or opposite, lanceolate, often caudate, $\frac{1}{2}$–1 inch broad, the edges serrated or lobed, with the lobes serrate, the two sides unequal, and the lower one at the base obliquely-truncate; texture coriaceous; rachis glabrous or fibrillose; veins very oblique; sori in long irregular lines reaching nearly to the margin. *Lam. Enc.* ii. 306. *Hook. Syn. Fil.* 208. *Bedd. F. S. I. t.* 143, as caudatum.

Madras Presidency, Western mountains; Ceylon; Malay Peninsula; Soonderbun; near Koolna in Jessore.

(Also in Australia, S. Africa and its islands, and Polynesia.)

18. ASPLENIUM MACROPHYLLUM. (*Swartz.*) As in falcatum, but the pinnæ generally larger and broader, and less cut. *Sw. Syn. Fil. p.* 77 *and* 261. *Hook. Syn. Fil. p.* 209. *Bedd. F. S. I. t.* 142.

Distinct enough from falcatum if typical specimens only are viewed, but quite passing into it if large suites of specimens are examined, it should, I think, only rank as a variety.

Localities much the same as falcatum. Mr. Clarke says not in Ceylon, but I have gathered many specimens there.

19. ASPLENIUM CAUDATUM. (*Forst.*) As in falcatum, but the sori generally confined to two parallel rows close to the midrib, or with a few other short oblique sori. *Forst. Prod. p.* 80. *Hook. Syn. Fil. p.* 209. Aspl. contiguum, *Bedd. F. S. I. t.* 140. *Probably only a variety of falcatum.*

S. India, on the Western mountains; Ceylon; Malay Peninsula. (Also in Australia, Africa, and Brazil.)

20. ASPLENIUM GARDNERI. (*Baker.*) Rhizome short, creeping; stipes grey, 2–6 inches with a few scattered small scales; fronds lanceolate, $\frac{1}{2}$–1 foot long, 3–5 inches broad, often gemmiparous; rachis not winged; pinnæ 8–10 pair, distinct, ascending, lanceolate, short-stalked, acute, central ones 2–3 inches long $\frac{1}{2}$–$\frac{5}{8}$ inch broad, toothed, square on the upper side, cuneate on the lower side at the base; veins erect-patent, forked, moderately close; sori regular, parallel, $\frac{1}{4}$–$\frac{1}{2}$ inch long. *Hook. Syn. Fil. p.* 485. *Bedd. Suppl. Ferns. t.* 355.

Closely allied to macrophyllum, and probably only a variety of it. I have specimens from North India (not gemmiparous), which I do not know whether to refer to this or to macrophyllum. My Ceylon specimens are all gemmiparous, and the texture is generally thinner and the veins further apart.

Ceylon; Khasya Mountains, Umwai, 3,000 feet elevation.

21. ASPLENIUM PARADOXUM. (*Blume.*) Stipe firm, erect, grey, slightly scaly; fronds 1–2 feet long, with a large oblong-rhomboidal terminal pinna, and 8–12 lateral ones on each side, the lowest of which are 5–6 inches long, 1–1$\frac{1}{2}$ inches broad, the apex acuminate and slightly toothed, the two sides unequal, the upper one narrowed suddenly almost at a right angle, the lower obliquely cuneate; texture coriaceous; rachis firm, erect, compressed, rather scaly; veins obscure, very oblique, usually once forked; sori reaching nearly from the midrib to the margin. *Bl. Fil. Jav.* 179. *Hook. Syn. Fil. p.* 209. Aspl. zamioides, *Hook. Sp. Fil.* iii. *p.* 114. *Bedd. F. B. I. t.* 193.

Penang. The compressed rachis and short broader almost entire pinnæ give this a very different look to Gardneri or macrophyllum. I have only seen two or three specimens and do not know how far it varies, but should not be surprised if it turned out to be only a variety of macrophyllum.

(Also in Java and Sumatra.)

22. ASPLENIUM FORMOSUM. (*Willd.*) Stipes tufted, very short, naked, polished, dark brown; fronds 12–16 inches long; pinnæ 20–31 pair (lower ones generally reduced), sessile, horizontal, ½ inch long, by 1½–2 lines deep, the upper edge deeply cut, the apex rather obtuse, the lower edge truncate in a straight line, so that about half the lower side is cut away; texture herbaceous; veins obscure, simple or forked; sori linear-oblong, short, oblique, confined to the lower side, or 1–4 on each side of the midrib. *Willd. Sp. Pl.* v. 329. *Hook. Syn Fil. p.* 210. *Bedd. F. S. I. t.* 136.

South India, abundant in moist woods at the higher elevations on the Nilgiris, Pulneys and Anamallays; Ceylon, rare.

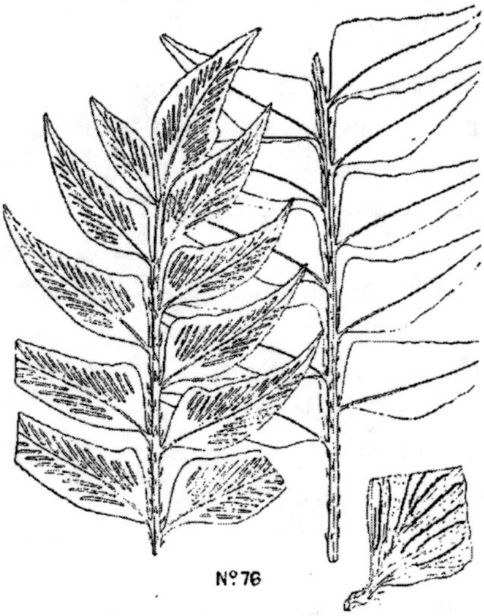

No. 76

ASPLENIUM PARADOXUM. (*Blume.*)

(Also in Tropical America, the West Indies, and Africa, Angola, and Congo.)

23. ASPLENIUM UNILATERALE. (*Lam.*) Stipes scattered slender, naked, dark brown, polished or grey, and opaque, 4–8 inches long; fronds 6–15 inches long, lanceolate-oblong; pinnæ 10–30 pairs sub-sessile horizontal 1–3 inches long, by ¼–1 inch broad, in shape almost dimidiate, two-thirds of the lower side being entirely cut away, the apex acute or bluntish, all except the truncate part incised, the upper half of the base narrowed nearly at a right angle; texture thinly-herbaceous; rachis usually polished like the stem, or green and

opaque ; veins once or twice forked; sori not reaching either midrib or margin, often quite allantodioid in South Indian examples. *Lam. Enc.* ii. 305. *Hook. Syn. Fil. p.* 210, under resectum. *Bedd. F. S. I. t.* 132, under resectum.

Madras Presidency, in all the Western forests up to 5,000 feet; Himalayas from Chumba to Bhotan 1,000–5,000 feet; common eastward of Nepal; Chittagong; Ceylon; Malay Peninsula.

(Also in the Malay Islands, Polynesia, Japan and Tropical Africa.)

VAR. β RIVALE. (*Bedd.*) Pinnæ 30–40 pairs, close set and much smaller than in the type, being only $\frac{1}{4}$ inch broad, less cut and almost a parallelogram in shape; sori confined to the apex; in habit resembling normale, var. β.

Pulney Hills and Anamallays, only in beds of rivers.

VAR. γ. UDUM. (*Atkinson.*) Pinnæ very transparent and membranaceous, smaller than in the type, very oblique, and the cutting often fimbriate. (*Bedd. Supp. Ferns. t.* 357, as var. decurrens.)

Himalayas; Dalhousie, 5,500 feet elevation, and other localities, pendant from dripping rocks.

VAR. δ DELICATULUM. (*Parish.*) Fronds and pinnæ, much smaller than in the type, the latter less obliquely cut away on the lower side, and the main vein further from the margin. *Bedd. Supp. Ferns. t.* 358.

Tenasserim, on trees, 3,000 feet elevation. I have only seen one specimen sent by Mr. Parish.

24. ASPLENIUM HETEROCARPUM. (*Wall.*) Stipes scattered, firm, erect chestnut-coloured, polished; fronds up to 2 feet, of which the stipe is 6–8 inches, membranaceous, glabrous, linear in outline, pinnæ numerous (40 or more), dimidiate, nearly the whole of the lower margin being cut away, about 1 inch long by $\frac{1}{2}$ inch broad; upper margin and apex deeply cut, the segments being again bifid; lower margin entire; sori confined to the segments and directed upwards. *Wall. Cat.* 218. *Hook. Syn. Fil. p.* 210. *Bedd. F. S. I. t.* 131.

Madras Presidency, not uncommon in the Western forests, 4,000–7,000 feet elevation; Himalayas from Nepal to Bhotan,

4,000–8,000 feet; Khasya, 3,000–5,000 feet; Malay Peninsula; Ceylon, central provinces, above 3,000 feet.

(Also in south-east China and Borneo.)

25. ASPLENIUM LACINIATUM. (*Don.*) Stipes and rachis with lanceolate or linear scales; fronds linear, up to nearly 2 feet long; pinnæ numerous, alternate or subopposite, linear-oblong or half ovate, very much cut away, and unequal at the base, slightly pinnatifid, with the segments serrated, or more or less deeply pinnatifid nearly to the rachis and the segments distant; texture subcoriaceous; veins very oblique; sori copious. *Don. Prod. Fl. Nep. p.* 8. *Hook. Syn. Fil. p.* 211. *Bedd. F. S. I. t.* 145. Aspl. planicaule (Wallich), *Hook. Syn. Fil.* 211. *Bedd. F. S. I. t.* 139.

The typical laciniatum of North India has the pinnæ elongated and much narrowed towards the apex, and deeply cut into distant segments; typical planicaule of S. India has very short, half ovate pinnæ, scarcely at all cut; there are however many connecting links, and it is impossible, I think, to separate them even as constant varieties. Var. depauperatum (*Clarke*) is also found in S. India, but is, I believe, only a starved form.

Madras Presidency, all the Western mountains, 3,000–8,000 feet; Himalayas, Gurwhal to Bhotan; Khasya; Ceylon.

(Also in Japan.)

VAR. CRINIGERUM. (*Bedd.*) Pinnæ all more deeply and finely cut than any typical laciniatum; stipe very short (½ inch), and very scaly; rachis densely scaly; pinnæ with long hair-like scales on the nerves beneath.

South India, on the Balarangam Mountains (Mysore), and on Myhendra Mountains near Ganjam, 3,000–4,000 feet elevation.

26. ASPLENIUM PUMILUM. (*Sw.*) Stipes tufted, 3–4 inches long erect, glabrous or sparingly pubescent; fronds 2–6 inches each way deltoid, the upper part sinuated only, the lower cut into distinct pinnæ, of which the lowest pair is much the largest and often pinnatifid nearly to the midrib; texture herbaceous; sori very oblique, the lower ones sometimes ¾–1 inch long. *Sw. Fl. Ind. Occ.* iii. 1610.

(West Indies and Central America.)

No 77.

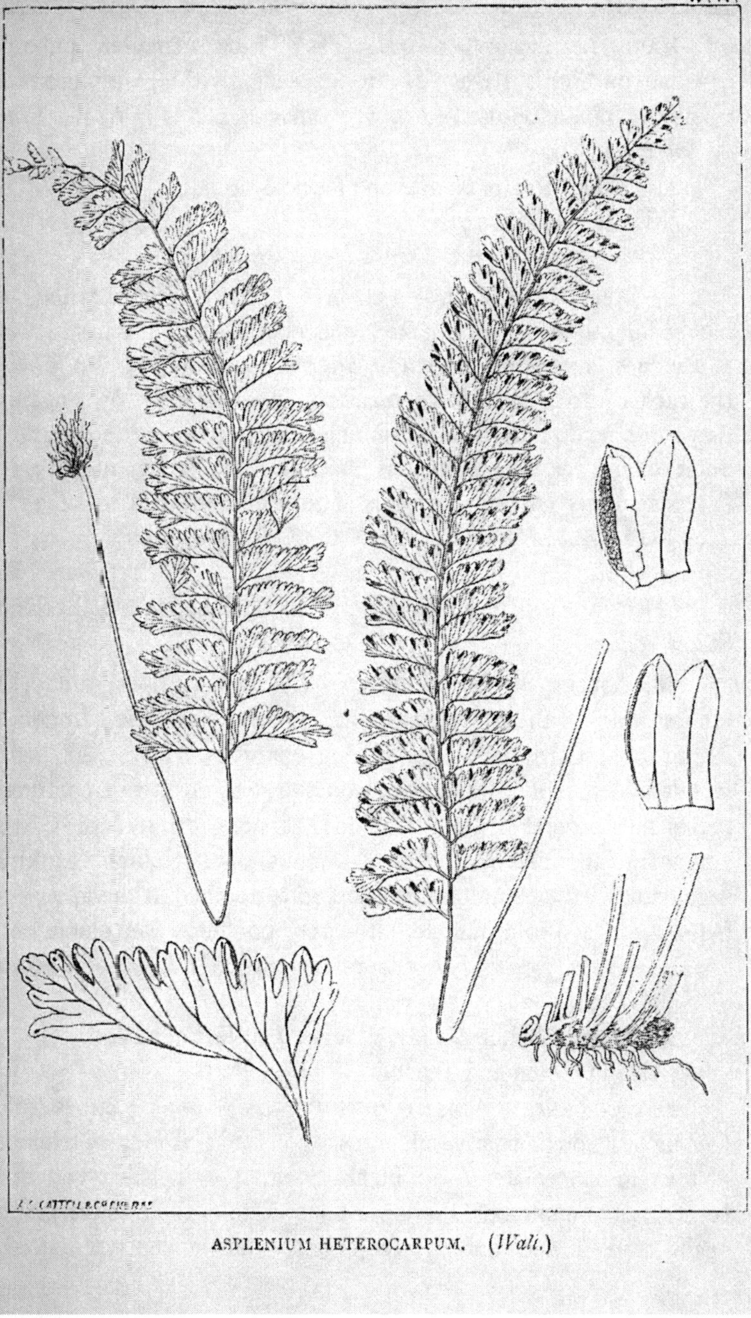

ASPLENIUM HETEROCARPUM. (*Wall.*)

VAR. HYMENOPHYLLOIDES. (*Fée.*) Fronds smaller, pubescent or ciliate on both surfaces; texture exceedingly thin, with prominent venation; pinnæ obtuse. *Fee, 7th. Mem.*. 54. *t.* 15. *f.* 1. *Clarke, N. India, p.* 482.

Mt. Aboo, Rajaputana, 4,000 feet elevation.

(Also in Abyssinia.)

* * * * *Fronds bi-quadripinnate.*

27. ASPLENIUM RUTA-MURARIA. (*Linn*) Stipes tufted, 2–4 inches long, slender, wiry, naked, ebeneous towards the base; fronds 1–2 inches long, about 1 inch broad, glabrous, deltoid, cut down to the rachis into a few pinnæ on each side, the lower ones again cut down into spathulate cuneate pinnules, which are serrated round the outer edge; texture coriaceous; rachis firm, green, naked; veins flabellate; sori copious; margin of indusium fimbriate. *Linn. Sp. Pl.* 1541. *Hook. Syn. Fil.* 213. *Bedd. F. B. I. t.* 61.

Kashmir.

(Also in Europe, North Africa, Thibet, Siberia, and the United States.)

28. ASPLENIUM PEKINENSE. (*Hance.*) Stipes tufted, 1–3 inches long, with a few linear scales near the base; fronds 2–6 inches long, narrowly oblong, shining, glabrous, with several lanceolate-deltoid pinnæ on each side, which are cut down to a compressed rachis into several ovate rhomboidal pinnules on each side, which are again pinnatifid (hence it is bipinnate sub-tripinnate), ultimate segments linear-cuneate, sharply forked or toothed at the apex, entire below; sori 2–6 to a pinnule, ultimately confluent; involucre entire. *Hance in Seem. Journ. Bot.* v. 262. *Hook. Syn. Fil. p.* 213. *Clarke, F. N. I. t.* 56. *f.* 2.

Kashmir; Jhelum Valley, 2,000–2,500 feet elevation.

(Also in China and Japan.)

29. ASPLENIUM ADIANTUM-NIGRUM. (*Linn.*) Stipes tufted, 6-9 inches long, nearly glabrous, polished; fronds bi-tripinnate, deltoid to lanceolate, 6–12 inches long, 4–6 inches broad at the base; pinnæ numerous, the lower ones deltoid, their lower pinnules again stalked and completely pinnate and lanceolate deltoid in

shape, the ultimate segments ovate or oblong, acutely serrate, texture coriaceous; veins obscure, oblique; sori copious, involucre with an entire margin. *Linn. Sp. Pl.* 1541. *Hook. Syn. Fil. p.* 214. *Bedd. F. B. I. t.* 62.

Kashmir, 5,000–8,000 feet, extending to Dalhousie and Chumba.

(Also in Europe, North Asia, North Africa, South Africa and its islands, and Sandwich Islands.)

30. ASPLENIUM FURCATUM. (*Thunb.*) Stipes tufted, 4–8 inches long, clothed with deciduous woolly hairs, as is the rachis; fronds coriaceous, 6–18 inches long, 4–6 inches broad; pinnæ 12–20 pair, lanceolate-deltoid, ¾–1 inch broad, cut down throughout nearly to the rachis into linear-cuneate pinnules, which are sharply serrated, on the outer edge; veins flabellate, deeply channelled; sori linear. *Thunb. Prod. Fl. P.* 172. *Hook. Syn. Fil. p.* 215. *Bedd. F. S. I. t.* 144.

South India, common on the higher Western mountains, Ootakamund, &c.; Ceylon, 5,000–7,000 feet.

(Also in Tropical America, Polynesian Islands, Australia, Cape Colony, Abyssinia, Mascareen Islands, and Canaries.)

31. ASPLENIUM AFFINE. (*Swartz.*) Stipes 6–12 inches long, firm, erect, grey, nearly naked; fronds 12–18 inches long, 6–12 inches broad; pinnæ numerous on each side, the lower ones lanceolate-rhomboidal, cut down to the rachis into numerous distinct rhomboidal pinnules, 4–6 inches long, 1½–2 inches broad, which are incised or deeply lobed; texture subcoriaceous; rachis firm, naked; veins subflabellate; sori copious, linear. *Sw. in Schr. Jour.* 1,800. 11. 56. *Hook. Syn. Fil.* 215. Asp. spathulinum (J. Sm.), *Bedd. F. S. I. t.* 226 (*probably taken from a specimen of furcatum and not from affine as represented at Kew.*)

Ceylon.

(Also in Mascareen Islands, Philippines, Borneo, Fiji, and Sandwich Islands.)

32. ASPLENIUM NITIDUM. (*Swartz.*) Stipes 1 foot long, firm, erect, greyish, naked; fronds 2–3 feet long, 1 foot broad; pinnæ numerous, lanceolate-deltoid, the lowest 6–9 inches long, 2–3 inches broad, cut down to the rachis into numerous stalked subdeltoid

pinnules, which are again cut down to the rachis into broad flabellate cuneate segments, serrated round the outer edge; texture subcoriaceous; rachis firm, grey, naked; veins channelled, flabellate; sori short, radiant. *Sw. Syn. Fil. p.* 280. *Hook. Syn Fil. p.* 215. *Bedd. F. S. I. t.* 148, 149. Aspl. laserpitiifolium, *Bedd. F. S. I. t.* 225.

Sikkim, Bhotan, Assam; Khasya, Cachar, 1,000–4,000 feet elevation; Ceylon; Madras Presidency in the Western forests; Malay Peninsula.

(Also in Malay Islands and S. Africa.)

33. ASPLENIUM FONTANUM. (*Bernh.*) Stipes tufted, 2–4 inches long, wiry, slender, glabrous; fronds 3–6 inches long, 1–1½ inches broad, oblong-lanceolate; pinnæ numerous, the lower ones reduced, often somewhat remote, pinnate, pinnatifid or only toothed; texture herbaceous, rachis and surfaces bright green; veins oblique; sori copious, covering nearly the whole segment. *Bernh. in Schrad. Neu. Jour.* 1 *pt.* ii. 26. *Hook. Syn. Fil. p.* 216. *Bedd. F. B. I. t.* 146.

Himalayas, from Kashmir to Gurwhal, 5,000–9,000 feet.

(Also in Europe.)

VAR. β EXIGUUM. Frondsless divided and more narrow, and an ebeneous rachis. Asp. exiguum, *Bedd. F. S. I. t.* 146.

Nilgiris, Kulhatty; Himalayas.

34. ASPLENIUM VARIANS. (*Hook and Grev.*) Stipes tufted, 1–3 inches long, slender, naked, greenish; fronds 4–6 inches long, 1 inch broad, oblong-lanceolate; pinnæ 8–12 pair, the lower ones subdeltoid ½–¾ inch long, ¼–⅜ inch broad, cut down to the rachis into a few cuneate flabellate pinnules, the lowest two lines across, sharply toothed on the outer edge; texture thin, herbaceous; rachis, slender, naked, green; veins, one carried into each tooth; sori copious. *Hook. Syn. Fil.* 216. *Bedd. F. S. I. t.* 129.

South India, common on the Nilgiris and the mountains on the west side, 3,000 feet upwards; Himalayas, 6,000–10,000 feet, rarer eastwards; Ceylon, 3,000 feet and upwards.

A form found at Kulhatty on the Nilgiris, quite runs into the European lanceolatum. Another form on the Tinnevelly hills west of

Courtallum has short deltoid fronds fully 2 inches across at the base, and broader pinnules.

(Also in South Africa, North China and Japan.)

35. ASPLENIUM BULBIFERUM. (*Forst.*) Stipes tufted, 6–12 inches long, firm, erect, scaly near the base, sometimes hairy throughout; fronds 1–4 feet long, oblong to ovate-lanceolate, 2–3 pinnate; pinnæ many pair, horizontal, often proliferous from the upper surface, the largest eight inches long, and two inches broad, cut down to a compressed winged rachis, into many lanceolate-deltoid pinnules which are cut into slightly toothed linear oblong flaccid segments; texture herbaceous; veins firm, pinnate; sori oblong, large, often filling the whole segment. *Forst. Fl. Ins. Aust. Prod.* 80. *Hook. Syn. Fil. p.* 218. *Bedd. F. B. I. t.* 65, as bullatum (Wall.)

Nepal, Sikkim, Bhotan, Khasya, 2,000–6,000 feet; Penang.

(Also in Australia, New Zealand, Mexico, New Caledonia, Natal, and the East African Islands.)

36. ASPLENIUM TENUIFOLIUM. (*Don.*) Stipes tufted, 3–6 inches long, slender, glabrous, or with a few hairs; fronds green, thinly herbaceous, up to 20 inches long, lanceolate, 3–4 pinnate; pinnæ many pair, the lower ones 3 inches long by ¾ inch broad, lower pinnule subdeltoid, cut down to a narrowly winged rachis into spathulate segments, quarter inch or less broad, sharply cut on the outer edge; veins solitary; sori 1–2 to a segment. *Don. Pr. Fl. Nep.* 8. *Hook. Syn. Fil. p.* 220. *Bedd. F. S. I. t.* 130.

South India, higher ranges of the Nilgiris, Pulneys, and Anamallays; Ceylon at Newera Elya; Himalayas, Nepal to Bhotan 5,000–9,000 feet; Khasya, 4,000–5,500 feet; Birma.

* * * * * *Ultimate division of the frond, narrow, linear; sori linear or linear-oblong, marginal or submarginal. Darea of authors.*

37. ASPLENIUM RUTÆFOLIUM. (*Kunze.*) Stipes tufted, 6–9 inches long, compressed, greenish, glabrous; fronds 6–15 inches long, narrowly oblong, glabrous, bipinnate, the rachis often prolonged, naked, and rooting at the apex; pinnæ 12–20 pair, the lowest sub-deltoid, two inches or more long, cut down to the rachis to many erect-patent distant pinnules on each side, the lowest on

No 78.

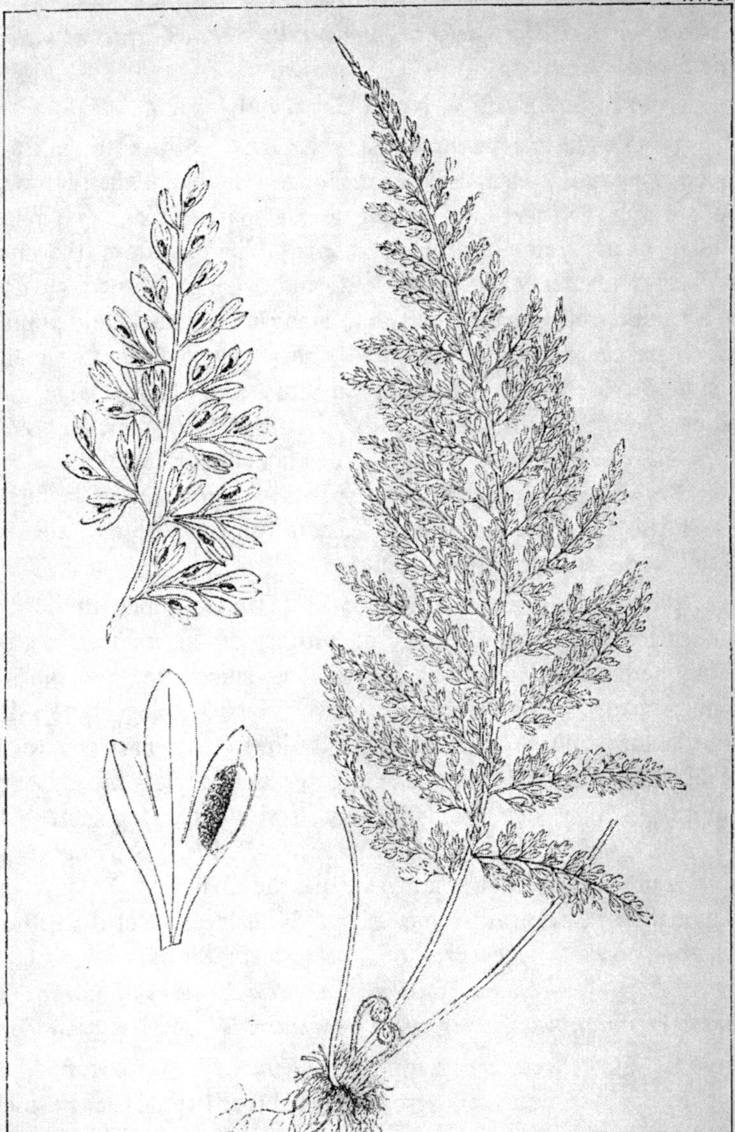

ASPLENIUM TENUIFOLIUM. (*Don.*)

the upper side agian cut into erect-patent linear segments, the lowest on the under side suppressed; texture coriaceous; rachis compressed; sori linear marginal. *Kze. in Linnæa*, x. 521. *Hook. Syn. Fil. p.* 222. *Bedd. F. S. I. t.* 138.

South India, on the Tinnevelly Mountains; Ceylon, Singhe Rajah Forest; Himalayas, Bhotan, and Mishmee; Khasya.

(Also in South Africa, Japan and Fiji.)

38. ASPLENIUM BELANGERI. (*Kze.*) Caudex short, stout, erect; stipes densely tufted, 4 inches to a span long, compressed upwards, greenish; fronds 1--1½ feet long, narrow-oblong (the sides almost forming a parallelogram), acuminated only at the apex, sparingly stellate-squamulose beneath, here and there proliferous, subchartaceous, pale green, bipinnate, primary pinnæ from 1-2 inches long, horizontally patent, singularly uniform in the whole length, linear obtuse, nearly sessile, again pinnated (or they may be said to be deeply pinnatifid), pinnules or segments 2-3 lines long, linear-clavate, or subspathulate, obtuse, straight, or a little curved, decurrent, with the rachis simple monosorous, or the lowest superior one is bifid or subpinnatifid; veins solitary central; sori large, conspicuous, occupying nearly the length of the pinnule, marginal; involucres of the same colour and texture almost of the frond; main rachis compressed, partial ones distinctly winged. *Hook. Sp. Fil.* iii. 209. *Syn. Fil. p.* 223. *Bedd. F. B. I. t.* 287.

The Malay Peninsula.

(Also in Java, Sumatra, and Borneo.)

GENUS XLI.—ATHYRIUM. (*Roth.*)

(*Derivation unknown.*)

As in Asplenium, but the involucres, or at least many of them, more or less curved, often horseshoe-shaped, rarely quite uniform as in Lastrea.

1. ATHYRIUM SPINULOSUM. (*Max.*) Stipes 6-12 inches long, scattered, firm, erect, straw-coloured, furnished more or less with pale brown lanceolate scales; fronds 6-12 inches, deltoid, as broad as long, 3-pinnate; pinnæ 9-12 pairs, lowest the largest, 2½-3 inches

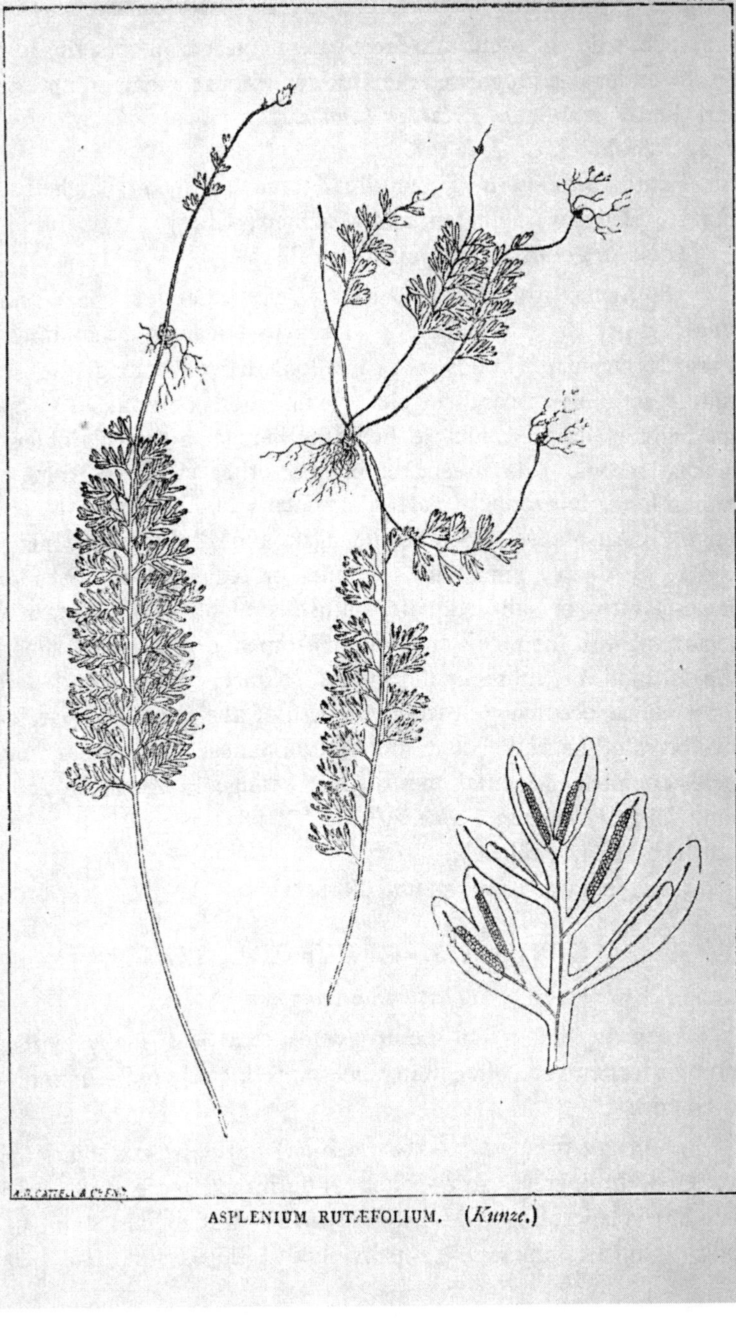

A.R. CATTELL & Co. ENG.

ASPLENIUM RUTÆFOLIUM. (*Kunze.*)

broad, ovate-lanceolate; pinnules lanceolate, cut down to the rachis on each side into 6–9 oblong rhomboidal segments two lines long, one line broad, which are sharply toothed or crenated; texture herbaceous; rachis naked or nearly so; sori 2–10 to a segment; indusium slightly curved, or horseshoe-shaped, very small and thin. Cystopteris, *Max. Fl. Amur.* 340. *Baker in Hook. Syn. Fil.* 225, under Asplenium. Athyrium subtriangulare (Hook), *Bedd. F. B. I. t.* 242. *The supposed species, or variety, subtriangulare, does not differ from spinulosum, except that the teeth are less spinulose; it cannot, I think, be considered even a variety.*

Sikkim 10,000–12,000 feet; Lachen, Samding, Yeumtong.

(Also in Manchuria, Amurland and Korea.)

2. ATHYRIUM ATKINSONI. (*Bedd.*) Stipes 6–12 inches long, erect, straw-coloured, furnished towards the base with a few long narrow pale-coloured scales; fronds 10–12 inches long, triangular, 10–12 inches broad at basal pinnæ, gradually narrowing upwards, tripinnate, with the tertiary pinnæ deeply pinnatifid; pinnæ 7–8 pairs, the lowest much the largest, about three inches broad; texture herbaceous, naked, secondary pinnæ with the rachis winged, but the pinnules (tertiary pinnæ) often distinctly petioled, at least in the lower portion of the pinnæ, pinnatifid $\frac{1}{2}$–$\frac{2}{3}$ down, the segments being more or less crenated; sori one to each segment on the basal vein, linear, curved or almost reniform, never double; veins terminating just within the margin. *Bedd. Fern. Sup. p.* 11, *t.* 359.

Sikkim at high levels.

(*Clarke's variety Andersoni is Athyrium fimbriatum, var. sphæropteroides.*)

3. ATHYRIUM HOHENACKERIANUM. (*Kze.*) Stipes tufted, 2–4 inches long, clothed throughout rather closely with linear-subulate scales; fronds 6–18 inches long, $1\frac{1}{2}$–3 inches broad, ovate-lanceolate; pinnæ in numerous pairs, lanceolate, 1–$2\frac{3}{4}$ inches long, cut nearly or quite to the rachis into ovate or oblong serrated pinnules; texture herbaceous; rachis naked upwards, scaly below; sori copious; involucre conspicuous, linear-oblong, curved or horseshoe-shaped. *Hook. Syn. Fil. p.* 225. *Bedd. F. S. I. t.* 151.

Madras Presidency in the Western Forests, from the plains up to 4,000 feet; Ceylon, Scinde.

4. ATHYRIUM FALCATUM. (*Bedd.*) Stipes 1–9 inches long with many linear golden scales at the base; fronds 6–14 inches long, with the rachis above dilated or winged, linear-lanceolate, narrowed at both ends, pinnæ 15–20 on each side, sessile, alternate, 1–1½ inch long, by ¼–⅓ inch broad, falcate-ovate, deflexed, obtuse or acuminate, generally with a large obtuse auricle at both the superior and inferior base, above pinnatifid almost half down to the costa; segments obtuse, crenated; sori numerous on each side cf the costa, at length confluent and covering the whole or nearly the whole of the under surface. *Bedd. F. S. I. t.* 151. Asplenium drepanophyllum, *Baker*, *Syn. Fil.* 226.

South India, Anamallay Hills, dry grassy places 5,000 feet. Myhenda Hill near Berhampore, 4,500 feet; Mahableshawer; Parasnath 4,000 feet.

ATHYRIUM FALCATUM. (*Bedd.*)

5. ATHYRIUM THELYPTEROIDES. (*Michx.*) Stipes 6–8 inches or more, furnished at the base with large lanceolate thin light coloured scales; fronds generally about 3 feet long and 8 inches broad, lanceolate, gradually narrowed towards the base; pinnæ numerous, erect-patent, ¾–1 inch broad, cut three-quarters of the way to the rachis or more into oblong blunt crenated segments; sori in close regular rows, short, oblong; indusium persistent. *Michx. Fl. Bor. Am.* II. 265. *Hook. Syn. Fil. p.* 226. A. allantodioides, *Bedd. F. B. I. t.* 221, *not F. B. I. t.* 68, *which is a form of* Diplazium sorzogonense.

Himalayas from Kashmir to Bhotan, common in many places. (Also in North America, Canada, Amur land.)

6. ATHYRIUM MACROCARPUM. (*Blume.*) Stipes 6–9 inches long, firm, erect, straw coloured, scaly below; fronds up to three feet long, generally lanceolate in outline; pinnæ 20–30 pair, very variable in size and cutting, sometimes less than one inch long, and only pinnatifid, usually about four inches, and sometimes 9–10 inches long, again pinnate, with the pinnules deeply pinnatifid, and as large or much larger than the whole pinnæ in the less compound forms; texture herbaceous, shining, striate beneath the lowest lobe on the upper side often larger; margin toothed; involucres very large, often reniform (as in Lastrea), but always mixed with some that are linear (asplenioid), and horseshoe-shaped, margin more or less fimbriate. Aspidium macrocarpum, *Bl. En. Fil. Jav.* 162. Asplenium, *Hook. Syn. Fil. p.* 227. *Bedd. F. S. I. t.* 152 *and* 153. A. squarrosum, *Wall. Cat.* 356.

South India, very common on the Western Mountains, above 3,000 feet; Ceylon; Himalayas, Gurwhal and Bhotan 2,000–9,000 feet; Khasya; Birma, and the Malay Peninsula.

Clarke's variety, Atkinsoni, is one of the simplest forms, and is very common on the Nilgiris, mixed with the more compound examples and connected by intermediate forms. Beddome's macrocarpum, var. β, *F. S. I. t.* 153, is at first sight very distinct looking, and is often collected as a Lastrea; it is, however, only a state in which the fructification is less and the lamina of the frond more developed than usual.

(Also in Malay Islands, China and Japan.)

VAR. β. 1-PINNATA. (*Clarke.*) Fronds linear; pinnæ short, slightly crenate, in shape much like some forms of the Polystichum auriculatum.

Khasya, 3,000–4,000 feet. I have only seen this in Mr. Clarke's collection, and it looks distinct from any of the simpler forms of macrocarpum from Southern India, the pinnæ being much less cut.

7. ATHYRIUM NIGRIPES. (*Mett.*) Caudex stout, often 2–3 inches out of ground; stipes tufted, firm, round, glabrous; fronds 8–30 inches long, quite deltoid, with the lowest pinnæ largest, to oblong, lanceolate, herbaceous, not plicate-striate beneath; pinnæ about 8 inches long, by 2½ broad, (but variable in size) pinnules often deeply pinnatifid to only a winged rachis; segments crenate or serrate, not spinulose; sori linear-oblong, only slightly curved in two oblique rows towards the midrib of the pinna; involucres persistent. *Mett. Farng. Aspl.* 195. *Hook. Syn. Fil.* 227, *not Bedd. F. S. I. t.* 157, *which is* selenopteris.

Himalayas, from Kashmir to Bhotan, 3,000–11,000 feet elevation, very common about Darjeeling; Khasya 2,000–6,000 feet. Not in Southern India or Ceylon, the former plant being selenopteris, (Kunze), the latter gymnogrammoides.

VAR. β CLARKEI. (*Bedd.*) Fronds linear-lanceolate, up to 3 feet long, and 3–4, rarely 6 inches, broad, gradually narrowed at both ends, generally rooting from a bud on the upper side of the rachis; rachis of pinnæ, costa, and veins, sometimes furnished with a few weak setæ. Athyrium Clarkei, *Bedd. Sup. Ferns, t.* 360.

Nepal, Sikkim, common at Surail near Darjeeling, 6,000 feet; Kulhoit Valley, 6,000–7,000 feet. I feel quite certain now that this is only an elongated variety of nigripes, and Mr. Clarke agrees.

(Mr. Clarke's nigripes, var. dissecta, appears to be typical nigripes rather more cut than usual.)

8. ATHYRIUM SELENOPTERIS. (*Kunze.*) Caudex stout, erect; stipes tufted, often 10 inches long, stramineous; fronds 10–20 inches long, lanceolate, somewhat attenuated towards the base, never deltoid; pinnæ 2–6 inches long, rather distant; texture rather flaccid, pinnatifid to a winged rachis in the smaller forms, or almost quite pinnate in the larger forms, the wing of the rachis being almost obsolete, the pinnules deeply pinnatifid, but with a somewhat decurrent base, the ultimate segments more or less crenated, or even serrated; sori oblong or curved. *Kunze, Mett. Farngatt. Asp.* 196. Asp. nigripes, var. selenopteris, *Clarke, F. N. I. p.* 491. Athyrium aspidioides, *Hook. Syn. Fil. p.* 228. (*in part*) *as far as the Nilgiri specimens are concerned,*

ATHYRIUM SELENOPTERIS. (*Kunze.*)

not the Madagascar plant of Schlecht. Athyrium pectinatum, *Bedd. F. S. I. t.* 155 (*not Wall.*) Athy. nigripes, *Bedd. F. S. I. t.* 157.

Madras Presidency, Western Mountains, Nilgiris, common at 6,000–8,000 feet. Pulneys, Tinnevelly Mountains; Ceylon at Newera Elya, and Maturatte, &c.

9. ATHYRIUM GYMNOGRAMMOIDES. (*Kl.*) Fronds large, 5–6 feet long, bi-tripinnate, primary pinnæ 12–16 inches long, oblong-lanceolate, secondary pinnæ up to 4½ inches long, by 1½ inch broad, either deeply pinnatifid to a winged rachis, or pinnate, the wing being obsolete; ultimate segment oblong, lobed one-third of the way down; sori near the midrib. *Mett. Aspl. p.* 193, *t.* 6, *fig.* 13–14. *Bedd. F. S. I. t.* 156. *Thw. En. Pl. Zey. p.* 385.

Ceylon, central provinces 5,000–6,000 feet, nearly allied to selenopteris. Mr. Baker includes this under nigripes, but it is not very near the Himalayan plant.

VAR. β ERYTHRORACHIS. (*Bedd.*) The naked stipes and rachis deeply channelled, bright purple; fronds deltoid, much smaller than the type, 6–10 inches long, without the stipe, lowest pinnæ 3–4 inches long, the partial rachis channelled and winged on the upper side, the pinnules petiolate, ⅝ inch long, auricled at the superior base and somewhat pinnatifid at the inferior base, crenate or subentire above, veins pinnate and forked terminating within the margin; sori asplenioid (never double), a few more or less curved. *Bedd. Sup. Ferns, p.* 12. Athy. nigripes, *Thw. En. Pl. Zey. p.* 384.

Ceylon, about Newera Elya.

This is probably a distinct species, it is included in the Kew bundle of nigripes, but is nearer to the Nilgiri selenopteris, some specimens of which are also in the Kew packet of nigripes, whilst others exactly similar are placed with the South African aspidioides. Mr. Thwaites has also referred it to nigripes, but he may not have seen the Himalayan plant.

10. ATHYRIUM FILIX-FŒMINA. (*Bernh.*) Fronds 1–4 feet, lanceolate, narrowed at both ends, membranaceous, green, bi-pinnate;

rachis soft, appearing triangular or furrowed when dry; primary pinnæ narrow linear-oblong, hardly narrowed at the base; secondary pinnæ $\frac{1}{4}$–1 inch, oblong, patent at right angles to the rachis of the primary pinnæ, sessile or decurrent, serrate or pinnatifid; margin bluntly or acutely toothed; involucres in two rows on the secondary pinnæ, short, oblong, subpersistent. *Bernh. in Schrad. Neu. Jour.* i. *pt.* 11. 26. *Clarke. F. N. I. p.* 491.

I follow Mr. Clarke here, as he has an intimate knowledge of this fern and its varieties in a growing state, he says that there are two main types of the Himalayan Filix-fœmina, viz.:—1st, with a succulent rachis, appearing triangular or grooved when dry, green, involucre subpersistent; 2nd, with a firm rachis, appearing round in the dried specimens, often red; involucre less persistent, often fugacious.

VAR. 1. DENTIGERA. (*Wall.*) Cutting nearly as in the European type (not nearly so fine as in pectinata), green, rachis succulent, grooved when dry; involucre subquadrate, or horseshoe-shaped, smaller and less persistent than in the European type. (Polypodium dentigerum, *Wall. Cat.* 334.)

Himalayas 6,000–11,000 feet, from Kashmir to Bhotan, common from Nepal westwards.

VAR. 2. PECTINATA. (*Wall.*) Very finely cut, tripinnate, 4-pinnatifid, bright green; rachis slender, but scarcely succulent or grooved when dry; involucre subquadrate, or short oblong, little horseshoe-shaped, subpersistent. *Wall. Cat.* 231. *Clarke, F. N. I. t.* 57. *Bedd. F. S. I. t.* 154, *small form.*

Himalayas, Sikkim to Gurwhal 2,000–5,000 feet elevation; Parasnath 4,000–5,000 feet; Mountains of the Godavery and Central India; Mahableshwar; Scinde; Mount Aboo.

VAR. 3. ATTENUATA. (*Clarke.*) 1-pinnate; base of the stipes densely clothed with broad lanceolate scales; rachis succulent when dry, grooved or triangular; fronds small, very narrow, much tapering at both ends; pinnæ patent, very close together, deeply regularly pinnatifid into oblong serrated segments, scarcely a quarter inch long;

involucre small, subquadrate, hardly ever horseshoe-shaped, not very fugacious. *Clarke, F. N. I. t.* 59. *fig.* 1.

Kashmir, 10,000–12,000 feet, north of the main valley; appears to be only a stunted form of dentigera.

VAR. 4. RETUSA. (*Clarke.*) 1–2-pinnate, rachis firm, round when dry; fronds red, never very large; involucre small, fugacious; sori, scattered, round. Cystopteris retusa, *Decne in Jacq. Voy.* 176, *t.* 177. *Clarke, F. N. I. t.* 59–2.

Himalayas 10,000–15,000 feet, from Kashmir to Bhotan.

VAR. 5. FLABELLULATA. (*Clarke.*) 2-pinnate; rachis firm, round when dry, fronds red, 1–3 feet; secondary pinnæ deeply pinnatifid; segments laciniate; involucre small, fugacious; sori scattered, round. *Clarke, F. N. I. t.* 60.

Sikkim, 13,000 feet; Yakla, Jongri, scarcely distinct from dentigera.

VAR. 6. POLYSPORA. (*Clarke.*) 2-pinnate, or sub-3-pinnate; rachis firm, round when dry; fronds red, 1–3 feet; involucre large, approximate, very persistent, often reniform; sori large, often ultimately thickly covering the whole of the pinnules. *Clarke, F. N. I. t.* 61. *fig.* 1.

N. W. Himalayas, 6,000–10,000 feet; Kumaon to Chumba.

Very distinct from the other varieties, and approaching oxyphyllum.

VAR. 7. PARASNATHENSIS. (*Clarke.*) 1-pinnate, sub-2-pinnate; rachis triangular when dry; fronds reddish, 1½ foot, narrow-oblong, scarcely attenuated at the base; primary pinnæ 1½ inch, broadest at the base; secondary pinnæ ¼–⅓ inch, acutely toothed, scarcely pinnatifid; involucre short, oblong, in two oblique rows, very persistent. *Clarke, F. N. I. t.* 61. *fig.* 2.

Parasnath 4,000 feet elevation; probably only a small stunted form of retusa.

11. ATHYRIUM OXYPHYLLUM. (*Hook.*) Stipes with many

reddish linear-lanceolate scales at the base; fronds up to 3 feet, oblong-lanceolate, generally 2-pinnaté, or in some forms only pinnate; slightly narrowed, never attenuated at the base, coriaceous, rigid, somewhat shining, striated when dry; primary pinnæ often falcate, sometimes only pinnatifid half-way to the rachis, $1\frac{1}{4}$–2 inches long, generally much larger; 2–$4\frac{1}{2}$ inches long, and pinnate, the pinnules more or less hastate from one or both of the basal lobes being enlarged or auricled, sub-entire to pinnatifid, and often sharply serrated, particularly at the apex; indusium small, fugacious or wanting. *Hook. Syn. Fil.* 228. *Bedd. F. B. I. t.* 67.

The exinvolucrate variety, called Kulhaitense by Clarke, is eberneum. (Wall.) It only differs in the absence of the involucre; the 1-pinnate form with short pinnæ looks different at first sight, but gradually runs into the larger and more compound forms.

Himalayas, from Gurwhal to Bhotan, 4,000–11,000 feet; Khasya 3,000–11,000 feet. I do not feel certain that the Khasya specimen called stramineum J. Sm. really belongs here, though it is so sorted in the Kew bundles; it is very like some of the Nilgiris forms of Athyrium selenopteris.

No. 82.

ATHYRIUM BREVISORUM. (*Wall.*)

12. ATHYRIUM BREVISORUM. (*Wall.*) Stipes $1\frac{1}{2}$ foot and more long stramineous-brown below, glossy; fronds $1\frac{1}{2}$–2 feet long, ovate-lanceolate, membranaceous, bi-tripinnate; primary pinnæ long-petiolate remote erect-patent, a foot and more long, broad-lanceolate, acuminate; secondary pinnæ 5–6 inches long, lanceolate, nearly sessile, pinnated; pinnules numerous, approximate, oblong-lanceolate, much acuminate, horizontally patent, 1–$1\frac{1}{2}$ inch long, coarsely serrated, rarely subpinnatifid, the serratures very acute, almost

mucronate, lowest pinnules more distant on short petiolules, intermediate ones more approximate, the lower base decurrent, upper ones confluent; veins pinnated; veinlets forked once or more; sori generally in two rows, oblique near the costule in the pinnules that are pinnatifid, extending to the lobes, small, short-linear, straight or lunate; involucres slightly convex, jagged at the margin; main rachis stramineous, glossy, flexuose. *Hook. Sp. Fil.* iii. 229. *Wall. n.* 220, (*not Mett.*) *Bedd. F. B. I. t.* 241.

Mishmee; Taongdong Mountains near Ava. The figure is taken from the Ava specimen collected by Wallich, which is bipinnate, the Mishmee specimen is tripinnate.

13. ATHYRIUM FIMBRIATUM. (*Wall. under Aspidium.*) Stipes stout, darkish brown, glossy, 1 foot and more long, copiously paleaceous, most so towards the base, with large glossy, tawny, lanceolate-subulate scales, fronds ample, 2–3 feet long, ovate or subdeltoid acuminate firm-coriaceous, 3–4-pinnate; primary pinnæ petiolate (as are the secondary and tertiary ones), 6–12 inches long, distant from a broad base, lanceolate, much acuminate; secondary ones also distant, of the same shape, but not acuminate, 1–1½ inches long, numerous; ultimate pinnules ovate-lanceolate, ¼ inch long, superior basal one the largest, acute, all pinnatifid with acute lobes, auricled at the superior base, terminal ones subconfluent; sori 2–5 on each pinnule, broad-oblong, or in age almost globose, very prominent and copious; involucre brown, membranaceous, broad, generally crescent-shaped or subreniform, fimbriated, extremely convex, soon forced back by sori; rachises all pale brown, glossy, more or less flexuose. *Wall. Cat.* 339. *Hook. Sp. Fil.* iii. 234. *Syn. Fil. p.* 229. *Bedd. F. B. I. t.* 295.

Himalayas, from East Kashmir to Bhotan, 5,000–12,000 feet.

VAR. β FOLIOSA. (*Wall.*) Rachis often very red and waved, glandular in the axis of the pinnæ, ultimate segments broader than in the type; sori small. *Wall. Cat.* 359. *Clarke, F. N. I. t.* 62. *fig.* 2.

Sikkim and Nepal at high levels.

No. 83.

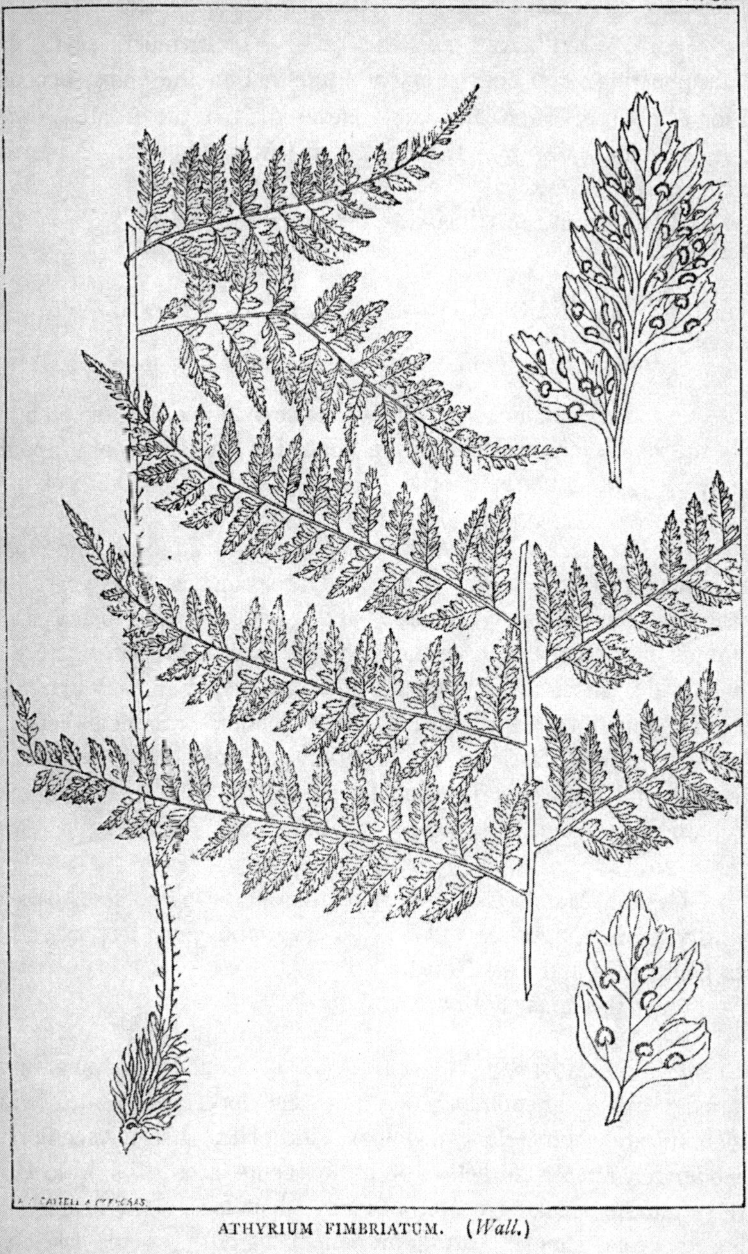

ATHYRIUM FIMBRIATUM. (*Wall.*)

VAR. γ. SPHŒROPTEROIDES. (*Clarke.*) Involucre small, early disappearing; sori both lateral and terminal on the veins, becoming soon globose, often appearing elevated from the frond. *Clarke, F. N. I. t.* 62, *fig.* 1. Asplenium Atkinsoni, var. Andersoni, *Clarke, F. N. I. t.* 57.

Throughout the Himalayas, 9,000–13,000 feet.

GENUS XLII.—DIPLAZIUM. (*Swartz.*)

(*Diplazo* to be double; the double indusia or involucres.)

As in Asplenium, but some of the sori double, *i.e.*, on each side of the vein, each furnished with a linear indusium, the one opening interiorly, the other exteriorly.

1. DIPLAZIUM LANCEUM. (*Thunb.*) Caudex long-repent, rooting sparingly, scaly, stipes distant 4 inches to a span long slender, thickened at the base, and paleaceous with black scales, fronds chartaceous, firm, opaque, longer than the stipes, rarely an inch wide, lanceolate, attenuated, and acuminated at each extremity, entire, sometimes a little repand; costa slender, prominent beneath; veins horizontal, fascicled, the superior, and sometimes the inferior, branch only fertile; sori linear, distant, remote from the costa, often diplazioid. *Thunb. Fl. Jap.* 333. *Hook. Sp. Fil.* iii. 235. *Bedd. F. S. I. t.* 227.

Ceylon, Matale East and Saffragram 2,000–3,000 feet, dies off in dry weather. Assam and N. E. Bengal 500–5,000 feet, extending to Chittagong and East Nepal.

(Also in China, Formosa, and Japan.)

2. DIPLAZIUM SUBSERRATUM. (*Bl.*) Caudex creeping, elongated; fronds membranaceous, 1½ feet long, 1–1½ inch wide, glabrous and satiny, elongate-oblong, lanceolate, sharply acuminate, moderately attenuated below, obtuse or acute at the base, towards the middle sinuate-crenate, coarsely dentate-serrated nearer the apex; costa slender, firm, prominent beneath; veins fascicled,

horizontal or nearly so, one to three of the exterior branches soriferous; sori distant, often curved; involucres often diplazioid, narrow-linear, occupying about two-thirds of the space between the costa and margin; stipes 1–2 inches long, slender, terete. *Bl. En. p.* 174. *Hook. Sp. Fil.* iii. 236. *Bedd. F. B. I. t.* 289.

Penang.

(Also in Java.)

3. DIPLAZIUM ZEYLANICUM. (*Hook.*) Caudex terete, repent, subterraneous, naked, black; stipes remote, solitary, 4 inches to a span long, paleaceous with lax dark subulate-lanceolate scales; fronds herbaceous, a span to a foot long, 1–2 inches broad, lanceolate acuminate, deeply pinnatifid in the middle, pinnate at the base, serrated only towards the apex, lobes and pinnæ horizontal, oblong, obtuse; veins pinnated, entire or forked; sori linear; involucres with the superior basal one principally diplazioid. *Hook. Sp. Fil.* iii. 237. *Bedd. F. S. I. t.* 228.

Ceylon, forests of Ambagamwa and Kotmallee.

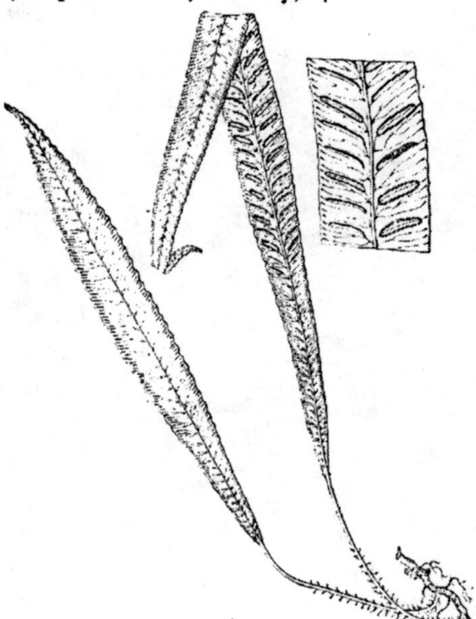

No. 84.

DIPLAZIUM LANCEUM (*Thunb.*)

4. DIPLAZIUM PALLIDUM. (*Bl.*) Stipes a foot or more long, stramineous, deciduously scaly at the base; fronds $1\frac{1}{2}$–2 feet long, ovate acuminate, subcoriaceous, often pale whitish-green when dry pinnated, pinnæ numerous, approximate, mostly petiolate, horizontal, 5–6 inches long, $\frac{1}{2}$–$\frac{3}{4}$ of an inch broad, from a somewhat rounded

or obliquely cuneated base, linear-oblong, acuminate, falcate, sharp'y and subspinulosely serrated, terminal one petiolate and similar to the rest, or larger and broad and pinnatifid at the base from being formed of dwarfed and confluent pinnæ, very coarsely serrated towards the finely acuminated apex; veins very patent, immersed, generally twice dichotomous, the lowest superior branch (arising from near the costa) bearing the linear sorus along its whole length, rarely diplazioid, and only from 1–3 at the superior and mostly truncated but not auricled base; involucres narrow, firm, membranaceous. *Bl. En. Fil. Jav.* 176. *Hook. Sp. Fil.* iii. 238. *Bedd. F. B. I. t.* 196.

Birma and the Malay Peninsula.

(Also in the Malay Islands and the Philippines.)

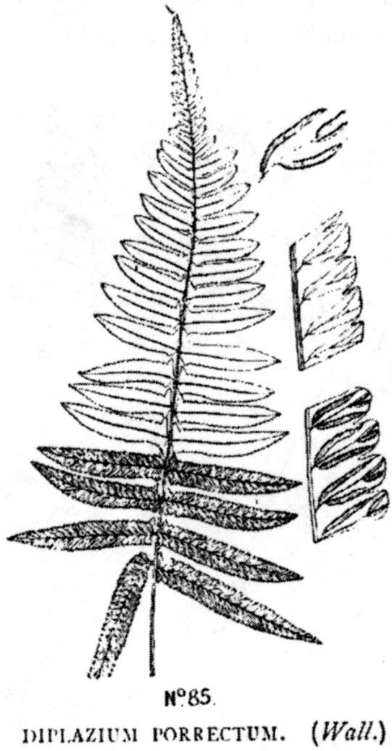

N°85.

DIPLAZIUM PORRECTUM. (*Wall.*)

5. DIPLAZIUM PORRECTUM. (*Wall.*) Caudex erect or ascending; stipes tufted, 6–12 inches long; fronds 8–10 inches to 1½ foot long deltoid-oblong, pinnate; pinnæ horizontal, numerous, 4–6 inches long, petiolate or sessile, and confluent at the acuminated pinnatifid apex, from a broad truncated and auricled or generally quite hastate base (having a distinct auricle above and below), linear-lanceolate, obtuse or acuminate, lower ones more or less deeply pinnatifid, intermediate ones obtusely dentate; uppermost ones entire at the margins; veins patent, pinnated in the auricles, the rest once or twice forked; sori linear, elongated, confined to the superior or basal veinlet, and extending its whole length, or on the two outer ones, mostly diplazioid; involucres membranaceous when young. *Wall. Cat.* 204. *Hook. Sp. Fil.* iii. 250. *Bedd. F. B. I. t.* 245.

The Malay Peninsula, Penang, &c.

(Also in the Malay Islands.)

6. DIPLAZIUM BANTAMENSE. (*Bl.*) Rhizome creeping; stipes 6–12 inches long, with lanceolate caducous scales; fronds up to 1½ foot long, simply pinnate; pinnæ generally 3–5 on each side, alternate or subopposite, with one terminal one, subcoriaceous, glabrous, generally sharply serrated towards the apex, otherwise nearly entire, 6–9 inches long, by 1–2 broad, somewhat narrowed at the base; apex acuminate or often caudate; veins pinnate; sori slender, irregular, starting from near the midrib and extending nearly to the margin, or only half-way towards it. *Bl. En. Fl. Jav. Fil.* 190–191. *Hook. Syn. Fil. p.* 231. D. fraxinifolium (Wall.), *Bedd. F. B. I. t.* 59.

Madras Presidency, on the Tinnevelly and Travancore Hills. Khasya Hills, 4,000 feet elevation; Cachar 500 feet elevation; Malay Peninsula.

(Also in Malay Islands and Southern China.)

N°86.

DIPLAZIUM BANTAMENSE. (*Bl.*)

7. DIPLAZIUM SYLVATICUM. (*Presl.*) Caudex decumbent; stipes 1 foot long, firm, erect, naked except at the base, where furnished with scales; fronds 1–3 feet long, simply pinnate, ovate-lanceolate in outline; pinnæ numerous, about 6 inches long by 1 inch broad, the apex acuminate or caudate, the margin nearly entire or slightly waved or serrated, particularly towards the apex, but not to more than one line deep (at least in the type); base truncate or narrowed; texture thin, herbaceous; veins pinnate, fine; sori long, linear. *Presl. Rel. Hænk.* 1–42, *under* Asplenium. *Hook. Syn. Fil.* 232. *Bedd. F. S. I.* 161, *a small specimen.*

Madras Presidency, throughout the Western forests up to 4,500 feet. Ceylon, central provinces; Malay Peninsula.

(Also in Mauritius, Fernando Po, Java, and Borneo.)

VAR. β PRESCOTTIANUM. (*Wall.*) Pinnæ narrower than the type, more deeply serrated or cut, and more or less lobed towards the base. *Wall. Cat.* 235. *Hook. Sp. Fil.* iii. 251. *Bedd. F. B. I. t.* 243.

Singapore and Penang (perhaps a distinct species).

8. DIPLAZIUM SPECIOSUM. (*Mett.*) Stipes tufted, 1 foot or more long, firm, erect, straw-coloured or brownish, nearly naked; fronds 1–2 feet long, 8–12 inches broad, with 10–20 pairs of pinnæ below the pinnatifid apex, the lower ones often stalked, 4–6 inches long, about ¾ inch broad, the apex much acuminated, the edge lobed, the lobes reaching down half to two-thirds of the way to the rachis, generally falcate acute, obscurely crenate; texture herbaceous but firm; rachis erect, naked; veins pinnate in the lobes; sori slender, reaching nearly to the edge; rachis 4-sided with sharp angles. A. acuminatum, *Wall. Mett.* (*non H. and A.*). *Hook. Syn. Fil. p.* 235. *Bedd. F. B. I. t.* 290.

The Malay Peninsula; Tinnevelly Mountains. Mr. Clarke considers it a form of sylvaticum.

9. DIPLAZIUM PINNATIFIDO-PINNATUM. (*Hook.*) Stipes 6–12 inches long, firm, erect, naked; fronds 9–12 inches long, 6–9 inches broad, pinnate, with a pinnatifid apex; pinnæ 3–4 only on each side, 3–4 inches long, 1 inch broad, the apex acute, the margin sharply serrated; base cuneate; texture coriaceous, drying a dull blackish colour; veins obscure, pinnate; sori irregular, beginning at midrib, not reaching the margin. *Hook. Syn. Fil.* 231. *Bedd. F. B. I. t.* 244.

Mishmee; Mr. Clarke has united it with the Philippine Lobbianum, of which there is only one authentic specimen at Kew, and though this does not represent the whole frond, it has numerous pinnæ of a lighter colour and more prominent venation; it appears to me to be quite a different plant.

10. DIPLAZIUM LONGIFOLIUM. (*Don.*) Caudex erect, small, densely clothed with the bases of old stipes, paleaceous, stipes tufted 5–6 inches long, fronds broad-lanceolate, acuminate, membranaceous, a span to 14 inches long, pinnated, pinnatifid at the apex, pinnæ, on slender petioles, 1½–3 inches long, very patent, broad-lanceolate, falcate, sharply acuminated, truncated and auricled at the superior base, inferior base excised, the margin more or less deeply lobed, lobes as well as the auricles spinulosely serrate; costa slender, flexuose, vein-like; veins in oblique fascicles corresponding to each lobe, dichotomous lowest superior branch only soriferous; sori mostly asplenioid, linear, neither attaining the costa nor the margin. *Don. Prod. Fl. Nep.* 7, *under* Asplenium. Diplazium lobulosum, *Bedd. F. B. I. t.* 247. *Hook. Sp. Fil. t.* 141. *Syn. Fil.* 234.

Mr. Clarke has placed this in Asplenium, but there are diplazioid indusia on my specimens, and on some of those at Kew. Asplenium trapeziforme (Roxb.), *Bedd. F. S. I. t.* 134, is not at all allied here, as suggested by Mr. Clarke.

No. 87.

DIPLAZIUM LONGIFOLIUM. (*Don.*)

Nepal and Kumaon, 6,000–8,000 feet.

11. DIPLAZIUM TOMENTOSUM. (*Hook.*) Caudex 1–2 inches, erect, sending down wiry black roots; stipes 6–9 inches long, firm, erect; fronds deltoid-lanceolate, 6–12 inches long, 3–4 inches broad at base and gradually narrowing upwards; pinnæ numerous, the lowest pair deflexed, the others horizontal, $\frac{3}{8}$–$\frac{5}{8}$ inch broad, narrow-oblong, somewhat falcate, usually auricled at base on the upper side, pinnatifid half or two-thirds down to the midrib in the larger fronds, subentire in the smaller ones; segments falcate, $\frac{1}{8}$ inch broad;

texture subcoriaceous, main rachis pubescent, rachis of pinnæ pubescent and veins beneath somewhat hairy; veins 3–4 on each side in the lobes; sori long. *Hook. Syn. Fil. p.* 234. *Bedd. F. B. I. t.* 195.

Birma and the Malay Peninsula; there is one specimen in the Kew Herbarium marked Khasya Griffith, but it is very probable that it came from Birma.

(Also in the Malay Islands.)

12. DIPLAZIUM JAPONICUM. (*Thunb.*) Rhizome creeping or suberect; stipes up to 18 inches long, pubescent or glabrous; fronds herbaceous, 8–18 inches long, 6–8 inches broad, deltoid to lanceolate pinnate; rachises and costa more or less woolly, with crisped hairs mixed with small scales, or almost quite glabrous; pinnæ 6–12 on each side, below the pinnatifid apex, alternate, subopposite, or the lower ones quite opposite, some of the lower ones petioled, upper ones sessile or decurrent, all pinnatifid either half-way to the rachis or quite down to a winged rachis; segments nearly entire, with a toothed rounded or falcate apex, or rather deeply pinnatifid; veins pinnate in the lobes; veinlets simple or forked, often somewhat hairy or with minute crisped scales; sori linear, commencing near the midrib and not quite reaching the margin. *Thunb. Fl. Jap.* 334. Diplazium Thwaitesii (A. Br.), *Hook. Syn. Fil.* 235. *Bedd. F. S. I* 291. D. lasiopteris (Mett.), *Hook. Syn. Fil.* 235. *Bedd. F. S. I. t.* 160. Diplazium decussatum (Wall.), *Bedd. F. B. I.* 292. D. polyrhizon, *Baker, Syn. Fil.* 490.

I have followed Mr. Clarke in reducing all these species to japonicum; the typical lasiopteris of Southern India has the fronds more hairy and generally lanceolate in shape, the lower pinnæ being reduced; but some Japan examples are quite as lanceolate in shape; typical decussatum has short very deltoid fronds, and Thwaitesii is only a large form of decussatum; if only examples from certain geographical areas are examined, lasiopteris and decussatum might well be looked upon as distinct species, but when large suites of specimens from an extended area are compared, is is impossible to keep up the supposed different species even as good varieties, they quite run one into the other; I have found typical decussatum with the rhizome creeping, though it is generally erect; in lasiopteris and Thwaitesii it is wide creeping. I have seen nothing like Mr. Clarke's variety chattagramica, with bipinnate fronds, the secondary pinnæ petioled and the rachis not winged, and can hardly fancy it belongs here, the specimen could not be found at Kew, but from the figure in Clarke's Review, it appears to be one of the numerous forms of latifolium and perhaps the same as the one he calls succulentum. Mr. Clarke is quite wrong in referring Schkuhrii Thwaites here, he did so on a specimen of my decurrens, wrongly named Schkuhrii, but decurrens (which is Thwaites's polypodioides var. *β c. p.* 3332, and Moore's dilatatum, var. *β* minor), can have no place here.

Madras Presidency, on the Western ghats, the supposed lasiopteris at Ootacamund, 7,000 feet, and Poombary on the Pulneys, 7,000 feet; decussatum on the Tinnevelly Hills and Jeypore Hills, West of Vizagapatam, 3,000–4,000 feet. Ceylon, central provinces; N. W. Himalayas; Nepal; Nynee Tal; Kangra; Kumaon; Khasya, 3,000 feet; Malay Peninsula.

(Also in Japan, China, and Polynesia.)

13. DIPLAZIUM SCHKUHRII. (*Thwaites.*) Caudex erect; scales dense, small, lanceolate, dark-brown; stipes 9–18 inches long, naked; fronds deltoid-lanceolate, up to 2 feet long, bipinnate below, bipinnatifid above; pinnæ alternate, lower ones distant, 6–8 inches long, by $1\frac{1}{2}$–2 inches broad; rachis winged; pinnules distant, sessile ligulate-oblong, all very regular in shape, $\frac{3}{4}$–$\frac{7}{8}$ inch long, $\frac{3}{8}$–$\frac{1}{4}$ inch broad, pinnatifid about $\frac{1}{3}$ down into rounded lobes; texture rather firm; surfaces glabrous, bright-green; veinlets simple or pinnated in the lobes; sori linear, generally reaching from the midrib to the sinus between the lobes, double or single. In younger plants or smaller specimens, the fronds are often pinnate only, *i.e.*, the primary pinnæ only pinnatifid half to two-thirds to the rachis. *Thw. En. Pl. Zey. p.* 385. (*Not Mett. or J. Sm. which is only a form of* sylvaticum.) *Hook. Syn. Fil. p.* 491. *Bedd. F. S. I. t.* 230.

Ceylon; central provinces.

14. DIPLAZIUM SORZOGONENSE. (*Presl.*) Stipes tufted, scaly

below; fronds up to 16 inches long, pinnate, with numerous pinnæ; pinnæ sessile, about 6 inches long, by 1¼ broad, cut down very regularly throughout two-thirds to the rachis into oblong blunt subentire lobes, which are of equal breadth, (¼ inch) throughout to the apex; texture firm; rachis slightly scaly; veinlets simple, each occupied in its entire length from costule to apex by a sorus. *Hook. Syn. Fil. p.* 236 (*in part.*) *Bedd. F. B. I. t.* 246.

Malacca and Penang; differs from the North India plant in its longer lobes with quite parallel edges, its simple veins, and its longer sori. The figure quoted above is from the Malay plant (though supposed at the time to be from North India), and there is another specimen of the same in the Kew Herbarium, labelled Khasya, Griffith, but it is probable that Griffith obtained it from Malacca.

15. DIPLAZIUM STOLICZKÆ. (*Bedd.*) Stipe and rachis glabrous or subglabrous; fronds 1–1½ feet long, by 10 inches broad, pinnate; pinnæ numerous, the lowest pair slightly the largest, and only a few of the upper ones gradually diminishing, the lower 2–3 pairs opposite or subopposite, the rest alternate; texture subcoriaceous; pinnæ very shortly petioled, 5–6 inches long, 1–1½ inch broad, gradually tapering towards the apex, cut down ⅔ to ⅝ of the way to the rachis, into oblong, rounded pinnules, which are more than ¼ inch broad, and very regularly crenated; main veins slightly wavy; veinlets simple or forked towards their apex or below their centre, all very conspicuous; sori 3–7 to each pinnule or segment (on the lower veins only), extending from the main vein ⅔ of the way to the margin. *Bedd. F. B. I. p.* 13 *and t.* 361.

North India (Dr. Jerdon), probably Khasya. This is not in the Kew Herbarium, and had not been seen by Mr. Clarke when he wrote his Review.

VAR. β HIRSUTIPES. Differs from the type by the stipes and often the rachis being very fibrillose, in the pinnæ being narrowed, and the lower ones generally more or less reduced, and in the pinnules being much less incised. Diplazium sorzogonense, *Hook. Syn.*

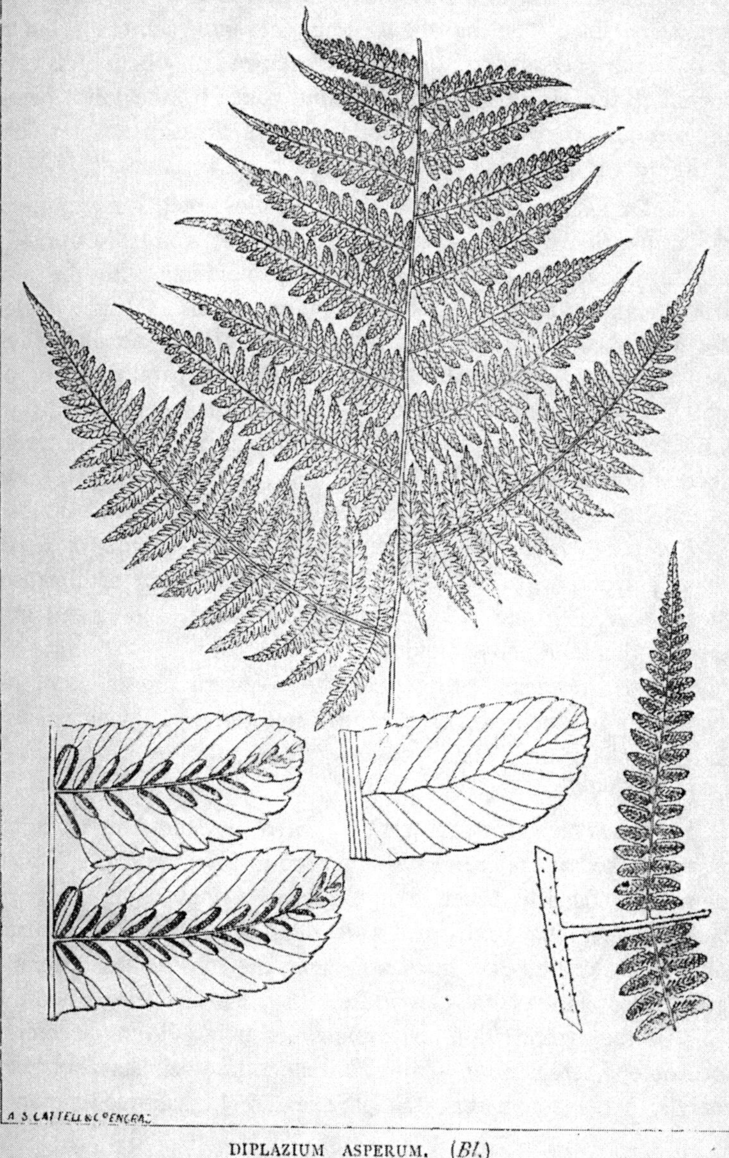

A. S. CATTELL & Co. ENGRA.

DIPLAZIUM ASPERUM. (*Bl.*)

Fil. 236 (*in part*). Diplazium Stoliczkæ, *Clarke, F. N. I. p.* 500. Diplazium thelypteroides, *Bedd. F. B. I. t.* 68.

Himalayas; Nepal to Bhotan, 7,000–10,000 feet; very abundant about Darjeeling. This and the type may run into each other, but as yet only one specimen of the type is known; they both look very different to the Malay sorzogonense, and differ by the lobes being more serrated, the veinlets being often forked, the sori never reaching the margin and being confined to the 3–4 lower veinlets.

16. DIPLAZIUM ASPERUM. (*Bl.*) Caudex erect, often quite a large trunk, (like Alsophila) stipes main and partial rachises prickly and scaly; fronds large, rather coriaceous, bipinnate with the pinnules pinnatifid nearly to the rachis, pinnules quite at right angles with the rachis, sessile or subsessile, 3–5 inches long, about 1 inch broad, segments very regular, forming an oblong parallelogram, or slightly falcate, obtuse, crenate, or serrate, often rather sharply; veinlets numerous, 8–12 in each segment, generally simple, rarely forked, all or nearly all generally soriferous; sori touching the costa but not the margin, generally only one of the lower ones double. *Bl. En.* 195. Diplaz. polypodioides, *Hook. Syn. Fil.* 238 (*in part*). Diplaz. polypodioides, *Bedd. F. S. I. t.* 163. Diplaz. sikkimense, *Clarke, F. N. I. p.* 500, *t.* 65, *fig.* 1, scarcely differs, and is certainly nearer to this than polypodioides.

Madras Presidency; throughout the Western forests, from no elevation up to 3,000 feet, often quite a tree fern; Cuddapa forests; Sikkim, banks of the Teesta, 500 feet.

(Also in Java.)

17. DIPLAZIUM POLYPODIOIDES. (*Mett.*) Caudex erect, stout, densely clothed at the crown with long brown fibrillose scales, 1 inch long; stipes densely tufted, stout, green, 1 foot or more long; fronds 3–4 feet long, and 2 feet wide, bipinnate, with 8–9 primary pinnæ on each side below the simple ones, the lower ones generally distant, secondary pinnæ 2–4 inches long, cut down nearly to the rachis in the typical form, but sometimes only $\frac{1}{3}$ down; segments short oblong, crenate or serrate, or subentire; veinlets about six, generally forked, sometimes simple; texture herbaceous; surfaces

N°89.

A. S. CATTELL SC. ENGRAV.

DIPLAZIUM POLYPODIOIDES. (*Mett.*)

glabrous or nearly so; sori in two oblique rows in the segments; indusium linear, commencing at the midrib, but generally falling well short of the margin, lower ones generally double. *Mett. Hort. Fil. Lips.* 78. *Hook. Syn. Fil.* 238 (excluding asperum (Bl.), which differs in its more coriaceous texture, much more regular segments, numerous veinlets, and its prickles.) *Bedd. F. B. I. t.* 293. Asplenium marginatum, *Wall. Cat.* 391, *type sheet.*

Madras Presidency, in the Western forests up to 6,000 feet elevation. North India, throughout the Himalayas and Khasya hills; Ceylon; the Malay Peninsula. Clarke's variety "vestita" has the rachises more or less villous or subtomentose, but does not otherwise recede from the type, he says it is confined to the central Himalayas. His variety "sublatifolia" runs into "latifolia," and rather belongs to that species, if the two are really distinct, which is very doubtful, his variety "effusior" is D. umbrosum, var. multicaudata.

(Also in Australia.)

VAR. β DECURRENS. (*Bedd.*) Pinnæ more deltoid in form with the secondary pinnæ few and distant, and more or less decurrent on the rachis, only cut down a third or half-way to the rachis; veinlets in the segments few, only 3–4; sori curved, generally occupying the whole length of the veinlets, and extending to the margin. Diplazium decurrens, *Bedd. F. S. I. t.* 229. Diplaz. polypodioides, var. β, *Thw. En. Pl. Zey. p.* 385. *c. p.* 3332. Diplaz. dilatatum, var. β minor, *Moore, Index Fil.* 327, *in part only.*

A very distinct looking fern, and I believe a good species, but I now prefer to follow Mr. Thwaites (who alone can have seen it growing), and consider it a variety of polypodioides. Sir W. Hooker, *Sp. Fil. t.* 258, has mentioned it under polypodioides as perhaps a distinct species. Mr. Baker has included it under maximum (Don.), which is otherwise, as far as the Kew bundle is concerned, one of the large forms of latifolium, and Mr. Clarke in his Review has named it Dipl. Schkuhrii, but this was owing to his having received a specimen of it so labelled (evidently by mistake), from Mr. Thwaites.

Ceylon; Ambagamwa.

18. DIPLAZIUM LATIFOLIUM. (*Don.*) Like polypodioides, only the secondary pinnæ are generally much less cut down, and often much broader, they are sometimes almost entire, or with only shallow serratures, when the fern has quite the appearance of "sylvaticum," only bipinnate instead of simply pinnate ; other forms have the secondary pinnæ 2 inches (or even more) broad at the base, cut down a third or half-way to the rachis; segments always more or less crenate or serrate; veinlets simple or forked, rather distant, their number depending on the size of the segments (never so numerous as in asperum, except when the segments are double the size of those of that plant); sori narrow, often occupying the whole length of the veinlet, and reaching the margin ; indusium sometimes obsolete or early caducous. *Don. Prod. Fl. Nep.* 8. *Hook. Syn. Fil.* 239. Dip. dilatatum, *Hook. Sp. Fil.* iii. 258. *Bedd. F. S. I.* 162, *a form running nearer to* polypodioides. Dip. maximum, *Hook. Syn. Fil.* 232, *in part.*

Madras Presidency, in all the Western forests. North India, throughout the Himalayas and Khasya Hills. Ceylon; Malay Peninsula; from very low altitudes up to 9,000 feet elevation.

(Also in Australia, China and the Philippines.)

If we only included here species with very broad secondary pinnæ, not cut more than half-way down to the rachis, this plant would be very distinct from "polypodioides," but I fear this is not possible, and in all large herbaria, I find specimens that it is very difficult to say which species they should be referred to. Diplazium torrentium and succulentum of Clarke cannot be made into distinct species, unless we also make many more, but they belong to types which, though generally referred here, must, from the deeper cutting of their secondary pinnæ, go into "polypodioides," if the two are to be kept distinct ; no figures and no description could enable any one to distinguish some of these forms as species, the only difference often being the extent of the cutting of the secondary pinnæ. D. decurrens unless a distinct species (which view its venation I think supports), should rather be referred here than to "polypodioides," but until the plant is better known, I think it safer to follow Mr. Thwaites's view.

Young plants of latifolium often produce simply pinnate fronds, which in some of the less cut varieties can scarcely be distinguished from sylvaticum, and I think Mr. Clarke's Sylhet specimens, referred by him to sylvaticum, belong to latifolium.

19. DIPLAZIUM TRAVANCORICUM. (*Bedd.*) A very large fern with trunk-like caudex, secondary pinnæ 20–24 inches long, lanceolate, somewhat attenuated at the base, the apex acuminate or caudate, quite pinnate towards the base, the lower pinnules being petioled, the upper ones gradually becoming sessile, then decurrent, and the pinnæ terminating with a long broad pinnatifid apex, which for the upper 8 inches or so is only very shallowly incised, lowest 2 or 3 pinnules smaller than the adjoining ones, next in order $2\frac{1}{2}$–$3\frac{1}{4}$ inches long, by about 1 inch broad, lanceolate in shape, very slightly serrated towards the apex; veins numerous, prominent and pinnate from a prominent central costa; texture subcoriaceous; surfaces glabrous and striated; sori commencing a little distance from the midrib, and not nearly reaching the margin.

Travancore Hills; Athraymally forests, a very fine new species.

20. DIPLAZIUM UMBROSUM. (*J. Smith, under Athyrium.*) Stipes 1 foot or more long, strong, erect, clothed often with dark scales, and sometimes muricate; fronds 3–5 feet long, 12–18 inches broad; primary pinnæ ovate-lanceolate to deltoid-lanceolate, up to 18 inches long; secondary pinnæ very various, sometimes small and only pinnatifid (in the simpler forms), to quite pinnate with the pinnules pinnatifid in the larger and more compound forms; texture herbaceous; veins pinnate; veinlets simple or forked; sori generally short and near the midrib; indusium very variable, often all asplenioid or diplazioid, often all allantodioid and mixed with very short sori. *Hook. Syn. Fil.* 229 and 489 (under Athyrium.)

I follow Hooker and Baker, and refer here a good many forms, firstly because I now believe they are so closely allied that they really are only varieties of one species, and that some of them run one into the other even in their restricted areas, and that others are geographical varieties which would not be constant in cultivation, and secondly, because I think any attempt to separate them into species would only add to the present confusion, it being a task that should only be undertaken after a cultivation of all the different forms.

Mr. Clarke has proposed the subgenus *Pseud.-Allantodia* for the species with allantodioid sori and free veins, but I am afraid these allantodioid sori are not constant or to be depended on, *Australe*, from the Nilgiris, has the sori often quite allantodioid as figured by me, *tab.* 158, *F. S. I.;* but I have specimens where all the sori are perfectly diplazioid; again, I have specimens of Asplenium resectum, from two different localities, with nearly all the sori allantodioid.

DIPLAZIUM UMBROSUM, VAR. AUSTRALE. (*R. Br.*)

VAR. AUSTRALE. (*R. Br.*) Stipes often muricate; fronds 3-pinnatifid, often rather flaccid in texture, ultimate segments broad and blunt, sori sometimes quite allantodioid, at other times quite asplenioid or diplazioid; rhizome creeping or erect. Athyrium australe, *Bedd. F. S. I. t.* 158. Diplaz. bellum, *Clarke, F. N. I. p.* 496. Diplaz. multicaudatum, var. tristis, *Clarke, l. c. p.* 512.

Sikkim, Bhotan; Khasya; Nilgiris and other mountain forests, 5,000–7,000 feet, in South India; Birma.

(Also in Australia and Tropical Africa.)

VAR. PROCERUM. (*Wall.*) Rhizome creeping; stipes muricate; fronds very large, moderately firm in texture, primary pinnæ up to nearly 2 feet long, secondary pinnæ 5–5½ inches, again pinnated with the pinnules about 1 inch long, and pinnatifid about half-way to, the rachis; segments oblong, crenate; veinlets in the segments once forked; sori mostly in two rows, near and parallel to the midrib, but other very short sori are scattered on the segments; indusium allantodioid. *Wall. Cat.* 2203. *Hook. Syn. Fil.* 489. Dipl. procerum, *Clarke,* 495.

Himalayas, Kumaon to Bhotan, 4,000–8,000 feet, very common; Assam; Khasya, 3,000–6,000 feet, very common.

VAR. MULTICAUDATUM. (*Wall.*) Rhizome creeping; fronds up to 3 feet; primary pinnæ up to 1 foot long; secondary pinnæ petioled, about 3 inches long and 1 inch broad, acuminate, cut down nearly to the rachis, the segments oblique to the rachis, $\frac{1}{2}$–$\frac{3}{4}$ inch long, rather narrow ligulate, more or less sharply serrated; veinlets forked or simple; sori oblong or subquadrate near the rachis; lower indusia diplazioid. *Wall. Cat.* 229. Dipl. Jerdoni, *Bedd. F. B. I. t.* 327. D. Griffithii, *Baker, Syn. Fil.* 239. *Bedd. F. B. I.* 328.

No. 91.
DIPLAZIUM UMBROSUM,
VAR. MULTICAUDATUM. (*Wall.*)

Himalayas, from Nepal to Bhotan, 1,000–5,000 feet, common. Khasya, 1,000–5,000 feet; Chittagong, 200–2,000 feet.

VAR. ASSIMILE. (*Endl.*) Fronds deltoid, membranaceous, flaccid, tripinnate, with the tertiary pinnæ (pinnules) very small, deeply pinnatifid; segments rounded entire, to slightly crenated; veins from pinnate to simple or forked, according to the size of the segments; sori oblique from the midrib towards the margin; indusia mostly diplazioid. *End. Fl. Norf.* 10. *Bedd. F. S. I t.* 294. Athyrium australe, *Thw. En. Pl. Zey. p.* 385. Perhaps a distinct species.

Ceylon, central provinces.

(Also in Norfolk Island and Australia.)

Mr. Clarke informs me that Müller has placed his Diplazium bellum in a new genus of Cyatheæ.

GENUS XLIII.—ANISOGONIUM. (*Presl.*)

(From *anisos*, unequal; *gonia*, an angle; the angles of the venation.)

As in Diplazium, but the veins anastomosing.

1. ANISOGONIUM CORDIFOLIUM. (*Mett.*) Stipes 6–12 inches long, firm, erect, scaly below; fronds 8–12 inches long, 3–4 inches broad, entire, caudate at the base, the point acuminate or subdeltoid, with a large terminal and 1 or 2 pairs of smaller but similar spreading lateral pinnæ; texture coriaceous; veins in close groups of about 4; anastomosing copiously in the outer half of the frond; sori reaching from the midrib to the edge. *Mett. Fil. Hort. Lips. p.* 74, *t.* 12. *f.* 6. *Hook. Syn. Fil.* 243. *Bedd. F. B. I. t.* 331 (the simple form.)

Malacca and Malay Peninsula.

(Also in Philippines and Malay Islands.)

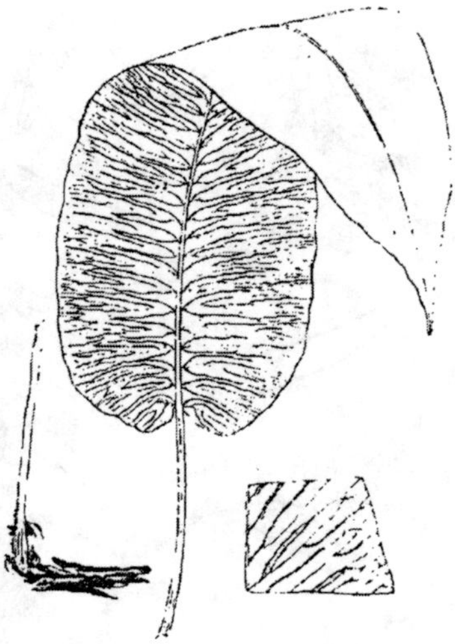

N° 82

ANISOGONIUM CORDIFOLIUM. (*Mett.*)

2. ANISOGONIUM LINEOLATUM. (*Mett.*) Stipe 6–9 inches long, firm, erect, grey, scaly below; fronds occasionally simple, usually with a terminal pinna and 3–6 pairs of lateral ones, which are 6–12 inches long, 2 inches or more broad, entire, often suddenly acuminate; texture coriaceous; rachis naked; veins 4–8 to a cluster, uniting slightly towards the edge. *Mett. l. c. p.* 74. *tab.* 11. *f.* 5. *Hook. Syn. Fil.* 243. *Bedd. F. B. I. t.* 330.

Malacca and Malay Peninsula.

(Also in Philippines and Malay Islands.)

3. ANISOGONIUM HETEROPHLEBIUM. (*Mett. MSS.*) Stipes 1 foot long, grey, scaly throughout; fronds 12–18 inches long, 8–9 inches broad, with 6–8 opposite pairs of pinnæ below the pinnatifid apex; the lowest 2 inches or more apart, 3–4 inches long, 1–1¼ inches broad, the edge undulated, the point acute, the base cordate

on both sides; texture thinly herbaceous, colour dark-green; rachis villose and fibrillose throughout; both surfaces naked; veins pinnate, the groups joining one-third of the way from the midrib to the edge, and the veins of the same and different groups anastomosing; sori not reaching the edge, copiously diplazioid. *Hook. Syn. Fil. p.* 243. *Bedd. F. B. I. t.* 329.

East Nepal to Mishmee, 4,000–6,000 feet elevation.

4. ANISOGONIUM ESCULENTUM. (*Presl.*) Caudex subarborescent, erect; stipes 1–2 feet long, strong, erect, tufted; fronds 4–6 feet long, occasionally simply pinnate only, but generally bipinnate; lower pinnæ 12–18 inches long, 6–8 inches broad; pinnules 3–6 inches long, ¾–1 inch or more broad, the apex acuminate, the edge more or less deeply lobed, the base narrowed suddenly, often auricled; texture subcoriaceous; rachis often pubescent; veins fine, copiously pinnated, 6–10 on each side in each lobe, with a distinct barren central midrib; the veinlets of the different clusters beginning to unite a short distance from the midrib, with lines of sori often on all the lateral veinlets. *Presl. Rel. Hœnk.* i. *p.* 45. *Hook. Syn. Fil.* 244. *Bedd. F. S. I. t.* 164, *as* Callipteris.

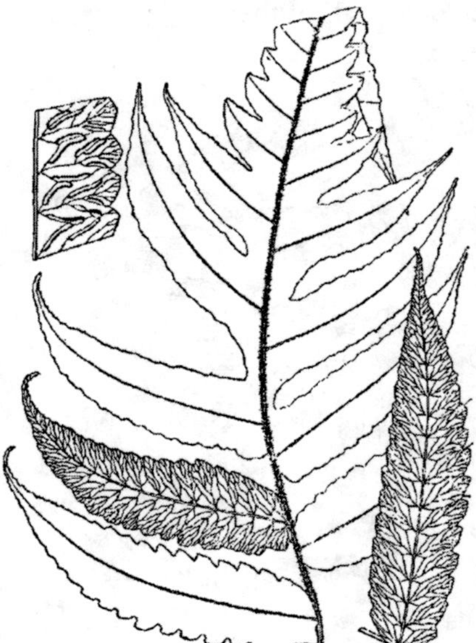

No. 93

ANISOGONIUM HETEROPHLEBIUM. (*Mett.*)

South India, common in the plains on the Western side and up to 3,000 feet. Bengal Plains; Ceylon; Malay Peninsula.

(Also in China, Formosa, and the Malay Islands.)

5. ANISOGONIUM SMITHIANUM. (*Baker.*) Caudex oblique, decumbent; stipes thick, 1 foot long, slightly scaly below, furfuraceous

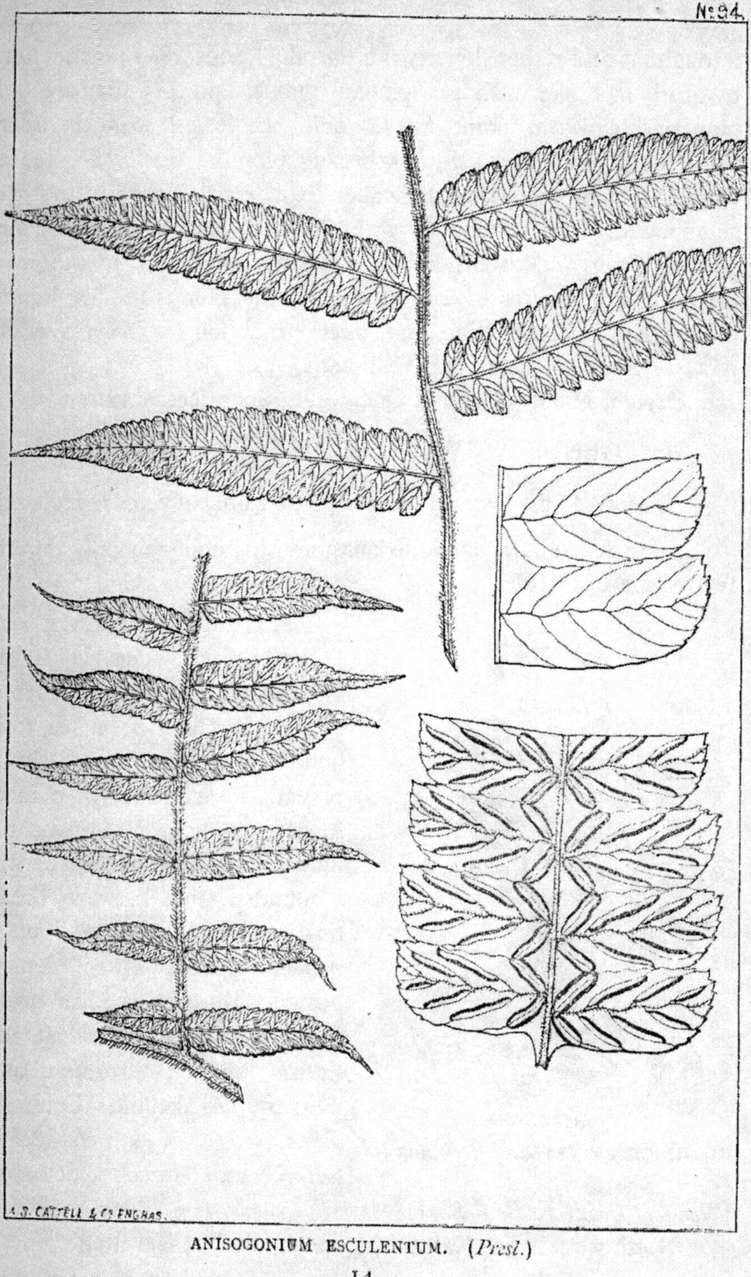

ANISOGONIUM ESCULENTUM. (*Presl.*)

throughout and rather densely muricated; fronds 18–24 inches long, by nearly as broad, with 4–5 pinnate pinnæ, and 4–5 that are only pinnatifid below the point on each side, the lowest 3 inches apart, about 9 inches long, 4 inches broad; pinnules sessile, 2–3 inches long, $\frac{5}{8}$–$\frac{3}{4}$ inch broad, the edge subentire, the point slightly toothed, acuminated, the base rounded on both sides; texture subcoriaceous; both surfaces and rachis naked, the latter muricated in the lower part; veins in groups of 2–3 on a side, the groups usually joining half-way across to the edge; sori often $\frac{1}{4}$ inch long. *Hook. Syn. Fil. p.* 245. *Bedd. F. B. I.* 332 (Callipteris).

Ceylon, Matale East and Oodawella, 3,000 feet elevation.

GENUS XLIV.—HEMIDICTYUM. (*Presl.*)

(*Hemi*, half; *diktyon*, net; outer portion only of veins reticulated.)

As in Asplenium, but veins anastomosing obliquely only towards the margin of the frond.

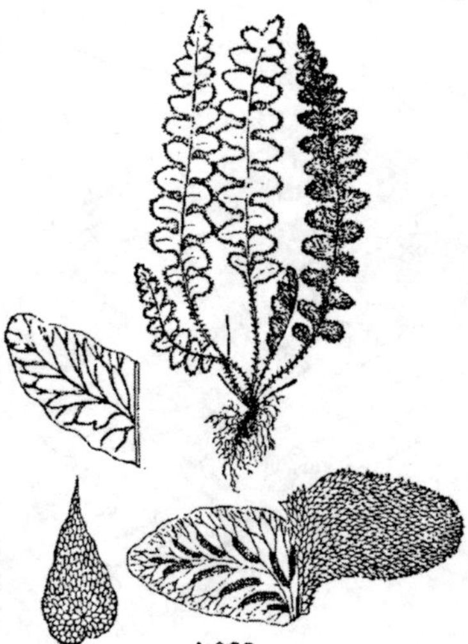

N°95.

HEMIDICTYUM CETERACH. (*Linn.*)

1. HEMIDICTYUM CETERACH. (*Linn.*) Stipes densely tufted, 1–3 inches long, wiry, ebeneous, chaffy; fronds 4–6 inches long, one inch or less broad, linear pinnatifid or scarcely pinnate, lobes alternate obtuse $\frac{3}{8}$–$\frac{1}{2}$ inch long, $\frac{1}{4}$–$\frac{3}{8}$ inch broad, with a rounded sinus between them; texture subcoriaceous, upper surface naked, lower densely coated with small reddish brown ovate membranous scales; sori linear oblique; involucre rudimentary. Asplenium Ceterach. *Linn. Sp. Pl.* 1538. *Hook. Syn. Fil. p.* 244. Ceterach officinarum (Willd.), *Bedd. F. B. I. t.* 71.

North-west India, Kashmir, 3,000–6,000 feet elevation.

(Also in Afghanistan, Western Asia, Europe, and North-west Africa.)

2. HEMIDICTYUM FINLAYSONIANUM. (*Hook.*) Stipes 6–9 inches long, green, subcompressed, nearly naked; fronds usually 1 foot long (often much more), 6–8 inches broad, occasionally simple and entire, generally pinnate with 2–6 opposite pairs of lateral pinnæ, the lower ones 4–8 inches long, $1\frac{1}{2}$–2 inches broad, the apex very acuminate, the base narrowed into a distinct petiole, the margin entire or irregularly lobed; texture leathery; veins subflabellate, very oblique, anastomosing slightly towards the margin, sometimes bounded by an irregular intramarginal line; sori often $1\frac{1}{2}$–2 inches long, rooting buds are often produced from the midribs of the pinnæ near the apex. *Hook. Syn. Fil.* 245. *Bedd. F. B. I. t.* 72.

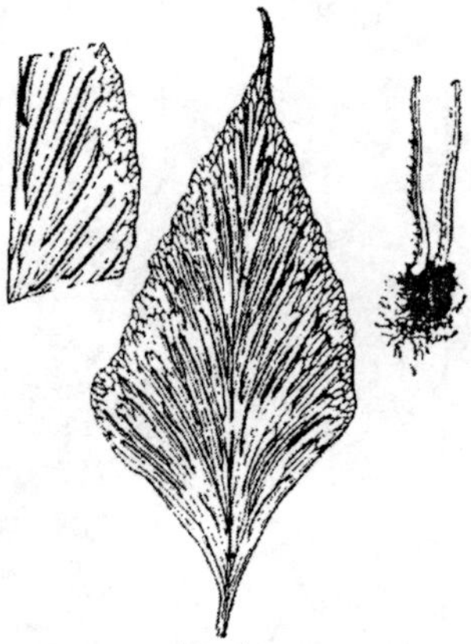

No. 96
HEMIDICTYUM FINLAYSONIANUM. (*Hook*).

North and East Bengal, with Assam, up to 3,000 feet, very common, especially in Khasya; Malay Peninsula.

GENUS XLV.—ALLANTODIA. (*Wall.*)

(*Allantos*, a sausage; form of indusium.)

Sori dorsal, linear-oblong, attached to the primary veins; indusium the same shape as the sorus and quite enclosing it, bursting in an irregular line down to the centre, or rarely asplenioid; veins anastomosing and forming several elongated areoles, smaller towards the margin, with free marginal clavate veinlets; fronds pinnate, very membranaceous, (the character of the indusium is not to be relied on, similar sausage-shaped indusia being found in species of true Asplenium and Diplazium.)

1. ALLANTODIA JAVANICA. (*Bl. under Asplenium.*) Fronds

No. 97

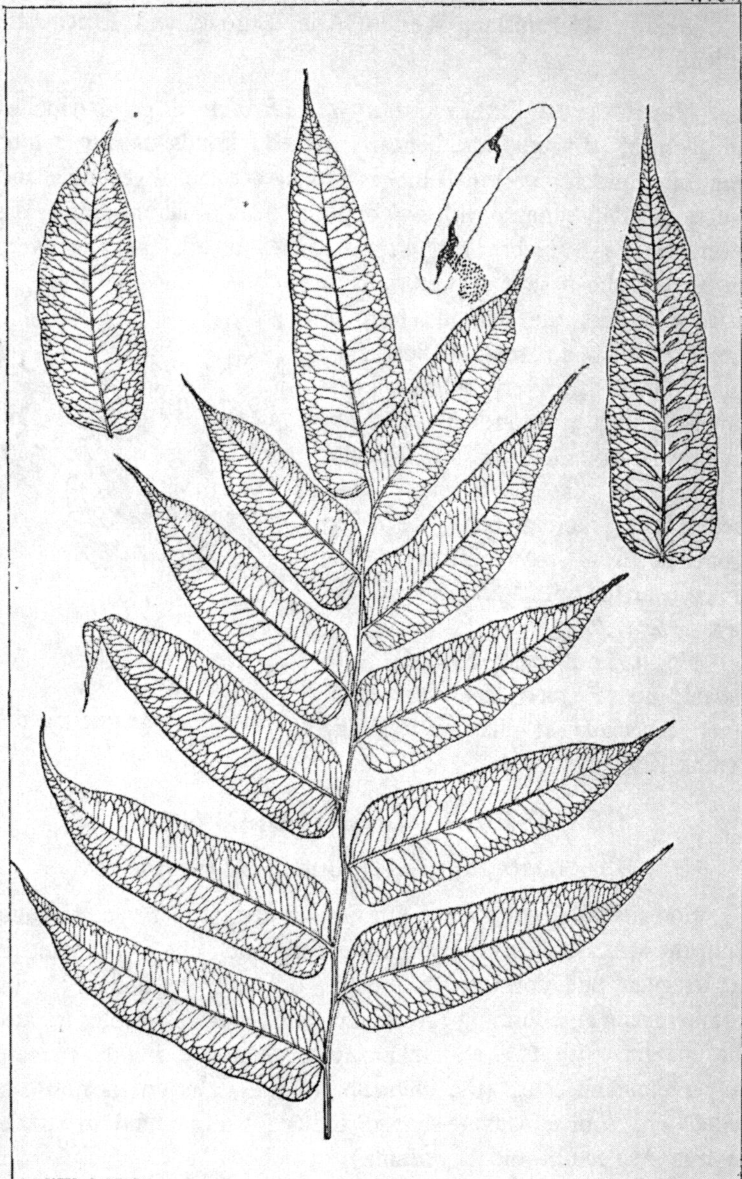

ALLANTODIA JAVANICA. (*Bl.*)

often 2 feet long, 1 foot broad, pinnæ 4–8 inches long, 1–1¾ inch broad, oblong, entire or slightly crenulate, particularly at the caudate apex, veins forked near the midrib, 2–3 of hexagonal areoles occupying the outer half of the space between midrib and margin; sori confined to the anterior vein of the first fork or areole. *Bl. En. Pl. Jav. Fil.* 175. Allant. Brunoniana (Wall.), *Hook. Syn. Fil. p.* 246. *Bedd. F. S. I.* 159.

Nepal and Bhotan, 4,000–7,000 feet elevation; Khasya, Mikir Hills; Ceylon.

(Also in Java and Samoa.)

GENUS XLVI.—ACTINIOPTERIS. (*Link.*)

(*Actin*, rays; *pteris*, a fern.)

Sori linear, elongated, submarginal; indusium the same shape as the sorus, folded over it, placed one on each side of the narrow segments of the frond opening towards the midrib: a single species like a miniature palm.

1. ACTINIOPTERIS DICHOTOMA. (*Forsk, under Acrostichum.*) Stipes densely tufted, 2–6 inches long; fronds like fans, 1–1½ inch deep, composed of numerous dichotomous segments which are rush-like in texture, not more than ½ line broad, the veins few and sub-parallel with the indistinct midrib, the segments of the fertile frond longer than those of the barren one. Acrostichum dichotomum, *Forskh. Fl. Ægypt. Arab.* 184. Actiniopteris radiata, *Hook. Syn. Fil. p.* 246. *Bedd. F. S. I. t.* 124.

Throughout India, especially the Peninsula in dry rocky places below 3,000 feet elevation; Ceylon.

(Also in North Africa, Mascareen Islands, Persia, Cabul.)

No. 98

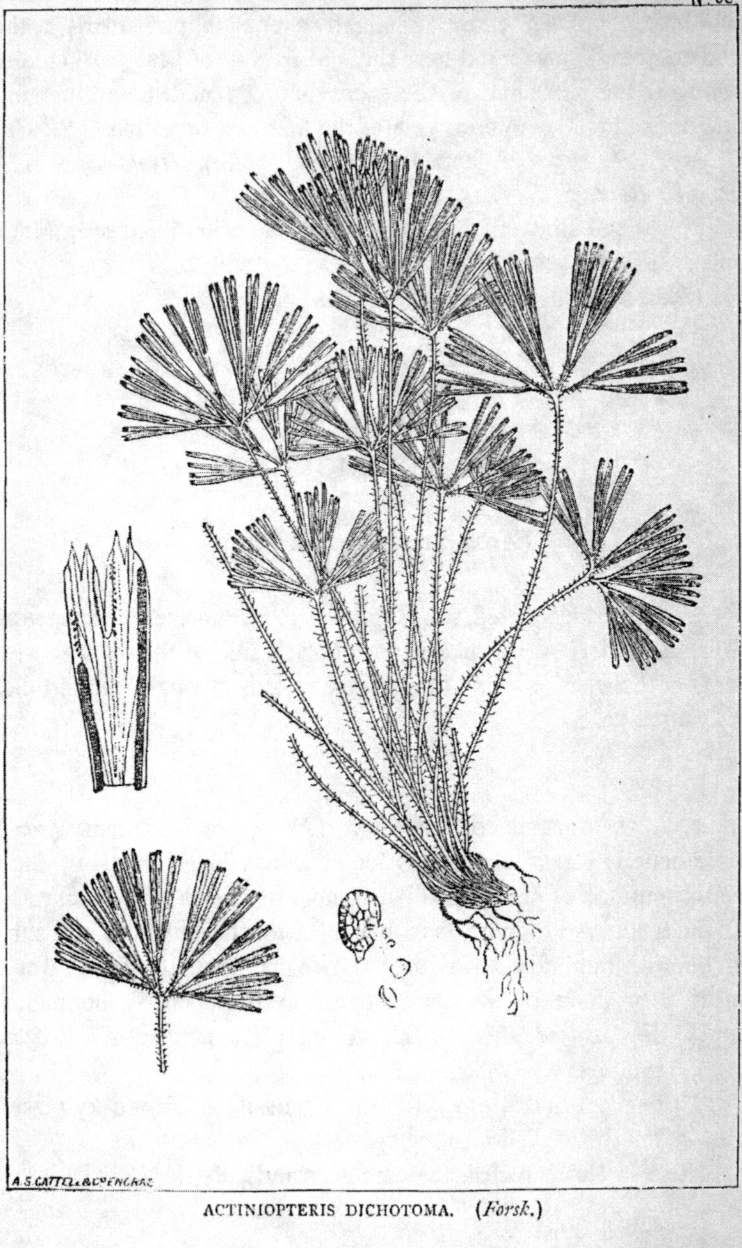

ACTINIOPTERIS DICHOTOMA. (*Forsk.*)

TRIBE IX.—ASPIDIEÆ.

Sori dorsal, subglobose, rarely elliptical; indusium superior, similar in shape to the sorus, fixed either by the centre or a sinus.

GENUS XLVII.—DIDYMOCHLÆNA. (*Desv.*)

(*Didymos*, double; *chlæna*, a cloak;—the double indusium.)

Sori elliptical, terminal on a veinlet, but distinctly intramarginal; indusium elliptical, marginate at the base, attached longitudinally to the linear receptacle, free all round the edge; veins subflabellate, free, their apices clavate; fronds bipinnate, pinnules articulate with the rachis.

1. DIDYMOCHLÆNA LUNULATA. (*Desv.*) Caudex erect, subarborescent; fronds densely tufted, 4–6 feet long, bipinnate; pinnules ¾–1 inch broad, dimidiate, subquadrangular, entire or slightly sinuated; texture subcoriaceous; veinlets forked or pinnate, their apices marked with white dots; sori 2–6 to a pinnule. *Desv. in Mem. Soc. Linn.* vi. *p.* 282. *Hook. Syn. Fil. p.* 248. *Bedd. F. B. I. t.* 15.

Birma and the Malay Peninsula.

(Also in Tropical America; East African Islands; Malay Islands; Fiji.)

GENUS XLVIII.—MESOCHLÆNA. (*R. Br.*)

(*Mesos*, middle; *chlæna*, cloak, attachment of the indusium.)

Sori and indusium of Didymochlæna, but habit and venation of Nephrodium, *i.e.*, the lower pair of veinlets anastomose, the others free, parallel; fronds bipinnatifid.

1. MESOCHLÆNA POLYCARPA. (*Bl. under Aspidium.*) Caudex erect; stipes tufted, short; fronds 2–3 feet long, 12–18 inches broad, pinnate; pinnæ close, very numerous, spreading, dwindling down below to mere auricles, the largest 6–9 inches long, ½ inch broad, cut down half-way or more to the rachis into linear-oblong lobes; rachis and lower surface villose; veins very close, pinnated,

No. 99

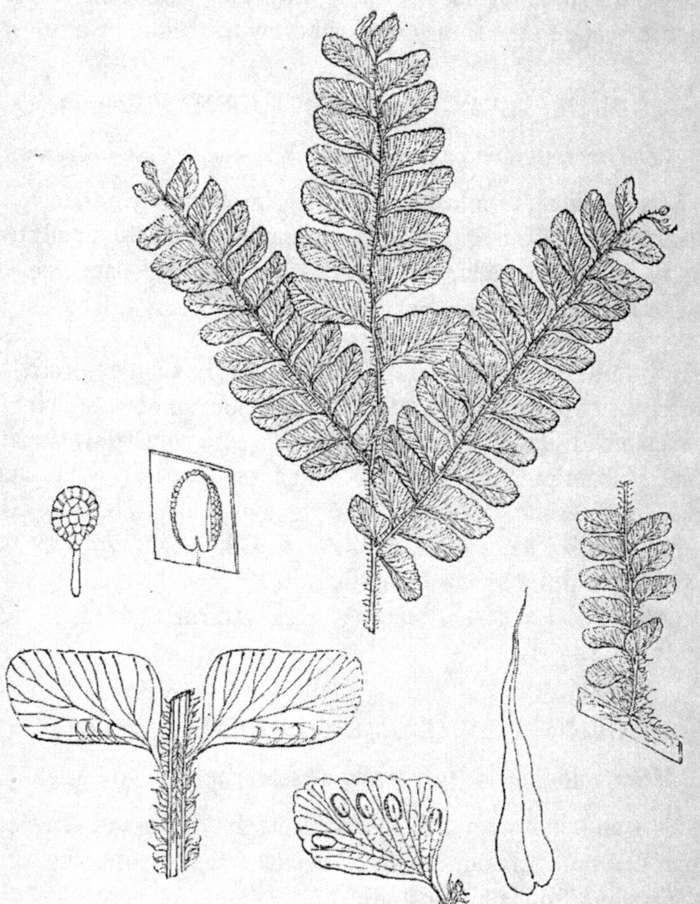

A. F. CATTELL & Co. ENG.

DIDYMOCHLÆNA LUNULATA. (*Desv.*)

twelve or more on each side in a lobe; sori small, close, ultimately confluent Aspidium polycarpum, *Bl. En. Fil. Jav.* 156. Didymochlæna *Hook. Syn. Fil. p.* 248. Mesochlæna polycarpa, *Bedd. F. B. I. t.* 344. Nephrodium javanicum, *Hook. Sp. Fil.* iv. *p.* 67.

In the *Syn. Filicum* this genus has been joined with Didymochlæna; but as Mr. Smith has pointed out, it is really a Nephrodium with the indusium elongated.

Malay Peninsula.

(Also in the Malay Islands.)

GENUS XLIX.—POLYSTICHUM. (*Roth.*)

(*Polys*, many; *stichos*, order.)

Sori subglobose, dorsal or terminal on the veinlets; indusium orbicular, fixed by the centre; veins all free; texture generally coriaceous and teeth generally awned.

1. POLYSTICHUM SEMICORDATUM. (*Sw.*) Stipes scattered, 6–12 inches long, fibrillose at the base; fronds 2–3 feet long simply pinnate; pinnæ 4–6 inches long, ½–¾ inch broad, nearly entire, acuminate, cordate or truncate at the base; texture herbaceous or somewhat firm; surfaces naked and rachis nearly so; veins pinnate, the lower ones ending short of the margin; sori in 1–3 rows on each side, the inner one the most constant and regular, close to the midrib. *Sw. Syn. Fil. p.* 45. *Hook. Syn. Fil.* 249. *Bedd. F. B. I. t.* 35.

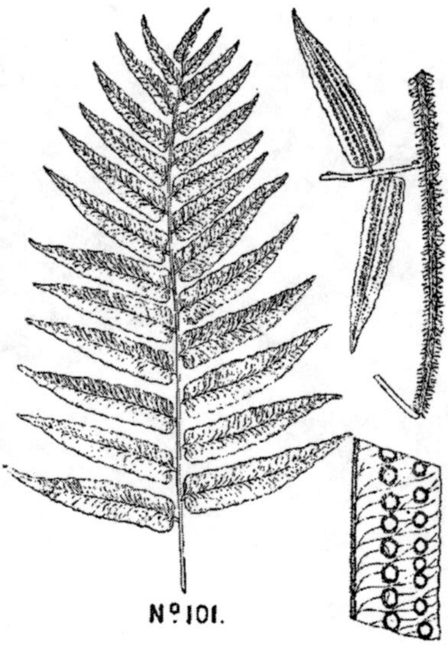

N°. 101.

POLYSTICHUM SEMICORDATUM. (*Sw.*)

Birma and the Malay Peninsula.

(Also in the Malay Islands, Philippines, and Tropical America.)

No. 105

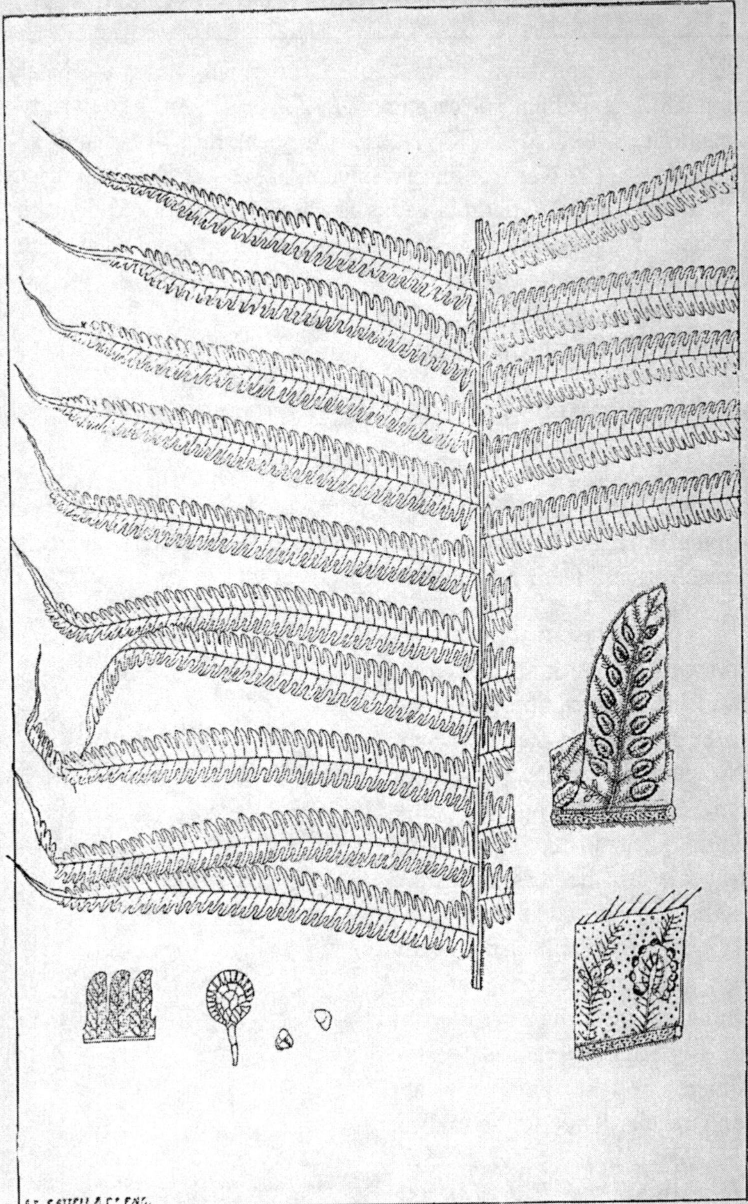

MESOCHLÆNA POLYCARPA. (*Bl.*)

2. POLYSTICHUM LONCHITIS. (*Linn. under Polypodium.*) Caudex short, stout oblique, densely paleaceous; stipes short paleaceous, lower portion of the rachis with ferruginous large scales; fronds 6–18 inches long, densely tufted, erect rigid, linear or lanceolate, tapering at both ends, pinnated; pinnæ numerous, approximate from a broad nearly sessile obliquely truncated base, ovate or lanceolate, falcate acute spinulose-serrate, the superior base truncated and auriculate; sori confined to upper portion of the frond in two or more series upon the pinnæ; indusium denticulate on the margin. *Hook. Sp. Fil.* iv. 8. *Sw. Syn. Fil. p.* 43. *Hook. Syn. Fil. p.* 250. *Bedd. F. B. I. t.* 128. Polypodium Lonchitis, *Linn. Sp. pl.* 1548.

North West Himalaya, Kashmir, Sonamurg 11,000 feet elevation. (Also in Arctic and Alpine Europe, Asia, and North America.)

3. POLYSTICHUM LACHENENSE. (*Hook.*) Rhizome very scaly; stipes very numerous, thick, densely tufted, scaly, 2–4 inches long; fronds narrow-linear, 4–8 inches long by ½–¾ inch broad, pinnate, the lower pinnæ remote but hardly reduced in size; pinnæ 2–3 inches broad, deltoid-ovate, subcoriaceous, lobed more or less or subentire, the apex blunt, the margins spinosely serrated or crenate-serrate; sori 6–12 to a pinna, often covering the whole under side; indusium incised. *Hook. Syn. Fil. p.* 250. *Clarke, F. N. I. p.* 506. *Bedd. F. B. I. t.* 32.

Sikkim, 13,000–16,000 feet, Lachen, Tungu, Samding, 7,000–15,000 feet; Kashmir, Palgram, 13,000 feet.

4. POLYSTICHUM ATKINSONI. (*Bedd.*) Rhizome small, scaly; stipes 2–3 inches long, thin, stramineous, and with the rachis furnished with a few chaffy scales; fronds 1–3 inches long, ½ inch broad, pinnate, the lower pinnæ not reduced; pinnæ ovate, very coriaceous, spinosely-serrated, the superior base often with an auricle; sori 1–3 to a pinna, generally on the upper half only. *Bedd. F. B. I. Suppl. t.* 362.

Sikkim, Yakla Pass 10,000 feet; Lachen 10,000 feet; Bhotan.

5. POLYSTICHUM AURICULATUM. (*Linn. under Polypodium.*) Stipes tufted, 4–6 inches long, scaly below, or throughout; fronds

12–18 inches long, 2–4½ inch broad, pinnate, not or only slightly attenuated at the base; pinnæ numerous, subsessile, oblong or narrowly oblong, auricular falcate, coriaceous, entire, or pinnatifid with the auricle sometimes quite free, lower veinlets in groups of threes; sori in two rows one on each side of the midrib, very variable in size; indusium often quite absent. *Linn. Sp. Pl.* 1548. *Hook. Syn. Fil.* 251.

Throughout India and Ceylon.

(Also in Formosa.)

TYPE. Pinnæ submembranaceous, lanceolate falcate, 2–2¼ inches long, serrate; upper base square, parallel with rachis and often auricled, lower base much cut away; involucre very fugacious or generally altogether absent. *Hook. Sp. Fil.* iv. 11, *t.* 218. *Bedd. F. S. I. t.* 120. Polypodium harpophyllum (Zenker), *Hook. Syn. Fil.* 511.

Nilgiris, Pulneys and other Western hills; Madras Presidency, at the higher elevations.

VAR. β MARGINATUM. (*Wall.*) Pinnæ very coriaceous, shining, scaly below, ovate-oblong, closely spinulose, often somewhat lobed; indusium conspicuous, sometimes very large. *Wall. Cat.* 366. *Don. Prod. Fl. Nep.* 3. *Bedd. Sup. Ferns, t.* 363. *Clarke, F. N. I.* 507.

North India; Kunawur to Bhotan, 7,000–10,000 feet elevation.

VAR. γ CŒSPITOSUM. (*Wall.*) Pinnæ short, ovate-oblong, margin scarcely spinulose or serrate, sometimes entire; texture scarcely coriaceous; indusium conspicuous, ciliate. *Wall. Cat.* 367. P. cœspitosum, *Bedd. F. B. I. t.* 33. Aspid. obliquum, *Don. Prod. Fl. Nep.* 3. *Clarke, l. c.* 507.

Khasya, 3,000–4,500 feet elevation. Himalayas, Bhotan to Kunawur, 4,000–8,000 feet.

VAR. δ LENTUM. (*Don.*) Pinnæ pinnatifid, serrate, usually spinulose, the auricle often nearly free. *Don. Prod. Fl. Nep.* 4. Var. sub-bipinnata (Hook.), *Bedd. F. B. I. t.* 136.

Throughout the Himalayas and Khasya, altitude 1,500–8,000 feet, very common.

No. 102

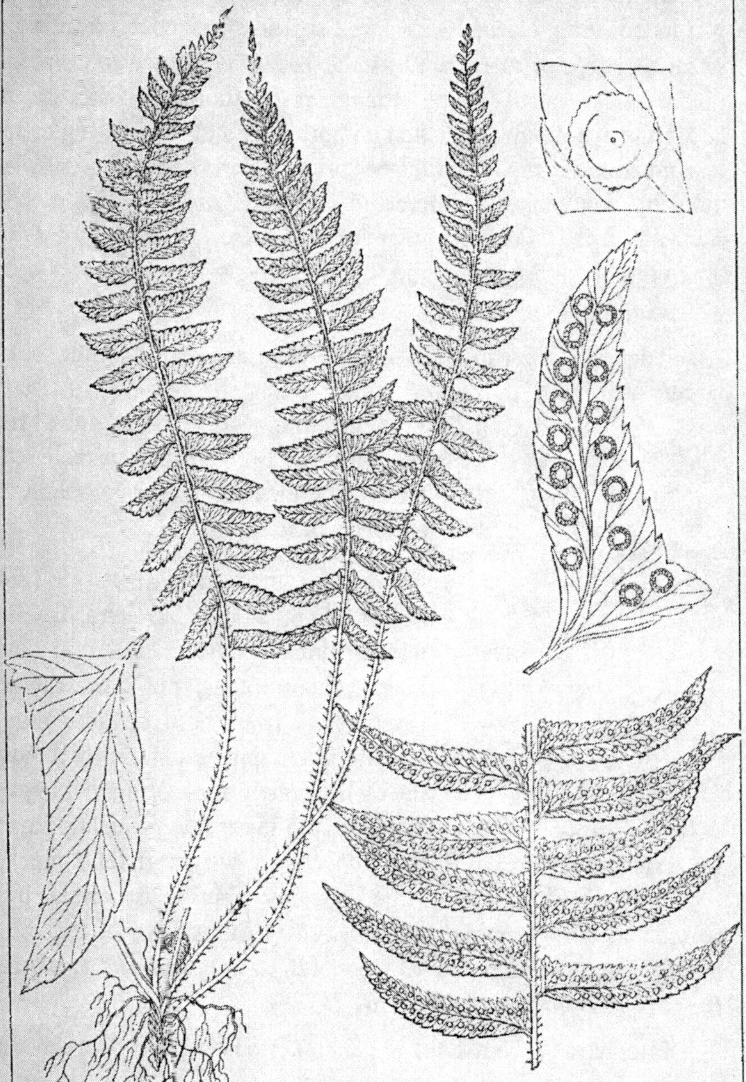

A. S. CATTELL & Co. ENGRAS.

POLYSTICHUM AURICULATUM. (*Linn.*)

6. POLYSTICHUM ILICIFOLIUM. (*Don.*) Stipes densely tufted, 2–4 inches long, clothed with large scales throughout; fronds linear or lanceolate, not attenuated at the base, very coriaceous, pinnate; pinnæ either small simple triangular or subrhomboidal, or much larger and again pinnate, naked on both sides and shining, angles spinulose-mucronate; rachis fibrillose; sori mostly in two rows, usually large; indusium peltate; veins immersed. *Don. Prod. Fl. Nep.* 3. *Hook. Syn. Fil.* 251. Polystichum stimulans (Kze.), *Bedd. F.B. I. t.* 31.

Himalayas, from Chumbra to Sikkim, 7,000–11,000 feet elevation.

The smaller forms with simple pinnæ are very distinct, but the larger ones with the pinnæ again pinnated, quite graduate into P. aculeatum, var. rufo-barbatum till it becomes quite indistinguishable from forms of that fern, and is probably only a variety of it.

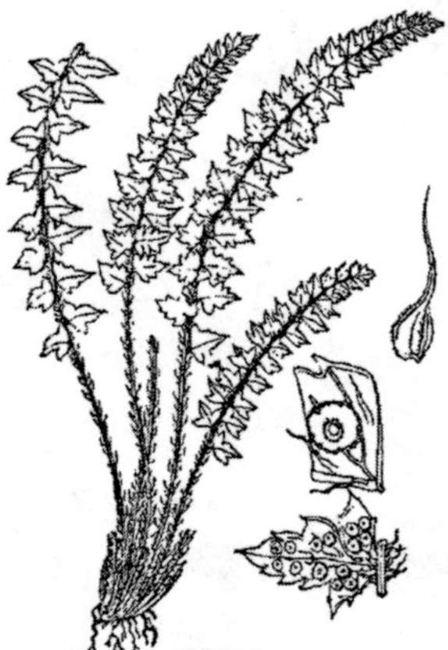

Nº103.
POLYSTICHUM ILICIFOLIUM. (*Don.*)

7. POLYSTICHUM THOMSONI. (*Hook.*) Stipes tufted, 2–4 inches long, fibrillose; fronds pinnate linear up to 7 inches long, subcoriaceous, not gradually attenuated at the base, both surfaces more or less fibrillose; pinnæ cut down almost to the rachis, bristly serrate, very unequal at the base, the lower margin being cut away, the upper with the basal lobe much enlarged; veins pinnate or forked in the segments; sori terminal on a veinlet; indusium peltate, bluntly crenated or subentire. *Hook. Syn. Fil. p.* 251, *and 2nd Cent. Ferns, t.* 25, *in part only*. *Bedd. F. B. I. t.* 126.

Himalayas; from Balti to Sikkim, 7,000–13,000 feet elevation.

Very near the smaller forms of Prescottianum, but the stipe is fibrillose, not scaly. Hooker's plate is taken from specimens of both species, and it is very probable that they are only varieties of the same plant.

VAR. β. GRACILIS. Fronds smaller, (3–5 inches long with the stipe by ½–¾ inch broad), margin of pinnæ crenate, with a sudden acumination (not bristly serrate), involucre reniform. *Clarke, F. N. I. t.* 508. Lastrea gracilis (Moore), *Bedd. F. B. I. t.* 198. Lastrea sparsa, var. gracilis, *Hook. Syn. Fil.* 498.

Sikkim, 11,500 feet elevation. A very doubtful species, which Mr. Clarke considers only a variety of Thomsoni, so I place it here pending further material. Mr. Clarke says that the involucre is polystichoid.

8. POLYSTICHUM ACULEATUM. (*Sw.*) Stipes tufted, 6–12 inches long, scaly and fibrillose below or throughout; fronds large, ovate-lanceolate, bipinnate, coriaceous, not attenuated at the base (or only slightly so in some forms); pinnæ numerous close lanceolate, pinnules oblong, unequal at the base, lower margin excised, upper generally more or less auricled, margins bristly or spinulose; texture more or less coriaceous, under surface generally fibrillose; veins pinnate or forked in the segments of the pinnules; sori towards the apex or at the apex of the lower veinlets. *Sw. Schrad. Journ.* ii. 37. *Hook. Syn. Fil. p.* 252.

Throughout the Indian region on the mountains.

(Also throughout the whole world.)

VAR. β LOBATUM. (*Eng. bot. t.* 1563.) Fronds narrowly lanceolate; pinnæ hardly pinnate, the lower secondary pinna sessile, or decurrent. *Clarke, F. N. I. p.* 509.

Throughout the Himalayas.

VAR. γ. RUFO-BARBATUM. (*Wall. Cat.* 369.) Fronds bipinnate, very coriaceous, usually reddish; stipes densely clothed with large red scales; rachis with red fibrillæ; pinnules naked and fibrillose beneath, in cutting like ilicifolium. P. aculeatum, *Bedd. F. S. I. t.* 121. Polyst. brachypterum, *Kunze, No.* 906.

Nilgiris and Western mountains of South India; Himalayas, from Kashmir to Bhotan.

VAR. δ. ANGULARE. (*Presl. Newm.* 173.) Lax and of thinner

POLYSTICHUM ACULEATUM, VAR. RUFO-BARBATUM. (*Wall.*)

texture, pinnules smaller, more numerous, orbicular, rhomboid, mostly auriculate, the serratures setiferous rather than spinulose. *Bedd. F. S. I. t.* 121.

Nilgiris and Western mountains of South India.

VAR. ζ SEMIFERTILE. Base of the frond fertile, upper one-third barren. (*Clarke, l. c.*)

Sikkim.

VAR. η BIARISTATUM. (*Bl. En. Pl. Jav. Fil.* 164.) Pinnules large, oblong-falcate, sparingly serrate or spinulose; sori generally round the margin.

Khasya; Ceylon; Malay Peninsula.

VAR. θ SETOSUM. (*Wall. Cat.* 371.) Lower surface of frond with very long fibrillæ; rachis with very large scales as well as fibrillæ, pinnules small, quite entire, except the spinulose apex or with very inconspicuous crenatures to represent the usual lobes; sori apical on the lower veinlet of the forked or pinnate vein of the segment (or what would correspond to the segment where the pinnule is entire).

Himalayas, from Kumaon to Sikkim, 5,000–8,000 feet elevation. A well marked form, considered a distinct species by some botanists.

VAR. ι ANOMALUM. (*Hook. Sp. Fil.* iv. 27.) Segments blunt or slightly mucronate; sori often, but not always, on the upper surface of the fronds. Polystichum anomalum, *Bedd. F. S. I. t.* 219.

Ceylon; Horton plains and Happootalee, 5,000–6,000 feet elevation.

VAR. κ TRAVANCORICUM. (*Bedd.*) Pinnæ rather distant, lower pair generally deflexed; pinnules prominently petioled, either subentire, large broad deltoid, with the lobing blunt not mucronate, or elongated up to 3 inches long, and pinnatifid or completely pinnate (except an indistinct wing to the rachis), the pinnules distant and again bluntly lobed, 3–4 pair below the pinnatifid apex; rachis and stipe scaly and fibrillose, under surfaces fibrillose.

Travancore and Tinnevelly mountains, 4,000–5,000 feet elevation. A distinct variety, but evidently a form of aculeatum, the more entire pinnules are nearest in shape and cutting to those of anomalum and biaristatum; the same frond will often have some pinnæ with the pinnules short and only slightly lobed, and others with them all elongate and pinnate or deeply pinnatifid.

VAR. λ MUCRONIFOLIUM. (*Bl. En. Pl. Jav. Fil.* 164.) Fronds 3-pinnate or sub-3-pinnate. (*Clarke, l. c.* 509.)

Khasya and Assam; this is very distinct looking, it is tripinnate like the last, but very different, being finely cut with small pinnules.

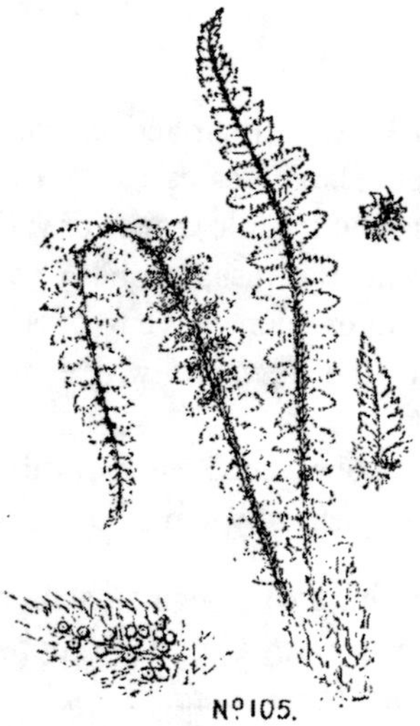

No 105.

POLYSTICHUM PRESCOTTIANUM. (*Wall.*)

9. POLYSTICHUM PRESCOTTIANUM. (*Wall.*) Stipes short, thick, flaccid, with many straw-coloured scales and fibrillæ; fronds from narrow to broad lanceolate, tapering at the base; pinnæ either short oblong, ½–1 inch long, more or less divided, but not to the rachis, or elongate, 2–3 inches long and deeply pinnatifid to the rachis or even pinnate; segments with the margin serrate and often hair-pointed, more or less fibrillose beneath. *Wall. Cat.* 363. *Bedd. F. B. I. t.* 34. *Hook. Syn. Fil.* 253.

Himalayas; from Kashmir to Bhotan, 10,000–13,000 feet elevation.

VAR. β BAKERIANUM. (*Clarke.*) Fronds large, very flaccid, broad-lanceolate, (9–10 inches broad), truncate at the base. *Clarke, F. N. I. t.* 66.

Sikkim; Yakla, 12,000 feet; very distinct-looking at first sight, but evidently only a flaccid variety of the above.

VAR. γ CASTANEUM. (*Clarke.*) Stipe round, naked, scales on the rachis blackish, pinnæ little pinnatifid.

Sikkim, 15,000 feet elevation.

GENUS L.—CYRTOMIUM. (*Presl.*)

(Derivation not known.)

Indusium orbicular, peltate; veins pinnate from a central costa, the lower anterior veinlets free, the rest angularly and irregularly anastomosing, forming unequal and subhexagonal areoles within which are 1–3 excurrent venules, or the upper veinlets only angularly anastomosing; fronds pinnate, coriaceous.

1. CYRTOMIUM FALCATUM. (*Sw.*) Stipes tufted, 6–12 inches long, densely clothed below with large dark scales; fronds 1–2 feet long, by 6–9 inches broad, pinnate; pinnæ numerous, the lower ones stalked, ovate-acuminate, falcate, 4–6 inches long, by 1–2 inches broad, the edge entire or slightly undulated, the upper side narrowed suddenly, sometimes auricled, the lower rounded or obliquely truncate at the base; texture coriaceous, both surfaces naked, the upper one glossy, primary veins from the midrib of the pinnæ parallel to each other nearly to the margin, throwing off pinnately 1–2–3 times inarching veinlets; sori small, copious, scattered. *Swartz, Syn. Fil. p.* 43. *Hook. Syn. Fil.* 257.

VAR. β CARYOTIDEUM. (*Wall.*) Pinnules larger, sharply toothed, sometimes deeply lobed towards the base, and generally with a long sharp auricle on one or both sides at the base. *Wall. Cat.* 376. *Bedd. F. S. I. t.* 119.

Nilgiris at the higher elevations. Himalayas from Gurwhal to Bhotan, 3,000–8,000 feet elevation. Khasya, 3,000–4,000 feet; Ceylon. There is also a variety common on the Nilgiris known as microptera, which has more numerous and much smaller pinnæ, scarcely at all auricled or lobed, but it graduates into caryotideum, though extreme forms look very distinct. The type of falcatum, which only differs slightly, is from China, Japan, South Africa, Sandwich Islands, and Madagascar.

2. CYRTOMIUM CADUCUM. (*Wall.*) Stipes tufted, 1 foot long, firm erect, stramineous, scaly below; main rachises sometimes

with a terminal rooting bud; fronds 1–2 feet long, 6–9 inches broad, pinnate; pinnæ petioled, numerous, narrow lanceolate acuminate, from subentire to deeply lobed; texture coriaceous; primary veins from the midrib of the pinnæ repeatedly dichotomous at an acute angle into nearly equally strong veins, not anastomosing usually till near the margin, many of them free to the margin; sori rather large and in two rows half-way between the rachis and the margin, or much smaller and scattered. *Wall. Cat.* 381. *Hook. Syn. Fil.* 257. *Bedd. F. B. I. t.* 45. *Clarke, F. N. I. p.* 512.

Himalayas; from Nepal to Bhotan, 4,000–7,000 feet; Khasya, 3,000–5,000 feet elevation.

GENUS LI.---ASPIDIUM. (*Swartz.*)

(*Aspidos*, the indusium being like a shield.)

Indusium orbicular or reniform, or sometimes irregular and abnormal, being linear and curved, or sometimes absent; veins compoundly anastomosing with generally free veinlets in the areoles, receptacles compital or often at the apex of the free veinlets; fronds very various, from simple to tripinnatifid, often membranaceous and flaccid.

1. ASPIDIUM SINGAPORIANUM. (*Wallich.*) Rhizome creeping; stipes subtufted, those of the fertile fronds 6–12 inches long, fronds 12 inches or more, 2–4 inches broad, oblong entire, acuminate at the apex, narrowed rather suddenly and then decurrent gradually at the base; texture herbaceous; primary veins distinct nearly to the edge, united by transverse arched ones, the areoles of which enclose netted veinlets, the ultimate ones free; sori numerous, close, 4–6 in a line between the main veins; indusium peltate orbicular. Nephrodium (Baker), *Hook. Syn. Fil.* 296. *Bedd. F. B. I. t.* 168.

Singapore and the Malay Peninsula.

(Also in the Malay Islands.)

2. ASPIDIUM VASTUM. (*Blume.*) Rhizome creeping, stipes scattered, narrowly winged often nearly or quite to the base, furnished with numerous linear subulate brown persistent scales; fronds

No. 106

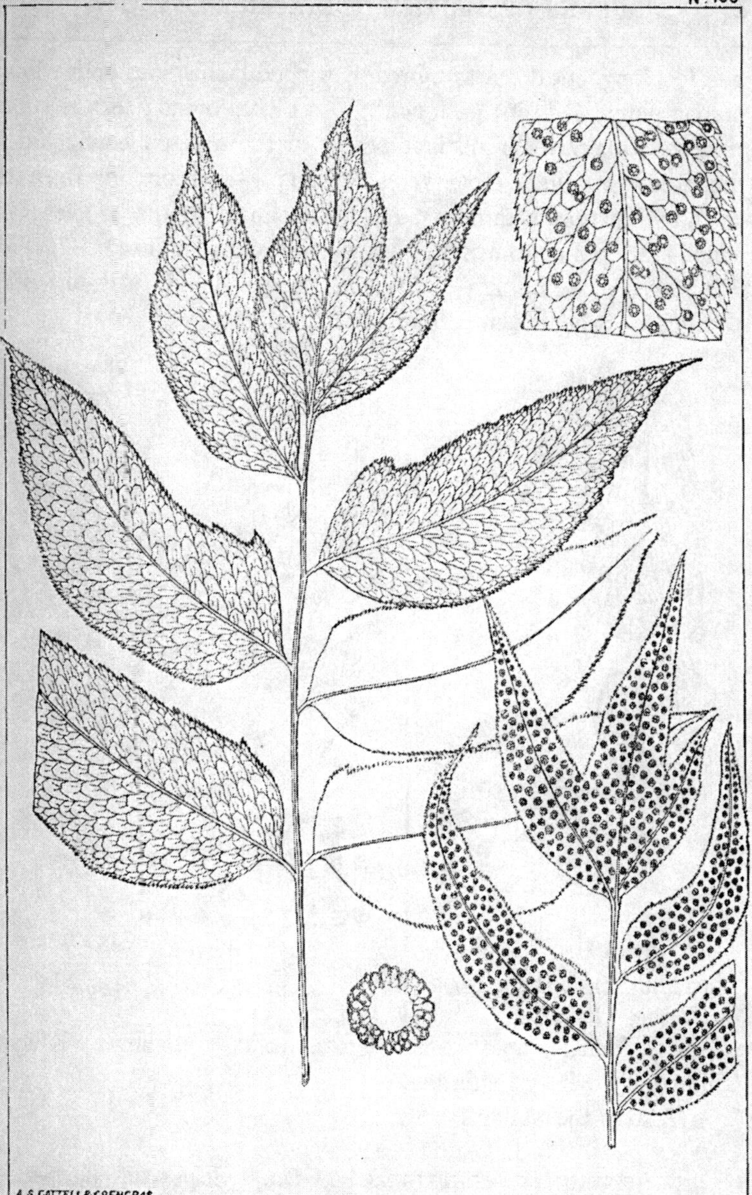

CYRTOMIUM FALCATUM, VAR. β CARYOTIDEUM. (*Wall.*)

2–4 feet long, cut down to a broadly-winged rachis, into entire linear oblong pinnæ 6–12 inches long, by 1–2 inches broad; texture subcoriaceous; main veins distinct nearly to the margin, connected by numerous prominent cross veins forming 7–8 areoles between the costa and margin, with netted and free veinlets in the areoles; sori small, scattered on the netted veins; indusium reniform. *Bl. En. Pl. Jav. Fil.* 142. *Hook. Syn. Fil.* 296. Aspid. alatum, *Wall. Cat.* 378. Sagenia alata, *Bedd. F. B. I. t.* 169.

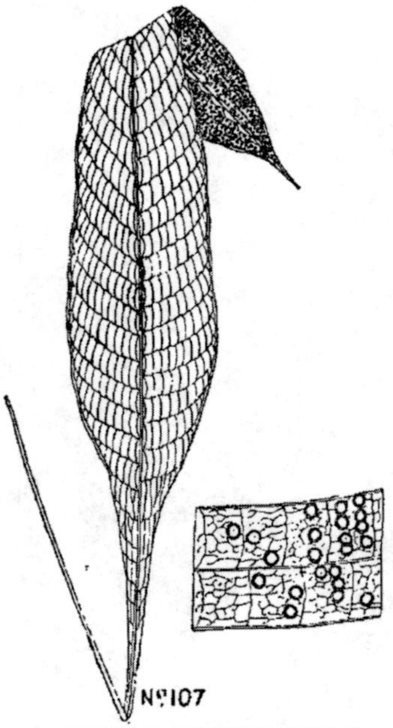

N°107

ASPIDIUM SINGAPORIANUM. (*Wall.*)

N°108

ASPIDIUM VASTUM. (*Blume.*)

East Bengal, up to 1,000 feet elevation; Mishmee; Khasya; Chittagong; Malay Peninsula.

(Also in the Malay Islands.)

3. ASPIDIUM SUBCONFLUENS. (*Bedd.*) Stipes tufted, 1–2 feet long, furnished with dark coloured linear-subulate scales; fronds about 1 foot each way, triangular in outline, tripartite, lateral pinnæ opposite or subopposite, shortly petioled, unequal sided with the

upper pinnules small falcate subentire, the lower ones much produced lanceolate acuminate, the 2–3 basal ones cut about one-third down into falcate lobes, terminal pinnæ deeply pinnatifid, lobes 3–6 inches, pinnatifid a quarter of the way down to the midrib; texture moderately firm, surface glabrous above, pubescent on the veins beneath; veins anastomosing with a few free included veinlets; sori scattered, small, generally on the netted veins; indusium variable, reniform, curved, horseshoe-shaped or nearly peltate, persistent. *Bedd. Sup. Ferns, t.* 364.

Khasya, 3,000–5,000 feet elevation, below Umwai.

No. 109.

ASPIDIUM SUBCONFLUENS. (*Bedd.*)

4. ASPIDIUM SEMIBIPINNATUM. (*Wall. under Polypodium.*) Stipes 1 foot or more long, pale brown, naked; fronds 12–18 inches long, 6–9 inches broad, terminal pinnæ linear-oblong, 6–9 inches long, 1 inch broad, entire, narrowed towards both ends, lateral pinnæ 4–6 on each side smaller, the lower one or two pairs tripartite; texture herbaceous; veins inconspicuous, the primary ones lost before they reach the margin, the rest variously anastomosing, the areoles with free included veinlets; sori minute, scattered, confined to the connected veinlets; indusium reniform and irregular as in the last. *Hook. Sp. Fil.* iv. 59, *t.* 231. *Syn. Fil.* 297. *Bedd. F. B. I. t.* 137. Polypodium semibipinnatum, *Wall. Cat.* 388.

Penang; nearly allied to some forms of polymorphum, but I think sufficiently distinct.

(Also in Borneo.)

5. ASPIDIUM SUBTRIPHYLLUM. (*Hook.*) Rhizome creeping;

stipes 1 foot or more long; fronds 12–18 inches long, 8–12 inches broad, subdeltoid with a large deeply pinnatifid apex, with lanceolate lobes; below this one or two pinnæ on each side, the lowest stalked, distant, forked at the base, or pinnatifid, the point lanceolate; texture herbaceous, surfaces somewhat hairy beneath and on the main veins above, main veins distinct to the edge, the others copiously anastomosing, with free veinlets included in the areoles; sori rather large, but scattered, confined to the connected veinlets; indusium reniform. *Hook. Sp. Fil.* iv. 52. *Syn. Fil.* 296. *Bedd. F. S. I. t.* 242, *and F. B. I. t.* 48.

No. 110.
ASPIDIUM SUBTRIPHYLLUM. (*Hook.*)

Ceylon and the Malay Peninsula. My Ceylon specimens are much smaller than those from Birma, but I believe they are the same species; in habit it is quite like variolosum, but the sori are always on the netted veinlets, instead of at the apex of free veinlets.

6. ASPIDIUM VARIOLOSUM. (*Wall.*) Rhizome suberect, stipes tufted, scaly near the base only, 12–18 inches long in the fertile, less in the sterile fronds, more or less dimorphous, deltoid in outline, herbaceous in texture, and somewhat puberulous, especially in the sterile ones; pinnæ about three pair below the pinnatifid apex, the lowest pair again pinnated with the pinnules often pinnatifid, the next pair often pinnatifid or pinnated in a less degree, the pinnæ of the fertile fronds generally narrower and often more divided, main veins not very distinct but more so in the fertile than in the sterile; areoles copious, with many free included veinlets; sori rather large, almost always at the apex of the free veinlets, very rarely on the netted veins; indusium peltate and reniform on the same frond. *Wall. Cat.* 379. *Bedd. Sup. Ferns, t.* 365 (*not F. B. I.* 170, *which is*

No. 111

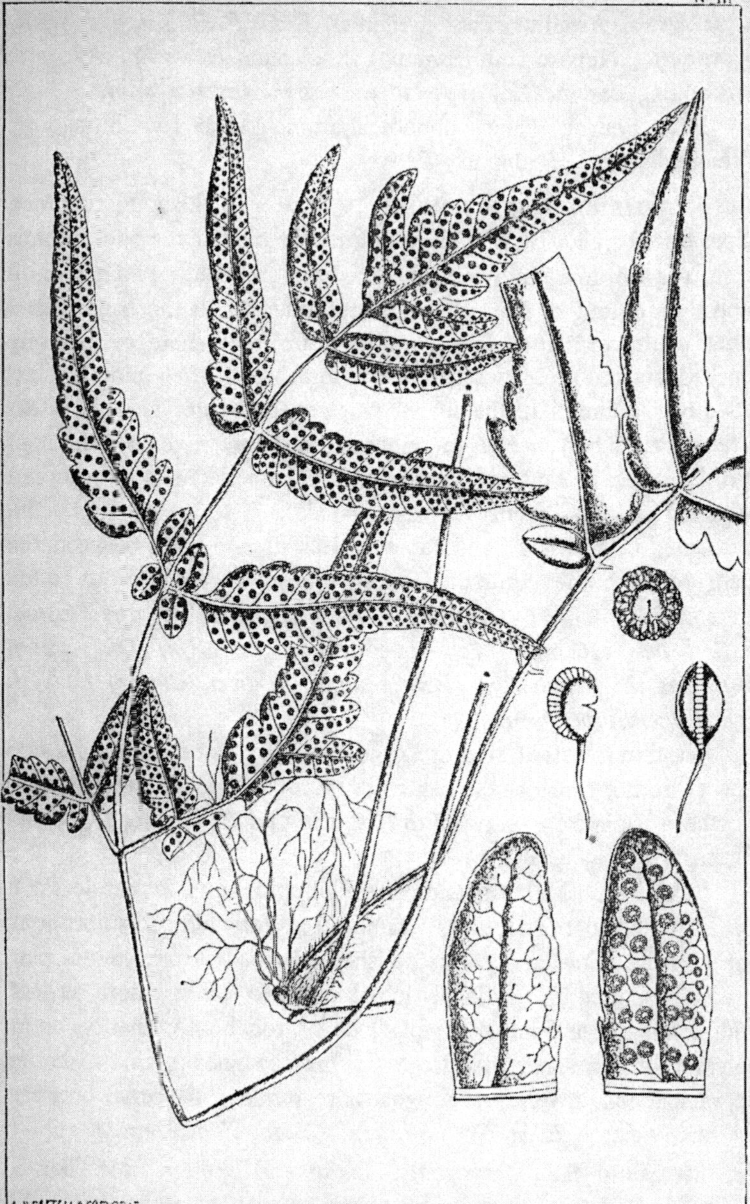

A. S. Cattell & Co. Engrav.

ASPIDIUM VARIOLOSUM. (*Wall.*)

cicutarium.) Aspidium Zollingerianum, *Bedd. F. B. I. t.* 251, *fertile frond only.* Nephrodium (Sagenia) variolosum, *Hook. Sp. Fil.* 298, *and* Zollingerianum (*l.c.*) *as far at least as the Birmese plant.*

East Bengal Plains, abundant from Assam to Chittagong; Tenasserim near Moulmein; Penang.

7. ASPIDIUM POLYMORPHUM. (*Wall.*) Rhizome suberect, stipes tufted, yellowish or brown, paleaceous only at the base; fronds large, 1–4 feet long, by 1 foot or more broad, pinnate; pinnæ 3–6 on each side, oblong or elliptic, acuminate, unequal at the base, sometimes contracted when fertile, quite entire to crenate or coarsely toothed, stalked or subsessile, the terminal one often more or less lobed or subpinnatifid, the lowest pair generally (not always) bifurcate; texture herbaceous to subcoriaceous; main veins prominent and distinct to the margin, with many free included simple or forked veinlets; sori on the netted veins, small and scattered in the uncontracted fronds, large and more or less in two rows between the main veins in the contracted ones; indusium reniform or often quite absent. *Wall. Cat.* 382. *Hook. Syn. Fil. p.* 297. *Bedd. F. S. I. tabs.* 116, 117. Sagenia siifolia, *Baker, Syn. Fil. p.* 299, *as far as the Courtallum plant.* Neph. Wightii, *Clarke, F. N. I.* 538, *the contracted form.*

Western forests of Madras Presidency, very common up to 4,000 feet. (I do not consider the contracted form even a constant variety.) Northern India from Gurwhal to Mishmee and Chittagong; Ceylon; Birma.

(Also in the Malay Islands, the Philippines and Fernando Po.)

8. ASPIDIUM SIMONSII. (*Baker.*) Very like polymorphum, but with the stipes and rachis polished blackish-purple, lowest pair of pinnæ pinnate below, deeply lobed upwards, others more or less bifurcate below and rather deeply lobed throughout, venation as in polymorphum; sori rather large (in my specimens), in two series between the main veins, or irregularly scattered sub-4-serial between the main veins. *Hook. Syn. Fil.* 504. *Bedd. Sup. Ferns. t.* 367.

Seetakand Hill, Chittagong; Sikkim, and Bhotan. Mr. Clarke, makes it a variety of polymorphum, and he may be right, but until more specimens are gathered, I consider it safer not to lump it with that. Mr. Clarke says he does not see how it differs from polymorphum, var. macrocarpum, but he has made a new species of that. Both Baker and Clarke make two sections of Sagenia, one with "sori in more than two rows between the principal veins, often irregularly scattered," the other with "sori in two rows between the principal veins," both forms occur in this species and in polymorphum, and more or less in semibipinnatum and other species, so the definition is only misleading.

9. ASPIDIUM HETEROCARPUM. (*Bedd.*) Rhizome creeping widely; stipes solitary, erect, with lanceolate-linear brown persistent scales at the base; pinnate, very much as in polymorphum, but lower pinnæ not bifurcate; pinnæ 4–8 inches long, narrow-lanceolate, entire, caudate at the apex, subsessile or very shortly stalked, gemmiparous in the axils; main veins distant to nearly the margin, areoles copious with free included veinlets; sori very small on the netted veins, much scattered; indusium reniform or horseshoe-shaped, or sometimes curved or linear, as in Athyrium and Asplenium. Sagenia heterocarpa, *Bedd. F. B. I. t.* 47. Sagenia heterosora (Baker), *Hook. Syn. Fil.* 504. *Clarke, l. c.* 537.

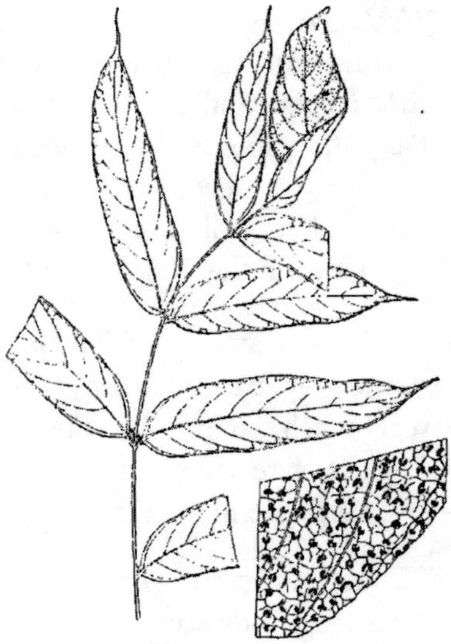

N°112

ASPIDIUM HETEROCARPUM. (*Bedd.*)

Assam and Chittagong, in wet flats near rivers, forming large groves about 6 feet high.

10. ASPIDIUM DECURRENS. (*Presl.*) Rhizome creeping; stipes winged nearly or quite to the base, furnished with numerous linear-subulate brown persistent scales; fronds often 3 feet long, dimor-

phous, the fertile much contracted, pinnatifid down to a broadly winged rachis into 3–4 pair of pinnæ or lobes on each side, 6–12 inches long, 1–2½ inches broad, lowest pair often bifurcate, margins quite entire in the sterile, more or less crenated in the fertile, subcoriaceous, glabrous on both sides; main veins distinct nearly to the margin, with cross veins forming series of large areoles in which are included netted veinlets and simple or forked free veinlets; sori large, generally in two pretty regular series between the main veinlets, nearly always at the apex of the free veinlets, often continued all down the wing of the stipes; indusium generally more or less reniform, sometimes elongated and irregular. *Presl. Rel. Hænck*, 28. *Hook. Syn. Fil.* 299. Sagenia pteropus, *Bedd. F. S. I. t.* 82.

Eastern Bengal at the foot of the hills, Assam, Cachar, Chittagong; South India in the Bolampatty Hills between Coimbatore and Palghat, 2,000 feet elevation; Tinnevelly and Travancore Hills, 2,000–2,500 feet; Ceylon; Malay Peninsula. In habit very like vastum, but fertile fronds contracted, and sori differently situated.

(Also in the Malay Islands, South China, Polynesia.)

VAR β MINOR. (*Bedd.*) Fronds very small (1 foot long only), sterile 3–5 partite rather thin pinnatifid, fertile deeply pinnatifid, very much contracted, the lobes or pinnæ being very narrow. Sagenia pteropus-minor, *Bedd. F. S. I. t.* 245.

Ceylon only, in the Doombera district at no great elevation.

11. ASPIDIUM CICUTARIUM. (*Sw.*) Stipes tufted, 1 foot or more long, with many scales close to the base; fronds very variable in size, from 8 inches up to several feet, deltoid in outline, apex pinnatifid, below which are 1–4 pair of pinnæ, which are either only lobed or completely pinnated with the secondary pinnæ deeply pinnatifid, or even again pinnated (*i.e.* tripinnate), with the tertiary pinnæ deeply pinnatifid (quadripinnatifid), the lowest pair of pinnæ are always deeply pinnatifid or pinnate on the lower margin, but the other pairs are generally much less so and often only lobed ⅓–½ down, texture thin, surfaces glabrous in some varieties, but in others hairy on the upper surface and puberulous on the costas and costules

No. 113.

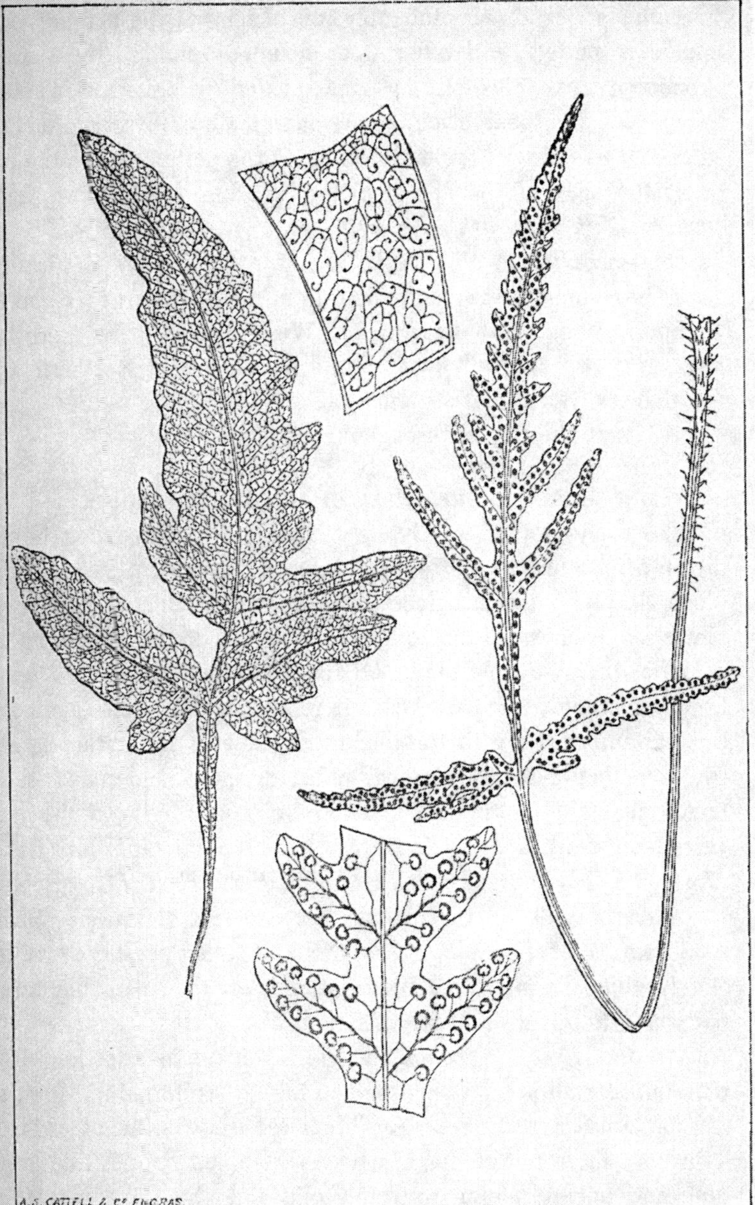

ASPIDIUM DECURRENS, VAR. β MINOR. (*Bedd.*)

beneath; principal veins tolerably conspicuous to the margin, others copiously netted with often free included veinlets (there are no prominent cross veins forming large well-defined areoles as in some of the species, and the free veinlets are often few only); sori rather large, in two rows between the main veins, on the netted veins (compital) or at the apex of the free veinlets; indusium reniform or peltate. *Swartz. Mett. Farngatt. Pheg. and Asp.* 117. *Hook. Syn. Fil.* 299. Sagenia coadunata (Wall.), *Bedd. F. S. I. t.* 81. *and t.* 170 (variolosa).

Throughout the Indian region, from the plains up to 5,000 feet. In South India (both Eastern and Western sides), the more hairy variety known as coadunata only is found, but in Northern India the glabrous variety is also common.

(Also in the tropics throughout the globe.)

12. ASPIDIUM MULTICAUDATUM. (*Wall.*) Stipes 1–3 feet, often densely clothed nearly its whole length with linear-subulate brown persistent scales; fronds 3–4 feet long, with a large terminal pinna deeply pinnatifid, lobes lanceolate acuminate, and several pinnæ on each side, the lowest deltoid 1 foot or more long and nearly as broad, deeply pinnatifid above and pinnate below; texture firm herbaceous, rachises beneath rusty; main veins distinct to the margin, areoles with free included veinlets; sori rather large in two rows between the principal veins, or more numerous and scattered, generally at the apex of free veinlets, rarely on the netted veins (compital). *Wall. in Herb.* Nephrodium Griffithii (Baker), *Hook. Syn. Fil.* 300. Sagenia Griffithii, *Bedd. F. B. I. t.* 337.

Khasya Hills, South side up to 1,000 feet elevation. Birma; Aspidium? *t.* 118, *F. S. I.*, is probably this species, or at least closely allied, it has twice been gathered in the Anamallay forests, but young fronds without fructification.

In the *Synopsis Filicum* Sagenia is kept up as a section of Nephrodium for all species supposed to have a reniform indusium, and Euaspidiumas a section of Aspidium for those with an orbicular indusium, the result of this has been that allied species like repandum and polymorphum (probably one and the same plant) and membranaceum and (Trimeni) giganteum (closely allied if not varieties one of the other), are placed far apart; it is a fact, however, that most of the species have both orbicular and reniform involucres, sometimes on the same individual, the involucres often varying much more than this, being athyrioid and asplenioid. Mr. Clarke has placed both Aspidium and Sagenia in Nephrodium, a genus widely different in habit.

GENUS LII.—PLEOCNEMIA. (*Presl.*)

(*Pleos*, full; *knemia*, rays; in allusion to the venation.)

Only differs from Aspidium in its less compound venation, only the lower veins anastomose arcuately forming one series of areoles near the costa (as in Campteria), without any free veinlets within them, the other veins generally all free, or some angularly anastomosing; sori generally at the apex of the free veinlets outside the areoles, but sometimes some are on the netted veins, (*i.e.*, compital).

1. PLEOCNEMIA THWAITESII. (*Bedd.*) Stipes tufted 1–1½ feet long, shining blackish-purple as is the rachis and main costa, basal scales linear dark-brown; fronds deltoid, 1½–2 feet each way, tripinnatifid; lowest pinnæ largest deltoid stalked, with several large lanceolate deeply pinnatifid pinnules; texture rather thick and opaque, the veins not conspicuous, glabrous beneath, and also above except the costa and veins which are scurfy or puberulous, lower veinlets forming elongate costal arches, no free included veinlets, the rest free with clavate apices, none reaching the margin; sori rather large in a single series on each side of the midrib of the segments, all at the apex of free veinlets; indusium reniform, with the lobes of the sinus broad and overlapping, so that it looks orbicular. Sagenia Thwaitesii, *Bedd F. S. I. t.* 244. Nephrodium (Sagenia) simulans (Baker), *Hook. Syn. Fil.* 300.

Ceylon, southern provinces near Galle, abundant on the Haycock Mountain. (*C. P.* 3331. *Thw. En. p.* 390.)

2. PLEOCNEMIA TRIMENI. (*Bedd.*) Stipes tufted, 1–1½ feet, grey, basal scales linear; fronds 1⅓–3 feet long, deltoid or deltoid lanceolate, pinnatifid at the apex, below pinnate with about 5–6 pair of lateral pinnæ, which are more or less stalked, and all pinnatifid

more than half-way to the rachis, about 8–9 inches long by 2 broad, and a much larger basal pair which are deltoid, again pinnated with the lower basal pinnules deeply pinnatifid, ultimate lobes bluntish, slightly crenated or nearly entire; texture rather thin; surfaces glabrous on both sides; costas and veins rusty above, less so or nearly glabrous beneath; lower veins forming elongated costal arches near the rachis of the pinnæ, with generally a second series of areoles formed by the veins again anastomosing angularly, veins of the segments only anastomosing near the midrib and forming one series of arches, the rest free, no free veinlets in the areoles; sori in a single row on each side of the midrib, those towards the margin and apex of the segments apical on the free veinlets, those lower down and nearer the costa of the pinnules generally on connected veins (*i.e.*, compital), indusium reniform. Sagenia gigantea, *Bedd. F. S. I. t.* 80 (*not the description.*) Pleocnemia gigantea (Baker), *Hook. Syn. Fil. 2nd Edit. p.* 503, *not Blume.*

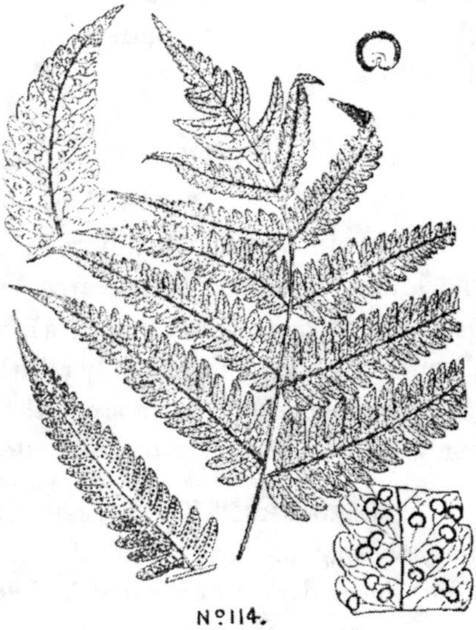

No. 114.

PLEOCNEMIA TRIMENI. (*Bedd.*)

The Kew packet of giganteum from which Sir W. Hooker took his description (*Sp. Fil.* iv. *p.* 50,) contains several different species; the Java specimen being a single pinna of Aspidium giganteum, a species distinct from this; the Birma and Assam specimens being multicaudatum (Wallich); and the Ceylon specimens being this plant, Pleocnemia membranacea, and P. Thwaitesii. This not being Blume's giganteum I have had to rename it.

Ceylon, central provinces, (*C.P.* 1357); South India, Anamallays, Palghat side, in the forests near the Nelliampady coffee estates.

3. PLEOCNEMIA MEMBRANACEA. (*Hook, under Aspidium.*) Stipes tufted up to 9 inches long, straw-coloured, basal scales linear; fronds up to about 18 inches long, deltoid, bi-tripinnate, pinnatifid at the apex, the lowest pair of pinnæ much the largest, long stalked, with the lowest secondary pinnæ stalked and again quite pinnate at the base, the pinnules being stalked and deeply pinnatifid, ultimate segments crenulate, upper pinnæ gradually less compound; texture thin, membranaceous, upper surface somewhat hairy towards the margins; costas and veins rusty or puberulous, under surface slightly puberulous; lower veins forming long costal arches, the rest free; sori at the apex of free veins; indusium both orbicular and reniform. *Hook. Syn. Fil. p.* 259. Sagenia gigantea, var. minor, *Bedd. F. S. I. t.* 243, *a small frond less compound than described above. Thw. En. Pl. Zey. p.* 390. (*C. P.* 1358.)

Ceylon; in the Doombera district at no great elevation. Mr. Thwaites had doubts whether this was a variety of the last, or a distinct species; the venation is quite that of the last species, but rather less compound, owing to the fronds being more cut and narrower; it is quite that of Pleocnemia, and I find some of the involucres reniform; it is of thinner texture, much more cut and less glabrous than the last, and, I think, may safely be considered a distinct species.

(Also in Java, Philippines, China, and Formosa.)

4. PLEOCNEMIA MEMBRANIFOLIA. (*Presl.*) Stipes tufted, furnished with black linear subulate scales more copious towards the base, up to about 1 foot long; fronds seldom more than 1 foot long, from deltoid to ovate, pinnate with a pinnatifid apex, lateral pinnæ few pairs opposite or subopposite, 2–4 inches long, $\frac{3}{4}$–$1\frac{1}{4}$ broad, more or less deeply pinnatifid, the segments rounded nearly entire, lowest pair of pinnæ much larger, deltoid, pinnatifid or almost pinnate, the lower basal segments being elongated and pinnatifid; main rachis and both surfaces more or less softly hairy, with multicelullar hairs; texture softly herbaceous; fertile fronds uniform with the sterile, or more or less contracted, often very much so, lower veins in the sterile and broad fertile fronds anastomosing and

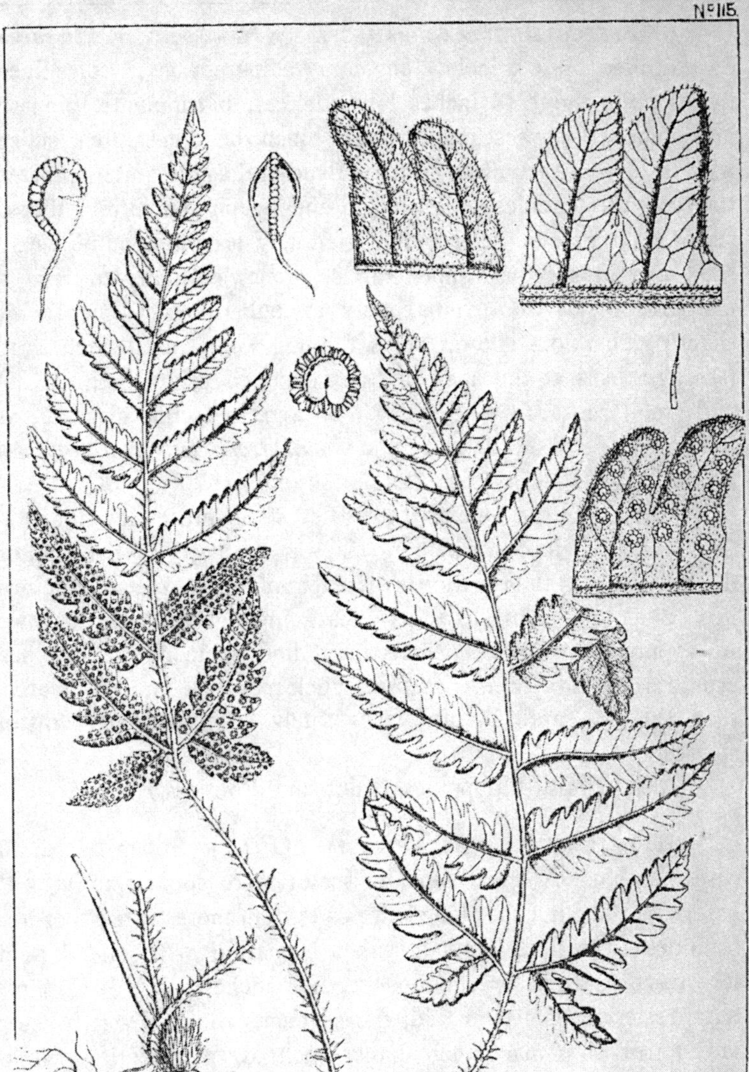

PLEOCNEMIA MEMBRANIFOLIA. (*Presl.*)

forming loops near the costa, sometimes very regularly, sometimes only occasionally, in the contracted fertile fronds all the veins free; sori generally apical on the free veinlets; involucre reniform. *Presl. Rel. Hænck.* 36, *t.* 5, *fig.* 3. Aspidium fuscipes, *Bedd. Sup. Ferns*, *t.* 366. Aspidium fuscipes, *Wallich*, *partly*, *but not the type sheet*, *which is* Lastrea sagenioides.

East Bengal Plains, extending into Assam, Cachar, and Chittagong. Khasya and Sikkim hills up to 3,000 feet elevation. Birma and the Malay peninsula. In habit much like small Aspidium cicutarium, but venation different, and easily known by the persistent black scales towards the base of the stipe; in the *Synopsis Filicum* it has been erroneously lumped with Lastrea dissecta by Hooker and Baker.

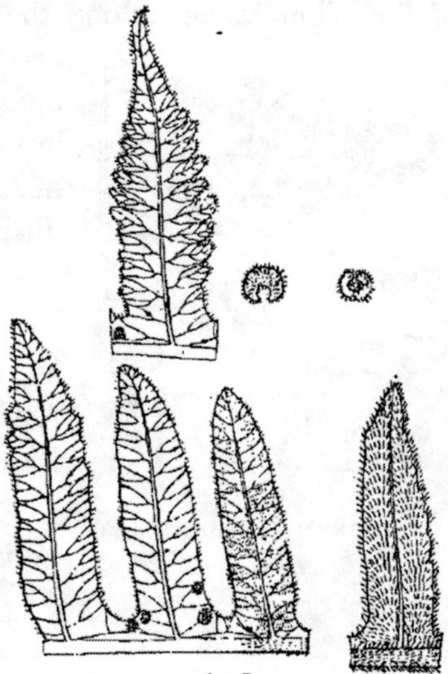

No. 116.

PLEOCNEMIA CLARKEI. (*Bedd.*)

5. PLEOCNEMIA CLARKEI. (*Bedd.*) Stipes and rachis slightly pubescent; fronds 2–3 feet long, lanceolate, narrowed at the base into distant auricles, softly shortly villous, herbaceous, pinnate; pinnæ numerous, alternate, $1\frac{3}{4}$–2 inches broad, pinnatifid nearly to the rachis, the pinnules lanceolate from a broad base, irregular as to length, and from subentire to deeply pinnatifid (on the same pinna) acute at the apex, lowest veins forming arcs along the costa of the pinnules from which proceed free veinlets; veins of the pinnules pinnate, or once or twice forked, the lowest veinlet of a group often looped with the next group; involucre kidney-shaped, hairy and ciliate. *Bedd. Sup. Ferns*, *t.* 368. Nephrodium artinexum, *Clarke*, *F. N. I. p.* 536.

Sikkim; near Dikeeling, 4,500 feet elevation.

6. PLEOCNEMIA LEUZEANA. (*Hook.*) Caudex subarborescent, densely scaly at the crown, stipes 2–3 feet long, stout, striated, shortly hirsute without scales; fronds up to 6 feet long, subdeltoid, bi-tri-pinnate; pinnæ 1–1½ foot long, 6–8 inches broad, simple, or the lowest with 2–3 large (12–14 inches long) secondary pinnæ from the lower side, which are again pinnate with the pinnules stalked, 2–4 inches long, and deeply pinnatifid, ultimate segments oblong-rounded, entire or denticulate, usually with a tooth in the sinus at their base; lower veins anastomosing in costal arches near the costa of the pinnules and along the midrib of the segments, other veins free and excurrent, or all the veins of the segment are free; sori copious, usually in single rows on each side of the midrib, mixed with yellow glandular hairs; indusium reniform, early fugacious. *Hook. Syn. Fil.* 295. *Bedd. F. B. I. t.* 134.

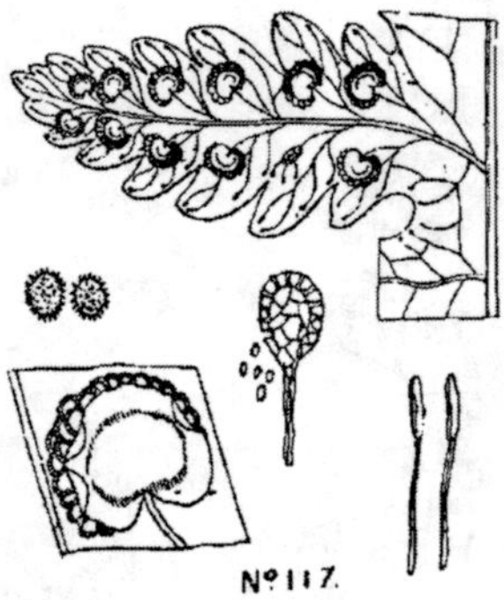

No. 117.
PLEOCNEMIA LEUZEANA.
(*Hook.*)

North and East Bengal, base of the hills up to 2,000 feet elevation, Sikkim, Assam, Cachar, Khasya, Chittagong; Birma, and Malay Peninsula.

(Also in Malay Islands, China, Polynesia, and North Australia.)

GENUS LIII.—LASTREA. (*Presl.*)

(After Chev. de Lastre, a French nobleman.)

Sori subglobose, dorsal or terminal on the veins; indusium reniform, attached by the sinus, or in the first four species sometimes orbicular; veins all free; fronds pinnate or compoundly 2–4 pinnate.

* *Indusium reniform or orbicular, texture more or less coriaceous.*

1. LASTREA AMABILIS. (*Bl. under Aspidium.*) Rhizome

creeping; stipes scattered, 6–12 inches long, slender, slightly scaly below; fronds about 1 foot long, by 6–9 inches broad, with a pinnate apex and 2–6 lateral pinnæ on each side, which are 1–1½ inch broad, all simply pinnated or the lowest sometimes slightly compound at the base, pinnules subrhomboidal with the lower side much cut away ½–1 inch long, cut down about a third or half-way to the costa into rounded lobes which terminate with a long bristle, sometimes being more or less serrated; texture subcoriaceous; rachis and both surfaces naked; veins pinnate in the lobes; sori submarginal; indusium reniform or orbicular. *Bedd. F. S. I. t.* 109. Aspidium amabile, *Bl. En. Pl. Jav. Fil. p.* 165. *Hook. Syn. Fil.* 254. Aspid. rhomboideum, *Wall. Cat.* 364.

I keep this species in Lastrea as I have always found the involucres reniform; they appear, however, to be sometimes orbicular, so that the species has equal right to be a Polystichum.

South India, on the Anamallays, Lower Pulneys, Travancore, and Tinnevelly Hills, 3,000–4,000 feet elevation; Ceylon, central provinces; North India, Nepal, Jaintea, about 4,000 feet, rare.

(Also in the Philippines and South China.)

2. LASTREA ARISTATA. (*Sw. under Aspidium.*) Rhizome long, creeping, very scaly; stipes scattered, about 1 foot long, more or less fibrillose, as are the main and partial rachises; fronds about 12–15 inches long, deltoid in outline, pinnate at the apex, below which are 5–6 lateral pinnæ on each side, which, except the lower pair, are generally simply pinnate or with a tendency to be bipinnate in their upper basal pinnules, lower pair bipinnate towards the base, the lower basal pinnules being much the largest and quite pinnated, pinnules subrhomboidal with the lower base cut away, more or less lobed, the upper basal lobe being the deepest, lobes copiously toothed, teeth aristate; texture more or less coriaceous; veins pinnate in the lobes, the veinlets being simple or forked; sori apical on the veinlets and well within the margin; indusium reniform or orbicular. *Bedd. F. S. I. t.* 101. Aspidium aristatum, *Sw. Syn. Fil.* 53.

South India, very general in the Western forests of the Madras Presidency; Ceylon; Birma.

I have always found the involucre strictly reniform, and Hooker has described it both under Polystichum and Lastrea (in the latter as Lastrea platypus); it is a much less divided fern than coniifolia, besides having an utterly different caudex; Mr. Clarke, who unites it with coniifolia, states, that he has never been able to see that a creeping caudex accompanies a less divided form, but Mr. Clarke's specimens are all typical coniifolia, and there is no aristata from the Himalayas in the Kew Herbarium, and only one poor specimen from Khasya, labelled Lastrea platypus.

(Also in Japan, Formosa, South China, Java, Luzon, and Norfolk Island.)

3. LASTREA AFFINIS. (*Wall.*) Very similar to aristata and amabilis, but the lower pinnæ less compound than in aristata and often quite similar to the upper ones; texture much more coriaceous and sori very large. *Wall. Cat.* 370. Lastrea aristata, var. Hamiltonii, *Bedd. Fern. Sup. pl.* 369. *Hook. Syn. Fil.* 256. Aspidium speciosum (Don.), Aspidium aristatum, var. affinis, and var. assamica, *Clarke, l. c.* 511.

I formerly considered this species a variety of aristata, I have never seen it growing, but Mr. Clarke tells that the rhizome is erect and not creeping, so I cannot consider it a variety of either aristata or amabilis.

Sikkim, Nepal, Assam, Jaintea.

4. LASTREA CONIIFOLIA. (*Wall.*) Rhizome erect; stipes tufted; fronds very large, ovate, 2–3 feet long, 4–5 pinnate, ultimate pinnules and segments small, coriaceous shining, aristate; sori large or small; indusium reniform or orbicular. *Bedd. F. B. I.* 261. Aspidium, *Wall. Cat.* 341.

I have always found the involucres reniform in their young stage, I have had both this and aristata in cultivation on the Nilgiris for many years, and they show no tendency to run one into the other.

LASTREA CONIIFOLIA. (*Wall.*)

A—Root of L. aristata.

Himalayas, Kumaon to Bhotan, 4,000–10,000 feet, Khasya, 3,000–6,000 feet; South India on the Western mountains; Ceylon; Malay Peninsula.

(Also in Natal, Samoa, and Australia.)

* * *Indusium always reniform.*

† *Pinnæ subentire or only slightly lobed (except in forms ν and δ of Walkeræ.)*

5. LASTREA CUSPIDATA. (*Mett. under Aspidium.*) Stipes about 1 foot long, reddish as is the rachis, scaly towards the base; fronds 1–3 feet long, pinnæ numerous, linear-lanceolate from a broad base, 4–6 inches long, ½–¾ inch broad, cuspidate at the base, very shallowly lobed (not ⅓ to the rachis), the lobes sharply serrated; texture scarcely coriaceous; rachis and both surfaces naked; veins pinnate with 3–4 veinlets on each side; sori towards the base of the veinlets; indusium reniform, fugacious. *Mett. Farngatt. Pheg. and Asp.* 92. Polypodium elongatum, *Wall. Cat.* 309. *Bedd. F. B. I. t.* 118. Nephrodium cuspidatum, *Hook. Syn. Fil. p.* 260.

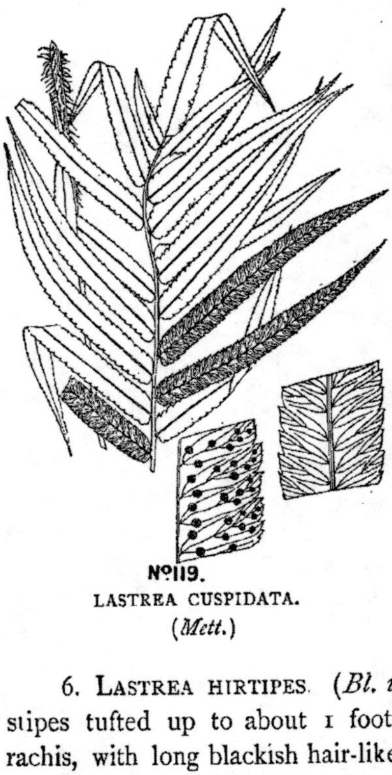

No. 119.
LASTREA CUSPIDATA.
(*Mett.*)

Khasya Hills, 3,000–4,000 feet elevation, near Shillong.

6. LASTREA HIRTIPES. (*Bl. under Aspidium.*) Caudex erect; stipes tufted up to about 1 foot long, densely clothed, as is the rachis, with long blackish hair-like scales; fronds up to 3 feet long, pinnæ numerous, linear-lanceolate from a broad base, 4–8 inches long, by nearly 1 inch broad, with broad shallow lobes reaching ¼ to ⅓ towards the rachis, lower ones not reduced; texture herbaceous;

surfaces naked; veins pinnate; veinlets 4–5 on a side; sori low down on the veinlets, indusium reniform. *Bl. En. Pl. Jav. Fil* 148. *Bedd. F. S. I. t.* 96. Asp. atratum, *Wall. Cat.* 380.

Himalayas, 5,000–9,000 feet, from Nepal to Bhotan, Khasya 4,000–6,000 feet; South India, Nilgiris, &c.; Ceylon; Birma.

(Also in the Malay Islands and Polynesia.)

7. LASTREA WALKERÆ. (*Hook under Polypodium.*) Stipes up to 1½ foot long, clothed with linear scales; fronds up to 3 feet long, oblong-lanceolate, pinnate; pinnæ linear-lanceolate, short-stalked, acuminate, slightly crenate along the margins, lower ones about 6 inches long, by about 1 inch broad, lower base cut away, upper base square; texture subcoriaceous, glabrous; veins in pinnate groups; sori 2–3 serial, between the midrib and the margin, dorsal on the veinlets; indusium reniform, very fugacious. Polypodium Walkeræ, *Hook. Syn. Fil. 1st ed. p.* 305. Lastrea, *2nd ed.* 493. *Bedd. F. S. I. t.* 234.

Ceylon.

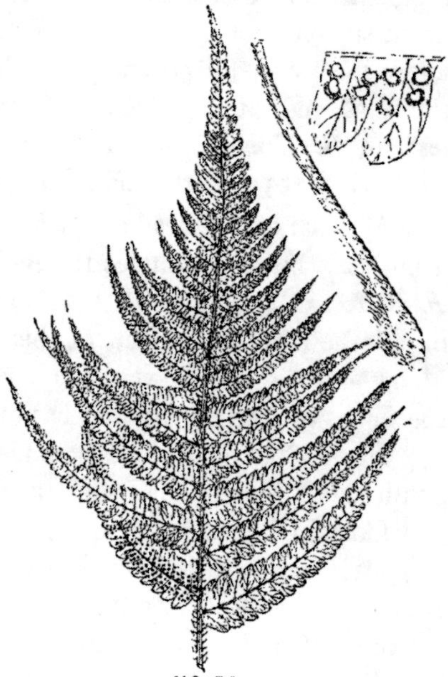

Nº 120

LASTREA HIRTIPES. (*Bl.*)

VAR. β MACROCARPA. Fronds very large, the pinnæ slightly lobed, often furnished with a large auricle at the superior base. *Bedd. F. S. I. t.* 235.

Ceylon.

VAR. γ PINNATIFIDA. Pinnæ pinnatifid nearly to the rachis, leaving only a broad wing along the rachis, lower ones sometimes pinnate. *Bedd. l. c. t.* 235.

VAR. δ BIPINNATA. Pinnæ sub-bipinnate. *Bedd. l. c. t.* 235. Ceylon.

† † *Pinnæ cut more than half-way to the rachis, compound in some forms of Filix Mas.*

A. Veins generally simple.

8. LASTREA GRACILESCENS. (*Bl.*) Stipes tufted, long, slender; fronds oblong-lanceolate, pinnate, lower pinnæ scarcely reduced, often deflexed, rachises pilose above, pinnæ cut down nearly to the rachis, segments narrow-oblong, obtuse, not much narrowed upwards, veins about six on each side of the costule, the two lowest terminating above the sinus, all generally simple, rarely forked, sori medial on the veins, indusium glabrous or minutely pilose. Aspidium gracilescens, *Bl. En. Pl. Jav. Fil.* 155. *Hook. Syn. Fil.* 262. *Bedd. F. B. I. t.* 253. *Clarke, F. N. I.* 513 *in part.*

Mr. Clarke includes here L. flaccida (Hooker), which is certainly a mistake; he also includes the Assam forms of L. immersa (*Bedd. F. B. I.* 252) united with the Malay Peninsula plant by Hooker; in this he may be correct, as this plant appears distinct from the Malay one, it is however, much larger than any of Mr. Clarke's specimens of gracilescens, and has more veins to the segments.

Nepal, Sikkim, 6,000–8,000 feet elevation, Khasya, 4,000 feet; South India, Mudumally forests, a small form.

(Also in China, Japan and Java.)

Mr. Clarke's variety decipiens (Darjeeling, 7,000 feet, and Khasya, Dingling, 5,000 feet) has the fronds shorter and more deltoid, and the veins often branched with the sorus subterminal on the upper branch; it is probably a distinct species. His variety hirsutipes only differs in having the stipes hirsute and in being of rather thicker texture (Khasya and Jaintea, 4,000–5,000 feet); his variety didymochlœnoides has longer narrower pinnæ with very large sori, but runs into the type.

9. LASTREA IMMERSA. (*Bl.*) Caudex creeping, stipes elongated 3–4 feet long, fronds rather coriaceous in texture, pinnate, ovate

oblong, or oblong in outline, pinnæ 6–10 inches long, sessile, about 1 inch broad, cut down close to the rachis, glabrous above on the segments, or with occasionally a few distant inconspicuous hairs on the viens, the rachis strigose, frosted beneath on the veins and rachis with minute yellow glandular dots; segments linear, rather distant; veins simple (or the lowest one very rarely forked), 12–14 or even more on each side of the costa; sori medial, one to each vein, much immersed, the depression plainest on the upper side, indusium large, persistent, reniform, but appearing orbicular from the overlapping at the sinus. Aspidium immersum, *Bl. En. Fil.* 156. Nephrodium immersum, *Hook. Sp. Fil.* 112. *Syn. Fil.* 263.

Malacca and the Malay Peninsula.

(Also in the Philippines and New Caledonia.)

Mr. Clarke considers that the Assam plant (*Bedd. F. B. I. t.* 252) should be referred to gracilescens, it is of a different texture, less cut down, and with much fewer veins.

10. LASTREA CALCARATA. (*Bl.*) Caudex erect, stout, stipes tufted, fronds lanceolate pinnate, sometimes with auricles below, up to about 2 feet long, pinnæ spreading 1–4 inches long by ½ inch to nearly 1 inch broad, cut down two-thirds or more towards the rachis into oblique falcate linear oblong segments, the upper basal one sometimes considerably longer than the others, rachis villous, under surface more or less villous, upper surface villous, or glabrous except the secondary rachis, veinlets 3–8 on a side, simple, sori medial, involucre glabrous or villous. Asp. calcaratum, *Bl. En. Fil. Jav. p.* 159. Lastrea calcarata, *Hook. Sp. Fil.* iv. 93, *and* falciloba, *p.* 108.

VAR. CILIATA, type (*Wall. Cat.* 351), texture herbaceous, lowest pinnules deflexed, no auricles on the stem; stipes rounded, pinnæ about 4 inches long, caudate at the apex, nearly 1 inch broad; indusium hairy or glabrous. Lastrea falciloba, *Bedd. F. S. I.* 105. Asp. ciliatum, *Wall. Cat.* 351, and Asp. canum, *Wall. Cat.* 387. Nephr. ciliatum, *Clarke, F. N. I.* 515, except syn. L. Bergiana (*Bedd.*), which is L. cana (*Baker*).

No. 121.

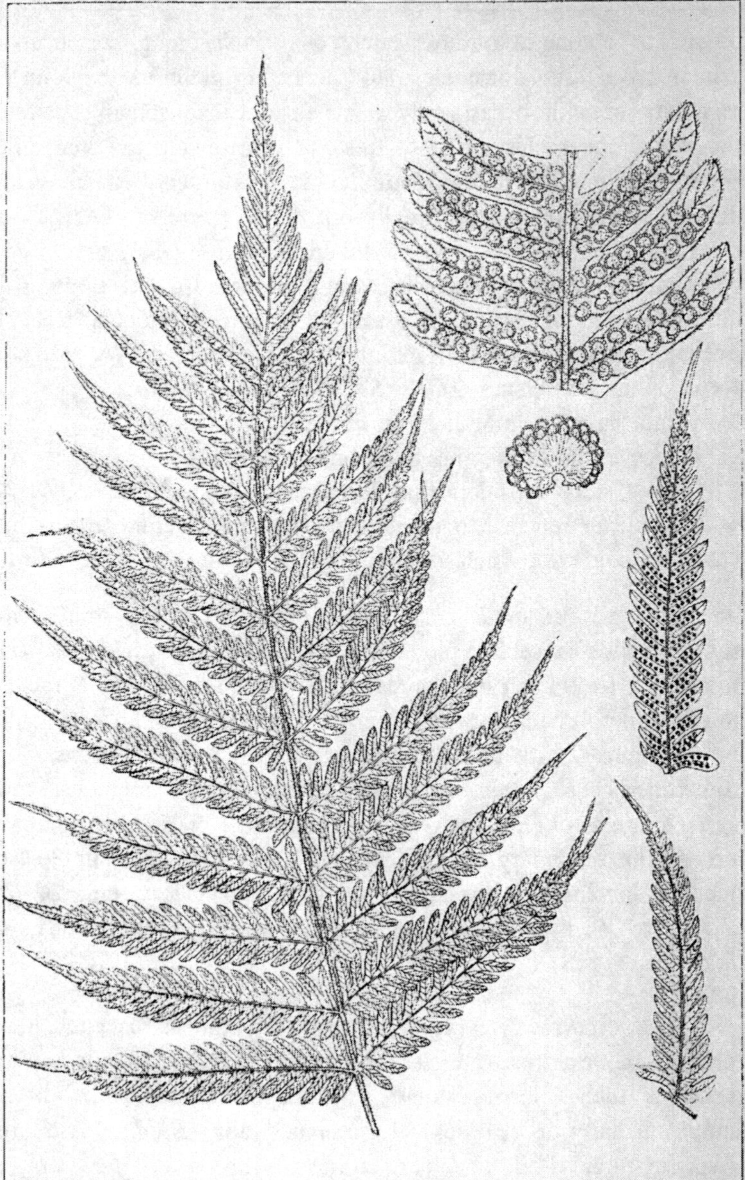

LASTREA CALCARATA, VAR. CILIATA. (*Wall.*)

South India, very common in all the Western forests; and in Ceylon (exactly corresponding with Wallich's two type sheets). Specimens sent from both these localities were partly referred by Hooker to his calcarata and partly to falciloba, but he doubted whether the two species were really distinct. Also in Khasya, the Himalayas; Birma.

ASP. CALCARATUM, VAR. β. *Thw. En.* 391, L. calcarata, *Bedd. F. S. I. t.* 246, is an abnormal form, with small narrow pinnæ tapering at both ends and less pinnatifid, except sometimes quite at the base, where the segments are almost free and distant; but, as Thwaites says, it passes into the type. A form from Birma also has very narrow pinnæ and is densely hairy.

VAR. β SERICEA. (*J. Scott, MS.*) Pinnæ short oblong, 1–2 inches long by ½–¾ inch broad, quite obtuse at the apex, or ending in a short sudden point (never caudate), involucre glabrous, otherwise as in the type. L. sericea, *Bedd. F. B. I. t.* 308. This is, perhaps, scarcely distinct as a variety from the type, but its geographical limits are curious, in North India it has only been found in Chittagong, elevation 200 feet, and in South India only on the Jeypore Hills west of Vizagapatam, elevation 2,000 feet. I have had it for several years in cultivation and it quite kept its character.

VAR. γ FALCILOBA. (*Clarke.*) Stipes angled and furnished with auricles below the frond; pinnæ more numerous and narrower, 4 inches long by ½ inch broad; texture subcoriaceous (more like ochthodes); indusium glabrous. Lastrea falciloba, *Hook. Sp. Fil.* iv. *p.* 108, in part only. Aspidium hirsutulum, *Wall. Cat.* 7083, type sheet example b, has no auricles on the stipe, and appears to me to belong to the type (ciliata), it only consists of a single small frond, and might belong to either, but I fear falciloba and ciliata are not well defined as varieties, but run one into the other. *Clarke, F. N. I.* 515, *excl. t.* 105, *Bedd. F. S. I.*

Khasya and Sikkim mountains up to 3,000 feet and river banks in the plains.

(Clarke's variety pubera does not belong here, *Wall. Cat.* 338, being Nephrodium arbuscula (typical), and from the Sirumallays near Dindigal, not from Nepal.

11. LASTREA VISCOSA. (*J. Sm.*) Stipes 6 inches or more long, firm, erect, reddish-brown, slightly scaly, finely villous; fronds 9–12 inches long, 4–5 inches broad, oblong-lanceolate, pinnæ close 2–3 inches long, the lower ones somewhat reduced and deflexed, cut nearly to the rachis into close spreading linear-oblong lobes under 1 line broad, textures herbaceous, colour dark green; rachis villous, under surface densely glandular, veinlets 5–6 on a side, sori medial. *Hook. Syn. Fil. p.* 264. *Bedd. F. B. I. t.* 334.

Malay Peninsula, at Malacca.

(Also in the Philippines and Borneo.)

12. LASTREA CRASSIFOLIA. (*Bl.*) Stipes tufted 1½ foot long, channelled above slightly hirsute; fronds deltoid ovate, firm herbaceous, pinnate, pinnæ pinnatifid, rachis, costa and costules beneath hirsute, the rest glabrous, pinnæ petiolate (petioles ¼ inch long) or subsessile, lower ones not reduced in size, pinnatifid nearly two-thirds down to the rachis, segments obtuse subfalcate subentire, basal ones reduced in size, costa deeply channelled above, veinlets simple, the lower pair free (as in Lastrea) or joining just before entering the sinus of the segments (as in Nephrodium) remaining ones simple (or rarely forked) sori one on, or a little below the centre of each vein, involucre reniform glabrous. Aspidium, *Bl. En. Fil. Jav.* 158. *Hook. Syn. Fil.* 266. Lastrea nephrodioides, *Bedd. F. B. I. t.* 199.

Birma and the Malay Peninsula. I also have a specimen collected in Sikkim, 3,000 feet elevation, by the late Mr. Atkinson, which I refer here, as it exactly corresponds in venation; the pinnæ, however, are subsessile, and the upper basal segment (or pinnule) somewhat enlarged.

(Also in the Philippines and Java.)

13. LASTREA CANA. (*Baker.*) Stipes densely tufted, 6–10 inches long, finely villous and often furnished with pellucid scales, chiefly towards the base; fronds 8–12 inches long, elongate lanceolate, not narrowed at the base, or suddenly or gradually narrowed into auricles on the stipe, pinnate with numerous pinnæ, central ones two inches long by ½ inch broad, cut down nearly to the rachis into close

crenated lobes, texture herbaceous, rachis slender, villous, and both sides slightly so, veinlets 6–8 on a side, simple (very rarely forked); sori small medial on the veins, indusium reniform, glabrous or pilose. *Baker, Hook. Syn. Fil.* 267, *not Wallich, Bedd. F. B. I. t.* 307. L. Bergiana, *Bedd. F. B. I. Suppl. t.* 370. Aspid. appendiculatum, *Wall. Cat.* 349, *type sheet only.* Aspid. eberneum, *Wall. Cat.* 389, *type sheet only.*

Himalayas near Simla, Sikkim, Yakla 8,000 feet elevation. Mr. Clarke thinks this may be only a variety of ochthodes, but it has no glands at the base of the pinnæ, the texture also is different, and it is more hairy.

14. LASTREA BEDDOMEI. (*Baker*). Rhizome slender, wide creeping; stipes 6–9 inches long, slender, glossy; fronds pinnate up to about 1 foot long, lanceolate elliptic, central pinnæ the largest, about $1\frac{1}{2}$ inches long, $\frac{3}{8}$ inch broad, cut down almost to the rachis into close rather acute entire segments under 1 line broad, lower pinnæ distant and dwindling down very gradually, texture rather firm, veins beneath furnished sparingly with longish white needle-like hairs, veinlets 4–5 on each side, simple sori near the margin. *Baker, Hook. Syn. Fil. p.* 267. L. gracilescens, *Bedd. F. S. I. t.* 110.

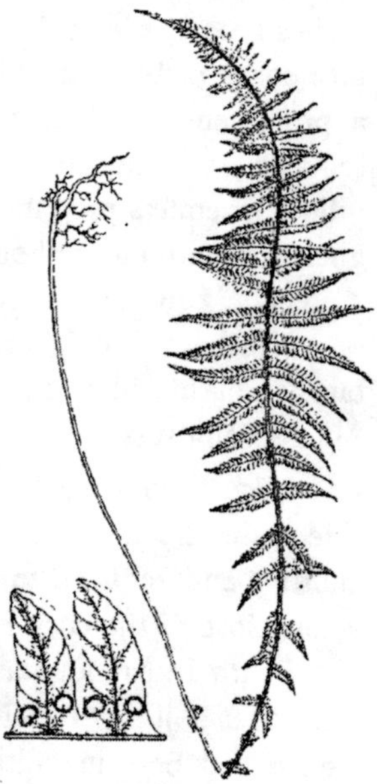

No. 122.
LASTREA BEDDOMEI.
(*Baker.*)

South India on the Travancore and Tinnevelly Mountains in swampy ground. Ceylon, common in swampy places about Newera Elya. A pretty delicate species much cultivated at Ootacamund.

15. LASTREA ELWESII. (*Baker.*) Stipe not seen, main rachis minutely pubescent; fronds oblong-lanceolate, narrowed from the midrib at both ends, 16 inches long, by $4\frac{1}{2}$ inches broad, glabrous, pinnate; pinnæ patent, subobtuse, cut down only one-half towards

the midrib; segments broad, short, obtuse, lower pinnæ much deflexed and gradually shorter; texture moderately firm, surfaces naked, bright green; veinlets distant, simple, about 4 on each side; sori small marginal; indusium small fugacious. *Hook. Syn. Fil.* 497. *Bedd. Fern. Sup. t.* 376.

Sikkim (Elwes, only once collected, and a single frond without stipe.)

16. LASTREA OCHTHODES. (*Kze.*) Caudex erect, stipes tufted, 1–2 feet long, firm, naked or nearly so; fronds 2–4 feet long, 8–12 inches broad; pinnæ ¾–1 inch broad, cut down nearly to the rachis into entire or bluntish, often falcate segments 1–1½ lines broad, with a prominent gland at the base beneath, the lower ones gradually reduced; texture subcoriaceous; rachis and underside more or less villous; veinlets prominent, simple 10–15 on a side; sori submarginal. Aspidium octhodes, *Kze. in Linnæa*, xxiv. 282. *Bedd. F. S. I. t.* 106. Nephrodium prolixum, *Baker, Syn. Fil.* 268.

Northern India, throughout the Himalayas and Khasya Mountains; South India and Ceylon, throughout the mountain forests; Malay Peninsula.

VAR. β TYLODES. (*Kze.*) More coriaceous, rachis and underside glabrous, lower pinnæ not gradually reduced, but suddenly abortive and reduced to tuberculated glands, sori at the base of the veins, close to the costules. *Bedd. F. S. I. t.* 107.

South India mountains, rare, and probably the same localities as ochthodes; it is, I believe, quite entitled to rank as a species. I have had both in cultivation for many years, and Mr. Thwaites, who cultivated them in Ceylon, considered them distinct species.

17. LASTREA FAIRBANKII. (*Bedd.*) Caudex long creeping, as thick as a crow quill, very black, glabrous, but furnished with a few scales, copiously rooting, stipes 8–20 inches long stramineous, black at the base, rachis channelled above, glabrous or slightly pubescent with weak glandular hairs; fronds coriaceous 6–10 inches or more long, narrow oblong pinnated, pinnæ opposite or alternate, sessile or nearly so, 1–1½ inches long, less than ½ inch broad, linear obtuse or acuminate at the apex, pinnatifid nearly to the rachis, the lower ones

reduced in size and often more distant, the partial rachis channelled and glabrous on the upper side, slightly pubescent or glabrous beneath, and there furnished with numerous broad-ovate or lunate very transparent scales, segments oblong to ovate entire much recurved at the margins; veins more or less undulate; veinlets simple excurrent at the margin; sori one on the centre of each veinlet; involucre reniform, fimbriate at the margin. *Bedd. F. B. I. t.* 254.

Pulney Mountains, in swamps about the south base of Peermall Malley, 4,000 feet elevation. It was also formerly found about the lake at Kodiekarnal on the same mountains, but has disappeared from that locality. In my Supplement I have reduced it to *thelypteris*, but now believe it to be distinct. In its reduced lower pinnæ it approaches *Beddomei*, but it is much more rigid in texture, and its scaly secondary rachis is quite unlike that fern. I hope it may be further collected. There is a specimen in the British Museum.

B. Veins forked.

18. LASTREA THELYPTERIS. (*Desv.*) Rhizome slender, wide-creeping, stipes about 1 foot long, slender stramineous; fronds 1–2 feet long, 4–6 inches broad, lanceolate, truncate at the base; pinnæ spreading, $\frac{1}{2}$ inch broad, cut down very nearly to the rachis into entire spreading linear oblong lobes, those of the barren frond the broadest, lower pinnæ equalling the others, veins forked (upper ones simple) texture herbaceous, rachis and both sides naked, sori small, not confluent, in rows near the recurved edge; indusium small inconspicuous. *Desv. in Mém. Soc. Linn.* 6. 257. *Bedd. F. B. I. t.* 44. *Hook. Syn. Fil.* 271.

South India, on the Nilgiris, swamps near Ootacamund; North India, Kashmir, Bandipoor, City Lake, 5,600 feet elevation, Kunawur, 6,000 feet.

(Also in Europe, North Asia, North America, Cape Colony and New Zealand.)

19. LASTREA GRISEA. (*Baker.*) Stipes firm, erect, grey, villous upwards; fronds $1\frac{1}{2}$–2 feet long, 8–9 inches broad, oblong-lanceolate;

pinnæ close, 3–4 inch long, $\frac{3}{4}$–$\frac{7}{8}$ inch broad, narrowed gradually from the base to the apex, cut down nearly to the rachis into blunt,

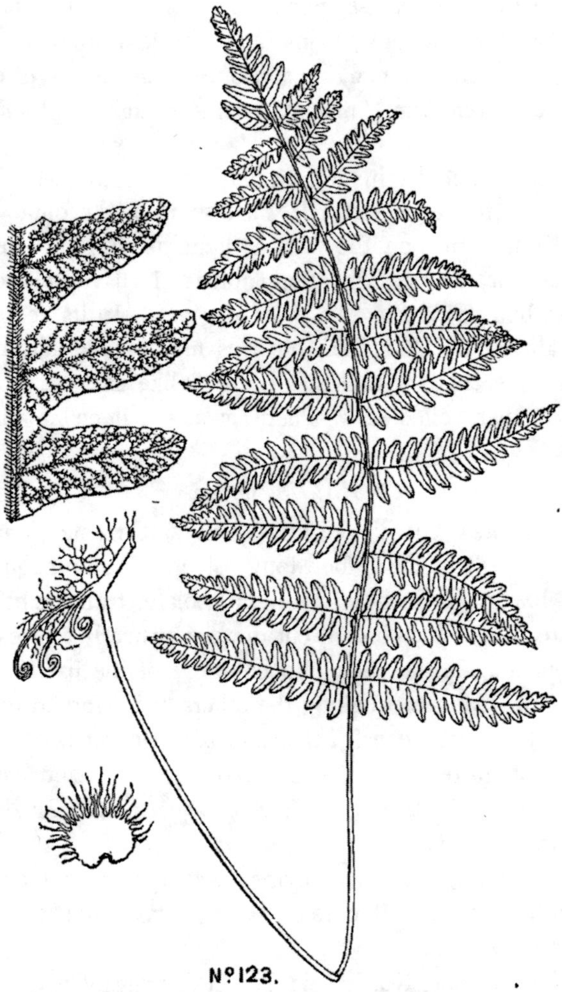

No. 123.

LASTREA THELYPTERIS. (*Desv.*)

entire lobes, 2 lines broad, with recurved edges; texture subcoriaceous; rachis villous, and veins beneath slightly so; veinlets about 10 on a side, mostly forked; sori small, submarginal; involucre ciliated. *Hook. Syn. Fil. p.* 271. *Bedd. F. B. I. t.* 335.

South India, near Cochin, only once collected.

20. LASTREA FUSCIPES. (*Wall.*) Stipes tufted, slender 6–12 inches long, dark purplish-brown, scaly below, fronds 12–24 inches long, 6–12 inches broad, oblong-lanceolate, pinnate; pinnæ 3–6 inches long, 1 inch broad, the lowest pair rather shorter than the others, and deflexed, and with some of its lower segments often elongated; segments cut down to a broadly-winged rachis, linear-oblong, blunt, entire or slightly crenate; texture herbaceous, rachis polished like the stipe; veinlets 6–8 on each side, simple

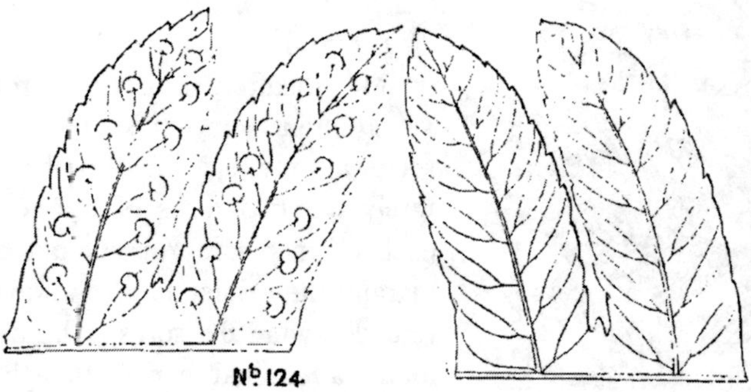

No. 124

LASTREA SYRMATICA.

or forked, generally excurrent when sterile, but terminating well within the margin when fertile; sori generally apical on a veinlet, sometimes well below the apex; indusium reniform fugacious. *Wall. Cat.* 361. Lastrea melanopus, *Hook. Sp. Fil.* iv. 110. *Bedd. F. B. I. t.* 38. L. sagenioides, *Hook. Syn. Fil.* 271. Polypodium obscurum, *Hook. Sp. Fil.* iv. 237. *Syn. Fil.* 308. *Bedd. F. B. I. t.* 230.

Birma and the Malay Peninsula.

(Also in the Philippine Islands.)

The type sheet of Aspidium fuscipes in Wallich's Herbarium, No. 361, *is this plant, but the other sheets are Pleocnemia membranifolia.*

21. LASTREA SYRMATICA. (*Willd. under Aspidium*). Stipes

tufted, 1–2 feet long, naked, straw-coloured; fronds up to about 5 feet long pinnate; pinnæ shortly stalked up to about 1 foot long by 1½ inch broad, cut down to a broadly winged rachis, the lower ones scarcely reduced; segments ¼ inch broad, slightly toothed, rather distant, with a tooth in the sinus between them, glabrous or subglabrous, scarcely coriaceous in texture; rachises glabrous on both sides; veins all forked 10–15 on each side; sori small in a single row on each side of the costule, nearer the margin than the costule, always medial on the superior veinlet (never terminal); indusium reniform glabrous. *Willd. Sp. Pl.* v. 237. *Hook. Syn. Fil.* 272. L. spectabilis, *Hook. Sp. Fil.* iv. 115. *Bedd. F. S. I. t.* 108.

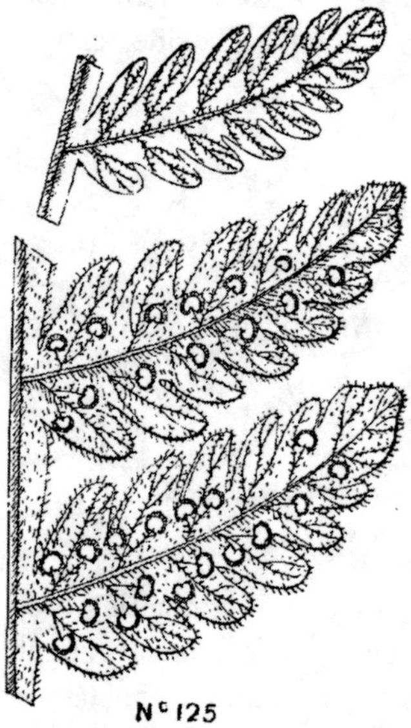

No 125

LASTREA FLACCIDA. (*Hook.*)

Mr. Baker says that the groups of veins often join, this I have not seen in my specimens; but very rarely the two forks of the vein join each other before running out at the margin; the veinlet is also always continued beyond the sorus, I have never found a terminal sorus, though they often appear to be so until the frond is held up to the light.

South India, not common; Carcoor ghat, 2,000–2,500 feet; Anamallays and Travancore Hills. Ceylon, forests of the central provinces; North India, Sikkim, Assam and Khasya, up to no great elevation; Birma and Malay Peninsula.

(Also in the Philippines.)

22. LASTREA FLACCIDA. (*Hook.*) Stipes tufted, about 1 foot long, slender, glabrous, fronds, 1–1½ feet long, pinnate; pinnæ very flaccid and membranaceous, 3–4 inches long by nearly 1 inch broad, cut down to the rachis, which has a very distinct narrow wing quite square with the rachis, between the pinnules; pinnules oblong from a very square

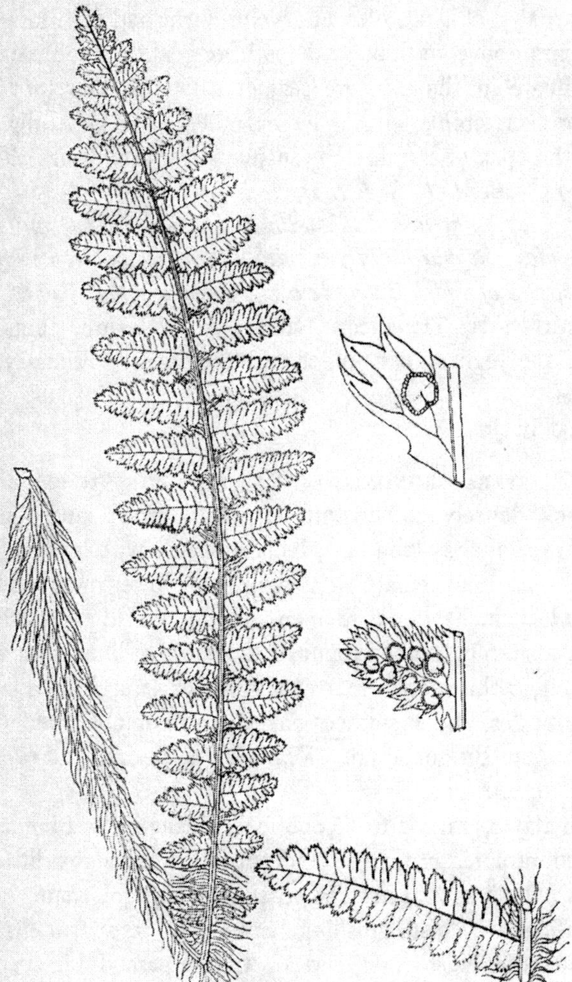

No. 126.

LASTREA BRUNONIANA. (*Wall.*)

base, and obtuse at the apex, rather deeply lobed (about half down); the segments being falcate, lower pinnæ somewhat distant and a little reduced in size, and sometimes deflexed; main rachis slightly hairy, partial rachis costules and veins furnished with longish weak brown hairs above, and beneath with long white needle-like hairs; veins pinnate in the ultimate segments in fully developed fronds, forked or even simple in smaller examples; sori generally terminal or near the apex of a veinlet; indusium small reniform. *Hook. Syn. Fil. p.* 274. *Bedd. F. S. I. t.* 250.

Mr. Clarke has joined this with L. gracilescens, but quite wrongly in my opinion, its real affinity is with L. tenericaulis, which it strongly resembles, and of which it may be a more simple form.

South India, Travancore Hills, rare. Ceylon, about Newera Elya and the highest part of central provinces. Himalayas up to 6,000 feet.

(Also in Java.)

23. LASTREA BRUNONIANA. (*Wall.*) Stipes tufted, 4–6 inches long, black, densely clothed with large dark-brown lanceolate scales, fronds 12–18 inches long, 2–4 inches broad, with numerous close subequal oblong-lanceolate blunt pinnæ, the lower ones reduced, the largest 1½–2 inches long, ¾ inch broad, cut down nearly to the rachis into sharply toothed rounded lobes 1½–2 lines broad, texture herbaceous, rachises ebeneous and more or less clothed with long fibrillose scales, under surfaces naked, sori copious, medial on the veinlets. Asp. Brunonianum, *Wall. Cat.* 344. *Hook. Syn. Fil.* 274. *Bedd. F. B. I. t.* 37.

Himalayas, 11,000 to 16,000 feet, Kashmir to Bhotan. Very like L. odontoloma in texture and cutting, knowing so little of the plant as I do, I should not like to suggest it is the same, but I had great difficulty in distinguishing between some specimens of these two in the Kew Herbarium, and Mr. Clarke named one specimen he gave me of this "odontoloma."

24. LASTREA BARBIGERA. (*Hook.*) Stipes tufted, 6–12 inches long, densely clothed with large bright-brown scales and soft silky

Nº 127

LASTREA BARBIGERA. (*Hook.*)

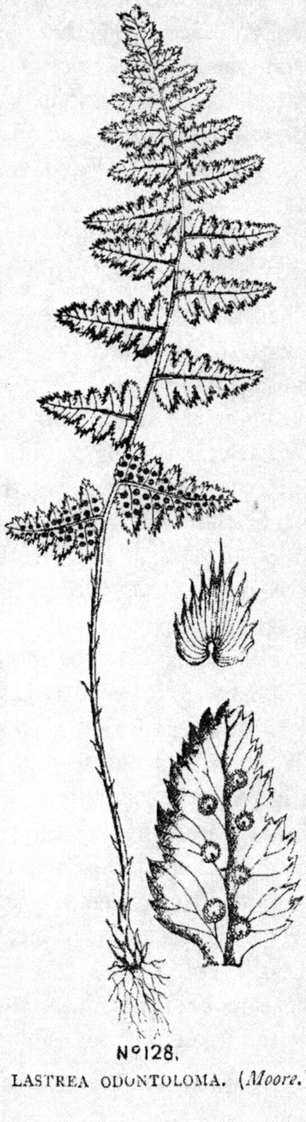

Nº 128.

LASTREA ODONTOLOMA. (*Moore.*)

hairs; fronds 2–3 feet long; pinnæ close, lanceolate, 4–6 inches long, 1–1⅛ inch broad, gradually reduced below; pinnules oblong, blunt, usually distinct, sometimes subpinnatifid, the segments with copious aristate teeth, the edge often incurved; texture herbaceous; rachises clothed like the stipe; midrib beneath rather scaly; sori in rows close to the midrib of the pinnules. *Hook. Syn. Fil.* 274. *Bedd. F. B. I. t.* 227. L. Falconeri, *Hook. Syn. Fil.* 277. *Bedd. F. B. I. t.* 41.

Himalayas; Kashmir to Sikkim, 11,000–15,000 feet elevation. Nearly allied to Brunoniana if it be really distinct, which I doubt.

25. LASTREA ODONTOLOMA. (*Moore.*) Stipes 6 inches, soft thick chestnut-coloured, with scattered deciduous lax lanceolate scales; fronds up to 10 inches long, by 6–8 inches broad, oblong-lanceolate, truncate at the base; pinnæ often widened at the base, 2-pinnate; secondary pinnæ elliptic-oblong, pinnatifid (sometimes deeply); segments rounded, sharply serrate; texture thin becoming hyaline towards the margin; venation subflabellate; involucre fimbriate. *Clarke, F. N. I. p.* 521. L. Filix-mas, var. odontoloma, *Hook. Syn. Fil. p.* 498. *Bedd. F. Sup. t.* 373, *not F. S. I. t.* 114 (*which is typical Filix-mas.*)

Himalayas, Chumba to Bhotan, 11,000–16,000 feet elevation.

I have followed Mr. Clarke in separating this from Filix-mas, but I fear I may be wrong in so doing, as specimens of Mr. Clarke's Filix-mas, var. panda seem to connect this with that protean species; but if it goes into Filix-mas, Brunoniana and barbigera must also be referred there. I find the greatest difficulty in distinguishing between this species and Brunoniana, the fimbriate involucre and the truncate base to the frond, seem the only reliable characters, the former, however, is of no specific value, and the latter I fear is not constant (unless I still confuse the species), as some specimens which I believe to be Brunoniana, and decided by Mr. Clarke to be such, have the fronds without reduced pinnæ at the base.

26. LASTREA FILIX-MAS. (*Linn. under Polypodium.*) Stipes tufted, more or less clothed with scales, fronds up to about 4 feet long, and about 1 foot broad pinnate to sub-bipinnate;

pinnæ lanceolate, cut down nearly (scarcely ever quite) to the rachis into close, blunt, regular segments which are subentire, crenate, or serrulate, lower pinnæ sometimes gradually reduced, sometimes not at all so; texture generally more or less coriaceous, rachis scaly or glabrous, under surface generally naked, sometimes fibrillose, veins forked, or the lower ones pinnate, sori medial, involucre large, reniform glabrous. Polyp. Filix-mas, *L. Sp.Pl.* 1551. *Hook. Syn. Fil. p.* 272; *Sp. Fil.* iv. 116. Lastrea odontoloma. *Bedd. F. S. I. t.* 11 (typical Filix-mas). *Clarke, F. N. I. p.* 519.

Throughout the Indian region, but generally confined to considerable elevations on the mountains.

(Also found throughout the world (in temperate places) except in Australia and America south of Peru).

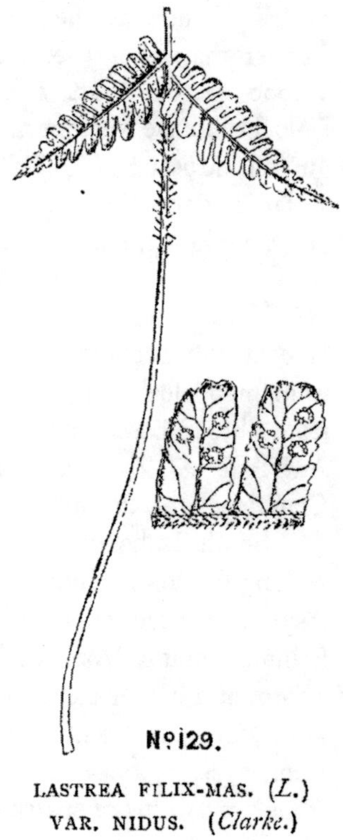

No. 129.

LASTREA FILIX-MAS. (*L.*) VAR. NIDUS. (*Clarke.*)

VAR. β PARALLELOGRAMMA. (*Hook. Sp. Fil.* iv. 116.) Pinnate, rarely sub-bipinnate, pinnæ often reduced towards the base, segments oblong-parallelogram, generally close and compact, entire, crenated or serrated.

I include under this as sub-varieties, patentissima, fibrillosa, apiciflora, nidus, and Clarkei. Taking patentissima (common throughout the Indian region) as the type, they all show very slight differences, and these are not constant; *apiciflora*, which has generally been made a distinct species, is remarkable on account of the sori being confined to the apex of its segments; Mr. Clarke has, however, found it frequently with the sori scattered, though he says it can be distinguished by being remarkably free from fibrillæ and hairs, but I have specimens which I gathered, near Darjeeling, with fibrillæ on all the veins beneath; the fronds are generally more truncate at the base than patentissima, but I have specimens where the pinnæ are gradually reduced; the involucre is reniform, or quite circular from the overlapping at the sinus. Himalayas, Nepal to Bhotan, 7,500–11,000 feet elevation, *Bedd. F. B. I. t.* 40.—*Nidus.* Tufts very circular, fronds small, lower pinnæ a little reduced and deflexed, segments few, sori scattered, but with a tendency to be apical. Sikkim, 9,000–12,000 feet. *Bedd. F. B. I. Sup. t.* 372.—*Clarkei.* Tufts circular, fronds tapering much at the base, almost down to the caudex; much smaller than the type, but quite running into it. Sikkim, 9,000–11,000 feet. *Bedd. Fern Sup. t.* 371. Colonel Dyas sent this from Dalhousie with the under surface very fibrillose (*vide* specimen in British Museum).—*Fibrillosa* differs only in having the under surfaces of the pinnæ copiously clothed with fibrillæ. N. W. Himalayas, 9,000–12,000 feet from Kumaon to West Kashmir.

VAR. γ ELONGATA. (*Hook and Grev. Ic. t.* 234.) Fronds truncate at the base, bi-tripinnate, or sometimes pinnate only in forms from high elevations, ultimate segments generally narrowed upwards from a broad base, rachises glabrous or scaly. *Hook. Sp. Fil.* iv. 117. *Bedd. F. S. I.* 112. Var. marginata, *Clarke, plate* 71. Aspid. Canariense, *A. Brown.*

South India on the Western mountains, 4,000–6,000 feet elevation; Ceylon; Himalayas and Khasya, 5,000–9,000 feet elevation. Aspidium rigidum (*Desv.*) seems quite to run into this. Asp. Schimperianum (*Hochst.*) [intermedia, *Bedd. F. S. I. t.* 113], is only a form at a higher elevation, 2-pinnate or 1-pinnate, with often very large sori; but it quite runs into the type. Nilgiris, higher elevations. Himalayas, 7,000–12,000 feet. This can always be distinguished from large forms of sparsa by the lower basal pinnules of the lowest pinnæ not being elongated.

VAR. δ COCHLEATA. (*Don.*) Fronds truncate at the base, generally dimorphic, pinnate or sub-bipinnate in the sterile, bipinnate in the fertile; involucres very large and completely covering the under surface of the contracted fertile pinnules, but the broader fronds are sometimes partially, or even wholly, in fructification;

rachises glabrous, or sometimes scaly. *Don. Prod. Fl. Nep.* 6 *Bedd. F. S. I. t.* 115. Arthobotrys macrocarpa, *Wall. Cat.* 395.

North India up to 4,000 feet elevation; South India, Western mountains 2,000–4,000 feet; Malay Peninsula. A very distinct looking plant in its typical form at low elevations, but running it to elongata at higher elevations (*vide* forms of my collecting on the Nilgiris and Brumagherries in the British Museum).

VAR. ε PANDA. (*Clarke, F. N. I. p.* 519, *t.* 68, *fig.* 1.) Fronds simply pinnate, truncate at the base, narrow oblong, pinnæ pinnatifid ⅓–⅔ towards the midrib, segments subspinulose.

Himalayas, Dhurmsala, 10,000–11,000 feet elevation. This has much the aspect of odontoloma, and it will probably prove to be a luxuriant form of that plant; if a variety of Filix-mas, it certainly connects odontoloma with it.

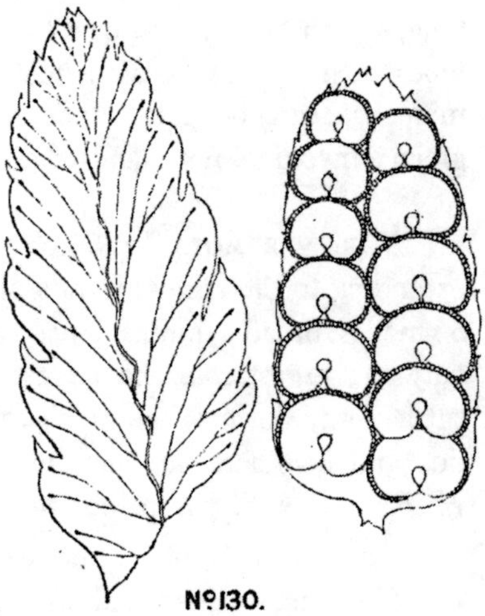

No. 130.
LASTREA FILIX-MAS. (*L.*)
VAR. δ COCHLEATA. (*Don.*)

††† *Fronds compound, 2–4-pinnate.*

27. LASTREA RIGIDA. (*Desv.*) Stipes tufted, 6 inches long, densely clothed below with large lanceolate or ovate scales; fronds up to 2 feet long, oblong-lanceolate, largest pinnæ 3–4½ inches long, 1–1½ inch broad, the pinnules of the lower half free ovate rhomboidal, cut down nearly to the rachis below, teeth mucronate; texture herbaceous; rachises usually scaly, under side naked or slightly glandular; veinlets subpinnate in the lower lobes of the pinnules; sori near the midrib; indusium firm prominent. *Hook. Syn. Fil. p.* 275. *Clarke, F. N. I. p.* 523.

Very near L. Filix-mas elongata, and I cannot say I know any character to distinguish it.

Himalayas, Kashmir to Kumaon 6,000–8,000 feet elevation. (Also in Europe, Caucasus, and Cabul).

28. LASTREA SPINULOSA. (*Desv.*) Stipes tufted, about 1 foot long, sparingly clothed with ovate concolorous scales; fronds 12–18 inches long, 6–8 inches broad, oblong-lanceolate; lower pinnæ sub-deltoid, 3–4 inches long, 1½–2 inches broad, the lowest pair about equal to the next; pinnules ovate-lanceolate, the largest about 1 inch long, ½ inch broad, cut down to the rachis below into close oblong lobes with copious aristate teeth; texture herbaceous; rachis stramineous, scarcely scaly; under surface not glandular; colour pale-green; involucre not gland-ciliated. *Hook. Brit. F. t.* 20.

VAR. γ REMOTA. (*A. Br.*) Scales lanceolate, concolorous, extending to the rachis; fronds oblong-lanceolate, about 2 feet long, 6 inches broad; pinnæ lanceolate, close; pinnules ovate-oblong, only the lowest free, the largest about 1 inch long, ½ inch broad, cut half-way down to the rachis or more, spinulose teeth few; under side and involucre not glandular. *Hook. Brit. F. t.* 22. *Bedd. F. B. I. t.* 336. Asp. eberneum, *Wall. Cat.* 389, *in part.*

Kashmir to Nepal, 6,000–9,000 feet elevation.
(Also in Northern and Alpine Europe, Asia and America.)

29. LASTREA SPARSA. (*Don.*) Rhizome short, suberect, densely covered with lanceolate-linear golden or reddish scales; stipes long, 1 foot or more, with scattered scales; main rachis generally glabrous or subglabrous; fronds ovate, 2–3 pinnate, lowest pinnæ the largest, deltoid, with their lower basal pinnules generally compound, pinnules deeply pinnatifid above, less so below, and more or less cut away at the base, ultimate segments oblong or somewhat trapezoidal, coarsely toothed and often quite sharply serrated; texture more or less coriaceous; veins pinnate in the segments terminating within the margin; sori either terminal on a veinlet or well below its apex; indusium reniform. *Don. Prod. Fl. Nep.* 6. *Bedd. F. S. I. t.* 103. *Hook. Syn. Fil.* 276. Aspidium marginatum, *Wall. Cat.* 291, *2nd sheet.*

No. 131.

A. S. CATTELL & Co. ENGRAS.

LASTREA SPARSA. (*Don.*) VAR. γ OBTUSISSIMA. (*Mett.*)

Himalayas and Khasya, 2,000–6,000 feet, very common ; South India, abundant on all the Western mountains and on the hills on the East side ; Ceylon ; Birma and Malay Peninsula.

(Also in the Malay Islands, China, and Mauritius.)

VAR. β NITIDULA. (*Wall. Cat.* 392.) Stipes and rachis red, lower pinnæ less divided, pinnules less cut ; indusium deciduous, *Bedd. F. Sup. t.* 374.

Nepal to Bhotan, 9,000–12,000 feet elevation.

VAR. γ OBTUSISSIMA. (*Mett.*) Base of stipe clothed with light brown broad chaffy scales, lower pinnæ similar to the others ; frond less cut, the ultimate segments broader, shorter and blunter, oblong to obovate. *Bedd. F. Sup.* 375. *Kuhn. Lin.* 36.

Ceylon, Nepal.

VAR. δ DELTOIDEA. (*Bedd.*) Fronds quite deltoid, the upper and lower basal pinnules being much reduced in size. *Bedd. F. S. I. t.* 248.

Ceylon.

VAR. ε MINOR. (*Thw.*) Fronds very small, often only 3 inches, simply pinnate, the pinnæ only ½ inch broad, but in fructification, larger specimens, however, running into the smaller forms of deltoidea.

Ceylon ; Simla, North Cachar.

VAR. ζ ZEYLANICA. (*Bedd.*) In texture and colour like obtusissima, but much more compound and the basal pinnules larger than the others, main secondary and tertiary rachises more or less matted with black adpressed flattish scales ; base of stipes a cushion-like mass of long narrow golden scales. L. pulvinulifera, var. β Zeylanica. *Bedd. F. Sup. p.* 17.

Ceylon, Blackpool.

VAR. η UNDULATA. (*Thw.*) Pinnæ deflexed, rachis and secondary rachis geniculate-flexuose. A very curious variety only found on the top of the hill over the Hackgalle Government Gardens,

Ceylon (near Newera Elya), 5,000 feet elevation. Lastrea undulata (*Thwaites*), *Bedd. F. S. I. t.* 271.

Mr. Clarke's variety latesquama, does not differ from what I consider the type of sparsa, which agrees exactly with *Wall. Cat.* 390, Asp. densum, and *Wall. Cat.* 7080, Asp. oppositum.

30. LASTREA PULVINULIFERA. (*Bedd.*) Stipe up to 30 inches long, furnished with a dense cushion-like mass of golden scales at the base (as in L. odorata), and clothed throughout (especially in the older specimens), as are the rachis and partial rachises, with numerous narrow black scales, which proceed from a broad base, and which are generally more copious at the axils of the pinnæ; fronds ample, up to 30 inches long (without the stipe) by 18 inches broad near the base, deltoid, tripinnate, coriaceous-herbaceous; pinnæ gradually decreasing in size from the base to the apex, lower pair opposite, large deltoid with the pinnules of the lower margin much the largest, remaining pinnæ alternate or rarely subopposite or opposite; pinnules up to 4 inches long in the basal pinnæ, with their secondary pinnules equal to the primary pinnules on the upper parts of the frond; segments obtusely rounded, entire or lobed, and occasionally dentate or crenate, glabrous on both sides, but sometimes furnished with a few weak setæ on the costules and veins on the upper side; veinlets inconspicuous, terminating within the margin; sori terminal on the lower veinlet; involucre reniform glabrous. *Bedd. F. B. I. t.* 333. Lastrea pulvinulifera (Baker), *Hook. Syn. Fil. p.* 500, *in part only. Clarke, F. N. I. p.* 525, *in part only.* Lastrea sparsa, var. squamulosa, *Clarke, l. c. p.* 524, *in part.*

Sikkim, very common about Darjeeling. Perhaps only a very compound form of sparsa.

31. LASTREA BUCHANANI. (*Baker.*) Stipes tufted up to 1 foot long, dark coloured at the base, straw-coloured upwards, densely clothed as is the rachis, with long spreading rather rigid black hairs; fronds ovate to deltoid, tripinnate, with the tertiary pinnules from subentire to pinnatifid, secondary rachis hairy, lowest pinnæ largest deltoid unequal sided from being more compound at the base,

No. 132.

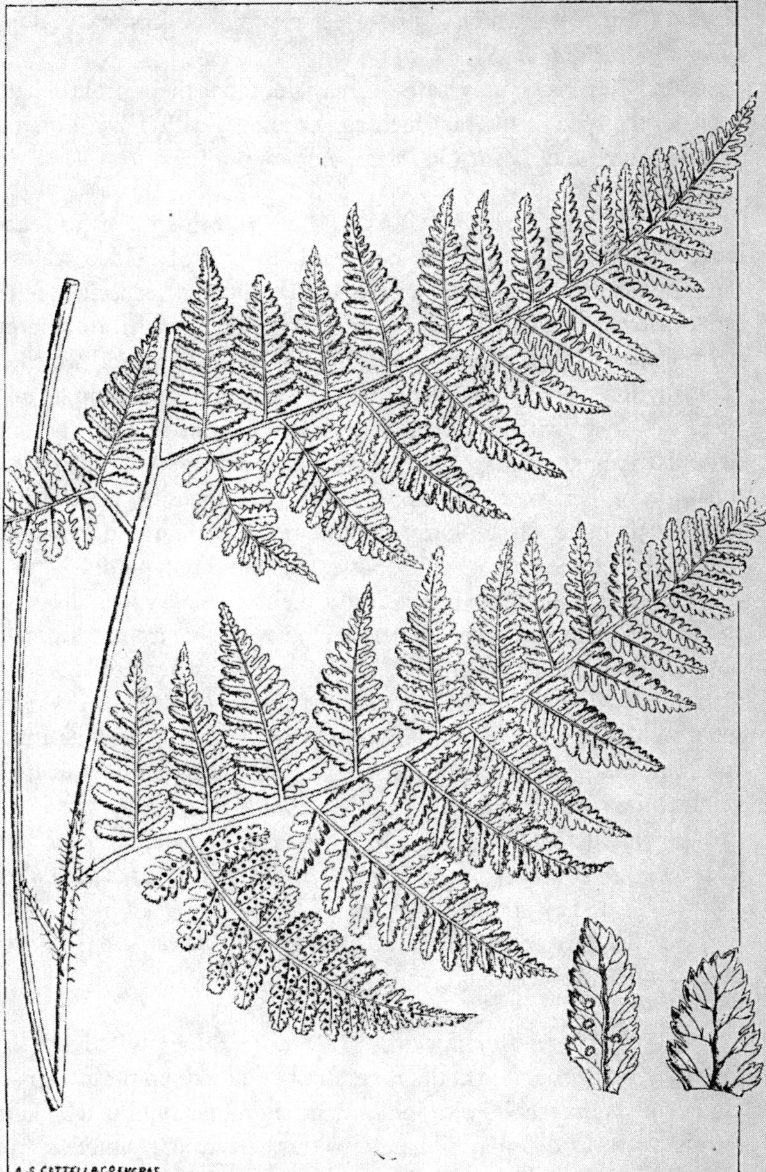

LASTREA SPECTABILIS. (*Wall.*)

tertiary rachis a little scaly, ultimate segments oblong blunt; texture subcoriaceous; veins pinnate or forked in the ultimate segments; sori below the middle of the veins and near the costules (never apical on a veinlet as in pulvinulifera); involucre reniform, glabrous, persistent. *Hook. Syn. Fil. p.* 498. Lastrea pulvinulifera, *Hook. l. c.* 500, *in part only.* Nephrodium pulvinulifera, *Clarke, F. N. I. p.* 525, *in part only.*

Himalayas, near Darjeeling, 7,500 feet elevation.

(Also in Natal and Bourbon.)

32. LASTREA SPECTABILIS. (*Wall. under Aspidium.*) Stipes 1–1½ foot long and with the rachises purple-coloured and furnished with patent linear subulate reddish-brown scales; fronds 2–4 feet long, more than 1 foot broad, subdeltoid, tripinnate with the tertiary pinnules deeply pinnatifid, and their segments again crenated or serrated, lowest pinnæ largest, deltoid, unequal-sided, the two lower basal secondary pinnæ being much produced; texture moderately firm, the costa of the pinnules and veins of the segments sparingly furnished with long weak setæ most copious on the upper side, otherwise glabrous, sori medial on the upper basal veinlet of the segment; involucre reniform. *Wall. Cat.* 372. *Clarke, F. N. I. p.* 526. Lastrea Hendersoni, *Bedd. Fern Sup. t.* 377.

Khasya on Shillong Hill 5,000–6,500 feet elevation; Nepal.

33. LASTREA DEPARIOIDES. (*Moore under Diclisodon.*) Stipes about 1 foot, long, firm, slightly scaly below; fronds up to 2 feet long, oblong-lanceolate, bipinnate with the pinnules deeply pinnatifid, pinnæ 4–6 inches long, 2 inches broad, lanceolate, the secondary rachis with a very narrow inconspicuous wing, pinnules stalked, deltoid, unequal sided, with broad blunt subquadrangular lower segments and prominent teeth, texture rather firm, rachis and both surfaces naked; sori terminal in the teeth which the convex involucres quite conceal. Diclisodon, *Moore, Index Fil.* 316. Lastrea deparioides, *Bedd. F. S. I. t.* 104. *Hook. Syn. Fil.* 277.

South India, on the Anamallay Hills, 2,000 feet elevation; Ceylon, southern provinces.

34. LASTREA THWAITESII. (*Baker.*) Quite like the last in general outline and habit, except that the pinnules are less cut and the segments bluntly lobed instead of having prominent teeth, and the sori just within the margin; it is probably only a variety of deparioides or the normal form of it, as that species is very abnormal in the genus. *Hook. Syn. Fil. p.* 277. L. concinna (*Thwaites*), *Bedd. F. S. I. t.* 246.

Ceylon, southern provinces, 2,000 feet elevation.

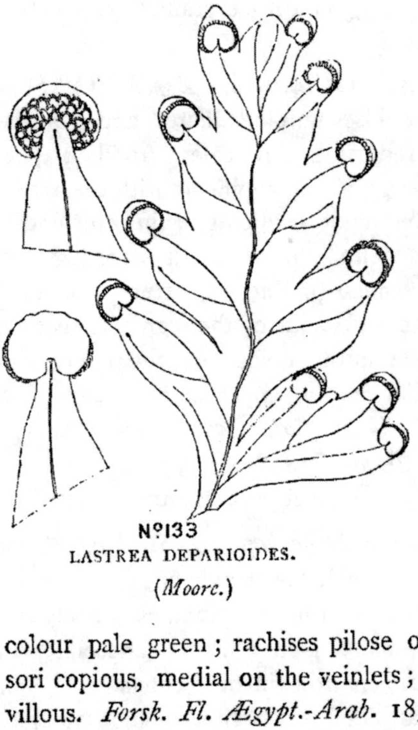

No. 133
LASTREA DEPARIOIDES.
(*Moore.*)

35. LASTREA CRENATA. (*Forsk under Polypodium.*) Stipes up 1½ foot long, straw coloured, glossy, densely clothed at the base with a tuft of golden lanceolate-linear scales, fronds up to 1½ foot long, 3–4-pinnate deltoid, lowest pinnæ much the largest deltoid, 6–9 inches long, 3–4 inches broad, pinnules lanceolate, often imbricated, with ovate or oblong pinnatifid segments, with blunt rounded lobes; texture herbaceous, colour pale green; rachises pilose or subglabrous, surfaces pilose; sori copious, medial on the veinlets; indusium large, pale coloured, villous. *Forsk. Fl. Ægypt.-Arab.* 185. Lastrea eriocarpa; (*Decne.*) *Hook. Sp. Fil.* iv. 141. *Bedd. F. S. I. t.* 95. Nephrodium odoratum (*Baker*), *Hook. Syn. Fil. p.* 280. Aspidium pilosulum, *Wall. Cat.* 337; and subdiaphanum, 343.

Himalayas from Gurwhal to Bhotan, 2,000–7,000 feet elevation, Khasya, 2,000–4,500 feet, Chota Nagpore, 2,000–3,000 feet; South India, on the Anamallays, Peringoonda Hill, 5,000 feet, and elsewhere on the western ghats, but rare; Ceylon; Malay Peninsula.

(Also in Tropical Africa; Mauritius; South China.)

36. LASTREA PARISHII. (*Hook.*) Caudex creeping, stipe 6–9 inches long, slender, naked, ebeneous, fronds small, 6–8 inches each way, deltoid, the lower pinnæ much the largest, lower pinnules larger than the others, which are oblong-lanceolate acuminate 1½–2 inches long by ½–¾ inch broad, cut down nearly to the rachis into close oblong-lanceolate crenated lobes, texture membranaceous, rachises and under surfaces pubescent; veinlets pinnate or forked in the lobes; sori in two rows, not far from the midrib, apical on a veinlet or situated well below the apex, indusium reniform. *Hook. Syn. Fil. p.* 281, *Bedd. F. B. I. t.* 43.

Birma, Moulmein, moist shady places on limestone rocks.

No 134.

LASTREA PARISHII. (*Hook.*)

37. LASTREA SIKKIMENSIS. (*Bedd. under Polystichum.*) Stipes and rachises rather copiously furnished with persistent ovate acute blackish scales, fronds ovate acuminate up to 3 feet long, subcoriaceous-membranaceous, bipinnate, primary pinnæ 4–6 inches long, oblong acuminate, secondary pinnules oblong, deeply pinnatifid, ½ inch to 1 inch long, tertiary pinnules sharply and deeply cut, with the segments acuminate and falcate, costa of the pinnules waved, veins simple or forked, terminating within the margin, sori generally one to each segment, terminal on a veinlet, involucre reniform. Polystichum sikkimense, *Bedd. F. B. I. t.* 127. Nephrodium, *Clarke, F. N. I. p.*525. *Hook. Syn. Fil.* 256.

Sikkim, Mon Lepcha, 10,000–12,000 feet elevation.

38. LASTREA BLUMEI. (*Hook.*) Stipes up to about 2 feet long, stout, very shaggy, with long linear rufous scales, rachises

rufous-pubescent, and copiously furnished with rufous scales, fronds very large ovate in outline, tripinnate, primary pinnæ 10–15 inches long, tertiary pinnæ 1-1¼ inch long, pinnatifid nearly to the rachis, the segments oblong entire or rarely rather deeply incised, sparingly hairy above, pubescent on the costa on both sides; veinlets forked or simple; sori small medial on the veinlets; involucre reniform, glabrous. Lastrea Blumei, *Hook. Sp. Fil.* iv., 135, *in part at least. Bedd. F. S. I. t.* 249. L. intermedia (*Baker*), *Hook. Syn. Fil. p.* 283. L. rhodolepis, *Clarke, F. N. I.* 526.

North India, Sikkim, Assam and Khasya 5,000–7,000 feet; Ceylon, common in the central provinces, 2,000–3,000 feet elevation.

(Also in Japan; Malay Islands; Polynesia.)

Mr. Clarke states that it is not the intermedia of Blume. I do not know whether he is correct in this, but in any case a new name is unnecessary, as it has been published and figured as Blumei, a name otherwise unoccupied.

39. LASTREA RECEDENS. (*J. Smith.*) Rhizome creeping, stipes erect, villous, clothed at the base with linear scales; fronds very large deltoid, 3-pinnate above, 4-pinnate below, with the quaternary pinnules deeply pinnatifid, lower pinnæ up to nearly 2 feet long, (in large specimens) secondary pinnæ on the lower side 9–10 inches long, quaternary pinnæ ¾ inch long, the ultimate segments entire or slightly crenated, texture herbaceous, rachises villous, under surface softly hairy on the veins, upper surface nearly glabrous except on the costules, veins forked, sori terminal on, or a little below, the apex of a veinlet. Phegopteris recedens (*J. Smith*), *Hook. Jour. of Bot.* iii. 394. Lastrea recedens, *Bedd. F. S. I. t.* 98, *two-thirds of a small frond.* Nephrodium, *Hook. Syn. Fil.* 281.

South India, on the lower Pulney Mountains, and Travancore and Tinnevelly Hills, 3,000–5,000 feet elevation; Ceylon, central provinces, 2,500–5,000 feet elevation.

(Also in the Philippines.)

40. LASTREA DISSECTA. (*Forst.*) Rhizome erect, stipes 1 foot or more long, a little scaly at the base, fronds deltoid to ovate, up to

nearly 3 feet long; texture herbaceous, pinnate above, with the pinnæ 6–9 inches long by 1¼ inch broad, pinnatifid two-thirds towards the rachis, bipinnate below, from some of the lower basal pinnules of the lowest pinnæ being stalked and much elongated and deeply pinnatifid, and equal to some of the upper primary pinnæ; ultimate segments crenulate, a little hairy above (on the lamina, not the veins), with scale-like hairs, quite glabrous below in South Indian examples, but with scale-like hairs in specimens from Ceylon; veinlets forked, always free, a forked veinlet often proceeds from the costa to the margin of the sinus, between the segments; sori apical on the superior veinlet, forming a single row on each side of the segments nearer the margin than the midrib, involucre reniform, glabrous; fertile portions of the frond often much contracted and frond often only partially seeding. Lastrea membranifolia, *Bedd. F. S. I. t.* 102, *a small frond.*

The descriptions of Lastrea dissecta in *Hooker's Syn. Fil.* and of L. membranifolia in *Hook. Sp. Fil.* includes this species, the variety ingens and Pleocnemia membranifolia.

Madras Presidency, Western mountains, common up to about 5,000 feet elevation; also in the N. Arcot and Vizagapatam Hills; Ceylon, up to 5,000 feet; Birma.

(Also in Malay Islands and Polynesia.)

VAR. INGENS. (*Clarke.*) A very large fern, stipe and main rachis pubescent, and with lax narrow-lanceolate sparse brown deciduous scales; fronds up to 9 feet long, the lower pinnæ 2 feet and more long, bipinnate above, the pinnæ about 1 foot long by 6 inches broad, the secondary pinnæ quite distinct but sessile from a very broad base and deeply pinnatifid, tripinnate below, the lower basal pinnules of the lowest pinnæ being stalked, elongated and again pinnated, their pinnules (tertiary pinnæ) being deeply pinnatifid, and equalling the secondary pinnæ above; ultimate segments entire, nearly glabrous above except on the costa, and costules, but there are a few scale-like hairs on the lamina, costa, costules and often the veins beneath furnished with white glistening multicellular patent hairs; texture, venation and sori exactly as in dissecta; involucre reniform, but the lobes of the sinus often overlapping, so that it appears to be circular; fertile portions of the frond often much contracted, and fronds often only partially seeding. *Clarke, F. N. I. p.* 526.

Himalayas, Sikkim, and Bhotan, 4,000–7,000 feet, very abundant between Darjeeling and Surail; Khasya, 3,000–5,000 feet.

Mr. Clarke says that it seeds but rarely, and then usually only very partially, this is an error, as I found many clumps near Darjeeling (end of November) with most of the fronds entirely covered with seed, and not in the least contracted. I had written out a full description, believing this to be a distinct species from dissecta, differing in having copious multicellular hairs beneath, the South Indian plant being glabrous; I have, however, since seen Ceylon specimens in the British Museum which have similar hairs beneath, so I can now only regard it as a variety; it only differs in its larger size, and in being more compound, and in the ultimate segments being more entire.

41. LASTREA SPLENDENS. (*Hook.*) Stipes 2–3 feet long, stout, polished bright chestnut coloured and scaly, as is the main rachis; fronds long-lanceolate up to 4 feet, by about 1½ broad, bipinnate, primary pinnæ narrow lanceolate, about 2 inches broad, and nearly the same breadth throughout; secondary pinnæ 20–30 pairs, about ¼ inch broad, lanceolate-oblong, rounded at the apex, cut about one-third towards the rachis into small lobes, the upper basal one being generally rather larger than the others, all more or less serrated; texture subcoriaceous, glabrous on both surfaces, or slightly scaly beneath; rachis of primary pinnæ deeply channelled above, and winged upwards glabrous above, often scaly beneath; veinlets pinnate or forked, not reaching the margins; sori well below the middle of upper veinlet, forming a row on each side of the pinnule near the costa. *Hook. Syn. Fil.* 282. *Bedd. F. B. I. t.* 42.

Sikkim and Bhotan, 6,000–7,000 feet elevation; Malay Peninsula.

42. LASTREA ANGUSTIFRONS. (*Moore.*) Rhizome wide-creeping; stipes 1–2 feet long, ebeneous, deciduously scaly; fronds 2 feet

by 6–8 inches, glabrous, elongate, 3-pinnate, pinnæ distant, erect-patent, flexuose, lanceolate, two inches broad; pinnules distant lanceolate, cut down to the rachis below into subquadrangular toothed segments (tertiary pinnæ) $\frac{1}{8}$ inch broad, texture subcoriaceous; rachis and both sides naked; veinlets forked; sori small, low down on the veins near the midrib of the pinnules. *Moore in Hook. Sp. Fil.* iv. p. 126. *Hook. Syn. Fil. p.* 283. *Bedd. F. B. I. t.* 226. L. splendens, var. β, *Hook. Sp. Fil.* 126.

Nepal, Sikkim (a little-known plant, perhaps abnormal Filix-mas or splendens).

43. LASTREA SCABROSA (*Kunze.*) Caudex stout, suboblique, densely paleaceous, stipes 1–3 feet long, densely paleaceous towards the base, scabrous above; fronds membranaceous, semitransparent, deltoid-ovate acuminate up to about 2 feet long, bipinnate, or subtripinnate above, tripinnate below, pinnæ alternate, distant 6–12 inches long, the lowest pair deltoid with some of the inferior basal secondary pinnæ enlarged to double the size of the others, which are generally $1\frac{1}{2}$–2 inches long and pinnatifid down to a winged rachis (or almost pinnate); the pinnules $\frac{1}{4}$–$\frac{1}{2}$ inch long, cut down one-third to half-way to the costa into more or less obtuse segments, veinlets prominent, one to each segment, simple or forked, terminating within the margin and clavate at the apex; costa and veins furnished with weak whitish

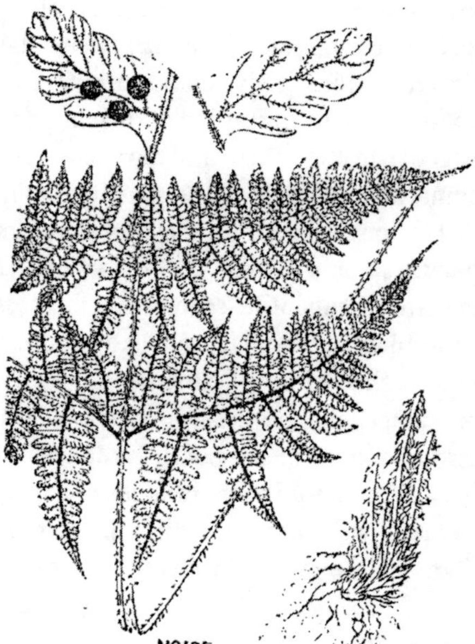

LASTREA SCABROSA. (*Kunze.*)

hairs on both sides; sori medial on the veinlets, one to each segment, becoming jet black when ripe, indusium (?) Aspidium scabrosum (*Kunze*), *Hook. Syn. Fil. p.* 283. Polypodium nigrocarpum, *Bedd. F. S. I. t.* 169.

Nilgiris, common in the sholas at the higher elevations, 6000–7,500 feet; in texture and habit the pinnæ much resemble those of Cystopteris setosa. I have never been able to detect any indusium even in the youngest stage, though I have long had it in cultivation; I suspect it is really a Phegopteris.

44. LASTREA FERRUGINEA. (*Bedd.*) Caudex short, stout, erect, stipes 1–1½ foot long, densely clothed throughout with broad-ovate very transparent scales and scabrous with tubercles; fronds 1–2 feet long, deltoid-ovate, tripinnate below, bipinnate tripinnatifid above, texture herbaceous, turning blackish when dried, pinnæ 8–10 inches long, spreading at a right angle, the lowest pair deltoid and larger than the others and more compound, its lower basal secondary pinnæ being elongated and pinnate, bipinnatifid; secondary pinnæ 1–2 inches long, pinnate in the lower and larger pinnæ, pinnatifid above, pinnules about ½ inch long, cut about half down into oblong rounded crenate or subentire segments; rachises and both sides ferruginous, with minute glandular scale-like pubescence, veinlets simple or forked, terminating within the margin and clavate at the apex, sori medial or subterminal on the veins, submarginal, one to each lobe of the tertiary pinnæ, in the South Indian plant confined to the upper lobes, in the Ceylon plant more lobes are seeded and the sori are not quite so marginal, indusium reniform, glabrous, persistent. *Bedd. F. S. I. t.* 100. *Hook. Syn. Fil.* 283. Lastrea obtusiloba (*Baker*), *Hook. Syn. Fil.* 284. *Bedd. F. S. I. t.* 296. Asp. Blumei, var.? *Thwaites, p.* 392.

South India, Nilgiris, rare in sholas between Avalanche and Sispara, 7,500 feet elevation, not observed elsewhere; Ceylon (C. P. 3142), about Newera Elya, 6,000 feet elevation. The Ceylon and South Indian plants are certainly the same; I had both in cultivation for a long time and could not have distinguished them except for the labels; it is nearly allied to scabrosa, but quite a different colour both living and dried, more ferruginous, and not scabrous.

Nº 136.

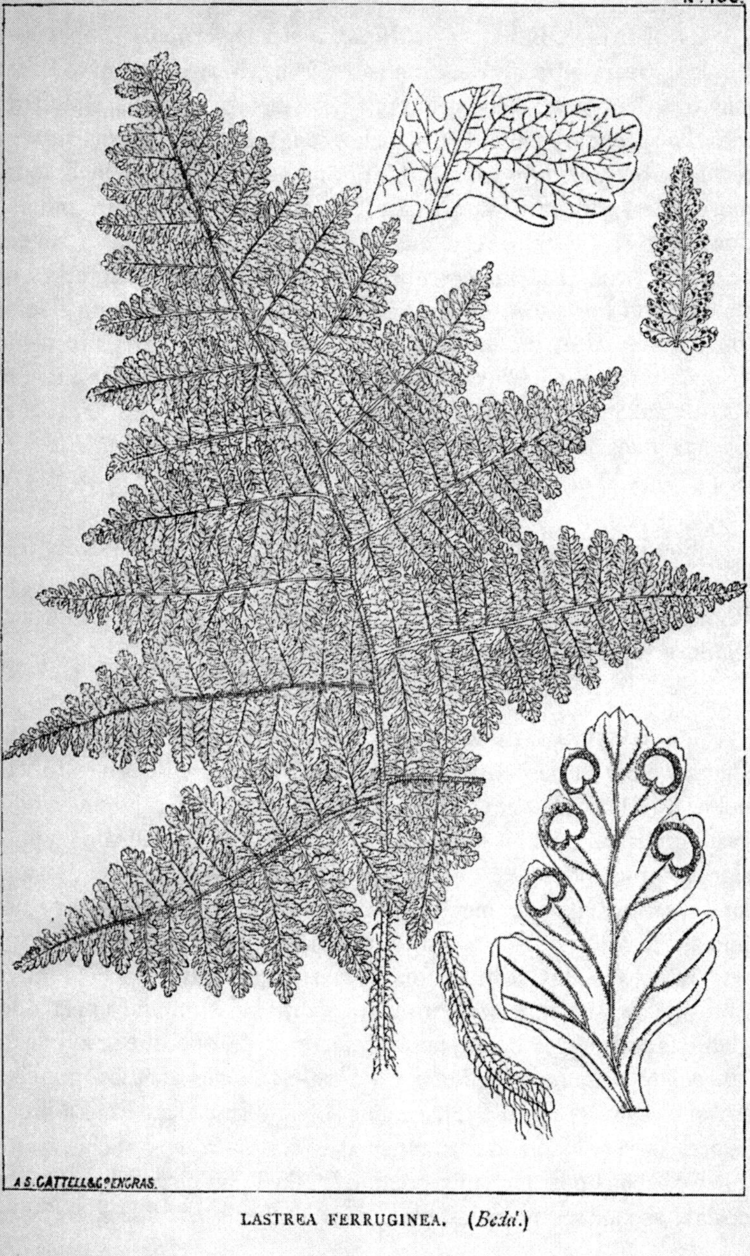

LASTREA FERRUGINEA. (*Bedd.*)

45. LASTREA BORYANA. (*Willd. under Aspidium.*) Stipes 2–3 feet long, sparingly scaly near the base; fronds very large, up to 8 feet long by 4 feet broad, herbaceous or almost membranaceous, bipinnate, with the secondary pinnæ ($3\frac{1}{2}$–6 inches long) pinnatifid down to a very regularly but narrowly winged midrib, pinnules blunt $\frac{1}{2}$–$\frac{3}{4}$ inch long, more or less wide apart at the base, pinnatifid about one-third or half-down into small entire segments; rachises and both surfaces naked, or with a little mealy pubescence and a few hairs; veins forked or simple; sori low down on the veins, in a single row on each side of the pinnules near the midrib, generally very small, large in some Himalayan examples, involucre often much lacerated on the margin, very fugacious. *Willd. Sp. Pl.* v. p. 285. *Baker, Syn. Fil.* 284. Lastrea divisa, *Hook. Sp. Fil.* iv. 133. *Wall. Cat.* 393. *Bedd. F. S. I. t.* 97. Polypodium subtripinnatum, *Clarke, F. N. I. p.* 545, *t.* 80, *fig.* 1.

South India, on the Western mountains, 3,000–7,500 feet elevation; Ceylon, central provinces; Himalayas, Gurwhal to Bhotan, 4,000–8,000 feet elevation; Khasya; Malay Peninsula. Clarke's variety microstegioides does not recede from the type.

(Also in Bourbon, Java, and China.)

46. LASTREA TENERICAULIS. (*Wallich under Polypodium.*) Caudex erect, furnished with numerous fibrous roots, stipes tufted, below a little scaly, above very glaucous, with a blueish bloom, which easily rubs off; rachis with a line of hairs on the sulcated upper side, glabrous beneath; fronds 1–3 feet and more long, broad ovate-lanceolate acuminate, membranaceous, bipinnate with the pinnules pinnatifid nearly to the costæ, pubescent with long white hairs on the costa and costules on both sides, rachis of the pinnules furnished with a very regular line of dense hairs on the upper side, glabrous and convex below, pinnæ rather remote, opposite or alternate, lanceolate acuminate, inferior ones 10–12 inches long by 3 inches broad; pinnules up to 2 inches long, oblong lanceolate from a broad adnate base (which is decurrent so as to form a winged rachis, particularly in the upper pinnæ), pinnatifid (in the lower pinnæ almost to the costa); secondary pinnules pinnatifid in the lower pinnæ, entire or

with the apex crenated in the upper portion of the frond; veins in the larger ultimate segments pinnate with veinlets simple, in the smaller segments veinlets once-forked only, all terminating a little within the margin; sori medial or terminal on the veinlets, 1–6 to each ultimate segment, involucre very deciduous. Polypodium tenericaule, *Wall. Cat.* 335. Lastrea flaccida, *Bedd. F. S. I. t.* 90. Polyp. Russellianum, *Wall. Cat.* 7077. Lastrea setigera, *Baker, Syn. Fil.* 284, *in part.*

Hooker's and Baker's descriptions of tenericaulis and setigera are made to include Phegopteris ornata, a very different fern. I have never been able to detect an indusium even in the youngest stage of our South Indian plant, and I should follow Wallich and include it in Phegopteris, only Mr. Clarke says it is present in the Bengal examples.

South India, on the Western mountains, 2,000–3,000 feet elevation, very common; Ceylon, 1,500–3,000 feet; North India, Himalays from no great elevation up to 4,000 feet; Malay Peninsula.

(Also in China, Australia, and Polynesia.)

GENUS LIV.—NEPHRODIUM. (*Schott.*)

(From *nephros*, a kidney; shape of indusium.)

Sori subglobose, dorsal on the veins; (often athyrioid in otaria) indusium reniform, sometimes wanting; veins pinnate, one or more pair anastomosing angularly with an excurrent veinlet from their junction which is either free or joined in the angle of the next superior pair; fronds always simply pinnate with pinnatifid pinnæ in the Indian species (rarely simple in species not Indian); caudex erect or creeping. Most of the supposed species of Goniopteris fall in here, as an indusium is often present in the very young stage though sometimes entirely absent.

1. NEPHRODIUM OTARIA. (*Kze.*) Rhizome creeping, stipes 6–12 inches long, pale-coloured; fronds 12–15 inches long, pinnate, lateral

pinnæ distant, 4–6 inches long, 1½ inch broad, linear-oblong, truncate at the base, caudate at the apex, coarsely but shallowly lobed, the lobes serrated; terminal pinna sometimes with larger lobes or auricles towards its base; texture thin herbaceous; rachis and surfaces smooth; veins pinnate in each lobe, 6–8 on each side, the lowest pair anastomosing angularly, with an excurrent vein which either runs out to the margin or occasionally joins one or even two of the superior veins (but the anastomosing is not so systematic as in the other species of the genus); sori medial on the veinlets, most of which are soriferous; fertile frond often contracted but not always; indusium reniform or often asplenioid and athyrioid. Aspidium otaria, *Kunze, Herb. Mett. Aspid. p.* 34. *Hook. Syn. Fil.* 288. Pleocnemia aristata, *Hook. Sp. Fil.* iv. 62. *Bedd. F. S. I. t.* 83. The sori are quite abnormal, the venation and position of the sori are not at all that of Pleocnemia.

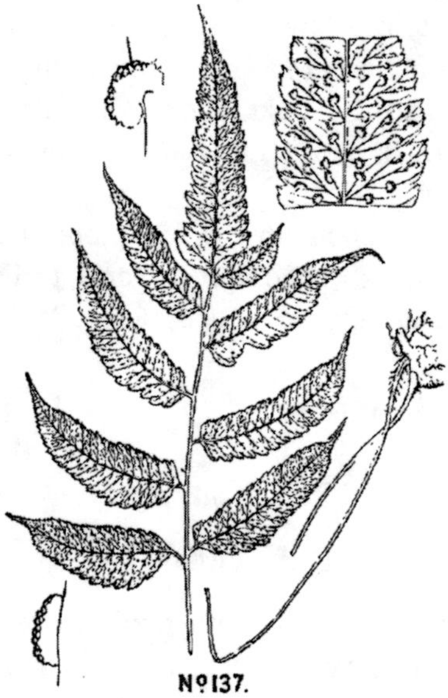

No. 137.

NEPHRODIUM OTARIA. (*Kze.*)

South India, Anamallay Hills, the dry teak forests, 1,000–3,000 feet elevation, appearing in the rainy season, Tinnevelly Hills and elsewhere on the Western ghats, but by no means general; Ceylon, 2,000–3,000 feet elevation.

(Also in Luzon.)

2. NEPHRODIUM UNITUM. (*Linn. under Polypodium.*) Rhizome creeping, stipes 1–1½ foot long, brownish naked; fronds about 2 feet long, pinnate, pinnæ numerous, 3–5 inches long, ½ inch broad, cut down about one-third, rarely more, into triangular acute entire or subentire lobes, lower pinnæ not reduced; texture coriaceous; veins pinnate in the lobes, 4–8 on each side, the lowest pair anastomose

angularly, with an excurrent veinlet which runs to the margin or joins one rarely two pair of the superior veins; upper surface glabrous, under surface generally very hairy; sori medial on the veins; indusium reniform, hairy. *R. Br. Prod. Fl. Nov. Holl.* 148. *Hook. Syn. Fil.* 289. Polypodium unitum, *Linn. Sp. Pl.* 1548, *in part.* N. propinquum, *Hook. Sp. Fil.* iv. 79. *Bedd. F. S. I. t.* 89.

Throughout the Indian region in swampy places and tanks.

(Also in Tropical Asia, Africa, Australia and America.)

3. NEPHRODIUM PTEROIDES. (*Retz. under Polypodium.*) Rhizome wide-creeping, stipes up to 2 feet long, slender, slightly scaly below; fronds up to 4 feet or rather more long and 2 feet broad, pinnate, pinnæ spreading ¾ to nearly 1 inch broad, apex acuminate, (lower ones not reduced), cut down only one-third, the lobes triangular, acute; texture herbaceous; rachis and upper surface nearly glabrous, under surface with minute glandular pubescence on all the veins, veins pinnate on the lobes, the lowest pair always anastomosing angularly with a free excurrent veinlet, the other veins, (7–9 pair,) always free; sori towards the apex of the upper veinlets always confined to the lobes or the apex of the lobes. Polypodium pteroides, (*Retz.*), *Hook. Syn. Fil.* 289. Nephr. terminans, *Wall. Cat.* 386. *Hook. Sp. Fil.* iv. 73. *Bedd. F. S. I. t.* 90.

Madras Presidency, Western mountains, 2,000–4,000 feet elevation; Ceylon, up to 3,000 feet; Birma; (not in N. India).

(Also in the Philippines.)

Very near extensum, but less cut, the anastomosis of the veins regular and the sori terminal.

4. NEPHRODIUM EXTENSUM. (*Bl.*) Rhizome creeping, stipes up to 2 feet, glabrous or slightly pubescent; fronds up to 4 feet long, and 1½ foot broad, pinnate; pinnæ about ¾ inch broad (lower ones not reduced), cut down two-thirds into linear oblong-falcate slightly crenulate lobes; texture herbaceous; rachis subglabrous, upper surface naked, or with a few distant hairs, under surface with minute glandular pubescence on the veins; veins pinnate in the lobes, 10–13 pair, the lowest pair anastomosing at an angle with a free excurrent

veinlet, or meeting just at the sinus without the excurrent veinlet, or the lowest pair is quite free (as in Lastrea), the other pairs always all free; sori towards the apex of the veins and present on all or all but the 1–2 lower ones, often much immersed and visible as punctiform dots on the upper surface. Asp. extensum, *Bl. En. Pl. Jav. Fil.* 156. *Hook. Syn. Fil.* 289, (*not Bedd. F. S. I. t.* 85, *which is large* molle). Asp. multijugum, *Wall. Cat.* 348, (*not* 355, *which is* truncatum). Nep. punctatum, *Bedd. F. B. I. t.* 131, (*not* punctatum, *Baker, Syn. Fil. p.* 513, *which is* Lastrea ochthodes, *vide specimen in Kew Herbarium.*)

South India, Tinnevelly Hills, rare; Ceylon, central provinces, 3,000–4,000 feet elevation; Birma, Penang, and Malay Peninsula (Khasya, 2 sheets of Griffiths in the Kew Herbarium, but not found by any one else in North India).

(Also in the Malay Islands.)

5. NEPHRODIUM MICROSORUM. (*Clarke.*) Rhizome wide creeping, stipes angled, furnished with linear-subulate long soft brown persistent scales towards the base, more or less softly pubescent as is the rachis; fronds about 2 feet long; pinnæ rather distant, sessile, about $4\frac{1}{2}$ inches long, by $\frac{7}{8}$ inches broad, the lower ones somewhat reduced or the stipe with auricles, deeply cut almost to the rachis into linear-oblong tongue-like entire or subentire segments, the upper and lower basal ones often considerably longer than the others; texture thinly herbaceous, both surfaces, especially the under one, furnished with scattered long white needle-like hairs; veins about 13 pairs, the lowest pair always regularly anastomosing at an acute angle very near the costa of the pinnæ with an excurrent vein, the other pairs always all free; sori minute, sometimes only near the costa of the pinnæ and scarcely extending to the lobes; involucre glabrous caducous. N. extensum, var. microsorum, *Clarke, F. N. I. t.* 530, and var. late-repens.

Sikkim up to 4,000 feet elevation, very abundant about Siligori, near the foot of the Darjeeling Pass.

6. NEPHRODIUM CUCULLATUM. (*Bl.*) Stipes about 1 foot

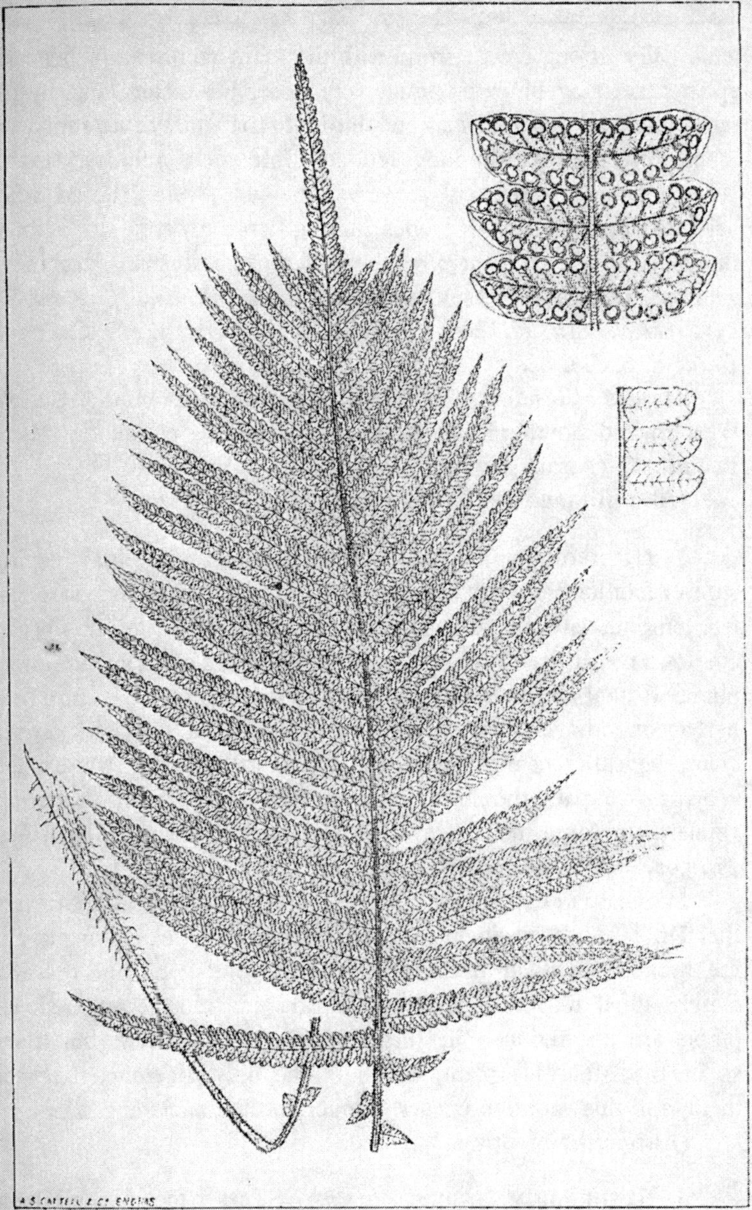

NEPHRODIUM CUCULLATUM. (*Bl.*)

long, hairy, strong erect; frond with the main rachis hairy beneath, up to 2 feet long, pinnate; pinnæ very close, 3–6 inches long, by $\frac{3}{8}$–$\frac{1}{2}$ inch broad, cut down scarcely one-third into triangular acute subfalcate lobes, lower pinnæ dwindling suddenly into mere auricles; texture very coriaceous, lower surface very pubescent; veins (raised when dry), 8–10 pair, 3–5 lower ones uniting; sori towards the apex of the veins, which are generally all soriferous; indusium prominent, glabrous, persistent. Aspidium cucullatum, *Bl. En. Pl. Jav. Fil.* 151. *Hook. Syn. Fil.* 290. N. unitum (*Sieber*), *Wall. Cat.* 358. *Bedd. F. S. I. t.* 88.

Madras Presidency, Western ghats, not common; Ceylon, Western and Southern provinces, marshy places, common; Malay Peninsula; (Assam doubtful.)

(Also in Mauritius, Malay Islands, and Polynesia.)

7. NEPHRODIUM ELATUM. (*Baker*) Rhizome wide-creeping, stipes 1 foot long, downy; rachis downy; fronds oblong lanceolate, 3–4 feet long, pinnate, pinnæ sessile, 9–15 inches long by 1–1$\frac{1}{2}$ inch broad, cut down nearly two-thirds into close rather falcate blunt lobes; lowest pinnæ distant and much reduced or not reduced at all, texture firm, herbaceous, above rachis of pinnæ strigose, and a few hairs on the veins, beneath costules and veins hairy, with longish white hairs, veins 13–16 pair, the lower 3–4 pair anastomosing with excurrent veinlets, sori large medial, involucre minute fugacious. *Baker, Syn. Fil.* 502. *Bedd. Fern. Sup. t.* 378.

Himalayas (Dr. Jerdon.) Mr. Clarke has stated in his Review that Dr. Jerdon's specimen is a Goniopteris, but on examining it with me, he acknowledged that it is unlike any Goniopteris, and that it is closely allied to, if not identical with, the Mauritius fern; the lower pinnæ are not reduced in Jerdon's specimen at Kew, but much so in the Mauritius plant, which is the only difference between them, and this variation occurs as much in others of the genus.

(Also in the Mauritius.)

8. NEPHRODIUM ARIDUM. (*Don.*) Stipes 1 foot or more long, erect, slightly pubescent; fronds 3–4 feet long 12–18 inches broad;

pinnæ rather distant, 6–9 inches long, $\frac{3}{4}$–1 inch broad, cut about one-third of the way down into subtriangular sharp pointed lobes; texture coriaceous; rachis and lower surface hairy; veinlets 8–10 on a side, 5–6 pair anastomose; sori in rows about midway between the midrib and edge; indusium naked, lower pinnæ reduced. Aspid. *Don. Prod. Fl. Nep. p.* 4. A. venulosum, *Wall. Cat.* 352, *type sheet.* A. obscurum, *Blume.* Neph. aridum, *Hook. Syn. Fil. p.* 291. *Bedd. F. B. I. t.* 297.

Throughout East Bengal abundant, from the Soonderbun to Assam and the Dehra Doon, up to 3,000 feet elevation.

Malay Peninsula (not in South India or Ceylon.)

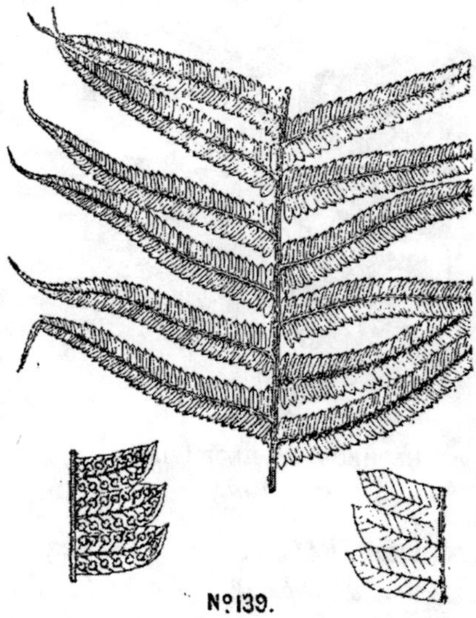

No. 139.

NEPHRODIUM ARIDUM. (*Don.*)

9. NEPHRODIUM GLANDULOSUM. (*Hook.*) Stipes approximate, main rachis closely villous, frond 1 foot long, adpressedly strigose on the upper surface; pinnæ truncate at the base, subentire, serrate or pinnatifid scarcely one-sixth the way to the midrib; veinlets beneath minutely hirsute, several pairs uniting, indusium reniform, elongate, prominent, firm; sori ultimately often confluent, *Hook. Sp. Fil.* iv. 76, *partly. Clarke, F. N. I. p.* 531, *t.* 74, *and fig.* 1. *Not Bedd. F. B. I. t.* 132, *which is* urophyllum.

The above is Mr. Clarke's diagnosis from Blume's specimens collected in Java, but there is an exactly similar specimen in the Kew Herbarium from Griffith, supposed to have been collected in Assam, but Mr. Clarke thinks it is probably from Malacca, but in either case it must be recorded in this work; it differs from the next in being strigose above, but I strongly suspect it is only a slight variety of it; it has glandular dots on the under surface, 6–7 pairs of veins, of which the four lower anastomose.

10. NEPHRODIUM UROPHYLLUM. (*Wall. under Polypodium.*) Rhizome short creeping; stipes approximate, 2 feet or more long, stout, erect, furnished with lanceolate-linear brown scales below; fronds up to about 4 feet long, pinnate; pinnæ narrow-oblong, subsessile or sessile, acuminate or caudate at the apex, 6–12 inches long by 1½–2 inches broad, the margin subentire, slightly crenated or with very short serratures; upper surface quite glabrous, or the rachis of the pinnæ a little strigose, under surface quite glabrous or with some minute pubescence on the veins, copious glabrous not glandular punctiform dots are present on both sides; texture subcoriaceous or herbaceous, veins 8–10 pair, rarely 14, all or nearly all anastomosing, the excurrent veinlets either free or joining the pair above; sori small, one to each vein, about its centre; indusium reniform, generally absent. *Wall. Cat.* 299. *Hook. Syn. Fil. p.* 314. Goniopteris, *Bedd. F. S. I. t.* 239. Nephrodium lineatum, *Presl. Epim. Bot. p.* 48. *Hook. Sp. Fil.* iv. 72. *Bedd. F. B. I. t.* 133. Asp. lineatum, *Bl. En. Fil. Jav.* 144, (*not Wall.*) Nephro. glandulosum, *Bedd. F. B. I. t.* 132, (*not Blume.*)

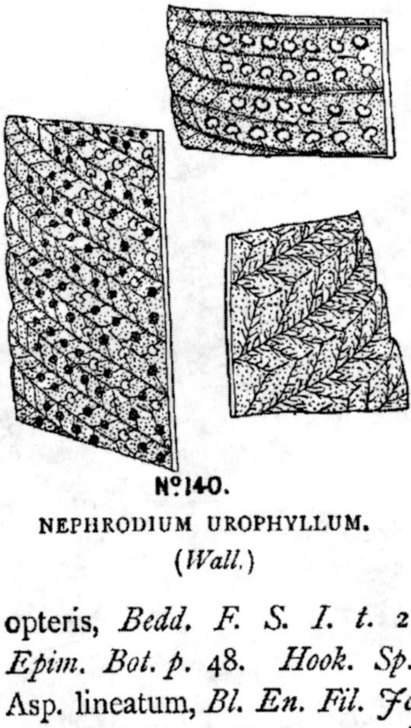

No. 140.

NEPHRODIUM UROPHYLLUM.

(*Wall.*)

Himalayas, from Gurwhal to Bhotan and Chittagong 1,000–5,000 feet elevation; Ceylon, Oodawella Forest; not in South India. There can be no doubt that this is a Nephrodium, and that involucres are often present, though Mr. Clarke has still kept it in Goniopteris. Sir W. Hooker described it both as a Nephrodium and as a Goniopteris.

(Also in Java and Philippines.)

11. NEPHRODIUM MOULMEINENSE. (*Bedd.*) Stipes firm, erect, 2 feet or more long; fronds up to 4 feet long, pinnate, pinnæ often with a large gland at base, numerous coriaceous, about 1 foot long and 1¼–1½ inch broad, narrow oblong, caudate at the apex, the margin with sharp serratures, which are falcate and only about one line deep, sometimes nearly obsolete or obscure, the frond being nearly entire, upper surface generally quite glabrous and shining, under surface with obscure hairs on the costa and veins; veins very prominent 16–21 pair, all but the upper 2–3 pair anastomosing with a zigzag excurrent veinlet united throughout; sori medial on the veins or often near their apex in a single row on each side of the costule; indusium reniform. *Bedd. F. Sup. p.* 18. Goniopteris lineata, *Bedd. F. B. I. t.* 3. G. multilineata, *Bedd. F. B. I. t.* 231, (not 232, Penangiana, *which is the next species*). Polypodium multilineatum (*Wall.*), *Hook. Syn. Fil.* 316. I have been obliged to rename this as it is a Nephrodium, and there is another Neph. multilineatum, *i. e.* Wallich's (our truncatum).

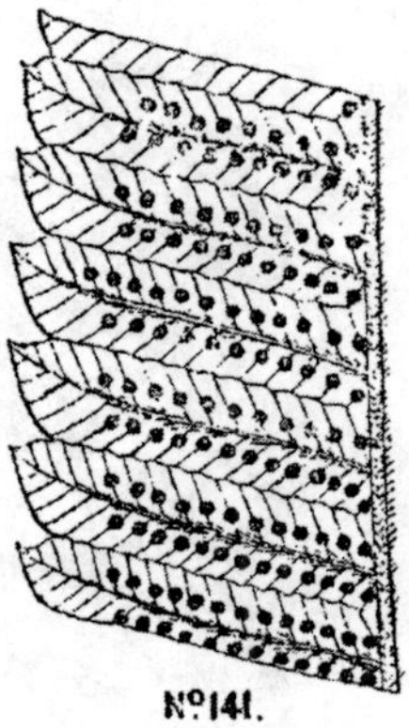

No. 141.

NEPHRODIUM MOULMEINENSE. (*Bedd.*)

South India, very common on the Golcondah Hills (west of Vizagapatam) 2,000–3,000 feet elevation, involucre distinct; (not on the Western mountains). Throughout North India, from the plains up to 5,000 feet elevation, very common; Birma, very common near Moulmein (involucre distinct); this differs from urophyllum in being more rigid in texture and in having many more veins.

12. NEPHRODIUM COSTATUM. (*Wall. under Polypodium.*) Stipes 1½ foot and more long, rather stout, scaleless, glossy, and as well as the rachis strongly tinged with red (rarely stramineous); fronds 1–3 feet long, broad-oblong or lanceolate coriaceous-submembranaceous pinnated glabrous, pinnæ numerous, rather distant, patent, sessile 5–8 inches long, ½ an inch or a little more broad (on sterile fronds sometimes exceeding an inch) from an obliquely cuneate truncate sessile

base (lower ones rather more attenuated and subpetiolate) lanceolate or elongate-oblong, finely acuminated at the apex, the margin coarsely and sharply submucronate-serrated, serratures pointing a little forward, uniform; costæ prominent beneath, of the same colour as the rachis and stipes, generally reddish, glabrous on both sides or obscurely hairy on the costa and veins beneath; veinlets about 6–8 pairs, of which all are connivent except 2–3 short pairs in the teeth of the serratures, sori in two series generally at the base of the veins close to the costules, but sometimes near the centre of the veins, involucres reniform, very fugacious and only to be detected on very young fronds. *Bedd. F. B. I. t.* 220. Polypodium costatum, (*Wall. Herb.*) *not Brack.* P. (Goniopteris) lineatum, *Coleb. in Herb. Wall. and Wall. Cat.* 300. *Hook. Sp. Fil.* v. 12. Polypodium penangianum, *Hook. Sp. Fil.* v. 13. *Bedd. F. B. I. t.* 232 (slightly broader in the pinnæ).

North India, Nepal to Kumaon at high elevations; specimens from Dr. Stuart (Gurwhal) have the involucre quite distinct; Penang.

Nº 142.

NEPHRODIUM ARBUSCULA. (*Desv.*)

13. NEPHRODIUM ARBUSCULA. (*Desv.*) Caudex small erect and trunk-like, stipes tufted, short, slightly pubescent; fronds 12–18 inches long, pinnate, lanceolate in outline, pinnæ numerous close, 2–3 inches long by about $\frac{3}{8}$ inch broad, very shortly petioled, rather blunt at the apex, generally auricled at the superior base, the margin with shallow serratures, lower ones gradually reduced to mere deltoid auricles; texture firm, herbaceous; veins 6–8 pair, the 3–4 lower pair

anastomosing, the upper ones free, rachis pubescent, upper surface glabrous in age, under surface more or less hairy on all the veins; sori solitary near the middle of the 3–4 lower veins, indusium small reniform. *Desv. Mém. Soc. Linn.* vi. *p.* 253. *Hook. Syn. Fil.* 292. *Bedd. F. S. I. t.* 87. Neph. falcilobum, var. pubera, *Clarke, F. N. I. p.* 515. *Wall. Cat.* 338, Asp. puberulum.

South India, Western forests, 2,000–4,000 feet, in beds of rivers; Ceylon, central provinces.

(Also in the Mascarene Islands.)

14. NEPHRODIUM PENNIGERUM. (*Bl.*) Caudex erect; stipes villous or subglabrous up to about 1 foot long; fronds large up to 4 feet long, pinnate, generally with the lower pinnæ more or less reduced, sometimes not so; pinnæ numerous, spreading 8–10 inches long, 1–1½ inch broad (the fertile sometimes much contracted), apex acuminate, margin cut down only about ¼ towards the rachis into oblong falcate lobes; texture herbaceous, rachis villous, upper surface strigose on the main costa, otherwise glabrous or often more or less strigose particularly near the margins, under surface villous on the veins; veins 8–12 pair, the 5–6 lower ones generally, rarely only 3, anastomosing; sori medial on the veins; involucre reniform, generally persistent Aspid. pennigerum, *Bl. En. Pl. Jav. Fil.* 153. *Hook. Syn. Fil.* 292. Neph. abruptum, *Bedd. F. S. I. t.* 86. Asp. multilineatum, *Wall. Cat.* 353. Neph. glandulosum, var. læte-strigosa, *Clarke, F. N. I. p.* 532. Neph. pennigerum var. multilineata, *Clarke. l. c. p.* 532. Neph. abortivum (*J. Sm.*), *Hook. Syn. Fil. p.* 292.

South India, common in all the Western mountain forests; Ceylon, central provinces, 2,000–4,000 feet; East Bengal, from Mishmee to Chittagong, at no great elevation. (Clarke's specimens of glandulosum var. læte-strigosa and pennigerum var. multilineata are quite the same as the South Indian plant.) Malay Peninsula.

(Also in the Malay Islands and Tropical Africa.)

15. NEPHRODIUM MOLLE. (*Desv.*) Rhizome tufted, or more rarely creeping; stipe and main rachis beneath pubescent, shortly

hairy or glabrous, with few or no scales; fronds oblong-lanceolate, 1–3 feet long, pinnate, pinnæ spreading generally about 4–6 inches long by ¾ inch broad, the lower ones generally more or less reduced, often into mere auricles, sometimes not reduced at all, generally cut down about half-way to the midrib into blunt subfalcate lobes; texture herbaceous, generally more or less pilose on both sides, sometimes glabrous or subglabrous, except in the costas and costules; veins 6–8 pair, pinnate in the lobes, the lowest pair (rarely two) anastomosing with an excurrent veinlet, involucres reniform glabrous or hairy. *Desv. Mém. Soc. Linn.* vi. 258. *Hook. Syn. Fil.* 293. *Bedd. F. S. I. t.* 84. *and* extensum, *t.* 85, *not Bl.* Polypodium parasiticum (*Linn.*) Asp. solutum, *Wall. Cat.* 350 *and* tectum, *Cat.* 394. Neph. didymosorum, *Bedd. F. B. I. t.* 200.

Throughout the Indian region from the plains up to 6,000 feet.

(Also throughout the world in tropical and subtropical regions.)

VAR. β AMBOINENSE. (*Presl.*) Fronds smaller, papyraceous, more glabrous, pinnæ smaller, less cut, being generally only slightly crenated or cut down about ⅛ to ¼, very gradually reduced towards the base, the lower ones often being hastate and very acuminate, veins 4–5 pairs, 2 rarely 3 lower pairs anastomosing; sori generally on 2–3 lower veins, sometimes confined to the lowest pair (didymosorous). Neph. amboinense, *Hook. Sp. Fil.* 292. Nephr. extensum, var. β minor, *Bedd. F. B. I. t.* 201. Evidently only a form of molle, sometimes confounded in herbaria with Arbuscula.

North India, Bengal, and Assam, near the foot of the hills; Ceylon, Ambagamoa. (*C. P.* 3390.)

NEPHRODIUM PROCURRENS is a name given by Baker (*Syn. Fil. p.* 290.) to molle with a creeping root, but there are no other characters to distinguish this form, as I have the very large form of molle with the lower pinnæ reduced to deltoid auricles (sent from Ceylon) with the root wide-creeping, as well as forms which have the fronds truncate at the base and no reduced lower pinnæ. (*Wall.* 349, 3rd sheet in this form.)

VAR. γ AUREUM. (*Clarke, F. N. I. p.* 533.) Differs by having the minute pubescence bright and golden, the fertile fronds longer than the barren, and the pinnæ sometimes contracted near the base; the frond truncate at the base, *i.e.*, the lower pinna not reduced. It is to be feared that none of these characters are permanent. It is a form from Sikkim and Bhotan, 1,000–4,000 feet elevation, and from Assam.

ASPIDIUM MULTIJUGUM. (*Wall. Cat.* 348.) Taken by Mr. Clarke in his type of *var. multijuga*, is typical *extensum* (*Bl.*)

VAR. DIDYMOSORUM. (*Parish*, *Bedd. F. B. I. t.* 200.) From Tenasserim; is a very hairy form of molle, lower pinnæ not at all reduced, sori twin, confined to the two lower veinlets (the latter character probably not constant.) *Wall. Cat.* 354, Asp. canescens, from Singapore, second sheet, is this plant.

Asp. tectum (*Wallich, Cat.* 394, in Linnæan Herb.) is a deltoid form of molle with no reduction of the lower pinnæ, and a creeping root.

16. NEPHRODIUM CRINIPES. (*Hook.*) Stipe up to 1½ foot long, stout, erect, clothed, as is the main rachis, with lanceolate-linear brown scales; fronds about 2–3 feet long, pinnate, dwarfed below into auricles; pinnæ horizontal, 4–6½ inches long, ½–¾ inch broad, cut down ½–¾ towards the midrib into oblong scarcely acute lobes, the upper basal one often somewhat enlarged; texture herbaceous; veins beneath minutely puberulous; costa, costules and veins sparingly furnished with longish hairs above; veins 6–8 on a side, the two lowest pair anastomosing; sori medial, but a little nearer the apex than the costule; indusium reniform glabrous persistent. *Hook. Syn. Fil.* 294. *Bedd. F. B. I. t.* 263.

North-east Bengal, up to 1,500 feet elevation, from Nepal to Assam and Chittagong; Malacca (Mr. Clarke's Nilgiri example is a portion of a contracted fertile frond of pennigerum.)

17. NEPHRODIUM FEROX. (*Moore.*) Stipe 1–2 feet long

strong, densely fibrillose, the hairs long black and leaving the stem rough when they fall; fronds 3–4 feet long, pinnate; pinnæ rather close spreading, up to 15 inches long, by $\frac{3}{4}$–$1\frac{3}{8}$ inches broad; apex very acuminate, cut down about one-third into lanceolate-falcate lobes; texture rigid coriaceous, both surfaces glossy; veins very prominent, 12–15 on each side, the lower (about 5) pairs anastomosing, the excurrent veinlet joined throughout and very prominent; sori basal on the veins close to the costule. *Hook. Syn. Fil.* 294. *Bedd. F. N. I. t.* 129.

Kumaon. (Mr. Clarke doubts the Himalayan locality, but there are specimens in Kew Herbarium supposed to have been collected there, and I received it from the Calcutta Herbarium as Himalayan.)

(Also in Java and the Philippines.)

18. NEPHRODIUM TRUNCATUM. (*Presl.*) Rhizome short, erect, stipes tufted stout erect up to 2 feet long, greyish naked or slightly pubescent; fronds pinnate up to 4 feet long, the lower pinnæ reduced often to mere auricles; rachis slightly pubescent or glabrous; pinnæ numerous up to 11 inches long by $1\frac{5}{8}$ inch broad, acuminate at the apex, sessile or subsessile and often somewhat contracted towards the base, cut down about half-way to the partial rachis into oblong lobes which are more or less square at the apex and crenated; texture herbaceous, upper surface generally glabrous, lower glabrous or slightly pubescent on the costa and veins, and sometimes with glandular dots; veins 6–9 pairs, generally the two, rarely 3–4 lower anastomose; sori small medial or nearer the costule than the margin; involucre reniform. *Presl. Tent. Pter.* 81. *Hook. Syn. Fil.* 294. Neph. eusorum (*Thw.*), *Bedd. F. S. I.* 130. Asp. prionophyllum, *Wall. Cat.* 355. Asp. multilineatum, *Wall. Cat.* 353, *from Singapore. Wall.* 352, *3rd sheet.*

South India, Tinnevelly and Travancore Hills; Ceylon, Central Provinces, 2,000–5,000 feet elevation; Cachar and Chittagong Hills at no elevation; Malay Peninsula.

(Also in Malay Islands, North Australia, and Polynesia.)

19. NEPHRODIUM BRACHYODON. (*Hook*) Stipes tufted, 1–2 feet long, greyish naked: fronds up to 3 feet long, pinnate; pinnæ petiolate, often contracted at base, 6–9 inches long, $1\frac{1}{2}$–$1\frac{3}{4}$ inches broad cut about one-third or half-way down into blunt slightly falcate lobes, lower pinnæ not much smaller than the others; texture sub-coriaceous; rachis naked or slightly pubescent, upper surface glabrous, except the partial rachis which is slightly hairy, under surface glabrous except the rachis and costules which are slightly hairy; veins 8–12, all free or the lower one anastomosing and with sometimes an excurrent veinlet, a single vein generally rises from the rachis of the pinnæ, between the pinnate groups of veins and runs to the margin; sori medial on the veins; involucre reniform. *Hook. Syn. Fil.*

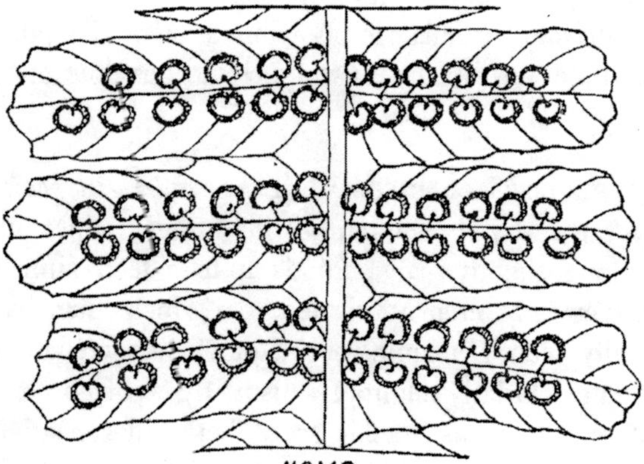

Nº 143.

NEPHRODIUM TRUNCATUM. (*Presl.*)

295. *Bedd. F. B. I.* 379. The lower pair of veins only occasionally anastomose in the Malay Peninsula plant, but in the West Indian plant several pairs generally join; the two plants, however, seem quite to run one into the other, and I am afraid they also connect Lastrea crassifolia.

Malacca and Malay Peninsula.
(Also in West Indies and Peru.)

Nephrodium multijugum (*Baker*), given as a Malay Peninsula

fern (*Syn. Fil.* 291) is, as far as the Kew specimen of Wall. Cat. 348 is concerned, Lastrea ochthodes. Aspidium multijugum, Wall. Cat. 348, in the Linnæan Herbarium is, however, Nephrodium extensum, typical, though referred by Clarke to molle as a variety. Nephrod. Hœnkianum (*Presl.*), given in Syn. Fil. p. 291, as a Ceylon fern, does not occur in that island or in our limits.

GENUS LV.—NEPHROLEPIS. (*Schott.*)

(*Nephros*, kidney; *lepis*, scale—the indusium kidney-shaped and scale-like.)

Sori round, arising from the apex of the upper branch of a vein, generally near the edge; indusium reniform or roundish; veins forked, free clavate; fronds simply pinnate with the pinnæ articulated at the base, furnished with white cretaceous dots on the upper surface.

1. NEPHROLEPIS CORDIFOLIA. (*Linn. under Polypodium.*) Caudex suberect, the wiry fibres often bearing tubers; stipes tufted, wiry, 1–4 inches long, slightly scaly; fronds up to 2 feet, pinnate; pinnæ numerous, crowded, often imbricated, 1–1$\frac{1}{4}$ inch long, by $\frac{1}{2}$–$\frac{5}{8}$ inch broad, usually blunt; margin entire or slightly crenate, the under side rounded or cordate, the upper distinctly auricled at the base; texture rather coriaceous; rachis scaly, both sides nearly glabrous; sori about half-way between the midrib and margin in a single row; indusium firm, persistent, lunate or reniform. Polypodium cordifolium, *L. Sp. Pl.* 1549. Nephrolepis tuberosa (*Presl.*), *Hook. Sp. Fil.* iv. 151. *Bedd. F. S. I. t.* 92.

Throughout the Indian region up to 5,000 feet elevation.

(Also in the tropics of the whole world, and in Japan and New Zealand.)

2. NEPHROLEPIS EXALTATA. (*Linn. under Polypodium.*) Rhizome suberect; stipes tufted, 4–6 inches long, firm, slightly scaly; fronds up to nearly 3 feet long, pinnate; pinnæ rather close,

No. 144.

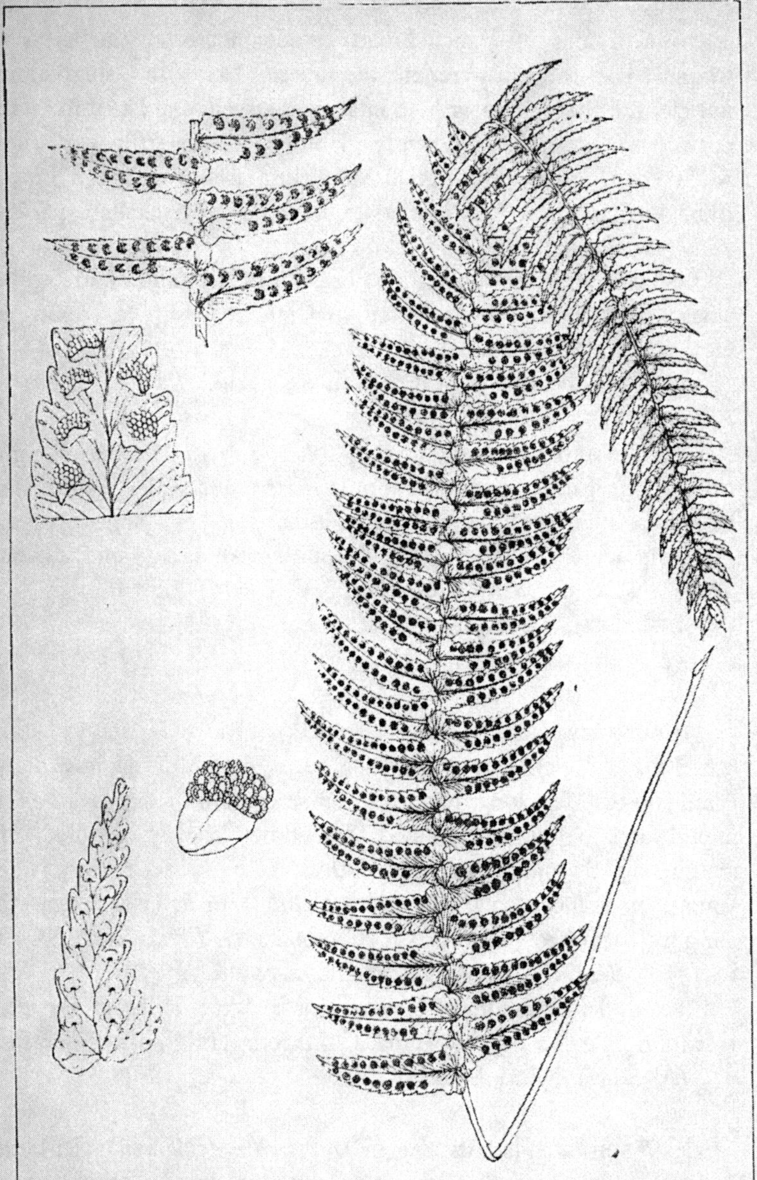

NEPHROLEPIS CORDIFOLIA. (*Linn.*)

2–3 inches long, $\frac{1}{4}$–$\frac{1}{2}$ inch broad, usually acute at the apex, the margin entire or slightly crenate, the superior base with a small narrow auricle, the lower base with a smaller rounded one; texture rather coriaceous, both surfaces nearly glabrous, or very scaly particularly when young; sori submarginal; indusium firm, reniform. Polypodium exaltatum, *L. Sp. Pl.* 1548. Nephrolepis exaltata (*Schott*), *Hook. Syn. Fil.* 301. *Bedd. F. S. I. t.* 93.

South India, the mountain forests of the Eastern and Western sides; East Bengal from Assam to Chittagong, up to 1,000 feet elevation; Ceylon; Malay Peninsula.

(Also in the tropics of nearly all the world.)

3. NEPHROLEPIS VOLUBILIS. (*J. Smith, MS.*) Rhizome climbing, up to 50 feet over trees, with adpressed chesnut scales on the short lateral distant spurs, whence spring clusters of stipes; pinnæ obtuse or not very acute; venation, sori, &c., as in exaltata. Aspid. exaltata, *Wall. Cat.* 1031, *partly*. *Clarke, F. N. I. p.* 541, *t.* 78.

Sylhet and Chittagong; Malacca.

(Also in Borneo.)

4. NEPHROLEPIS ACUTA. (*Presl.*) Rhizome short; stipes tufted up to 8 inches or more long, firm, naked or slightly scaly; fronds up to 8 feet long, pinnate; pinnæ up to 8 inches long and 1$\frac{3}{8}$ inch broad, oblong acuminated, sometimes shortly petioled, the margin slightly crenated; texture thin, both surfaces hairy when young, as is the rachis, but quite glabrous in age; sori near the margin; involucre reniform to suborbicular. *Presl. Hook. Sp. Fil.* iv. 153. *Bedd. F. S. I. t.* 94. Neph. biserrata (*Schott*).

South India, common on the North Arcot Hills, at no great elevation; Ceylon; North India, Chittagong Hills, up to 1,000 feet.

(Also in Tropical Africa.)

5. NEPHROLEPIS RAMOSA. (*Beauv. under Aspidium.*) Rhizome slender, wide-creeping; stipes very short, scattered; fronds up to 12 inches long, 1–3 inches broad, pinnate; pinnæ $\frac{1}{2}$–1$\frac{1}{2}$ inch long,

$\frac{1}{4}$–$\frac{1}{2}$ inch broad, slightly crenate, the upper edge auricled and truncate, parallel with the stem, the lower oblique; texture papyraceous, rachis villous, both surfaces slightly villous or glabrous in age; sori near the margin; involucre cordiform, roundish fugacious. *Beauv. in the Flore d'Oware. Hook. Syn. Fil.* 301. Neph. obliterata (*Hook*), *Bedd. F. S. I.* 251.

Ceylon, central provinces, 2,000–5,000 feet, climbing on trees; Malay Peninsula.

(Also in Tropical Africa; Philippines; Australia; Fiji.)

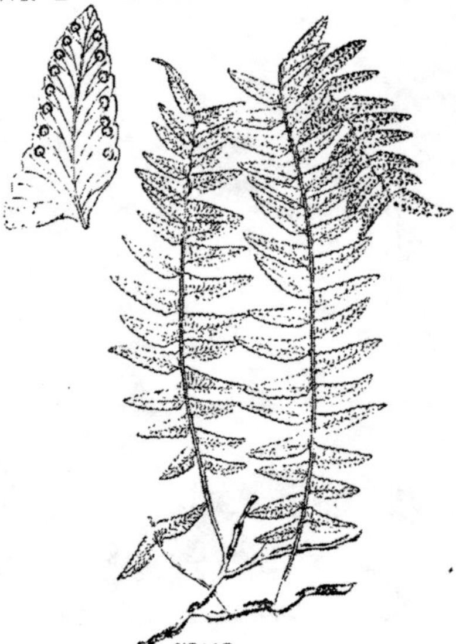

NEPHROLEPIS RAMOSA. (*Beauv.*)

GENUS LVI.—OLEANDRA. (*Cav.*)

(Resemblance to the Oleander.)

Sori round, inserted in a row near the base or below the centre of the compact free veinlets; involucre reniform; fronds entire lanceolate-elliptical, stems jointed, rhizome wide-creeping.

1. OLEANDRA NERIIFORMIS. (*Cav.*) Shoots woody, wide-creeping but often suberect, clothed with short adpressed scales which are often deciduous; stipes short, seldom 1 inch long, with the joint below the middle; fronds 4–8 inches long, $\frac{1}{2}$–1$\frac{1}{2}$ inch broad, in opposite pairs or often in terminal whorls, or more rarely scattered, from narrow-linear to oblong-acuminate; texture subcoriaceous, both sides glabrous or hairy underneath; sori in two rather irregular rows near the midrib. *Hook. Fil. Exot. t.* 58. *Syn. Fil.* 302. *Bedd. F. B. I. t.* 264.

Himalayas from Nepal eastwards; Khasya; 2,000–5,000 feet elevation.

(Also in Central America.)

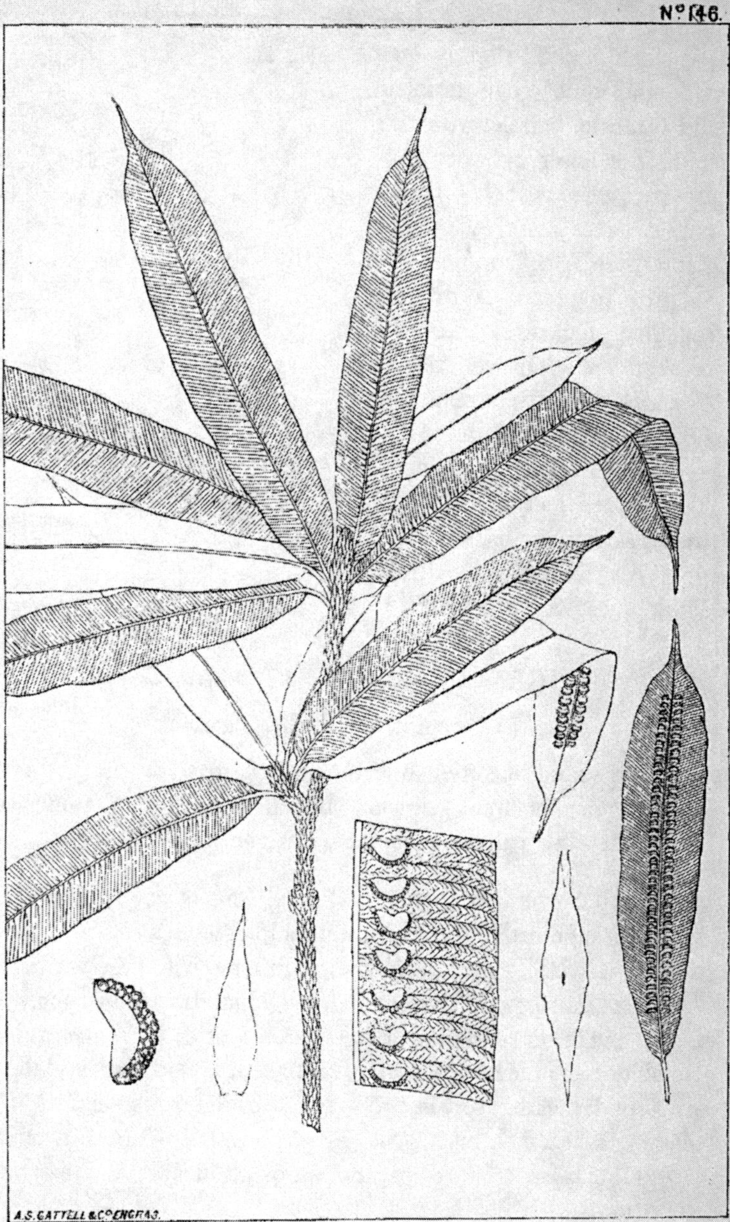

OLEANDRA NERIIFORMIS. (*Cav.*)

2. OLEANDRA MUSÆFOLIA. (*Kunze.*) Shoots firm, wide-creeping, clothed with long golden scales which are not deciduous; fronds generally single, scattered, or more rarely in tufts, 12–20 inches long, by about 1½ inch broad, narrow oblong acuminate on stipes which are 1–2 inches long and jointed close to the base; texture thin, a little hairy on both sides and the midrib scaly below; sori in two irregular rows near the midrib. *Mett. Fil. Ind. p.* 240. *Hook. Syn. Fil.* 302. Oleandra neriiformis, *Bedd. F. S. I.* 91.

South India on the Western mountains, particularly abundant in Coorg, rare elsewhere; Ceylon, central provinces. Mr. Clarke considers this species not distinct from the last; they appear to me as distinct as the others; all four, however, are so closely allied that they might be all considered varieties of one species.

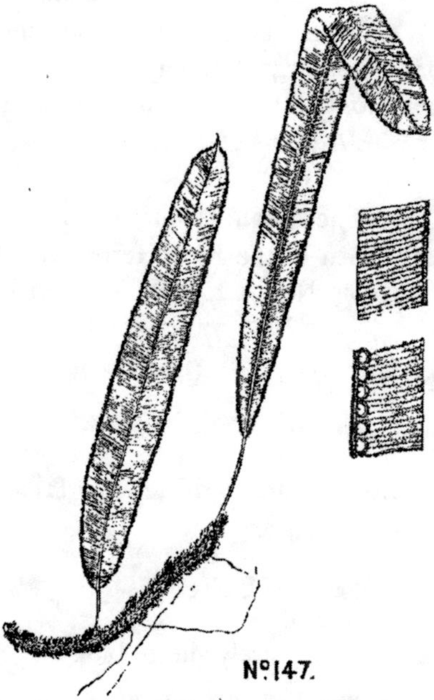

No. 147.

OLEANDRA WALLICHII. (*Presl.*)

3. OLEANDRA WALLICHII. (*Presl.*) Caudex creeping, rooting, thicker than a goose-quill, densely clothed with subulate crisped ferruginous, spreading and often reflexed scales thickly tufted at the extremity of the branches; stipes distant ½–3 inches long and sometimes paleaceous, jointed close to the base, so that the very short lower articulation is concealed among the scales; fronds 6–14 inches long, membranaceous soft, more or less hairy, subelliptical-oblong, the sides parallel, the base often obtuse and rounded, the apex suddenly and sharply acuminate; sori compact, almost imbricated in a continuous line close to and parallel with the costa on each side; involucres reniform, ciliated, opening towards the margin.

Presl. Tent. Pter. p. 78. *Hook. Sp. Fil.* iv. 158. Aspid. Wallichii, *Hook. Ex. Fl.* i. *p.* 6. *t.* 5. *Bedd. F. B. I. t.* 265.

Birma and the Malay Peninsula.

4. OLEANDRA CUMINGII. (*J. Sm.*) Caudex creeping, scarcely so thick as a writing pen, clothed with close-pressed subulate imbricated scales, stipes subterminal and subaggregated 2–7 inches long, slightly downy, articulated within ½–3 inches from the base; fronds 1–1½ foot long, firm membranaceous, elongate lanceolate acuminate, very much attenuated and gradually decurrent at the base, pubescent-villous on the costa and veins, sori rather large, forming a single and scarcely interrupted line very near to and on each side the costa. *J. Sm. in Hook. Jour. Bot.* iii. 413. *Hook. Sp. Fil.* iv. 158. *Bedd. F. B. I. t.* 135.

Birma and the Malay Peninsula. The Assam locality is doubted by Mr. Clarke, who thinks the specimen in the Kew Herbarium of Griffith's was collected at Malacca. The Nilgiri locality is an error, the specimen being musæfolia (*Kze*).

(Also in the Philippines and Canton.)

B. EXINVOLUCRATÆ. — Sori without an indusium. Tribes Polypodieæ to Acrosticheæ.

TRIBE X.—POLYPODIEÆ.

Sori on the back of the lobes, round or rarely short-oblong.

* *Desmobryoid series, habit and mode of growth of Aspidieæ, the stems continuous with the caudex; sori generally medial on the veins.*

GENUS LVII.—PHEGOPTERIS. (*Fée.*)

(*Phegos*, beech—the beech fern.)

Sori round, veins forked or pinnate, veinlets free; fronds from pinnate to decompound. Habit of Lastrea, and only differing from that genus in wanting an indusium.

1. PHEGOPTERIS SCOTTII. (*Bedd.*) Caudex suberect, stout tufted, clothed with brownish-black subulate scales as is the base of the stipe; fronds pinnate, oblong, with the stipe 10–12 inches long, by about 3 inches broad, rachis furnished with hair-like scales; pinnæ alternate 6–7 approximated pairs, with a terminal one, lower pair not much decreased in size, all short oblong or ovate obtuse from a square unequal base about $1\frac{1}{2}$ inches long, by a little less than 1 inch broad, and furnished with falcate acute serratures, glabrous on both sides, but with a few weak setæ or scales on the costa and veins, especially beneath; veins in pinnate groups, the lower veinlet or the two lower not reaching more than half-way to the margin, upper ones terminating in a dot within the margin; sori medial on the lower 2–3 veinlets. *Bedd. F. B. I. t.* 345.

Near Darjeeling, Valley of the Rungbee, 2,000 feet elevation (perhaps an abnormal form of Lastrea cuspidata or hirtipes).

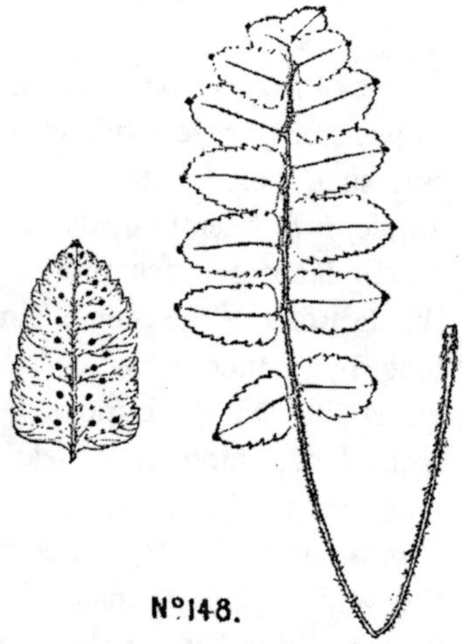

N°148.

PHEGOPTERIS SCOTTII. (*Bedd.*)

2. PHEGOPTERIS ERUBESCENS. (*Wall. under Polypodium.*) Stipes tufted 1–2 feet and more long, stout, as well as the rachis and costa more or less purplish-tawny, fronds in general ample but varying from 1 to 4 feet in length and from 6 inches to more than 2 feet in breadth, firm, sub-coriaceous, broad-ovate acuminate, pinnate, pinnæ 3–16 inches long, $\frac{1}{2}$–$1\frac{1}{2}$ inch wide, approximate, sessile, elongate-oblong, the sides parallel for a long way and then gradually acuminated to a serrated apex, deeply nearly to the costa pinnatifid, segments oblong, subfalcate, rather acute, entire or obscurely serrated, glabrous above, beneath sparingly furnished with longish white needle-like hairs on the rachis and costas and sometimes on the veins; veins approximate, simple free, two lowermost opposite pair meeting but scarcely uniting at the sinus,

soriferous always at the very base, so as to form two lines or series (at length confluent) one on each side and close to the costa, not extending to the apex of the segment; main rachis stout with a broad groove on the upper side (when dry.) *Wall. Cat. n.* 330. *Hook. Sp. Fil.* iv. 236. *Bedd. F. B. I. t.* 213. *Hook. Syn. Fil.* 306.

Himalayas, Kashmir to Bhotan, Khasya, 3,000–7,000 feet elevation; Malay Peninsula. It is very like Lastrea tylodes.

(Also in Malay Islands.)

3. PHEGOPTERIS AURICULATA. (*Wall. under Polypodium.*) Stipes stout, densely villous, with white matted hairs (as is the rachis), furnished below with numerous ovate black shining scales; fronds ample, firm, membranaceous, 3 feet and more long, 16 inches broad, oblong-lanceolate acuminate, generally gradually attenuated below by the dwarfing of the pinnæ, pinnated, pinnæ numerous, about 8 inches long by 1 inch broad, sessile and furnished at the base on the under side with a curious hooked gland, sometimes nearly quarter inch long, pinnatifid nearly to the rachis, segments broad oblong, very obtuse, entire, subfalcate, costa costules and veins villous, and the segments sparingly hairy on both sides between the veins; veins pinnate, simple, extending to the margin, lowest pair entering the margin above the sinus, soriferous below the middle, spore cases furnished with a few long weak hairs. Polypodium auriculatum, *Wall. Cat.* 314. *Hook. Syn. Fil.* 306. *Bedd. F. B. I. t.* 203.

Himalayas, from Gurwhal to Bhotan, 5,000–8,000 feet elevation, common about Darjeeling, Khasya, Myrung wood, 5,000 feet elevation. Polypodium appendiculatum, *Bedd. F. B. I.* 256, is only a state of this with the pinnæ not reduced at the base.

(Also in Java.)

4. PHEGOPTERIS VULGARIS. (*Mett.*) Rhizome slender creeping;

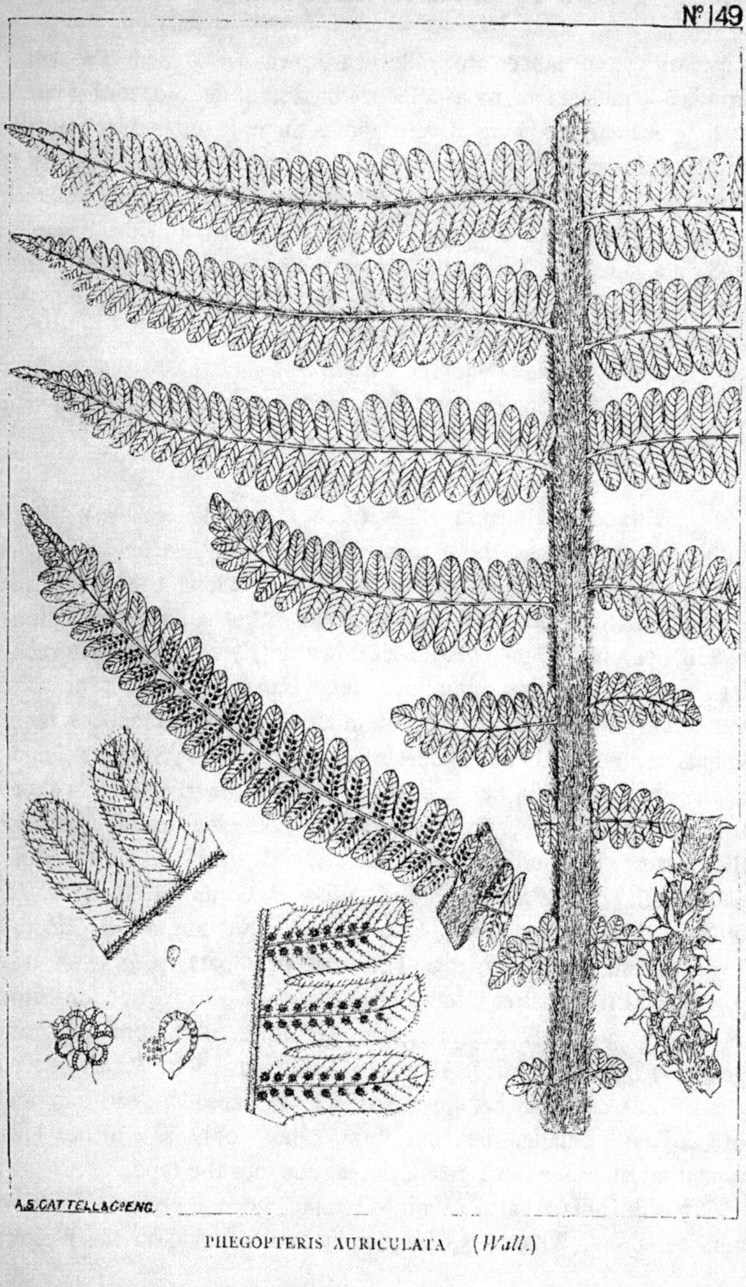

PHEGOPTERIS AURICULATA (*Wall.*)

stipe with large lanceolate yellowish-brown scales near the base fronds 6–9 inches long by 4–6 inches broad, subdeltoid, lowest pinnæ as long or nearly as long as any above them, main rachis beneath, with small ovate scales, pinnæ $\frac{1}{2}$–$\frac{3}{4}$ inch broad, cut down nearly to the main rachis, lobes oblong blunt or scarcely acute, entire or slightly crenate, $1\frac{1}{2}$–2 lines broad, more or less pilose on both sides; veinlets 6–8 on a side, the lower ones forked; sori nearer the margin than the midrib. *Mett. Fil. Hort. Lips.* 83. Polypodium Phegopteris, *Hook. Syn. Fil.* 308. *Clarke, F. N. I.* 544.

Cashmir, above Sonamurg, 11,000 feet elevation.

(Also in North Europe, Asia, and America; Caucasus and Japan.)

5. PHEGOPTERIS DISTANS. (*Don. under Polypodium.*) Stipe tufted, squamose near the base up to 2 feet long, yellowish or dark purplish-brown, glossy; fronds up to about 3 feet long, the lower pinnæ generally reduced and distant, sometimes not at all reduced, pinnæ 6–8 inches long, $1\frac{1}{2}$ inch broad, cut down nearly or quite to the rachis into deeply pinnatifid pinnules $\frac{1}{4}$ inch broad, with blunt or acute toothed or subentire lobes, the base dilated, texture herbaceous, rachis villous or rarely glabrous, undersurface a little hairy; veinlets pinnate in the ultimate lobes, pellucid; sori generally on the lower veinlets below the apex, or rarely apical, the veinlet not being continued beyond the sorus. Polypodium, *Don. Prod., Fl. Nep.* 2. Polypodium paludosum (*Bl.*), *Bedd. F. S. I. t.* 168. P. Griffithii, *Hook. Sp. Fil.* iv. 236. P. longipes, *Wall. Cat.* 316. P. adnatum, *Wall. Cat.* 328. P. brunneum, *Wall. Cat.* 333. This variety "adnata," *Clarke, F. N. I. p.* 544 (which is Lastrea microstegia, *Hook. Sp. Fil.* iv. 119 and *Bedd. F. B. I. t.* 39) only differs in being a little more compound and generally bipinnate, but it runs into the type. Var. "glabrata" of Clarke only differs in being somewhat more glabrous. Var. "minor" of Clarke is a smaller, less cut form, pinnæ only 1–2 inches long, pinnatifid only one-third down, but it runs into the type.

North India, from Kashmir to Bhotan, 3,000–8,000 feet elevation, very common; Khasya, 3,000–5,000; South India, on the Western mountains, 5,000–8,000 feet, very abundant; Ceylon; Malay Peninsula.

6. PHEGOPTERIS RUFESCENS. (*Blume, under Polypodium.*) Caudex creeping, furnished with appressed scales and wiry roots, stipe 8–16 inches long and together with the main and partial rachises slightly asperous; fronds 12–18 inches long by 9–12 inches broad, subdeltoid, subcoriaceous, puberulous beneath, with minute yellow hairs, bi-tripinnatifid, *i. e.* lower pair of pinnæ often bipinnatifid, upper ones pinnatifid, pinnules oblong obtuse, spinulose-serrate; veins pinnate, 3–4 on a side, veinlets simple or forked, reaching to the margin; sori medial on the veinlets. Polypodium, *Bl. Fil. Jav. p.* 194, *t.* 91. *Hook. Sp. Fil.* iv. 257. *Syn. Fil.* 309. *Bedd. F. S. I. t.* 236.

Ceylon, central provinces, 3,000–5,000 feet elevation.

(Also in Java, New Caledonia and Queensland.)

No. 150

PHEGOPTERIS RUFESCENS. (*Blume.*)

7. PHEGOPTERIS DRYOPTERIS. (*Linn. under Polypodium.*) Rhizome creeping; stipe with lanceolate subulate scales near the base; fronds 3–8 inches long and broad, deltoid, 3-pinnate, thin green, nearly glabrous, often glandulose, lower pinnæ largest, pinnules lanceolate, only the lowest free, oblong slightly crenate, texture thin herbaceous, rachis glabrous; veins pinnate in the lobes, veinlets forked or simple; sori submarginal a little below the apex of the veinlet. Polypodium Dryopteris, *Linn. Sp. Pl.* 1555. *Hook. Syn. Fil.* 309. *Bedd. F. B. I. t.* 74. Polypodium Robertianum, *Milde, Fil. Eur.* 99.

Kashmir, 7,000–11,000 feet elevation, and eastwards to Kumaon. (Also in Arctic and Alpine Europe, Asia and America.)

8. PHEGOPTERIS ORNATA. (*Wall. under Polypodium.*) Caudex erect; stipe, main and partial rachises with lanceolate-linear scales and muricate or scabrous from their persistent bases, not pilose, viscous or glaucous; fronds very large up to 15–20 feet long, tripinnate, except that there is a very regular wing to the rachis, pinnæ generally 2 feet or more long and about 1 foot broad, secondary pinnæ 1–2 inches broad,

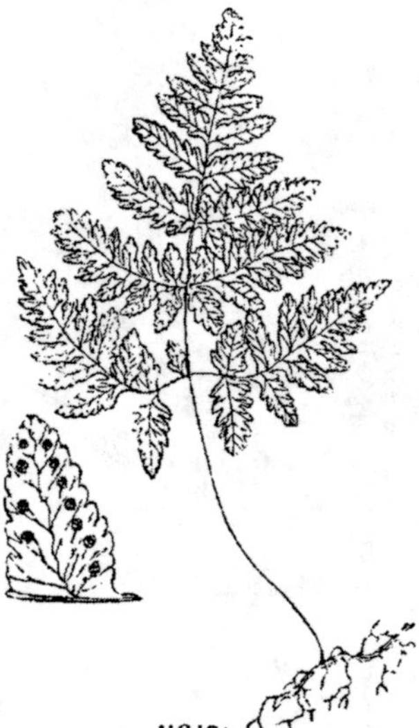

No. 151.

PHEGOPTERIS DRYOPTERIS. (*Linn.*)

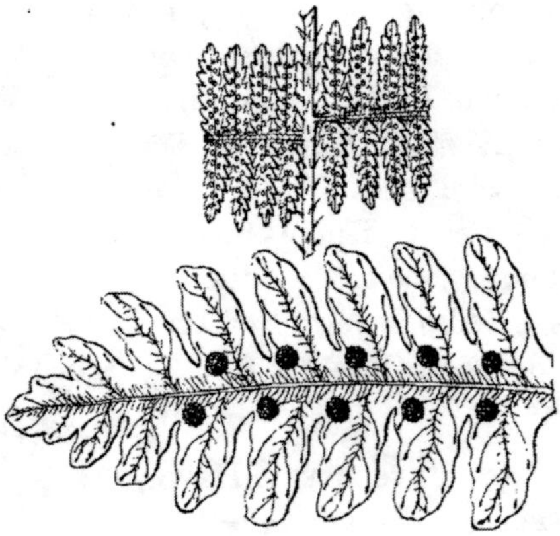

No. 152.

PHEGOPTERIS ORNATA. (*Wall.*)

their rachis also scabrous and scaly and furnished with long white needle-like hairs, tertiary pinnules up to $\frac{1}{4}$ inch broad, linear-oblong from a sessile square base, resting on the wing of the tertiary rachis, rather distant from each other, acute or blunt at the apex, deeply often nearly to the costa pinnatifid, the costa and often the veins furnished with needle-like hairs, texture thin herbaceous; veinlets simple or forked; sori medial. *Wall. Cat.* 327. *Bedd. F. S. I. t.* 171. Lastrea tenericaulis, *Hook. Sp. Fil.* iv. *t.* 269, *not the description which partly refers to* Lastrea tenericaulis. Phegopteris pallida (*Brack.*), *Hook. Sp. Fil.* iv. 266.

Himalayas, from Kumaon to Bhotan, in tropical valleys up to 2,000 feet elevation, common in Chittagong Hills, 500 feet elevation; South India, Carcoor ghat, Malabar and elsewhere along the Western ghats, but not common; Malay Peninsula.

One of the handsomest of Indian ferns, and much in cultivation, it may be a Lastrea (if Phegopteris is to be kept distinct from that genus, the propriety of which I doubt), but no one has yet detected an indusium, in any case it is quite distinct from Lastrea tenericaulis.

(Also in North Australia and Polynesia.)

9. PHEGOPTERIS PUNCTATA. (*Thunb. under Polypodium.*) Rhizome firm, wide-creeping, villous; stipes scattered 1–2 feet long and with the lower part of the main rachis more or less viscous-pubescent; fronds 1–4 feet long, tripinnate, pinnæ up to about 2 feet long, lanceolate to deltoid, secondary pinnæ 4–6 inches long, tertiary pinnæ sessile on the rachis, which is not winged, blunt at the apex, and pinnated two-thirds down into short rounded crenated lobes, more or less furnished on both sides with scurfy hair-like scales, the margins often somewhat reflexed, as in Hypolepis; sori copious towards the apex of the veinlets and near the margin. *Thunb. Fl. Jap.* 337. Phegopteris punctata, *Hook. Syn. Fil. p.* 312. Polypodium rugulosum, *Hook. Sp. Fil.* iv. 272. *Bedd. F. S. I. t.* 170. Polyp. rugulosum, *Labill. Fl. Nov. Hol.* ii. 92 *t.* 241. Hypolepis hostilis, *Presl.* (*as to the Nilgiri plant.*)

Himalayas, from Chumba to Bhotan and Chittagong, 1,000–5,000 feet elevation; South India, common on the Western mountains at the higher elevations; Ceylon, about Newera Elya; Malay Peninsula.

(Also almost throughout the tropics and south temperate zone, extending to Japan, New Zealand, St. Helena, and Chili; not from continental Africa.)

10 PHEGOPTERIS SUBDIGITATA. (*Blume, under Polypodium.*) Stipes tufted, firm, continuous with the rachis, furfuraceous, or

nearly naked; fronds very large, 3 feet or more long, broad lanceolate to deltoid, 3–4 pinnate, the rachis furfuraceous, pinnæ 8–10 inches long, often with clusters of viviparous buds in their axils, secondary pinnæ petiolate about 2 inches long; tertiary pinnæ petiolate $\frac{3}{8}$–$\frac{1}{2}$ inch long, pinnatifid, and generally pinnate at the base, the lower lobes incised, the upper ones generally entire, texture thin membranaceous, drying quite green, glabrous; veinlets forked or simple, pellucid, terminating well within the margin and clavate at the apex; sori small below the apex of the veinlet. Polypodium subdigitatum, *Bl. Fl. Jav. Fil.* 196. *t.* 93. *Bedd. F. B. I. t.* 229. *Hook. Syn. Fil. p.* 340. Phegopteris davallioides (Mett.), *Hook. Sp. Fil.* iv. 256. Polypodium coniifolium, *Wall. Cat.* 326.

Himalayas, from Nepal to Bhotan, 6,000–9,000 feet elevation, common; Malay Peninsula.

(Also in the Malay Islands.)

GENUS. LVIII.—GONIOPTERIS. (*Presl.*)

(*Gonia*, angle; *pteris*, fern—the veinlets meeting and forming angles.)

Habit and venation of Nephrodium, *i.e.*, veins pinnate, the lowest or several pairs of veinlets of contiguous groups anastomosing at an angle from which proceeds an excurrent veinlet; stipes continuous with the rhizome; fronds pinnate, in fact, all the characters as in Nephrodium, except that there is no indusium to the sorus.

All the supposed Indian species except the following have been proved to possess an indusium in a young stage or under certain conditions, so that they have been transferred to Nephrodium, the following species deviates somewhat from the habit of Nephrodium in its elongated proliferous non-seeding fronds, and in being often copiously branched from the axils, the sori are often those of Meniscium rather than Goniopteris.

1. GONIOPTERIS PROLIFERA. (*Roxb.*) Rhizome stout, wide-creeping; fronds 1–2 feet long, pinnate, often flagelliform and much elongated but then non-seeding, with pinnæ more or less dwarfed and rooting from the apex or some of its axils, often also

No. 153.

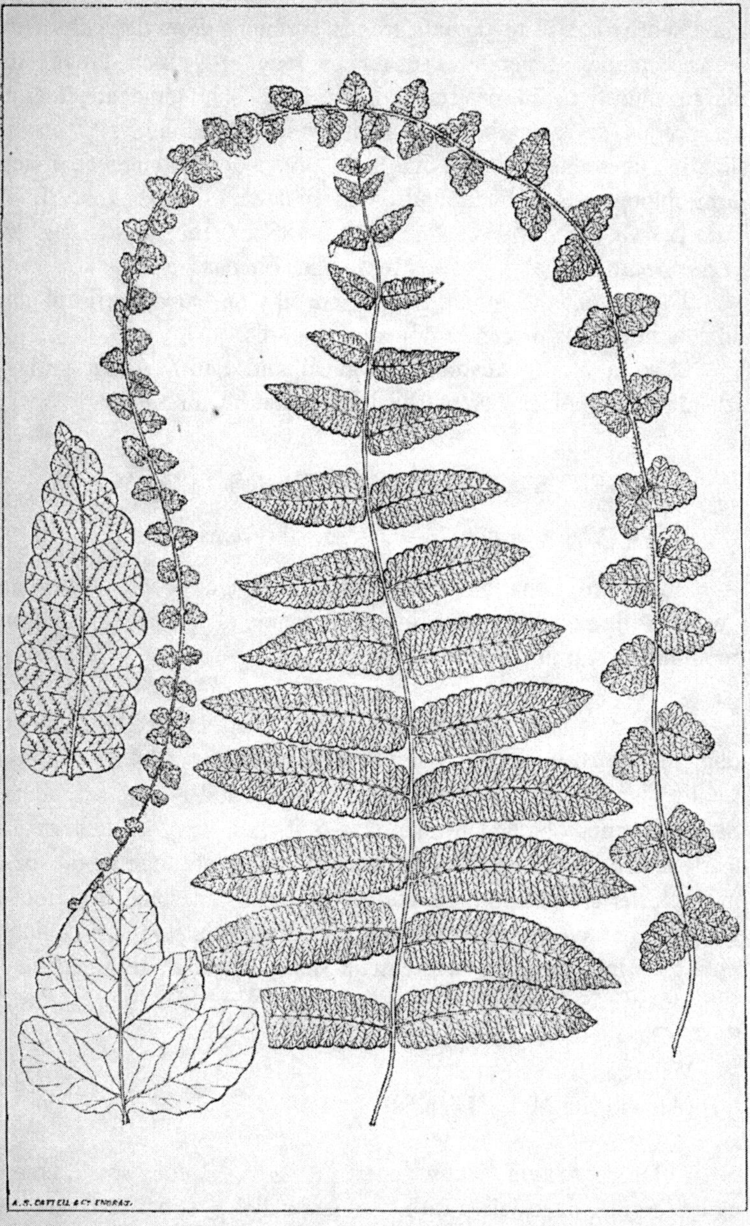

A. S. CATTELL & Co. ENGRAV.

GONIOPTERIS PROLIFERA. (*Roxb.*)

branched by complete pinnate fronds springing from the axils of the pinnæ, pinnæ generally 4–6 inches long, ½–¾ inch broad, the margin bluntly lobed or crenated, the apex blunt or acute, texture herbaceous or subcoriaceous, rachis and under side glabrous or slightly pubescent; veinlets fine, 6–10 on a side; sori medial, punctiform oblong or even linear and often confluent in age. *Roxb. Wall. Cat.* 312, *in Calc. Journ. Nat. Hist.* iv. 489. *t.* 32. *Hook. Syn. Fil.* 315. *Bedd. F. S. I. t.* 172. Meniscium, *Swartz.*

Throughout the Indian region generally on banks of rivers and ditches in the plains or low down on the hills.

(Also in North Australia, Tropical and South Africa and its Islands; Philippines; New Caledonia; South China.)

GENUS LIX.—DICTYOPTERIS. (*Presl.*).

(*Diktyon*, a net; *pteris*, fern—the veins netted.)

Habit and venation of Aspidium, *i.e.*, veins copiously anastomosing with or without free included veinlets, only differing from Aspidium in wanting an indusium.

1. DICTYOPTERIS BARBERI. (*Hook.*) Stipes tufted, 6–12 inches long, slightly scaly at the base; fronds palmately 5-lobed or more usually pinnate with a large terminal segment and 1–4 pairs of pinnæ, the upper ones oblong-lanceolate, 4–6 inches long, 1 inch broad, nearly entire, the lowest pair with a deep lanceolate lobe at the base on the lower side, texture subcoriaceous, both sides naked; areoles rather large and regular, with copious free veinlets; sori copious, principally in two rows near the main veins, dorsal or terminal on a vein or veinlet. *Hook. Sp.* v. *p.* 100. *Syn. Fil.* 317. *Bedd. F. B. I. t.* 322.

Malacca.

(Also in the Malay Islands.)

2. DICTYOPTERIS TENERIFRONS. (*Hook.*) Caudex small, creeping underground, scaleless with very few radicles, stipes few, remote,

slender, glossy, stramineous, the base very tomentose with a few sparse scales partly subterraneous, attached to the caudex by a small point; fronds thin, membranaceous pale-green, glabrous, subpuberulous on the veins, 6–9 inches long, quite as broad as long, cordate-deltoid, subternate or pinnated with 3–9 subfalcate pinnæ, lateral ones nearly opposite, petiolate, lowest pair half ovate, acuminate, 4–6 inches long, lobate-pinnatifid, those of the superior margin with broad ovate nearly equal subdenticulate blunt lobes, the inferior ones much elongated and acuminated, the basal ones again lobate pinnatifid, intermediate pinnæ ovate-lanceolate, pinnatifid, terminal pinna long petiolate, broad-ovate acuminate, deeply pinnatifid especially at the base; veinlets uniformly reticulated, areoles with no included free veinlets, costular areoles large; sori rather irregularly scattered, dorsal or compital. *Hook. Sp. Fil.* v. 104. *Bed. F. B. I. t.* 4.

Moulmein; very like small specimens of Aspidium cicatarium in habit and outline, but there are no free veins, and the sori are more scattered and larger, and show no signs of an indusium.

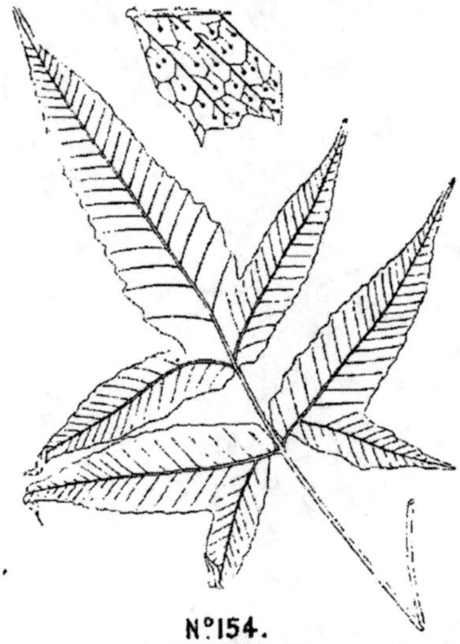

No. 154.
DICTYOPTERIS BARBERI. (*Hook.*)

3. DICTYOPTERIS CHATTAGRAMICA. (*Clarke.*) Rhizome short, stout; stipes 10–12 inches long, tufted, long, black with small scales near the base; fronds deltoid, distinctly dimorphic, pinnate below, pinnatifid upwards about 10–12 inches long by 6–7 inches broad, lower pinnæ deltoid with the lower basal lobes much enlarged, margins pinnatifid, surfaces pubescent, the margin with minute golden multicellular hairs; sori naked, medial or terminal on the veins. *Clarke, F. N. I. p.* 548, *t.* 81.

Chittagong at no elevation, very general.

4. DICTYOPTERIS DIFFORMIS. (*Bl. under Polypodium.*) Caudex stout ascending, stipes tufted, 4 inches to 1½ foot in length, black setaceous-paleaceous at the base; fronds subcoriaceous, minutely pellucid-punctulate glabrous, often subglaucous beneath, pinnate with very numerous pinnæ, from 6 inches to a foot long, 1–3 inches wide, more or less petiolate, broad-oblong, acuminated, the lowest pair half-ovate, unequally bipartite, lowest segments deflexed and sometimes free, and 5–6 inches long, all of them more or less deeply lobed, often to within one-third of the costa, the lobes oblong, acute, or acuminate entire or sinuate-lobate, terminal pinna petiolate pinnatifid, costule one to each lobe, the veins anastomose copiously, forming elongated areoles, which are longest near the costæ and costules, areoles frequently including a free veinlet; sori dorsal or compital, or rarely terminal on the free veins, copious but rarely approaching the costa. Polypodium difforme, *Bl. Fil. Jav.* 135. *Hook. Syn. Fil.* 318. Dictyopteris irregularis (*Presl.*), *Hook. Sp. Fil.* v. 101. *Bl. Fil. Jav.* 164, *t.* 72. *Bedd. F. B. I. t.* 77. Polypodium confluens, *Wall. Cat.* 325.

No. 155.
DICTYOPTERIS CHATTAGRAMICA. (*Clarke.*)

The Malay Peninsula, Tenasserim, Malacca.

(Also in the Malay Islands.)

5. DICTYOPTERIS POLYCARPA. (*Mett. under Phegopteris.*) Stipe 6 inches long, reddish yellow, slightly pilose upwards; frond deltoid bipinnatifid, 6–15 inches long, pinnæ 6 pairs, lowest largest deltoid unequal sided, stalked tripartite, central ligulate acuminate crenate,

No. 156

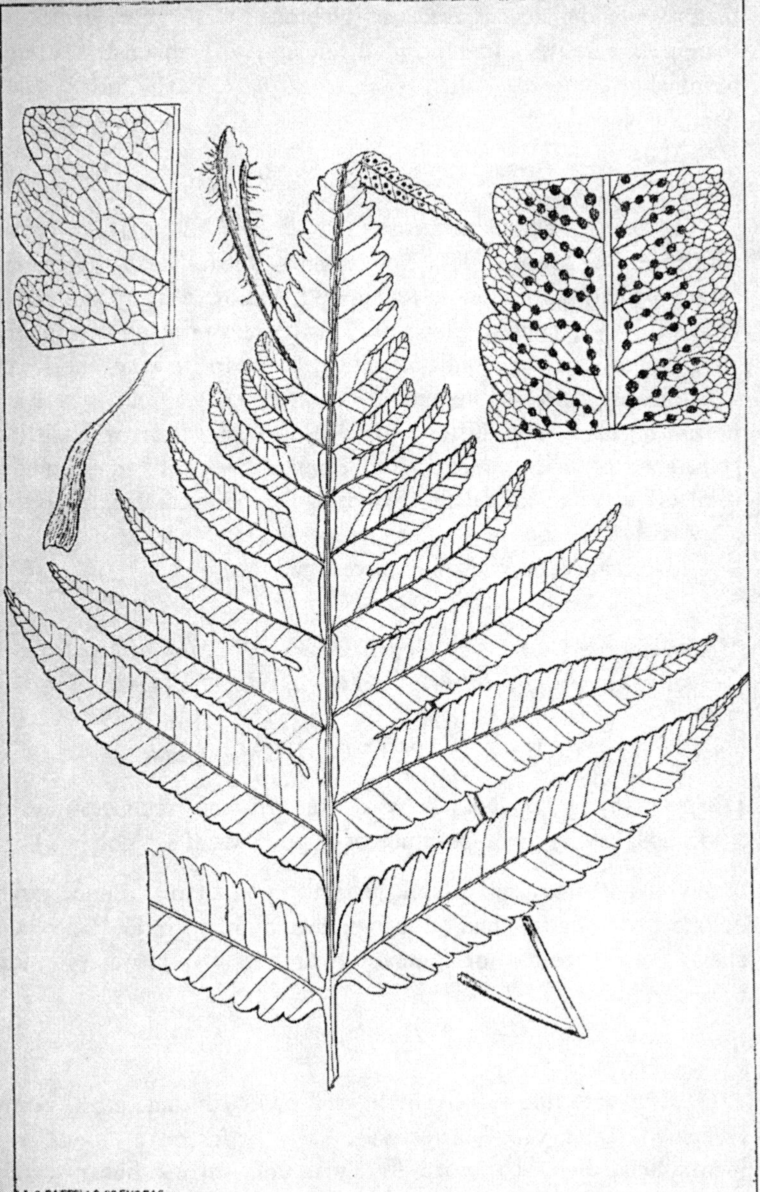

A. S. CATTELL & Co ENGRAS.

DICTYOPTERIS DIFFORMIS. (*Bl.*)

texture membranaceous, surfaces glabrous; main veins distinct to margin; areoles with free included veinlets; sori copiously scattered, terminal or compital. *Mett. Kuhn. Lin.* 36, *p.* 124. *Baker, Hook. Syn. Fil.* 506.

Malacca.

6. DICTYOPTERIS HETEROSORA. (*Baker.*) Stipe short brown, with spreading linear scales; fronds oblong-spathulate, 2–3 feet long, simply pinnatifid, the lowest foot only a narrow wing to the rachis, above this 3–4 pairs of distant oblong-lanceolate acuminate pinnæ, 1½–2 inches broad at middle, confluent in a narrow wing, the lowest simple or bipartite, texture thin but firm, surfaces glabrous, ribs naked brownish; main veins distinct to edge, 3–4 lines apart with distinct arches between them, and copious small areoles with free included veinlets; sori very abundant, small irregular, often confluent. *Baker, Hook. Syn. Fil.* 506.

Malacca, (habit of Aspidium vastum.)

** *Eremobryoid series. Stems articulated at the point of junction with the rhizome; sori generally, not always, terminal on the veins.*

GENUS LX.—POLYPODIUM. (*Linn.*)

(*Polys*, many; *pous*, foot; *polypus*,—the rhizome when destitute of fronds, having the appearance of some kinds of sea polypus.)

Veins all free; sori naked, generally punctiform, round, rarely oblong, generally terminal on the veinlets, or more rarely below the apex; fronds simple or pinnatifid or rarely pinnate or more compound.

* *Fronds entire.*

1. POLYPODIUM PARASITICUM. (*Mett.*) Rhizome erect, rarely creeping; stipes tufted, subsessile, hairy or fuscous, fronds 2–3 inches long, ¼–⅜ inch broad (rarely more), narrow linear (rarely abnormally pinnatifid), blunt at the apex, gradually narrowed at the

base, the margin entire or slightly undulated, texture herbaceous to subcoriaceous, both sides more or less clothed with long hairs; veins more or less immersed, forked; sori often mixed with copious hairs, round or linear, at the apex of the superior veinlet forming a single row on each side of the costa. *Hook. Syn. Fil. p.* 319. *Bedd. F. S. I. t.* 165. P. mediale (*Baker*), *Hook. Syn. Fil. p.* 507.

South India, common on the Nilgiris and other Western mountains at the highest elevations; Ceylon. (This includes P. mediale of Baker, the sori often being linear and globose on different fronds of the same plant, as in my figure quoted above). Mr. Wall sends some specimens from Ceylon with a creeping root, but I never saw it creeping in the Nilgiri plant.

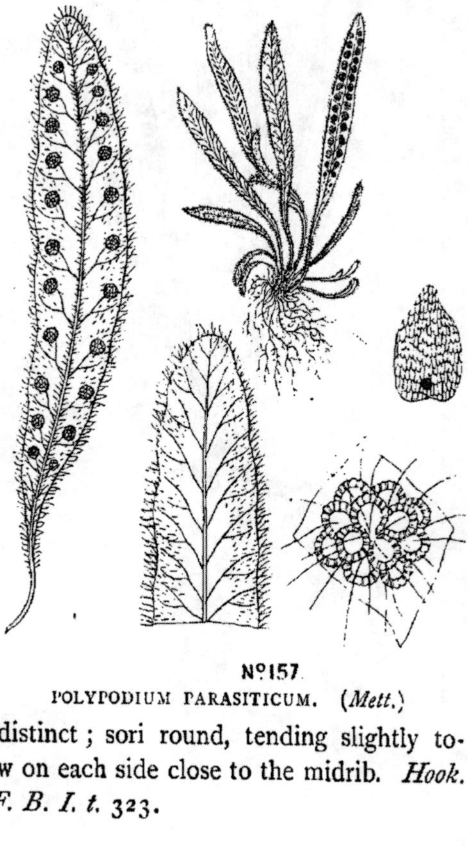

No. 157.
POLYPODIUM PARASITICUM. (*Mett.*)

2. POLYPODIUM SUBEVENOSUM. (*Baker.*) Stipes tufted, very short, black wiry; fronds 3–4 inches long, ⅛ inch broad, ligulate, the point bluntish, the lower part narrowed very gradually, the edge slightly repand, texture subcoriaceous, colour bright green, the rachis black, slightly furfuraceous below; veins simple, very short and indistinct; sori round, tending slightly towards oblong, in a long row on each side close to the midrib. *Hook. Syn. Fil. p.* 320. *Bedd. F. B. I. t.* 323.

Penang.

3. POLYPODIUM ZEYLANICUM. (*Mett.*) Rhizome strong, wide-

No. 158

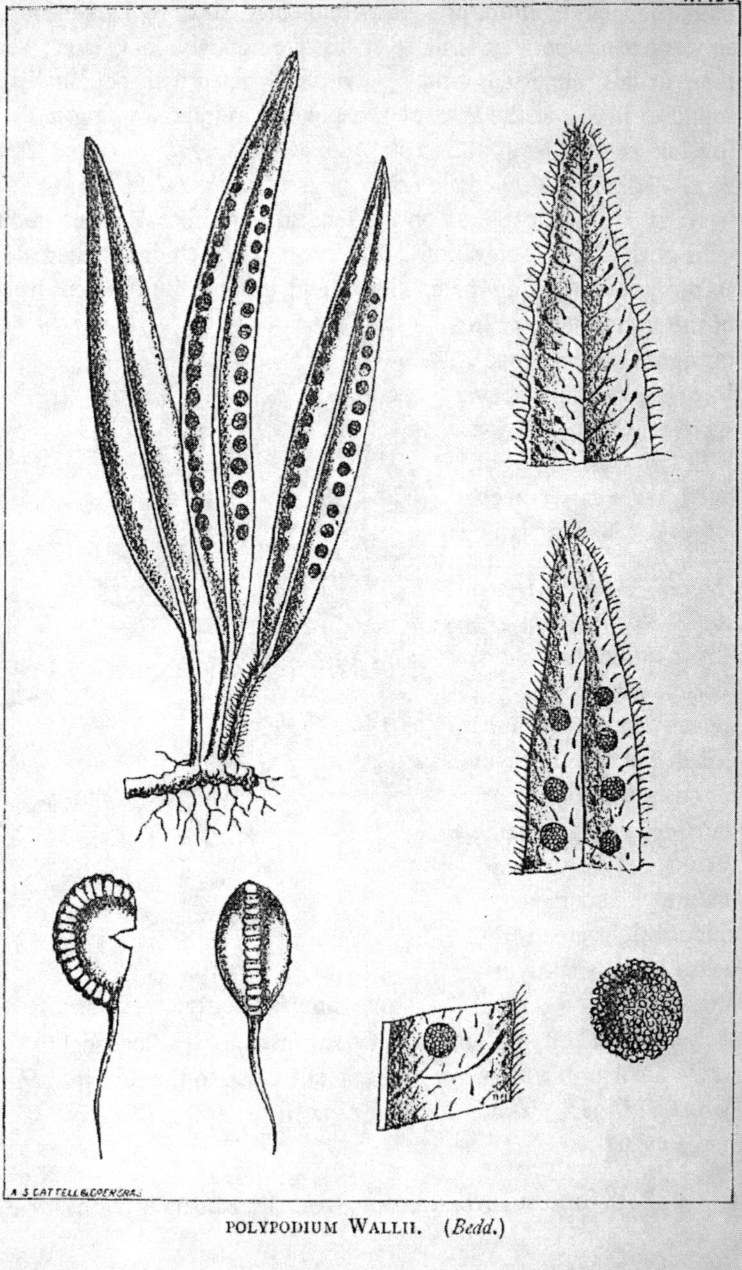

POLYPODIUM WALLII. (*Bedd.*)

creeping, clothed with broad grey scales; stipe 1 inch or more long, clothed with soft spreading hairs; fronds 8–12 inches long, $\frac{1}{4}$–$\frac{3}{8}$ inch broad, acuminate, the base narrowed very gradually, the margins slightly undulated; texture subcoriaceous, both sides naked; veins forked oblique, rarely simple; sori round, at the apex of the upper veinlet, or at the apex of the vein when simple, forming a single row on each side of the costa. *Hook. Syn. Fil.* 321. *Bedd. F. S. I. t.* 237.

Ceylon, Newera Elya, on rocks and trees.

4. POLYPODIUM WALLII. (*Bedd.*) Rhizome creeping, scaly, furnished with numerous thick black wiry roots; stipes 3–6 lines long, scaly and hairy; fronds linear-lanceolate with a blunt apex 3 inches long by $\frac{1}{2}$ inch broad, thick, coriaceous, the veins quite hidden, more or less clothed on both sides and on the margins with delicate black hairs; veins thick, forked (or simple towards the apex of the frond); sori large, round, terminal on the superior veinlet and forming a regular row on each side about midway between the costa and the margin. *Bedd. Fern Sup. t.* 380. Polypodium parasiticum, var. pilosiusculum, *Thw. MS. C. P.* 3921.

Ceylon, Adam's Peak; allied to parasiticum, but much larger and of much thicker texture.

5. POLYPODIUM HIRTELLUM. (*Bl.*) Caudex small ascending, scaly above; stipes tufted $\frac{1}{2}$–$1\frac{1}{2}$ inch long, slender, filiform, villous, with spreading reddish-brown hairs, fronds firm-membranaceous, linear-oblong to lanceolate, 1–4 or more inches long, $\frac{1}{8}$–$\frac{1}{3}$ of an inch broad, quite entire at the margin, attenuated at the base, rather densely villous and ciliated with similar hairs to those of the stipes; veins spreading, simple or often forked near the base; sori in a single regular series close to the costa; veins when simple soriferous near their base, when forked, soriferous at the apex of the short fork. *Bl. En. Fil. Jav. p.* 123. *Hook. Sp. Fil.* iv. 166. Polypodium hirtum, *Hook. Sp. Fil.* iv. 170, (*not Mett.*). *Bedd. F. B. I.* 212. P. lasiosorum (*Hook.*), *Bedd. F. B. I. t.* 172.

Ceylon.

(Also in Java and Luzon.)

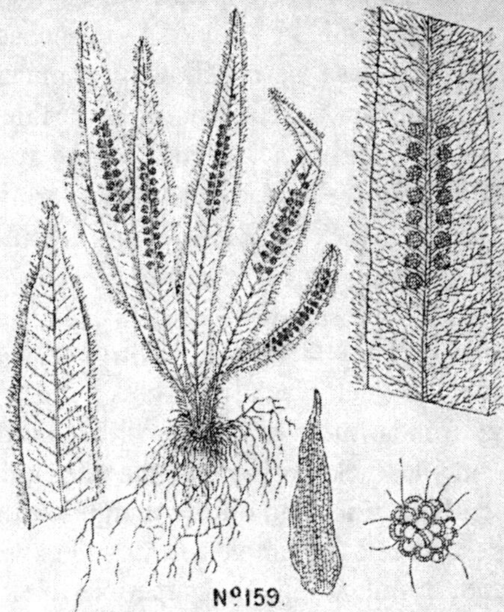

No. 159.

POLYPODIUM HIRTELLUM. (*Bl.*)

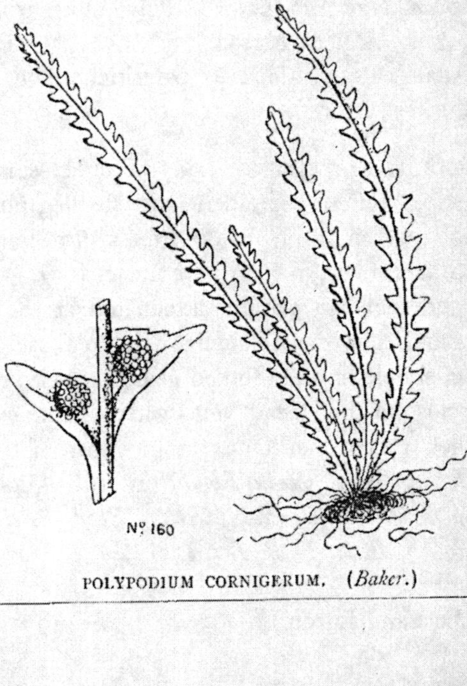

No. 160

POLYPODIUM CORNIGERUM. (*Baker.*)

6. POLYPODIUM SESSILIFOLIUM. (*Hook.*) Caudex small, erect or ascending, scaly; stipes scarcely any; fronds tufted, membranaceous, firm, 3–9 inches long, 2–3 lines wide, linear, scarcely acuminated, obtuse, attenuated at the base; veins oblique, approximate, forked; sori oblong, parallel with the costa in lines or series intermediate between the costa and the margin, medial on the upper veinlet. *Hook. Fil.* iv. 168. *Syn. Fil. p.* 322. *Bedd. F. B. I. t.* 119.

Penang.

(Also in the Philippines.)

** *Fronds pinnatifid.*

7. POLYPODIUM CORNIGERUM. (*Baker.*) Fronds tufted, subsessile, erect ligulate, 3–4 inches long, 2–2½ lines broad, pinnatifid or subpinnate, lobes 20–30 jugate, diminishing in size from middle of frond both ways, almost triangular, subacute, repand on the upper edge; texture subcoriaceous, surfaces glabrous; veins one to each lobe, forked, falling far short of the margin; sorus large round, solitary at fork close to main rachis, and medial on the vein. *Hook. Syn. Fil.* 503. *Bedd. Fern Sup. t.* 381.

Ceylon, Horton plains, rare, (C. P. 4005.)

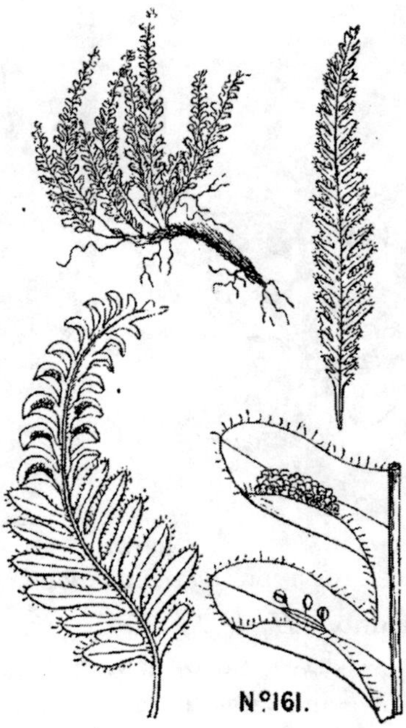

No. 161.

POLYPODIUM CUCULLATUM. (*Nees.*)

8. POLYPODIUM CUCULLATUM. (*Nees.*) Caudex very small, ascending; stipes densely tufted 1–3 lines long, naked; fronds subcoriaceous or somewhat membranaceous, 3–5 inches long, 2–3 lines broad, flaccid, linear-lanceolate acuminate, deeply nearly to the costa pinnatifid; the lobes linear-

oblong $\frac{1}{2}$–$\frac{3}{4}$ line broad, those of the upper half fertile, broader and with the edges upcurved so as to clasp the large solitary sorus; costa and sometimes the frond deciduously pilose. *Hook. Syn. Fil.* 324. Calymmodon cucullatus (*Presl.*), *Bedd. F. S. I. t.* 233.

Ceylon, on rocks and trees, central and southern provinces, 3,000–5,000 feet elevation.

9. POLYPODIUM KHASYANUM. (*Hook.*) Stipes tufted, very short, fringed with soft hairs; fronds up to about 14 inches long, by 1½ inch broad, flaccid, cut down nearly to the rachis into linear-oblong entire or slightly undulated blunt lobes 2–3 lines broad, texture thick subcoriaceous; rachis and both sides sparingly hairy; veinlets simple; sori apical on the veinlets, sunk in an oval cavity (having an elevation on the upper side of the frond) in rows of 4–6 on each side of the midrib. *Hook. Syn. Fil.* 325. *Bedd. F. B. I. t.* 173.

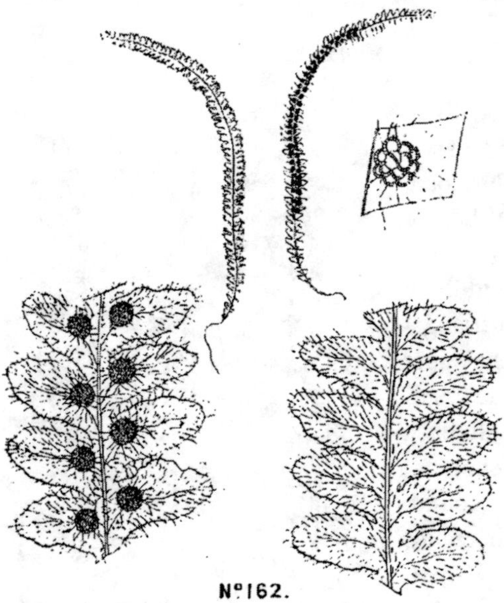

Nº 162.

POLYPODIUM TRICHOMANOIDES. (*Sw.*)

Khasya 3,000–4,000 feet, near Cherra; Assam, from Cherra to Jowye and Jarain in Jaintea, 3,000–4,000 feet elevation, not plentiful anywhere.

10. POLYPODIUM TRICHOMANOIDES. (*Sw.*) Caudex short, erect, paleaceous above, densely rooting with wiry fibres; stipes short, $\frac{1}{2}$–1 inch long, densely tufted, patent-villous with long fibrous hairs, fronds 3–4 inches to a span long, 2–4 lines wide, rigid-membranaceous,

linear, attenuated at both extremities, deeply nearly to the costa pinnatifid or almost pinnate (quite so at the very base), lobes horizontally patent from a broad base, ovate or oblong entire, sub-concave beneath, sub-deciduously ciliated with long fibrous or blackish patent hairs; veins solitary in each lobe, simple or forked, each lobe having a single sorus near the base of the veins and the costa. *Hook. Sp. Fil.* iv. 178; *Syn. Fil.* 326. *Bedd. F. B. I. t.* 2.

Sikkim, 9,000–12,000 feet elevation.

(Also in South America, Brazil and Ecuador; and Cuba.)

11. POLYPODIUM GLANDULOSUM. (*Hook.*) Caudex small, indistinct, clinging to the bark of trees by copious rooting fibres, the rest of the plant all over pilose-glandulose, most so beneath; stipes tufted 1–3 lines long, fronds 2–4 inches long, ¼ inch broad, linear obtuse, scarcely attenuated at either extremity, rather firm-membranaceous, sub-succulent, deeply nearly to the rachis pinnatifid; segments ovate, sub-acute, horizontally patent, decurrent at the base, lowermost ones free, all of them serrate-pinnatifid, costule, and rather distant few and oblique simple veins indistinct; sori 1–6 to each segment globose. *Hook. Sp. Fil.* iv. 193. *Syn. Fil.* 327. *Bedd. F. S. I. t.* 238B.

No. 163. POLYPODIUM GLANDULOSUM. (*Hook.*)

Ceylon, in the central provinces, Rambodde, and summit of Wattakelia Hill.

12. POLYPODIUM THWAITESII. (*Bedd.*) Caudex creeping, clothed with lanceolate scales; fronds sessile or subsessile, subcoriaceous, perfectly glabrous, 2–4 inches long by about 1 inch broad, lanecolate or oblanceolate, deeply almost to the rachis pinnatifid; lobes 1–2 lines broad, lanceolate, blunt, rather ascending, more or less repand or sinuate-pinnatifid, the lower reduced gradually to a narrow wing; veinlets distant, erect-patent, simple or more rarely forked, where simple soriferous at the apex, where

forked the superior veinlet only is soriferous; sori round, slightly immersed. *Bedd. F. B. I. t.* 188. *Baker, in Hook. Syn. Fil. p.* 508.

Ceylon, about Dickoya, on trees, very sweet scented (C.P. 3,900).

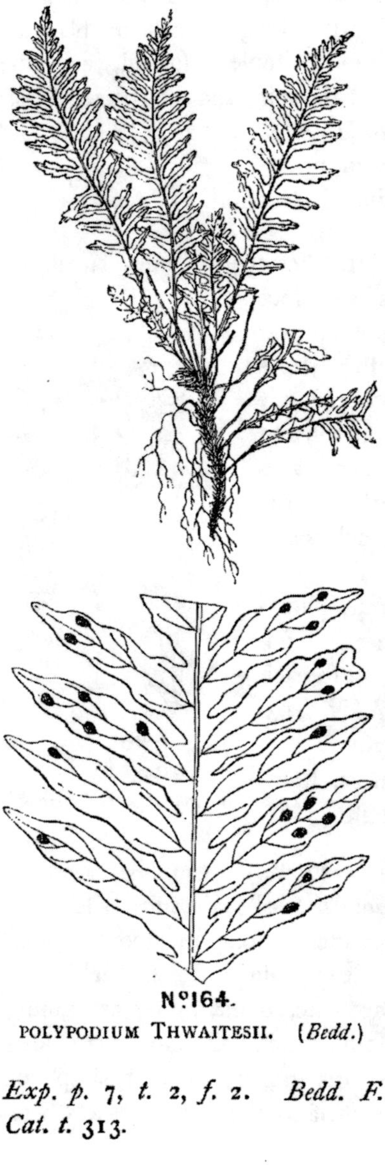

No. 164.
POLYPODIUM THWAITESII. (*Bedd.*)

13. POLYPODIUM DECORUM. (*Brack.*) Caudex short, rather thick, creeping, densely ferruginous-squamose, stipes approximate, sub-terminal on the caudex, 2–4 lines long; fronds coriaceous, glabrous, 6–12 inches long, ½–1 inch broad, narrow-lanceolate, much and almost caudate-acuminate, the base very gradually attenuated into the short stipe, deeply and nearly to the rachis pinnatifid, segments horizontally patent, narrow-oblong obtuse, quite entire, below gradually becoming shorter and broader and forming shallow elongated lobed wings at the base; costa glabrous or pilosulous, costule and veins quite sunk and inconspicuous; sori oblong, 2–8 in a row, on each side of the costule, and apical on the short veins, which do not nearly reach the margin, partially sunk in a hairy cavity (but with no raised border). *Hook. Sp. Fil.* iv. 179. *Brack. Fil. Un. St. Exp. p.* 7, *t.* 2, *f.* 2. *Bedd. F. B. I. t.* 238A. P. serra, *Wall. Cat. t.* 313.

South India, on the Tinnevelly Mountains, near Courtallum; Ceylon, Singhe Rajah Forest; Singapore and Mount Ophir; North-west India, near Mandal (Edgeworth).

(Also in Borneo, Luzon, Tahiti.)

14. POLYPODIUM FUSCATUM. (*Bl.*) Stipes tufted, 1–3 inches long, densely clothed with soft spreading hairs; fronds 3–6 inches long, ½–1 inch broad, cut down nearly to the rachis throughout into close entire obtuse pinnæ, ½ line broad, the lower ones shorter and broader, texture subcoriaceous, rachis and both sides thinly clothed with soft hairs; veins obscure, simple; sori forming a close row on each side the midrib, at last filling nearly the whole surface. *Hook. Syn. Fil. p.* 331. *Bedd. F. B. I. t.* 324.

Ceylon.

(Also in Java.)

* * * *Fronds pinnate.*

No. 165.

POLYPODIUM DECORUM. (*Brack.*)

15. POLYPODIUM OBLIQUATUM. (*Bl.*) Stipes tufted, 1 inch or more long, rigid, naked or villous; fronds up to 15 inches long and 2 inches broad, pinnate, being cut down to the rachis throughout into entire close subhorizontal linear pinnæ, 1–1½ lines broad, dilated at the base, the lower ones dwarfed, texture subcoriaceous; rachis naked or hispid, both sides naked; veinlets simple, not reaching the margin; sori sunk in a cavity 4–6 on each side, apical on the veinlets; the edges of the

No. 166.

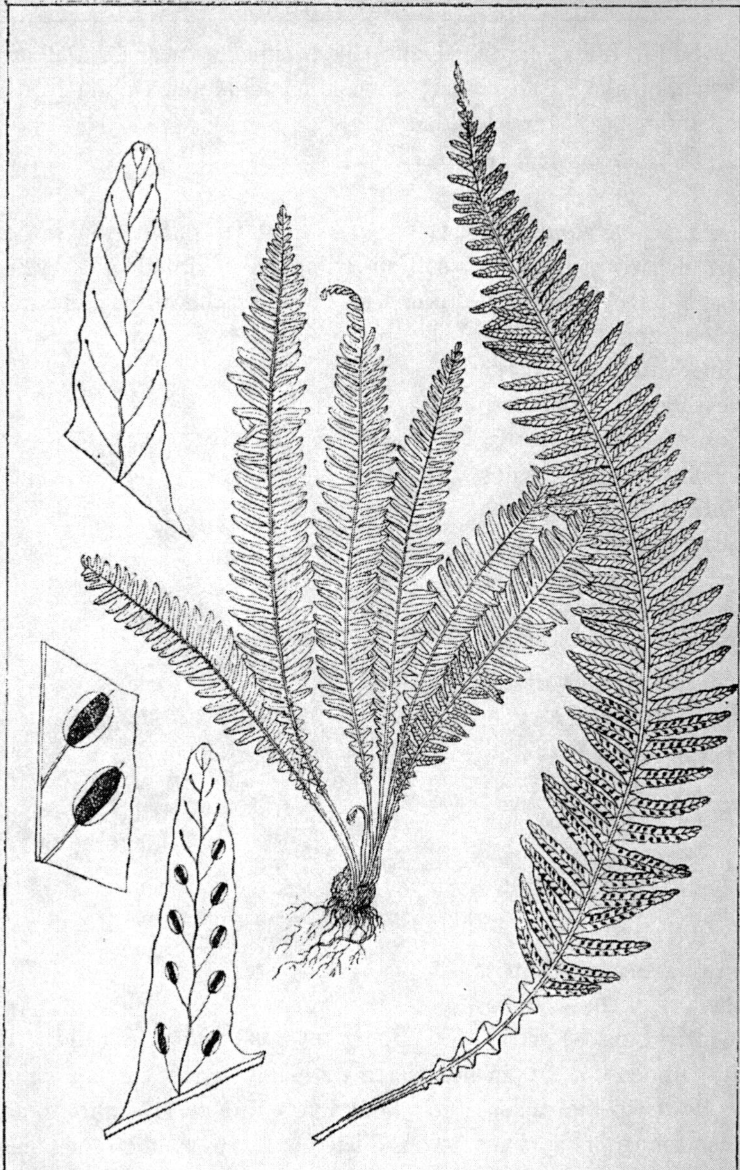

A. S. CATTELL & Co. ENGRAS.

POLYPODIUM OBLIQUATUM. (*Bl.*)

fertile pinnæ sometimes undulated. *Hook. Syn. Fil.* 328. *Bedd. F. S. I.* 167. Cryptosorus, *Fée.* Cœlopteris, *A. Br.*

South India, Anamallay Mountains, up the Toracadu River, 4,000–5,000 feet elevation, Tinnevelly and Travancore Hills; Ceylon, common on trees about Newera Elya.

16. POLYPODIUM REPANDULUM. (*Mett.*) Caudex stout, erect, with densely matted roots; stipes tufted, very short, naked or hairy; fronds 4–6 inches long, about 1 inch broad, cut down to the rachis throughout, into erect-patent blunt crenated pinnæ $\frac{1}{2}$–$\frac{3}{4}$ lines broad; texture subcoriaceous; rachis naked, or with a few very long hairs; surfaces naked, or with long hairs beneath on the costa; veinlets simple, falling short of the margin; sori slightly immersed, filling nearly the whole space between the midrib and the margin, and apical on the veinlets. *Hook. Syn. Fil.* 328. Polypodium subfalcatum, var. *β*, *Bedd. F. B. I. t.* 189B. Polyp. minutum (*Baker*), *Hook. Syn. Fil.* 328, *as far as the Ceylon plant is concerned. C. P.* 3073.

No. 167.

POLYPODIUM REPANDULUM. (*Mett.*

Ceylon, higher parts of central provinces, on trunks of trees.

17. POLYPODIUM SUBFALCATUM. (*Bl.*) Rhizome erect; stipes densely tufted, clothed with soft spreading hairs; fronds 2–10 inches long, by ½–1 inch broad pinnate, *i.e.* cut down to the rachis into close spreading pinnæ; pinnæ hairy on both sides, soft in texture, rather sharply toothed sometimes one-third or half-down, decurrent at the base, the lower ones gradually reduced; veinlets simple, not reaching the margin; sori apical on the veinlets one to each tooth or lobe of the pinnæ. *Bl. Fil. Jav.* 186, *t.* 87. *A. B. Hook. Syn. Fil.* 328. Polyp. parvulum, *Bedd. F. S. I. t.* 166, *not Bory*. P. subfalcatum, *Bedd. F. B. I.* 189, *fig. A.* (*not fig. B.*) P. parvulum, *Thw. En. Pl. Zey. p.* 394 *in part*, *C. P.* 1290, *not* 3073. It differs from the last in being soft in texture instead of coriaceous, in being much more hairy (repandulum being generally quite glabrous), in being serrate instead of crenulate, and in the sori not being immersed. Mr. Thwaites included them both under his parvulum, and Mr. Baker has the former both under repandulum and minutum in the *Synopsis Filicum*.

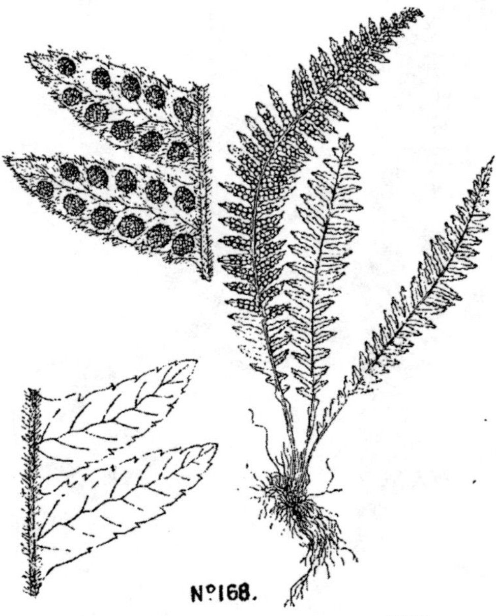

No. 168.

POLYPODIUM SUBFALCATUM. (*Bl.*)

South India, Nilgiris Lamb's Rock near Conoor, Anamallays banks of Toracadu river, 4,5000 feet; Ceylon, central provinces; North India, Himalayas from Gurwhal to Bhotan, 5,000–9,000 feet elevation; Khasya. Mr. Clarke says that some of the Khasya specimens are as small as P. trichomanoides, but that species has only one sorus to each pinna, whilst this has the pinna polysorus, or

N°169.

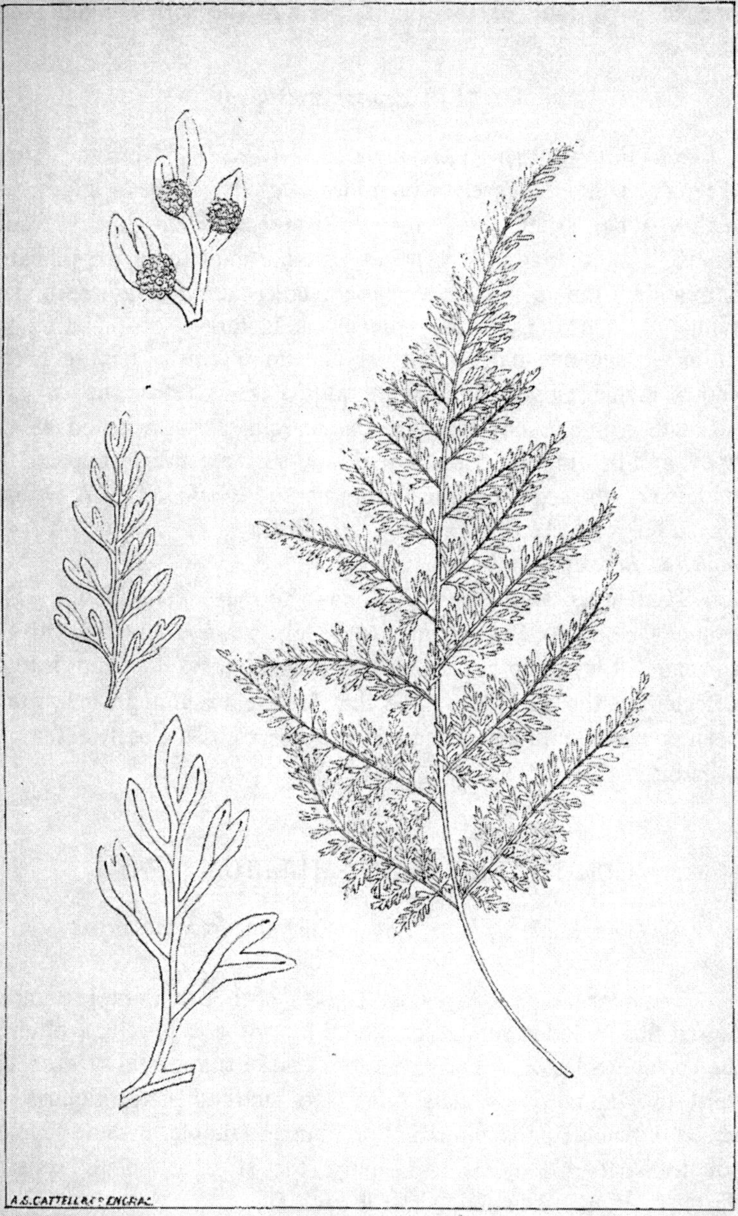

A.S. CATTELL & C° ENGRA.

POLYPODIUM DAREÆFORME. (*Hook.*)

one to each lobe of the pinna, besides the sori are differently situated.

* * * * *Fronds compound.*

18. POLYPODIUM DAREÆFORME. (*Hook.*) Rhizome stout, creeping, clothed densely with filiform golden scales; stipes 6–9 inches long, articulated on the rhizome, naked, glossy; fronds 12–18 inches long, 8–12 inches broad, sub-deltoid, 3–4-pinnate; Darea-like; pinnæ 1–2 inches broad, lanceolate deltoid; secondary pinnæ ¾ inch long, tertiary pinnæ small, forked or pinnate; the ultimate segments narrow, almost filiform bluntish, texture herbaceous, rachis glossy, both sides quite naked; veins one to each ultimate segment, not reaching the margin, and thickened at the apex, and bearing the sorus low down; sori extending beyond the margins of the segments; indusium none. *Hook. Sp. Fil.* iv. 256, *Syn. Fil.* 339. Acrophorus Hookeri, *Bedd. F. B. I.* 95 (*not Moore, which is Leucostegia Hookeri.*)

Himalayas and Khasya, 4,000–5,000 feet elevation. This cannot belong to Phegopteris as the stipes are articulated with the rhizome; it is very probably a Leucostegia, but no indusium is to be detected in the many examples that I have examined; it has long been confused with Leucostegia Hookeri, which it closely resembles in habit.

GENUS LXI.—GONIOPHLEBIUM. (*Presl.*)

(*Gonia*, angle; *phebes*, veins—the veins forming angles.)

Veins forming ample regular areoles, each with a simple or rarely forked free included veinlet, on which the sorus is terminal, often in the costal areoles only, but sometimes also in the second or even the third row, marginal veinlets free; sori non-indusiate, globose or rarely oblong; fronds pinnatifid or pinnate (simple in some species not Indian); rhizome wide-creeping, the stipe articulate on the rhizome; pinnæ articulate with the rachis.

* *Fronds pinnatifid or somewhat pinnate at the base only.*

1. GONIOPHLEBIUM AMÆNUM. (*Wall.*) Caudex creeping, stout, densely paleaceous, with ferruginous subulate scales, which are sub-adpressed, never hair-pointed; stipes a span to a foot or more long, stramineous or brown; fronds 1 to nearly 2 feet long, 6–10 inches wide, glabrous or sub-pubescent, ovate, terminating in a lanceolate-acuminate subentire segment, deeply pinnatifid to within 2–3 lines of the costa, segments horizontal, more or less approximate, 3–8 inches long, $\frac{1}{4}$–$\frac{1}{3}$ inch wide, subfalcate from a broad base, ensiform gradually acuminate, entire, or coarsely dentate-serrate, lowest pair deflexed, veins forming one costal series of moderately sized soriferous areoles, and sometimes two (the second not soriferous), marginal veinlets free, soriferous veinlet always arising from the vein at a distance from the costa; sori subglobose sunk (papillose on the upper side.) *Hook. Sp. Fil.* v. 24. *Wall. Cat. n.* 290. *Bedd. F. B. I. t.* 5.

Himalayas, from Gurwhal to Bhotan, 4,000–11,000 feet elevation, common; Khasya 3,000–6,000 feet. (Clarke's var. tonglensis from Tonglu near Darjeeling, appears only to differ in the pinnæ being blunt at the apex, there is, however, only one poor specimen known of it.)

2. GONIOPHLEBIUM SUBAMÆNUM. (*Clarke.*) Rhizome slender, densely clothed with grey-brown lanceolate-subulate scales, which are subadpressed, never hair-pointed, near the base of the main rachis are sometimes ovate or lanceolate scales; stipes about 2 inches long; fronds 6 inches long, deeply pinnatifid nearly to the rachis, lower segments much abbreviated and deflexed, all serrated at the margins; costal arches of the main rachis continued nearly or quite to the base of the frond; main rachis above glabrous or puberulous. *Clarke, F. N. I. p.* 550, *t.* 82, *f.* 2.

Very nearly allied to amænum, and perhaps only a form of it, differs in its slender rhizome and small size.

Himalayas, on the ridge between Sikkim and Nepal, 11,000–12,000 feet elevation, very abundant.

No. 170.

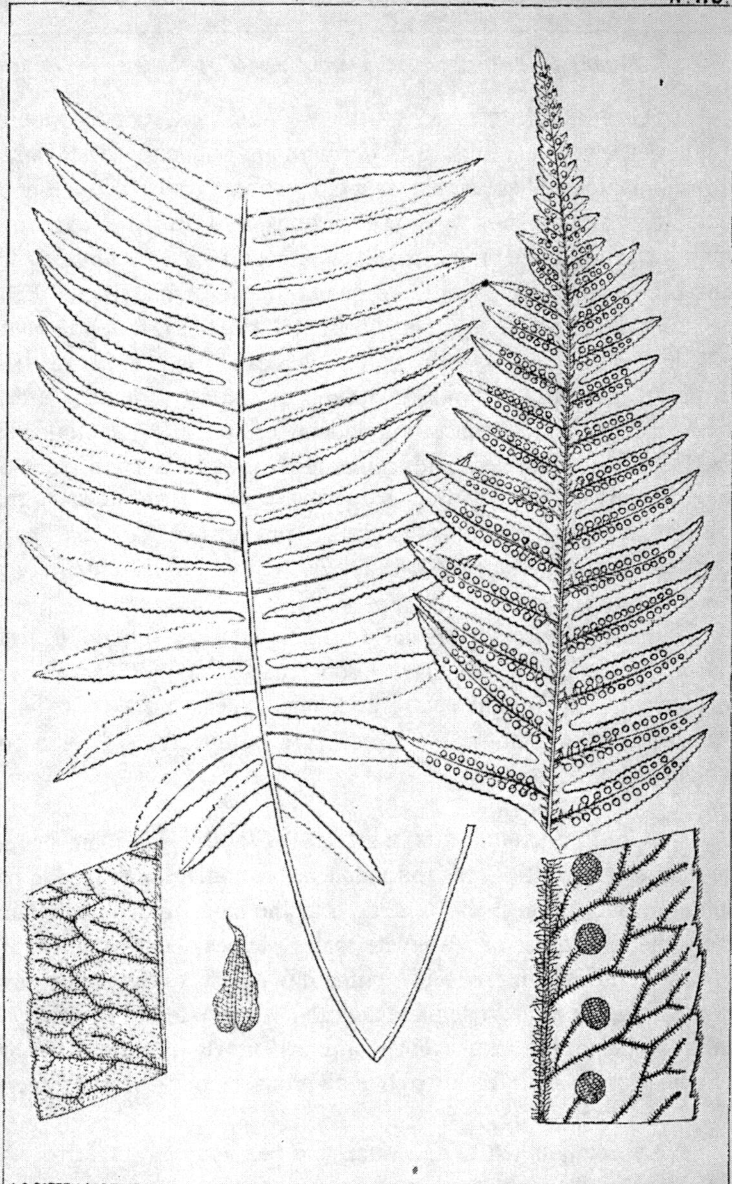

A. S. CATTELL & Co ENGRAS.

GONIOPHLEBIUM AMÆNUM. (*Wall.*)

3. GONIOPHLEBIUM LACHNOPUS. (*Wall.*) Rhizome more slender than in amænum, densely clothed with hair-pointed brown-black scales spreading from small bases; base of the rachis often with a few similar scales; stipe 2–4 inches long, slender naked; fronds flaccid, 12–18 inches long, 3–4 inches broad, cut down nearly to the rachis into spreading slightly-toothed segments ¼ inch broad, texture herbaceous, both sides naked, or the rachis beneath slightly scaly, and pubescent above; costal areoles in a single series (never two as sometimes occurs in amænum), or rarely the veins are all free (not forming areoles); sori in a single series in the areoles, or at the apex of the forked veinlet when there is no anastomosis. *Wall. Cat.* 310. *Hook. Syn. Fil.* 342. *Bedd. F. B. I. t.* 163. *Clarke, F. N. I. p.* 551.

Himalayas, from Kashmir to Bhotan, 2,000–3,000 feet elevation, very common. Khasya, 3,000 – 5,000 feet elevation.

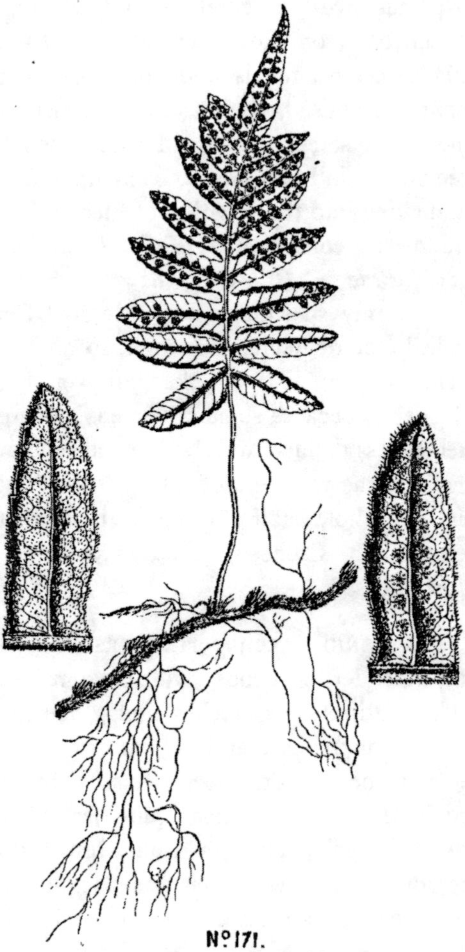

No. 171.
GONIOPHLEBIUM ERYTHROCARPUM. (*Mett.*)

4. GONIOPHLEBIUM ERYTHROCARPUM. (*Mett.*) Rhizome ½ line thick, glaucous, firm, wide-creeping, scales lanceolate, dark-castaneous,

minute, not hair-pointed; stipe 3–4 inches long, naked, stramineous, very slender; frond oblong-deltoid, 3–4 inches long, 1½–2 inches broad, pinnatifid nearly to the rachis, lobes 5–10 jugate, ligulate blunt, 3–4 lines broad, obscurely repand, adnate, only the lowest narrowed at the base, on the lower side scarcely shortened, texture rigidly subcoriaceous; rachis and costas below and under surface pilose; main veins raised, very distinct to nearly the edge, costal areoles in one or two series, the second series when present generally without a free veinlet in lower areole, sometimes forked, or rarely netted and graduating into the venation of Pleopeltis; sori in a single series in the lower areoles. *Mett. Kuhn. Linn.* 36, *p.* 135. *Hook. Syn. Fil.* 511. *Bedd. F. B. I. Sup.* 382.

All my specimens from Messrs. Clarke and Atkinson have typical Goniophlebium venation, so also have nearly all the specimens at Kew. Mr. Clarke, however, has removed the species to Pleopeltis, because some specimens gathered by him have the costal areoles less defined and the veinlets somewhat netted and graduating into the venation of Pleopeltis. I look upon these as abnormal, the whole habit of the plant being that of Goniophlebium.

Sikkim, Lacheen, 9,000–11,000 feet elevation, Yakla valley, 8,000 feet.

5. GONIOPHLEBIUM HENDERSONI. (*Atkinson, MS.*) Rhizome very slender, glaucous, wide-creeping, clothed with hair-pointed scales; stipes 3–4 inches long, naked or scaly, very slender, grey, stramineous; fronds narrow-lanceolate 8–10 inches long, 1½–2 inches broad, deeply nearly to the rachis pinnatifid, or the lower lobes or pinnæ quite free; pinnæ or lobes 20–30 pair, patent lanceolate acute, 3–4 lines broad, distantly incised, all except the lowest dilated at their base, texture moderately firm, surfaces green, naked; areoles and sori uniserial, the latter near the midrib, not crowded, occasionally the veins are all or nearly all quite free and not anastomosing, or forming areoles, costal arches of the main rachis prominent, very long and narrow, absent of course at the base of the larger fronds, where it is pinnate, not pinnatifid. *Hook. Syn. Fil. p.* 511. *Bedd. F. B. I. t.* 383.

No 172.

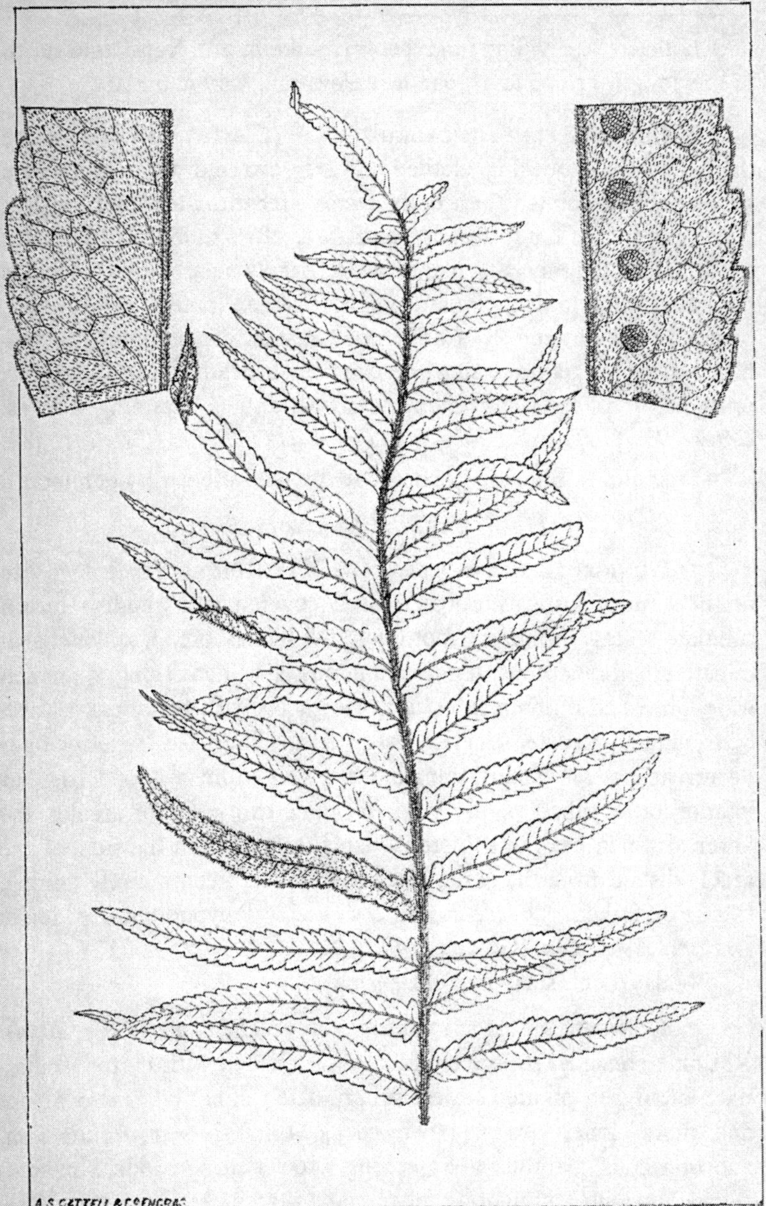

GONIOPHLEBIUM MOLLE. (*Bedd.*)

Himalayas, dividing ridge between Sikkim and Nepal, and north of the Jongri, 11,000 to 13,000 feet elevation, very abundant.

6. GONIOPHLEBIUM MICRORHIZOMA. (*Clarke.*) Rhizome 1 line thick, firm wide-creeping, clothed with grey-brown ovate or lanceolate scales, not hair-pointed; base of the rachis often with a few similar scales; stipes 4–5 inches long; fronds lanceolate, often caudate at the apex, about 1 foot long by 3–4 inches wide, deeply nearly to the rachis pinnatifid, the lowest pinnæ sometimes free; pinnæ 20–30 pair, patent lanceolate acute, 3–4 lines broad, distantly incised, texture herbaceous, rachis glabrous above, castaneous beneath; areoles and sori uniserial, or all the veins often quite free, and not forming areoles. *Clarke, F. N. I.* 551. *Hook. Syn. Fil. p.* 511. *Bedd. F. B. I. t.* 384.

Kashmir to Bhotan, 5,000–8,000 feet elevation, very common.

* * *Fronds distinctly pinnate throughout.*

7. GONIOPHLEBIUM MOLLE. (*Bedd.*) Rhizome creeping, size of the stem of a tobacco pipe, densely covered with reddish brown subulate scales; fronds 1½ foot long, 7–8 inches broad, oblong acuminate membranaceous, pinnæ numerous, 3–4 inches long, ½ an inch wide, furnished on both sides as is the rachis with soft weak whitish hairs, sinuate-crenate, superior base often subauricled, superior ones decurrent on the rachis, remainder sessile from a broad base, or inferior ones subpetiolate; veins forming two series of areoles, the lower of which has the soriferous veinlet arising from the side of the areole distant from the costa, marginal veinlets free or rarely uniting, simple or forked. *Bedd. F. B. I. t.* 206. Polypodium Beddomei (*Baker*), *Hook. Syn. Fil. 2nd Edit.* 344.

Malay Peninsula, in Tenasserim.

8. GONIOPHLEBIUM SUBAURICULATUM. (*Bl. under Polypodium*). Rhizome creeping, stoloniferous, densely clothed with narrow acuminate, often hair-pointed scales, subpruinate; stipes a span to a foot and more long, sparingly paleaceous, rufous-brown; fronds firm, subcoriaceous, glabrous, 2–6 feet long, a foot and more wide, pinnated, pinnæ horizontal, numerous yet remote, 3–10 inches long, ¼ to nearly ½ an inch wide, shortly petioled and jointed on the rachis from a

somewhat cordate or truncated and occasionally auricled base, linear-lanceolate, finely and gradually acuminated, serrated ; veins forming a double costular series of areoles, including a free venule, of which the lower series is soriferous, marginal veinlets free ; sori in a single series forming slightly elevated pustules on the superior side. *Bl. Fil. Jav. p.* 177, *t.* 83. *Hook. Sp. Fil.* v. 32. *Bedd. F. B. I. t.* 78.

Khasya, 3,000–5,000 feet elevation ; Malay Peninsula.

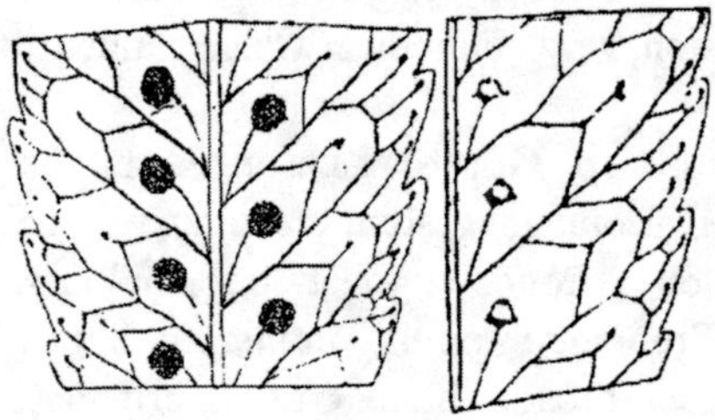

No. 173.
GONIOPHLEBIUM SUBAURICULATUM. (*Bl.*)

(Also in Malay Islands and Queensland.)

9. GONIOPHLEBIUM ARGUTUM. (*Wall. under Polypodium.*) Rhizome thick as a writing-quill, squarrose with ovate-acute short blackish or brown glossy spreading scales, stipes 3–4 inches to a span long, brown glossy ; fronds firm-membranaceous, glabrous, 1–2 feet long, 8–10 inches broad, pinnated, pinnæ distant sub horizontally patent, 4–6 inches long, $\frac{1}{2}$–$\frac{3}{4}$ inch wide, from a broader but obtusely and oblique cuneated or subtruncated base (rarely rotundate-auricled) elongate-oblong, acuminate, rather obtusely serrated, lower ones often opposite, the rest alternate, superior ones more or less adnate and decurrent, terminal one similar to the rest, veins forming a costal series of large oblong soriferous areoles ; marginal veins ending in a thickened apex within the margin all free ; sori super-

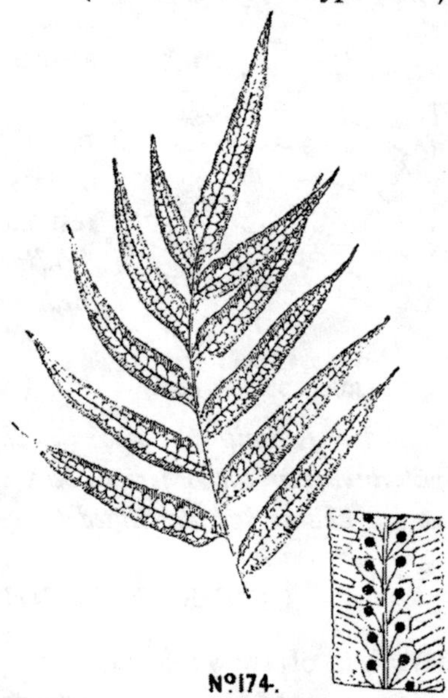

No. 174.
GONIOPHLEBIUM ARGUTUM. (*Wall.*)

ficial at the apex of the free veins in the costal areoles. *Wall. Cat. n.* 308. *Hook. Sp. Fil.* v. 32. *Bedd. F. B. I. t.* 6.

Himalayas, from Kashmir to Bhotan, 4,000–9,000 feet elevation, very common. Closely allied to the last species.

10. GONIOPHLEBIUM VERRUCOSUM. (*Wall. under Polypodium.*) Rhizome long, stout creeping, very paleaceous; stipes 1½ foot and more long; fronds 2–3 feet long, oblong-acuminate, firm-membranaceous, drooping; pinnæ numerous but distant, 6–9 inches long, 1–1½ inch broad, oblong costate, articulate upon the rachis, suddenly and shortly cuspidate-acuminate entire or serrated chiefly towards the apex, nearly sessile, the base obliquely cuneate; primary veins slender but straight and parallel costuliform, forming with the anastomosing veins four or five series of areoles each with a free included veinlet, but of which the lowest series only is soriferous; sori in a single series next the costa sunk in a deep cavity, having a corresponding pustule on the upper side. *Wall. Cat. n.* 296. *Hook. Sp. Fil.* v. 31. *Bedd. F. B. I. t.* 257.

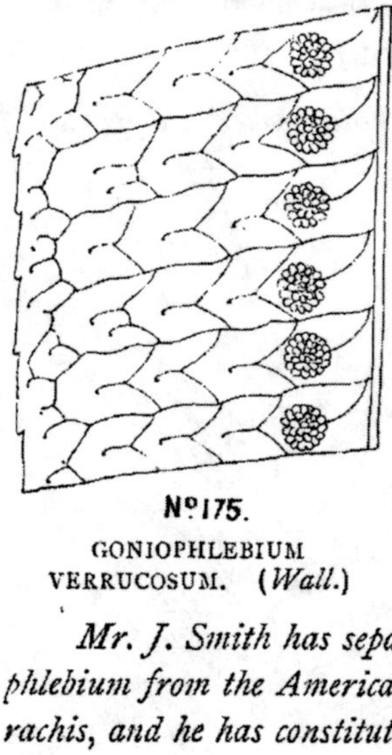

No. 175.
GONIOPHLEBIUM VERRUCOSUM. (*Wall.*)

Malacca and Penang.
(Also in the Philippines.)

Mr. J. Smith has separated these East Indian species of Goniophlebium from the American because the pinnæ are articulated with the rachis, and he has constituted the genus Schellolepis for them.

GENUS LXII.—NIPHOBOLUS. (*Kaulf.*)

(*Niphos*, of snow; *bolus*, a large pill—the snow-like scales and round sori.)

Fronds on their under surface matted with woolly or cottony tomentum; sori globose or elliptic, superficial or immersed, buried in the tomentum; veins internal, obscure, pinnate, prominent or uniform from a central costa, venules anastomosing sometimes transversely parallel, forming parallelogrammoid areoles, with excurrent free or occasionally connivent or anastomosed veinlets, sometimes uniting in roundish or oblong hexagonal unequal oblique areoles, with variously directed simple or divaricately forked veinlets, the veins of the fertile frond when contracted less developed; fronds simple or rarely lobed, rigid, coriaceous, opaque, the fertile often contracted.

1. NIPHOBOLUS ADNASCENS. (*Sw. under Polypodium.*) Rhizome wide-creeping, paleaceous with lanceolate-setaceous scales; stipes distant, 1–2 inches long, furnished at the base with lanceolate-linear often hairy scales; fronds dimorphous, carnose-coriaceous, dark green above, but hoary with sparse stellated pubescence beneath, and paler and even white with more copious compact hairs; sterile fronds, 2–4 inches long, spathulate or elliptical-lanceolate, obtuse; fertile ones 6–8 inches long, linear or oblong obtuse or acute, both kinds tapering below into the stipe, costa sub-carinate, costules sunk obscure, their areoles including four (sometimes only three or two) veinlets, which are generally free with clavate apices, though they sometimes anastomose; sori deep sunk in the tomentum and in the substance of the frond on each side of the costa, arranged 5–6 in obliquely transverse series, capsules long stalked, mixed with long stalked stellated scales. *Sw. Syn. Fil. pp.* 25 and 228. *Hooker. Sp. Fil.* v. 47. *Bedd. F. S. I. t.* 184. *Wall. Cat.* 268. Polyp. verrucosum, *Wall. Cat. n.* 267. P. vittarioides, *Wall. Cat. p.* 270. P. pertusum, *Wall. Cat.* 267.

Throughout India from the plains up to 4,500 elevation; Ceylon; Malay Peninsula.

(Also in China; Fiji; Mascareen Islands, Cameroon Mountains.)

2. NIPHOBOLUS LÆVIS. (*J. Sm.*) Rhizome slender, wide-creeping, clothed with linear setaceous scales; stipes distant, somewhat hairy ½ inch to nearly 2 inches long, furnished with a tuft of scales at their base; fronds coriaceous, linear-lanceolate, much narrowed towards the apex, 2½–6 inches long, ¼–¾ inch broad, glabrous above, hairy with stellate pubescence beneath; venation obscure, costules thin, areoles in three series between the costa and margin, with one,

No. 176.

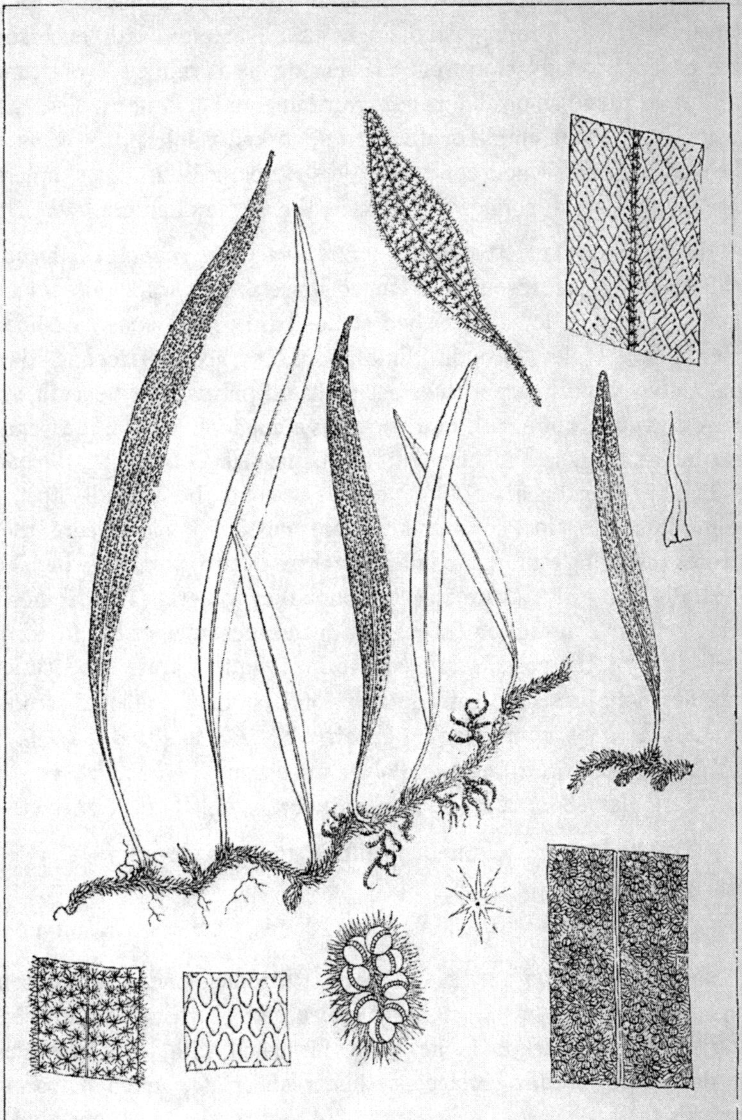

A. S. CATTELL & Co. ENGRS.

NIPHOBOLUS ADNASCENS. (*Sw.*)

two or three clavate veinlets in each, which are variously directed, free or rarely joined to the base of the areole above; sori large, partially sunk in the tomentum, often confined to the apex of the frond, or scattered, or covering nearly all the under surface. *Bedd. F. B. I. t.* 161. P. Niphobolus jaintense, *Clarke, F. N. I. p.* 552, *t.* 82.

Khasya hills, Jaintea, Jarain, 3,500 feet elevation. Considered a variety of adnascens by Mr. Baker, but sufficiently distinct in its venation, I think, to rank as a species.

3. NIPHOBOLUS ACROSTICHOIDES. (*Sw.*) Rhizome wide-creeping, branched, younger portions squarrose, with rather large bright ferruginous lanceolate scales; stipes 1–3 inches long furnished at the base with obtuse scales; frond hard coriaceous, 1–2 feet and more long, ½–1 inch wide, glabrous above, beneath whitish or tawny, stellate-tomentose (tomentum very deciduous) elongate-lanceolate or linear obtuse; sterile fronds generally the broadest; areoles 5–7 between the costa and margin, each with 3–6 veinlets free and simple, or variously forked and anastomosing; sori rather small, prominent, very compact, generally occupying the upper part of the frond, arranged in 6–8 oblique very close series between the costules. *Sw. Syn. Fil. p.* 29 *and* 225. *Hook. Sp. Fil.* v. 44. *Bedd. F. B. I. t.* 81. Polyp furfuraceum, *Wall. Cat. n.* 278.

Birma and the Malay Peninsula generally. I have specimens from Tenasserim 2 feet long and only ½ inch wide.

4. NIPHOBOLUS HETERACTIS. (*Mett.*) Rhizome wide-creeping, the scales copious lanceolate-linear, not adpressed golden; stipes distant up to 7 inches long, more or less scaly; fronds oblong, with a long acumination about 6 inches long by 1¾ inches broad, coriaceous, the fertile not generally contracted, upper surface glabrous, lower clothed with close compact stellate scales, the rays of which are broad, with filamentous hairs admixed; areoles in 8–9 series between the costa and margin, each including 2–3 veinlets, which are generally forked and more or less anastomosing; sori rather large and prominent. *Mett. Kuhn in Linn.* 36, 140. *Clarke, F. N. I. p.* 535. N. Lingua, *Hook. Syn Fil.* 350, *in part, and p.* 512. *Bedd. F. Supt. t.* 385.

Sikkim and Bhotan, 4,000–6,000 feet elevation; Khasya, 3,000–5,000 feet. This is very near the Japan Lingua, but it appears to differ sufficiently to be considered a species, besides the filamentous hairs radiating round the scales, which it requires a magnifying glass to detect, the habit is somewhat different and the scales of the rhizome more free and copious.

5. NIPHOBOLUS PANNOSUS. (*Mett.*) Rhizome wide-creeping, slender, scales linear, dark coloured, closely adpressed; stipes up to 6 inches long, stellately scaly; fronds lanceolate up to 6 inches long by 1½ inch broad, narrowed at both ends, coriaceous, glabrous above, at least in age, beneath densely matted with stellate scales, the rays of which are hair-like; areoles in about seven series between the costa and margin, each including 2–4 veinlets which are simple, forked, free, or variously anastomosing; sori crowded, rather small, 5–6 in a row between the main veins, not reaching the margins. *Mett. Kuhn. Linn.* 36, *p.* 141. *Hook. Syn. Fil.* 512. Niphobolus Lingua, *Bedd. F. S. I. t.* 240.

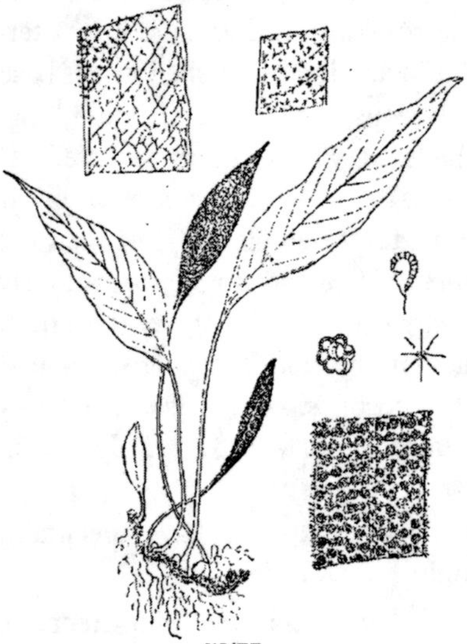

No 177.

NIPHOBOLUS PANNOSUS. (*Mett.*)

Ceylon, up to 3,000 feet elevation; Tenasserim.

6. NIPHOBOLUS STIGMOSUS. (*Sw.*) Rhizome wide-creeping, stout rufous-paleaceous with slender subulate scales; stipes subaggregate, 1–6½ inches long, angled; fronds a span to 1½–2 feet and more long, 1–2–3 inches and more broad, firm, coriaceous, in age glabrous above, beneath densely stellate-tomentose and subfurfuraceous (tomentum forming a close coat), lanceolate or suboblanceolate acuminate,

gradually tapering below and decurrent upon the stipes, costules distinct, elevated on the under side; sori immersed, very minute and numerous, arranged in compact closely placed lines or series between the costules and in equally-compact series transversely with them; areoles in about 10 series between the costa and margin, each including many veinlets which are much branched and anastomosing. *Sw. Syn. Fil.* 29, 226. N. costatus, *Hook. Sp. Fil.* v. 50. *Wall. Cat. p.* 265. *Bedd. F. B. I. t.* 120.

Himalayas, from Gurwhal to Bhotan, 2,000–6,000 feet elevation, Khasya, 2,000–3,000 feet, Parasnath, 2,500 feet; Tenasserim; Golcondah Hills West of Vizagapatam. My Birma specimens have very long stipes and the frond scarcely decurrent, my Himalaya and Vizagatam specimens have the frond very much decurrent, and the stipe very short.

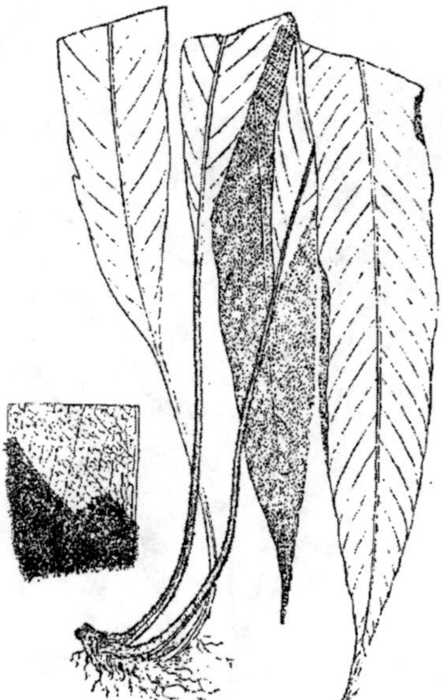

No. 178.

NIPHOBOLUS STIGMOSUS. (*Sw.*)

7. NIPHOBOLUS SUBFURFURACEUS. (*Hook.*) Rhizome short, branched, creeping, the younger branches paleaceous with ferruginous subulate scales, stipes subaggregated, 4–5 inches long, nearly glabrous, fronds 24–30 inches long, 4–5 inches wide, broad-lanceolate or oblanceolate, sharply acuminated below, gradually and much attenuated upon the stipes, glabrous above, minutely sellate-tomentose beneath, the tomentum thin, firm and close so as to appear subfurfuraceous or compactly pannose of a whitish colour, costa stout, costules evident but not elevated; venation indistinct, quite that of true Campyloneuron, the areoles from 15–20 in a series between the costa and the margin, each with numerous (8–9) included free or scarcely anastomosing soriferous veinlets; sori rather small, elevated, subglobose (not in the least sunk),

forming as many arched series between the costules as there are areoles. *Hook. Sp. Fil.* v. 52. *Bedd. F. B. I. t.* 259.

Bhotan and Mishmee. The areoles are much more numerous than in stigmosus, and the included veinlets also more numerous, but much less anastomosing, the fronds in my specimens are of thinner texture, the veinlets being visible (without soaking the frond).

8. NIPHOBOLUS FISSUS. (*Bl.*) Rhizome creeping, paleaceous with ferruginous scales, stipes aggregated short scarcely any or 3–5 inches long, and then winged or margined to the base; fronds carnose-coriaceous 6 inches to a foot and more long, ½ an inch to 1–1½ inch wide, lanceolate or linear-lanceolate or even linear, often finely acuminated, the margin quite entire (or rarely spuriously and very unequally pinnatifid with remote long and narrow segments), from near the middle gradually attenuated downwards to the caudex, at first wholly tomentose with ferruginous stellated hairs, at length glabrous on the upper side and depressed-punctate, the dots corresponding with the sori; venation quite sunk, veins pinnate but not prominent, venules transversely parallel and forming with the veins parallelogrammoid areoles (about five between costa and margin), with two, sometimes only one, excurrent free clavate veinlets in each areole; sori copious and at first quite sunk among the tomentum appearing in the form of small tubercles, at length a circular opening appears, but the sori scarcely rise above the surface of the tomentum, arranged in series. *Bl. Fil. Jav. p.* 58, *t.* 24. Niph. porosus, *Hook. Sp. Fil.* v. 48. *Bedd. F. S. I. t.* 183.

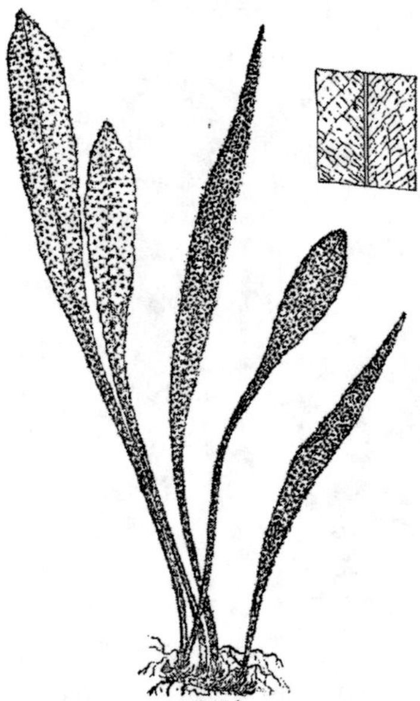

NIPHOBOLUS FISSUS. (*Bl.*)

Polypodium porosum, *Wall. Cat. n.* 266. Niph. Schmidianus, *Kze. Bot. Zeit.* vi. *p.* 121. Polyp. mysurense (*Heyne*), *Wall. Cat.* 269. Niph. floccigerus (*Mett.*), *Bedd. F. Sup. t.* 386.

South India, Western mountains, 3,000–8,000 feet elevation; Ceylon, central provinces; Himalayas and Khasya, 2,000–7,000 feet elevation; Malay Peninsula. (The Khasya floccigerus only differs in the fronds being narrower.)

9. NIPHOBOLUS FLOCCULOSUS. (*Don.*) Rhizome short, stout densely scaly, especially at base of stipes, with finely subulate golden scales; stipes 2–8 inches long, aggregated, clothed as are the fronds with dense whitish or brownish stellate tomentum; fronds 4–16 inches long by $\frac{3}{4}$–$1\frac{1}{2}$ broad, carnose-coriaceous, lanceolate, finely acuminate, subsinuate, moderately attenuated and decurrent, or broad and unequally hastate at the base, in age glabrous above and blackish punctate, venation immersed, costules indistinct, areoles 9–16 each with 3–5 included veinlets which are generally free, simple or forked, more rarely anastomosing with a veinlet from the top of the areole; sori scarcely sunk, small but slightly elevated above the tomentum, very copious, arranged in regular rows between the costules. *Don. Prod. Fl. Nep.* 1. N. detergibilis, *Hook. Sp. Fil.* v. 49. *Bedd. F. B. I t.* 162. P. costatum, *Wall. Cat.* 265, *partly*.

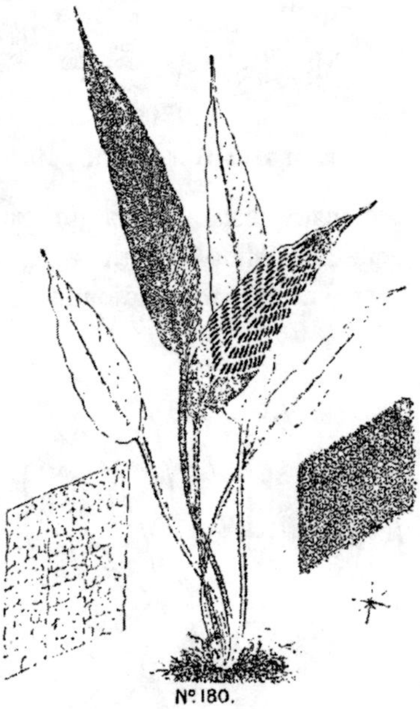
Nº 180.
NIPHOBOLUS FLOCCULOSUS. (*Don.*)

Himalayas, Gurwhal to Bhotan, up to 5,000 feet elevation, Khasya, extending into the Sylhet plains.

10. NIPHOBOLUS GARDNERI. (*Metten.*) Rhizome short-creep-

ing, the younger portions densely ferrugineous-paleaceous; stipes approximate, arising from a scaly branch of the caudex, 2–4 inches long; fronds about a foot long, carnose-coriaceous lanceolate, obtusely acuminate, gradually attenuated upon the stipes, densely clothed with a very compact firm sub-furfuraceous mass of whitish or ferruginous stellated tomentum, costa and primary veins or costules slightly elevated beneath, venation of Campyloneurum, secondary transverse veins more obscure, areoles about 7 between the main costa and margin, each including 2–4 veinlets, which are generally simple with a clavate apex, rarely forked and rarely anastomosing with adjoining veinlets; sori superficial (not sunk) in 3–4 series, parallel with the costules and 10–12 transverse series between the costa and the margin. *Metten. Polypod. p.* 129. *Hook. Sp. Fil.* v. 51. *Bedd. F. S. I. t.* 241.

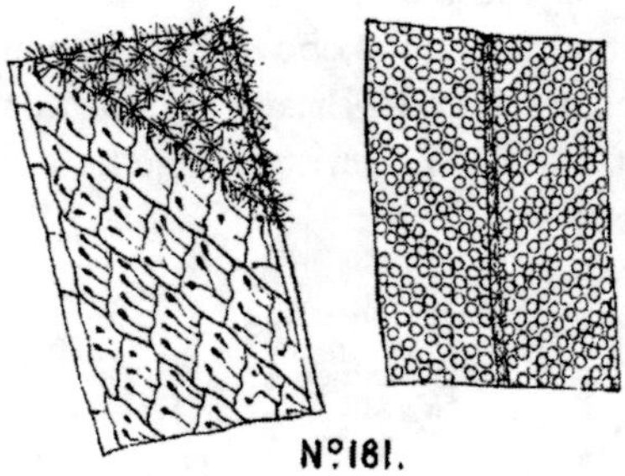

No. 181.

NIPHOBOLUS GARDNERI. (*Mett.*)

Ceylon, rocks and trees in central and southern provinces up to 3,000 feet; South India, Anamallay Hills, 5,000 feet elevation.

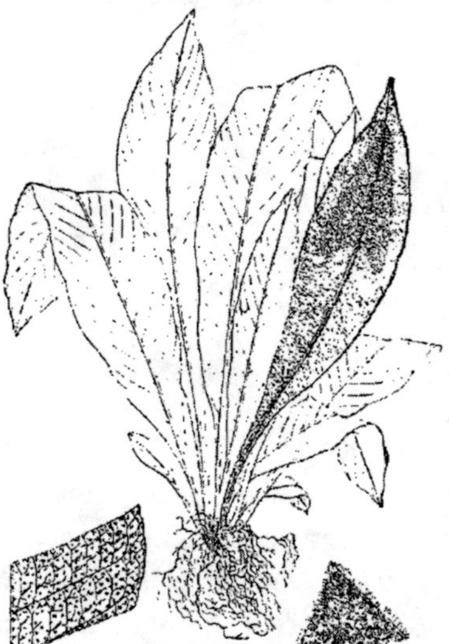

No. 182.

NIPHOBOLUS PENANGIANUS. (*Hook.*)

11. NIPHOBOLUS PENANGIANUS. (*Hook.*) Rhizome short-creeping; stipes scarcely any; fronds submembranaceous, $1\frac{1}{2}$ foot and more long, $2\frac{3}{4}$ inches wide, oblanceolate finely acuminate, the base much and gradually attenuated, sessile, the margin irregularly sinuated, glabrous above (at least in maturity), beneath thinly clothed with fuscous stellated hairs, venation internal, but manifest

when viewed between the eye and the light, costules not elevated, areoles 10–12 between the costa and the margin, including 2–4 simple or forked clavate soriferous veinlets; sori prominent (not sunk), forming a broad mass in the disk of the upper half of the frond, not reaching the margin; capsules mixed with long stipitate peltate stellated scales. *Hook. Sp. Fil.* v. 52. *Hook. Ic. Pl. t.* 203. *Gen. Fil.* 83, *Polycarpium, Pr. Bedd. F. B. I. t.* 121.

Penang, Tenasserim (Parish).

12. NIPHOBOLUS BOOTHII. (*Hook.*) Rhizome short with lanceolate-linear golden scales; stipes 8–16 inches long, and stout in proportion, tawny brown, paleaceous, with imbricating ferruginous lanceolate scales only at the very base; frond carnose-coriaceous, 16–24 inches long, 3–4 inches wide, elliptic-lanceolate, obtusely acuminate, moderately attenuated, glabrous, and punctated above with minute blackish dots (probably corresponding with the receptacles of the sori), beneath covered with a dense velvety mass of ferruginous stellated tomentum; primary costular veins evident but not prominent, united by transverse arched veins, forming many series of areoles, each with few included veinlets, which are much branched or anastomosing; sori small, partially sunk in the tomentum forming transverse lines between the costules and as many as there are areoles. *Hook. Sp. Fil.* v. 53. *Bedd. F. B. I. t.* 258.

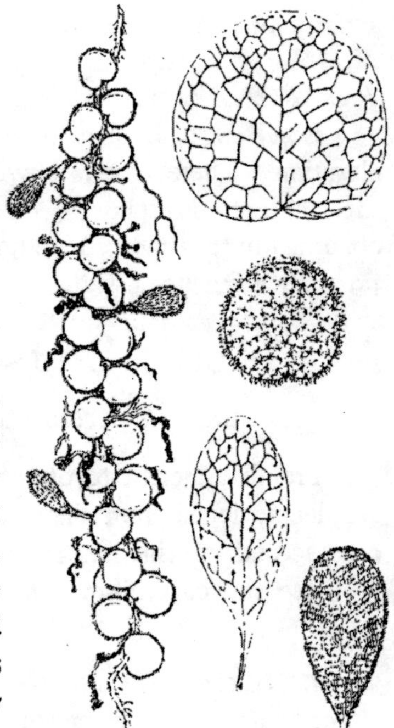

NIPHOBOLUS MUMMULARIÆFOLIUS. (*Mett.*)

Bhotan.

13. NIPHOBOLUS NUMMULARIÆFOLIUS. (*Sw. under Acrostichum*). Rhizome slender wide-creeping, filiform, clothed with bright ferruginous lanceolate fibrillose scales; fronds dimorphous, carnose-coriaceous, the barren ones roundish or elliptical, subsessile ½–1 inch each way, the fertile ones longer and narrower, 1½–2 inches long. ¼–⅓ inch broad, upper surface naked, at least in age, lower densely coated with loose ferruginous woolly tomentum; veins forming areoles irregular in size and shape, empty or with one free veinlet, marginal veinlets free; sori close, scattered, sometimes covering the whole surface. *Sw. Syn. Fil.* 191, 419 *to* 2. Polyp. nummulariæfolium. *Mett. Farngatt Polyp.* 122, *t.* 3. *Hook. Sp. Fil.* v. 54. *Syn. Fil.* 351. *Bedd. F. B. I. t.* 320. Galeoglossa, *Presl.*

East Bengal, Bhotan, Assam, Khasya, Cachar, up to 2,500 feet elevation. There is a variety from Khasya (obovatum, Mett.) with the sterile fronds obovate on a ¾ inch petiole. This species is abnormal in the genus, I do not think it is a Niphobolus at all, but probably a Drymoglossum.

GENUS LXIII.—DIPTERIS. (*Reinw.*)

(*Di*, two; *pteris*, fern—the fan-like fronds in two parts.)

Fronds adherent to the caudex, flabellate in two halves which are deeply lobed from their circumference in the direction of the base, secondary veins forming many areoles, including free or netted veinlets; sori punctiform, numerous, scattered small, or in a single series.

1. DIPTERIS WALLICHII. (*Br.*) Rhizome stout, creeping, clothed with appressed copious black hard subulate setaceous scales wrinkled at the back; stipes 1–2 and more feet long, smooth and polished, distant erect; fronds coriaceous, 1–2½ feet long and much wider than long, dark-green above, whitish or ferruginous beneath, flabelliform bipartite into two nearly equal broad-cuneate portions which are palmately and dichotomously divided, ultimate segments 6–10 inches long, 1½–2 inches wide, oblong acuminate; costæ from the summit of the stipes dichotomously branched through the

No. 184.

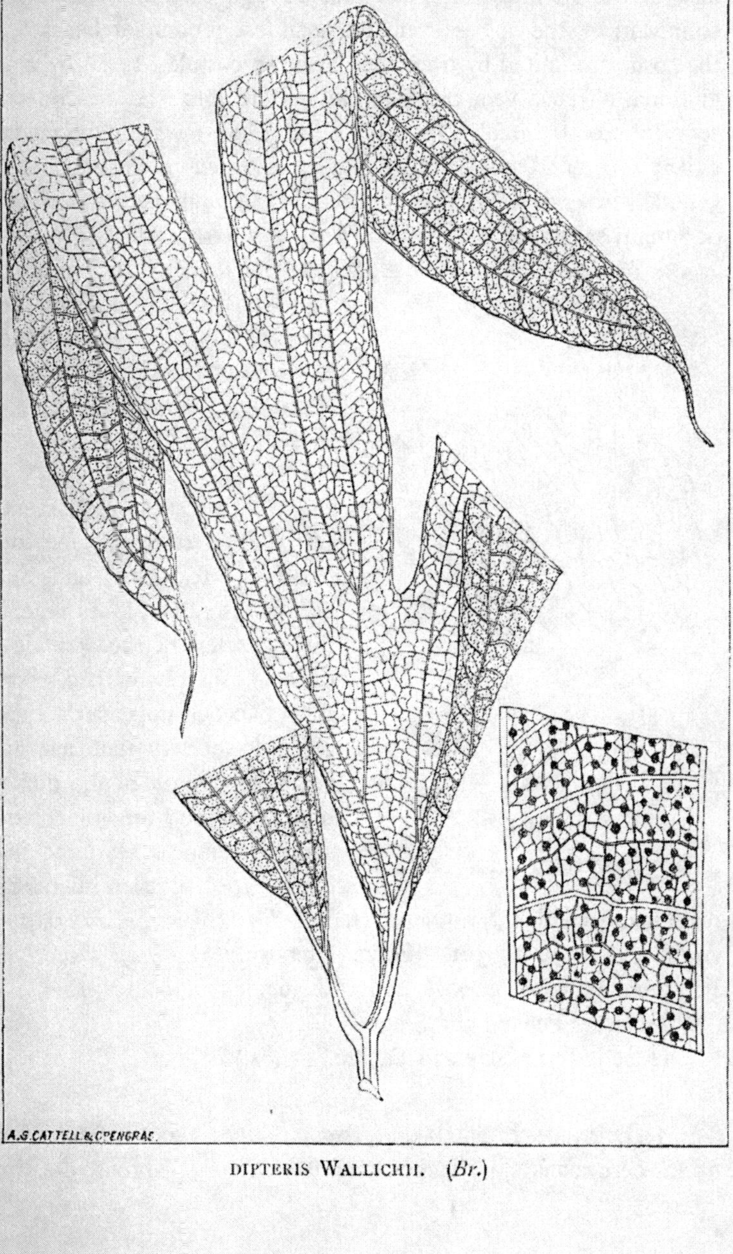

A. S. CATTELL & Co. ENGRAS.

DIPTERIS WALLICHII. (*Br.*)

disk of the frond, a single pair runs through each terminal segment connivent at the apices; venation manifest prominent beneath, all the costæ are united by transverse flexuose costules, these by a longitudinal flexuose vein through the middle into two nearly equal series of costular areoles, then again into lesser ones all subquadrangular; sori small, superficial copious, scattered in the areoles, but generally in series more or less perfect and accompanied by a resinous or gummy substance. *R. Br. in Hook. and Grev. Ic. Fil. t.* 168–9. *Hook. Sp. Fil.* v. 99. *Wall. Cat. n.* 287. *Bedd. F. B. I. t.* 80.

Khasya, up to 4,000 feet, Borpani, 2,000 feet, and elsewhere, Cachar, at Luckipoor, 250 feet elevation, Jaintea, Sylhet station in the plains.

No. 185.

DIPTERIS HORSFIELDII. (*Br.*)

2. DIPTERIS HORSFIELDII. (*Br.*) Stipe strong, 3–5 feet long; frond 1–3 feet long, and much broader, the main lobes reaching three-quarters of the way down, the edges sharply toothed, texture subcoriaceous, upper surface dark-green, lower very glaucous, main veins very prominent, dichotomously forked; areoles copious; sori very minute, scattered irregularly, especially plentiful near the main veins, confluent, not gummy. *R. Br. Hook. Sp. Fil.* v. *p.* 99. *Bedd. F. B. I. t.* 321. Polyp. conjugatum, *Kaulf.* (*not Lam.*) Polyp. Dipteris (*Bl.*), *Hook. Syn. Fil.* 362.

Malacca, Penang and Singapore.

(Also in the Malay and Pacific Islands.)

3. DIPTERIS LOBBIANA. (*Hook.*) Stipes 1 foot and more long; fronds coriaceous, 8–12 inches long, flabelliform, glabrous, 3–4 times

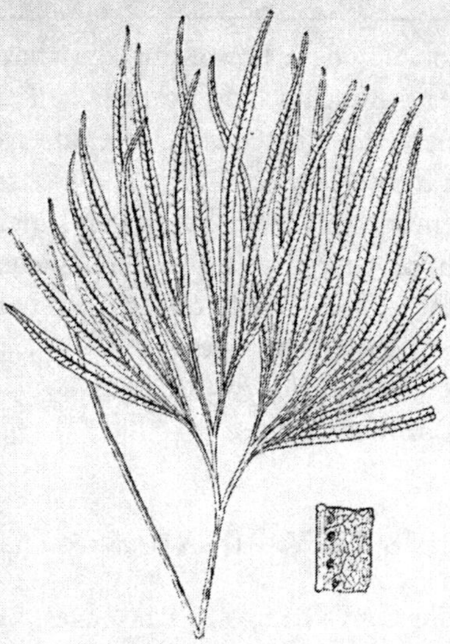

N°. 186.

DIPTERIS LOBBIANA. (*Hook.*)

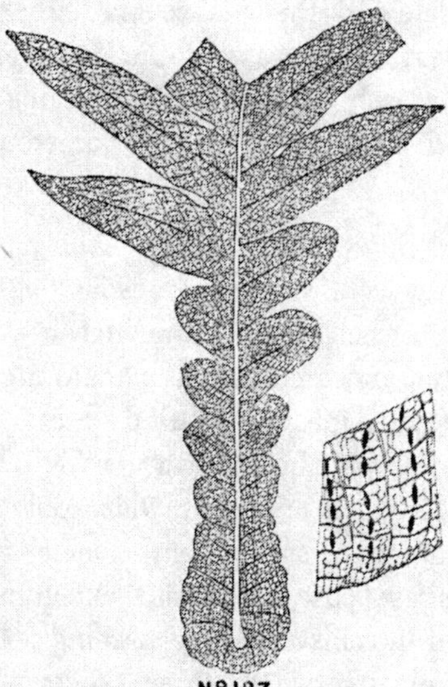

N°. 187.

DRYNARIA CORONANS. (*Wall.*)

digitately dichotomous, dark brownish-green above, pale and tawny beneath, segments 4–8 inches long, scarcely half an inch wide, linear-sublanceolate, finely acuminated costate entire; venation manifest, the costules form a costal series of large soriferous areoles, the rest of the veins unite, constituting lesser areoles and include free veinlets; sori 1–2 in each primary areole (sometimes confluent) in a single series very near the costa. *Hook. Sp. Fil.* v. 100. *Hook. in Kew Gard. Misc.* v. *p.* 300, *t.* xi. *Bedd. F. B. I. t.* 233. Polypodium bifurcatum, *Baker in Syn. Fil. p.* 362.

Malacca, on Mount Ophir.

GENUS LXIV.—DRYNARIA. (*Bory.*)

(*Dryads*, the sterile fronds being like oak-leaves, a tree sacred to the Dryads.)

Fronds articulate with the caudex, with either a separate sterile frond like an oak leaf, or the base of the frond pinnatifid and oak-leaf-like; veins copiously anastomosing, forming quadrate or hexagonal areoles; sori small, round or oval, numerous

1. DRYNARIA CORONANS. (*Wall.*) Rhizome thick, creeping, branched and interwoven, villous-paleaceous with golden scales; fronds large uniform, when growing arranged in a circle, firm, coriaceous, but rather thin and translucent, two and more feet long, from a broad sessile cordate, lobate-pinnatifid base (then suddenly contracted), lanceolate, deeply almost to the rachis pinnatifid, segments 8–12 inches long, $\frac{3}{4}$–1 inch and more wide, oblong-lanceolate, acuminate, lower ones gradually shorter, entire, incrassated at the margin; venation very manifest, costules parallel extending to the margin, these are connected by transverse veins forming 5–6 soriferous areoles and then again generally two or three others which include free veinlets; sori oval, often confluent longitudinally, solitary in the primary areoles, forming an eccentric series always nearer one costule than the opposite one. *Wall. Cat. n.* 288. *Hook. Sp. Fil.* v. 94

Bedd. F. B. I. t. 13. D. conjugata, *Hook. Syn. Fil.* 366 (*not Lam.*)

Himalayas, Nepal to Bhotan, 1,000–4,000 feet elevation, rare, Khasya, 1,000–3000 feet common, Chittagong Hills, 500 feet elevation; Tenasserim and Malay Peninsula.

(Also in Hong Kong and Formosa.)

2. DRYNARIA SPLENDENS. (*Hook.*) Rhizome woody, the scales grey, fibrillose, adpressed; fronds subsessile, 2–3 feet long, 1 foot or more broad, the lower part barren, cut down nearly or quite to the rachis into erect-patent entire acute lobes 4–8 inches long, 1–2 inches broad, the upper fertile pinnæ distant, ligulate, 4–8 inches long, $\frac{1}{4}$–$\frac{1}{2}$ inch broad; main veins distinct, with distinct transverse veinlets and copious intermediate ones and free veinlets; sori oblong or subquadrangular, filling up the whole of the fertile pinnæ except the midrib. *Hook. Sp. Fil.* v. 96. *Syn. Fil.* 367. *Bedd. F. B. I. t.* 316. Dryostachyum, *J. Sm.*

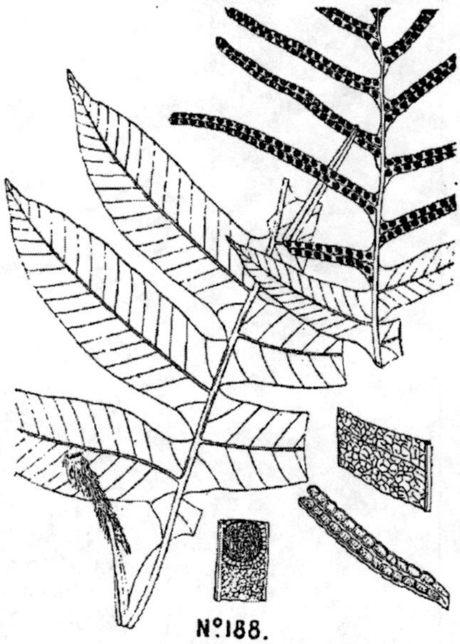

No. 188.
DRYNARIA SPLENDENS. (*Hook.*)

Singapore.

(Also in the Philippines.)

3. DRYNARIA PROPINQUA. (*Wall.*) Rhizome stout, creeping, the scales lanceolate-linear pubescent; fronds glabrous dimorphous, the barren ones 4–9 inches long, 3–4 inches broad, cut half or three-quarters down into bluntish or acute lobes, the fertile ones 1$\frac{1}{2}$–3 feet long, often 1 foot broad, with a distinct stem, the lobes 4–6 inches long, $\frac{1}{2}$–$\frac{3}{4}$ inch broad, reaching down nearly or quite to the rachis,

No 189.

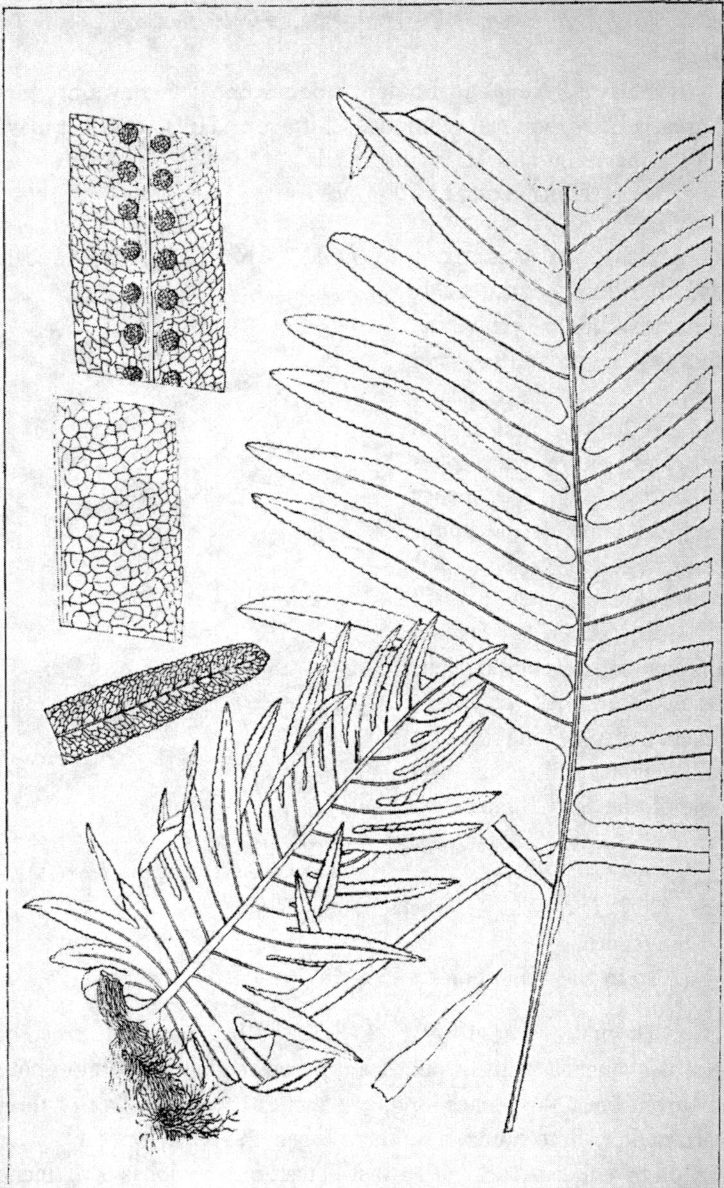

DRYNARIA PROPINQUA. (*Wall.*)

obscurely serrated, texture subcoriaceous; main veins of the fertile fronds ramifying, not carried in distinct parallel lines to the margin, areoles copious, the free veinlets few and variously directed; sori in a single row near the midrib, placed at the point of union of several veinlets. *Wall. Cat.* 293. *Hook. Syn. Fil.* 367. *Bedd. F. B. I. t.* 160. Pleopeltis Parishii, *Bedd. F. B. I. t.* 125.

Himalayas, from Gurwhal to Bhotan, 2,000–7,000 feet elevation, Khasya, very common; Birma and Malay Peninsula.

(Also in Java.)

4. DRYNARIA MOLLIS. (*Bedd.*) Rhizome creeping, clothed with subulate golden transparent ciliated scales; fronds firm-membranaceous dimorphous; sterile ones 4–6 inches long, sessile ovate glabrous, deeply pinnatifid with the sinuses very narrow and the segments sometimes overlapping each other, fertile fronds very shortly stipitate (the dwarfed lower segments often extending nearly to the base of the rachis), ovate-lanceolate up to 1½ feet long, 2–4 inches broad, furnished with soft hairs on both sides and ciliated, deeply almost to the rachis pinnatifid, segments lanceolate 1–2 inches long, ⅓–½ inch broad, nearly horizontal, rather distant, the sinus being very broad, the lower ones dwarfed and gradually reduced to a decurrent wing; venation very prominent in the sterile fronds, but much less so in the fertile ones than in D. propinqua; veins forming three or four series of rather regular areoles in which are sometimes included free veinlets; sori forming only a single series close to the costa, each sorus being on the vein between the first and second areole. *Bedd. F. B. I. t.* 216. Polyp. (Drynaria) rivale, *Mett. in Hook. Syn. Fil. p.* 367, *a later name.*

Himalayas, Nynee Tal, Gurwhal, Kumaon, 6,000–9,000 feet elevation.

5. DRYNARIA QUERCIFOLIA. (*L.*) Rhizome creeping, short, stout, densely clothed with red-brown satiny lanceolate-subulate soft scales, which have a cordate base, and are ¼–½ inch long; fronds coriaceous or subcoriaceous of two kinds, sterile ones varying in

No.190.

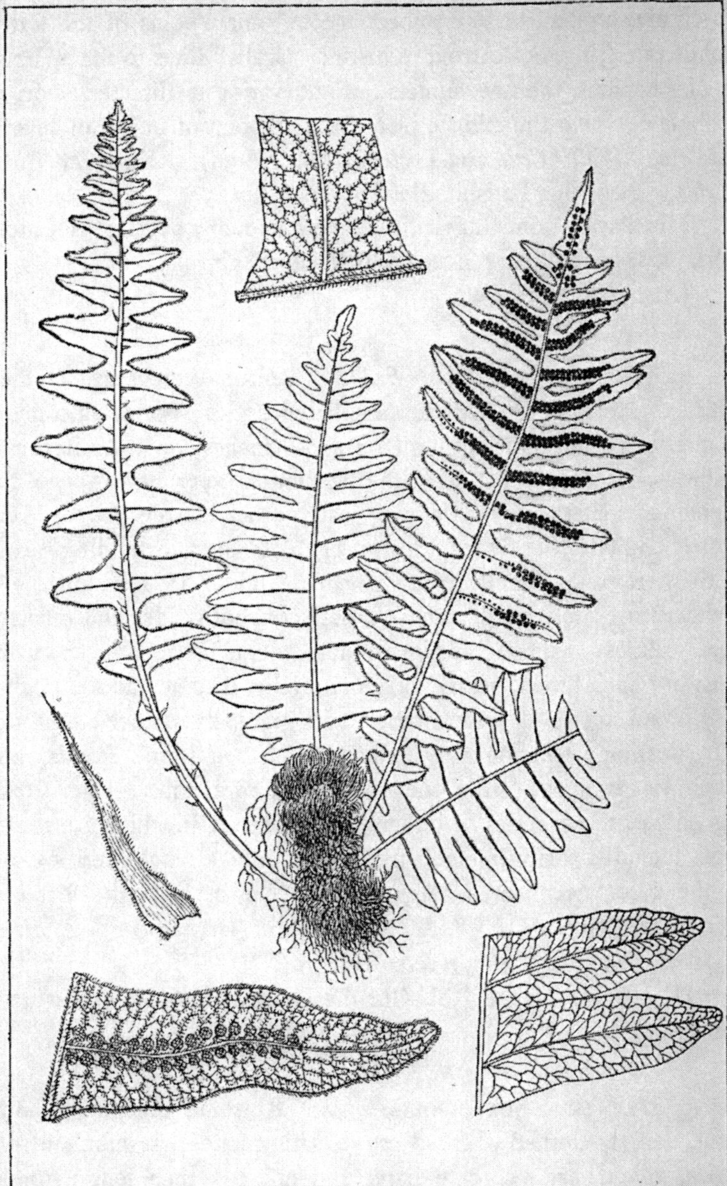

A. S. CATTELL & Co. MADRAS.

DRYNARIA MOLLIS. (*Bedd.*)

size from 3–12 inches and more long, and 7–8 inches wide, green when very young, but soon turning dark-brown, glossy, cordate-ovate variously lobate-pinnatifid, sometimes half-way down to the costa; fertile ones 2–3 feet long, long-petiolate broad-ovate deeply nearly to the rachis pinnatifid, segments 5–9 inches long, 1–1½ inch wide, oblong acuminate, entire; venation manifest, costules distinct rather distant, united by transverse veins forming 4–6 primary soriferous areoles filled up with a net-work of small quadrangular areoles with or without free veins; sori compital small, numerous, two in each primary areole, consequently in two series between and parallel with the costules. Polypodium quercifolium, *Lin. Sp. Pl. p.* 1547. *Hook. Sp. Fil.* v. *p.* 96. *Bedd. F. S. I. t.* 187.

Throughout the Indian region in the plains, or very low down on the mountains, on trees or rocks.

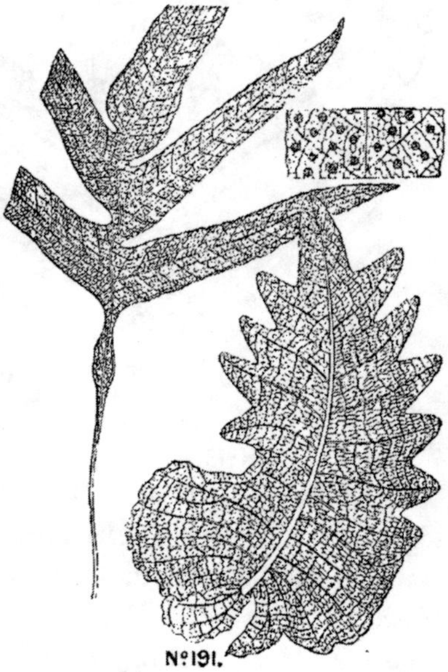

No. 191.

DYRNARIA QUERCIFOLIA. (*Linn.*)

6. DRYNARIA LINNÆI. (*Bory*) Rhizome stout, the scales 1–2 lines long from a peltate base, broadly ovate obtuse, with a deciduous acumen; fronds dimorphous the barren ones sessile, brown rigid, bluntly lobed, the fertile ones long-stalked 2–3 feet long, 6–12 inches broad, cut down nearly to the rachis, into entire erect-patent lanceolate lobes, texture rigid, both sides naked; main veins distinct to the edge with copious irregular areoles between them, with copious small scattered sori. *Bory. Ann. Sc. Nat.* i. v. *p.* 464, *t.* 12. *Hook. Syn. Fil.* 368. *Bedd. F. B. I.* 315.

Ceylon; Malay Peninsula. Very like quercifolia, but the scales on the rhizome are quite different and the sori smaller and more scattered, it may be only a variety and is united with it by Bentham.

I have seen no specimen from South India, but without critical examination it might be passed by in the field or in the herbarium as quercifolia.

7. DRYNARIA RIGIDULA. (*Sw.*) Rhizome stout creeping, the the scales fibrillose dark-brown, fronds dimorphous, the barren ones sessile, 6–9 inches long, rarely more, 3–4 inches broad, cut down $\frac{1}{3}$–$\frac{1}{2}$ towards the rachis into blunt lobes, or rarely quite pinnate at the apex, the fertile 2–4 feet long, 12–18 inches broad, long-stalked pinnate, pinnæ one inch or more apart, narrowed or stalked at the base, 6–12 inches long, $\frac{1}{4}$–$\frac{3}{8}$ inch broad, the point acuminate, the edge more or less deeply incised, crenate, texture rather coriaceous; rachis and both surfaces naked, main veins not distinct to the edge, areoles copious, free veinlets few; sori immersed in a single row half-way between the edge and midrib. *Sw. Syn. Fil.* 230. *Hook. Syn. Fil.* 368. Drynaria diversifolia (*R. Br.*), *Hook. Sp. Fil.* v. 98. *Bedd. F. S. I. t.* 314.

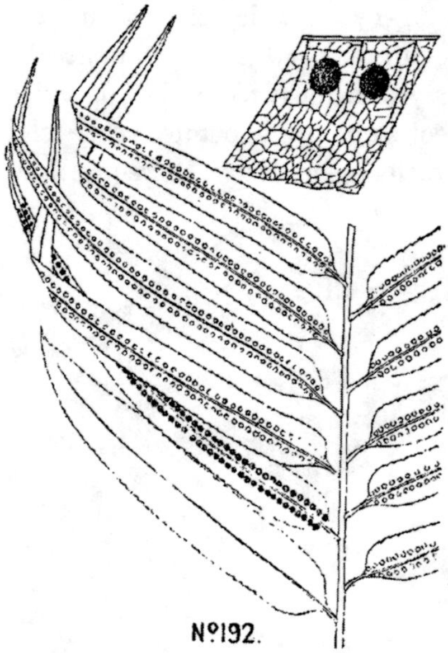

No. 192.

DRYNARIA RIGIDULA. (*Sw.*)

Malacca.

(Also in tropical Australia, Malay Islands, the tropical Pacific Islands.)

GENUS LXV.—PLEOPELTIS. (*H. & B.*)

(*Pleos*, full; *peltis*, shield—the sori often furnished with round scales.)

Veins copiously anastomosing, forming copious irregular areoles, with generally free included veinlets spreading in various directions, the sori various in position, generally on the back of united veinlets; fronds simple, pinnatifid or pinnate, articulate with the caudex. In the *Synopsis Filicum* Phymatodes is the name adopted for this genus (or subgenus only in that work); this name, however, is of much later date than Pleopeltis, having been instituted by Presl. in 1836, Pleopeltis by Humboldt and Bonpland in 1810. Some authors split the genus up into many genera.

* *Fronds simple* (*also* 3–5 *lobed in pteropus.*)

A. *Main veins not distinct to the edge.*

1. PLEOPELTIS ACCEDENS. (*Bl.*) Rhizome wide-creeping, slender filiform, scarcely paleaceous, attached to the bark of trees by copious woolly radicles, stipes scattered 2–5 lines long; fronds sub-coriaceous, opaque, glabrous entire, sterile ones 1–1½ inch long, oblong ovate obtuse, fertile ones 2–3½ inches long, from a broad cuneate base, long-acuminate; venation obscure, costules indistinct, veins forming three large areoles (in each of which is one large forked veinlet) and a smaller marginal areole; sori large for the size of the plant on the acuminated portion in a single series on each side of the costa. *Bl. En. Fil. Jav. p.* 121. *Hook. Sp. Fil.* v. 66. *Bedd. F. B. I. t.* 215.

Malacca.

(Also in the Philippines, the Malay Islands, Polynesia.)

2. PLEOPELTIS ROSTRATA. (*Hook.*) Rhizome very slender, wide-creeping, furnished with lanceolate-linear scales, stipes distant ¼–2 inches long, naked; fronds lanceolate-acuminate, somewhat dimorphic, the barren often being broader, coriaceous glabrous, the margin entire; veins immersed, main veins indistinct, areoles irregular, including simple or forked free veinlets; sori in a single row on each side close to the midrib. *Hook. Syn. Fil.* 353. *Bedd. F. B. I. t.* 159.

Sikkim and Bhotan, 6,000 feet elevation, abundant; Khasya 4,000–5,000 feet elevation.

3. PLEOPELTIS LINEARIS. (*Thunb.*) Rhizome wide-creeping, woody, the scales lanceolate dull-brown, never with hairs, stipes from a few lines to 2 inches long, rarely with any scales; fronds 6–12 inches long, rarely more, ½–¾ inch broad, entire, narrowed gradually at both ends, texture coriaceous, both sides naked or nearly so; areoles

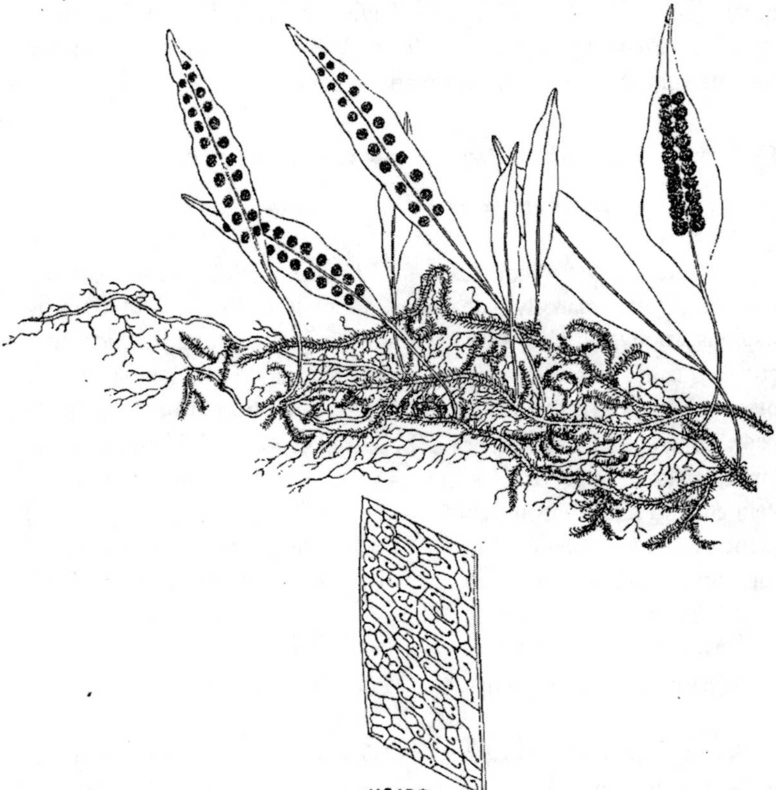

No. 193
PLEOPELTIS ROSTRATA. (*Hook.*)

irregular with forked free veinlets; sori superficial or scarcely immersed, never sunk in a cyst, large prominent, forming a single row half-way between the costa and margin, when young covered with copious thin peltate scales. *Thunb. Fl. Jap.* 335. *Hook. Syn. Fil.* 354. Polyp. loriforme, *Wall. Cat.* 271, *2nd sheet* (*typical.*) P. Wightianum, *Wall. Cat.* 2222, acutissimum, 4727, gladiatum, 279.

Pleopeltis nuda, *Hook. Exot. Fl. t.* 63. P. Wightianum, *Bedd. F. S. I.* 180. (P. loriforme, *Wall. Cat.* 271, *type-sheet*, belongs here, I believe, and not to simplex, it has larger fronds, but they are narrow and coriaceous and the veins hidden.)

Himalayas, 1,000–10,000 feet elevation, very common, Khasya; throughout South India; Ceylon; Malay Peninsula.

(Also in the Malay Islands, China, Japan, Central and South Africa and its Islands.)

VAR. STENISTE. (*Clarke.*) With the fronds only 1–1½ lines broad and the sori projecting beyond the margin, but always superficial, is only a form of linearis, and it quite graduates into the type, his var. "polymorpha" is an abnormal form of linearis with the fronds pinnatifid (such as occurs in many other ferns.)

4. PLEOPELTIS SIMPLEX. (*Sw.*) Very like linearis, only the fronds are of thinner texture and much larger, up to 2 feet long by 1–2 inches broad, the veins more distinct, the sori always more or less deeply sunk and forming pustules on the upper side of the fronds, sometimes quite sunk in a cyst with visible margins, but never nearly so prominent as in stenophylla, which also differs in its smaller size, much more rigid texture and fewer veins. *Sw. Syn. Fil.* 27. Polyp. excavatum (*Bory.*), *Willd. Sp. Pl.* v. 158. P. Grevilleanum, *Wall. Cat.* 5169. P. sesquipedale, *Wall. Cat.* 275. P. lineare, var. β simplex, *Hook, Syn. Fil.* 354.

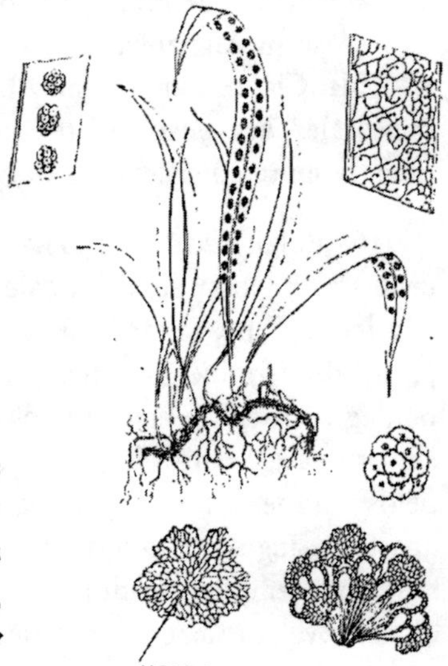

No. 194.

PLEOPELTIS LINEARIS. (*Thunb.*)

Himalayas, confounded by *Hooker* (in his *Sp. Fil.*) and by *Clarke* with linearis, but kept distinct by all other botanists, and made a distinct variety of linearis by Mr. Baker in the *Syn. Fil.*, but Mr. Baker now agrees that it should be made a distinct species; the scales of the rhizome differ from those of "normalis," but the fronds are almost exactly similar to that species, and I had previously confounded it with that (not with linearis.)

5. PLEOPELTIS CLATHRATA. (*Clarke.*) Rhizome short creeping, with ovate acute, often hair-pointed scales; fronds small, stipe often as long as the frond; sori mixed with sessile irregularly peltate and lacerate clathrate scales. *Clarke, F. N. I. p.* 559, *t.* 82, *fig.* 1.

Kashmir, Pir Pinjul, 11,000–12,000 feet elevation.

(Also in Afghanistan.)

Mr. Clarke thinks it may be high level form of linearis, but that the scales are peculiar, the texture thinner, the venation consequently more conspicuous, and the stipe longer.

6. PLEOPELTIS STENOPHYLLA. (*Bl.*) Rhizome creeping, paleaceous, with glossy subulate pale imbricated ferruginous scales, stipes 1–2 inches long, distant; fronds firm-coriaceous, very rigid, glabrous polished, 4–9 inches long, $\frac{1}{4}$–$\frac{1}{2}$ inch, or rarely more wide, linear-oblong obtuse, the margin thickened and subreflexed, broadly crenate-sinuate, rarely narrowing upwards, but much and gradually attenuated below on the stipes; costa prominent beneath, costules none, veins anastomosing so as to form oblong, hexagonal oblique areoles, generally quite empty or with rarely a free included veinlet; sori rather distant oval, arranged in a series close to the margin, deeply sunk in a cyst, forming elevated pustules on the upper side one to each crenature, the margin of the cavity elevated. *Bl. Fil. Jav. p.* 135, *t.* 55, *f.* 1. *Hook. Sp. Fil.* v. 65. *Mett. Polyp. p.* 99, *t.* 1, *f.* 31–34 *venation*. *Bedd. F. B. I.* 234.

Mr. Clarke states that this comes between "linearis" type and his variety "steniste," but both these ferns have different venation, and neither have the sori sunk in cysts; this has the sori always much nearer the margin than the midrib even in the broader forms.

Malacca.

(Also in the Philippines.)

7. PLEOPELTIS SINUOSA. (*Wall.*) Rhizome much branched, long-creeping or scandent on trees, sparingly radiculose, half an inch to two inches thick, almost woody when dry, carnose when recent, studded, as it were, with large conical processes upon which the stipes are or have been articulated, and which appear to increase much in size after the fronds have fallen, the whole densely covered (as it were tessellated) with nearly orbicular appressed whitish peltate scales with a dark spot in the centre, stipes 1-2 inches long, glabrous and scaleless; fronds sub-dimorphous, subcoriaceous glabrous, sterile ones 3-6-7 inches long, ¾-1 inch broad, subelliptical, oblong obtuse entire, fertile ones longer, sometimes 1 foot-16 inches long, ½-¾ of an inch wide, linear-oblong obtuse, the margins more or less sinuated, the base in both attenuate-decurrent; venation copiously anastomosing, forming large very irregular areoles filled with lesser ones (formed by more slender veins), and these include branched or simple veinlets which occasionally again anastomose; sori remote, large, oblong, immersed in cysts, which form pustules on the upper side arranged in a single series nearer the margin than the costa. *Wall. Cat. n.* 2231. *Hook. Sp. Fil.* v. 61. *Bedd. F. B. I. t.* 8.

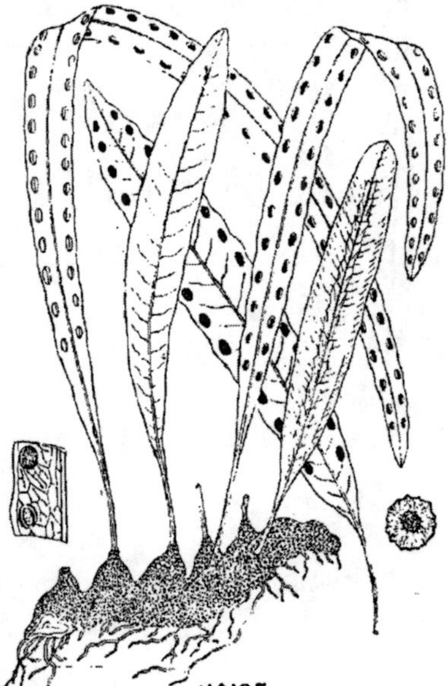

No. 195.

PLEOPELTIS SINUOSA. (*Wall.*)

Malacca.

(Also in the Solomon Islands, Amboyna and New Hebrides.)

8. PLEOPELTIS LONGIFOLIA. (*Metten.*) Rhizome horizontal, creeping, thick squamose, stipes approximate, 2-3 inches long; fronds 1-2-3 feet long, ¾-1¼ inch wide, thick, carnose-coriaceous,

glabrous, linear-lanceolate, obtusely acuminate, gradually long attenuated below on the stipes, entire, the margins subrevolute, venation internal, very indistinct, costules veniform, united by transverse veins into rather large areoles then into irregular lesser ones, which include free veinlets; sori compital oblong, forming a line or series near the margin rather close placed, sunk in cysts, and forming a corresponding elevated line on the upper surface, capsules mixed with long-stipitate scales. *Metten. Polyp. p.* 87. *Hook. Sp. Fil.* v. 60. *Bedd. F. B. I. t.* 7. P. contiguum, *Wall. Cat.* 285.

Birma and the Malay Peninsula generally, Mergui, Singapore, &c.; North India, Kumaon.

(Also in the Philippines and Malay Islands.)

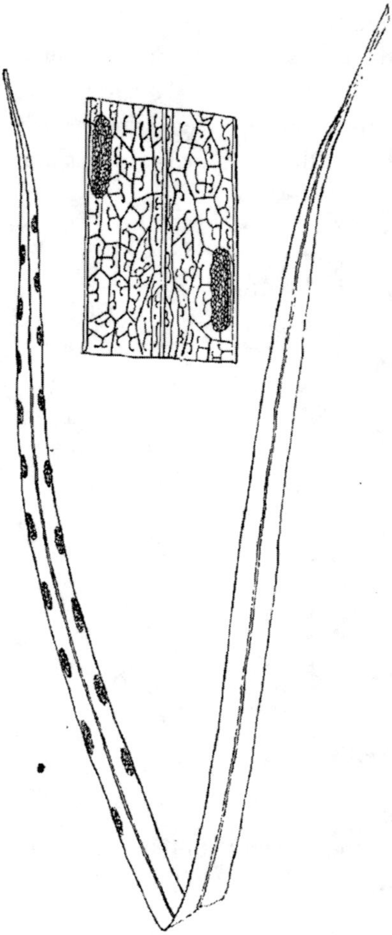

No. 196.

PLEOPELTIS LONGIFOLIA. (*Mett.*)

9. PLEOPELTIS SUPERFICIALIS. (*Bl.*) Rhizome wide-creeping, thick as a crow-quill, the scales ovate and lanceolate acute, spreading, brown shining, stipes up to six inches long, often curved, sometimes with ovate scales; fronds lanceolate-linear (often forked at the apex), subcoriaceous, narrowed gradually at both ends, the margins entire, 6–12 inches long, by ½–2 inches broad, glabrous; areoles numerous with free veinlets; sori

copious scattered irregularly, compital, large or small. Polypodium superficiale, *Bl. En. Pl. Jav. Fil.* 123. *Hook. Syn. Fil.* 355. *Bedd. F. B. I. t.* 75.

Khasya Hills, 4,000–6,000 feet elevation, extending to the Naga country to the east, and to Bhotan and Mishmee; Malay Peninsula.

(Also in South China.)

10. PLEOPELTIS LANCEOLATA. (*L.*) Rhizome long-creeping, paleaceous, with lanceolate ferruginous scales, stipes remote, 1–2–4 inches long; fronds coriaceous, 3–9 inches long, $\frac{1}{4}$–$\frac{3}{4}$ inch wide, lanceolate, more or less acuminate, long and gradually attenuated at the base, copiously furnished with orbicular ovate, small appressed peltate scales dark in the centre, pale in the circumference and denticulate; veins immersed indistinct, the primary veins form large obliquely elongated areoles, which include very irregular and different sized areoles, and a few free veinlets which are rarely forked; sori generally very large and often exceedingly prominent, pulvinate globose or oval, stalked scales mixed with the spore cases. Polyp. lanceolatum, *Linn. Sp. Pl.* 1082. P. lepidota, *Hook. Sp. Fil.* v. 56. *Willd. in Schlecht Adunbr., p.* 17. *Bedd. F. S. I. t.* 181. P. angustata var. depauperata, *Clarke, F. N. I. p.* 559.

Nilgiris and higher mountains on the West side of the Madras Presidency; Assam (one poor specimen in Kew Herbarium); Ceylon, Ambawalla estate.

(Also in Tropical America and the West Indies, South Africa and its islands; St. Helena; Sandwich Islands.)

11. PLEOPELTIS ANGUSTATA. (*Sw.*) Rhizome long-creeping, branched, paleaceous with falcate subulate-setaceous scales, stipes remote, 1$\frac{1}{2}$–4 inches long; fronds 5 inches to a span or more long $\frac{3}{4}$–2 inches wide, tapering below into a petiole, glabrous above, clothed beneath with cottony tomentum which is deciduous, coriaceous, oblong-lanceolate; venation sunk obscure, costular areoles with free or branched and more or less connected veinlets; sori very large, subglobose oval, partially sunk in the frond, very convex,

No. 197

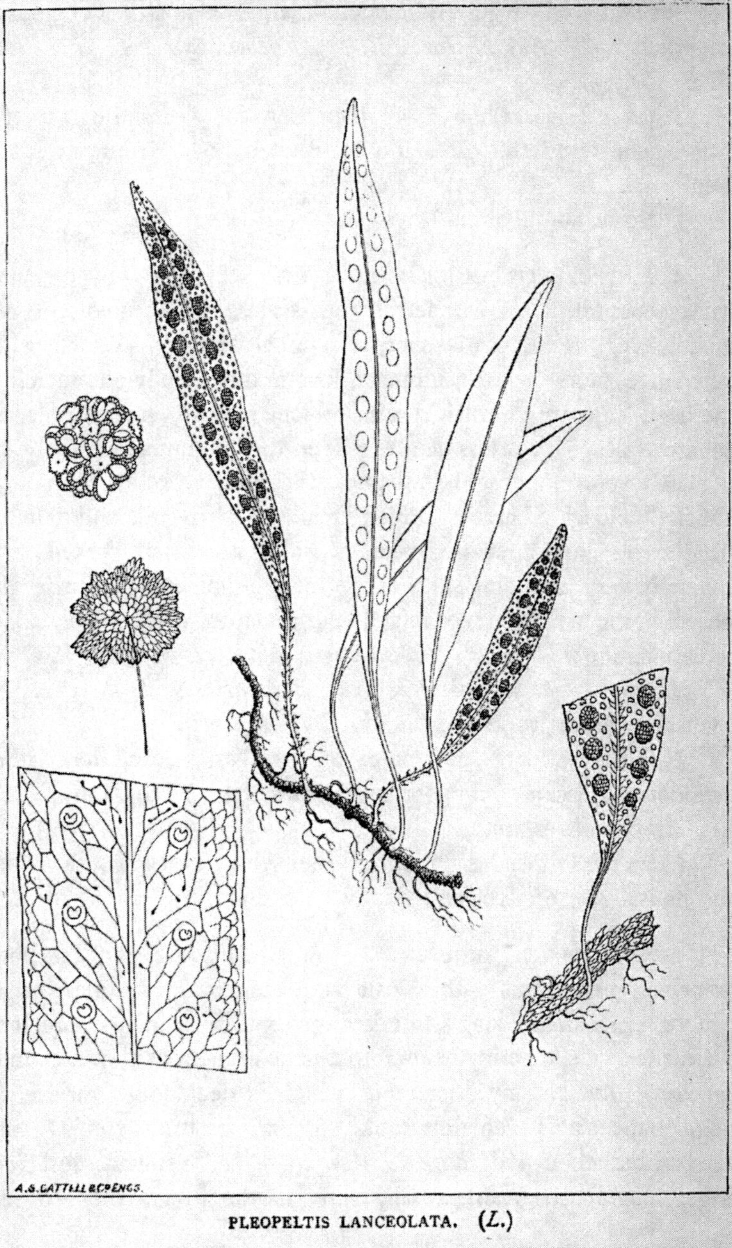

PLEOPELTIS LANCEOLATA. (*L.*)

forming a single series on each side between the costa and margin, generally towards the apex only, sometimes longitudinally confluent. *Sw. Syn. Fil. pp.* 27 *and* 224. Niphobolus angustatus, *Hook. Sp. Fil.* v. 43. *Bedd. F. S. I. t.* 185. Niphopsis, *J. Sm.* Pleopeltis macrosora, *Presl.* Polypodium sphærocephalum, *Wall. Cat. n.* 272.

Malay Peninsula, Singapore, Malacca, and Penang. South India (?) I have never detected it, though I have a specimen said to have been collected on the Nilgiris, and Hooker gives Tranquebar as a locality.

(Also in the Malay Islands and North-east Australia.)

12. PLEOPELTIS NORMALIS. (*Don.*) Rhizome scandent, thick as a crowquill, with ovate or lanceolate almost hair-pointed adpressed scales, which carry erect from their backs tufts of linear stiff black-red bristles; fronds narrowed much at the base, sometimes to the very foot of the stipe, usually broadest near the middle, 1–2 feet long, by 1–2 inches broad, submembranaceous glabrous, a few scattered ovate close-adpressed scales often present on the stipes and near the base of the main rachis beneath; venation as in linearis, main veins very indistinct and areoles with free included veinlets; sori large, superficial or a little immersed, often in several rows, or irregularly in one row, or rarely regular in one row. *Don. Prod. Fl. Nep.* 1. *Clarke, F. N. I.* 558. *Hook. Syn. Fil.* 358, *in part. Bedd. F. B. I. t.* 10. P. longifrons, *Wall. Cat.* 274.

Himalayas, Nepal to Bhotan, 4,000–8,000 feet elevation, Khasya, 3,000–5,000 feet; Tenasserim on Mooleyit 5,000 feet elevation.

B. *Main veins distinct to the edge, or nearly to the edge.*

13. PLEOPELTIS RHYNCOPHYLLA. (*Hook.*) Rhizome creeping, slender, paleaceous, subsquarrose with subulate ferruginous scales, stipes scattered, slender, 1–2 inches long of the sterile frond, 2–4 of the fertile one; fronds firm, subcoriaceous, glossy, slightly thickened, remotely crenate, sterile ones 1–2 inches long, elliptical, or subovate, obtuse, fertile ones 3–6 inches long, lanceolate from near the base,

gradually and long-acuminated, below attenuated; venation distinct, slightly prominent, the costules connected by transverse veins forming areoles which enclose free veinlets, which latter sometimes unite with opposite veins; the sori mostly confined to the narrow acuminated apex, and when mature very large in a single series on each side of the costa. *Hook. Sp. Fil.* v. 65. *Hook. Ic. Plant.* 655 (*or t.* 55 *of Cent. of Ferns.*) *Bedd. F. B. I. t.* 9.

Khasya, 4,000–5,500 feet elevation; Tenasserim on Mooleyit, 5,000 feet elevation.

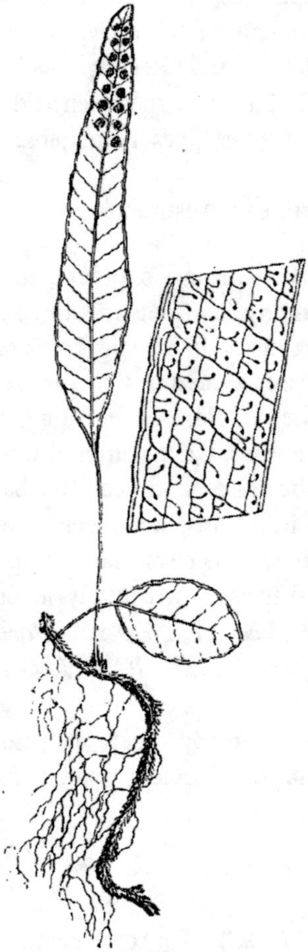

No. 198.
PLEOPELTIS RHYNCOPHYLLA.
(*Hook.*)

14. PLEOPELTIS GRIFFITHIANA. (*Hook.*) Rhizome wide-creeping, as thick as a crowquill, the scales dense, lanceolate-subulate, brown, spreading; stipes 3–6 inches long, firm, erect; fronds 6–8 inches long, up to $2\frac{1}{4}$ inches broad, coriaceous, lanceolate or ovate-lanceolate, the apex acute, the margin more or less repand, the base rounded or suddenly narrowed; main veins very distinct to the edge, areoles fine, hidden with copious free simple or forked veinlets; sori large, one between each main vein in a single row close to the costa, often extending more than half-way to the base of the frond. *Hook. Syn. Fil. p.* 359. *Bedd. F. B. I. t.* 158.

Sikkim and Bhotan, 6,000–9,000 feet elevation. Khasya, 4,000–5,000 feet.

15. PLEOPELTIS OVATA. (*Wall.*) Rhizome wide-creeping,

thick as a crowquill, scales lanceolate-linear, brown spreading; stipes 4–8 inches long, firm, erect, slightly scaly below; fronds 6–12 inches long, up to 3 inches broad, ovate-lanceolate, the apex acute, the margin entire, the base narrowed suddenly, texture herbaceous, both sides glabrous; main veins distinct to nearly the edge, with copious areoles including free forked veinlets; sori large irregularly scattered near the costa. Polypodium ovatum, *Wall. Cat.* 276. *Hook. Syn. Fil.* 359. *Bedd. F. B. I. t.* 157.

Sikkim, Chundaghiri, Bhotan, Khasya, 4,000 feet elevation, at Bishop's Falls, Shillong, rare.

16. PLEOPELTIS MEMBRANACEA. (*Don.*) Rhizome short-creeping, stout, the younger portion paleaceous, with blackish-green ovate acuminate scales; stipes distant or subaggregated, 1–5 inches long, if longer winged above with the decurrent base of the frond; fronds 6 inches to 2–3 feet long, by less than an inch to 6 inches broad, thin membranaceous and translucent, lanceolate or oblong-lanceolate, or oblanceolate, acuminate, the base long attenuated and much gradually decurrent upon the stipes, glabrous, the margin entire (or rarely more or less deeply sinuate-lobate or pinnatifid, and even fimbriated throughout the whole length with long narrow unequal segments); venation very distinct, main veins horizontal or nearly so, slender, usually remote, connected by transverse veins which form the primary areoles, and these are filled up with irregular net-work, of which the areoles are very unequal and include copious free veinlets; sori compital, rather small, usually in two series between the costules, more or less numerous according

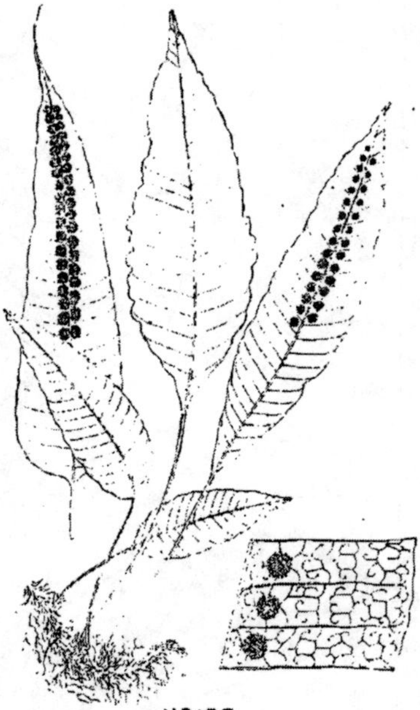

Nº 199.

PLEOPELTIS GRIFFITHIANA. (*Hook.*)

No. 200.

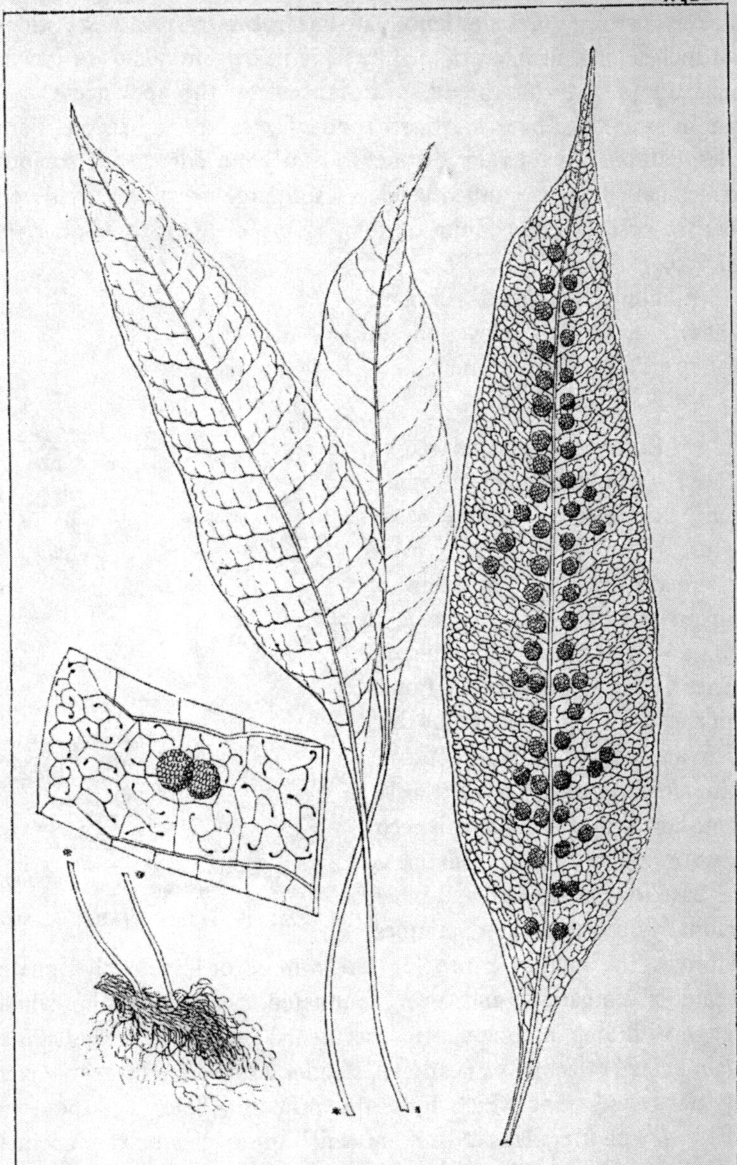

PLEOPELTIS OVATA. (*Wall.*)

to the width of the frond, rarely reduced to one sorus near the costa, where a single series parallel with the costa is formed, not unfrequently there are 3–4–5 series (not very regular) between the costa, (in one instance a single series only appears between the costules, and those of a very large size and abnormal in form, often oval or oblong and lying parallel with the costules). *Don. Prod. Fl. Nep. p.* 2. *Hooker Sp. Fil.* v. 70. Polyp. grandifolium, *Wall. Cat. n.* 282. P. heterocarpum, *Bl. Fil. Jav. p.* 167, *t.* 75. *Bedd. F. S. I. t.* 177.

Himalayas, from Gurwhal and Bhotan, 3,000–8,000 feet elevation, Khasya, 2,000–5,000 feet, Chota Nagpore, Parasnath; South India, mountainous tracts on both sides of the Presidency, 2,000–5,000 feet elevation; fronds varying from ½ inch to 5 inches in breadth; Ceylon. It only appears with the rainy season and dies down in November.

17. PLEOPELTIS ZIPPELLII. (*Bl.*) Rhizome slender, creeping shortly, scales lanceolate acute; fronds lanceolate, often quite caudate at the apex, narrowed gradually at the base into a short stipe (or more rarely there is a stipe about 2 inches long), subcoriaceous, margin entire or a little undulate, lower part of the rachis beneath sometimes with a few scales; primary veins prominent and near the margin, areoles copious, with free included simple of forked veinlets; sori compital in two rows between the primary veins and in about four rows between the costa and margin. *Bl. Pl. Jav. Fil.* 172, *t.* 80. *Hook. Sp. Fil.* v. 72. Pleopeltis heterocarpa, *Hook. Syn. Fil. p.* 360, (*not Bl.*) *Bedd. F. B. I.* 319, (*venation not correct, as not showing the free veinlets.*)

Himalayas, Dalhousie (Dyas), Sikkim and Bhotan, 2,000–6,000 feet elevation, Khasya, 2,000–4,000 feet elevation, (not in Ceylon as stated by Clarke).

(Also in Java and Philippines.)

18. PLEOPELTIS PUNCTATA. (*Linn. under Acrostichum.*) Rhizome scarcely creeping, stout, clothed with brownish ovate or lanceolate scales; fronds 1–3 feet long, 1–3 inches broad, lanceolate, subsessile,

gradually narrowed at the base, acute or blunt at the apex, carnose-coriaceous, very glabrous; venation immersed (visible in a dried state), main veins fine but distinct to the margin, areoles copious, including smaller areoles, in which are free simple or forked veinlets, with clavate apices; sori compital, very small and scattered very irregularly, generally only on the upper half of the frond. *Linn. Sp. Pl.* 1524. *Sw. in Schr. Jour.* 1800, ii. 21. Pleopeltis irioides, *Hook. Syn. Fil.* 360. *Bedd. F. S. I. t.* 178. *Wall. Cat.* 281, glabrum, *and* 273, polycephalum.

South India, Western mountains up to about 3,000 feet elevation; Ceylon; North India, in the Bengal plains, and up to 3,000 feet elevation; Malay Peninsula.

(Also in China, Malay Islands, North Australia, Polynesia, Southern and Central Africa and the islands.

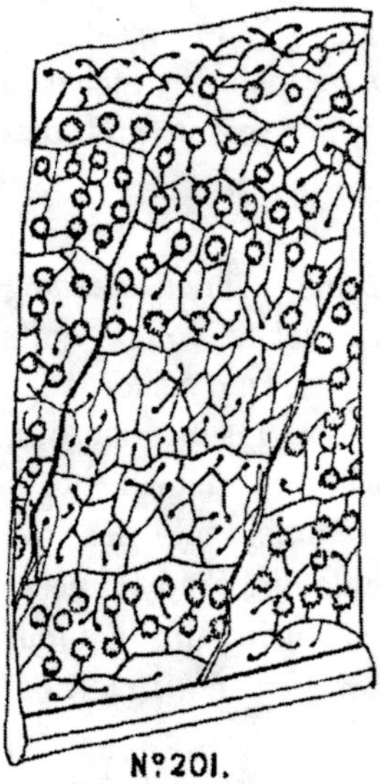

No. 201.
PLEOPELTIS PUNCTATA. (*Lin.*)

Bedd. F. B. I. t. 317.

Malacca.

(Also in the Malay Islands.)

19. PLEOPELTIS MUSÆFOLIA. (*Bl.*) In every way like punctata, so that the same description will do for both, except that the texture in this is, like that of nigrescens and hemionitidea, thin and papery, with the veins very prominent, whilst punctata has fleshy leaves, in texture like Thamnopteris Nidus. *Bl. Fil. Jav. p.* 171, *t.* 79. *Hook. Syn. Fil.* 360.

20. PLEOPELTIS HEMIONITIDEA. (*Wall.*) Rhizome creeping, scaly, furnished with wiry scaly fibrous roots; stipes scaly, winged upwards; fronds 6 inches to 1½ foot long, 1–2 inches broad, membranaceous subchartaceous, subtransparent very dark shining green, broad lanceolate, gradually acuminated into a fine point at the apex

and gradually attenuated at the base, being winged nearly all down the stipe, entire glabrous, costa slightly scaly beneath near the base; venation very prominent, main veins blackish, pinnate nearly horizontal, areoles in about five series, subquadrate, in which are free veinlets which are either simple or forked, but without clavate apices; sori compital, rather large, forming one series between the main veins very irregular in shape and size, subglobose or oblong, or even (by confluence) linear. *Wall. Cat. p.* 284. *Hook. Sp. Fil.* v. 73. *Bedd. F. B. I. t.* 182.

South India, on the Western mountains, rather common in Coorg, 3,000 feet elevation, rare elsewhere. Himalayas, Nepal, Bhotan, 2,000–7,000 feet elevation, Khasya, 1,000–5,000 feet elevation, Chittagong, 1,000 feet elevation.

(Also in South China and Malay Islands.)

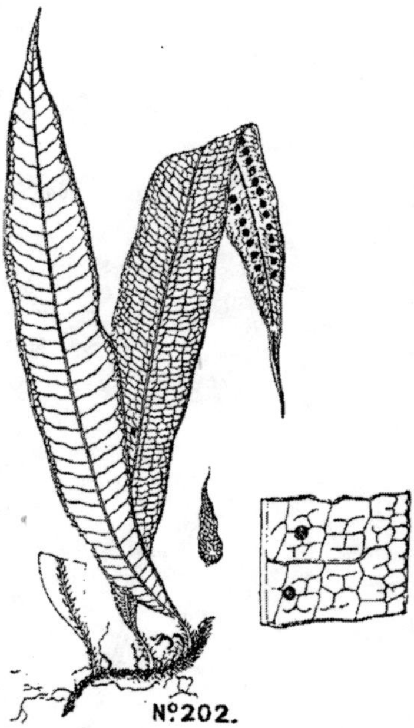

No. 202.

PLEOPELTIS HEMIONITIDEA. (*Wall.*)

21. PLEOPELTIS PTEROPUS. (*Bl.*) Aquatic, rhizome creeping, branched, the young apices only paleaceous, with blackish lanceolate-subulate scales; stipes more or less apart, 1–3–4 inches to 1 foot long, winged upwards, and as well as the back of the costa and costules furfuraceous-squamose; fronds 2–3–9 inches long, $\frac{3}{4}$–$1\frac{1}{2}$ and 2 inches wide, firm membranaceous, very dark dirty green (when dry often black), lanceolate acuminate entire, or 3-lobate, or 3-partite, or 5-lobed, terminal lobes up to 8 inches long, lateral ones 3–5 inches, below long-tapering into a gradually decurrent wing upon the petiole, glabrous above, margin entire; venation very conspicuous, main veins prominent beneath, rather wide apart, extending about two-thirds of the way to the margin, then uniting and forming large costal

No. 203.

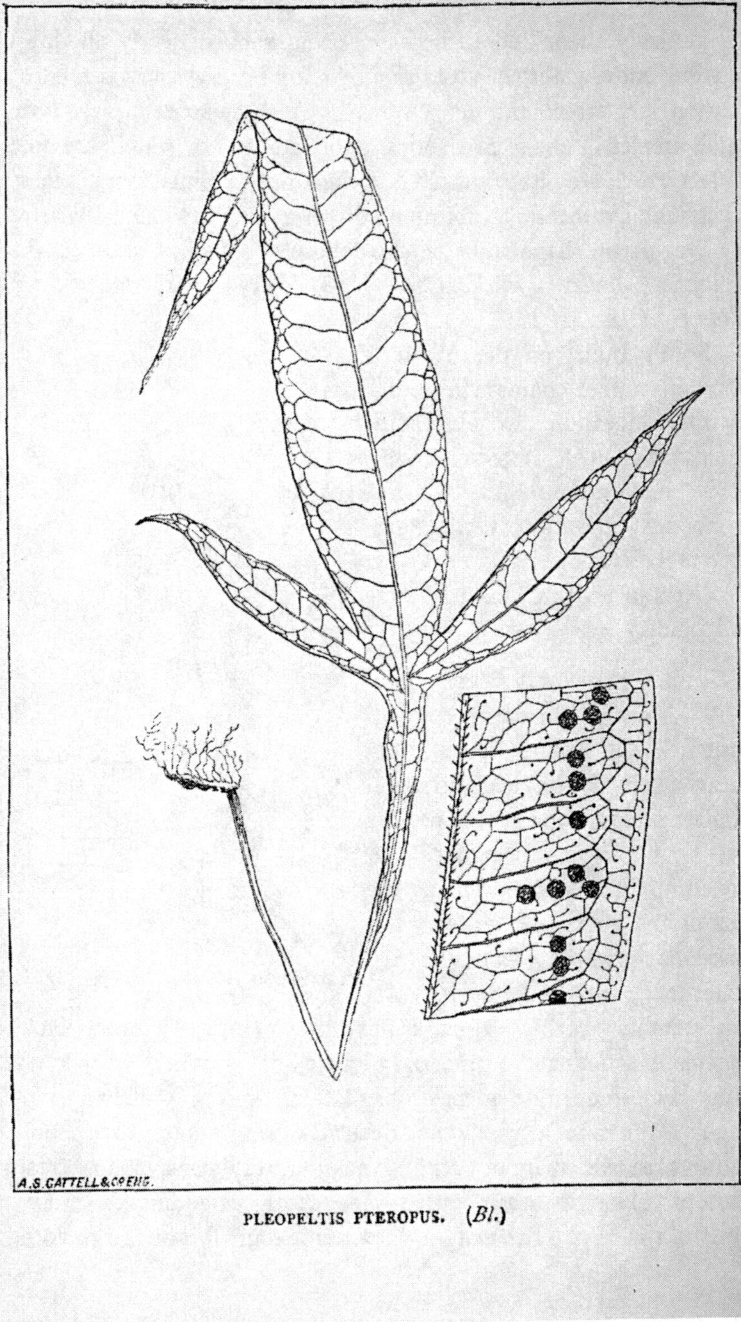

A. S. CATTELL & Co ENG.

PLEOPELTIS PTEROPUS. (*Bl.*)

areoles, within which the sori have their origin, a second series of smaller areoles is formed nearer the margin, and these and the rest of the frond are filled up with a net-work of smaller irregular areoles, including free simple or forked veinlets which have clavate apices; sori small not very numerous, 1–3 in each large areole, compital upon the secondary veins of the primary areole, often confluent into transverse, oblong or linear (grammitoid) sori. *Bl. Fl. Jav. Fil.* 168, *t.* 76. Polypodium tridactylon, *Wall. Cat. n.* 315. *Hook. Sp. Fil.* v. 75. *Hook. et Grev. Ic. Fil. t.* 209. *Bedd. F. B. I. t.* 11.

North India, Sikkim and Bhotan, 1,000–4,000 feet elevation; Khasya from no elevation up to 4,000 feet, in the plains at Mymensingh, Chittagong, plains up to 1,000 feet; Malay Peninsula.

(Also in the Philippines and South China.)

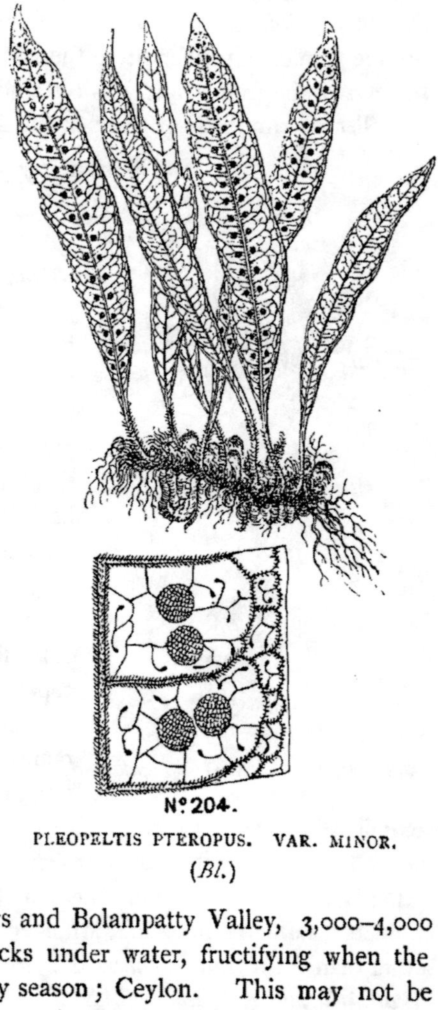

No. 204.

PLEOPELTIS PTEROPUS. VAR. MINOR.

(*Bl.*)

VAR. MINOR. Fronds always small and simple 3–4 inches long, by ½–¾ inch broad, never lobed. *Bedd. F. S. I. t.* 179.

South India, Anamallays and Bolampatty Valley, 3,000–4,000 feet elevation, in rivers on rocks under water, fructifying when the water subsides after the rainy season; Ceylon. This may not be entitled to rank as a permanent variety, as Mr. Clarke says the North

Indian plant is small and simple at the higher elevations; but I never saw 3-lobed examples in South India or Ceylon, or fronds more than about 4 inches long.

VAR. ZOSTERÆFORMIS. (*Wall. Cat.* 280.) Fronds very narrow and ribbon-like, 4–7 inches long, by 1–3 lines broad. *Hook. Syn. Fil.* 357. *Bedd. F. B. I. t.* 123. Baker is wrong in saying there are no free veinlets; it differs from the last in no way except in the narrowness of the fronds, and it is certainly only a local variety.

Tenasserim, beds of rivers at the foot of Mooleyit.

** *Fronds deeply pinnatifid.*

N°205.

PLEOPELTIS HASTATA. (*Thunb.*)

22. PLEOPELTIS HASTATA. (*Thunb.*) Rhizome creeping, stout, paleaceous with dense subulate or hair-pointed falcate ferruginous scales; stipes 2–5 inches long; fronds coriaceous, 2–12 inches and more long, deltoid-ovate acuminate, trifid or deeply pinnatifid to within half an inch of the rachis, with 5–11 segments, which are 3–6 inches long, ½ to 1 inch wide, very patent from a broad base oblong-lanceolate, very finely acuminated entire or repand or denticulate, thickened at the margin, the lowest ones cuneate-decurrent, terminal segment often the longest and most narrowly acuminated; venation conspicuous, main veins often prominent beneath, distant, united by transverse veins forming 3–4 series of primary areoles, which are filled up by lesser ones including free veinlets; sori large not sunk, arranged in a single series nearer the costa than the margin. *Thunb. Fl. Jap.* 335. Polypodium oxylobum, *Wall. Cat.* 294. *Bedd. F. S. I. t.* 175. Pleopeltis trifida, *Don.*

Prod. Fl. Nep. 3. *Hook. Syn. Fil.* 363. Pleopeltis malacodon, *Bedd. F. Sup. t.* 387.

Young rhizomes often produce only very small fronds, which are simple or trilobate only; (var. Thunbergii, *Clarke*). This fern can at once be known from malacodon by the base of the lowest pair of pinnæ (*i.e.*, base of the frond) being always a little decurrent on the apex of the stipe, (not scooped out and subcordate) and in being subentire or only a little denticulate instead of acutely serrulate; Mr. Clarke, however, is wrong in saying that it is always quite entire, my specimens (looked at under a lens) are always more or less toothed.

Throughout the Indian region on the mountains; in South India between 5,000–8,600 feet elevation; in the North 2,000 to 10,000 feet.

23. PLEOPELTIS MALACODON. (*Hook.*) In all respects like hastata, only that the base of the frond is scooped out and subcordate (instead of being a little decurrent), and the margins are acutely serrulate, the teeth mucronate or spinescent. *Hook. Sp. Fil.* v. 87. P. Stewartii, *Clarke, F. N. I. p.* 563, *a variety less serrated.* Mr. Baker and Mr. Clarke both protest against this being considered a variety only of hastata, otherwise I should have so placed it, the differences being those of a variety rather than of a species.

Himalayas, Nepal to Bhotan, 10,000–13,000 feet elevation.

VAR. β MAJUS. (*Hook. Sp. Fil.* v. 88.) Base of the frond cordate or sometimes decurrent; pinnæ (or rather segments) narrower and longer, and much more erect (*i.e.* pointing upwards); margins less prominently serrated, scales of rhizome blacker. Pleopeltis Stewartii, *Bedd. F. B. I. t.* 204, *and Baker, Syn. Fil.* 513 (*not Clarke*). Pol. propinquum, var. *Wall.* P. crytolobum, *J. Smith, MS. Clarke, F. N. I. t.* 83.

Nepal to Bhotan, 9,000–12,000 feet elevation (pendant from trees). I think that Sir W. Hooker may be safely followed in considering this only a variety of malacodon.

24. PLEOPELTIS EBENIPES. (*Hook.*) Rhizome stout creeping,

elongated and knotted with short frondiferous branches, everywhere densely imbricated with intensely black polished ovate lanceolate subcoriaceous concave scales, fuscous-pubescent at the margins, and not hair-pointed; stipes 6–9 inches long, glabrous, glossy; fronds 6–18 inches long, 8–10 inches broad, cut down to a broadly winged rachis into 6–20 pair of pinnæ or segments, $\frac{1}{2}$–1$\frac{1}{8}$ inch broad, the lowest pair generally deflexed, and either a little decurrent on the stipe, or scooped out and subcordate at their bases, sometimes quite patent as are the other pinnæ, all a little serrulate, finely acuminate, glabrous, except the rachises which are generally puberulous, and the main rachis sometimes scaly beneath; main veins distinct to the margin, areoles with copious free veinlets; sori in a single row near the midrib. *Hook. Sp. Fil.* v. 88. *Bedd. F. B. I.* 138. I cannot separate Clarke's variety "Oakesii" from the type; his variety "Parishii" is a Drynaria as far as the Moulmein plant is concerned; Jerdon's Khasya specimen being a single small sterile frond without rhizome, which may be ebenipes or hastata. Ebenipes, though closely allied to hastata, seems to be sufficiently distinct as a species in its peculiar rhizome, the fronds both in it and in malacodon, var. majus, are sometimes cordate, sometimes decurrent at the base; in malacodon type (in very many specimens examined) they are always cordate, and in hastata always decurrent.

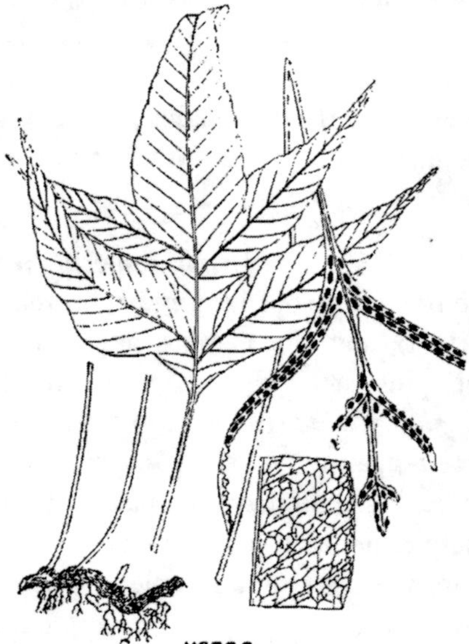

No. 206.

PLEOPELTIS INCURVATA. (*Bl.*)

Himalayas, from Ghurwal to Bhotan, 6,000–12,000 feet elevation.

25. PLEOPELTIS INCURVATA. (*Bl.*) Rhizome creeping, paleaceous, with adpressed scales; stipes scattered, a span to a foot long

of the sterile frond, 2 feet of the fertile, glossy brown; fronds firm-coriaceous glossy dimorphous, sterile ones 6–10 inches long, 8 inches to 1 foot wide, hastate, tripartite, simply ovate or pinnatifid with 4–6 lateral lobes, lobes ovate-acuminate entire horizontal, terminal one very large, all thickened at the margin; main veins distinct, but immersed, other veins internal and very indistinct; areoles with free included simple or forked veinlets; fertile fronds very long-stipitate, 10 inches to a foot long, nearly as much wide, very broad-ovate deeply pinnatifid nearly to the rachis, below subpinnate, segments 5–15, 4–8 inches long, very remote, linear and acuminate, decurrent at the base; sori large, copious, oval, sunk into a very deep cavity which forms a circular elevated truncated tubercle on the opposite side, occupying the space between the costa and the margin in a single series. *Bl. Fil. Jav. p.* 151, *t.* 65. *Hook. Sp. Fil.* v. 77. *Bedd. F. B. I.* 124.

Malacca.

(Also in the Malay Islands.)

No. 207.

PLEOPELTIS INSIGNIS. (*Bl.*)

26. PLEOPELTIS INSIGNIS. (*Bl.*) Rhizome short-creeping, paleaceous, with deciduous ferruginous scales; stipes 1–2 inches or more long (according to the length of the decurrent wing of the frond); fronds subtriangular-ovate, membranaceous, glabrous, 4–9 inches long (independent of the decurrent wing), and nearly as much broad, subdeltoid, deeply pinnatifid, with 5–9 lanceolate spreading acuminate segments; the base of the fronds subcuneate and decurrently attenuated so that the stipes is winged for the

greater part or even the whole of its length; venation distinct, main veins slender, united by transverse veins, forming 3–4 series of areoles, including free divaricating veinlets; sori very small, compital, generally two on each transverse veinlet, but appearing to be irregularly scattered. *Bl. Fil. Jav. p.* 166, *t.* 74. *Hook. Sp. Fil.* v. 78. *Bedd. F. B. I. t.* 214.

Malacca.

(Also in the Philippines and Java.)

27. PLEOPELTIS PHYMATODES. (*L.*) Rhizome very wide-creeping, woody, the scales dark brown fibrillose; stipes 3–12 inches long, firm, erect, glossy; fronds varying from simple oblong lanceolate 6 inches long, to deeply pinnatifid and 3 feet long, lobes numerous entire, acuminate, lanceolate oblong, 4–8 inches long by 1–1½ inch broad, texture coriaceous, both sides glabrous; no distinct main veins, areoles fine with copious free veinlets; sori large, more or less immersed, 1–2 serial or scattered. *Linn. Mant. p.* 360. *Hook. Syn. Fil.* 364. *Bedd. F. S. I.* 173. Polyp. alternifolium, *Wall. Cat.* 289, *type sheet.*

Ceylon; Malabar and Travancore, cultivated only (?); Malay Peninsula.

(Also throughout the tropics of the old world, the continent of India excepted.)

28. PLEOPELTIS LONGISSIMA. (*Bl.*) Rhizome wide-creeping; the scales ovate adpressed; stipes 3–4 feet long, glossy straw-coloured; fronds 1–4 feet long, 6–12 inches broad, cut down very nearly to the rachis (often leaving only the narrowest sign of a wing) into 3–20 erect-patent acuminate linear subentire segments or pinnæ, which are ¼–¾ inch broad, texture papery, both sides glabrous; primary veins not very distinct, areoles numerous, with free included simple or forked veinlets, with slightly clavate apices; sori in close single rows near the midrib, deeply sunk and forming papillæ on the upper surface. *Bl. En. Pl. Jav. Fil.* 127. *Hook. Syn. Fil.* 366. *Bedd. F. Sup.* 388. *Wall. Cat.* 289, *3rd sheet* (alternifolium, var. polyphyllum).

Assam, Gowhatty, Sylhet, Furidpore (floating in jheels.) (Also in the Philippines, Formosa, and Malay Islands.)

29. PLEOPELTIS NIGRESCENS. (*Bl.*) Very like longissima, but the wing to the rachis broader and the pinnæ broader (1–1½ inches), rather more crisp in texture and the veins more prominent; it is perhaps only a variety, but I have never seen longissima in a wild state. *Bl. En. Fil. Jav.* 127. P. longissima, *Bedd. F. S. I.* 176. *Wall. Cat.* 289, *2nd sheet* (alternifolium).

South India, on rocks, about the foot of the Western mountains, (foot of Sispara and Carcoor ghats), not ascending the mountains to any elevation, and never growing in water; Ceylon. An exceedingly handsome fern.

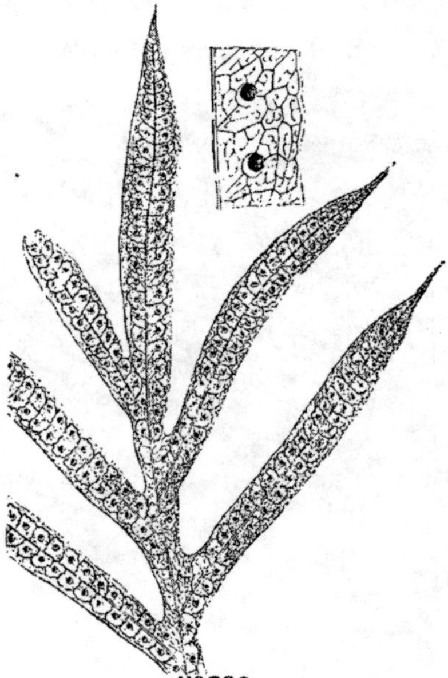

No. 208.
PLEOPELTIS NIGRESCENS. (*Bl.*)

30. PLEOPELTIS DILATATA. (*Wall.*) Rhizome stout creeping, paleaceous with ovate reticulated scales; stipes 1½ foot and more long, but strongly winged the whole length by the decurrent base of the frond; fronds ample 1½–2 and 3 feet long, a foot and more wide, membranaceous, light-green, glabrous, oblong-ovate, pinnatifid to within ½–1 inch of the rachis (less towards the base), segments 6–11, 5–8 inches long (shorter towards the apex), ¾–1½ inch wide, oblong-lanceolate acuminate, subentire, suddenly decurrent; main veins wavy, forming large primary areoles which extend two-thirds of the way to the margin and include the sori, these and the rest of the segments are occupied by lesser irregular areoles including many free veinlets, their branches moderately divaricating; sori numerous, very small, often oval or more or less elongated, compital on

the secondary veins and veinlets. *Wall. Cat. n.* 295. *Hook. Sp. Fil.* v. 85. *Bedd. F. B. I. t.* 122.

North India, from Nepal to Bhotan, 3,000–8,000 feet elevation, Khasya, 2,000–6,000 feet; Ceylon, forests above Telgamma, 4,000 feet elevation; Tenasserim and Malay Peninsula.

(Also in Samoa.)

*** *Fronds pinnate.*

31. PLEOPELTIS PALMATA. (*Bl.*) Rhizome stout, the scales large lanceolate; stipes 6–12 inches long, firm, erect, glossy; fronds 6–18 inches long, 8–12 inches broad, with a linear or linear-oblong entire or slightly toothed or repand terminal lobe, and 1–6 similar ones on each side, which are ½–1½ inch broad, narrowed or dilated, always slightly adnate at the base, long caudate at the apex, those of the barren frond the broadest, texture subcoriaceous, both sides glabrous; main veins distinct to the edge, areoles fine, hidden, including free incurved clavate veinlets; sori rather large in a single row, midway between the costa and margin. *Bl. Fil. Jav. p.* 150, *t.* 64. *Hook. Syn. Fil.* 368. *Bedd. F. B. I. t.* 156.

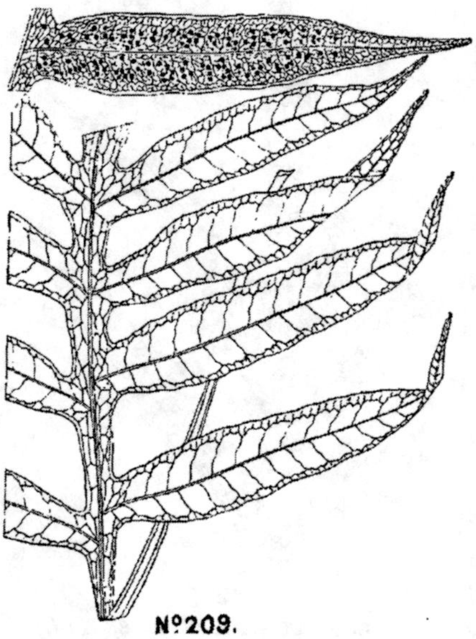

No. 209.

PLEOPELTIS DILATATA. (*Wall.*)

Malay Peninsula, Singapore, Penang and Malacca.

(Also in the Malay Islands and Philippines.)

32. PLEOPELTIS JUGLANDIFOLIA. (*Don*). Rhizome stout creeping, with many spreading lanceolate subulate bright-ferruginous scales; stipes 1 foot or more long, firm, erect, glossy; fronds 1½–2 feet long, 1 foot or more broad; pinnæ 8–10 on a side in pairs, which are 1–2

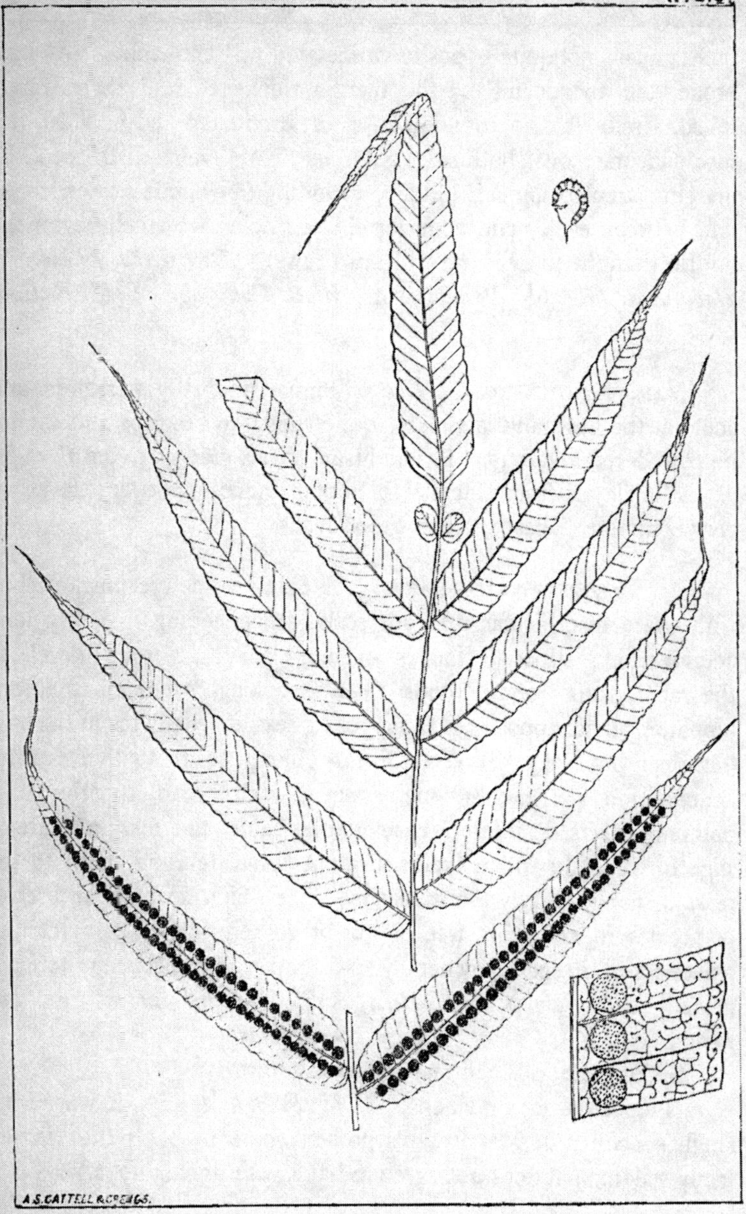

PLEOPELTIS JUGLANDIFOLIA. (*Den.*)

inches apart, not quite opposite, articulated with the rachis, 1–1½ inch broad, the apex caudate; the margin thickened and wavy, rarely lobed, sessile from a rounded base, or attenuated and petioled, texture subcoriaceous, both sides glabrous; main veins distinct to the margin; areoles copious, hidden, including free veinlets; sori large, one between each main vein, forming a single row, much nearer the midrib than the margin (rarely in two rows). *Don. Prod. Fl. Nep.* 3. *Hook. Syn. Fil.* 368. P. capitellata, *Wall. Cat.* 306. *Bedd. F. B. I. t.* 12.

VAR. TENUICAUDA. (*Hook.*) Pinnæ gradually narrowed and acute at the base and petiolate, quite runs into the type and cannot be considered a variety. P. leiorhizon, *Wall. Cat.* 303, *3rd sheet.*

Himalayas, from Gurwhal to Bhotan, 2,000–9,000 feet elevation, very common, Khasya, 2,000–5,000 feet.

33. PLEOPELTIS LEHMANNI. (*Mett.*) Rhizome creeping, clothed with ovate or orbicular glabrous scales, each ending in a very long acumination; stipes 8 inches or more long, glabrous as well as the rachis and frond; fronds 1½–2 feet long, submembranaceous pinnate; pinnæ opposite or subopposite, sessile, articulated at the base (terminal one long petioled), linear oblong entire, with a caudate acumination 4–6 inches long, about ¾ inch broad, superior base obliquely excised, inferior base amplexicaule, the margin entire or slightly repand; main veins evident not extending quite to the margin, connected by the transverse veins which form about 4 series of areoles in which are free simple or forked veinlets with clavate apices; sori irregular, generally 4–6 in two rows between the main veins. *Mett. Poly. p.* 229. *Bedd. F. B. I. t.* 260. *Hook. Syn. Fil. p.* 369.

Sikkim, 4,000–8,000 feet elevation; Birma.

(Pleopeltis moulmeinensis, *Bedd. F. B. I. t.* 205, drawn from a single specimen in Mr. Parish's possession, is probably this, imperfectly seeding; it does not agree in habit with juglandifolia.)

34. PLEOPELTIS HIMALAYENSIS. (*Hook.*) Rhizome glaucous

No. 211.

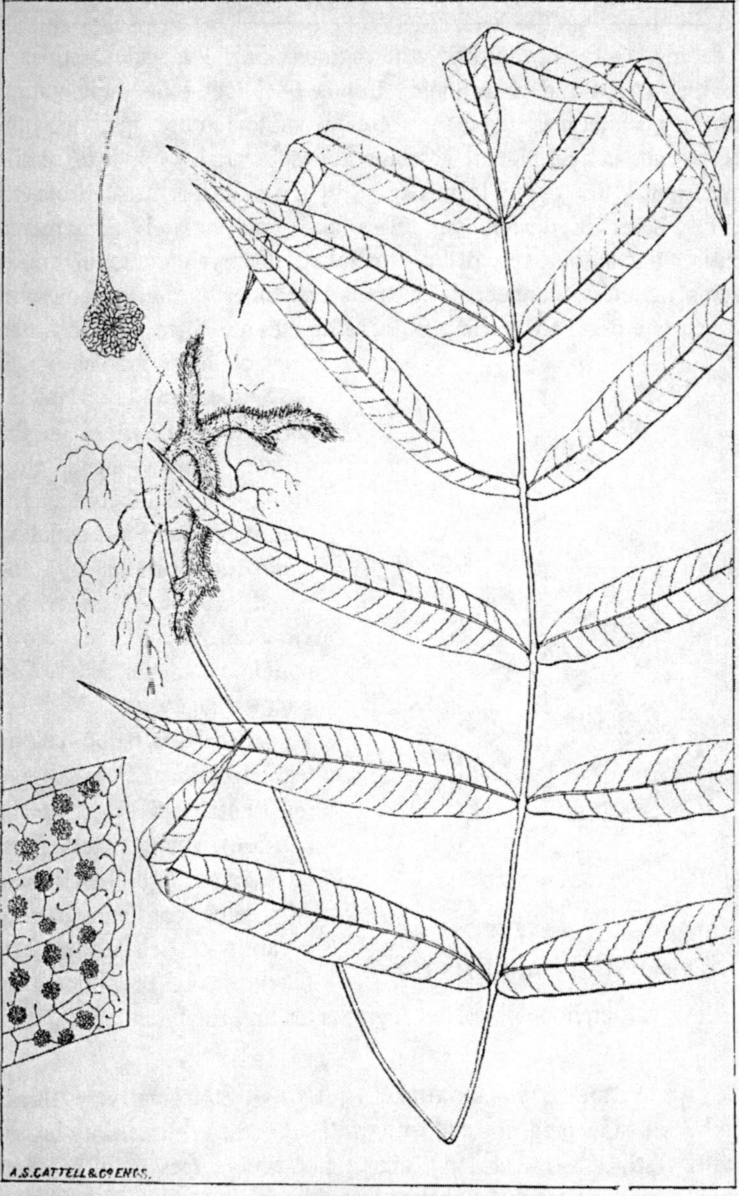

A. S. CATTELL & Co. ENGS.

PLEOPELTIS LEHMANNI. (*Mett.*)

creeping, clothed with bright ferruginous hair-like scales; stipes a span to 1 foot and more long; fronds 1–1½ foot long, submembranaceous, sometimes pubescent or even subtomentose, glabrous subcoriaceous in age, pinnated, pinnæ almost invariably opposite, sessile in distant pairs 5–8–9 inches long, by 1½–2 inches broad from an obtuse base, elliptical-oblong, finely and long-caudately acuminated entire, but with a very distinct membranous hyaline margin; main veins manifest, connected by transverse ones forming areoles, of which one or all are soriferous, these areoles are filled up with a network of lesser areoles which have free included veinlets; sori often large, 1–2 in the primary areoles, hence they are 1–2 serial between the main veins, and 3–4 serial in a direction parallel with the costa. *Hook. Sp. Fil.* v. 91. *Bedd. F. B. I. t.* 318. Polypodium venustum, *Wall. Cat.* 305, *not of Desv.*

No. 212

PLEOPELTIS HIMALAYENSIS. (*Hook.*)

Himalayas, 6,000–10,000 feet elevation, from Nepal to Bhotan, Khasya Hills (Jerdon), young plants often have simple or 3-lobed fronds. Mettenius considers it only a variety of Lehmanni. Mr. Clarke calls the tomentose variety, var. niphoboloides, but it graduates into the type.

35. PLEOPELTIS LEIORHIZA. (*Wall.*) Rhizome very thick, fleshy, wide-creeping, covered with ovate adpressed peltate, slaty-brown scales; stipes 1–2 feet long, erect; fronds 2–4 feet long, 1–2 feet broad; pinnæ narrow lanceolate-linear coriaceous acuminate at the apex, margins entire, sessile and rather decurrent at the base, or

attenuated and petioled, both sides glabrous; main veins scarcely more prominent than the rest, areoles with copious free veinlets; sori large, in a single row, a little nearer the midrib than the margin. Polypodium, *Wall. Cat.* 303, *type-sheet. Hook. Syn. Fil.* 369. *Bedd. F. S. I.* 174.

South India, common on all the Western mountains, 2,000–4,000 feet, on rocks; North India, from no elevation up to 4,000 feet.

TRIBE II.—GRAMMITIDEÆ.

Sori on the back of the lobes, more than twice as long as broad, usually linear.

GENUS LXVI.—NOTHOLÆNA. (*R. Br.*)

(*Nothos*, spurious; *lænos*, wool—the scales on back of frond pseudo-woolly.)

Sori marginal, at first oblong or roundish, soon confluent into a continuous marginal line, without a distinct involucre, but with the edge of the frond frequently inflexed; veins free; fronds adherent to the caudex, pinnate or bipinnate.

1. NOTHOLÆNA MARANTÆ. (*L. under Acrostichum.*) Rhizome stout, horizontal, densely paleaceous with soft silky ferruginous finely pointed subulate scales; stipes generally stout purplish-black, 3–10 inches long, aggregated, setosely and densely hirsute, as well as the rachis; fronds 4–10 inches long, 2–2½ inches wide, oblong-lanceolate, coriaceous, glabrous above, beneath densely clothed with ferruginous oblong-lanceolate imbricated scales, bipinnate, primary pinnæ petiolate or sessile from a broadish obtuse base, oblong-acuminate, pinnules not numerous, approximate, sessile, 2–3 lines long, very obtuse entire, upper ones confluent at the base (as are the terminal primary pinnæ), the edge scarcely reflexed; sori forming a broad border extending some way from the margin towards the costule,

N°213.

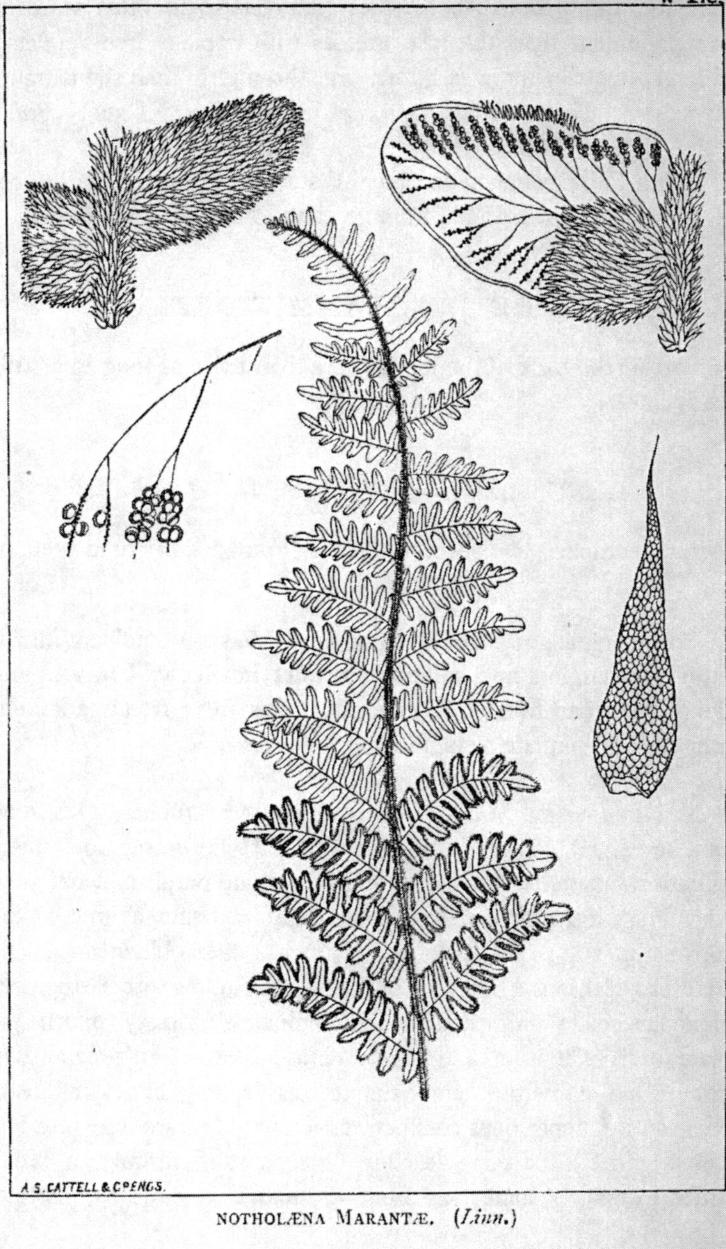

A. S. CATTELL & C° ENGS.

NOTHOLÆNA MARANTÆ. (*Linn.*)

much concealed by the paleaceous covering. *Linn. Sp. Pl.* 1527. Notholæna Marantæ, *R. Br.* Nothochlæna, *Hook. Sp. Fil.* v. 120. *Bedd. F. B. I. t.* 1.

Alpine Himalayas, from Kashmir to Kumaon, rare; Sikkim, 9,000–15,000 feet elevation, Lachen Valley.

(Also in South Europe and the Mediterranean region, from Macaronesia to the Caucasus and Abyssinia.)

2. NOTHOLÆNA VELLEA. (*R. Br.*) Stipes densely tufted, woolly, wiry, short; fronds 8–9 inches long, 1–1½ inch broad, oblong-lanceolate, bipinnate, pinnæ close lanceolate, the central ones the largest, with close roundish or oblong entire or 3-lobed pinnules, texture herbaceous but thick, both sides, especially the lower, coated with whitish or subferruginous tomentum, rachis bright chesnut-brown, more or less woolly. *R. Br. Prod. p.* 146. N. lanuginosa, *Desv. Hook. Syn. Fil. p.* 370.

Pangi and Lahul in Chumba, Cashmire.

(Also in Afghanistan, South Europe, Madeira, Cape Verd Isles, Algiers.)

GENUS LXVII.—MONOGRAMME. (*Schk.*)

(*Mono*, one; *gramme*, a line—sori in a single line on each frond.)

Sori subimmersed, linear elongated close to the midrib on one or both sides, the receptacles formed of a portion of the costa; veins consisting only of a costa; fronds small, grass or rush-like, simple or forked, rhizome creeping.

1. MONOGRAMME PARADOXA. (*Fée.*) Rhizome creeping, hairy; fronds linear filiform, grass-like, 2–12 inches long, ¼–½ line broad; sori within a vaginiform expansion of the costa, one side of which is larger than the other. *Fée. Vitt. p.* 38. M. Junghuhnii, *Hook. Sp. Fil.* v. 123. *Bedd F. S. I. t.* 210.

Ceylon, 3,000–5,000 feet elevation, not very common.

(Also in Java, Philippines, Queensland and Polynesian Islands.)

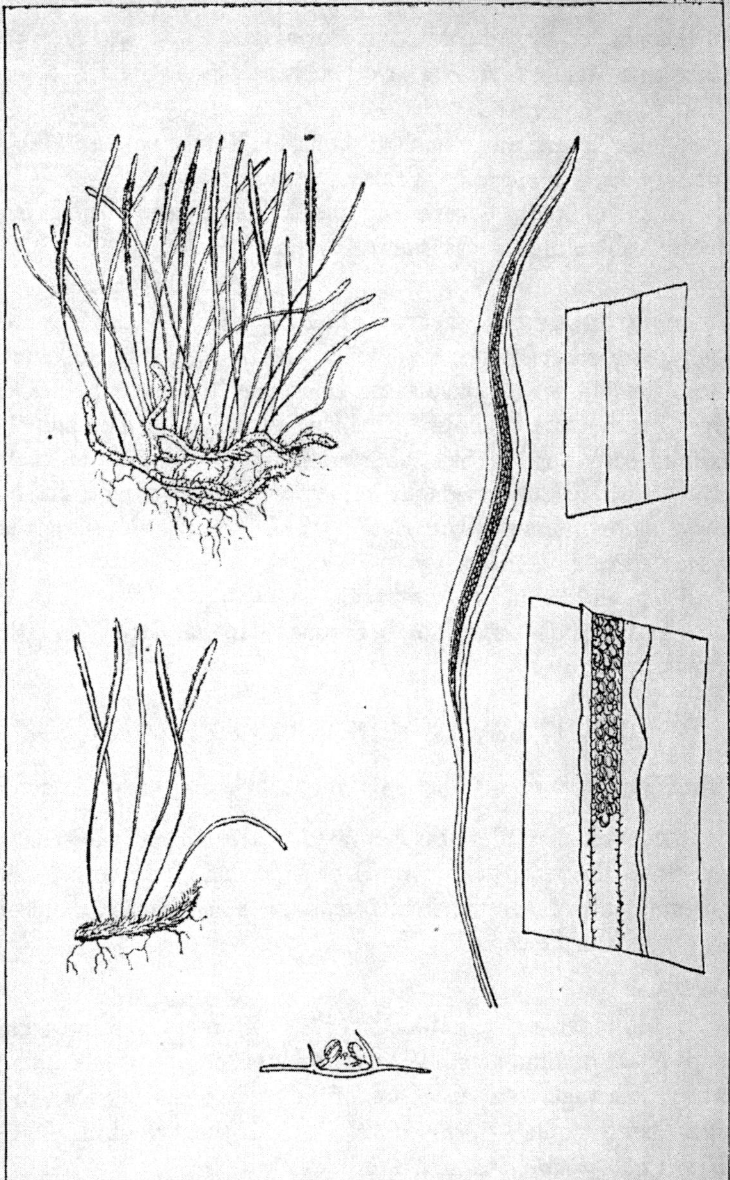

A.S. CATTELL & C°. PHOTOGRAV.

MONOGRAMME PARADOXA. (*Fée*).

GENUS LXVIII.—LEPTOGRAMME. (*J. Sm.*)

(*Leptos*, slender; *gramme*, a line.)

Sori arising from the veins over the under surface of the frond, linear or linear oblong, simple; veins free; fronds bi-tripinnatifid, adherent to the caudex, habit and mode of growth of Phegopteris and Lastrea, and only differing from the former in its elongated sori.

1. LEPTOGRAMME TOTTA. (*Schl.*) Rhizome scarcely creeping, stipes subtufted, 6–12 inches long, pilose, below scaly; fronds 12–18 inches long, 6–8 inches broad, pinnate, both sides pilose, pinnæ lanceolate, ¾–1 inch broad, pinnatifid half-way to the midrib, lobes blunt, entire or subentire, 1½–2 lines broad, herbaceous in texture; veinlets simple 5–7 on each side with the linear oblong sori medial. *Schlecht, Adumbr.* 15, *t.* 6. *Hook. Syn. Fil.* 376. Grammitis Totta, *Bedd. F. S. I. t.* 49.

South India, very common on the mountains on the west side at the highest elevations; Ceylon at the highest elevations; North India, North-west Himalayas, Kashmir to Bhotan, 6,000 feet elevation, rare, Khasya, 3,000–5,000 feet elevation, common.

(Also in Java, China, Japan, and Africa and its islands.)

2. LEPTOGRAMME AURITA. (*Hook.*) Rhizome extensively creeping; stipe 1 foot long, naked, glossy, the base curved and furnished with a few deflexed ovate acute scales; fronds up to 2 feet long, and 1 foot broad, pinnate, pinnæ in distant pairs pinnatifid nearly or quite to the rachis into lanceolate entire or crenate lobes, the lowest on one or both sides longer than the others and pinnatifid, the others sometimes unequal, texture subcoriaceous, rachis glossy, both surfaces generally glabrous; veinlets mostly forked; sori oblong. *Hook. Syn. Fil.* 377. Gymnogramme, *Hook. Sp. Fil.* v. 141. Grammitis aurita, *Bedd. F. B. I. t.* 152.

Sikkim and Bhotan, 3,000–6,000 feet elevation, Assam, Khasya, 2,000–5,000 feet elevation.

VAR. LEVINGII. (*Clarke.*) Fronds weak and flaccid, pinnæ 1½ inch

No. 215.

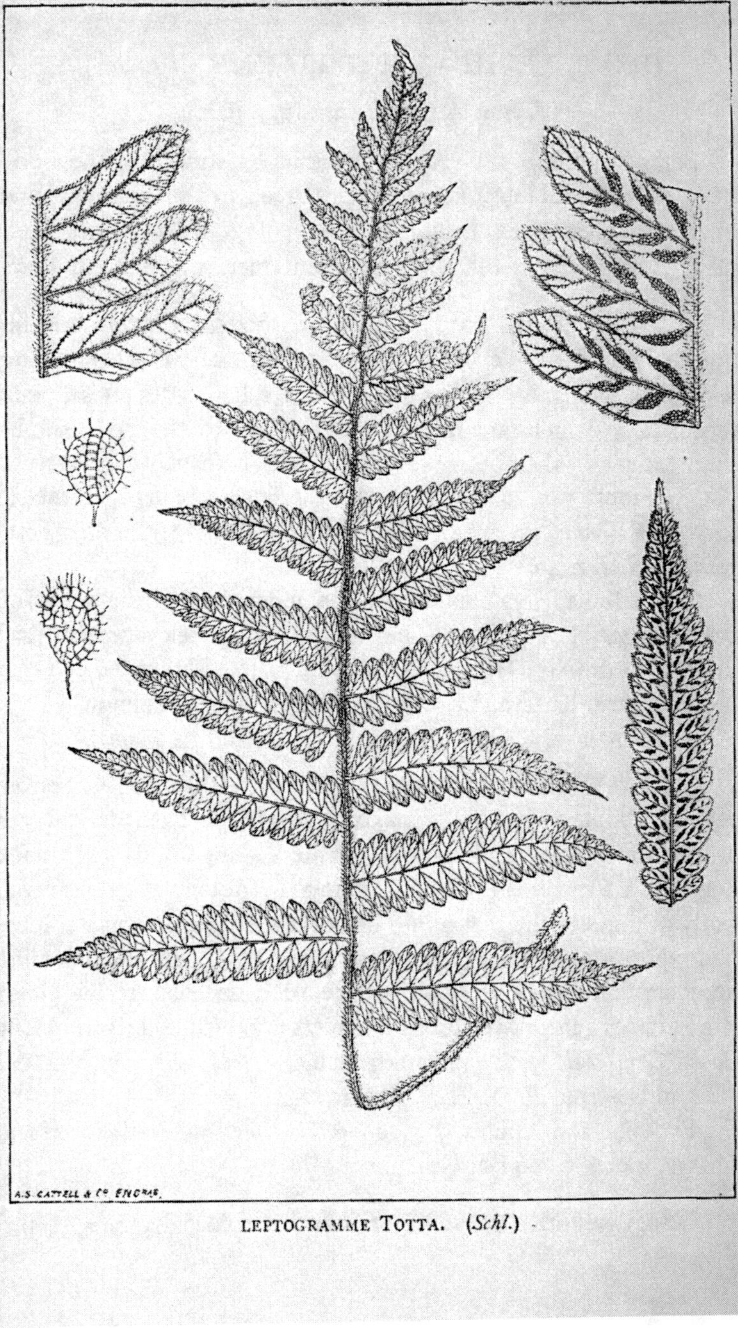

LEPTOGRAMME TOTTA. (*Schl.*)

long only, and ⅜ inch broad, not auriculate, lower ones very distant, all sparingly covered on both sides with long needle-like weak hairs. *Clarke, F. N. I. p.* 568.

Kashmir, Jhelum and Chittapani valleys, 4,000–7,000 feet elevation (Levinge), Sutlej, 9,000 feet elevation (Stewart).

3. LEPTOGRAMME OPACA. (*Spr.*) Stipes 1½ and more feet long, tufted, scaly near the base; fronds 2 feet and more long 12–15 inches

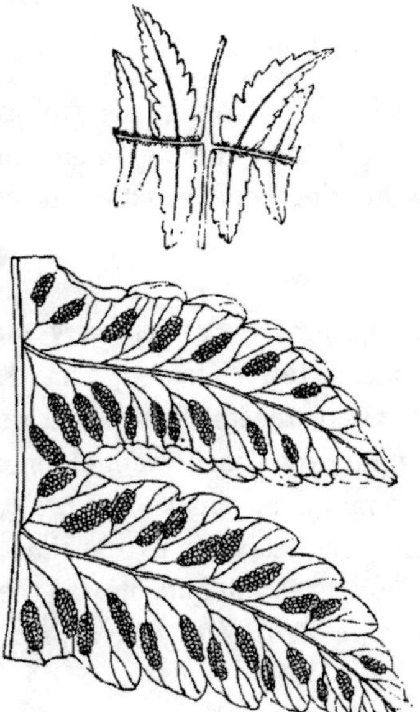

No. 216.

LEPTOGRAMME AURITA. (*Hook.*)

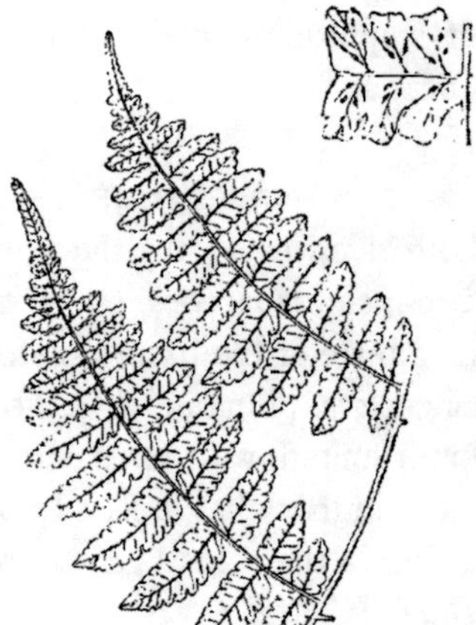

No. 217.

LEPTOGRAMME OPACA. (*Spr.*)

wide at base, subdeltoid-ovate acute membranaceous, pubescent on the rachises and costæ, bipinnate, lower primary pinnæ petiolate 6–8 inches long, 3–4 inches wide, oblong-ovate, their pinnules an inch wide, oblong sessile and adnate, and slightly decurrent at the base, obtuse or acute, pinnatifid, the lobes retuse or emarginate and toothed; veins pinnate in each lobe of the pinnules or large segments, veinlets forked or simple, soriferous towards the base of the lower branches; sori oblong. *Hook. Syn. Fil.* 378. Gymnogramma, *Hook. Sp. Fil.* v. *p.* 143. *Spr. Syst. Veg.* iv. 39. *Bedd. F. B. I. t.* 238. Gynnogramma obtusata, *Bl. Fil. Jav. p.* 97, *t.* 43. *and Hook. Sp. Fil.* v. 143.

Nepal to Bhotan, 4,000–7000 feet elevation; Khasya, 3,000–5,000 feet elevation.

(Also in Java.)

GENUS LXIX.—STEGNOGRAMME. (*Bl.*)

(*Stegnos*, a cover; *gramme*, a line.)

As in Leptogramme, only the veinlets of contiguous groups uniting as in Nephrodium, fronds pinnate; habit and mode of growth of Nephrodium and Goniopteris, only differing from the latter in its linear sori.

1. STEGNOGRAMME ASPIDIOIDES. (*Hook.*) Fronds hairy on both sides, especially the veins, ovate-lanceolate acuminated, pinnate, firm-membranaceous, pinnæ opposite or alternate, sessile subtruncate or adnate at the base, 3–4 inches long, rarely an inch wide, oblong-lanceolate, pinnatifid $\frac{1}{4}$–$\frac{1}{3}$ the way to the midrib; veins 5–6 pair, 2–5 lower united, with an excurrent spurious vein reaching to the sinus, those in the lobes free, all soriferous; sori linear-oblong, nearly the length of the veins. *Hook. Sp. Fil.* v. 150. *Bl. Fil. Jav. p.* 172. *Bedd. F. B. I. t.* 149.

Khasya, 4,000–6,000 feet elevation; Ceylon (?)

(Also in Java.)

GENUS LXX.—GYMNOGRAMME. (*Desv.*)

(*Gymnos*, naked; *gramme*, a line.)

Sori arising from the veins over the under surface of the frond; linear or linear-oblong, forked or sometimes simple; veins forked, veinlets free; fronds various, adherent to the caudex, habit and mode of growth of Cheilanthes.

No. 218.

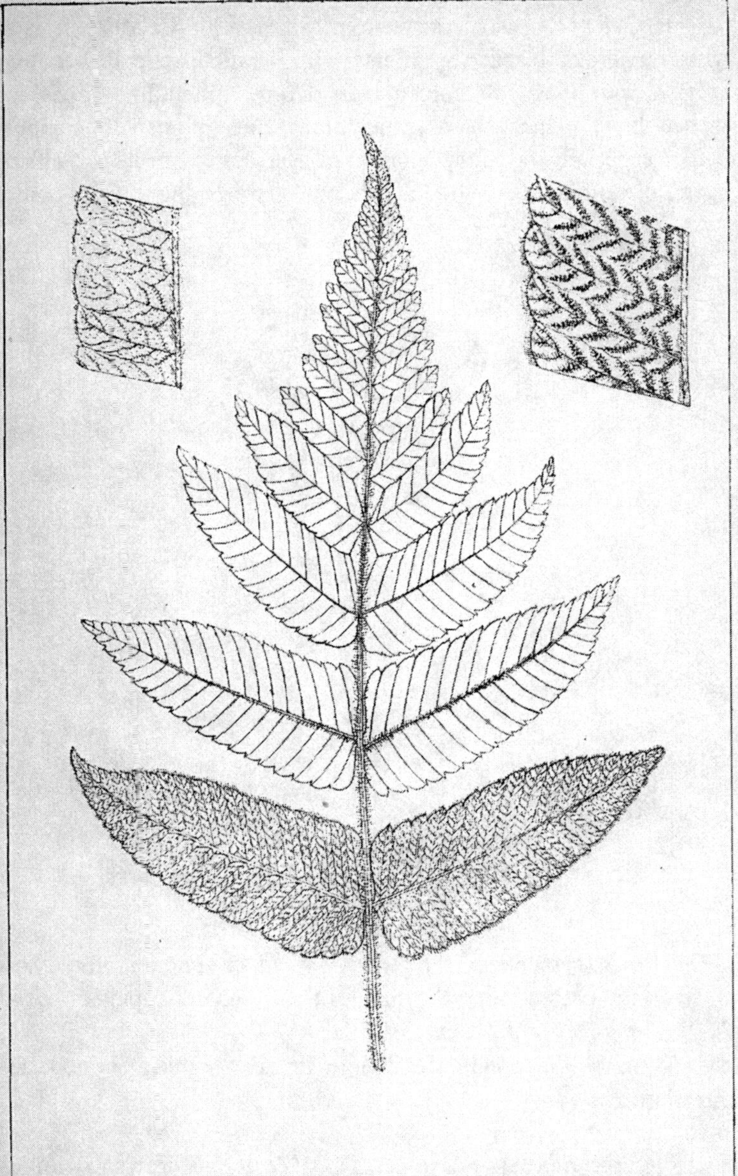

A. S. CATTELL P. C. ENGR.

STEGNOGRAMME ASPIDIOIDES. (*Hook.*)

1. GYNNOGRAMME ANDERSONI. (*Bedd.*) Caudex furnished with numerous black wiry roots; stipes tufted, 1–2 inches long, shaggy, with long soft golden hairs; fronds (including stipes) 1–4 inches long, ½ inch broad, membranaceous pinnated, copiously hairy, especially beneath, pinnæ sessile, cordate-ovate or oblong-ovate, pinnatifid or crenated; costa not very prominent, veins pinnate

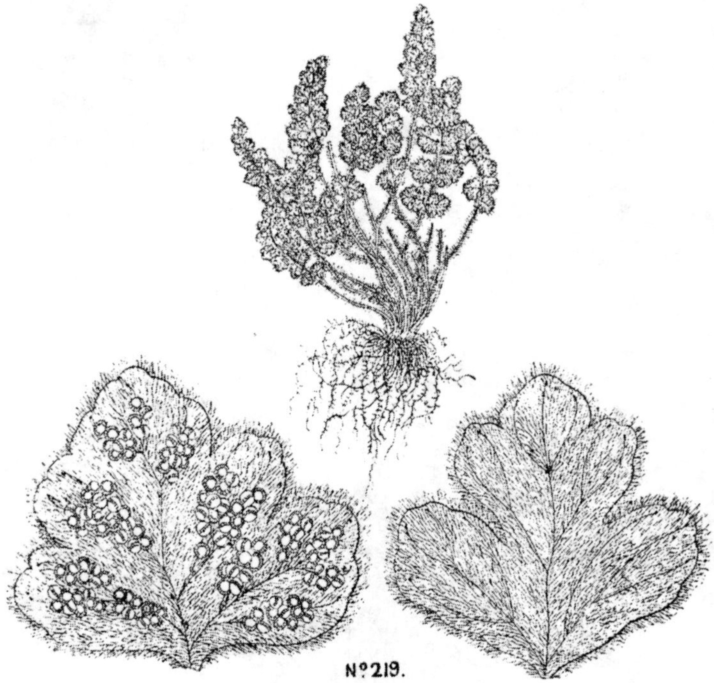

Nº 219.

GYMNOGRAMME ANDERSONI. (*Bedd.*)

in the lower segments of the pinnæ, forked or simple in the others, all free and not reaching the margin; sori forked copious. *Bedd. F. B. I. t.* 190. *Hook. Syn. Fil.* 380.

Kumaon, Soondadunga Valley, on dry rocks, 13,000 feet elevation.

2. GYMNOGRAMME LEPTOPHYLLA. (*Desv.*) Root a small annual

tufted mass of fibres; stipes tufted, glossy brown, slender, filiform, 1–4 inches long; fronds small 2–4 inches long, 1–1½ inch broad, delicate, membranaceous very transparent, ovate or deltoid, all fertile, varying from reniform crenated to variously pinnate or bi-tripinnate, those on the shorter stipes being less compound, pinnæ spathulate to obovate, decurrent, deeply crenated, lobes entire or serrulate; veins simple or forked, not reaching the margin; sori

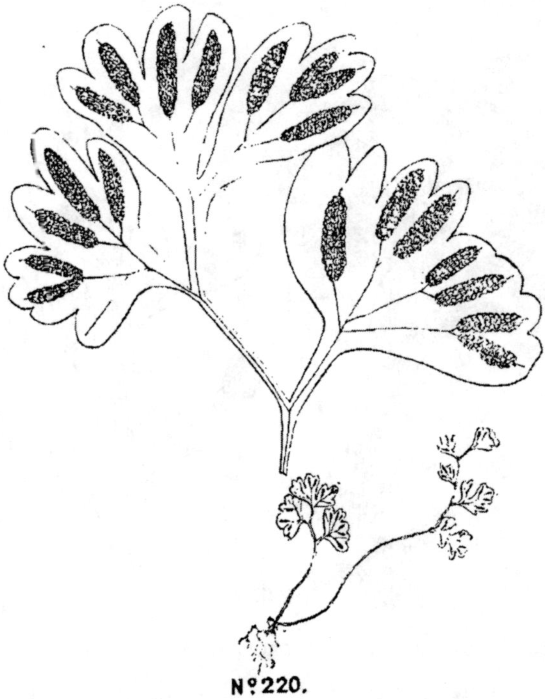

No. 220.

GYMNOGRAMME LEPTOPHYLLA. (*Desv.*)

oblong, simple or forked. *Desv. Journ. Bot.* i. *p.* 26. *Hook. Sp. Fil.* v. 136. *Bedd. F. S. I. t.* 270. Anogramma, *Link.*

Western ghats of the Peninsula of India, Ootacamund, Mahableswar, Suttara Fort walls.

(Also in Europe, the Azores, Madeira, Canaries, Africa, Persia, Australia, New Zealand, South America.)

3. GYMNOGRAMME MICROPHYLLA. (*Hook.*) Stipes densely tufted, 2–4 inches long, slender, fragile, glossy brown; fronds $1\frac{1}{2}$–3 inches long, deltoid quadripinnatifid, pinnæ close, the lower ones deltoid, pinnules deltoid, ultimate segments $\frac{1}{6}$–$\frac{1}{8}$ of an inch, obovate-oblong, texture pellucid-herbaceous; veins and sori one to each ultimate segment. *Hook. Syn. Fil.* 383. *Bedd. F. B. I. t.* 148, (habit of leptophylla, but not annual.)

GYMNOGRAMME MICROPHYLLA. (*Hook.*)

Khasya, Surareen, 5,000 feet elevation, Sikkim, Tonglo, 7,000–10,000 feet elevation, Sinchal, 8,000 feet elevation, Dikeeling, 7,500 feet elevation.

GENUS LXXI.—SYNGRAMME. (*J. Sm.*)

(*Syn* to unite; *gramme*, a line—sori often in united lines.)

Sori long linear, arising from the veins and veinlets on the under surface, veins forked close to the midrib or higher up, veinlets parallel

No. 222

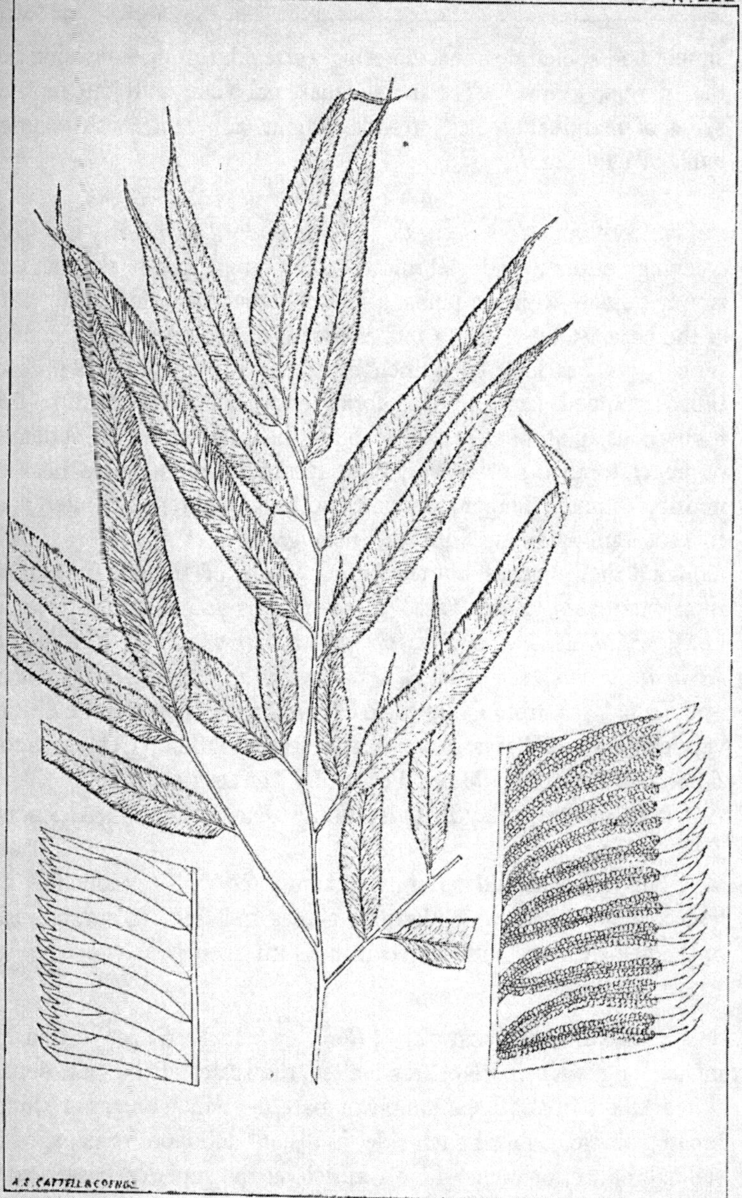

SYNGRAMME FRAXINEA. (*Don.*)

simple and sometimes anastomosing, or regularly anastomosing near the margin, forming a continuous marginal vein, with one or more series of marginal areoles; fronds various, adherent to the caudex; habit of Diplazium.

1. SYNGRAMME FRAXINEA. (*Don. under Diplazium.*) Rhizome creeping; stipes naked, glabrous, 1–4 feet long; fronds 1–4 feet long, simply pinnate with the pinnæ a foot or rather more long, attenuated at the base, stalked, and 2 inches broad, or bipinnate, the secondary pinnæ 3 inches long by $\frac{5}{8}$ inch broad, sessile or subsessile with a broad rounded base, in both forms finely acuminate, texture firm-herbaceous, glabrous, or a little pilose beneath, entire or subentire, or finely toothed; veins very close, forked from the base near the midrib, or much higher up, one or both of the branches often again forked, rarely joining with the next group of veins; sori running along all the branches, but stopping far short of the margin. Diplazium fraxineum, *Don. Fl. Nep.* 12–13. Gymnogramma javanica, (*Bl.*), *Bedd. F. S. I. t.* 232, *the pinnate form. F. B. I. t.* 57, *the bipinnate form.* G. serrulata, *Bl. Pl. Jav. Fil.* 113. *Wall. Cat.* 3 *and* 11.

Himalayas, from Chumba to Bhotan, 1,000–8,000 feet elevation, very common; Khasya, 1,000–5,000 feet elevation; Ceylon, 5,000–6,000 feet elevation; Malay Peninsula, Tenasserim, &c.

(Also in the Malay Islands; South Pacific Islands, Africa and Japan.)

This Fern should certainly be associated with "Wallichii" and "alismæfolia," with which it quite agrees in habit, the anastomosing of the veins is rare, but I detect it in all my specimens.

2. SYNGRAMME VESTITA. (*Wall. Cat.* 12.) Stipes tufted 3–6 inches long, wiry, more or less matted, the scales at the base densely tufted, silky; fronds linear, simply pinnate, 6–12 inch long, 1–1½ inches broad; pinnæ 7–14 on each side, in distant subopposite pairs, ovate, stalked, entire, or often with an auricle at the superior base, texture thick but flaccid, the rachis and both sides, but more especially the under, densely coated with fine velvety ferruginous hairs; veins

forked or pinnate, where pinnate the lower branches generally anastomose; sori universal on the veins. *Bedd. F. B. I. t.* 154. Grammitis vestita, *Wall. Cat.* 12. Gymnogramme vestita, *Hook. Syn. Fil.* 379

Himalayas from Chumba to Nepal, 6,000–9,000 feet elevation.

(Also in China.)

3. SYNGRAMME WALLICHII. (*Hook.*) Stipes tufted up to 20 inches long, firm, glossy brown, fibrillose near the base; fronds up to one foot long by 2½ inches broad, elliptic-lanceolate, simple, acuminate, entire at the margin, the base narrowed very gradually, texture subcoriaceous, both sides glabrous; veins fine parallel, simple, or forked from the base or much higher up, rarely joining with the contiguous group about the centre, but all anastomosing near the margin and forming 2–3 small oblong hexagonal areoles; sori on all the straight veins, but scarcely extending to anastomosing ones near the margin. *Bedd. F. B. I. t.* 153, Gymnogramme, *Hook. Sp. Fil.* v. *p.* 155, *t.* 302

No. 223.

SYNGRAMME VESTITA. (*Wall.*)

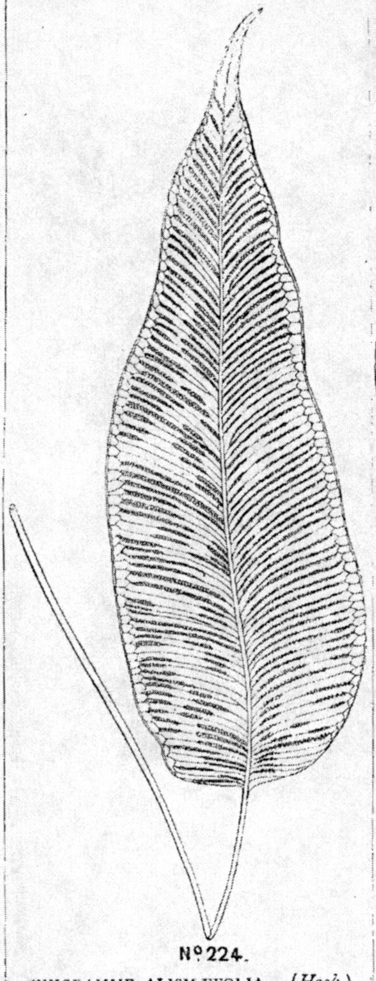

No. 224.

SYNGRAMME ALISMÆFOLIA. (*Hook.*)

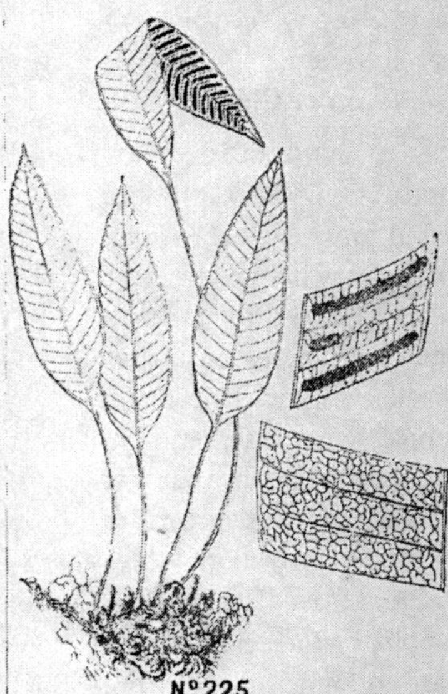

No. 225.

SELLIGUEA FEEI. (*Hook.*)

Singapore.
(Also in Borneo.)

4. SYNGRAMME ALISMÆFOLIA. (*Hook.*) Caudex creeping; stipes a span to a foot and more long, blackish-purple; fronds subcoriaceous, simple 5–8 inches long, 2½ inches wide near the base, from a rounded base, ovate or ovate-lanceolate, finely acuminated; veins numerous, approximate, simple or forked, anastomosing near the margin into 1–2 series of oblong hexagonal areoles; sori narrow-linear on all the straight veins, but scarcely extending to the anastomosing ones. *Bedd. F. B. I. t.* 240. Gymnogramme, *Hook. Sp. Fil.* v. 155.
Singapore.

GENUS LXXII.—SELLIGUEA. (*Bory.*)

(After Selligue, a Frenchman.)

Veins prominent, compound, anastomosing, with free included veinlets in the areoles; sori long linear; fronds simple, pinnatifid or rarely pinnate, articulate with the caudex; habit and mode of growth of Pleopeltis, from which genus it only differs in the sori being long linear.

* *Fronds simple.*

1. SELLIGUEA FEEI. (*Hook.*) Rhizome firm, wide-creeping, the scales bright brown, fibrillose; fronds dimorphous, the sterile ones 3–4½ inches long, 1½–2½ inches broad, on stems 3½–6 inches long, the fertile ones narrower and more contracted at the base on stems 6–10 inches long, both acute, entire, very coriaceous and glabrous; main veins very prominent to the margin, ¼ inch apart, veinlets obscure, forming copious areoles, with free included clavate venules; sori linear immersed in single rows, rarely interrupted, between the main veins, not quite reaching the margin. *Hook. Syn. Fil.* 389. *Sp. Fil.* v. 158. *Bedd. F. B. I. t.* 151.
Malay Peninsula, Penang, Singapore.
(Also in the Malay Islands.)

2. SELLIGUEA HAMILTONIANA. (*Wall.*) Rhizome wide-creeping, woody, the scales brown, linear; fronds dimorphous, the sterile ones 4–6 inches long, 2½–4 inches broad, elliptic oblong, entire, glabrous, acuminate, very gradually tapering at the base, the stipes 2–5 inches long, winged towards the apex by the decurrent base of the frond, fertile ones 4–8 inches long by 1–1½ inch broad, on stipes more than 1 foot long, texture rather thin, with the venation conspicuous; main veins very distinct to the edge, with copious intermediate areoles, with free included veinlets; sori in broad continuous rows, one between each main vein and parallel with them. Grammitis Hamiltoniana, *Wall. Cat.* 9. Gymnogramme, *Hook. Sp. Fil.* v. 160. *Bedd. F. B. I. t.* 239.

North and East Bengal, from Nepal to Mishmee and Chittagong, the plains up to 4,000 feet elevation.

(Also in Yunan.)

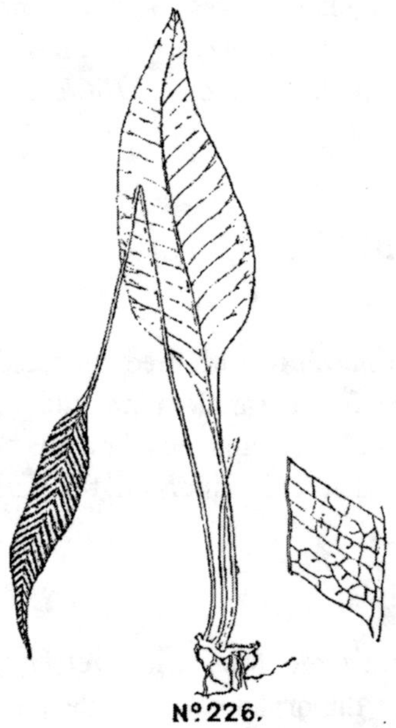

No. 226.
SELLIGUEA HAMILTONIANA.
(*Wall.*)

3. SELLIGUEA CAUDIFORMIS. (*Hook.*) Rhizome woody, creeping, the scales large, pale-brown, lanceolate; stipe 6–9 inches long, firm, erect, glossy, pale-brown; frond 6–9 inches long, ovate-oblong, acuminate, the sterile ones 3–4, the fertile ones 1–2 inches broad, texture coriaceous, both sides naked; main veins distinct to the edge, areoles with copious free clavate veinlets; sori in one continuous or interrupted row between the main veins. *Hook. Sp.* v. *p.* 158. *Bot. Mag. t.* 5328. *Syn. Fil.* 389.

The Malay Peninsula, Tenasserim and Mergui, (*nearly allied to Feei.*)

(Also in the Malay and Polynesian Islands and New Caledonia.)

No. 227.

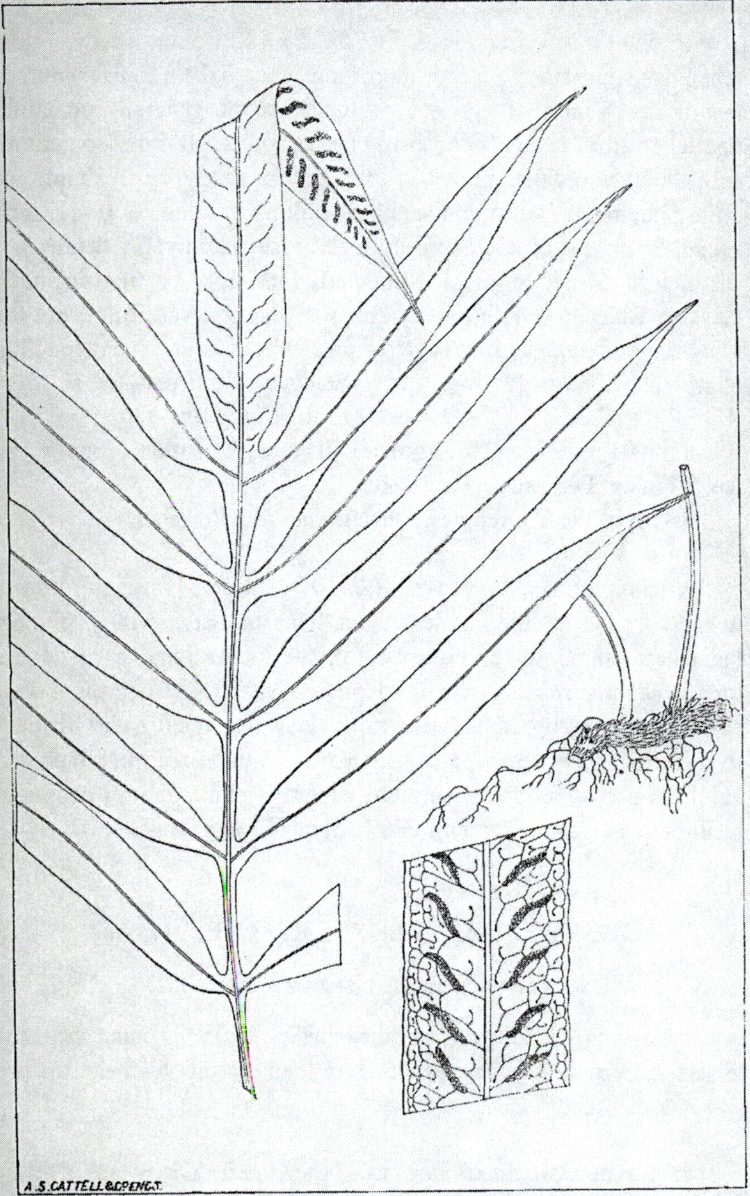

A. S. CATTELL & CO. ENG.

SELLIGUEA ELLIPTICA. (*Thunb.*)

* * *Fronds compound.*

4. SELLIGUEA ELLIPTICA. (*Thunb.*) Rhizome woody, wide-creeping; stipes up to 2 feet or more long, erect, naked, straw-coloured; fronds 12–18 inches long, by 6–12 inches broad, generally pinnatifid nearly to the rachis into 4–10 pinnæ on each side, sometimes subpalmately divided into 3–5 lobes, more rarely quite simple, or quite pinnate; lobes or pinnæ linear-oblong acuminate, $\frac{1}{2}$–$1\frac{1}{2}$ inch broad, texture subcoriaceous, quite glabrous; main veins slender not distinct to the edge, areoles unequal, with copious free included clavate veinlets; sori linear oblique, reaching the midrib but not the margin, sometimes interrupted and punctiform. Polypodium ellipticum, *Thunb. Fl. Jap.* 335. Selliguea decurrens, *Hook. Syn. Fil.* 389. *Bedd. F. B. I. t.* 150. *Wall. Cat.* 5 *and* 776.

Himalayas, Nepal to Bhotan; Khasya, elevation 2,000–5,000 feet; Malay Peninsula, Tenasserim.

(Also in the Philippines, Queensland and Formosa.)

5. SELLIGUEA MAINGAYI. (*Baker.*) Stipe $1\frac{1}{2}$ feet, dull brown, naked; fronds deltoid, under 1 foot long pinnate, with 5 oblong-lanceolate pinnæ, the end one largest, 5–6 inches long, 2–$2\frac{3}{4}$ inches broad, slightly repand, narrowed gradually at the base, the lowest pair distant, texture membranaceous, glabrous, main veins distinct to the edge, $\frac{1}{4}$ inch apart, areoles copious, minute, with free included veinlets; sori very copious, minute irregular, punctiform or confluent in lines or curves. *Baker in Hook. Syn. Fil. p.* 517.

Malacca.

GENUS LXXIII.—LOXOGRAMME. (*Presl.*)

(*Loxos*, oblique; *gramme*, a line.)

Characters of Selliguea, but differing in the fronds being adherent to the caudex (not articulate), and in their flaccid leathery texture and hidden venation.

1. LOXOGRAMME LANCEOLATA. (*Sw. under Grammitis.*) Rhi-

zome slender, wide-creeping; scales small, linear, brown; fronds 6–8 inches long by $\frac{1}{6}$–$\frac{3}{4}$ inch broad, linear lanceolate, the apex acute, the margin entire, the lower third narrowed gradually into a very short stipe, texture thick, coriaceous but flaccid, both sides glabrous; venation obscure, costal areoles numerous, small, without, or more rarely with, free included veinlets, the midrib much more slender than in *involuta;* the sori shorter and often nearly parallel, or quite parallel, with the midrib. Grammitis lanceolata, *Sw. Syn. Fil.* 22, 212, *t.* 1, *fig.* 4. Selliguea, *Hook. Syn. Fil.* 387. *Sp. Fl.* v. 156. Loxogramma lanceolata, *Bedd. F. S. I. t.* 51.

Southern India, Nilgiris and the higher Western mountains, 6,000–8,000 feet elevation, (rare compared with *involuta*). Ceylon, above Newera Elya, rare; Khasya, 4,000–5,000 feet elevation.

(Also in China, Japan, Fiji, Samoa, and Africa, with its eastern islands.)

2. LOXOGRAMME INVOLUTA. (*Don. under Grammitis.*) Rhizome stout, creeping, the scales lanceolate, brown; fronds 8–18 inches long, by 1–2½ inches broad, lanceolate, the apex acuminate, the margin entire, the lower part narrowed very gradually into a short broad compressed stipe; texture thick coriaceous, but flaccid, both sides glabrous; venation obscure, areoles copious with free included veinlets; sori in long parallel very oblique lines reaching from the midrib nearly to the margin. *Don. Fl. Nep.* 14. Selliguea, *Hook. Sp. Fil.* v. 155. *Syn. Fil. p.* 387. Loxogramma involuta, *Bedd. F. S. I. t.* 50. *Wall. Cat.* 6, 7 *and* 10.

Very common on the mountains throughout the Indian region; Himalayas, 2,000–7,000 feet elevation; Southern India and Ceylon, 5,000–8,000 feet.

Perhaps only a large form of *lanceolata.* Baker says there are no free included veinlets, but I find them always present in this plant, (Sir J. Hooker says sometimes), generally absent though sometimes present in lanceolata.

(Also in the Malay Islands and Polynesia.)

3. LOXOGRAMME AVENIA. (*Baker.*) Rhizome creeping; stipe

Nº 228.

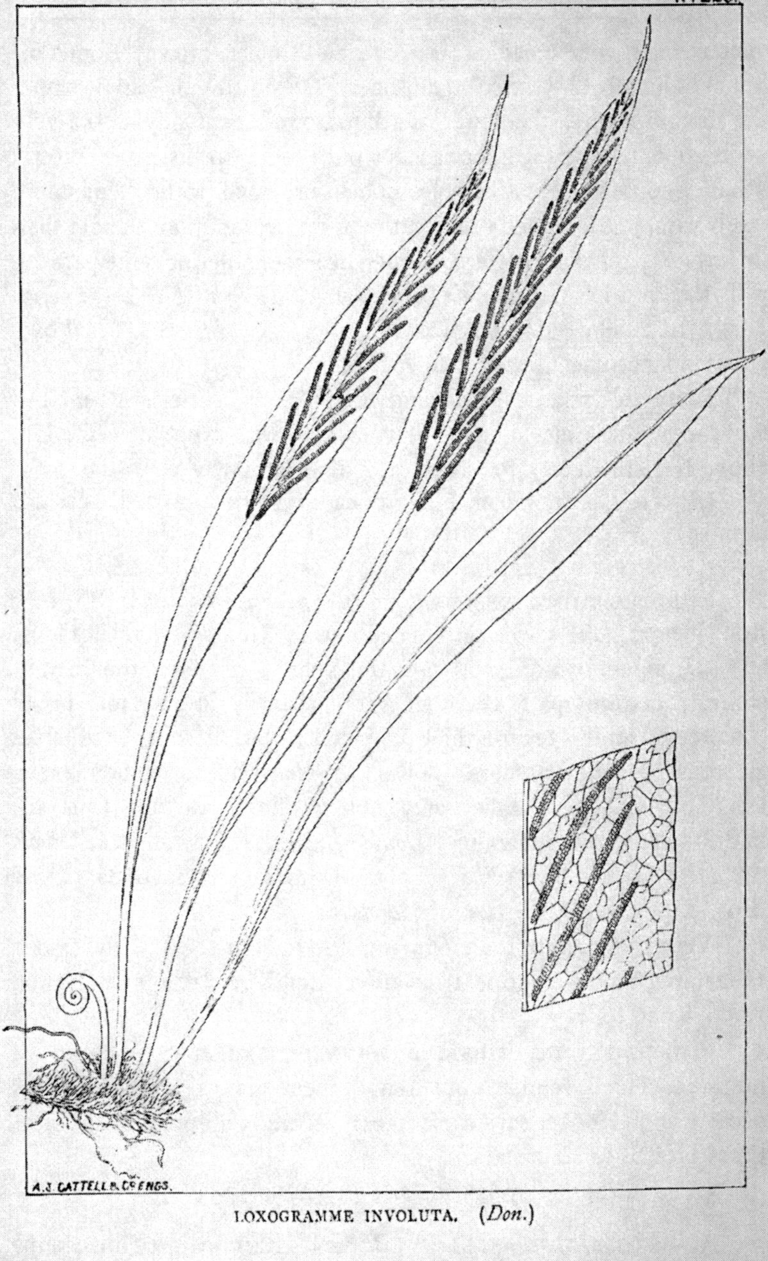

LOXOGRAMME INVOLUTA. (*Don.*)

about 1 inch long, fronds glabrous, coriaceous, 18–20 inches long, linear-oblong, spathulate, broader upwards, but narrowed and acute at the apex, about 3 inches wide in the widest part, glabrous on both sides, texture less coriaceous than in the last two; venation more evident, reticulated with free veinlets in some of the areoles, no prominent costules though the primary veins are slightly thicker than the others; sori in narrow linear more or less flexuose, parallel lines in the upper portion of the frond not touching the costa nor extending to the margin. *Baker, Syn. Fil. p.* 388. *Bedd. F. B. I. t.* 266.

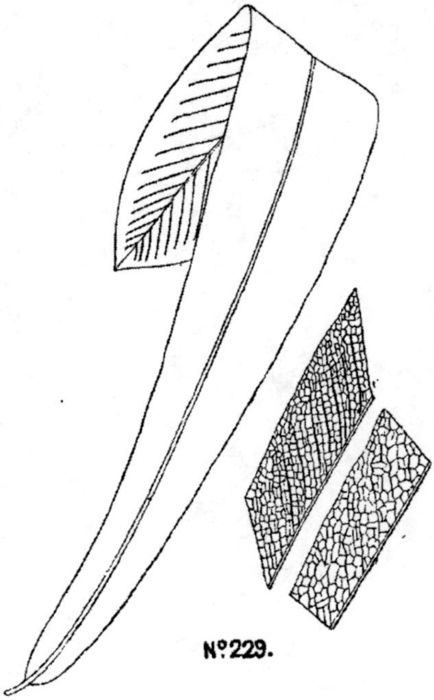

N°229.

LOXOGRAMME AVENIA. (*Baker.*)

The Malay Peninsula, Penang.

(Also in the Malay Islands.)

GENUS LXXIV.—BRAINEA. (*J. Sm.*)

(After C. Braine who first introduced the fern.)

Sori linear, simple or branched, usually on the veins which form the costal areoles and on the bases of the free transverse ones, often more extended and confluent; veins united so as to form one series of oblong or triangular costal areoles, the rest free, simple or forked, and generally all free towards the apex of the pinnæ; caudex erect, arborescent; fronds pinnated continuous with the caudex.

1. BRAINEA INSIGNIS. (*Hook.*) Caudex as thick as a man's

No. 230

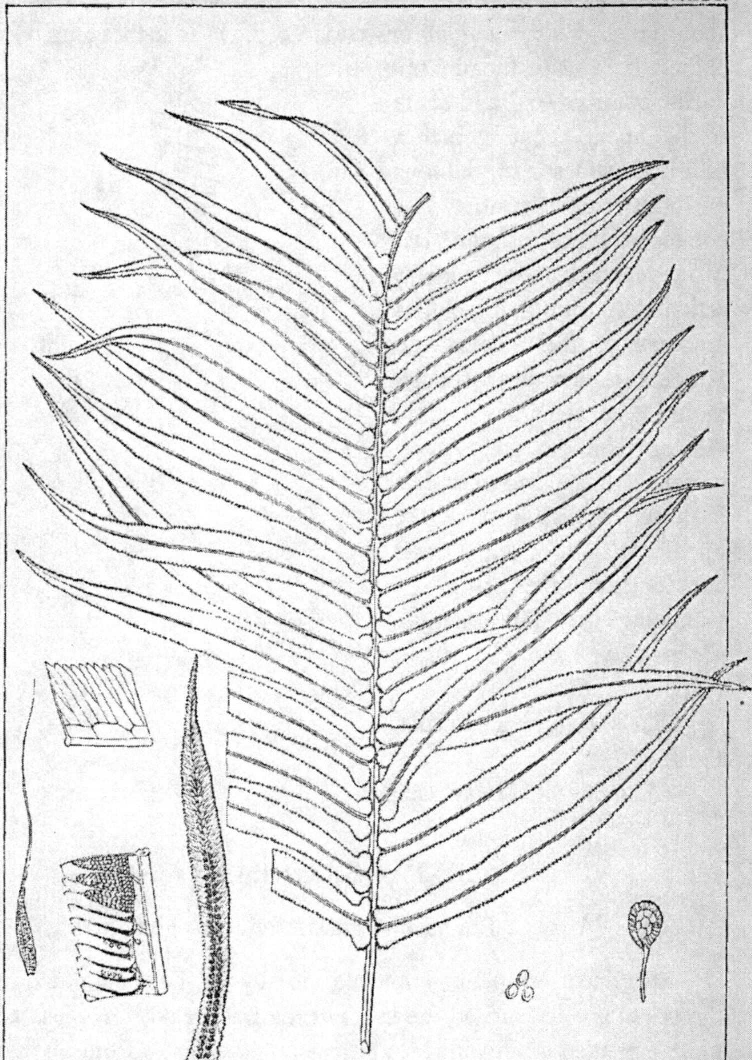

BRAINEA INSIGNIS. (*Hook.*)

arm, clothed with shaggy dark-brown ferruginous subulate-lanceolate scales, $\frac{3}{4}$–1 inch long; stipes stout, firm, 3-4 inches long, scaly only at the base; fronds coriaceous bright-green (Lomaria-like), pinnate, or occasionally below partially bipinnate; pinnæ numerous, close, horizontal, 5–6 inches long, 4 lines broad, base cordate, linear-oblong, acuminate, finely serrate. *Hook. Syn. Fil.* 390. *Bedd. F. B. I. t.* 139.

Khasya Hills, 3,000–4,000 feet elevation, Pomrang and Jainka; Malay Peninsula, in Tenasserim, the fir forests (Parish), on Mooleyit, 4,000 feet (Beddome.)

(Also in Hong Kong.)

GENUS LXXV.—MENISCIUM. (*Schreb.*)

(*Meniskos*, cresent; shape of fructification,)

Sori naked, oblong or linear, occupying the transverse connivent veinlets; veins pinnate, veinlets numerous, the opposite ones uniting in an arc or angle, and sending out from the angle a free or continuous venule; fronds simple or pinnate, (only differs from Goniopteris in the shape of the sori.)

1. MENISCIUM TRIPHYLLUM. (*Sw.*) Rhizome firm, wide-creeping, with chesnut lanceolate-linear scales at the extremities; stipes slender, slightly pubescent, of the fertile frond 1 foot long or more, of the sterile often shorter; fronds 3-foliate or with 5 or more pinnæ, the terminal one much the largest, all oblong-lanceolate with a broad base and acute apex, about 4–6 inches long by $\frac{3}{4}$–1$\frac{1}{2}$ inch broad, stalked or subsessile, margin entire or subrepand, the fertile ones often narrower, texture herbaceous, slightly pubescent beneath; areoles 6–9 between midrib and margin. *Sw. Syn. Fil.* 19, 206. *Hook. Syn. Fil.* 391. *Bedd. F. S. I. t.* 56. *Wall. Cat.* 61.

South India, Bolampatty Valley, Anamallays, Travancore, 2,000 –3000 feet elevation, gregarious and forming very large beds, nearly always trifoliate, rarely 5–foliate; Ceylon, Matale and Saffragam, 2,000–3,000 feet; North India, Eastern Bengal, Cachar, Chittagong, Sikkim, at no great elevation; Malay Peninsula.

(Also in China and Philippines.)

Nº 231.

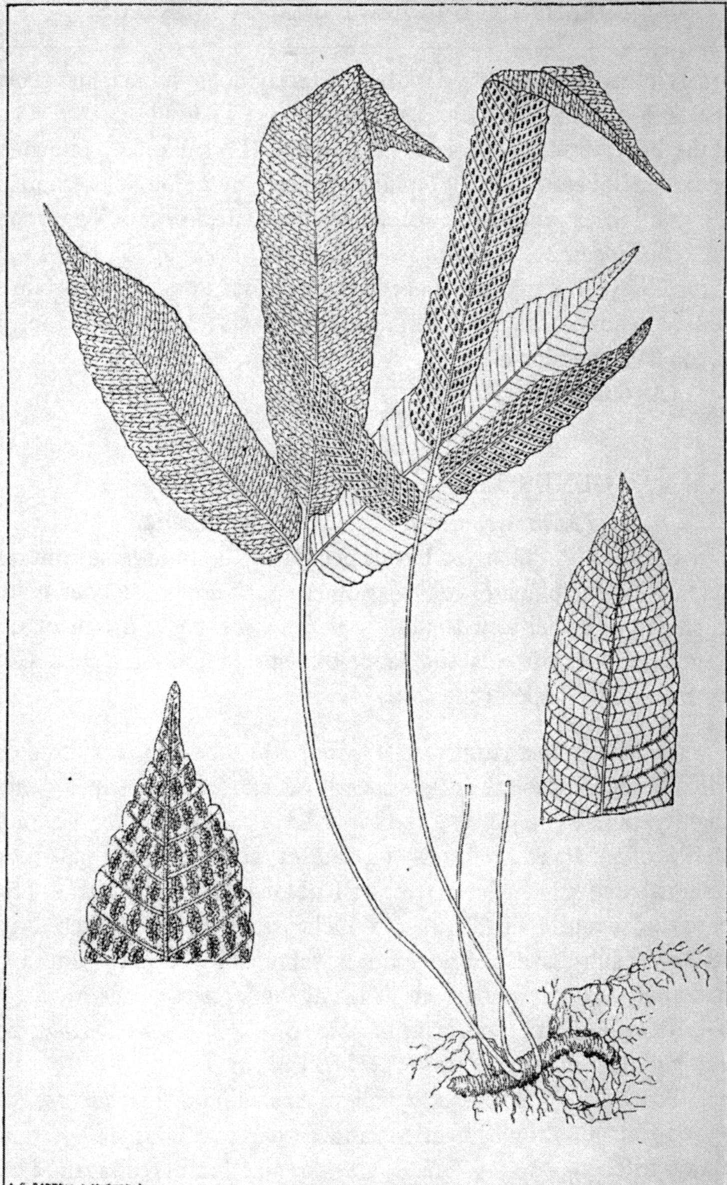

A. C. CATTELL & Cº ENGRᴿˢ

MENISCIUM TRIPHYLLUM. (*Sw.*)

VAR. β PARISHII, pinnæ 9–13, Tenasserim and Mishmee. *Bedd. F. B. I. t.* 184; this probably runs into the type, but there is nothing like it in South India.

2. MENISCIUM THWAITESII. (*Hook.*) Rhizome wide-creeping, thick as a crowquill, stipes 9–12 inches long, angled, naked except at the base, fronds 8–10 inches long, 4–6 inches broad at base, deltoid or subdeltoid, the apex acuminate and more or less pinnatifid, below which are several linear oblong rather deeply crenated

N°232.

MENISCIUM THWAITESII. (*Hook.*)

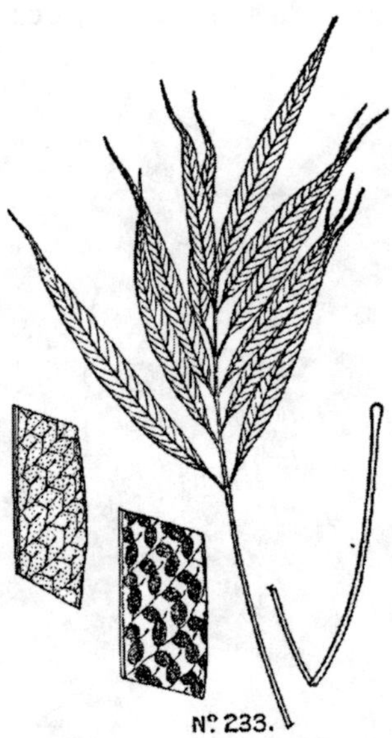

N° 233.

MENISCIUM SALICIFOLIUM. (*Wall.*)

pinnæ, the lowest stalked, the others sessile or subsessile, ½–1 inch broad, often suddenly narrowed at the base, texture herbaceous, below a little pubescent, above glabrous or nearly so, except the costa; areoles generally 5 series between the costa and margin. *Hook. Syn. Fil. p.* 391. *Bedd. F. S. I. t.* 223.

South India, Nilgiris, west slopes below Sispara, 3,000 feet elevation; Ceylon, Matale, 3,000 feet elevation.

3. MENISCIUM SALICIFOLIUM. (*Wall.*) Stipe 1 foot or more long, stramineous or pale-brown, glossy; fronds 12–18 inches long,

and up to 1 foot broad; pinnæ numerous $\frac{3}{4}$–$1\frac{1}{2}$ inch apart, 4–8 inches long by $\frac{1}{4}$–$\frac{3}{4}$ inch wide, narrowed very gradually from the middle to both ends, the apex being long acuminate, the margins entire or nearly so, texture subcoriaceous, rachis and both sides glabrous, main veins oblique, 1 line apart, areoles 4–5 between the midrib and margin, excurrent venules generally free; sori oblong, formed of two confluent rounded ones. *Wall. Cat. n.* 63. *Hook. Syn. Fil.* 391. *Bedd. F. B. I. t.* 207.

Malay Peninsula, Penang and Singapore.

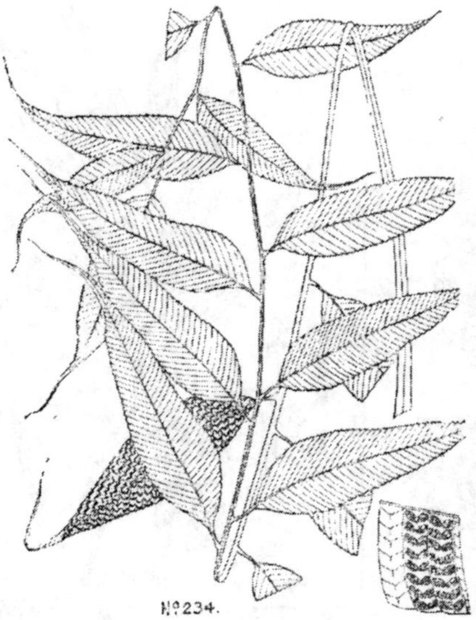

MENISCIUM CUSPIDATUM. (*Bl.*)

4. MENISCIUM CUSPIDATUM. (*Bl.*) Stipes 1–2 feet long, stout, naked; fronds 2–4 feet long, pinnate, pinnæ numerous up to about 18 inches long and 3 inches broad, oblong or elliptic lanceolate, the apex long acuminate or caudate, the margin subentire or crenated, the base gradually or suddenly narrowed, generally somewhat stalked, texture subcoriaceous, rachis and both sides glabrous or slightly pubescent; main veins prominent, areoles 6–20 between the midrib and the margin. *Bl. En. Pl. Jav. Fil.* 114. *Hooker, Syn. Fil.* 392. *Bedd. F. B. I. t.* 309. M. longifrons, *Wall. Cat.* 60.

North India. The plant figured is the same as Blume's type, with narrower more attenuated pinnæ and comparatively few areoles; it is from Sylhet, 250 feet elevation, and from Jaintea, Jowye, 4,000 feet elevation, it is not common in North India, also inhabits Java and the Philippines. The variety with broader pinnæ and about 20 areoles (Wallich's type of longifrons) is very common on the

Himalayas and Khasya, from 500–4,000 feet, and Mr. Clarke makes it a separate variety, under the name of longifrons; it, however, graduates into the type, I believe it is not separated at Kew, nor are there any characters to distinguish it; they both have the costa very red sometimes, Mr. Clarke also gathered small specimens with simple fronds (not in fruit, however).

(Mr. Clarke is quite wrong in referring Gymnopteris costata, var. deltigera, to this genus, it has quite different venation.)

GENUS LXXVI.—ANTROPHYUM. (*Kaulf.*)

(*Antron*, a cave, hollow; *phyo*, I grow.)

Sori reticulated or interrupted, carried along the veins in line, the receptacles immersed and forming grooves, or superficial; veins uniform reticulated; fronds adherent to the caudex, simple, with or without a defined midrib, fleshy-coriaceous in texture, all the species closely allied.

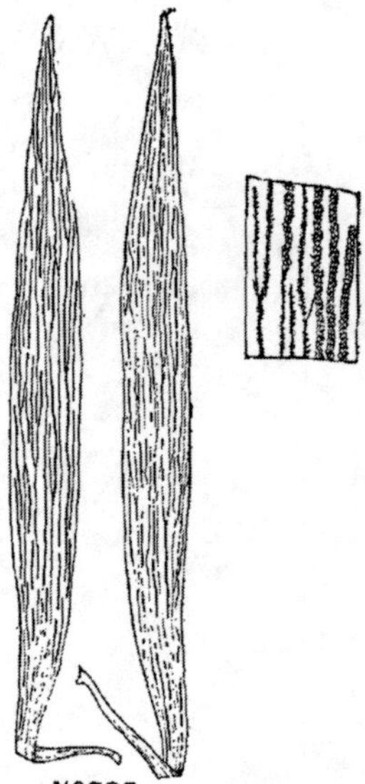

No. 235.
ANTROPHYUM RETICULATUM. (*Kaulf.*)

1. ANTROPHYUM RETICULATUM. (*Kaulf.*) Stipe none or very short, the frond being decurrent down to the base; fronds 6–15 inches long, by 1–1½ inch broad, linear-lanceolate or acuminate, very gradually narrowed downwards; midrib none or sometimes present towards the base of the frond, the areoles very long and narrow and distinctly raised on the upper surface; sori immersed, sometimes confluent. *Kaulf, Fée, 3rd Mém. Foug.* 14. *Bedd. F. S. I. t.* 231. Ant. coriaceum, *Wall. Cat.* 43. Ant. semicostatum (*Bl.*), *Hook. Syn. Fil.* 393.

All the South Indian, Ceylon, and North Indian specimens seem to me to belong to one species; "coriaceum" is said to differ

No. 236.

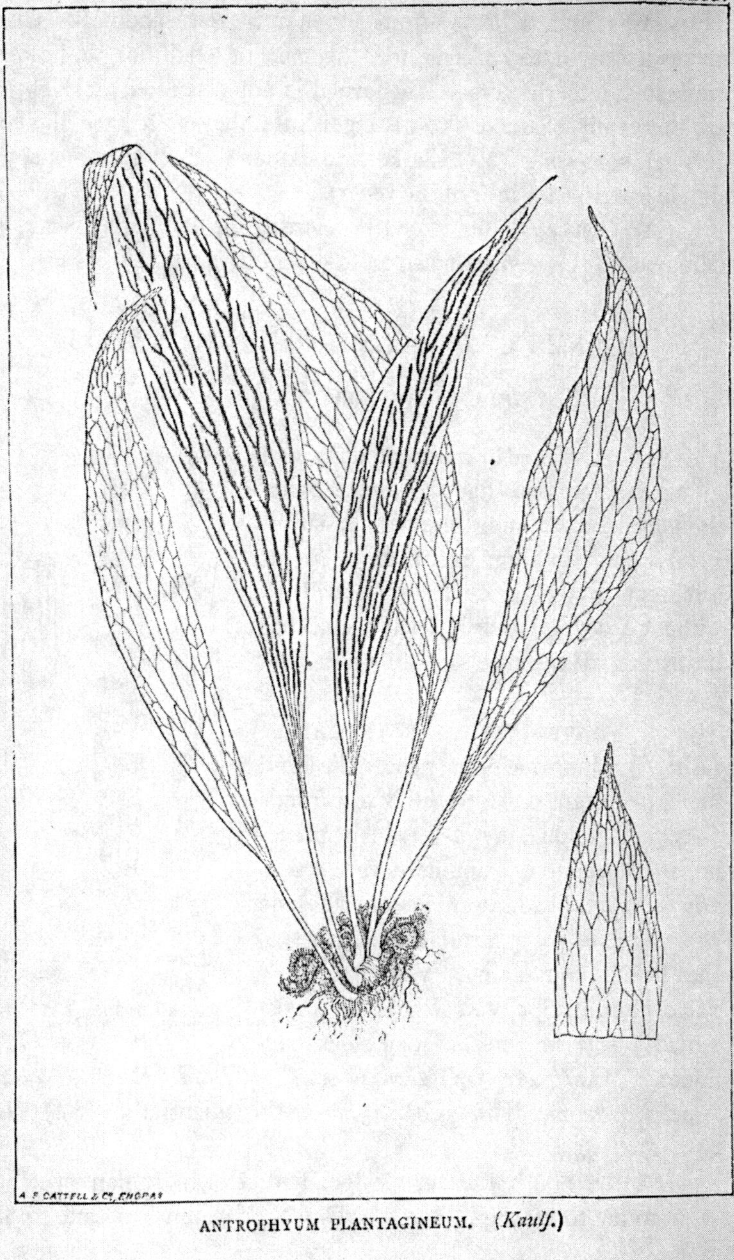

ANTROPHYUM PLANTAGINEUM. (*Kaulf.*)

by being plicate on the upper surface, but this peculiarity occurs also in the South Indian plant and is not a specific character; reticulatum can always be distinguished from "plantagineum" by its longer and narrower fronds, and generally also by the presence of numerous barren sporangiastra.

South India, rare, on the Tinnevelly and Travancore Mountains, 3,000 feet elevation; Ceylon, southern and central provinces, up to 4,000 feet; Himalayas and Khasya, up to 5,000 feet; Malay Peninsula.

(Also in Polynesia and Queensland.)

VAR. β PARVULUM. (*Bl.*) Fronds very small, 1–4 inches long, by $\frac{1}{6}$–$\frac{1}{3}$ inch broad. Antr. parvulum (*Bl*), *Fil. Jav.* 78, *t.* 34. *Hook. Sp. Fil.* v. 170. *Bedd. F. B. I. t.* 267.

Sikkim, Yoksun, 4,500 feet, Khasya; Penang.

(Also in Java.)

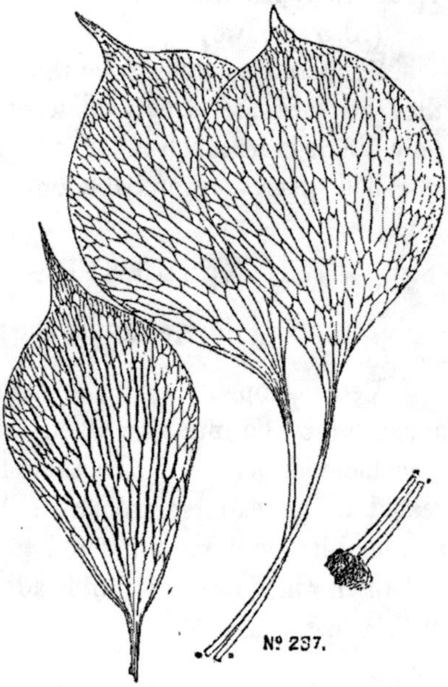

Nº 237.

ANTROPHYUM LATIFOLIUM. (*Bl*)

2. ANTROPHYUM PLANTAGINEUM. (*Kaulf.*) Stipe distinct, 1–4 inches long; fronds oblong, broadest towards the apex, then suddenly narrowed into an acute point, 4–10 inches long, and up to 2 inches broad, no midrib or an inconspicuous one towards the base; sori deeply immersed, sometimes distinctly raised on the upper surface making the frond plicate above. *Kaulf, Bory. in Voy. de la Coq. Bot. Cryp. t.* 28. *Bedd. F. S. I. t.* 52 (reticulatum).

South India, on the Western mountains, 2,000–5,500 feet

elevation, not very common; Ceylon, central provinces; Himalayas and Khasya up to 5,000 feet; Malay Peninsula.

(Also in the Malay Islands, Philippines and Polynesian Islands.)

3. ANTROPHYUM LATIFOLIUM. (*Bl.*) Stipe long up to 7 inches; fronds large, broadly obovate or round, up to 4¾ inches wide, acuminate or acutely lobed at the apex, no midrib; sori superficial or immersed, with the frond plicate above. *Bl. Fl. Jav. Fil.* 75. *Bedd. F. B. I. t.* 176.

Sikkim and Bhotan, 2,000–6,000 feet; Assam and Khasya 1,000–4,000 feet elevation.

(Also in Java.)

Supposed to differ from the last by the sori being superficial; they however are deeply immersed in some of my specimens, so it only differs in its much broader frond and longer stipes; all the three so-called species are probably only varieties of one plant.

GENUS LXXVII.—VITTARIA. (*Sm.*)

(*Vitta*, a riband, the riband-like frond.)

Veins simple, forming an acute angle with the midrib, their apices prolonged into a transverse marginal vein, which becomes the receptacle, or veins forked without the transverse marginal vein; sori seated in an extrorse groove of the margin, or in a slightly intra-marginal line with the unaltered edge of the frond produced beyond and often rolled over it; fronds adherent to the caudex, linear, grass- or tape-like.

1. VITTARIA ELONGATA. (*Sw.*) Rhizome creeping, scales many, with black hair-like points; fronds up to 2½ feet long, generally only ¼ inch broad, acuminate, grass-like, but rather firm in texture, mid-rib generally more or less distinct beneath; veins simple, oblique, immersed, parallel, connected by an intramarginal veinlet; sori quite sunk in an extrorse marginal groove. *Sw. Syn. Fil.* 109, 302. *Wall. Cat.* 144. *Bedd. F. S. I. t.* 21.

No. 238.

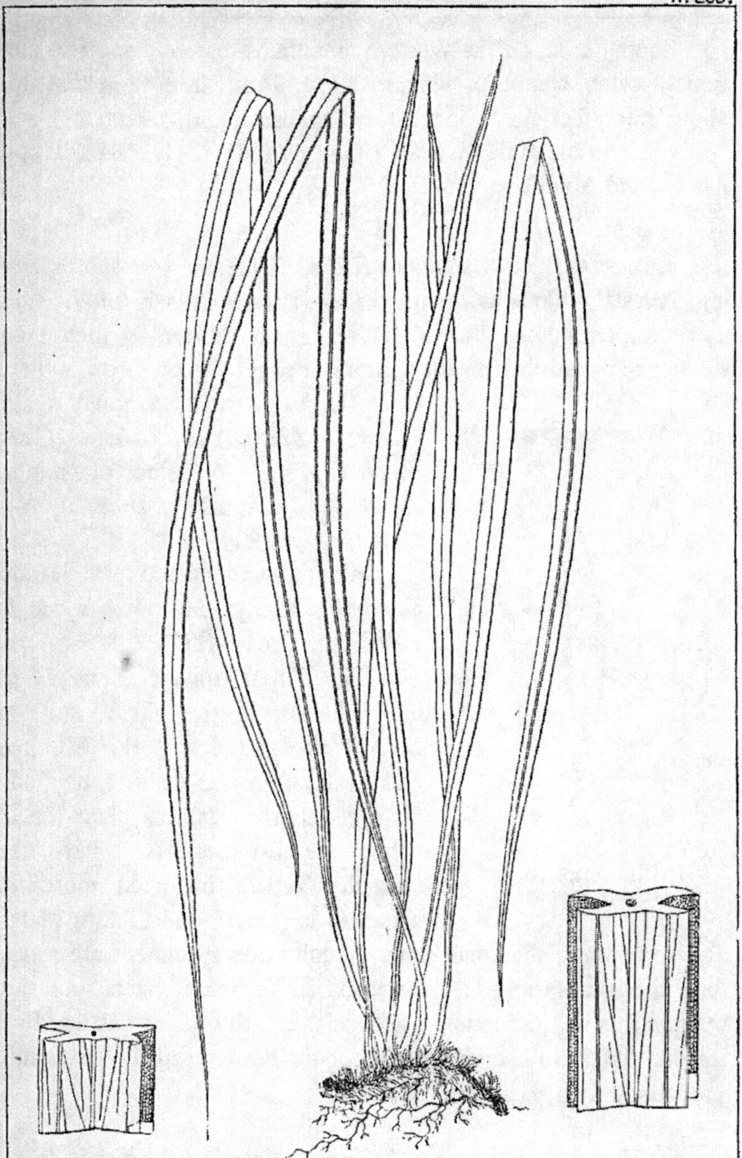

VITTARIA ELONGATA. (*Sw.*)

South India, on the Western mountains, 2,000–5,000 feet elevation; Ceylon, central provinces; North India, from the plains up to about 4,000 feet elevation; Malay Peninsula, Birma, &c.

(Also in the Malay Islands; Queensland; Polynesia; Tropical Africa, and Mauritius.)

2. VITTARIA SIKKIMENSIS. (*Kuhn.*) Rhizome very shortly creeping, with slaty-rufous hair-pointed scales; stipes densely tufted; fronds up to 4 inches long, but often very much shorter, $\frac{1}{20}$ inch broad, subobtuse; midrib beneath obscure or slightly depressed; sori sunk in a large extrorse marginal furrow. *Kuhn in Linnæa* xxxvi. 66. *Clarke, F. N. I. p.* 574. V. minor var. minima, *Hook. Sp. Fil.* v. 183. *Bedd. F. B. I. t.* 56 (*not minor of Fée*).

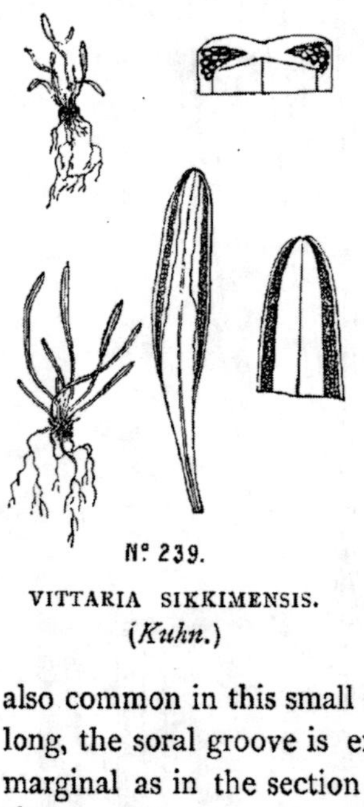

N° 239.

VITTARIA SIKKIMENSIS. (*Kuhn.*)

Sikkim, 2,000–6,000 feet elevation, common; Khasya, Mowlong, 2,500 feet elevation; Tenasserim.

The Tenasserim specimens are certainly the same as the Sikkim, and when Mr. Clarke stated that the Moulmein and Malay fern was distinct, he had in his eye only the Malacca plant (*i.e.* falcata or the next species). I have never seen the Tenasserim plant more than 2 inches long, and the Sikkim plant is also common in this small state, though other specimens are 4 inches long, the soral groove is extrorse as in Vittaria elongata (not intramarginal as in the section Tæniopsis) and this plant can hardly be said to differ from elongata except in its very small size, and is probably only a variety of it.

3. VITTARIA FALCATA. (*Kunze.*) Fronds 4–5 inches long, $\frac{1}{8}$ inch broad, the apex blunt, the lower part narrowed gradually to the base, texture leathery and very thick; a distinct raised midrib

attaining the apex in the barren fronds, but lost in the fertile ones; veins short, oblique, parallel, immersed; sori quite sunk, in deep intramarginal grooves. *Kunze. Hook. Syn. Fil.* 395. *V. falcata and minor Fée 3rd. Mém. Foug.*

Malacca.

(Also in the Philippines.)

4. VITTARIA AMBOINENSIS. (*Fée.*) Fronds 4–5 inches long, by 3–4 lines broad, smooth, submembranaceous, falcate acuminate, tapering below into a petiole; costa slender, disappearing below the apex; veins curved equal approximate; sori closely marginal, cuticle of the margin resembling a false involucre; caudex flexuose, contorted scaly, scales cancellate, rigidly toothed at the margin. *Fée, Vittar. p.* 44, *t.* 1, *f.* 1. (*not Mett.*) *Hook. Sp. Fil.* v. 177. *Bedd. F. B. I. t.* 117.

Martaban. This seems as distinct a species as most of this group, though it is possible it may be a small form of scolopendrina, the veins are combined where fertile by an intramarginal vein which runs along the centre of the receptacle.

(Also in Amboyna).

5. VITTARIA LINEATA. (*Sw.*) Rhizome very short creeping; stipes tufted, scales acuminate with caudate points; fronds up to 8 inches long, $\frac{1}{8}$–$\frac{1}{3}$ inch broad, narrowed gradually downwards to the stout compressed stipe, the margin often reflexed, texture thick, a distinct raised midrib from the base to the apex; veins simple, immersed, parallel, very oblique; sori in a broad intramarginal shallow furrow, the edge of the frond distinctly beyond the furrow and at first wrapped over it. *Sw. Syn. Fil.* p. 109. *Hook. Syn. Fil.* 396. Tæniopsis lineata, *Bedd. F. S. I. t.* 54. Fée separated the Indian plant from the American under the name of flexuosa, and Mr. Clarke has adopted that name, but the two plants seem identical.

South India, on the Western mountains, 2,000–6,000 feet elevation; Ceylon, central provinces, common; Himalayas, 2,000–12,000 feet elevation, from Gurwhal to Bhotan, Khasya, 1,000–6,000 feet elevation; Malay Peninsula.

(Also in Tropical America, and the West Indies, Africa and its Eastern Islands.)

No. 240.
VITTARIA SULCATA. (*Kuhn.*)

6. VITTARIA SCOLOPENDRINA. (*Presl.*) Caudex creeping, paleaceous with subulate scales; fronds linear lanceolate acuminate, membranaceous, gradually attenuated at both ends, 16–28 inches long by 1 inch broad, glabrous on both sides, scarcely stipitate; midrib thick; sori sunk in a furrow within the margin of the upper portion of the fronds, inner margin of the furrow winged, margin of the frond revolute over the fructification diaphanous or subindusiate. Haplopteris scolopendrina, *Pr. Tent. Pter. p.* 141. *Hook. Syn. Fil. p.* 396. Tæniopsis, *Bedd. F. S. I. t.* 212. Vitt. Zeylanica, *Fée.*

Ceylon, southern and central provinces, on rocks up to 3,000 feet elevation; Himalayas, Sikkim, Assam, Bhotan.

(Also in New Guinea, Philippines, Malay Islands, Seychelles, and Mozambique.)

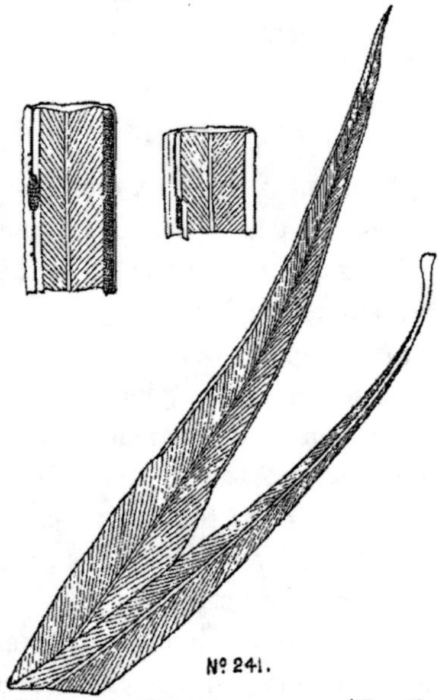

No. 241.
VITTARIA SCOLOPENDRINA. (*Presl.*)

7. VITTARIA SULCATA. (*Kuhn.*) Rhizome short creeping, scales dense lanceolate, pale-brown; fronds crowded, ligulate, obtuse, sessile, narrowed to the base, 2–4 inches long, $\frac{1}{8}$ inch broad; sori in an intramarginal deep furrow confined to the very much thickened upper half of the frond, where the midrib and veins

No. 242.

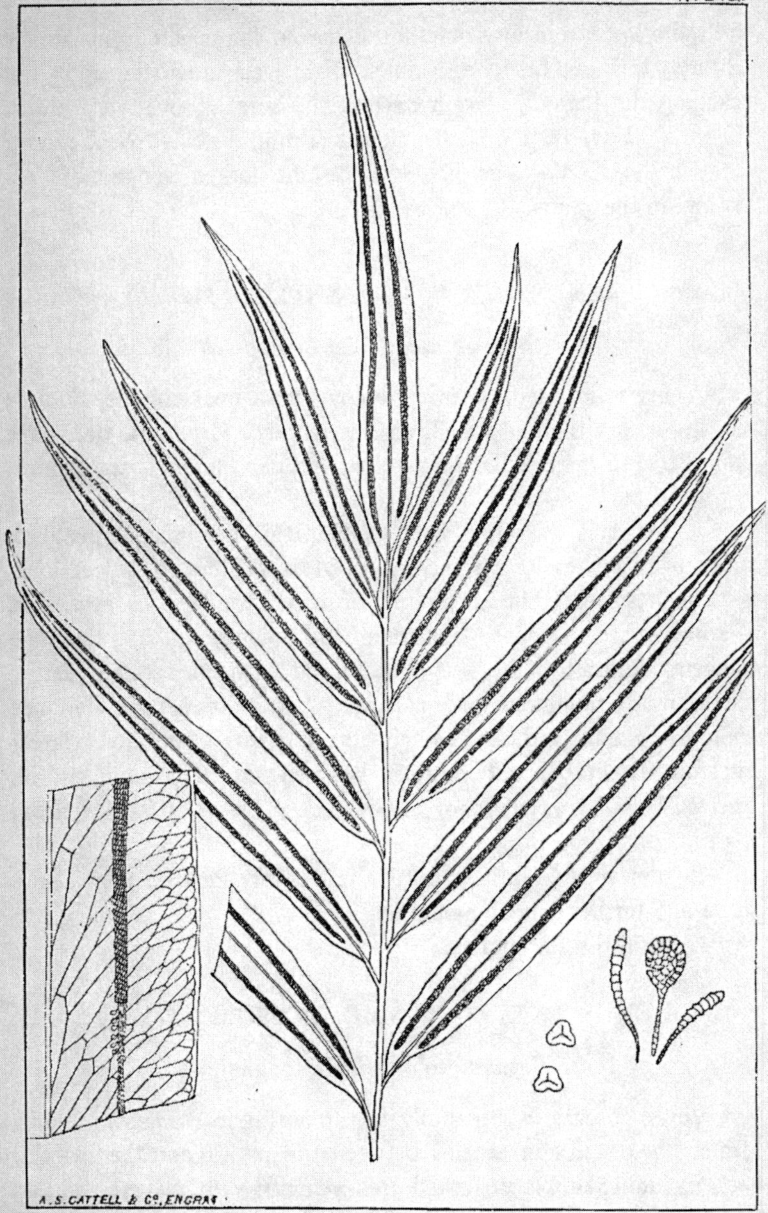

TÆNITIS BLECHNOIDES. (*Sw.*)

are quite lost; midrib visible in the barren lower half, veins forked or rarely with two branches, veinlets slightly clavate at the apex not reaching the margin, margin beyond the soral groove very thick. *Kuhn, Linnæa*, 36, *p.* 68. Tæniopsis falcata, *Bedd. F. B. I. t.* 175.

Ceylon, 4,000–5,000 feet elevation, the forked venation is abnormal in the genus.

GENUS LXXVIII.—TÆNITIS. (*Willd.*)

(From *tainia*, a fillet or ribbon.)

Veins reticulated, forming oblong hexagonal oblique areoles; sori linear, but the line sometimes interrupted, forming a transverse band between the midrib and margin; fronds adherent to the caudex.

1. TÆNITIS BLECHNOIDES. (*Sw.*) Rhizome creeping, setose; stipes 8–12 inches long, firm, naked, glossy; fronds 1–2 feet long, 8–12 inches broad, pinnate; pinnæ of barren frond 2–3 on each side, 1–2 inches broad, oblong-lanceolate, the point acuminate, the edge thickened and wavy, the base cuneate, the lower ones stalked, fertile pinnæ more numerous and narrower, texture coriaceous, areoles copious, oblique, without free veinlets; sori in a continuous (rarely interrupted) line, about midway between the edge and midrib. *Swartz, Syn. Fil.* 24 *and* 220. *Hook. Syn. Fil.* 397. *Bedd. F. B. I. t.* 54.

Ceylon, in the forests about Galle; Malay Peninsula, in Tenasserim and further south; Sylhet (?).

(Also in the Philippines.)

GENUS LXXIX.—DRYMOGLOSSUM. (*Presl.*)

(*Drymos*, wood; *glossa*, tongue).

Veins obscure, compoundly anastomosing in the sterile fronds, forming 3–4 series of areoles between the midrib and the margin, each including simple or forked free veinlets, with clavate apices; fronds articulate with the caudex, dimorphous, the sterile broad and short, the fertile long and narrow; sori linear, scarcely immersed, central or submarginal often at length confluent and covering the whole underneath surface of the frond; caudex wide-creeping on trees.

1. DRYMOGLOSSUM CARNOSUM. (*Hook.*) Rhizome long, filiform, wiry, clothed with peltate lanceolate-linear toothed scales, which are often hair-pointed; stipes 2 lines to 1 inch long, distant slender; fronds simple, of two kinds, sterile one from ½ an inch, (and then generally orbicular or sub-cordate) to 2 and even 3 inches long, and then elliptical or obovate or spathulate, or even lanceolate and acuminate, thick and fleshy, coriaceous when dry, faintly costate on the under side; veins anastomosing, the areoles including free veinlets, fertile fronds 1–2½ inches long, linear-spathulate obtuse; sori linear continuous forming a line intermediate between the costa and the margin, soon confluent, and representing one broad band, nearly as broad as the frond, when young covered by numerous peltate pedicellated scales. *Hook. Sp. Fil.* v. 189. Nothochlæna? (Tænitis?) carnosa, *Wall. Cat. n.* 138. *Bedd. F. B. I. t.* 55.

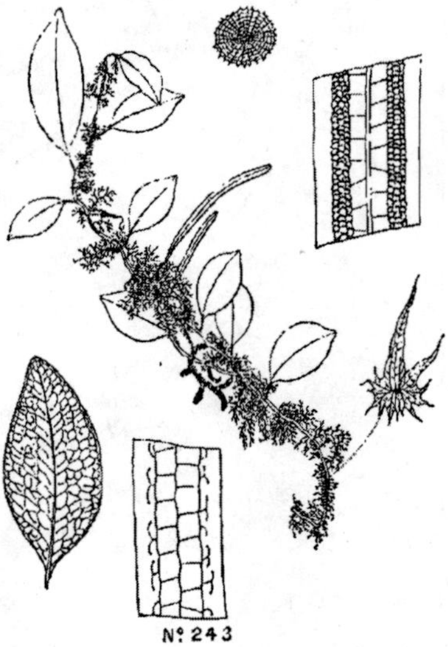

Nº 243

DRYMOGLOSSUM CARNOSUM. (*Hook.*)

Nepal, Sikkim, Bhotan, 2,000–5,000 feet elevation, common. (Also in China and Japan.)

2. DRYMOGLOSSUM PILOSELLOIDES. (*Presl.*) Rhizome long filiform, wiry, clothed with adpressed, diamond shaped peltate laciniated scales, which are sometimes hair-pointed; stipes about 2 lines long in the sterile, often about 1 inch long in the fertile fronds, fronds dimorphous, the barren ones roundish or obovate, ½–2 inches

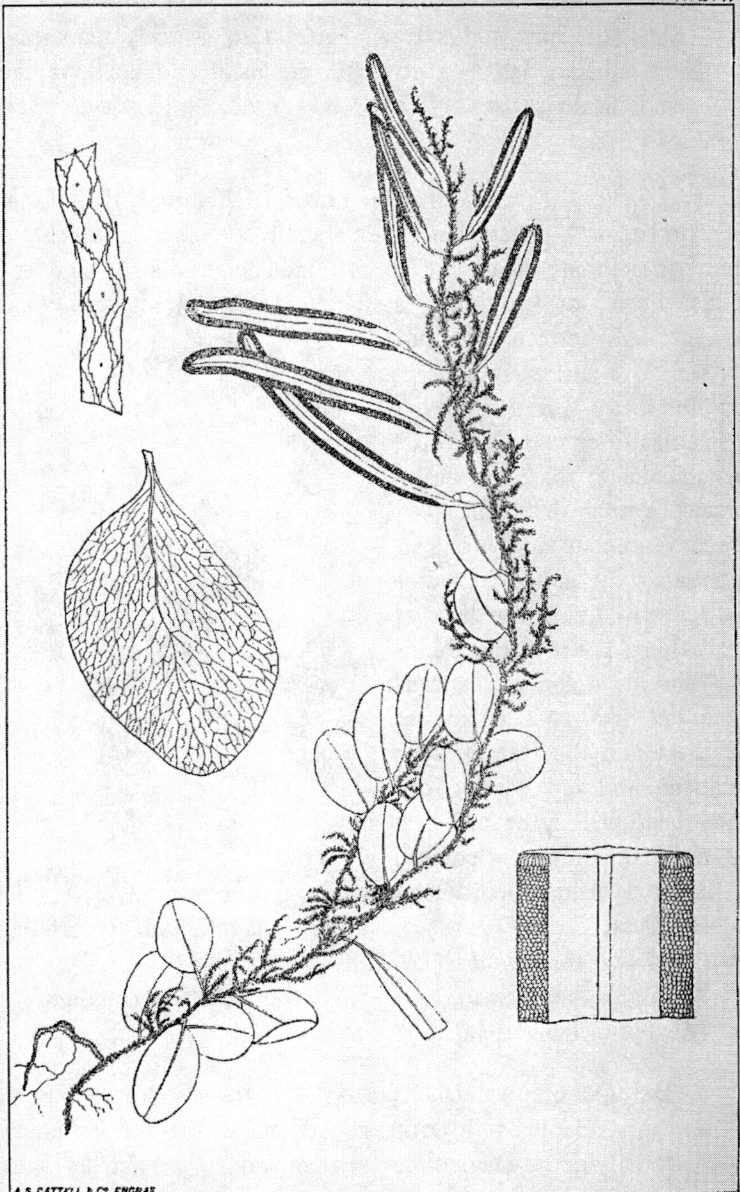

A. S. CATTELL & Co. ENGRAV

DRYMOGLOSSUM PILOSELLOIDES. (*Presl.*)

long, $\frac{3}{4}$ inch broad, very thick and fleshy, and when young more or less covered with stellate hairs, the fertile ones, 2–4 inches long $\frac{1}{8}$–$\frac{1}{4}$ inch broad; veins immersed, areoles with copious free veinlets; sori in broad continuous marginal lines often at length confluent and covering the whole under surface, capsules mixed with a few stellate paraphyses. *Presl. Tent. Pterid.* 227, *t.* 10. *Bedd. F. S. I. t.* 55 *and F. S. I. t.* 186 (Niphobolus nummularifolius).

Bengal Plains; Birma; Ceylon; South India, common in the Malabar plains, (Calicut, &c. on trees), also on the mountains, up to about 2,000 feet elevation, (Anamallays, Wynad, Coorg, &c.)

(Also in Java Philippines and Japan.)

VAR. β BEDDOMEI. Mr. Clarke proposes the name Beddomei for a specimen from the Anamallays figured by me (*tab.* 186, *F. S. I.*) because the fronds have stellate hairs and the scales of the rhizome are more pointed, but I find this stellate pubescence is always more or less present on the young fronds of Himalayan examples, and the rhizome scales are quite as hair-pointed in some specimens from Java, Philippines, and Japan, the fertile fronds are shorter and narrower in this South Indian form, and the broader usually sterile fronds sometimes fructify towards the apex, but I am not inclined to consider it even a permanent variety, as I believe it runs into the type with longer fertile fronds, which is also found in Southern India.

(Niphobolus nummularifolius, though I have included it in that genus, rather belongs here, it has exactly similar venation.)

GENUS LXXX.—HEMIONITIS. (*L.*)

(*Hemionos*, a mule—the mule fern.)

Sori continuous along the veins and copiously reticulated; veins copiously anastomosing, forming numerous areoles which have rarely a free veinlet in them, which when present is also soriferous; fronds adherent to the caudex, simple, pinnatifid, or pinnate.

1. HEMIONITIS ARIFOLIA. (*Burm. under Asplenium.*) Caudex

No. 245.

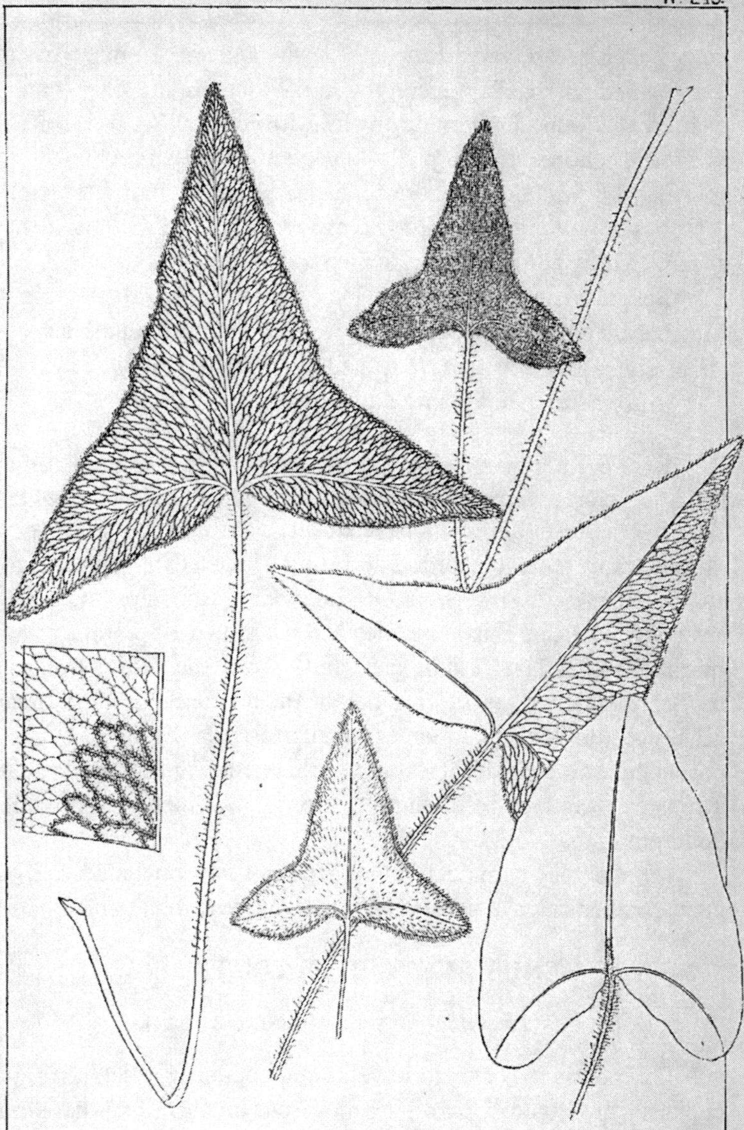

HEMIONITIS ARIFOLIA. (*Burm.*)

erect, short; stipe of the barren frond, 2–4 inches long, of the fertile often 1 foot long, dark chesnut-brown, glossy densely fibrillose towards the base; fronds 2–3 inches each way, cordate-hastate, the barren ones bluntish at the apex, with generally rounded (rarely pointed) basal lobes and a deep sinus, the fertile ones with the lobes more produced and pointed, texture more or less coriaceous, glabrous above, somewhat villous beneath; areoles oblique, numerous, free veinlets none or very rare. *Burm. Fl. Ind.* 231. H. cordifolia (*Roxb.*), *Bedd. F. S. I. t.* 53.

South India, common in the plains and on the mountains up to nearly 3,000 feet elevation; East Bengal plains; Ceylon; Birma.

(Also in the Philippines.)

2. HEMIONITIS GRIFFITHII. (*Hook. Fil. et Thoms.*) Rhizome short creeping; stipes paleaceous and coarsely hirsute, 8–12 inches long; fronds 12–16 inches long, 6–10 inches broad, subdeltoid, pinnatifid or pinnate with 2–4 pinnæ on each side, which are 1–1½ inch broad, entire or crenated, acuminate, texture herbaceous, rachis and both surfaces hairy on the venation; main veins prominent, generally barren, the veinlets reticulated into copious areoles all soriferous, rarely there are free included veinlets, which are also soriferous. *Hook. Sp. Fil.* v. 192. Dictyocline Griffithii (*Moore*), *Bedd. F. B. I. t.* 155.

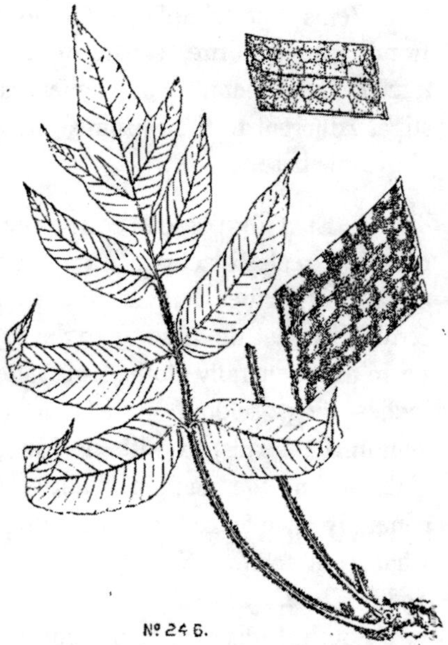

No. 246.
HEMIONITIS GRIFFITHII.
(*Hook. et Thoms.*)

Khasya, Cherra, 4,000–5000 feet elevation.

(Also in Formosa.)

TRIBE XII.—ACROSTICHEÆ.

Sori spread in a stratum over the under surface, or rarely over both surfaces of the frond, not confined to the veins only.

GENUS LXXXI.—ELAPHOGLOSSUM. (*Schott.*)

(*Elaphos*, a stag ; *glossa*, tongue.)

Veins free, simple or forked, their apices sometimes clavate, fronds simple, entire, sessile or stipitate, the fertile somewhat contracted and generally sporangiferous over the whole under surface ; stipes adherent to the rhizome, but generally pseudo-articulate a little above the base.

1. ELAPHOGLOSSUM CONFORME. (*Sw.*) Rhizome woody, wide creeping, scales blackish, ovate, jagged, not hair-pointed ; stipes firm erect, 2–3 inches long in the sterile, and often much more in the fertile, black at the base up to the pseudo-articulation, where it breaks off in age, generally clothed with sheathing scales ; sterile fronds 2–9 inches long, seldom more than 1 inch broad, narrow-lanceolate acuminate, furnished with deciduous scales on both sides, quite glabrous in age, margin slightly revolute in age ; veins hidden, generally once-forked, just reaching the margin ; fertile fronds somewhat contracted. *Sw. Syn. Fil.* 10, 192, *t.* 1. *Bedd. F. S. I. t.* 198. *Hook. Syn. Fil.* 401.

South India, Western mountains, at the higher elevations, very common ; Ceylon ; Malay Peninsula ; Sikkim and Nepal, 6,000–9,000 feet elevation, Khasya, 4,500–6,000 feet elevation.

(Also in Australia, Central and South Africa, Queensland, Polynesia, and the Malay Islands.)

2. ELAPHOGLOSSUM LATIFOLIUM. (*Sw.*) Rhizome woody, wide-creeping, scales bright chesnut or golden, lanceolate and more pointed than in conforme ; stipes longer than in conforme and the deciduous scales not sheathing ; fronds much larger than in conforme, and generally over 2 inches broad, margin diaphanous and much

No. 247.

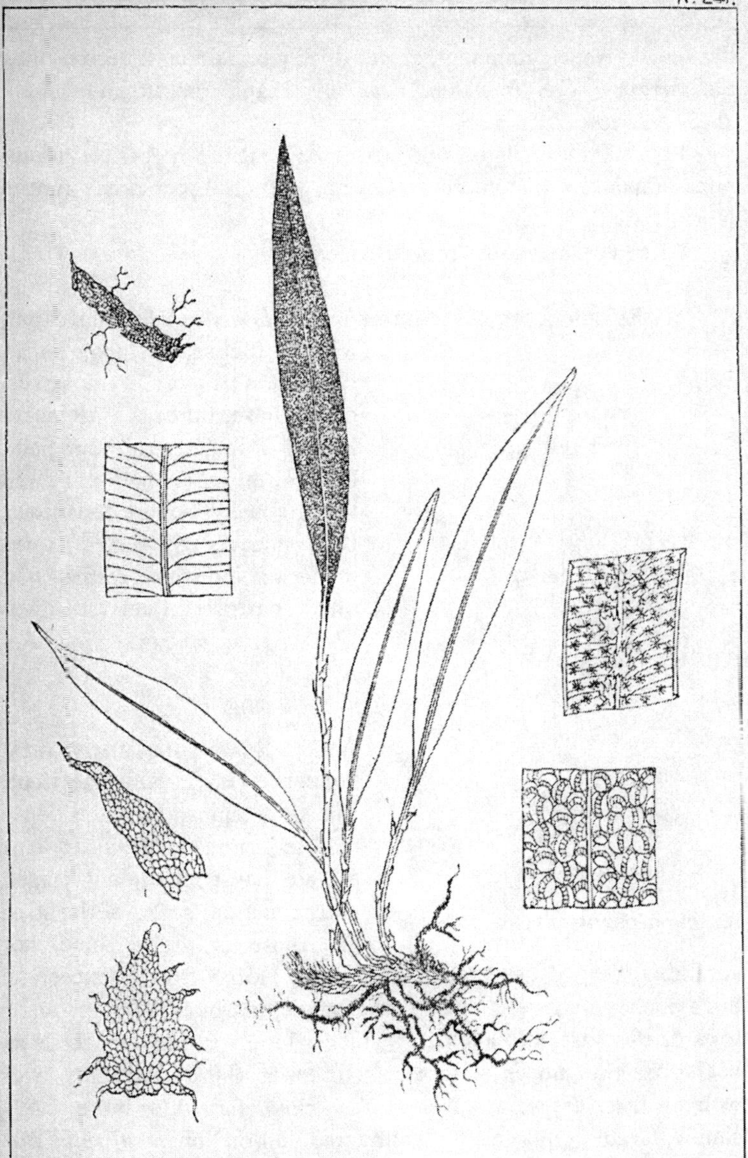

ELAPHOGLOSSUM CONFORME. (*Sw.*)

thickened; veins prominent, apices thickly clavate, and not reaching the margin. *Sw. in Schrad. Journ.* Elaph. laurifolium, *Bedd. F. S. I. t.* 200.

South India, Nilgiris, and Anamallays, at the higher elevations, rare compared with conforme; Ceylon, in central provinces; (not in North India.)

(Also in Cuba and Tropical America.)

3. ELAPHOGLOSSUM NORRISII. (*Hook.*) Rhizome stout, woody, the scales long, linear, dull-brown; barren frond sessile, or nearly so, tufted, 12–18 inches long, $\frac{3}{4}$–1 inch broad, the point blunt, the lower half narrowed very gradually, texture coriaceous, both sides nearly naked; veins immersed, indistinct; fertile frond much narrower than the other. *Hook. Sp.* v. *p.* 215. *Syn. Fil. p.* 401.

Penang.

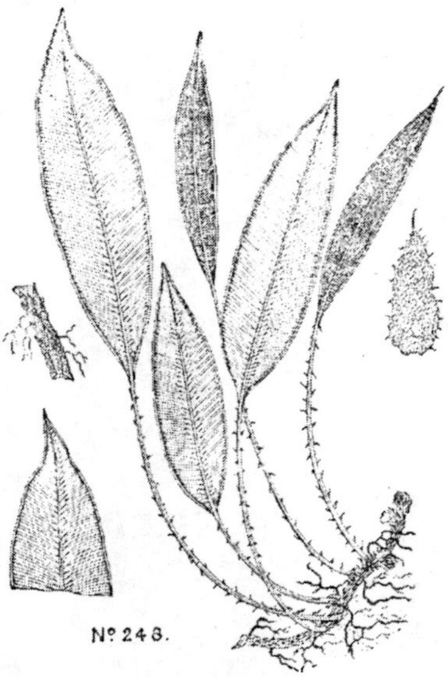

No. 248.

ELAPHOGLOSSUM LATIFOLIUM. (*Sw.*)

4. ELAPHOGLOSSUM STIGMATOLEPIS. (*Fée.*) Rhizome stout, woody, creeping, the scales dense reddish-brown, long linear lanceolate, hair-pointed, not jagged on the margin, scales of the stipe like those of the rhizome, not sheathing, very dense towards the base; barren fronds lanceolate, 8–12 inches long, $\frac{3}{4}$–1 inch broad, acute, narrowed very gradually towards the base into a stipe 1–3 inches long, texture coriaceous as in the last two, upper surface naked, lower thickly scattered over with small scales; veins apparent, fine, close, forked, or more rarely simple, fertile fronds smaller, contracted and on longer stipes. *Fée, 2me Mém. Foug. t.* 25. *Bedd. F. S. I. t.* 199. *Hook. Syn. Fil. p.* 521.

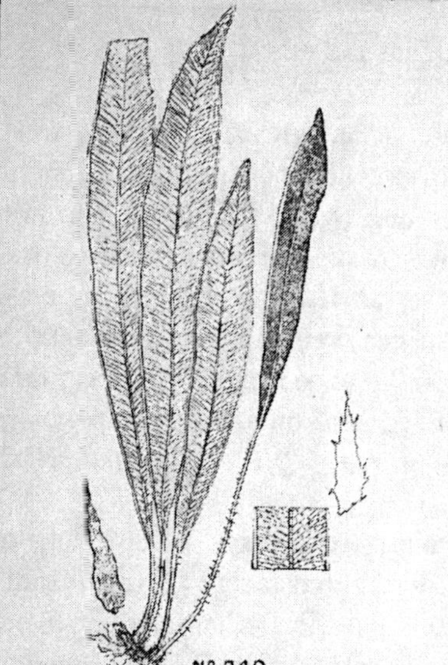

Nº 249.

ELAPHOGLOSSUM STIGMATOLEPIS. (*Fée.*)

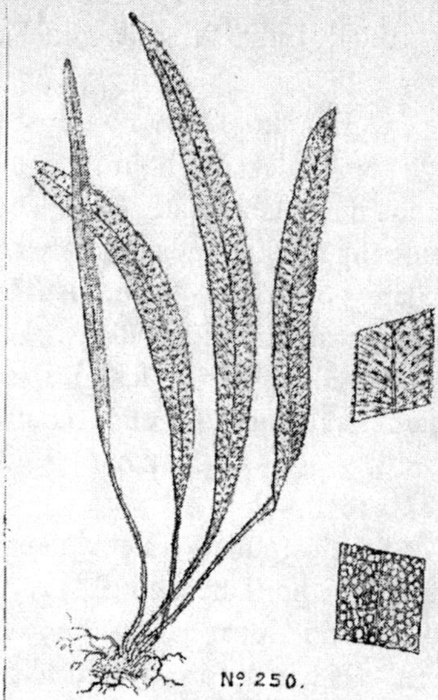

Nº 250.

ELAPHOGLOSSUM VISCOSUM. (*Sw.*)

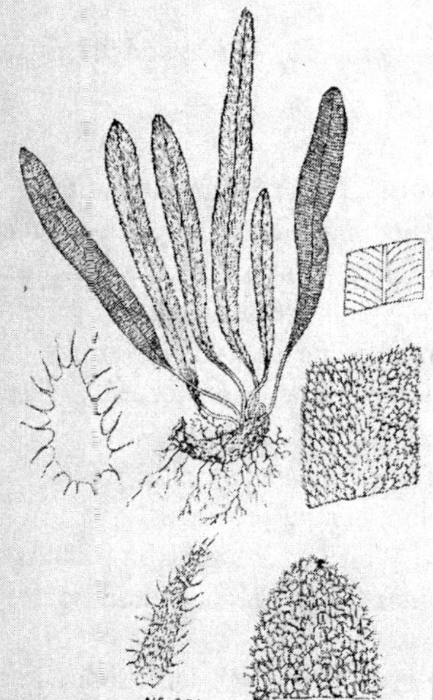

Nº 251

ELAPHOGLOSSUM SQUAMOSUM. (*Sw.*)

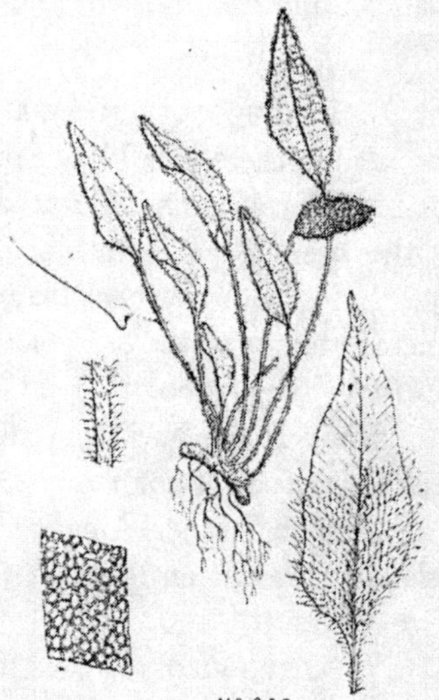

Nº 252

ELAPHOGLOSSUM SPATHULATUM. (*Sw.*)

South India, Nilgiris, and Palghat Hills.

5. ELAPHOGLOSSUM VISCOSUM. (*Sw.*) Rhizome woody, creeping, the scales bright-brown, narrow, linear, hair-pointed; sterile fronds linear-lanceolate, 6–9 inches long, by ½–¾ inch broad, narrowed gradually at both ends, densely covered on the under surface with stellate pubescence, glabrous above, at least in age, its stipe 2–3 inches, scaly and with stellate pubescence; veins apparent, their clavate apices well within the margin, generally once forked, rarely the forks again forked, fertile fronds contracted and on a longer stipe. *Sw. Syn. Fil.* 10, 193. *Bedd. F. S. I. t.* 196. E. stelligerum, *Wall. Cat.* 2167.

South India, Western mountains, Anamallays 4,000 feet, on rocks up the Toracadu River, Coorg, Travancore; North India, Sikkim and Nepal, 6,000–8,000 feet elevation, Khasya, 4,000–6,000 feet. (It has been proposed to separate the South Indian plant from the Himalayan under the name of stelligerum, but I cannot distinguish them.)

(Also in Tropical America; Tropical Africa; and its eastern islands; and the Malay Islands.)

6. ELAPHOGLOSSUM SQUAMOSUM. (*Sw.*) Rhizome short creeping, scaly; the scales black margined and ciliate; stipes 1–2 inches long, very scaly, fronds linear-lanceolate obtuse, gradually attenuated at the base, 4–12 inches long, ½–¾ inch broad, densely covered on both sides with velvety ciliated scales, fertile fronds often not contracted, texture flaccid; veins hidden, simple or forked. *Sw. in Schrad. Journ.* 1800, ii. *p.* 11. *Bedd. F. S. I. t.* 197.

South India, Nilgiris, Anamallays, Travancore hills, 3,000–4,000 feet elevation, not common; Ceylon, central provinces.

(Also in Tropical America and West Indies; Sumatra; Sandwich Islands; Mascareen Islands; Guinea Coast; Madeira and Azores.)

7. ELAPHOGLOSSUM SPATHULATUM. (*Sw.*) Rhizome short, creeping, densely scaly, furnished with numerous wiry roots; stipes 2–4

inches long, densely covered with reddish setaceous scales, fronds linear-lanceolate to rhomboid-lanceolate 1–2 inches long, covered on both sides with numerous hair-like scales, fertile fronds broad ovate, smaller than the sterile ones. *Sw. Syn. Fil. p.* 10. *Bedd. F. S. I. t.* 213. Acrostichum piloseloides, var. δ spathulatum. *Hook. Sp. Fil.* v. 228.

Ceylon, about Newera Elya, and in the southern provinces.

(Also in Tropical America and West Indies; Natal and Mascareen Islands; and Tristan d'Acunha.)

GENUS LXXXII.—STENOCHLÆNA. (*J. Sm.*)

(*Stenos*, narrow; *chlœna*, cloak; the narrow involute margin.)

Fronds simply pinnate, the fertile contracted and very narrow, the sterile with the habit of Lomaria; veins simple or forked, fine and close, generally quite free to the margin, or rarely the two forks or even two separate veins anastomose; stipes adherent to the rhizome; pinnæ articulate with the rachis. (In palustre, the rachis or costa of the sterile pinnæ is winged, particularly towards the apex, which wing has been called an obscure transverse vein, anastomosing in loops; the same occurs in Pteris patens, and some Athyriums (very apparent in Athy. fimbriatum, var. sphœropteroides) and it can scarcely be called a true vein.

1. STENOCHLÆNA PALUSTRE. (*Linn. under Polypodium.*) Rhizome scandent, (often reaching the tops of the highest trees), fronds glabrous, shining, of hard texture, pinnate, 1–4 feet long, pinnæ articulated numerous, alternate or opposite, lanceolate acuminate, pungently serrate towards the apex, oblique at the base, and furnished with a marginal gland on the upper edge, 5–10 inches long, 1–1½ inch broad, fertile fronds very much contracted; veins simple or forked, generally free to the thickened margin, rarely the forks or two separate veins anastomose in the middle of, or towards the margin of the pinnæ; rachis of sterile pinnæ winged, particularly towards the margin, and forming a pseudo vein parallel with it

No. 253.

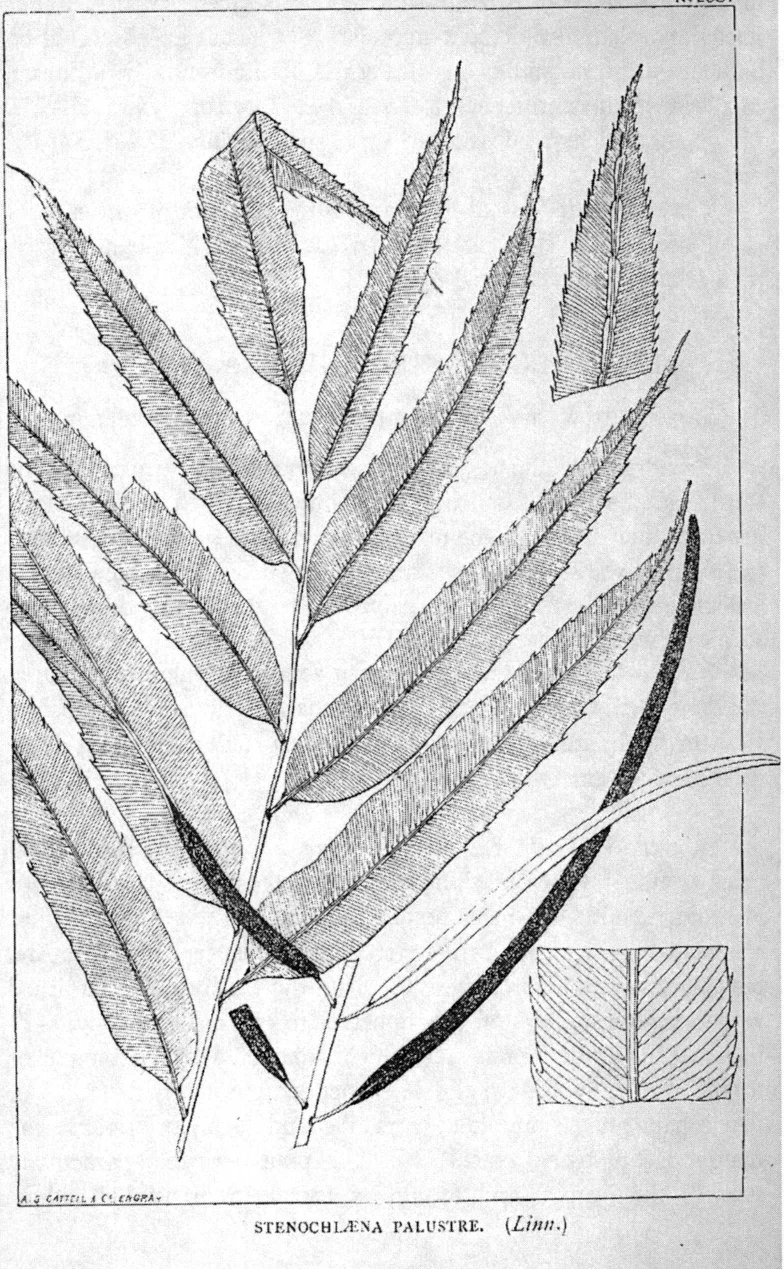

STENOCHLÆNA PALUSTRE. (*Linn.*)

Burm. Fl. Zey. 234. S. scandens, *J. Smith, in Hook. Journ. of Bot.* iii. 401. *Bedd. F. S. I. t.* 201. Lomaria scandens, *Willd. Sp. Pl.* 293.

South India, in the plains on the West Coast and up the mountains to about 3,000 feet elevation; Ceylon. North India in the plains of Bengal and at low elevations on the hills; Malay Peninsula. (Davallia achilleifolia, *Wall.* Teratophyllum aculeatum, *Mett. Ann. Mus. Lug. Bat.* 4, 296. *Bedd. F. B. I. t.* 209, is an abnormal form of this plant, showing clearly a winged partial rachis.)

(Also in South China; Queensland; and Fiji.)

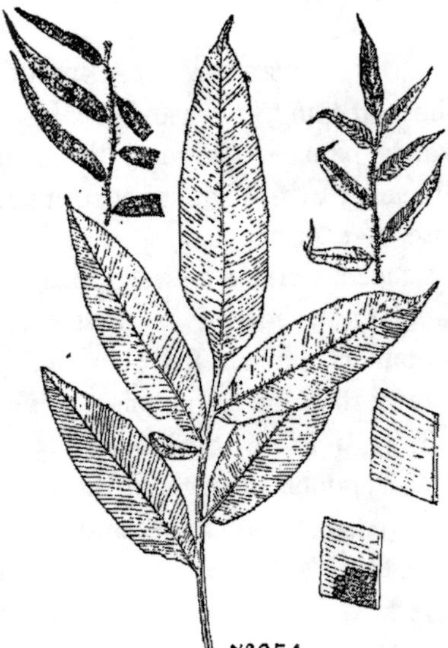

STENOCHLÆNA SORBIFOLIA. (*L.*)

2. STENOCHLÆNA SORBIFOLIA. (*L.*) Rhizome thick, woody, often 40 feet long, clasping trees like a cable, sometimes prickly, scales lanceolate-subulate, large; fronds up to 18 inches long, simply pinnate, barren pinnæ 3–8 inches long, about 1 inch broad, bluntly pointed, margin entire or toothed, 3–20 on each side, articulated at the base, texture subcoriaceous, glabrous, or nearly so on both sides, rachis often winged, fertile pinnæ smaller, much contracted, about ¼ inch broad. Acrostichum sorbifolium, *Linn. Sp. Pl. p.* 1526. Lomariopsis, *Hook. Syn. Fil. p.* 412. *Bedd. F. B. I. t.* 192.

The Malay Peninsula, Tenasserim, Malacca.

Bedd. F. B. I. t. 210, is an abnormal bipinnate form of this plant in which the rachis of the pinnæ is very broadly winged with small pinnules resembling the leaves of Feronia elephantum. Lomaria limonifolia, *Wall. Cat.* 35, is the same form.

(Also in Tropical America and West Indies; Fiji; Samoa;

New Caledonia; Philippines; Cochin China; Mascareen Islands, and Tropical Africa.)

GENUS LXXXIII.—POLYBOTRYA. (*H. B. K.*)

(*Poly*, many; *botrys*, bunch—in allusion to the fructification.)

Fronds pinnate, bipinnatifid or subbipinnate, the sterile not lomarioid in habit, generally viviparous, fertile much contracted; veins pinnate, all free; stipes adherent to the rhizome.

1. POLYBOTRYA APPENDICULATA. (*Willd.*) Rhizome thick, short-creeping, stipes and rachis scaly, scales linear, not adpressed; fronds pinnate, glabrous, the sterile ones viviparous at the apex; pinnæ 25 to 50 pair, subopposite or alternate, oblong-lanceolate, obtuse, 2–3 inches long, ½ an inch broad, rather deeply crenated with a setaceous bristle between each crenature, superior basal crenature the largest, inferior base cuneate and slightly unequal; veins not prominent, pinnate free; fertile fronds much contracted, pinnæ much shorter than the sterile ones. *Willd. Sp. Pl.* 114. *Bedd. F. S. I. t.* 194. *Wall. Cat.* 28 *and* 2685.

Common throughout the Indian region.

(Also in Philippines and Hong Kong.)

The above description only relates to the type, but there are several varieties more or less permanent.

VAR. β MAJOR. Stipes and rachis very thick, ¼ inch or rather more in diameter, rough with dense adpressed scurfy scales; pinnæ 1 inch in breadth, not auricled at the superior base or cuneate and unequal at the inferior; main veins very prominent and straight and costa-like veinlets more numerous and very prominent.

Sikkim; a very large fern, unlike any forms in Southern India or Ceylon.

VAR. γ ASPLENIIFOLIA. (*Bory.*) Rachis with copious linear patent scales, fronds seldom proliferous at the apex; pinnæ very

No. 255

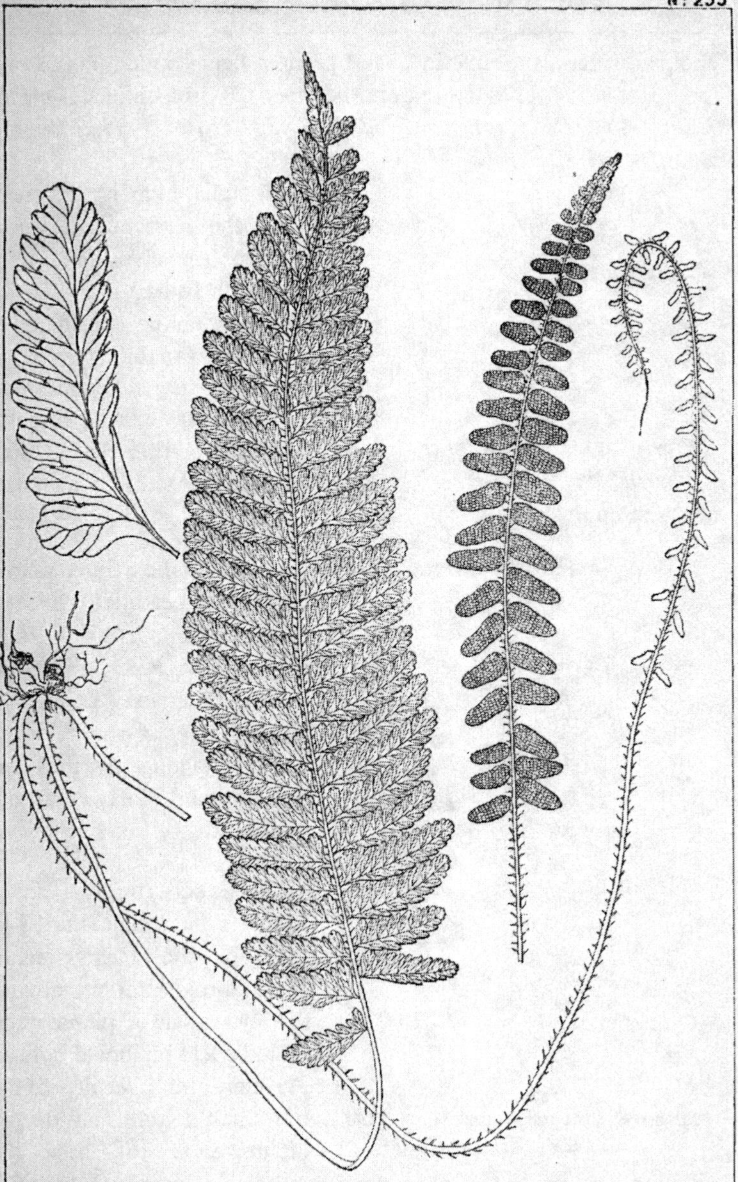

A. S. CATTELL & Co. ENGS.

POLYBOTRYA APPENDICULATA. (*Willd.*) VAR. γ ASPLENIIFOLIA.

unequal sided, the inferior basal portion being much cut away, the upper side deeper cut than in the type. P. aspleniifolia, *Bory, in Belang. Voy. Bot.* 23, *t.* 3. *Bedd. F. S. I. t.* 195. Acrost. Wightianum, *Wall. Cat.* 2163.

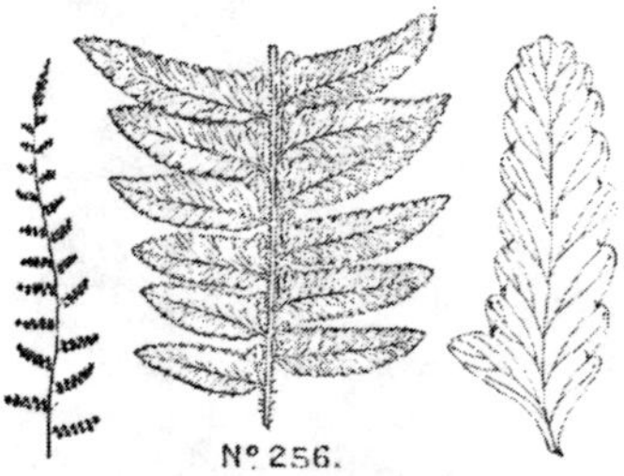

Nº 256.

POLYBOTRYA APPENDICULATA. (*Willd.*) VAR. δ HAMILTONIANA.

South India, in moist evergreen forests on the western side, up to nearly 4,000 feet elevation. (Not found in North India.)

This can only be considered a variety of this variable species, it looks, however, very different when growing, being a much brighter green and a far prettier species than the type, it is constant to its characters in cultivation.

VAR. δ HAMILTONIANA. (*Wall.*) Fertile pinnæ interrupted, the sori in bead-like clusters. *Wall. Cat.* 29. *Bedd. F. B. I. t.* 111, *the lower* 3 *figures.* Polyb. Helferiana (*Kze*), *Schk. Supp.* 2 *p.* 47. *t.* 114.

Chittagong, Assam; Tenasserim, and Malay Peninsula generally.

Nº 257.

POLYBOTRYA APPENDICULATA. (*Willd.*) VAR. ε COSTULATA.

VAR. ε COSTULATA. (*Hook.*) Sterile pinnæ pinnatifid $\frac{1}{2}$–$\frac{3}{4}$ down to the rachis; main veins costulate and prominent, the lowest pair of pinnæ often more or less bipinnate both in the sterile and fertile, sometimes half deltoid and deeply bipinnate at the base, the pinnules up to $3\frac{1}{2}$ inches long, and again deeply pinnatifid.

Hook. Sp. Fil. p. 252. *Bedd. F. B. I. t.* 110, *and* 111 *right hand top fig.*

Tenasserim; Khasya; Jeypore Hills, West of Vizagapatam. This variety can at once be distinguished by the much more deeply pinnatifid pinnæ, and by its costulate main veins, but the bipinnate character is not so constant; some specimens from Birma (*vide Bedd. F. B. I. t.* 110) have the lowest pinnæ deeply bipinnate in both sterile and fertile; and some specimens from Khasya and Jeypore are only slightly bipinnate in the sterile only, whilst other specimens from Birma have the lowest pinnæ quite unchanged (*vide Bedd. F. B. I. t.* 111, *right-hand top figure.*)

VAR. ζ SUBINTEGRA. Pinnæ almost entire, of a very dull colour and more coriaceous than in the type, not at all or very slightly auricled at the superior base, and the inferior base rounded and not at all unequal. *Bedd. F. B. I. t.* 111, *left-hand top fig.*

Birma only.

GENUS LXXXIV.—ACONIOPTERIS. (*Presl.*)

(*Akon*, a point, and *pteris;* the veins forming pointed angles near the margin.)

As in Elaphoglossum, only the veins are combined near the margin by a straight or zigzag vein.

1. ACONIOPTERIS GORGONEA. (*Kaulf.*) Rhizome very short, with ovate-lanceolate obtuse, brown-red scales; stipes tufted, scarcely an inch long, being usually winged near the base by the decurrent frond; barren fronds simple entire narrowly elliptic, tapering at both ends, 3–5 inches long, by $\frac{3}{4}$–$1\frac{1}{4}$ inch broad; glabrous, but with peltate flat scales, sparingly scattered on the surface beneath; midrib strong, texture firm, but diaphanous; veins parallel, above simple or furcate, the marginal vein more distinct, and further from the margin than in examples from Polynesia. *Kaulf. En. Fil.* 63. *Clarke, F. N. I. p.* 578.

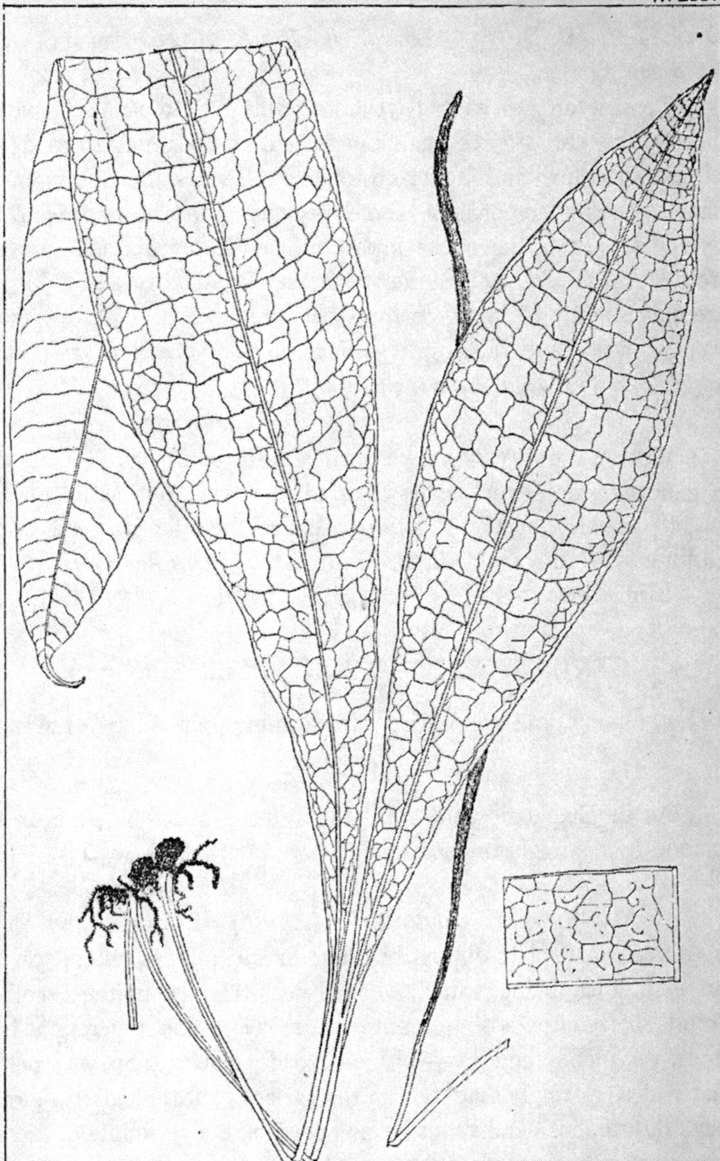

GYMNOPTERIS VARIABILIS. (*Hook.*)

Khasya, above Shaila, 2,500 feet elevation, lately discovered by Mr. Clarke, but only in a barren state, so it is doubtful whether it is this species, though it must be closely allied.

(Also in the Sandwich and Society Islands.)

GENUS LXXXV.—GYMNOPTERIS. (*Bernh.*)

(*Gymnos*, naked; *pteris;* seeding naked.)

Veins copiously anastomosing with free veinlets in the areoles; the primary veins costæform or obsolete; fronds simple or pinnate, generally dimorphous the fertile much contracted, or rarely simple uniform and bearing the sori on the contracted apex; stipes adherent to the rhizome.

1. GYMNOPTERIS VARIABILIS. (*Hook.*) Rhizome more or less creeping, squamose, with ovate or lanceolate scales; sterile fronds membranaceous to subcoriaceous, generally about 1 foot or a little more long and 1–2½ inches wide, ovate-lanceolate acuminate, often long decurrent on the stipe nearly to its base; costules generally more or less distinct, sometimes very prominent, zigzag or quite straight; areoles copious with free included veinlets; fertile fronds contracted and narrow, and normally entirely covered with sori, but in some cases the broader fronds are dotted all over with large polypodioid sori. *Hook. Sp. Fil.* v. 277. *Bedd. F. B. I. t.* 272.

Sikkim, Bhotan, Assam, Khasya, Cachar, up to 4,000 feet elevation. South India (rare, compared with the variety lanceolata) Tinnevelly mountains, fronds very thin and membranaceous and decurrent nearly to the base of the stipe, main veins wavy, but very prominent, Jeypore Hills (Vizagapatam), texture thicker and colour deeper green, very decurrent, main veins very prominent and nearly straight, polypodioid sori over many of the broad fronds; Birma.

VAR. β LANCEOLATA. (*Hook.*) Main veins none, or more or less indistinct. Gymnopteris lanceolata, *Hook. Sp. Fil.* v. 276. G. Féei (*Moore*), *Bedd. F. S. I. t.* 48.

Very common throughout the Western forests of the Madras Presidency and Bombay; Ceylon; Birma. Also in Chota Nagpore, and on Parasnath: in typical forms there are no main veins, and all the venation is indistinct, but other forms run too closely into variabilis for it to be considered a distinct species; the fronds are often quite rounded at the base, but at other times nearly as decurrent as in variabilis, the seeding is normally over the whole of the under surface of the fertile frond, but sometimes it is in a broad line on each side of the costa, leaving a considerable margin of the laminæ without sori, or at other times the seeding is punctiform or grammitoid (*Bedd. F. B. I. t.* 274), or the upper half of the frond is contracted and soriferous, as in Gymnopteris spicata, (Hymenolepis of authors). In South Canara and Coorg there are forms with both sterile and fertile fronds 3-lobed (*Bedd. F. B. I. t.* 273), and in Ceylon, pinnatifid forms (*Bedd. F. S. I. t.* 211) with often as many as five distinct pinnæ on each side the rachis, with only a narrow wing, but as the ordinary form is sometimes mixed with these even on the same root they can only be considered abnormal forms, not distinct varieties.

No. 259

GYMNOPTERIS MINUS. (*Mett.*)

VAR. γ AXILLARIS. (*Cav.*) This is a name given to a variety with a long slender tortuous rhizome, which creeps up trees, but it scarcely differs otherwise, the main veins are less prominent than in variabilis, but more so than in lanceolata. *Cav. Prælect.* 1801, *n.* 582. *Hook. Sp. Fil.* v. 276. *Bedd. F. B. I. t.* 271.

South India, in all the western forests; Plains of Bengal and Assam; Birma.

2. GYMNOPTERIS MINUS. (*Metten.*) Small, rhizome creeping,

thick as a sparrow's quill, scaly at the apex, scales lanceolate ; stipes remote, slender, 1–3 or in those of the fertile frond 4 inches long; sterile fronds membranaceous, $1\frac{1}{2}$–2 inches long, oblong or broad-lanceolate, costate, tapering into a stipe $2\frac{1}{2}$ inches long; costules indistinct, areoles with a free included clavate veinlet, smaller towards the margin; fertile fronds 2 inches long, linear obtuse. *Metten. Fil. Hort. Lips. p.* 20. *Hook. Sp. Fil.* v. 277. *Bedd. F. B. I. t.* 116.

Khasya Hills, 2,000–4,500 feet, in river sands, perhaps only a small form of variabilis var. lanceolata.

3. GYMNOPTERIS WALLII. (*Baker.*) Rhizome slender, wide-

No. 260.

GYMNOPTERIS METALLICA. (*Bedd.*)

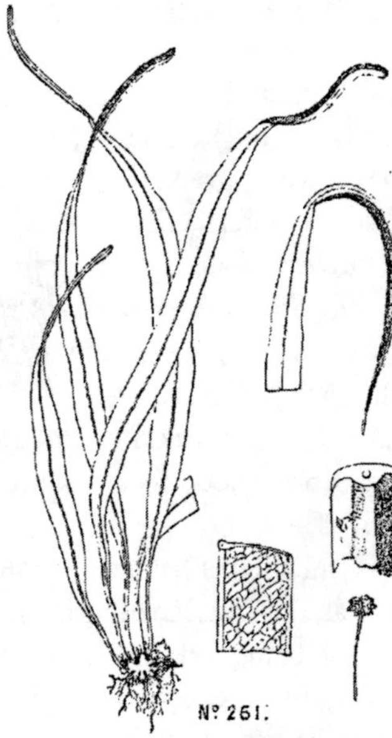

No. 261.

GYMNOPTERIS SPICATA. (*L. f*)

creeping, scales minute, grey, lanceolate acuminate; sterile fronds linear, subsessile, 8–9 inches long, under $\frac{1}{4}$ inch broad, narrowed to both ends, obscurely repand, texture thin but rigid, surfaces naked, bright green; midrib stramineous, veins slender, immersed, forming a single costal row of long areoles, usually with a free decurved veinlet springing from the outer border; fertile frond filiform, 6–8 inches long, long-stalked, fructification often interrupted. *Baker in Hook. Syn. Fil. p.* 523. *Bedd. F. B. I. Sup. t.* 389.

Ceylon, southern provinces, Mooroowa, rocky ravines.

4. GYMNOPTERIS METALLICA. (*Bedd.*) Fronds quite sessile, 3–7 inches long, up to nearly 1 inch broad, of a deep shining metallic blue; main veins not prominent and often not distinguishable from the others; fertile fronds only soriferous towards the apex. *Bedd. F. Sup. t.* 390.

Ceylon, Haycock Mountain near Galle, in dense forests on rocks, 2,000 feet elevation.

5. GYMNOPTERIS SPICATA. (*L. f.*) Rhizome woody, short, creeping; stipes 1–2 inches long, firm; fronds 6–18 inches long, ½–1 inch broad, the upper part for 4–6 inches, suddenly or gradually contracted and fertile, the edge entire, the lower part narrowed very gradually, texture subcoriaceous, surfaces naked; no distinct main veins, areoles uniform, hexagonal, with copious free, simple or forked veinlets; sori mixed with peltate sporangiasters. *Linn. Fil. Sup.* 444, *under Acrostichum.* Gymnopteris, *Presl. Tent. Pter.* 244, *t.* 11. Acrostichum, *Hook. Syn. Fil.* 424. Hymenolepis spicata, *Bedd. F. S. I. t.* 46.

North India, Sikkim and Bhotan, 4,000–7,000 feet elevation, Khasya 3,000–7,000 feet; South India, on the Western mountains; Ceylon.

(Hymenolepis has been proposed as a genus or subgenus for this species, as the fructification is on the contracted apex of the fronds, instead of being on a separate frond, the same peculiarity occurs constantly in other species, and I have similarly contracted fronds of G. variabilis var. lanceolata, which if separated from their rhizomes and other fronds could not be distinguished from this species, so I do not think the genus can hold good.)

6. GYMNOPTERIS QUERCIFOLIA. (*Retz.*) Rhizome stout, creeping, scales linear, hair-pointed; stipe of the barren frond 1–2 inches long, clothed with soft spreading ferruginous hairs; barren frond 3–4 inches

long, 1½–2 inches broad, the terminal pinna with blunt rounded lobes reaching sometimes ¼ of the way to the rachis, below this usually a single pair of small sessile ovate blunt auriculate lateral ones, texture thin, herbaceous, veins beneath hairy; main veins sometimes distinct to the edge, at other times hardly distinguishable from the other veins, with copious areoles, including free veinlets; fertile fronds with a terminal pinna, 1–2 inches long, ⅛ inch broad, and a pair of smaller lateral ones, the stipe slender, 6–9 inches long, naked except at the base. Acrostichum quercifolium. *Retz. Obs. Bot.* 6, *p.* 39. *Hook. Syn. Fil. p.* 418. *Bedd. F. S. I. t.* 47.

Tinnevelly and Travancore Hills, up to 2,000 feet elevation, Anamallays; Ceylon, about Colombo.

No. 262.
GYMNOPTERIS QUERCIFOLIA. (*Retz.*)

7. GYMNOPTERIS FLAGELLIFERA. (*Wall.*) Rhizome short, terrestrial, or scandent several feet up trees, strong, densely scaly with brown lanceolate scales at the extremities, and throwing out rootlets encircling the boughs; stipes often densely scaly, fronds simple or 3-foliate or pinnate with 5–11 pinnæ, the terminal pinna often much prolonged and rooting at the apex; pinnæ stalked entire or repand, or even lobed, 4–5 inches long by 2 inches broad; main veins very prominent to the margin, areoles copious with or without free veinlets; fertile pinnæ more or less contracted, generally without any free veinlets in the areoles, wholly soriferous or partially covered with meniscioid sori; texture herbaceous, drying a dull brown colour. *Wall. Cat.* 25. *Clarke, F. N. I. p.* 579. Pæcilopteris flagellifera, *Bedd. F. B. I. t.* 112.

North India, Sikkim and Assam, Cachar and Chittagong up to 3,000 feet elevation; Birma. Some of my Birma specimens have all the fronds simple, and are then hardly distinguishable from "varia bilis" (type) except by the peculiar colour and scaly stipe, others have the fronds all 3-foliate and the pinnæ often deeply lobed, particularly the two lower ones, these simple and 3-foliate fronds grow on the same rhizome, the broad sterile fronds are often partially seeded, particularly on the long terminal cauda. I have only seen pinnate fronds on North Indian examples.

Sir W. Hooker in his *Sp. Fil.* gives Malabar for a locality and quotes Rheede, Hort. Malab. xii. 11, which plate is Drynaria quercifolia; Pl. 19 is probably intended, which however is Gymnopteris subcrenata. On one of Wallich's sheets of this fern (25, No. 3) there is written, Rheede, Malab. xii. t. 19.

8. GYMNOPTERIS SUBREPANDA. (*Hook.*) Rhizome woody, wide-creeping; stipes of barren fronds stout erect, nearly naked; barren fronds varying from simple, 1 foot long, 1½–2 inches broad, to 2 feet long, 1 foot broad, copiously pinnate, with several linear-oblong entire or subrepand pinnæ on each side, which are sometimes 6–9 inches long, 2 inches broad, texture subcoriaceous, surfaces and rachis naked; main veins distinct nearly to the edge, with copious areoles, with free veinlets between them; fertile fronds like the others, but smaller. *Syn. Fil. p.* 419. *Hook. Sp. Fil.* v. *p.* 275. *Bedd. F. B. I. t.* 339.

Penang.

This is nearly allied to the more pinnate varieties of flagellifera. Dodgson's specimen from the Himalayas referred here in the Kew Herb. certainly belongs to flagellifera.

9. GYMNOPTERIS TRICUSPIS. (*Hook.*) Rhizome creeping, clothed with subulate setaceous ferruginous scales; stipes 1 foot long, 1½ of the fertile frond; sterile frond subcoriaceous, subtriangular-caudate, 8–10 inches long, 10–12 inches wide at the base, including the spread of the lateral lobes, deeply trilobate or 4-lobed, lateral lobes 5 inches or more long, 1½ inch wide, horizontally patent, intermediate one 6 inches and more long, 2 inches wide, all of them oblong-lanceolate acuminate, entire unicostate; venation manifest, costules distant, indistinct, connected by transverse irregular curved veins forming large areoles enclosing lesser ones which have copious

free branched and divaricating veinlets; fertile fronds much elongated but contracted, tripartite nearly to the base, segments scarcely ½ an inch wide, linear strap-shaped acuminate, lateral ones 9–10 inches long, erect-subpatent, intermediate one a foot and more long, sori generally universal except on the costa, or sometimes the terminal lobe only is soriferous, or rarely the apex only of one or more lobes is contracted and soriferous as in Gymnopteris spicata. *Hook. Sp. Fil.* v. 272. *Bedd. F. B. I. t.* 53.

Sikkim, at Goke below Darjeeling, 1,500 feet elevation.

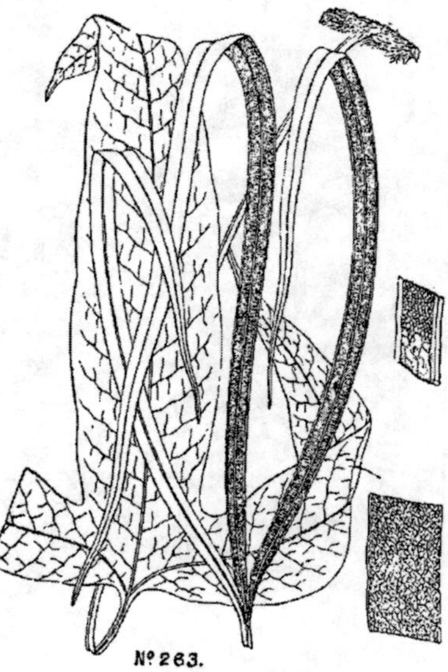

No. 263.
GYMNOPTERIS TRICUSPIS. (*Hook.*)

10. GYMNOPTERIS CONTAMINANS. (*Wall.*) Rhizome thick, short creeping; stipes scaly, fronds glabrous, pinnate, 1–2 feet long, of which the stipe is about ⅓; rachis generally more or less winged sometimes prominently, more or less scaly, pinnæ 11–30 alternate sessile or very shortly petiolate, lanceolate from nearly entire to slightly crenated or pinnatifid one-third down, with the segments serrated, terminal pinnæ often more or less elongated, generally vivaparous (the lateral ones rarely so); primary veins rather distant more or less conspicuous two-thirds of the way to the margin, areoles broad, in 3–4 series, the costal ones without any veinlets, the others with generally several veinlets irregulary disposed, mostly joining with the areole above, but some free with clavate apices; fertile pinnæ much contracted, entire or sinuate pinnatifid according to the form of the sterile, generally wholly soriferous, rarely only partially contracted into seed. Acrostichum contaminans, *Wall. Cat.* 22, and crispatulum, *Cat.* 24. Pæcilopteris repanda, *Bedd. F. S. I. t.* 202. Semicordata, *Baker, Syn. Fil.* 422. *Bedd. F. B. I. t.* 270. Blumeana, *Hook. Syn.*

No. 264.

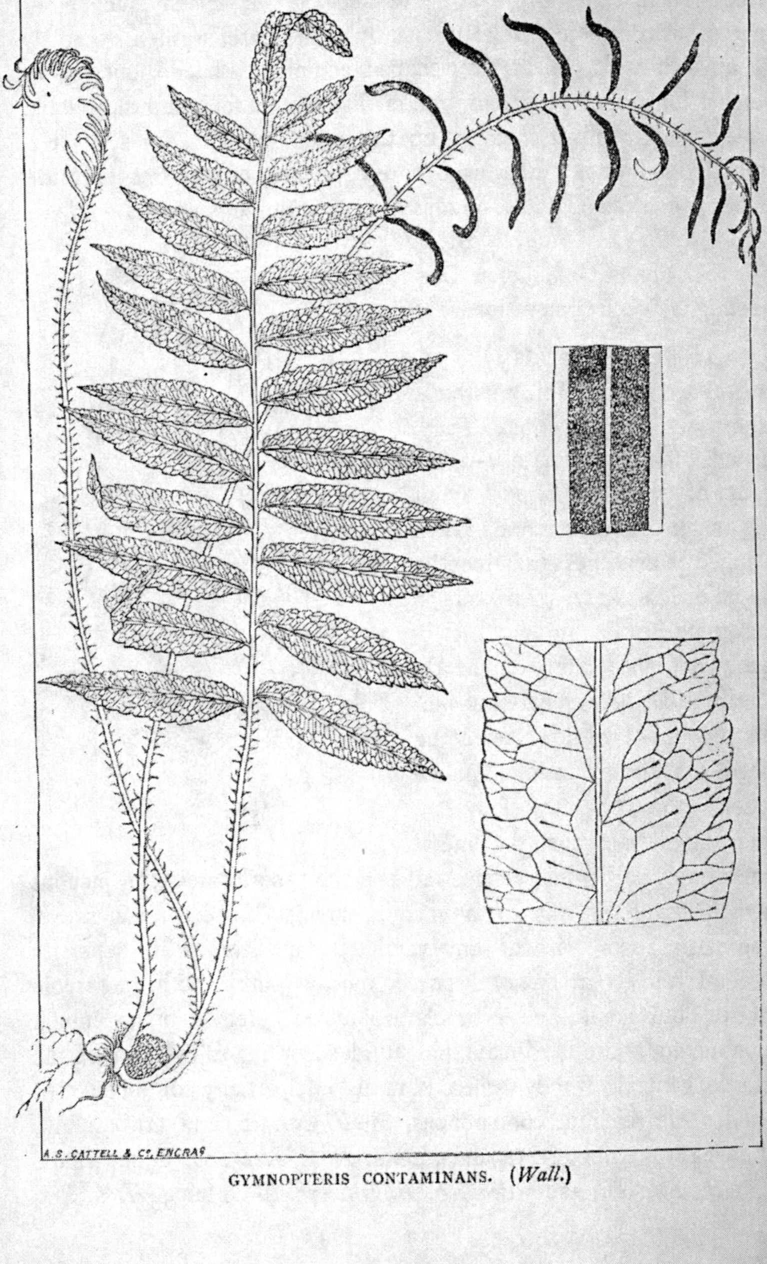

A. S. CATTELL & Co. ENGRAs

GYMNOPTERIS CONTAMINANS. (*Wall.*)

Fil. p. 423 (*at least as far as the North Indian specimens are concerned*). Acros. terminans, *Wall. Cat.* 2168.

South India, most abundant in all the Western coast moist forests from the plains up to about 4,000 feet; East Bengal, the lower hills up to 3,000 feet elevation; Ceylon (repandum of *Thw. En.*); Birma, common.

11. GYMNOPTERIS SUBCRENATA. (*Hook. and Grev. under Acrostichum.*) Rhizome thick, fronds glabrous pinnate, 1–4 feet, of which the stipe is sometimes nearly half; stipes and rachis furnished with a few scales; sterile fronds, pinnæ 4–12 alternate or sub-opposite petiolate, broad lanceolate sinuate or waved, with a longish serrated acumination, terminal pinnæ much the longest (sometimes 2 feet long), proliferous at the apex; primary veins close, costate and conspicuous nearly to the margin, veinlets anastomosing pretty regularly at right angles, from which proceed one or two generally free veinlets with clavate apices; fertile fronds conform to sterile, but much contracted. *Hook and Grev. Ic. Fil.* 110. Pæcilopteris terminans, *Bedd. F. S. I. t.* 203 (*not Wall.*). P. Hookerianum, *Moore, Thw. En. p.* 380, prolifera. *Hook. Ic. Pl. t.* 681–2. *Rheede, Hort. Malab.* xii. 19.

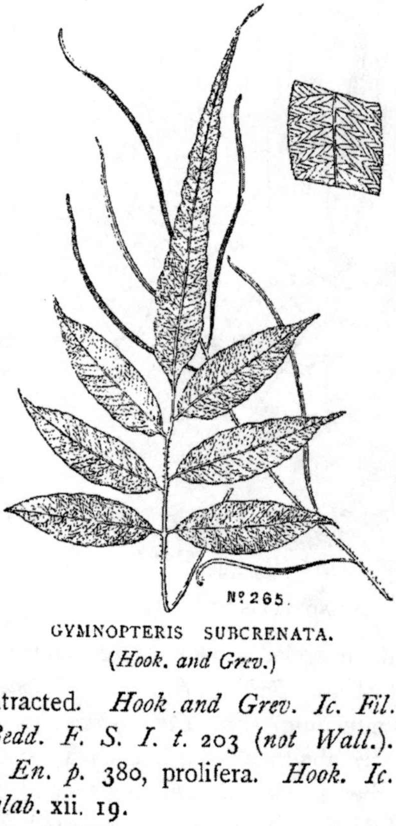

No. 265.

GYMNOPTERIS SUBCRENATA. (*Hook. and Grev.*)

South India, not uncommon in the Western moist forests of the Madras and Bombay Presidencies, up to about 4,000 feet elevation; Ceylon, central provinces.

This fern is not known from North India (Mr. Clarke's Chittagong specimens being costata), it has generally fewer and larger pinnæ than contaminans, sometimes up to 2 inches broad, and they are never quite sessile, the venation differs considerably, the primary veins are much more conspicuous or closer together, the areoles narrow and generally with an acute apex, the lowest ones empty, the others with often only one free excurrent veinlet (and then the venation is quite that of Meniscium), there are, however, often two or sometimes three excurrent veinlets, which are very irregular, free or anastomosing amongst themselves, or with the superior areole.

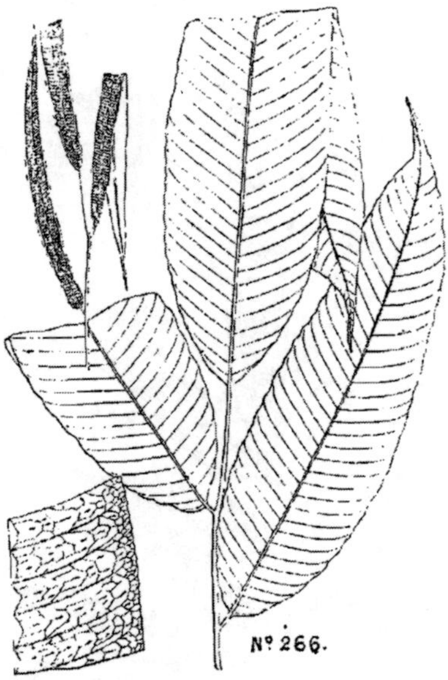
GYMNOPTERIS COSTATA. (*Wall.*)

12. GYMNOPTERIS COSTATA. (*Wall.*) Rhizome creeping, furnished with subulate scales; stipes up to 1½ feet long; fronds up to 2 feet long or more, pinnate, pinnæ up to 14 inches long by 3 inches broad, petiolate, acuminate, margin entire, sinuate, or crenate; primary veins very prominent and generally much raised, close together, areoles numerous, but varying with the breadth of the pinnæ, costal ones small (sometimes obsolete) empty, several excurrent veinlets from all the other areoles which are irregular, sometimes free and sometimes anastomosing. *Wall. Cat.* 26. *Bedd. F. B. I.* 113. *Hook. Sp. Fil.* v. 262, deltigerum and undulatum, *Wall. Cat.* 59 *and* 140. *Bedd. F. B. I.* 114 *and* 115, are only abnormal forms, such as occur more or less in nearly all the other species of Gymnopteris and cannot be recorded as varieties. (Mr. Clarke has again transferred the former, which was Meniscium of Wallich, to that genus, but he now acknowledges that he was wrong, and that the venation is different to Meniscium, the same

meniscioid sori being very common in flagellifera). Sir W. Hooker in his *Sp. Fil.* quite correctly described this species and its varieties; but he lumped subcrenata with contaminans, though he had formerly distinguished it, first under the name of subcrenata, and afterwards as prolifera. Mr. Baker, not understanding the three species, lumped them all in his edition of the Synopsis; and Mr. Clarke, not knowing subcrenata, has puzzled pteridologists with a lot of varieties which do not exist; I have had subcrenata and contaminans (very common South Indian plants) for many years in cultivation, and costata (not South Indian) I have seen in abundance in Birma, and know them to be three distinct species without any permanent varieties, though all three variable, as are nearly all other Gymnopteris.

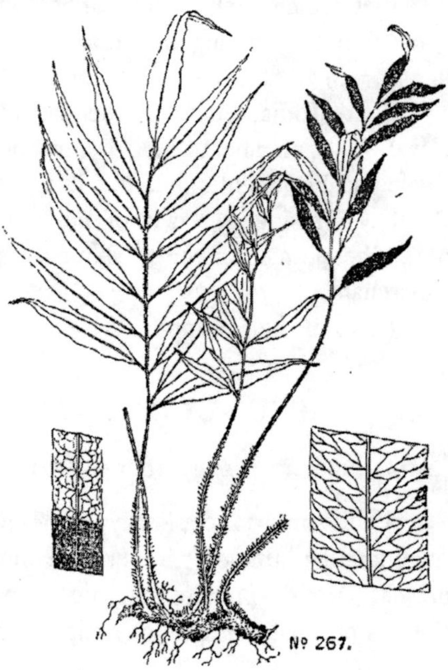

No 267.

GYMNOPTERIS PRESLIANA. (*Hook.*)

North India, Nepal and Chittagong, up to 3,000 feet elevation; Birma. (Some of the larger forms turn very red in drying.) The meniscioid form (deltigera) is common in Sikkim and Assam, the undulate form (formerly described as a genus, Jenkinsia) is, I believe, only from Birma.

Acros. virens. *Wall. Cat.* 1033, from Tavoy, is a blank sheet, so it is impossible to say whether the fern intended to be represented was this species or contaminans; it could not be subcrenata, as it does not grow in Birma.

13. GYMNOPTERIS PRESLIANA. (*Hook.*) Rhizome stout creeping, paleaceous with narrow attenuated lanceolate scales; stipes 6–10

inches long, more or less scaly, as is the rachis and petioles, fronds 6–12 inches long, pinnated glabrous, pinnæ submembranaceous, remote, subopposite, petiolate, 2–4 inches long, ½ an inch wide, narrow lanceolate acuminated at both ends, rachis more or less winged, specially towards the apex of the frond; fertile fronds generally longer stipitate, pinnæ much contracted, wholly or sometimes only partially fertile, costules indistinct, connected by generally 2 pairs of opposite veinlets, which meet at an acute angle, from which proceed a veinlet, which is either free or joined to the veins above, marginal veins free, terminating in a dot within the margin. *Hook. Sp. Fil.* v. 265. *Syn. Fil.* 420. *Bedd. F. B. I. t.* 269 (under Pæcilopteris.)

South India, Coorg, at the foot of the Bhagamandal ghat at no elevation, Concan (Law). I have only found this species in the single locality mentioned, but it is probably more common in the Bombay Presidency; it is of much thinner texture than contaminans, the pinnæ differently shaped, and the venation more that of subcrenata.

(Also in the Philippines.)

GENUS LXXXVI.—ACROSTICHUM. (*L.*)

(*Akros*, highest; *stichos*, order—fructification at the top of the frond.)

Veins uniform, copiously anastomosing, forming numerous subquadrangular areoles without free included veinlets, no main veins present; fronds pinnate, the upper pinnæ smaller and wholly soriferous on the lower surface; stipes adherent to the caudex.

1. ACROSTICHUM AUREUM. (*L.*) Caudex erect; stipe 1–2 feet long, tufted, strong, erect, glossy; fronds 2–6 feet long, 1–2 feet broad, pinnate, the upper pinnæ fertile and slightly smaller than the barren ones which are usually stalked, ligulate-oblong, ½–3 inches broad, the apex acute or blunt, sometimes retuse with a mucro, the edge quite entire, the base subcuneate, texture coriaceous, rachis and surfaces glabrous; areoles very small and copious without free veinlets. *Linn. Sp. Pl.* 1525. *Bedd. F. S. I. t.* 204.

No. 268.

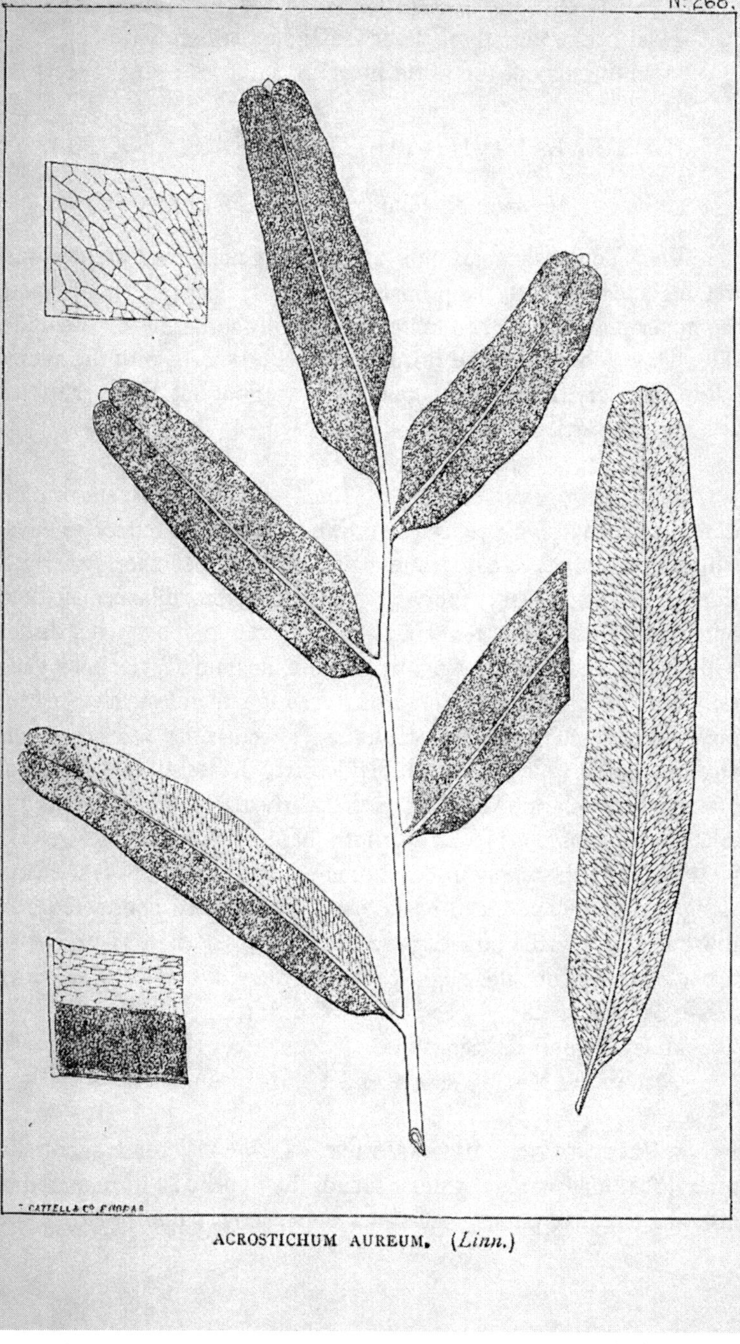

ACROSTICHUM AUREUM. (*Linn.*)

Tidal backwaters throughout the Indian region.
(Also throughout the world in warm countries near the sea.)

GENUS LXXXVII.—PHOTINOPTERIS. (*J. Sm.*)

(*Photeinos*, shining; *pteris*, a fern.)

Veins copiously anastomosing, forming numerous areoles with free included veinlets, the primary veins costæform; fronds pinnate, the upper pinnæ much contracted and wholly soriferous on the under side; stipe adherent to the rhizome, pinnæ articulate with the rachis. (Very like Drynaria in its pinnæ and venation, but the vernation is adherent not articulate.)

1. PHOTINOPTERIS RIGIDA. (*Wall.*) Rhizome repent or scandent, paleaceous, with elongated brown subulate fringed scales mixed with hair-like ones in age, white glaucescent; stipes short, nearly as thick as a writing pen; fronds $1\frac{1}{2}$–3 feet long, broad-lanceolate, very hard-coriaceous glossy, pinnate; sterile pinnæ long-petiolate, distant 3–6 inches and more long, broad ovate, acuminate, the apex generally caudate and curved upwards; venation manifest, elevated on both sides, costules subflexuose, united by transverse veins into four-angled areoles, which are again divided into lesser areoles including branched free clavate veinlets; petioles articulated on the rachis and dilated into a large orbicular scutiform base; sometimes these sterile pinnæ occupy the whole frond, more frequently the rachis is suddenly elongated at the apex, and bears 1–13 distant very contracted narrow-linear and fertile pinnæ, 5–12 inches long, soriferous except on the costa and on the slightly revolute margin. *Wall. Cat. n.* 27. *Hook. Sp. Fil.* v. 281. *Bedd. F. B. I. t.* 211.

Malay Peninsula; Singapore.
(Also in the Malay Islands, and Philippines.)

2. PHOTINOPTERIS DRYNARIOIDES. (*Hook.*) Fronds subsessile, several feet long, 1 foot or more broad, the upper part with numerous distant Lomarioid pinnæ, sometimes 1 foot long, 1 line broad, below

Nº 269.

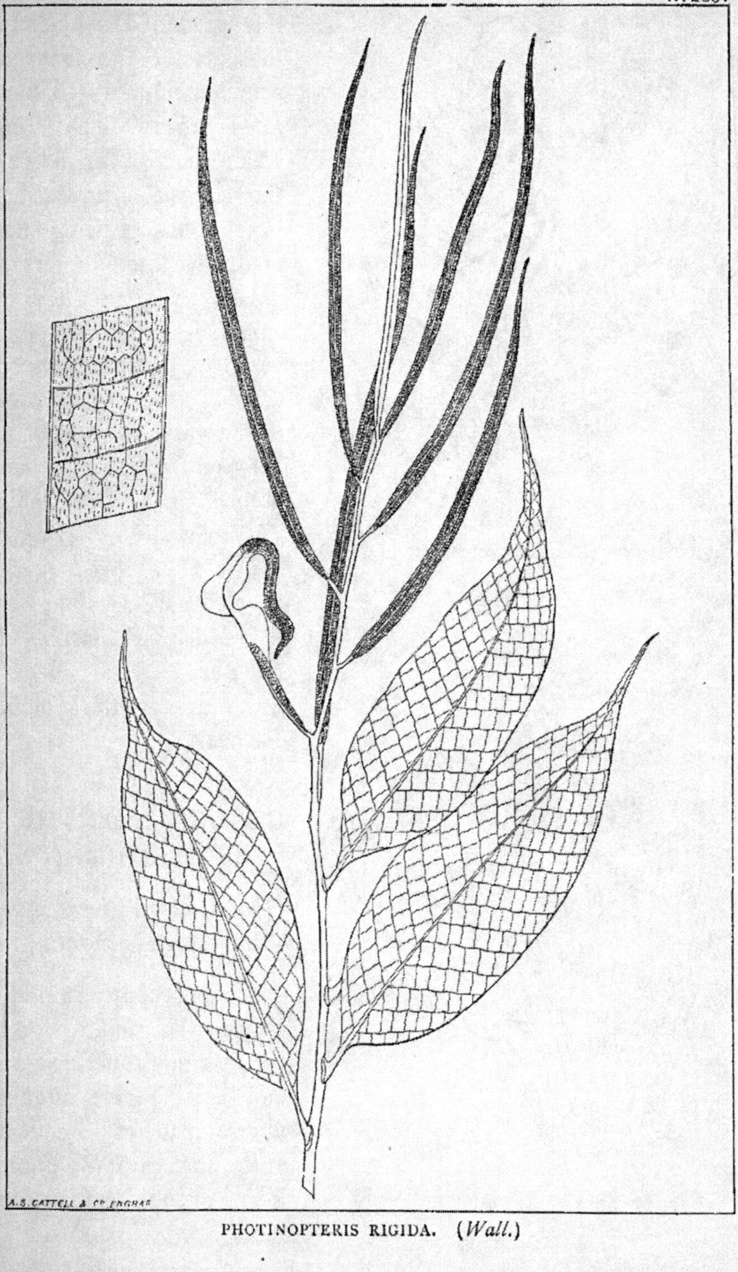

PHOTINOPTERIS RIGIDA. (*Wall.*)

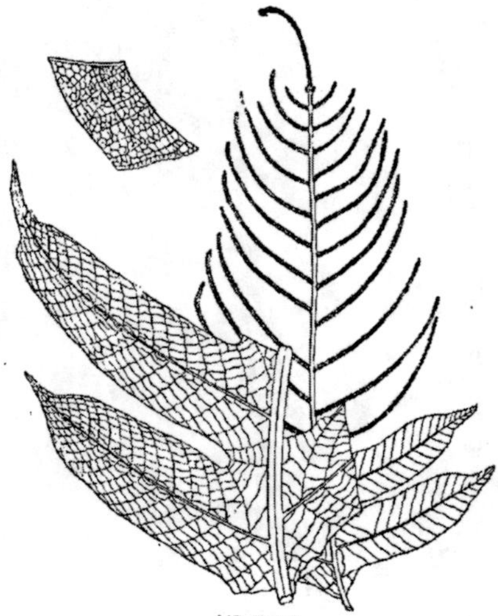

Nº 270

PHOTINOPTERIS DRYNARIOIDES. (*Hook.*)

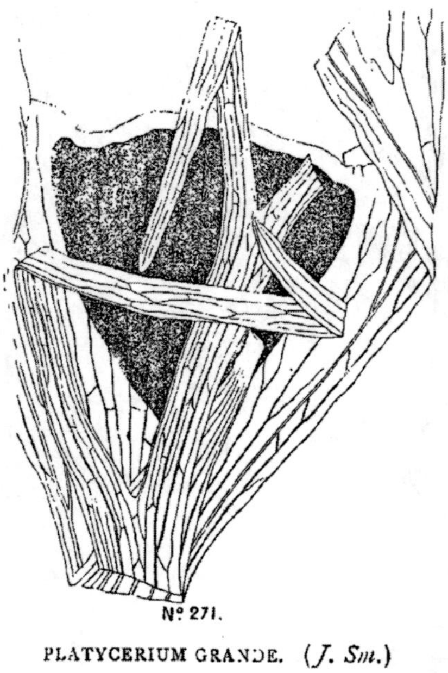

Nº 271.

PLATYCERIUM GRANDE. (*J. Sm.*)

this pinnatifid, with numerous close entire lanceolate acuminate lobes 4–6 inches long, 1¼–1¾ inch broad which reach down nearly to the rachis, all articulated, the lower ones passing down gradually into a mere undulated wing to the rachis, which is continued to its very base; texture very coriaceous; main veins raised, with transverse veinlets, and between them copious small areoles with free veinlets. *Hook. Syn. Fil. p.* 425. *Sp. Fil.* v. 282. *Bedd. F. B. I. t.* 325.

Malay Peninsula, Penang.

(Also in the Solomon Islands.)

GENUS LXXXVIII. — PLATYCERIUM. (*Desv.*)

(*Platys*, broad; *keros*, a horn —stag's-horn fern.)

Sori occupying a portion only of the under side of the disk of the fertile fronds and forming large, often reniform patches, frequently at the sinuses of the primary lobes; main veins costæform, prominent, furcate, free or anastomosing, veinlets copiously anastomosing, forming large oblong areoles, usually with free included simple or forked veinlets; fronds dimorphous, the sterile sessile, oblique, reniform, round or elongated, the fertile dichotomously forked with stag-horn-like divisions, in texture and pubescence resembling Niphobolus; articulate with the caudex.

1. PLATYCERIUM GRANDE. (*J. Sm.*) Barren fronds very large, suborbicular, convex or the upper ones erect, deeply laciniated with spreading or inflexed divisions; fertile fronds 4–6 feet long, pendent in pairs, the disk broad-cuneate, with the sorus against the upper edge, occupying the disk only, with an elongated dichotomously forked division beyond it at each corner; both surfaces green and smooth. *J. Sm. in Hook. Journ. Bot.* iii. *p.* 402. *Hook. Syn. Fil. p.* 425. *Bedd. F. B. I. t.* 326. There is only one soriferous patch to each frond.

Singapore.

(Also in Philippines and North Australia.)

2. PLATYCERIUM WALLICHII. (*Hook.*) Fronds ample, bifarious, at length glabrous; sterile ones imbricated below, irregularly sinuate-lobate, above elongated, dilated deeply and much dichotomously pinnatifid, segments patent-inflexed; fertile fronds geminate, very broadly flabellate-cuneate, twice dichotomous suddenly narrowed at the base, each primary division or segment bears a sorus on the disk (hence there are two sori on each frond), which is semicircular and very much produced in the sinus itself, the terminal segments beyond the soriferous disk are several times dichotomous and pendent, primary veins dichotomous, parallel elevated here and there, anastomosing into broad elongated areoles which are occupied by lesser ones with numerous free-branched included veinlets. *Hook. Sp. Fil.* v. 284. Acrostichum alcicorne, *Wall. Cat. n.* 19, (*not Linn.*) *Bedd. F. B. I. t.* 108.

Malay Peninsula, Tenasserim.

3. PLATYCERIUM BIFORME. (*Bl.*) Fronds ample, bifarious, at

No. 272.

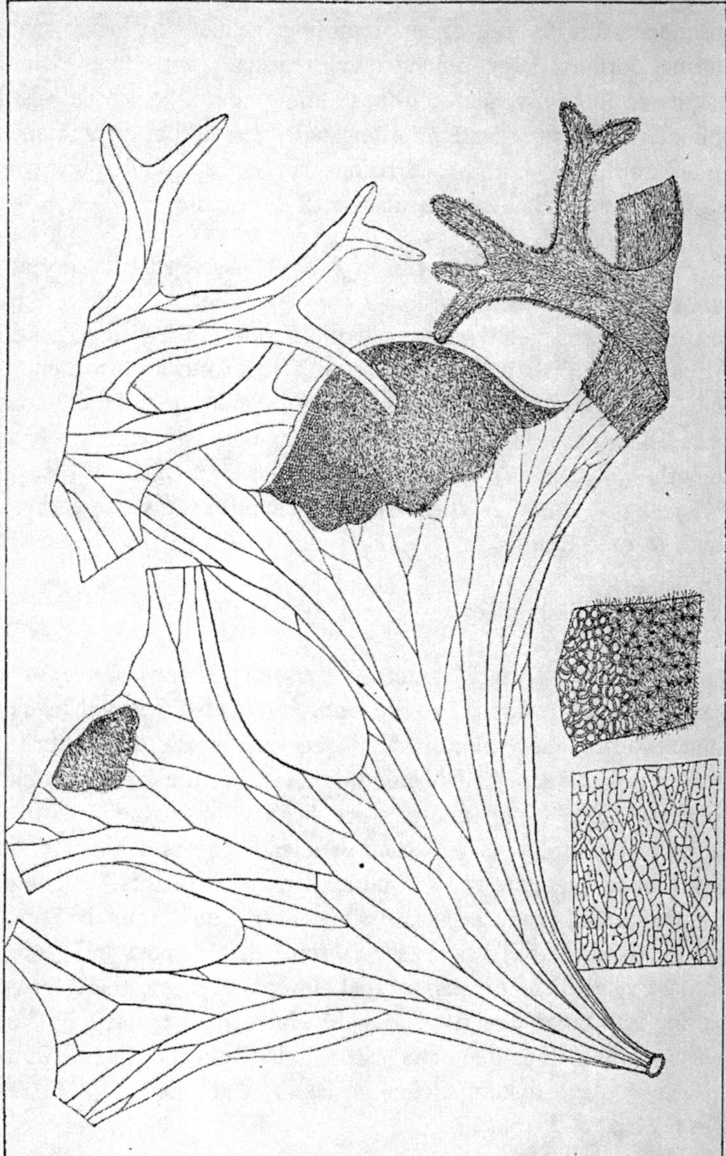

A. S. CATTELL & Co. ENGRAVERS

PLATYCERIUM WALLICHII. (*Hook.*)

length glabrous; sterile ones imbricated, very thick and corky towards the base, subrotund but very varied in circumscription, obed and sinuated at the margin, coarsely-reticulate-venose; fertile fronds rather long-stipitate of great size, 5–15 feet long, from a subcuneate base, repeatedly dichotomous, the segments loriform, flaccid and pendent, fertile segments quite different from the rest, forming a large reniform, stipitate, shield-like receptacle, 6–8 inches or more in diameter, wholly soriferous beneath, except at the margin. *Bl. Fil. Jav. p.* 14, *t.* 18. *Hook. Sp. Fil.* v. 285. *Bedd. F. B. I. t.* 109 *and* 224. A. fuciforme, *Wall. Cat. n.* 20.

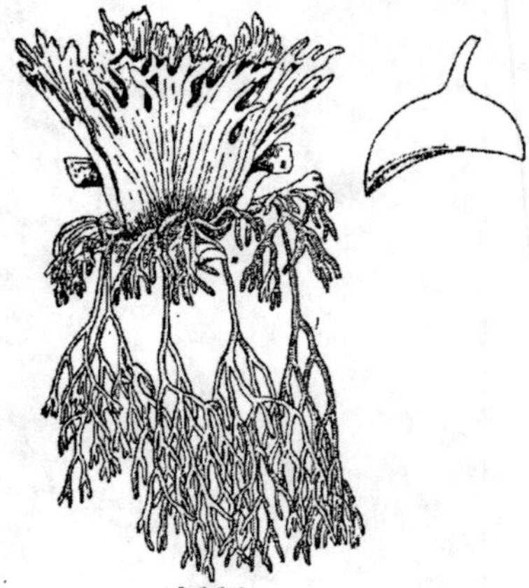

No. 273.
PLATYCERIUM BIFORME. (*Bl.*)

Malay Peninsula, Tenasserim, Mergui, Singapore. (Also in the Malay Islands and Philippines.)

SUB-ORDER III.—OSMUNDACEÆ.

Capsule 2-valved, opening across the apex, furnished with a short horizontal wing; vernation circinate.

GENUS LXXXIX.—OSMUNDA. (*Lin.*)

(*Osmunder*, one of the names of Thor, a Celtic divinity.)

Fertile frond wholly, on the upper or middle portion, contracted, forming simple or compound sporangiferous panicles; veins forked, free; fronds pinnate or bipinnate, articulated with the rachis.

1. OSMUNDA JAVANICA. (*Bl.*) Stipes tufted, 6–12 inches long, firm erect, naked; fronds up to 3 feet long, 8–12 inches broad, simply pinnate, the lower or central pinnæ fertile; barren pinnæ 4–8 inches

No. 274.

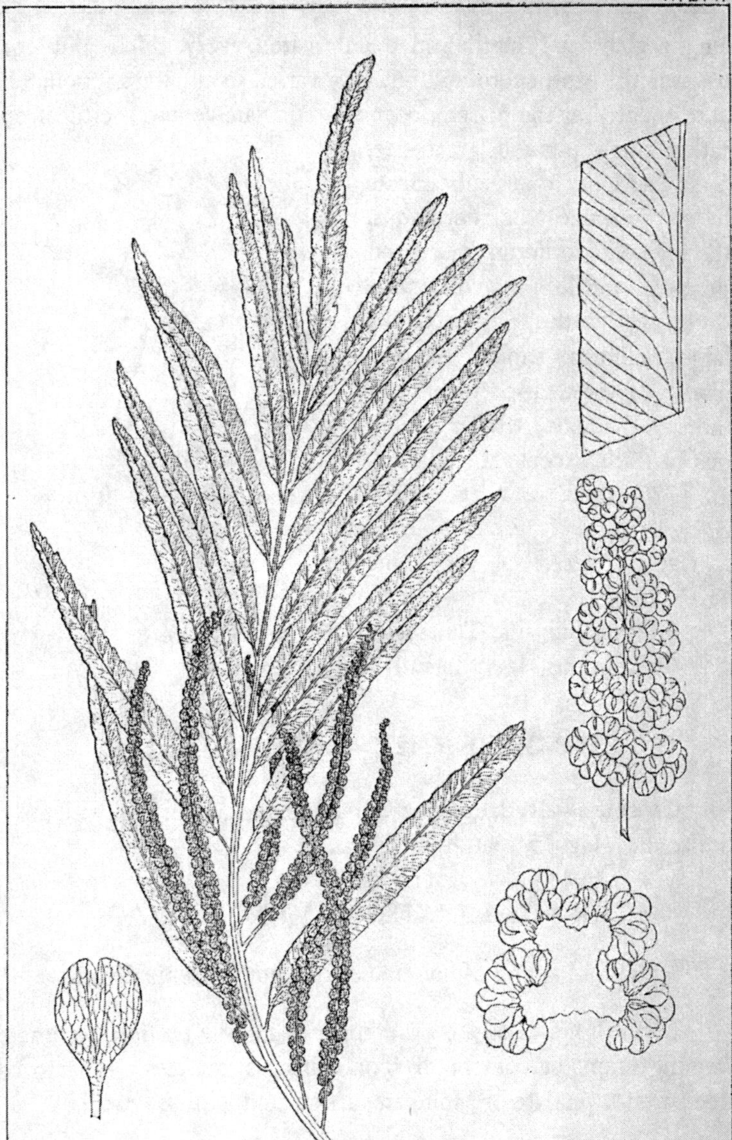

A. S. CATTELL & Co. ENGRAV.

OSMUNDA JAVANICA. (*Bl.*)

long, $\frac{3}{8}$–$\frac{3}{4}$ inch broad, cuneate at the base, and often slightly stalked, the edge entire or sharply toothed; texture coriaceous, rachis and both sides glabrous; fertile pinnæ shorter, made up of numerous close but distinct oblong sessile clusters. *Bl. Enum. p.* 252. *Bedd. F. S. I. t.* 77.

Ceylon, about Newera Elya; South India, cultivated only (?); Malay Peninsula; Tenasserim, banks of rivers in the plains. This is commonly in cultivation in Southern India, but I very much doubt if it is wild; I have never found it myself, though I have specimens said to have been collected in the Western ghats.

(Also in Java.)

Nº 275.

OSMUNDA CLAYTONIANA. (*L.*)

Nº 276.

OSMUNDA REGALIS. (*L.*)

2. OSMUNDA CLAYTONIANA. (*Lin.*) Stipes tufted, 1 foot or more long, clothed with loose woolly ferruginous tomentum when young, at length glabrous; fronds 1–2 feet long, 8–12 inches broad, simply pinnate; pinnæ deeply pinnátifid, the uppermost and lowest barren, some of the intermediate fertile, barren ones lanceolate, 4–6 inches long, 1 inch or more broad, the lobes oblong, entire, texture

herbaceous, fertile pinnæ shorter, pinnules dense cylindrical. *Lin. Sp. Pl.* 1521. *Bedd. F. B. I. t.* 187.

Himalayas from Kashmir to Bhotan, 6,000–10,000 feet elevation. Khasya, 4,500–6,000 feet.

(Also in North America.)

3. OSMUNDA REGALIS. (*L.*) Stipes tufted, 12–18 inches long, firm, erect, naked; fronds 2–4 feet long, 1 foot or more broad, bipinnate, the barren and fertile separate, or the frond barren below and fertile above, barren pinnæ 6–12 inches long, 2–4 inches broad, pinnules sessile or slightly stalked, 1–2 inches long, $\frac{1}{2}$–$\frac{3}{4}$ inch broad, oblong, blunt, often unequal at the base, the edge finely serrulate, texture subcoriaceous, rachis and both sides naked, fertile pinnules cylindrical, forming a copious panicle. *L. Sp. Pl.* 152. *Bedd. F. S. I. t.* 76.

South India, common on the Western mountains at the higher elevations; North India, Kumaon, Bhotan, Khasya, 4,000–6,000 feet, (small, the fertile and barren fronds generally separate.)

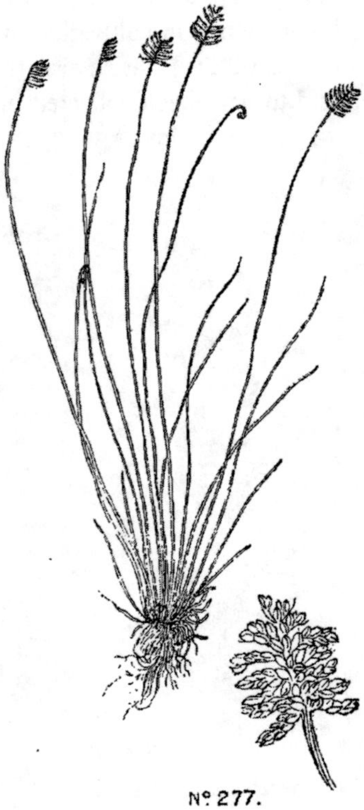

No. 277.
SCHIZÆA MALACCANA. (*Baker.*)

SUB-ORDER IV.—SCHIZÆACEÆ.

Capsule 2-valved, opening down the side, crowned by a complete operculiform ring; venation circinate.

No. 278.

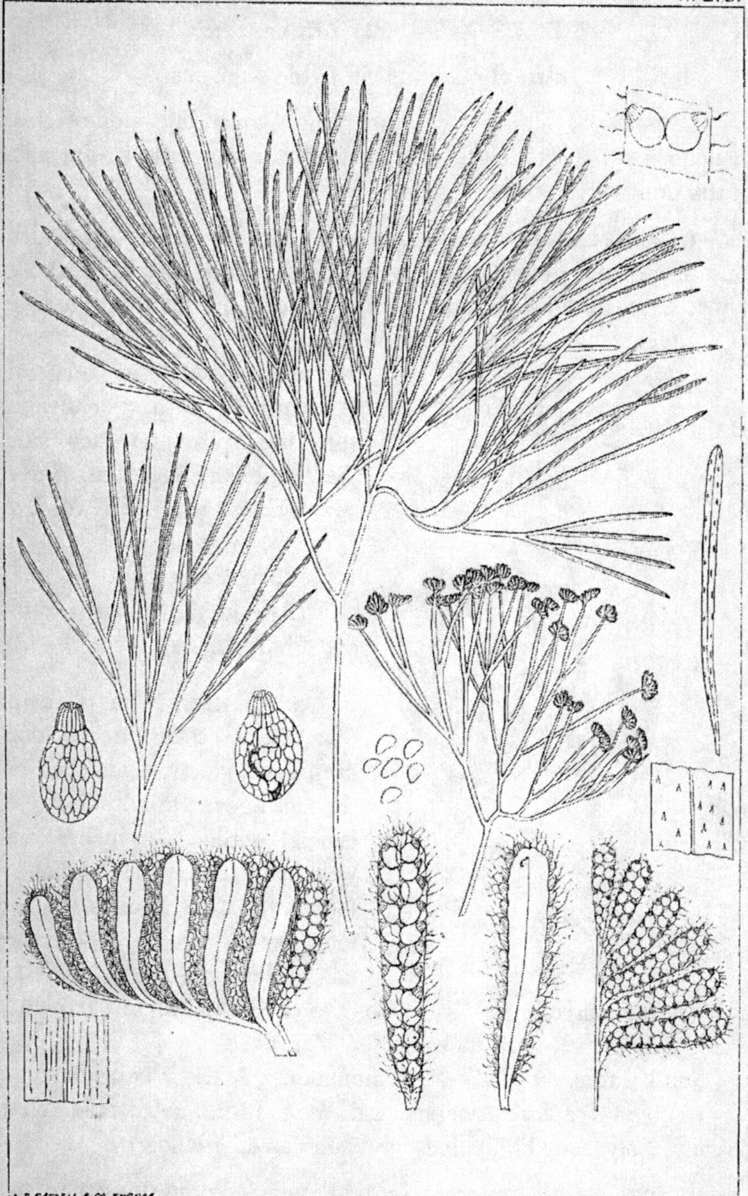

SCHIZÆA DICHOTOMA. (*Sw.*)

GENUS XC.—SCHIZÆA. (*Smith.*)

(*Schizo*, I cut; the cut fertile segments.)

Capsules sessile in 2–4 rows which cover one side of close distichous spikes, which form separate fertile segments at the apex of the fronds; veins free.

1. SCHIZÆA MALACCANA. (*Baker.*) Stipes dense, not distinguishable from the frond, which is 4–8 inches long, weak, flexuose, subterete, channelled in front not more than $\frac{1}{6}$ line thick, the barren and fertile ones similiar; fertile segment erect, often bilateral, $\frac{1}{4}$ inch deep with 3–6 slender spreading spikes on each side, the lowest 2–2$\frac{1}{2}$ lines long. *Baker, Syn. Fil. p.* 428. *Bedd. F. B. I. t.* 255.

Malay Peninsula.

(Also in the Malay Islands and Philippines.)

2. SCHIZÆA DICHOTOMA. (*Sw.*) Stipes 6–18 inches long, firm, erect, glossy, channelled on the face above; fronds fan-like in general outline, 6–9 inches each way, many times dichotomously forked, the ultimate divisions $\frac{1}{2}$–1 inch broad, with 1 fertile segment to each, $\frac{1}{4}$–$\frac{1}{2}$ inch long, the rachis often curved with 4–10 close spreading spikes on each side. *Hook. Syn. Fil. p.* 430. *Bedd. F. S. I. t.* 65.

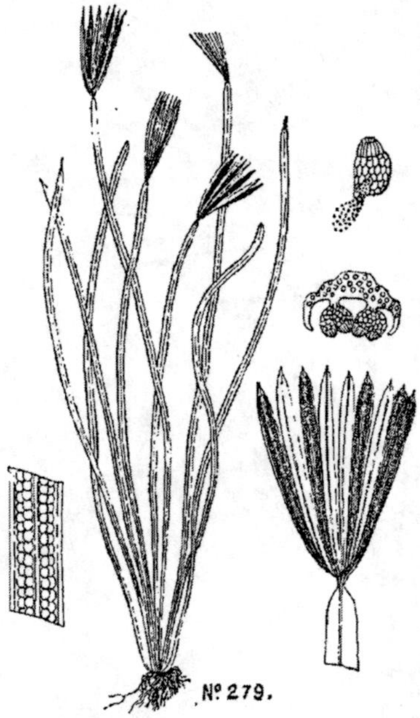

Nº 279.

SCHIZÆA DIGITATA. (*Sw.*)

South India, on the Western mountains; Malay Peninsula.

(Also in Tropical America and West Indies; Australia, New Zealand, Polynesia, Philippines, and Mascareen Islands.)

3. SCHIZÆA DIGITATA. (*Sw.*) Fronds long, linear, grass-like,

10–15 inches long by 2–3 lines broad, bearing a digitate fertile crest at the apex; crest 8–14, parted to the base, segments 1 inch long by a line broad; sori in 4 series (*i.e.*, 2 series each side the costa). *Sw. Syn. Fil.* 150, 380, *t.* 4. *Bedd. F. S. I.* 268.

North India, Khasya and Chittagong; Ceylon; Malay Peninsula. (Also in the Malay Islands; Fiji and Philippines.)

GENUS XCI.—ANEMIA. (*Sw.*)

(From *aneimon*, naked—the naked spikes.)

Capsules small, very abundant, forming a copiously branched panicle quite distinct from the leafy part of the frond; fronds pinnate or bi-tripinnatifid; veins free.

1. ANEMIA TOMENTOSA. (*Sw.*) Stipes 6–12 inches long strong, erect, clothed with deciduous ferruginous hairs; fronds ternately divided, the two lateral branches fertile, the terminal one spreading, sterile bipinnate, with the pinnules variously lobed or pinnatifid, texture herbaceous, rachis and both surfaces pilose; veins fine, flabellate. *Hook. Syn. Fil.* 433. Anemia Wightiana (*Gard.*), *Bedd. F. S. I. t.* 66.

South India, Nilgiris (Sispara ghat), Anamallays, Pulney Hills, Travancore Hills, 3,000–4,000 feet elevation.

(Also in Mexico, Peru and West Indies.)

GENUS XCII.—LYGODIUM. (*Sw.*)

(*Lygodes*, flexible—the climbing habit.)

Capsules solitary (or casually in pairs), in the axils of large imbricated clasping involucres, which form spikes either in separate pinnæ or in lax rows along the edge of the leafy ones; fronds scandent, pinnæ conjugate palmate-lobed, pinnatifid or pinnate; veins forked, free.

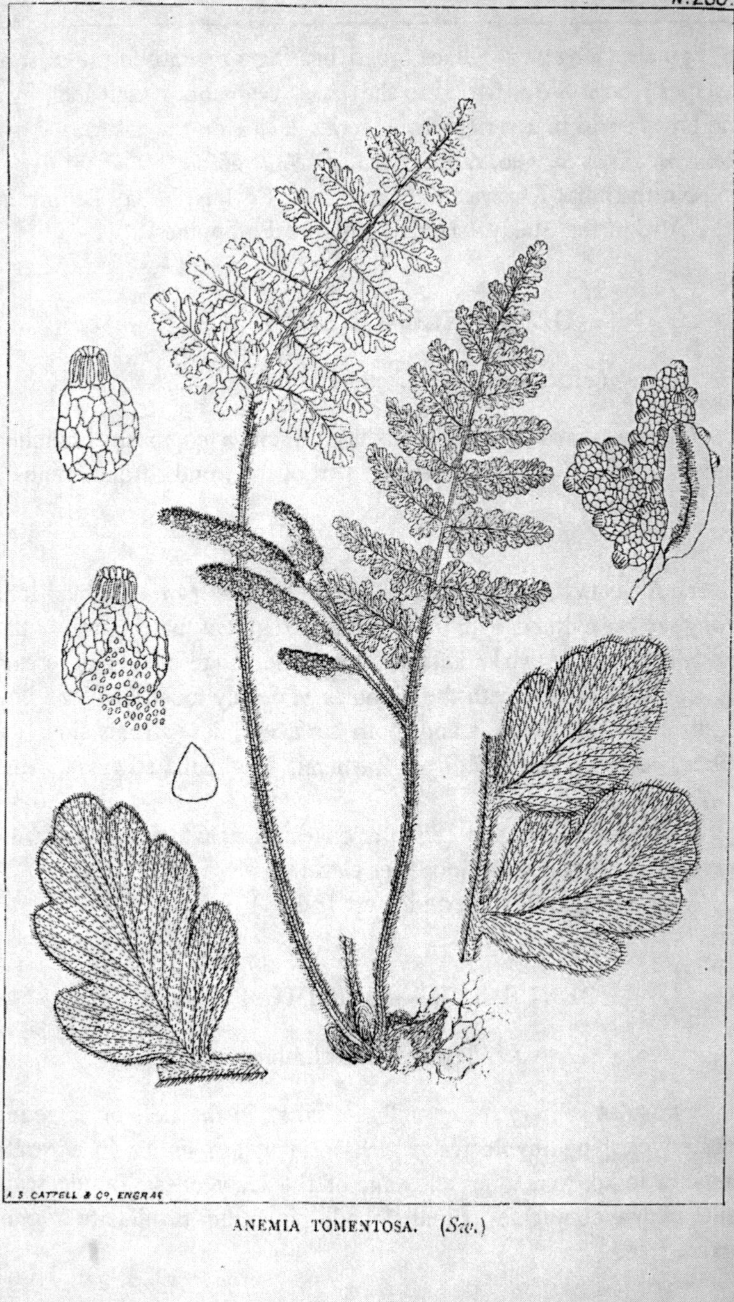

ANEMIA TOMENTOSA. (*Sw.*)

1. LYGODIUM CIRCINATUM. (*Sw.*) Fully developed barren frond, bipartite into 2 palmate lobes or simply palmate, primary petiole so much reduced that the fork seems almost to spring from the main rachis, secondary petiole 1–2 inches long, firm, naked, pinnules digitate, with 5–6 long lanceolate lobes, reaching nearly down to the base, or once or even twice-forked, ultimate barren divisions 4–12 inches long, $\frac{1}{2}$–$\frac{3}{4}$ inch broad, the fertile ones contracted sometimes so much so, that the lamina is nearly lost, the spikes 1–2 lines long, in close marginal rows, texture subcoriaceous, surfaces naked. *Sw. Syn. Fil.* 153. *Thw. En. Pl. Zey. p.* 379. pedatum, *Sw.* 154. L. dichotomum, *Bedd. F. S. I.* 62. *Wall. Cat.* 176. *Hook. Syn. Fil.* 437.

North India, Chittagong Hills; Ceylon, western, central, and southern provinces, up to 2,000 feet elevation; Malay Peninsula.

(Also in the Malay Islands; Philippines; Hong Kong and Chusan.)

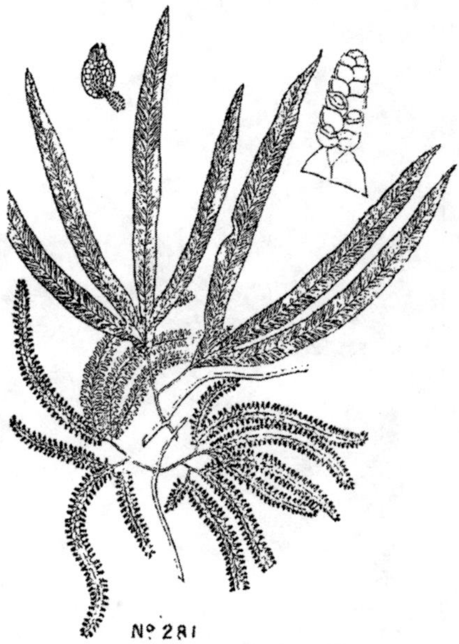

No. 281

LYGODIUM CIRCINATUM. (*Sw.*)

2. LYGODIUM MICROPHYLLUM. (*R. Br.*) Fronds simply pinnate, pinnules petioled, 3–4 on each side of the zigzag rachis, with a terminal one which is more or less lobed, barren pinnæ ovate-oblong, blunt, the margin subentire or rarely somewhat lobed, the base rounded or cordate, fertile ones short, deltoid, with generally a very rounded apex, and a square base and lobed round the margin. *R. Br. Prod.* 162. *Wall. Cat.* 174. L. scandens, *Bedd. F. S. I. t.* 61.

South India, Malabar and West Coast generally, very common in the plains, and also in the Wynad, up to about 3,000 feet eleva-

No. 282.

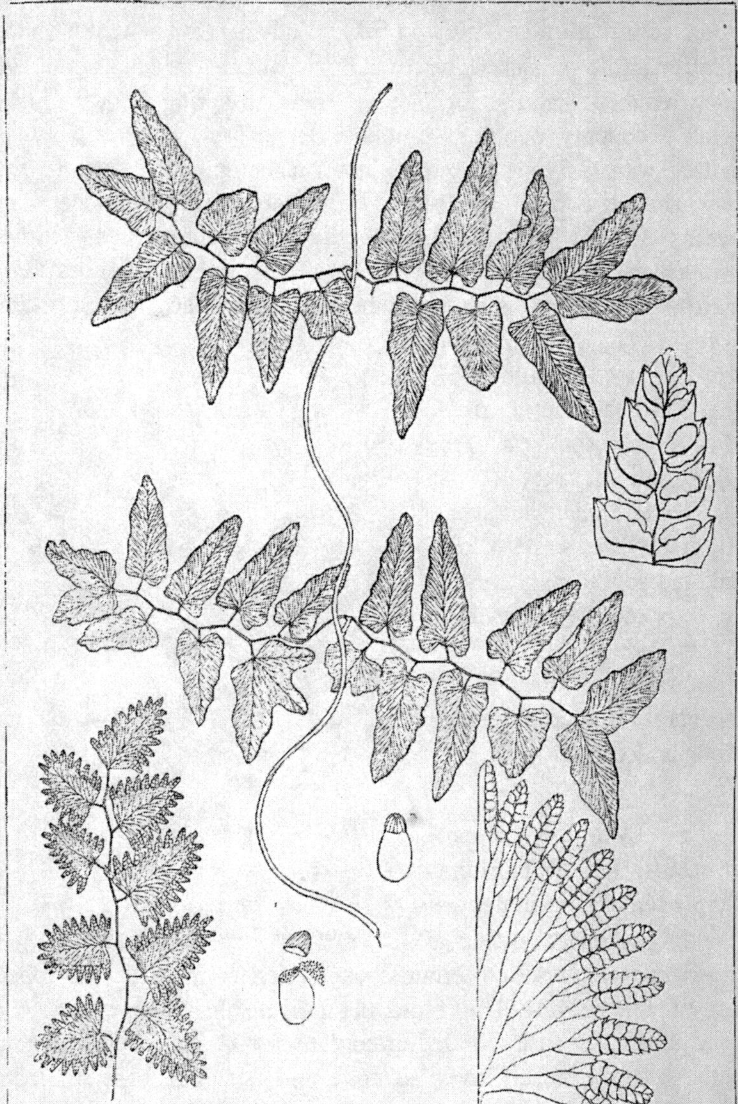

A. S. CATTELL & CO. ENGRA.

LYGODIUM MICROPHYLLUM. (*R. Br.*)

tion; Ceylon, abundant; North India, Bengal plains, rare; Malay Peninsula.

(Also in the Malay Islands.)

3. LYGODIUM FLEXUOSUM. (*Sw.*) Fronds glabrous or slightly hairy, pair of fronds stipitate-pinnate with the pinnules again pinnate or variously lobed, or subpalmate, all serrulate; sori protruding from the margin; texture subcoriaceous. *Sw. Syn. Fil.* 153. *Bedd. F.*

Nº 283.

LYGODIUM FLEXUOSUM. (*Sw.*)

Nº 284.

LYGODIUM POLYSTACHYUM. (*Wall.*)

S. I. t. 63. L. pinnatifidum, *Sw.* 153. L. longifolium, *Wall. Cat.* 175.

South India, on both sides of the Madras Presidency, common up to about 4,000 feet elevation; North India, plains, and up to 5,000 feet on the Himalayas; Ceylon; Malay Peninsula.

(Also in the Malay Islands; Philippines; North Australia, and Tropical Africa.)

4. LYGODIUM JAPONICUM. (*Sw.*) As in flexuosum, only that

the pinnæ are much smaller, with the pinnules smaller and finely cut, the fertile ones often so contracted that there is little or no lamina present. *Sw. Syn. Fil.* 154. *Bedd. F. S. I. t.* 64. *Wall. Cat.* 2201.

North India, abundant, extending west to Kashmir, up to 5,000 feet elevation; South India, Western mountains, rare. It is probably only a form of flexuosum.

(Also in Japan, China, Australia, Malay Islands and Philippines.)

5. LYGODIUM POLYSTACHYUM. (*Wall.*) Stem creeping, slightly pilose; fronds conjugate pinnate, membranaceous, pinnæ petiolate, furnished with a tufted gland at the apex of the petiole, deltoid-ovate to lanceolate, glandular-pilose on the rachis of the pinnæ costa and veins, pinnatifid more than half-down to the costa, segments with a rounded apex, entire or slightly crenate; costa of the pinnæ and central vein (or costule) of segments flexuose, veinlets simple or forked; fertile segments contracted. *Hook. Syn. Fil.* 438. *Bedd. F. B. I. t.* 300.

Malay Peninsula, Tenasserim.

SUB-ORDER V.—MARATTIACEÆ.

Capsule opening by a slit down one side or a pore at the apex, without a wing, usually joined together in concrete masses (synangia); vernation circinate.

GENUS XCIII.—ANGIOPTERIS. (*Hoffm.*)

(*Angio*, open; *pteris*, fern—the open sporangia.)

Capsules opening by a slit down the side, sessile, very close to one another, but not concrete, arranged in a linear-oblong or boat-shaped band of sporangia near the edge of the frond; veins simple or forked, free; fronds very large, bipinnate, springing from between two fleshy stipulæform appendages; the base of the stipes clavate, pseudo-articulate with the axis; pinnæ and pinnules articulate with the rachis.

№ 285.

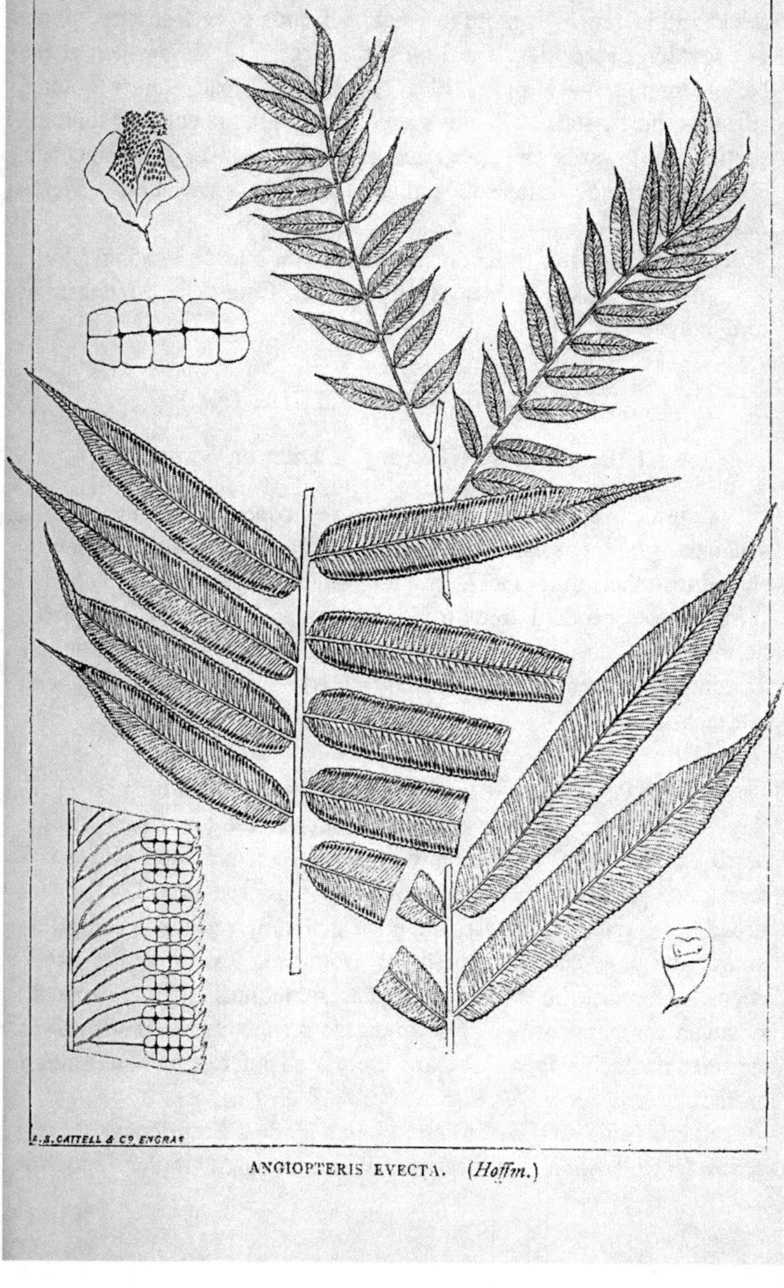

L.S. CATTELL & Cº ENGRAS

ANGIOPTERIS EVECTA. (*Hoffm.*)

1. ANGIOPTERIS EVECTA. (*Hoffm*) Caudex erect, often 2 feet thick, and as much or more in height; fronds 6–20 feet long, pinnæ 1–3 feet long, spreading, the lowest the largest, rachis swollen at the base, pinnules 4–12 inches long, ½–1½ inch broad, linear oblong, sessile or shortly stalked, the apex acuminate, the edge entire or toothed, particularly towards the apex, texture herbaceous to subcoriaceous, glabrous, shining; veins subparallel; sori of 8–15 capsules. *Hoffm. Schk. Krypt. Gew. t.* 151. *Bedd. F. S. I. t.* 78.

Throughout the Indian region up to 7,000 feet elevation.

(Also in Japan, Tropical Australia, New Caledonia, Madagascar, and Polynesia.)

GENUS XCIV.—MARATTIA. (*Sm.*)

(After Maratti of Tuscany, a writer on Ferns.)

Capsules sessile or stalked, 4–12 concrete in boat-shaped synangia, which consist of two opposite rows of capsules and open by slits down their inner faces, with or without an inferior involucre; veins simple or forked, free; fronds bi-tripinnate, large, springing from between two fleshy stipulæform appendages (which sometimes assume the character of abnormal fronds); pinnules articulate with the rachis.

1. MARATTIA FRAXINEA. (*Smith.*) Stipes 1–2 feet long, 1–1½ in. thick, smooth deciduously scaly or swollen in the lower part; fronds up to 15 feet long, bipinnate, or sometimes tripinnate; pinnæ 1–2 feet long, pinnules oblong-lanceolate, 4–6 inches long ½–1½ inches broad, the apex acuminate, the edge generally serrate, more rarely entire, the base cuneate, or slightly rounded, texture rather coriaceous, glabrous, the rachis of pinnæ sometimes slightly winged; synangia submarginal, in close rows, the receptacle linear with 6–12 capsules on each side, an obscure fimbriated inferior involucre often present. *Hook. Syn. Fil.* 440. *Bedd. F. S. I.t.* 79.

South India, Western forests of the Madras Presidency, 4,000–6,000 feet elevation (not nearly so common as Angiopteris which it

N°286

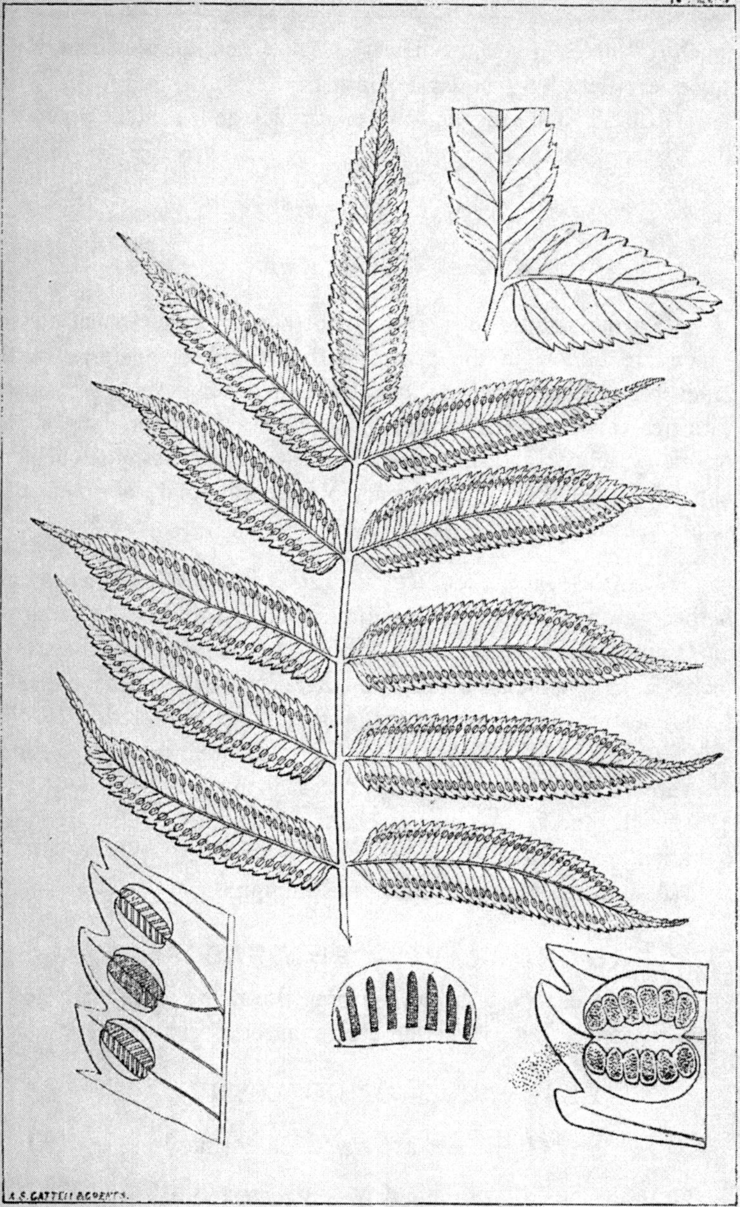

MARATTIA FRAXINEA. (*Sm.*)

much resembles in general habit); Ceylon, central provinces, above 5,000 feet elevation; Malay Peninsula.

(Also all round the world in the tropics and a little beyond in the southern zone.)

GENUS XCV.—KAULFUSSIA. (*Blume.*)

(After Kaulfuss, of Halle, a writer on Ferns.)

Capsules sessile, 10–15, quite concrete, in raised circular masses, which are hollow in the centre, with the oblong apertures on the inner face; veins costæform, parallel veinlets copiously anastomosing with free venules in the areoles; fronds 2–3 feet high, long stipate palmately lobed, and springing from two short fleshy stipulæform appendages; lobes of the fronds oblong elliptical; a genus of a single species.

1. KAULFUSSIA ÆSCULIFOLIA. (*Bl.*) Stipes 12–18 inches long, herbaceous, auricled at the base; fronds digitate (like a chesnut leaf), or ternate; the central pinnæ the largest, oblong, spathulate, 6–12 inches long, 3–4 inches broad, the others smaller, margins entire or lobed, texture fleshy-herbaceous; sori copious scattered. *Bl. En. Pl. Jav. Fil.* 260. *Bedd. F. B. I. t.* 185, (free included veinlets not shown). K. assamica, *Griff. Not.* l. ii. 628.

North India, Assam, Cachar, Chittagong Hills, 250 feet elevation.

(Also in the Malay Islands and Philippines.)

SUB-ORDER VI.—OPHIOGLOSSACEÆ.

Capsule deeply 2-valved, opening down the side nearly to the base, without a ring; vernation erect; terrestrial or epiphytic.

GENUS XCVI.—OPHIOGLOSSUM. (*L.*)

(*Ophis*, a snake; *glossa*, a tongue.)

Capsules sessile, arranged in two rows, forming a narrow close spike, which arises from the base or centre of the barren segment;

No. 287.

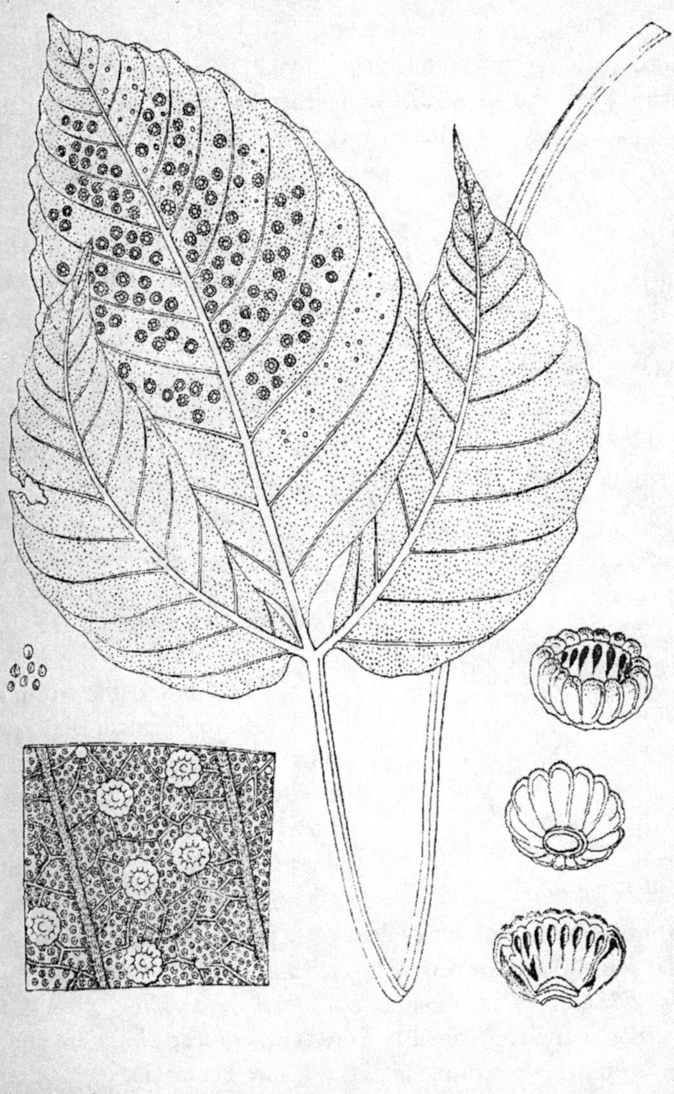

A. S. CATTELL & CO. ENGRAVERS

KAULFUSSIA ÆSCULIFOLIA. (*Bl.*)

rarely distinct, rising direct from the corm; veins reticulated; fronds simple entire, rarely palmate.

1. OPHIOGLOSSUM VULGATUM (*L.*) Rhizome not tuberous, short, or elongated, producing annually 1–2 fronds; fronds 6–9 inches long, the sterile division generally placed about the middle 2–4 inch long, ¾–2 inches broad, ovate or ovate-oblong, without a distinct haft, texture stouter than in the others, the midrib usually indistinct; fertile spike 1 inch long or rather more, on a peduncle 2–4 inches long, and considerably overtopping the sterile division when fully mature. *Lin. Sp. Pl.* 1518.

Sikkim, Goke, 4,000 feet elevation, Rungait camp, below Darjeeling, 2,000 feet elevation.

(Widely spread in Europe; Africa, and its eastern islands; America; Japan; Australia; New Zealand, and Sandwich Islands.)

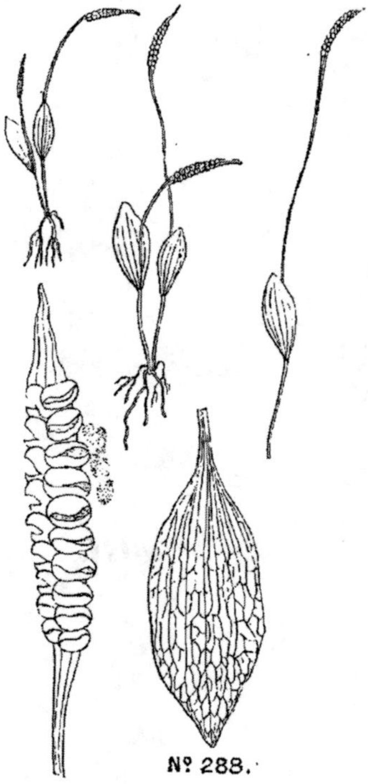

No. 288.

OPHIOGLOSSUM NUDICAULE. (*L. f.*)

2. OPHIOGLOSSUM NUDICAULE. (*L. f.*) Rhizome small, slightly tuberous; fronds 1 inch or more long, the sterile division placed not far from the base, ½–1 inch long, 2–5 lines broad, linear to ovate, without a haft, or with only a slight one, the texture thin but with no evident costa and veins not distinct; fertile spike ½ inch long, the peduncle often 2 inches long, very slender. *Sw. Syn. Fil. t.* 4. O. parvifolium, *Hook. and Grev. Bedd. F. S. I. t.* 71.

South India, Anamallay Forests, 2,500 feet elevation, and elsewhere on the Western mountains; Malay Peninsula.

(Also in America from United States southward to Brazil, New Caledonia, and Tropical Africa.)

3. OPHIOGLOSSUM FIBROSUM. (*Schum.*) Rhizome a large round white bulb with numerous fibrous rootlets; stipe very short with the sterile division close to its base, the latter 1½–2 inches long, by ¾ inch broad, lanceolate, acute or obtuse, the texture thick and opaque; midrib prominent, venation indistinct (except when dried), fertile spike 1½–2 inches long on a spike 4–5 inches long. *Schum. K. Dansk. Vid. Afh.* iv. 226. O. Wightii, *Hook and Grev. Bot. Mis.* iii. 218. O. brevipes, *Bedd. F. S. I. t.* 72.

South India, Anamallay teak forests, 2,000–3,000 feet elevation.

(Also in Tropical Africa, Guinea Coast; Ascension Island.)

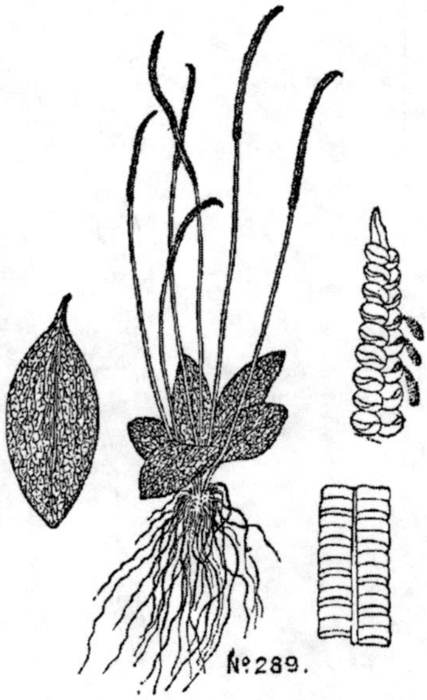

OPHIOGLOSSUM FIBROSUM. (*Schum.*)

4. OPHIOGLOSSUM RETICULATUM. (*L.*) Rhizome cylindrical, elongated with many fibrous rootlets; fronds 6–12 inches long, the sterile division placed a little below the middle, 1½–3 inches long, by 1–2 inches broad, with a distinct haft, and distinctly cordate at the base, the apex blunt or acute, texture thin; veins prominent, but usually no midrib; fertile spike 1 inch or more long on a slender peduncle, 2–4 inches long. *Linn. Sp. Pl.* 1518. *Hook. Syn. Fil. p.* 446. *Bedd. F. S. I. t.* 70. O. cordifolium (*Roxb.*), *Wall. Cat.* 47.

South India, Nilgiris and Anamallays, 2,000 feet elevation and upwards; Ceylon, Newera Elya; Himalayas; Malay Peninsula.

(Also in Malay Islands; Polynesia; Tropical America; Africa, Mascareen Islands; Philippines.)

5. OPHIOGLOSSUM PENDULUM. (*L.*) Epiphytic on trees;

No. 290.

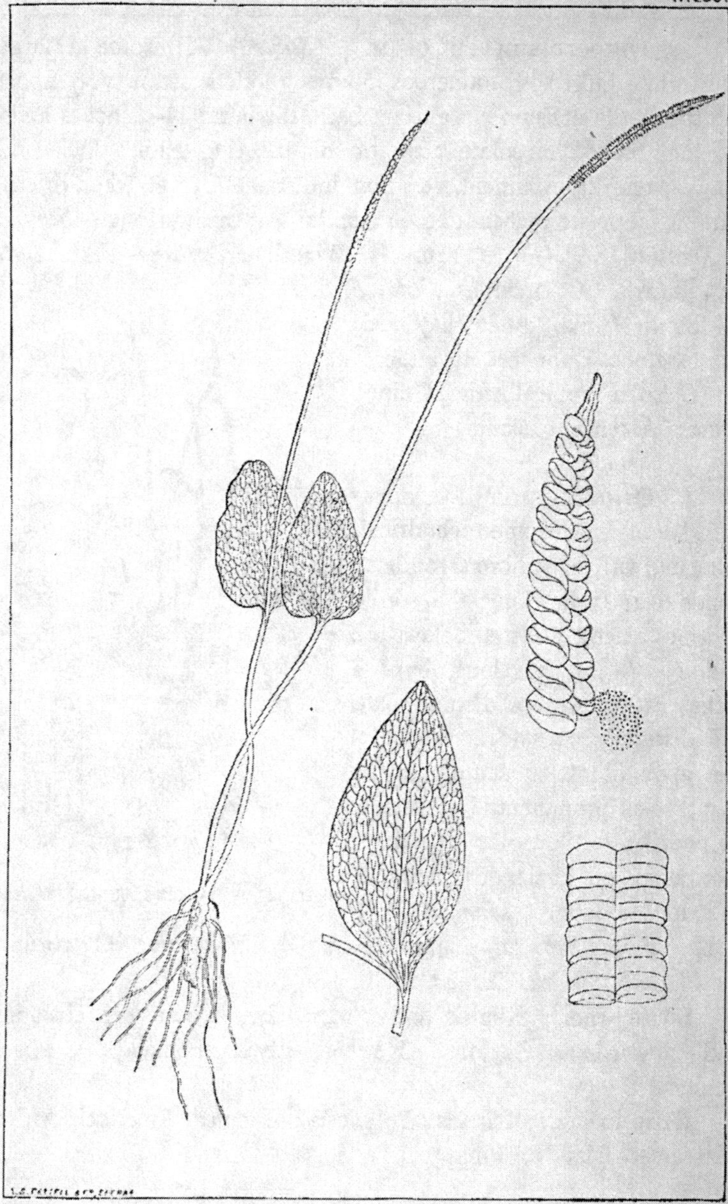

OPHIOGLOSSUM RETICULATUM. (*L.*)

fronds pendulous, ribbon-like, without a distinct stem, 1–3 feet long, 1–3 inches broad, simple or forked, texture fleshy; no midrib and the veining not distinct; fertile spike single, arising low down on, but above the base of, the sterile segment, 2–6 inches long, on a peduncle shorter than itself. *Linn. Sp. Pl.* 1518. *Bedd. F. S. I. t.* 269.

Ceylon, at no great elevation; Malay Peninsula; Assam (?)

(Also in Malay and Polynesian Islands; Mauritius; Australia; Philippines.)

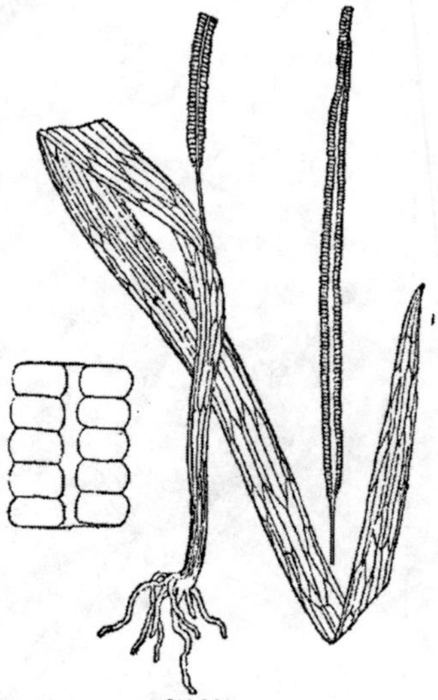

No. 291.

OPHIOGLOSSUM PENDULUM. (*L.*)

GENUS XCVII.—HELMINTHOSTACHYS. (*Kaulf.*)

(*Helminthos*, a worm; *stachys*, a spike.)

Capsules in long crested clusters which form a long loose spike; veins forked, free; fertile spike rising from the base of the leafy segment; fronds stipate, sterile segments foliaceous, digitate. A genus of a single species.

1. HELMINTHOSTACHYS ZEYLANICA. (*Linn. under Osmunda.*) Rhizome thick, fleshy, creeping; stipes often 1 foot long, barren segment palmately pinnate, often in three principal divisions which are stalked, and again forked or pinnate, the ultimate divisions linear-oblong, 3–4 inches long, ¾–1 inch broad, the apex acuminate, the edge slightly toothed or entire, texture herbaceous; fertile spike solitary, arising from the base of the barren segment, 3–4 inches long, ½ inch broad, the firm peduncle about as long as the fructification. *Linn. Sp. Pl.* 1519. *Hook. and Bauer, Gen. Fil. t.* 48B. *Bedd. F. S. I. t.* 69.

No. 292

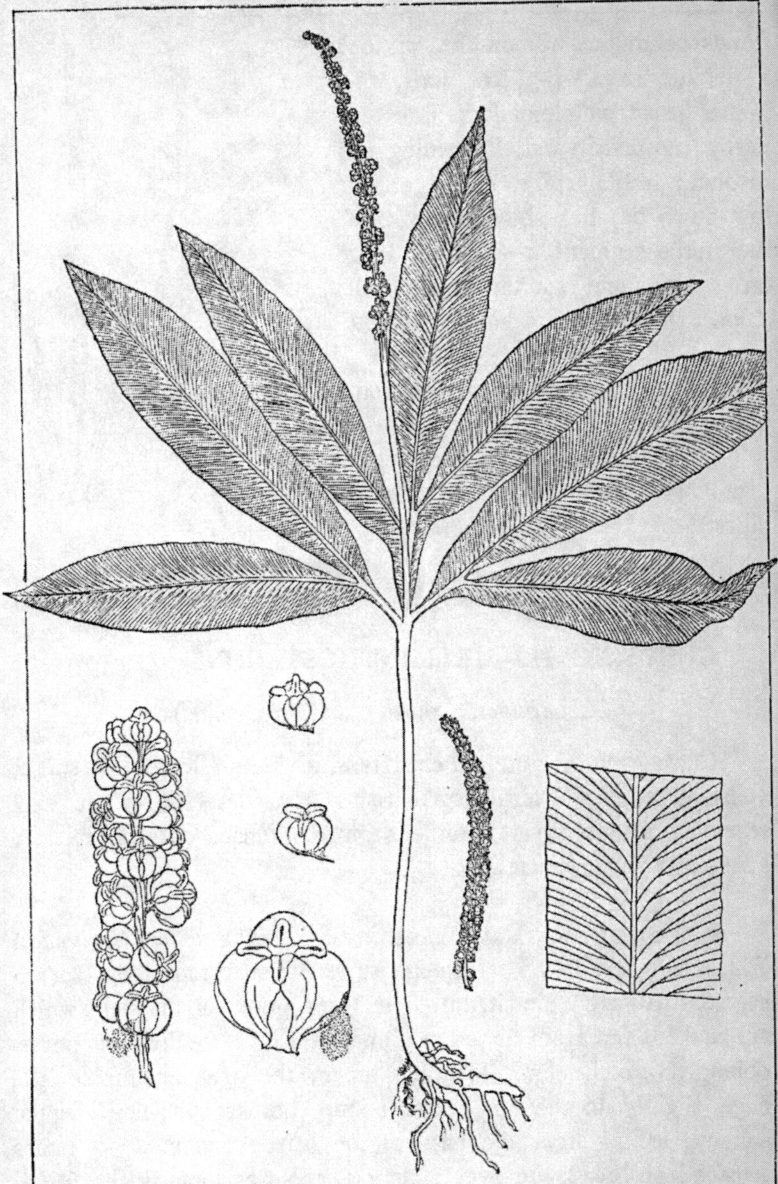

HELMINTHOSTACHYS ZEYLANICA. (*Linn.*)

South India, Western forests in swampy places up to 3,000 feet elevation; Ceylon, about Colombo and other parts of Western and Southern provinces; North India, Bengal plains to Assam and Cachar; Malay Peninsula.

(Also in Tropical Australia, Malay Islands, Philippines and New Caledonia.)

GENUS XCVIII.—BOTRYCHIUM. (*Sw.*)

(*Botrys*, a bunch; fructification like a bunch of grapes.)

Capsules sessile, arranged in two rows, on the face of spikes which form a compound panicle; veins forked, free; fronds erect, the sterile segments foliaceous, deltoid, bi-tripinnatifidly compound, rarely pinnate; fertile segments rachiform, compound paniculate.

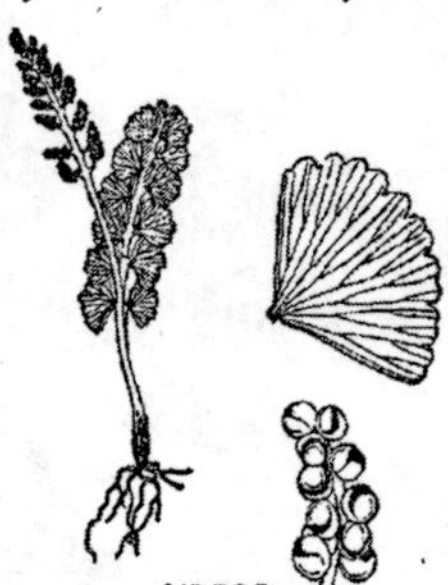

No. 293. BOTRYCHIUM LUNARIA. (*L.*)

1. BOTRYCHIUM LUNARIA. (*L. under Osmunda.*) Rhizome small, scarcely thickened, enclosed by brown sheaths furnished with stoutish fleshy brittle branched roots; stipes erect, smooth, cylindrical, hollow, succulent, vernation plicate or folded straight, the fertile branch clasped by the sterile before unfolding, fronds solitary, 3–10 inches high, firm, stout fleshy, sterile branch oblong, pinnate smooth, pinnæ 4–7 pairs flabellate or lunate, the margins crenate (rarely partially fertile) fertile branch pinnate or bipinnate; venation (barren pinnæ) flabellately-furcate, *i.e.* the vein enters at the base and is repeatedly forked, veins not quite extending to the margin. *Linn. Sp. Pl.* 1519. *Sw. Syn. Fil.* 171. *Bedd. F. B. I. t.* 208.

North India, Sikkim, Lachen, 11,000–13,000 feet elevation, Kumaon, 12,000 feet.

(Also the arctic and cold temperate zone, extending to South Europe; Patagonia; Australia.)

2. BOTRYCHIUM DAUCIFOLIUM. (*Wall.*) Stipes stout, 6–12

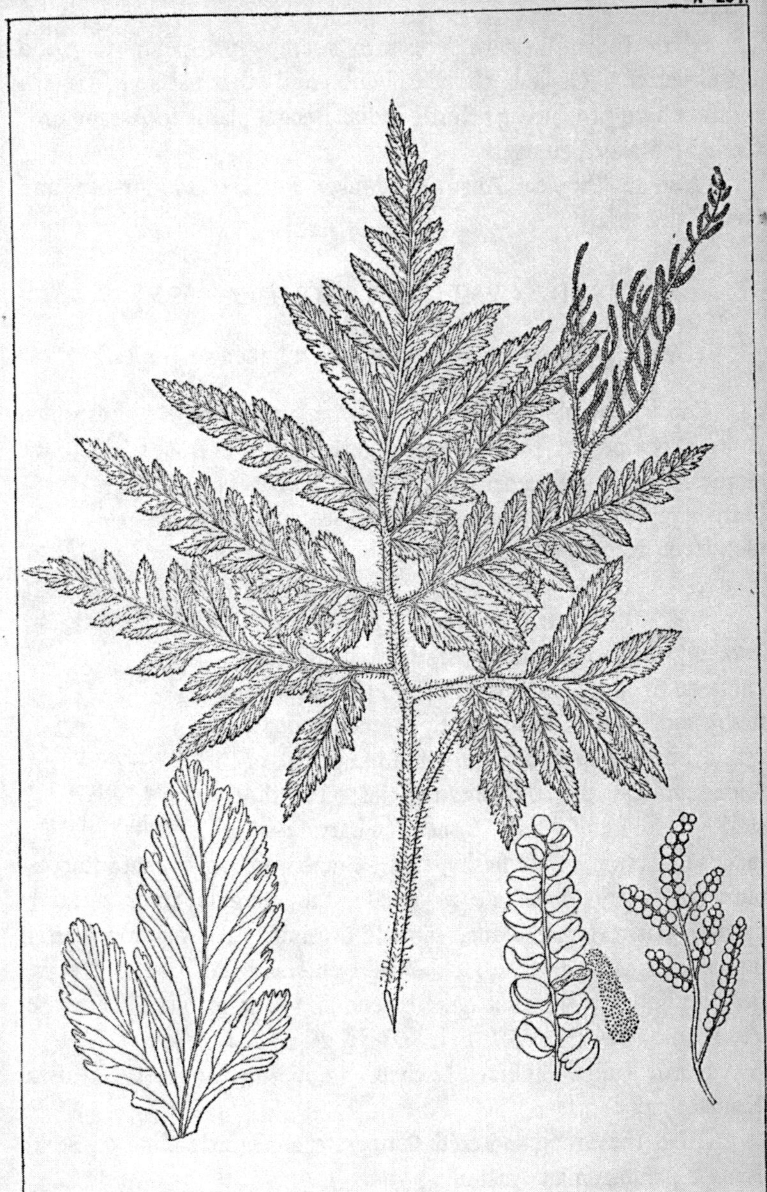

A. S. CATTELL & SPENCE.

BOTRYCHIUM DAUCIFOLIUM. (*Wall.*)

inches long, the sterile portion with a stalk, 1–6 inches long, *i.e.* prolonged beyond the fertile spike, 6–12 inches each way; deltoid, tripinnatifid or tripinnate; the lower pinnæ much the largest; segments lanceolate-oblong, $\frac{1}{4}$–$\frac{3}{8}$ inch broad, finely toothed; fertile segments about equalling the sterile segment when mature; panicle 2–4 inches long tripinnate, not very close. *Wall. Hook. and Grev. Ic. Fil. t.* 161. B. subcarnosum, *Wall. Cat.* 49. *Bedd. F. S. I. t.* 69.

Throughout the Indian region, up to 8,000 feet elevation.

(Also in Java and Polynesia.)

3. BOTRYCHIUM VIRGINIANUM. (*L. under Osmunda.*) Stipes 3–18 inches long, sterile portion not prolonged beyond the fertile spike 4–12 inches each way; deltoid, quadripinnatifid, lower pinnæ much the largest, pinnules ovate-oblong, close cut down to a broadly winged rachis into finely cut linear-oblong segments, both sides naked or slightly hairy; fertile branch of the rachis springing from the base of the sterile portion (*i.e.* sterile portion, sessile), or from the middle of it. *Linn. Sp. Pl.* 1519. *Sw. Syn. Fil.* 171.

No. 295.

BOTRYCHIUM VIRGINIANUM. (*Sw.*)
VAR. LANUGINOSUM.

VAR. β LANUGINOSUM. (*Sp. Wall. Cat.* 48.) Fertile branch arising from the middle of the sterile portion. *Bedd. F. S. I. t.* 67. *Moore, Ind. Fil.* 213. *Hook. Gard. Ferns, t.* 29. In the typical American plant, the fertile branch arises from the base of the sterile portion, and the latter is quite glabrous; in the Indian plant the fertile branch always springs from well above the base, and the sterile portion is more or less hairy, they are, however, only considered varieties.

South India, at the higher elevations on the Western mountains (only appearing in the rains); Ceylon, about Newera Elya; North India, on the Himalayas, Kumaon to Bhotan, 5,000–8,000 feet elevation, Khasya, 4,000–6,000 feet elevation.

(The typical plant is widespread in Europe, America and Japan.)

No. 298

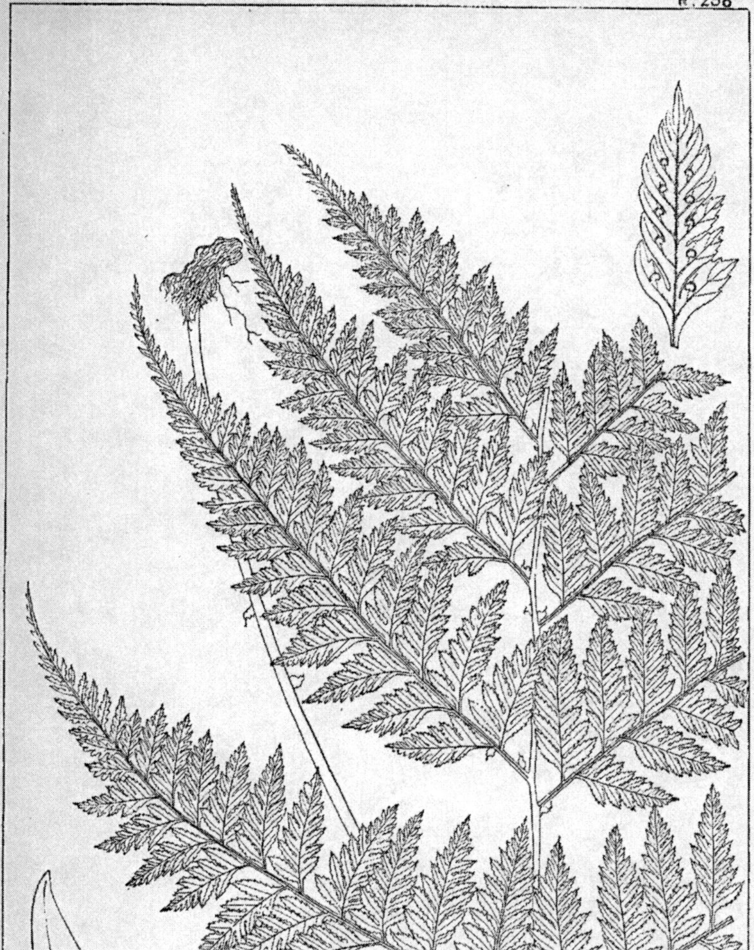

LEUCOSTEGIA MULTIDENTATA. (*Wall.*)

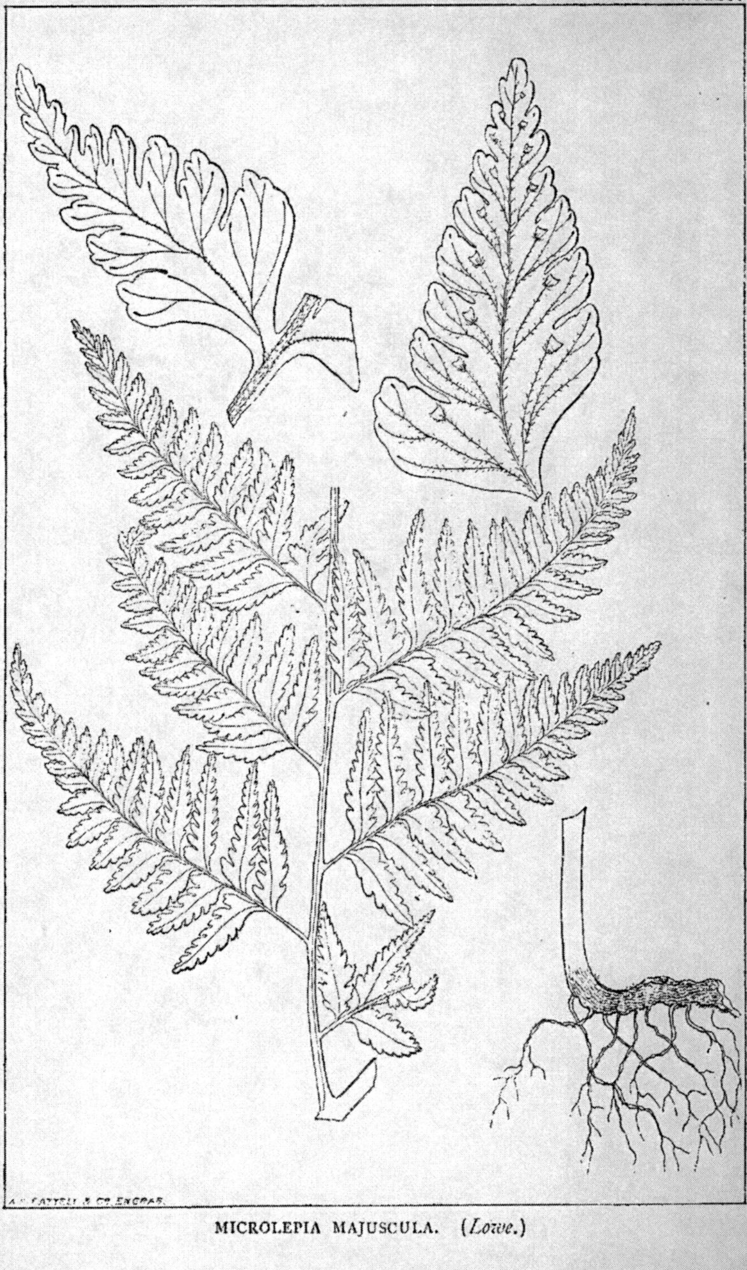

MICROLEPIA MAJUSCULA. (*Lowe.*)

ADDITIONS AND CORRECTIONS.

At page 16, after No. 10, insert :—

ALSOPHILA KINGI (Clarke MS. in Kew Herb.), a tree fern, 10 feet high, main rachis purplish shining glabrous, rachis of pinnæ purplish glabrous and somewhat glaucous, pinnæ 20-24 inches long, pinnules about 3 inches long by half inch broad, coriaceous, of a blueish glaucous tint, the rachis very scaly beneath and hairy above, cut down nearly to the base into oblong crenated segments, the midrib much raised and very prominent (particularly in the fertile pinnules) and scaly; veins once forked from a little above the base, or more rarely simple, receptacles much raised and very prominent.

Malay Peninsula at Laroot, in Perak, at 5,000 feet elevation, lately discovered by Dr. King's collectors.

At page 20, line 15, for 900—1,200, *read* 9,000—12,000.

At page 28, for plate 14, *read* plate 15.

At page 29, for plate 15, *read* plate 14.

At page 292, 9th line from bottom, for *This variety*, read *The variety*.

At page 295, 11th line from bottom, for *rugulosum Labill*, read *rugosulum Labill.*

At page 439, 4th line from bottom, for *as it* read, *as that.*

INDEX TO THE PLATES.

INDEX TO THE SPECIES AND SYNONYMS,

THE LATTER BEING IN ITALICS.